Philosophical Perspectives 19, 2005
Epistemology

PHILOSOPHICAL PERSPECTIVES
Edited by John Hawthorne

Managing editor: David Manley

Previously Published Volumes
(Volumes 1 through 9 are available from Ridgeview Publishing Company, Box 686, Atascadero, CA 93423.) Volume 1, Metaphysics, 1987; Volume 2, Epistemology, 1988; Volume 3, Philosophy of Mind and Action Theory, 1989; Volume 4, Action Theory and Philosophy of Mind, 1990; Volume 5, Philosophy of Religion, 1991; Volume 6, Ethics, 1992; Volume 7, Language and Logic, 1993; Volume 8, Logic and Language, 1994; Volume 9, AI, Connectionism, and Philosophical Psychology, 1995.

Volume 10, Metaphysics, 1996
Volume 11, Mind, Causation, and World, 1997
Volume 12, Language, Mind, and Ontology, 1998
Volume 13, Epistemology, 1999
Volume 14, Action and Freedom, 2000
Volume 15, Metaphysics, 2001
Volume 16, Language and Mind, 2002
Volume 17, Language and Philosophical Linguistics, 2003
Volume 18, Ethics, 2004

Additional titles to be announced.

Philosophical Perspectives 19, 2005
Epistemology

Edited by
JOHN HAWTHORNE

Blackwell Publishing, Inc.
350 Main Street
Malden, MA 02148 USA

Blackwell Publishing, Ltd.
108 Cowley Road
Oxford OX4 1JF
United Kingdom

Library of Congress Cataloging-in-Publication Data has been applied for.

ISBN 1-4051-3939-0
ISSN 1520-8583

Philosophical Perspectives, 19, Epistemology, 2005

Contents

Call for Papers

Philosophical Perspectives invites submissions for these upcoming volumes:

Volume 20, Metaphysics. (Papers due March 1, 2006)

Volume 21, Philosophy of Mind. (Papers due March 1, 2007)

Up to a third of the papers in each volume will be drawn from submissions. Send papers in duplicate and prepared for blind review to:

John Hawthorne, editor
Philosophical Perspectives
26 Nichol Ave
New Brunswick, NJ
08901-1411

Philosophical Perspectives, 19, Epistemology, 2005

DOUBT, CIRCULARITY AND THE MOOREAN RESPONSE TO THE SCEPTIC.

Jessica Brown
University of Bristol

1. Introduction

Sceptics argue that one lacks knowledge of ordinary propositions such as the claim that one has hands. A sample sceptical argument might run as follows. One does not know that one is not a handless brain in a vat (BIV); if one does not know that one is not a BIV, one does not know that one has hands; so, one does not know that one has hands. Moore famously offered the following style of response: one does know that one has hands, one knows that one has hands only if one knows that one is not a BIV, so one knows that one is not a BIV. (From now on, I will set aside the subtleties of Moore's historical position and focus on this response to the sceptic, calling it the M-response.)

There is widespread dissatisfaction with the M-response to the sceptic. Here I focus on one recent diagnosis of this dissatisfaction, offered in a series of papers by Davies and Wright. Since their views have undergone recent changes[1], I will focus on the views expressed in Davies 1998, 2000 and 2003, and Wright 2000, 2002, and 2003. Davies and Wright argue that there is a failure of transmission of warrant across the following key inference, (henceforth 'the BIV inference'):

BIV1) I have hands.
BIV2) If I have hands then I am not a BIV.
So, BIV3) I am not a BIV.

More specifically, they argue that warrant fails to transmit across the BIV inference on two grounds: that the inference cannot be used to rationally overcome doubt about the conclusion and that it cannot be used to strengthen one's epistemic position with respect to the conclusion.

One could dispute Davies's and Wright's diagnosis, attempting to argue that the BIV inference can be used to rationally overcome doubt about the conclusion, and can strengthen one's epistemic position with respect to the conclusion. For instance, in their different ways, Pryor and Sillins have argued that the inference can strengthen one's epistemic position with respect to the conclusion[2]. That is not my project here. Instead, I will assume for the sake of argument that the inference can neither rationally overcome doubt nor strengthen one's epistemic position with respect to the conclusion, and critically examine the consequences that Davies and Wright draw from these claims.

2. Transmission, Closure and Warrant

Widely differing definitions of 'closure' and 'transmission' can be found in the literature. Indeed, some define 'closure' to mean roughly what others mean by 'transmission'.[3] As a result, my use of these terms will be partly stipulative. However, my use will not be wholly stipulative. I am interested in trying to capture some of the ideas which Davies and Wright associate with what they call 'transmission'.

Before exploring the notion of transmission further, we need to clarify the notion of warrant at issue. I use 'warrant' as a synonym for justification, allowing that warrant may be either evidential or non-evidential. Epistemologists standardly distinguish the notions of having a warrant to believe that p and warrantedly believing that p. One may have a warrant to believe that p yet not believe that p. Further, even if one has a warrant to believe that p and believes that p, one's belief might not be warranted if it is based on some other poor reason to believe that p. Davies and Wright do not explicitly state which notion they are concerned with. Both notions are interesting for different purposes. Here, I focus on the notion of having a warrant to believe that p. Throughout the paper we are examining the efficacy of the M-response to the sceptic. The most radical sceptic is not best characterised as holding that one lacks a warranted belief that one is not a BIV. That denial is compatible with one's having warrant to believe that one is not a BIV but failing to believe it, or having such a warrant and believing that one is not a BIV but not on the basis of that warrant. Neither of these possibilities gets to the heart of the sceptic's argument. Rather, the sceptic is best understood as denying that one has warrant to believe that one is not a BIV. Given this understanding of scepticism, it seems that the crucial question to ask of the M-response is whether one can have warrant to believe that one is not a BIV via the BIV inference. Of course, one would also like one's belief that one is not a BIV to constitute a warranted belief. But, the prior question is whether one has warrant to believe that one is not a BIV.

With this background in place, we can start to distinguish the notion that warrant to believe transmits across a known entailment from the idea that warrant to believe is closed across such an entailment. I will take closure as the following claim:

> Closure: if one has warrant to believe that p, and knows that p entails q, then one has warrant to believe that q.

Notice that, so-defined, closure merely states that if one has warrant to believe that p and knows that p entails q, then one has warrant to believe that q; it is silent on how one has warrant to believe that q. Wright holds that transmission is a stronger notion than closure, saying 'Transmission...says more: roughly, that to acquire a warrant for the premises of a valid argument and to recognise its validity is *thereby* to acquire—possibly for the first time—a warrant to accept the conclusion' (2002: 332; see also 2000: 141, 2003: 57). Elsewhere, he says, 'a transmissible warrant should make for the possible advancement of knowledge, or warranted belief' (2002: 331–32; see also 2000: 140–41, 2003: 58). One of Wright's ideas, then, is that in having warrant to believe that p and knowing that p entails q, one thereby has warrant to believe that q (see also Davies 1998: 325 and 2000: 393–4). The force of the 'thereby' becomes apparent when we contrast closure and transmission. Closure states that if one has warrant to believe that p and knows that p entails q, then one has warrant to believe that q; it is silent on how one has warrant to believe that q. So an inference could satisfy closure if it is a condition for having warrant to believe the premises that one has a prior warrant to believe the conclusion which is independent of the inference. However, it does not follow, indeed Wright denies, that such an inference would satisfy transmission, which requires that one has warrant to believe the conclusion in one particular way, namely in virtue of one's warrant to believe the premises. Further, Wright holds that a transmissible warrant allows for the possible strengthening of one's epistemic position. One way in which an inference may strengthen one's epistemic position with respect to the conclusion is by providing one with warrant to believe it for the first time. However, it could also do so by strengthening an existing warrant to believe the conclusion. Thus, we can draw from Wright's remarks the two following notions of transmission of warrant, which I will call first-time (or FT) transmission, and advancement (or A) transmission:

> First-Time Transmission (FT): if one has warrant to believe that p, and knows that p entails q, then one thereby has warrant to believe that q, potentially for the first time.
>
> Advancement Transmission (A): if one has warrant to believe that p, and knows that p entails q, then one thereby has warrant to believe that q, potentially strengthening one's warrant to believe that q (either by providing first-time warrant to believe that q, or by strengthening an existing warrant to believe that q).

FT and A-transmission clearly place distinguishable conditions on a transmissible warrant, that it potentially provide first-time warrant to believe that q, or that it potentially strengthen one's warrant to believe that q either by strengthening an existing warrant to believe that q, or by providing a first-time warrant to believe that q. Given the definitions, any inference which satisfies FT-transmission also satisfies A-transmission, for providing first-time warrant to believe that q is one way of strengthening one's warrant to believe that q.

Although FT and A-transmission place distinguishable conditions on a transmissible warrant, Wright does not explicitly distinguish them and his main focus is implicitly on the notion of FT-transmission. Wright uses the notion of a failure of transmission of warrant in his diagnosis of the felt dissatisfaction with the M-type response to the sceptic. Wright argues that there is a class of valid arguments, including the BIV inference, across which warrant fails to transmit, those which fit his so-called 'disjunctive template'.[4] His key claim is that an argument fitting this template has the following property, one has warrant to believe one of the premises only if one has prior and independent warrant to believe its conclusion (2000:155, 2002: 343, 2003:63). If one has warrant to believe one of the premises of an argument only if one has prior and independent warrant to believe its conclusion, then the argument cannot provide one with warrant to believe the conclusion for the first time, and is a counterexample to FT-transmission. In the case of the BIV inference, Wright's claim is that one's sensory experience as of having hands constitutes warrant to believe that one has hands only if one has prior and independent warrant to believe that one is not a BIV. So, the BIV inference cannot provide first-time warrant to believe that one is not a BIV.

It seems that Wright thinks that arguments fitting his disjunctive template are also counterexamples to A-transmission. For instance, he says of the goal argument that 'you don't get any additional reason for thinking a game is in process [the conclusion] by having the warrant for [premise] i)...'. Regarding another putative example of a failure of transmission, Wright says that warrant for the premise is not to be reckoned as among the subject's reasons for accepting the conclusion, 'either as bestowing a first such reason, or as enhancing reasons already possessed (2000: 142–43). However, it is not clear whether an inference's being a counterexample to FT-transmission entails that it is a counterexample to A-transmission. To examine the issue, let us consider an inference which is a counterexample to FT-transmission. Suppose, then, that a warrant, w, to believe that p does not FT-transmit across the known entailment to q for Wright-style reasons, namely it is a condition of having warrant to believe that p that one already have prior and independent warrant to believe that q. Would it follow that w cannot potentially strengthen one's warrant to believe that q? Someone might defend a positive response by arguing that if it is a condition of having warrant to believe that p that one already have prior and independent warrant to believe that q, then one's warrant to believe that p cannot be stronger than one's prior and independent warrant to believe that q. But, it may be said, if one's warrant to believe that p cannot be stronger than one's prior and independent warrant to believe that q, then one cannot strengthen that prior warrant to believe that q by appeal to one's warrant that p and one's knowledge that p entails q. This line of thought may tempt some. Still, the crucial conditional claim needs defending, namely that if it is a condition of one's having warrant to believe that p that one already have prior and independent warrant to believe that q, then one's warrant to believe that p cannot be stronger than one's prior and independent warrant to believe that q. The issue is complicated by the fact that, at least on Wright's view, in the relevant cases, the prior and independent warrant to believe that q takes the form of a non-evidential entitlement, whereas the warrant to believe that p is evidential.[5] For instance, in the case of the BIV inference, Wright holds that one's sensory experience as of hands constitutes warrant to believe the premise that one has hands only if one has prior and independent non-evidential entitlement to believe the conclusion that one is not a BIV. Given that the warrant to believe the premise and conclusion are of such different types—evidential and non-evidential—it is not clear that the former cannot be stronger than the latter. I will not attempt to settle the issue of whether an argument's being a counter-example to FT-transmission entails that it is a counterexample to A-transmission, although the issue turns out to be important in section 4.

Many have rejected Wright's claim about the class of arguments across which warrant fails to transmit, arguing that inferences fitting the disjunctive template can provide first-time warrant to believe the conclusion (e.g., Brown 2003, McLaughlin 2003, Pryor 2004).[6] Since my aim is to examine the consequences of Wright's view, I will not address the issue of whether he's correct to think that the BIV inference cannot provide first-time warrant to believe its conclusion. I will grant both that the BIV inference cannot provide first-time warrant to believe the conclusion, and the further claim that it cannot strengthen one's warrant to believe the conclusion. My focus will be on the consequences Wright draws from these claims. Before doing so, we will examine Davies' rather different diagnosis of the M-type response to the sceptic.

3. Davies and Doubt

In a series of papers, Davies suggests that warrant fails to transmit across the BIV inference because it cannot be used to rationally overcome doubt about its conclusion (see Davies 1998, 2000, and 2003; but see 2004 for a change of view)[7]. Davies adopts Jackson's account of when an inference is unable to rationally overcome doubt about the conclusion, namely when it is such that 'anyone—or anyone sane—who doubted the conclusion would have background beliefs relative to which the evidence for the premises would be no evidence' (Jackson 1987:111). More specifically, Davies's idea is that if one were to doubt the conclusion of the BIV inference and think one were a BIV, one would not take one's sensory experiences as of hands to warrant the first premise of the inference, namely that one has hands. In fact, I'll suggest that an inference's inability to rationally overcome doubt is not best thought of as a failure of transmission. To see this, it is useful to consider the relation between doubt about the conclusion of the BIV inference, that one is not a BIV, and one's having warrant to believe its first premise, that one has hands. There are two possibilities to consider: 1) one's doubt that one is not a BIV prevents one's sensory experience as of having hands from constituting warrant to believe that one has hands; and 2) one's doubt that one is not a BIV is compatible with one's sensory experience as of having hands constituting warrant to believe that one has hands. I will argue that, on either option, the fact that the BIV inference cannot be used to rationally overcome doubt about its conclusion is not best thought of as a failure of transmission of warrant.

Suppose that one doubts the conclusion of the BIV inference, namely that one is not a BIV. This may prevent one's sensory experience as of having hands from constituting warrant to believe that one has hands. This would happen if one has good grounds to doubt that one is not a BIV, say if one were given plausible evidence that many ordinary people have recently been envatted. In this case, one's sensory evidence as of having hands cannot be used to rationally overcome doubt about the conclusion; rather, it ceases to constitute warrant to believe the premise that one has hands. But if one's doubt about the conclusion prevents one's sensory evidence from constituting warrant for the first premise, then this cannot be a case in which one has a warrant to believe the premise but one which fails to transmit to the conclusion. Given that our two transmission principles are conditional claims whose antecedents state that one has warrant to believe that p, a case in which one lacks warrant cannot constitute a counterexample to either claim. For instance, FT-transmission states that if one has warrant to believe that p, and knows that p entails q, then one thereby has warrant to believe that q, potentially for the first time. A case in which one lacks warrant to believe that p cannot provide a counterexample to this principle. (See Beebee 2001, Pryor 2004.)

Now consider the possibility that one's doubt about the conclusion does not prevent one's sensory evidence from constituting warrant to believe that one has hands. This may occur if one's doubt that one is not a BIV is groundless and one has no reason to think that one is a BIV. In a case in which one's doubt about the conclusion is compatible with one's sensory experience as of hands constituting warrant to believe that one has hands, there seems no reason to suppose that the BIV inference is a counterexample to either of our two transmission principles. One does have warrant to believe the premise that one has hands, and one knows that one's having hands entails that one is not a BIV. So, it seems that nothing prevents one from thereby having warrant to believe that one is not a BIV, potentially strengthening one's warrant to believe the conclusion, or providing first-time warrant to believe it. Of course, one's warrant to believe that one has hands would be ineffective in overcoming one's doubt that one is not a BIV. Given that one doubts that one is not a BIV, one would not take one's sensory experience as of hands to constitute warrant to believe that one has hands. Further, although one's doubt is groundless, it seems that given that one thinks one may well be a BIV, it would be irrational for one to take one's sensory experience to constitute warrant to believe that one has hands. Since one's doubt is groundless is could be classed as irrational. Still, as Pryor puts it, one's groundless doubt 'rationally obstructs' one from taking one's experiences as of hands to constitute warrant to believe that one has hands.

It seems, then, that even if the BIV inference cannot rationally overcome doubt about its conclusion, this is not best thought of as a counterexample to the transmission of warrant. Despite this, it might still be suggested that the felt dissatisfaction with the M-type response to the sceptic stems from the fact that the BIV inference cannot be used to rationally overcome doubt about its conclusion. From now on, I will assume that the BIV inference cannot be used to rationally overcome doubt about its conclusion and, in the next section, consider whether that undermines its use in an anti-sceptical response.

4. Scepticism and transmission

It is a controversial matter what constraints an adequate response to scepticism should meet. However, many of the most influential responses to scepticism deny that an adequate response should answer sceptical doubts or use only principles which the sceptic would accept. If this view is correct, then that the BIV inference cannot rationally overcome doubt does not show that it cannot be part of an adequate anti-sceptical response. A variety of reliabilist and contextualist views respond to scepticism by providing accounts of how one can have knowledge where these accounts rely on the truth of the claim that the BIV possibility is a far away, or irrelevant, possibility. One's belief that one has hands would not meet Nozick's tracking conditions for knowledge if there were a nearby world in which one is a BIV. DeRose, Sosa, and Williamson claim that one's belief that one has hands and one's belief that one is not a BIV constitute knowledge because these beliefs are safe, i.e. in the actual and nearby worlds one has these beliefs only if they are true. But, that requires that there is no nearby world in which one is a BIV. Similarly, relevant alternative theories have the consequence that one knows that one has hands only if the BIV world is not relevant (e.g., Dretske 1970 and Stine 1976). None of these theorists attempt to justify the assumption that the BIV world is far away or irrelevant. Rather, they aim to show how, given the truth of this assumption, one can have knowledge. Thus, these accounts do not attempt to resolve doubt about whether one is a BIV or convince someone who doubts this that she has knowledge. Rather, they attempt to use part of our conception of the world to show how, despite the sceptical argument, we can have knowledge. As Nozick says

> Our task here is to explain how knowledge is possible. . .In doing this, we need not convince the sceptic, and we may introduce explanatory hypotheses that he

would reject. What is important for our task of explanation and understanding is that *we* find those hypotheses acceptable or plausible... (1981: 197–98.)

Of course, sceptics are likely to regard these responses as question begging. In reply, non-sceptics point out that they aim to counter the sceptical claim that scepticism follows from our own intuitions and assumptions. In answering this sceptical challenge, it is entirely legitimate to draw on some of our assumptions to show that scepticism does not follow from our intuitive world view. As DeRose says, 'if the sceptic is marshalling deeply felt intuitions of ours in an attempt to give us good reasons for accepting his scepticism, it's legitimate to point out that other of our beliefs militate against his position, and ask why we should give credence to just those that favour him.' (1995: 215. For similar remarks, see Cohen 1988: 113.)

It seems, then, that many influential responses to scepticism deny that an adequate response to scepticism must answer sceptical doubt about whether one is a BIV. If this denial is correct, then whether the BIV inference can rationally overcome doubt is irrelevant to whether a non-sceptic can use the inference as part of an adequate reply to the sceptic.

Now consider Wright's claim that the M-type response to scepticism is inadequate because the BIV inference fails to provide first-time warrant to believe the conclusion, or strengthen one's warrant to believe the conclusion. It seems that it would be preferable if an anti-sceptical response showed that one had warrant to believe that one is not a BIV all along rather than providing one with first-time warrant to believe it. If a reply to the sceptic provides warrant to believe that one is not a BIV for the first time, then prior to that response being given, no one had warrant to believe that he is not a BIV and, assuming that knowledge requires warrant to believe, no one knew that he is not a BIV. Further, even after the response has been given, those who are ignorant of the response would still lack warrant to believe and so knowledge. This would be a deeply damaging conclusion if the response to scepticism involves complex philosophical arguments known by only a few. Assuming closure for warrant to believe, these problems also extend to ordinary propositions, such as that one has hands. Given closure for warrant to believe, if a response to scepticism provides first-time warrant to believe that one is not a BIV, it also provides first-time warrant to believe such ordinary claims as that one has hands. So, before the reply to scepticism is given, or if one is ignorant of that reply, one lacks warrant to believe, and so knowledge of, such ordinary claims. Similar points hold for the notion of strengthening one's warrant to believe that one is not a BIV. If the reply to the sceptic strengthens one's warrant to believe that one is not a BIV, then it is compatible with that reply that, prior to that reply being given, or if one is ignorant of that reply, one has a very weak warrant to believe that one is not a BIV, perhaps so weak that one does not know that claim. (For analogous points concerning knowledge, see DeRose 2000.)[8]

It seems, then, that it would be preferable if a reply to the sceptic showed that, all along, we were in a good epistemic position with respect to the denial of the BIV hypothesis, rather than providing first-time warrant to believe it or strengthening our warrant to believe it. An analogous point about knowledge is implicitly accepted by a wide range of responses to scepticism, including contextualist and reliabilist responses. For example, Stine (1976) argues that one can know that sceptical hypotheses are false without evidence since they are not normally relevant. Plausibly, if sceptical hypotheses are normally irrelevant then this has always been the case and, thus, the account shows how one always knew their falsity. (It is logically possible that a sceptical hypothesis, such as the BIV hypothesis, could be irrelevant now but used to be relevant, say because there used to be lots of BIVs around. But, this hardly seems likely.) DeRose, Sosa and Williamson argue that one knows that one is not a BIV since one's belief is safe (it is safe because it is true at the actual world and nearby possible worlds). But, plausibly, if one's belief that one is not a BIV is safe, then this has always been the case. Indeed, DeRose (2000) explicitly denies that the anti-sceptic need develop a 'heroic' response which provides first-time knowledge that sceptical hypotheses are false, and instead recommends a 'non-heroic' response which attempts 'not to show how to gain knowledge in the face of the sceptical argument, but rather to show how the sceptical argument never worked in the first place' (p.129).

It seems, then, that an adequate response to the sceptic need not provide first-time warrant to believe that one is not a BIV, or strengthen one's warrant to believe that claim. This initially suggests that even if the BIV inference cannot provide first-time warrant to believe its conclusion, nor strengthen one's warrant to believe the conclusion, this is no objection to the idea that, as part of an anti-sceptical response, one can argue that one has warrant to believe that one is not a BIV via the BIV-inference. However, in fact matters are more complex for, as I'll now argue, if the BIV inference can neither provide first-time warrant nor strengthen one's warrant to believe the conclusion, this may prevent the inference from meeting a certain desideratum for an adequate reply to the sceptic, namely that it provide an account of how one has warrant to believe that one is not a BIV.

The sceptic claims that one lacks warrant to believe various ordinary claims since, she says, one lacks warrant to believe that one is not a BIV. Given this, an anti-sceptical reply would not be adequate if it merely asserted that one does have such warrant. Rather, an adequate response should provide an account of how one has warrant to believe. The analogous point about knowledge is widely accepted: an adequate reply to the sceptic should provide an account of how one has knowledge, rather than merely asserting that one has knowledge (e.g. Stroud 1984, ch. 3). Even though the examples of relevant alternatives and safety-based views considered above are not best thought of as providing first-time knowledge that one is not a BIV, they do provide an account of how one knows that one is not a BIV. However, I'll now argue that, if the BIV inference neither provides first-time warrant nor strengthens one's warrant to believe the conclusion, then it cannot provide an account of how one has warrant to believe that conclusion.

Suppose that the BIV inference cannot provide first-time warrant to believe that one is not a BIV for Wright-style reasons, namely, that one has warrant to believe the premise that one has hands only if one has prior and independent warrant to believe that one is not a BIV. On this view, one can provide an account of how one has warrant to believe the premises of the inference only by providing an account of how one has warrant to believe that one is not a BIV independent of the inference. This would be compatible with the BIV inference playing a non-redundant role in the account of how one has warrant to believe that one is not a BIV if it could at least strengthen one's prior and independent warrant to believe that one is not a BIV. Earlier we saw that it is unclear whether an argument that cannot provide first-time warrant to believe its conclusion can strengthen one's warrant to believe its conclusion. Wright's main claim is that the BIV inference cannot provide first-time warrant to believe its conclusion. It is not obvious whether it follows from this that the BIV inference cannot strengthen one's warrant to believe its conclusion. Still, it seems that Wright holds that the BIV inference cannot strengthen one's warrant to believe its conclusion. If the BIV inference can neither provide first-time warrant to believe its conclusion, nor strengthen one's warrant to believe its conclusion, it seems to follow that the inference cannot play a non-redundant part in an account of how one has warrant to believe that one is not a BIV. For one could show how one has warrant to believe its premises only by providing an account of how one has warrant to believe that one is not a BIV which is independent of the inference. Further, even if one had such an account, the inference would not strengthen one's warrant to believe that one is not a BIV.

It seems, then, that the question of whether the BIV inference can be used as part of a response to the sceptic is rather more complex than initially appeared. While the BIV inference cannot rationally overcome doubt about its conclusion, an adequate response to scepticism need not answer the sceptic's doubts. Wright claims that the BIV inference cannot provide first-time warrant to believe its conclusion. By itself, this claim does not undermine the use of the BIV inference in a reply to the sceptic. For, an adequate response to the sceptic is not required to provide first-time warrant to believe that one is not a BIV. Further, if the BIV inference's inability to provide first-time warrant is compatible with its being able to strengthen one's warrant to believe that one is not a BIV, then the BIV inference may be a non-redundant part of the account of how one has warrant to believe that one is not a BIV. Wright further claims that the BIV inference cannot strengthen one's warrant to believe that one is not a BIV. If Wright is correct in thinking that the BIV inference can neither provide first-time warrant, nor strengthen one's warrant to believe the conclusion, then this would undermine the use of the BIV inference in a reply to the sceptic. This is not because an adequate response to the sceptic need strengthen one's warrant to believe that one is not a BIV or provide first-time warrant to believe it; an adequate response need do neither. However, an adequate response should provide an account of how one has warrant to believe that one is not a BIV. I have argued that if the BIV inference can neither provide first-time warrant to believe that one is not a BIV, nor strengthen one's warrant to believe that one is not a BIV, then it is redundant in an account of how one has warrant to believe that one is not a BIV.

5. Conclusion

A Moorean style response to the sceptic employs what I have called the BIV inference, BIV1) I have hands, and BIV2) If I have hands, then I am not a BIV, so BIV3) I am not a BIV. Davies and Wright argue that this style of reply to the sceptic is unsatisfactory because warrant fails to transmit across the BIV inference. In more detail, they claim that the BIV inference cannot rationally overcome doubt about its conclusion and cannot strengthen one's warrant to believe its conclusion. For the purposes of this paper, I have assumed with Davies and Wright that the BIV inference can neither rationally overcome doubt about its conclusion, nor strengthen one's warrant to believe its conclusion, and examined the consequences of this assumption for the use of the BIV inference in a reply to the sceptic. I have argued that even if the BIV inference cannot rationally overcome doubt about its conclusion, on an influential and plausible view, an adequate response to the sceptic is not required to answer sceptical doubts. So, this first motivation provides no reason to think that the BIV inference cannot be used as part of an adequate response to scepticism. Wright argues that the BIV inference cannot provide first-time warrant to believe the conclusion. By itself, this does not undermine the use of the BIV inference in a reply to the sceptic. For, an adequate response to the sceptic is not required to provide first-time warrant to believe that one is not a BIV. Further, if the inference's inability to provide first-time warrant is compatible with its being able to strengthen one's warrant to believe that one is not a BIV, then it may be a non-redundant part of the account of how one has warrant to believe that one is not a BIV. Wright further claims that the BIV inference cannot strengthen one's warrant to believe that one is not a BIV. If Wright is correct in thinking that the BIV inference can neither provide first-time warrant, nor strengthen one's warrant to believe the conclusion, then this would undermine the use of the BIV inference in a reply to the sceptic. However, the reason for this is not immediately apparent. An adequate response to the sceptic need not strengthen one's warrant to believe that one is not a BIV, nor provide first-time warrant to believe that. However, an adequate reply to the sceptic should provide an account of how one has warrant to believe that one is not a BIV.

I have argued that if the BIV inference can neither provide first-time warrant to believe that one is not a BIV, nor strengthen one's warrant to believe that one is not a BIV, then it is redundant in an account of how one has warrant to believe that one is not a BIV.[9]

Notes

1. See especially Davies 2004.
2. Pryor (2004) argues that the inference can yield warrant to believe the conclusion, whereas Sillins (forthcoming) argues that it can yield warranted belief in the conclusion.
3. Williamson (2000) and Hawthorne (2004) seem to define 'closure' to mean roughly what Davies and Wright mean by 'transmission'. Pryor (2004) defines transmission in terms of the notion of warrant to believe whereas Sillins (forthcoming) defines it in terms of the notion of warranted belief.
4. An argument of form [A, (if A then B), B] fits the disjunctive template if 1) A entails B; 2) there is a proposition C incompatible with A; 3) my warrant for A consists in my being in a state which is subjectively indistinguishable from a state in which C would be true; 4) C would be true if B were false (Wright 2000: 155). The BIV inference fits Wright's template with A = I have hands; B = I am not a BIV; and C = I am a BIV. In particular, condition iii) holds: what initially seems to warrant claim A (I have hands) is my experience as of hands, but I could be in an indistinguishable state were C true: I am a BIV.
5. Cohen (1999) considers the view that one has evidential warrant for BIV1) only if one has prior and independent non-evidential entitlement for BIV3). Interestingly, he suggests that even though the prior entitlement for the conclusion is not sufficient for knowledge of it, the warrant yielded by the inference is so sufficient. This suggests that, at least in that paper, Cohen was tempted by the view that an inference could satisfy A but not FT-transmission. However, Cohen has not defended this view in his later papers.
6. McLaughlin (2003) objects that Wright's view has the result that warrant fails to transmit across an absurdly wide class of arguments. Sillins (forthcoming) argues that arguments meeting the disjunctive template can provide first-time warranted belief in the conclusion.
7. In commenting on Moore's famous proof of the external world, Davies says that 'anyone sane who doubted the conclusion Moore(3), [An external world exists] would have background beliefs relative to which the perceptual evidence for Moore(1) [Here is one hand and here is another] that is offered for borrowing would be no evidence' (2000: 401). Wright argues that 'a transmissible warrant should make for the possible advancement of knowledge, or warranted belief and the overcoming of doubt or agnosticism' (2003: 331–32).
8. My focus is on warrant to believe, not warranted belief. However the strongest anti-sceptical reply would not only show that, all along, one had warrant to believe that one is not a BIV but also that, all along, one's belief that one is not a

BIV constituted a warranted belief. If a reply to the sceptic provided warranted belief for the first time then, prior to that reply being given or for those ignorant of the reply, one lacked warranted belief that one is not a BIV. Assuming that knowledge requires warranted belief, one also lacked knowledge that one is not a BIV.

9. I have given versions of this paper at a number of places including Bristol, Glasgow, Oxford and Stirling. Thanks to audiences on these occasions for their useful comments. Thanks too to Duncan Pritchard for helpful comments on an earlier draft.

References

Beebee, Helen. 2001. 'Transfer of Warrant, Begging the Question and Semantic Externalism.' *Philosophical Quarterly* 51: 356–74.

Brown, Jessica. 2003. 'The Reductio Argument and the Transmission of Warrant.' In Nuccetelli 2003.

Cohen, Stewart. 1988. 'How to be a Fallibilist.' *Philosophical Perspectives* 2: 91–123.

——— 1999. 'Contextualism, Scepticism, and the Structure of Reasons.' *Philosophical Perspectives* 13: 57–89.

Davies, Martin. 1998. 'Externalism, Architecturalism, and Epistemic Warrant.' In Wright, C., Smith, B.C., and Macdonald, C. (eds.) *Knowing Our Own Minds*, OUP, Oxford, 1998, 321–61.

——— 2000. 'Externalism and A Priori Knowledge.' In Boghossian, P. and Peacocke, C. (eds.), *New Essays on the A Priori*, OUP, Oxford, 2000, 384–432.

——— 2003. 'The Problem of Armchair Knowledge.' In Nuccetelli 2003, 23–57.

——— 2004. 'On Epistemic Entitlement; Epistemic Entitlement, Warrant-Transmission and Easy-Knowledge.' *Proceedings of the Aristotelian Society*: 213–245.

DeRose, Keith. 1995. 'Solving the Sceptical Problem.' *Philosophical Review* 104: 1–52.

——— 2000. 'How Do We Know We're Not Brains in a Vat?' *Spindel Supplement to the Southern Journal of Philosophy* XXXVIII: 121–48.

Dretske, Fred. 1970. 'Epistemic Operators.' *Journal of Philosophy* 67: 1007–23.

Jackson, Frank. 1987. *Conditionals*. Blackwell: Oxford.

Hawthorne, John. 2004. *Knowledge and Lotteries*, OUP: Oxford.

McLaughlin, Brian. 2003. 'McKinsey's Challenge, Warrant Transmission, and Scepticism.' In Nuccetelli 2003: 79–96.

Nozick, Robert. 1981. *Philosophical Explanations*. OUP: Oxford.

Nuccetelli, Susana (ed.). 2003. *New Essays on Semantic Externalism, Scepticism, and Self-Knowledge*. MIT Press: Mass.

Pryor, James. 2004. 'Is Moore's Argument an Example of Transmission Failure?' *Philosophical Perspectives* 18.

Sillins, Nicholas. Forthcoming. 'Transmission Failure Failure'. *Philosophical Studies*.

Sosa, Ernest. 1999. 'How to Defeat Opposition to Moore.' *Philosophical Perspectives* 13: 141–54.

Stine, Gail. 1976. 'Scepticism, Relevant Alternatives and Deductive Closure.' *Philosophical Studies* 29.

Stroud, Barry. 1984. *The Significance of Philosophical Scepticism*. OUP: Oxford.

Williamson, Timothy. 2000. 'Scepticism and Evidence.' *Philosophy and Phenomenological Research* 60: 613–28.

Wright, Crispin. 2000. 'Cogency and Question-Begging: Some Reflections on McKinsey's Paradox, and Putnam's Proof.' *Philosophical Issues* 10: 140–63.

——— 2002. 'Anti-Sceptics Simple and Subtle: Moore and McDowell.' *Philosophy and Phenomenological Research* LXV: 330–48.

——— 2003. 'Some Reflections on the Acquisition of Warrant by Inference.' In Nuccetelli 2003: 57–78.

——— 2004. 'On Epistemic Entitlement; Warrant for Nothing (and Foundations for Free?)' *Proceedings of the Aristotelian Society*: 167–212

Philosophical Perspectives, 19, Epistemology, 2005

PLURALISTIC SKEPTICISM: ADVERTISEMENT FOR SPEECH ACT PLURALISM

Herman Cappelen
University of Oslo

Even though the lines of thought that support skepticism are extremely compelling, we're inclined to look for ways of blocking them because it appears to be an impossible view to accept, both for intellectual and practical reasons. One goal of this paper is to show that when skepticism is packaged right, it has few problematic implications (or at least fewer than is often assumed). It is, for example, compatible with all the following claims (when these are correctly interpreted):

- We can say something true by uttering sentences of the form "S knows that p"; that is, our ordinary, reflective, intuitions about the truth-value of knowledge attributions can be respected.
- The beliefs expressed by utterances of sentences of the form "S knows that p" can be true.
- Knowledge is the norm of assertion.

Skepticism is compatible with these claims when combined with a view I call *Speech Act Pluralism*. Speech Act Pluralism is a theory about the content of speech acts—it's a general theory about the relationship between semantic content and speech act content. It's motivated by considerations that have nothing specifically to do with skepticism or epistemology. In other words, this is not an *ad hoc* solution to problems involved in accepting skepticism. It is, rather, a theory that anyone who thinks about the nature of linguistic content should adopt. It just so happens that it lends support to skepticism.

A wide range of philosophical arguments in all areas of philosophy appeal to the intuitions that competent speakers have about the content of sentences, what's said by utterances of sentences, and the truth-conditions of such utterances. Proponents of Speech Act Pluralism claim that many such arguments are fundamentally flawed because they are based on mistaken assumptions about the nature of speech act content (i.e. the nature of what's said, asserted, claimed, etc by utterances) and the relation between speech act content and semantic content. Much work done in epistemology (especially the debates that focus on the semantics for "know") provides a good illustration of this contention. Many of the central arguments against skepticism appeal to intuitions we allegedly have about what's said and asserted by utterances of knowledge attributions. If Speech Act Pluralism is correct, these arguments uniformly fail.

There's a lot that I'm not doing. In particular:

- **I don't** provide new arguments for skepticism—I take familiar skeptical arguments at face value, i.e. as showing that skepticism is true. I then defend that view from various objections. Of course, indirectly, this is an argument for skepticism because if I'm right, some of the central obstacles to accepting skepticism are removed.
- **I don't** present direct arguments against alternative semantics for "know". In particular, I don't present all the data that show that "know" is not a context sensitive term.[1] However, indirectly I provide an argument against contextualism because if I'm right, all the evidence that's alleged to support contextualism is better explained by my version of skepticism.
- **I don't** defend Speech Act Pluralism. I present the view, provide some illustrations, and refer the reader to the various places where the arguments for it are developed in greater detail. The goal here is to illustrate the philosophical significance and usefulness of Speech Act Pluralism, not to present all the arguments for it.

The paper has three parts. Part One presents Pluralistic Skepticism in more detail. Part Two shows how it can account for speakers intuitions about sentences containing "know". Part Three is about the relationship between Pluralistic Skepticism and the knowledge account of assertion.

1. Pluralistic Skepticism

Pluralistic Skepticism (PS) has three central components:

a. Semantic invariantism: the view that the semantic value of "know" is invariant between contexts of utterance.
b. Skepticism: the view that it is extremely hard to know anything. The semantic content of utterances of sentences of the form "S knows that p" are almost never true. We don't know most of what we take ourselves to know. We stand in the knowledge relation to few, if any, propositions.
c. Speech Act Pluralism: the view that in uttering a sentence one (literally) asserts indefinitely many propositions (only one of which is the proposition semantically expressed.) As a result, it doesn't follow from a. and b.

that one can't (literally) say something true by uttering a sentence of the form "A knows that p".

Before I present this view in more detail, I'll give a brief overview of how it is related to some other positions one might hold about the semantics for "know".

First, PS is opposed to ***traditional versions of skepticism***[2]. According to this view, skeptical arguments reveal that what's literally said by utterances of sentences of the form "A knows that p" is always (or almost always) false. Our intuitions to the effect that such utterances are true are explained away either as a mistake (i.e. as the result of being mistaken about how hard it is to obtain knowledge) or as the result of confusing warranted assertability with true assertion (i.e. confusing the truth of an assertion with its warranted assertability.)

It is the (c) component of PS that distinguishes PS from this kind of skepticism. According to PS, our intuitions about the truth-value of utterances of sentences (relative to circumstances of evaluations) are intuitions about what's saliently asserted by those utterances. When what's saliently asserted by an utterance of "S knows that p" is not the proposition semantically expressed (and typically it isn't), we will have the *correct* intuition that this utterance said something true (even though the semantic content is false.)

Second, PS is opposed to ***contextualism*** about "know".[3] According to contextualists, the semantic value of "know" shifts from one context of utterance to another—know belongs in the same semantic category as "she", "that", and "you". The primary motivation for contextualism is the kinds of intuitions we have about variability of what's said (and the truth-values of what's said) by utterances of knowledge attributions. According to PS this is best explained, not as semantic variability, but by variability in what's saliently asserted from one context of utterance to another (and from one context of interpretation to another.)

Third, PS is opposed to various versions of ***non-skeptical invariantism***[4]. The non-skeptical invariantists agree with PS that the semantic value of "know" is invariant between contexts of utterance. They differ from PS'ists in claiming that the semantic content of utterances of "S knows that p" is true (in (most of) the cases where we intuitively think it is true). The non-skeptical invariantists try to find a stable semantic value for "know" that doesn't make all knowledge attributions false. They do that (at least in part) because they try to respect our intuitions about what speakers say (and the truth-value of what they say) when they utter sentences containing "know". Again, this is, according to PS, a mistaken strategy—it is an attempt to give a semantic account of variability in speech act content.[5]

Note that there is something the last two opponents of PS agree on: there is data about our intuitions about what's said by utterances of knowledge attributions that it seems difficult for a skeptic to account for. That's one reason why both the contextualist and non-skeptical invariantist go to great lengths fixing up the semantic value of 'know' (the former by making it context sensitive, the latter by making it, for example, *subject sensitive*.). A central thesis of this paper is that the contextualist and the non-skeptical invariantist make the same mistake: they try to account for variability in speech act content by tinkering with the semantics.

Before showing how PS deals with the kind of data that makes contextualists and non-skeptical invariantists opposed to skepticism, I need to say a bit more about two components the version of skepticism I'm defending: the skepticism part and the speech act pluralism part.

1.1. Skepticism

The arguments for skepticism are familiar, but two points are important to emphasize in order to prepare the defense of PS: the effects of skeptical arguments and the relationship between skepticism and semantic competence. I discuss these in turn.

The Effects of Arguments for Skepticism

One way to think about skepticism is as the view that the semantic value of "know" is such that extremely high standards must be met in order for the proposition semantically expressed by a positive knowledge ascription to be true. According to this view, the propositions semantically expressed by all (or almost all[6]) utterances of sentences of the form "A knows that p" are false. The arguments for this are old and familiar; they typically involve evil demons, brains in vats, or so-called lottery propositions. Here's an illustration of the latter:

> I think I know that there's a computer in my office at the University of Oslo. However, when I ask myself (sitting at home) whether I know that no one has broken into my office the last 20 minutes and stolen my computer, I'm inclined to say that I don't know. UiO is a relatively safe campus, but burglaries do happen, and I can't rule out that today I was the unlucky one. This leads me to think that I don't stand in the knowledge relation to the proposition *that no one has broken into my office in the last 20 min and stolen my computer* (call this proposition 'the lottery proposition') The proposition that I know that there's a computer in my office, entails the lottery proposition. Realization that I don't know the lottery proposition leads me towards the conclusion that I don't know what I thought I knew, (that there's a computer in my office).

Two points about this kind of argument are important for what follows:

a. Skeptical arguments of this kind intuitively *generalize* in three important ways:
   i. They make me conclude not just that I don't know that there's a computer in my office (right now), but more generally, that I know very little of what I though I knew. As Hawthorne puts it: "These considerations generate a powerful pressure towards a skepticism that claims that we know little of what we ordinarily claim to know. For when confronted with the data, we philosophers feel a strong inclination to stick to our judgment about the lottery proposition and retract our original judgment about the ordinary proposition" (Hawthorne, (2004), p. 6)[7]
   ii. They make me draw conclusions about my epistemic state *at other times*. I don't just conclude that I know very little *now*—I conclude that I *never* did.
   iii. Finally, they make me conclude that *others* who claim that I have knowledge are wrong. I don't draw conclusions just about my own self-ascriptions—anyone who says about me that I know that p (where p is one the propositions I now have figured out that I don't know) is wrong.
b. Skeptical arguments are accompanied by a sense of *discovery*—by a sense of having understood something new about our epistemic condition. A theory of knowledge should account for this sense of discovery that accompanies skeptical arguments. Below I argue (what might seem obvious) that no non-skeptic theory can do that.

I take (a) and (b) to be data about the effects skeptical arguments have on people when they first encounter them. An adequate theory should explain why those arguments have those effects and that can be done in one of two way: either explain these reactions away as some sort of confusion, or take them at face value and adjust your theory of knowledge accordingly. The skeptic pursues the latter option.

Skepticism and Understanding of "know"

According to PS, non-philosophical speakers *don't* know that skepticism is true—it is not a necessary condition on understanding "know" that speakers know that the semantic content of utterances of sentences containing "know" typically are false. That's something they find out by thinking about philosophical arguments. This is connected to point (b) above: Skeptical arguments wouldn't be accompanied by a sense of discovery if linguistic competence with "know" required knowledge of the truth of skepticism.

This is not a surprising feature of the verb "know". For any term F, there will be important truths of the form *something is F just in case G*, knowledge of which is *not* required for understanding F. An analogy might clarify this point:

there are no doubt many truths of the form *A loves B only if* ... knowledge of which are not required in order to understand and be a competent user of the term "love". No sensible semanticist would assume that the semantics for English must include all such truths—the semantics for English will not include a theory of love (or, for that matter, of power or justice.) And that's fortunate, for if it did, none of us would be competent English speakers. The same goes for "know": you don't need to know a theory of knowledge in order to understand English—in particular, you don't need to know that skepticism is true.[8] [9]

1.2. Speech Act Pluralism (SPAP)

The most distinctive part of PS (what distinguishes it from other versions of skepticism) is that it incorporates Speech Act Pluralism (SPAP). SPAP is not a view that most philosophers are familiar with, so I need to go into some detail to present its main components. As mentioned above I will not present detailed arguments for the view here.[10] Instead, I'll present three components of SPAP that will be of importance in explaining how PS accounts for allegedly anti-skeptical data.

SPAP Elaboration 1: Pluralism

SPAP is the view *that any utterance of a sentence S in a context C says (asserts, claims) many propositions other than the semantic content of S relative to C.* An important corollary is *that it is not the case that if an utterance of S in a context C says (asserts, claims) that p, then p is the semantic content of S relative to C.*
Two Illustrations:

Illustration #1: The Dresser (from Cappelen and Lepore (1997)):
Imagine an utterance of (3).

3. A: At around 11 p.m., I put on a white shirt, a blue suit, dark socks and my brown Bruno Magli shoes. I then got into a waiting limousine and drove off into heavy traffic to the airport, where I just made my midnight flight to Chicago.

According to SPAP, (4)–(6) are all true descriptions of what's said by an utterance of (3) (note that 4–6 are all different propositions):

4. A said that he dressed around 11 p.m., went to the airport and took the midnight flight to Chicago.
5. A said that he dressed before he went to the airport.
6. A said that he put on some really fancy shoes before he went to the airport.

The extent to which 4–6 will seem natural will depend on the circumstance of the report, so arguments for SPAP are accompanied by small stories that describe the context for the report. Having argued that these reports are literally true (not just appropriate or warranted), SPAP proponents conclude that in uttering 3. A (literally) said the complement clause of 4–6. And that's just a tiny sample of what was said in uttering 3.

Illustration #2: The Terrorist: Here's a similar example from Scott Soames (2002): "A terrorist has planted a small nuclear device in a crowded stadium downtown. There is no time to evacuate the building or the surrounding area. In speaking to the negotiator, he says "I will detonate the bomb if my demands are not met," knowing that it is obvious that if he does so, thousands of people will die, and intending to communicate precisely that. The negotiator reports to his superior that the terrorist said that he will kill thousands of people if his demands are not met."[11]

Our intuition is that all of 7, 8–8.2 are true (these are my elaborations):

7. He says that he will kill thousands of people if his demands are not met.
8. He says that he will detonate the bomb if his demands are not met.
    8.1. He says says that he will create mayhem downtown if his demands are not met.
    8.2. He says that he will inflict great damage on our community if we don't do as he says.

Cappelen and Lepore (1997) summarizes these point as follows: "... indirect reports are sensitive to innumerable non-semantic features of reported utterances and even on the context of the report itself. As a result, typically there will be indefinitely many correct indirect reports of any particular utterance" (Cappelen and Lepore (1997), p. 291). Soames draws a related conclusion:

> [The phenomenon of many propositions being expressed by an utterance of a sentence] "... is an extremely general one that has nothing special to do with proper names, indexicals or any of the semantically contentious issues that are of special concern here. On the contrary, the phenomenon of asserting more than the semantic content of the sentence one utters in a context is all but ubiquitous. ... what an assertive utterance of a sentence s counts as asserting depends not only on the semantic content of s, but also on the obvious background assumptions in the conversation and the speaker's intention about how the speaker's remarks is to be interpreted in the light of them." (Soames, 2002 pp. 76–78)[12]

SPAP can be developed in many different ways. Two issues are particularly important for how one thinks about the semantics for "know": the various kinds of contextual variability that affects *what is said* and the role of semantic content. I discuss these in turn.

SPAP Elaboration 2: Contextual Variability of Speech Act Content

According to SPAP, three kinds of contextual variability influence speech act content:

V1 *Variability in what is asserted/said by an utterance of S from one context of utterance to another*: All versions of SPAP agree that the set of propositions asserted by an utterance of a sentence, S, can vary from one context of utterance to another. The set of propositions said and asserted by utterances of, for example "A will detonate the bomb if his demands are not met" will vary from one context to another.[13]

V2 *Variability in what is said/asserted by an utterance of S from one context of interpretation to another.* A more radical version of SPAP claims that what's said by an utterance u of a sentence S in a context of utterance C, will vary between contexts of interpretation. On this version of SPAP, what's said by utterance, u of S in C, relative to a context of interpretation C′, might be different from what's said by u relative to another context of interpretation C″. This is the view endorsed by Cappelen and Lepore (1997) and considered, but not endorsed, by Soames (2002) and Cappelen and Lepore (2005).

V3 *Variability in what is saliently said/asserted from one context of interpretation to another.* Not all proponents of SPAP agree to the kind of content relativism described in V2 above. However, all versions of SPAP would agree that what is *saliently asserted* by an utterance u (in a context of utterance C) relative to one context of interpretation CI′ might be different from what's saliently asserted by u from relative to another context of interpretation, CI″. Any version of SPAP will need a theory about why one part of the speech act content becomes salient in a context of interpretation. According to SPAP an utterance asserts many propositions. One (maybe several) of these will be more salient than the others to the speaker and interpreter. Whether or not a SPAP proponent accepts V2, she will accept the view that the saliently asserted proposition might vary from one context of interpretation to another.

One of the main objections to skepticism is that it can't account for intuitions we have about what speakers say and the ways these intuitions vary between contexts of utterance. In responding to those kinds of objections appeals to V1-V3 will prove useful (more about that below).

SPAP Elaboration 3: Role of Semantic Content

According to some versions of SPAP, any utterance of a sentence S says/asserts the semantic content of S (even though that proposition might not be saliently asserted relative to all contexts of interpretation). According to other versions of SPAP, this is not the case—there are utterances of S that do not assert the semantic content of S. In what follows, I'll assume that the semantic content is *always* asserted.

Summary: SPAP and "know"

Applied to sentences of the form "S knows that p" these three elaborations of SPAP have the following implications. Let u be an utterance of a sentence of the form "S knows that p" in a context of utterance C. According to PS:

a) One proposition said/asserted by u is the proposition semantically expressed (call this proposition p). p is false (that's the implication of endorsing skepticism).
b) u might assert many propositions, $p_1 \ldots p_n$ in addition to p.
c) If you endorse V2 above, $p_1 \ldots p_n$ will vary with the context of interpretation: i.e. interpreted from context of interpretation CI the set of propositions asserted by u might be different from the set of propositions asserted relative to another context of interpretation, CI*.
d) Even for those who don't endorse V2 above, it follows from V3 that the *salient* component of the speech act content will vary from one context of interpretation to another, i.e. which one of $p \ldots p_n$ is salient will depend on the context u is interpreted from.

I've gone into this much detail about the SPAP component of PS because it is an unfamiliar view and because it is at the center of the defense of skepticism presented below. In what follows, I first respond to the charge that skepticism implies some kind of error theory about intuitions about the semantic content of our views. In the last part of the paper I respond to the charge that skepticism is incompatible with the knowledge account of assertion.

2. Pluralistic Skepticism, Linguistic Intuitions, and Contextual Variability

Our linguistic behavior, our intuitions about what speakers say and our intuitions about the truth-value of what they say seem to be sensitive to contextually variable features in a way that might seem difficult for a skeptic to explain. Derose says:

> "In some contexts, "S knows that P" requires that S have a true belief that P and also be in a very strong epistemic position with respect to P, while in other contexts, the same sentence may require for its truth, in addition to S's having a true belief that P, only that S meet some lower epistemic standards" (Derose (2001), p. 182).

What makes for this difference? In the examples favored by the contextualist it is various practical factors (such as what is practically *at stake*) that vary between contexts of utterance. In other words, this sensitivity to contextual standards is not just brought out when thinking about skeptical possibilities—it is not just when speakers are in philosophical contexts that their standards shift. As Derose points out:

> "To make the relevant intuitions as strong as possible, the contextualist will choose a "high standards" case that is not as ethereal as a typical philosophical discussion of radical skepticism ... it makes the relevant intuitions more stable if the introduction of the more moderate skeptical hypothesis and the resulting raise in epistemic standards are tied to a very practical concern, and thus seem reasonable given the situation." (Derose (2002), p. 191.)

There are two kinds of variability that the skeptic is asked to account for:

i. Let S be the sentence "A knows that p (at t)", and let u and u' be two utterance of S in C1 and C2, respectively. Let C1 be a so-called *low standard context* and C2 a *high standard context*. According to the contextualist our intuitions about the truth-values of u and u′ might differ. We can, for example, have the intuition that u is true while u′ is false. This can't be explained by a change in A's epistemic position (both utterances are about A at time t). The relevant difference, according to the contextualist, can be found in the attributors' practical situation. The only relevant difference between the contexts might be, for example, that the speakers have different practical concerns, no philosophizing or strange skeptical possibilities need enter into the story.
ii. Our intuitions about *what is said* by utterances u′ and u′ of S can varies (let S, u and u′ be as in (i) above). Our intuition might tell us that u′ says *that S has a true belief that p and is in a very strong epistemic position with respect to p*, while u says *that S has a true belief that p and is in a less strong epistemic position with respect to p*[14]. Again, the only difference between the contexts is that the speakers have different practical concerns.

The problem for the skeptic is supposed to be this: If the semantic content of "know" invokes a super-high standard and this is invariant between contexts of utterance, the skeptical invariantist will be unable to explain these kinds of variability. And, it is assumed, these are the kinds of intuitions that a semantic theory for English *should* account for.

2.1. Reply: How PS Deals with Contextual Variability

Not only can PS easily explain this kind of data, but it can do so better than any alternative theory. The assumption has been that the skeptic has to say that these intuitions are, somehow, *mistaken*, i.e. has to defend some kind of large-scale error theory about speakers' intuitions. A skeptic who endorses PS, however, is not committed to an error theory. According to PS, we assert many different propositions when we utter sentences of the form "A knows that p". We do not just assert the proposition semantically expressed. So a proponent of PS will hold that some of the propositions asserted (said, claimed, etc) by an utterance of a positive knowledge attribution can be true even though the proposition semantically expressed is false. She will also hold that the totality of asserted propositions can vary from one context of utterance to another, and from one context of interpretation to another. So there are plenty of resources in PS to account for the kind of variability appealed to by contextualists. PS, by virtue of incorporating SPAP, predicts exactly this kind of variability.

Before going into more detail about how PS accounts for (i) and (ii), one important methodological remark: if SPAP is correct, it's a dangerous simplification to talk simply about *the intuitions we have about what's said by an utterance u in a context C* (or about *our intuitions about the truth-value of what was said by an utterance u in a context C.*) All such intuitions must be *relativized* to a context of interpretation. We should always talk about our intuitions about u *from a context of interpretation C.* Not doing so gives the impression there's some neutral and (possibly) privileged semanticist's point of view from which we can have intuitions about utterances. If SPAP is correct, there is no such privileged standpoint.

To see how PS deals with these kinds of cases, I distinguish (as the contextualist does) between three kinds of epistemic standards that can be invoked: *low-standards* (LS), *ordinary-high standards* (OHS) (not the super-high philosophical standards, but the kinds of standards that, according to contextualists, are invoked by raising ordinary non-philosophical/practical stakes), and *Super-High Standards* (SHS) (the kinds of standards triggered by skeptical arguments.)

The challenge is to explain why our intuitions vary between contexts in the way described by (i) and (ii). Here are some schematic explanations, using the resources of PS—in all the cases below let S be the sentence "k knows that p (at time t)".

- *Intuitions about utterances in LS-context of utterance from LS-context of Interpretation*: Let u be an utterance of S by A in an LS-context C. Assume B interprets u from a similarly LS context of interpretation C′. Suppose B has the intuition that what A said in uttering u was true. PS will explain this as follows. Relative to C′, A saliently asserted a proposition that's true. We can assume, for example, that relative to C′, A asserted the proposition *that k knows that p relative to a low standard.*[15] This proposition is true. Of course, in uttering u the speaker also asserted the proposition semantically expressed (and it is false), but it was not saliently asserted relative to C′ so it does not affect our intuitions about u from C′.
- *Intuitions about utterances in OHS-contexts from OHS-contexts of interpretation*: Let u be an utterance of S by A in a OHS-context of utterance.

B interprets u from a similarly OHS-context of interpretation, C′. Suppose that B has the intuition that what A said in uttering u was false. PS-Explanation: relative to C′, A saliently asserted a proposition that's false. For example, relative to C′, A asserted the proposition *that k knows that p relative to an ordinary high (but not super-high) standard.* This proposition is false. Of course, in uttering u the speaker also asserted the proposition semantically expressed, but it is not saliently asserted relative to C′ and it is not the proposition our intuitions track.

- *Intuitions about any utterance from a SHS-Context of interpretation*: let u be an utterance of S by A in *any* kind of context (low, ordinary-high or super-high). If B interprets u from a SHS context of interpretation C′, she'll have the intuition that what S said in uttering u was false. PS-explanation: In a SHS Context of interpretation it is the proposition semantically expressed that's salient, and this proposition is false. Super-high standards make us focus on the proposition semantically expressed (and this proposition is expressed by *all* utterance of positive knowledge attributions from all contexts of interpretation.) In SHS Contexts, the proposition semantically expressed by all utterances of all sentences of the form "S knows that p" is salient. That is why skeptical arguments generalize as described in section 1.1 above.

In general, the strategy is this: if an informed observer in a context of interpretation CI has an intuition to the effect that an utterance u (by A of sentence S in a context of utterance C) said something true (or false), we should take that as evidence that A in uttering u in C saliently asserted a proposition that's true relative to CI.

PS and Warranted Assertability Maneuvers

Derose and Stanley[16] assume that someone who denies the semantic import of the kinds of intuitions discussed above will have to appeal to what Derose calls a *warranted-assertability maneuver (WAM)*. Here's what Derose says about WAMs:

> "Such a maneuver involves explaining why an assertion can seem false (or at least not true) in certain circumstances in which it is in fact true by appeal to the fact that the utterance would be improper or unwarranted in the circumstances in question. Going the other way, an intuition that an assertion is true can be explained away by means of the claim that the assertion, while false, is warranted, and we mistake this warranted assertability for truth." (Derose (1999), p. 201)

Derose argues that misuse of such maneuvers will make semantics impossible:

> "It's an instance of a general scheme that, if allowed, could be used to far too easily explain away the counterexamples marshaled against any theory about the truth conditions of sentence forms in natural language. Whenever you face an apparent counterexample—where your theory says that what seems false is true, or when it says that what seems true is false—you can very easily just ascribe the apparent truth (falsehood) to the warranted (unwarranted) assertability of the sentence in the circumstances problematic to your theory. If we allow such maneuvers, we'll completely lose our ability to profitably test theories against examples. By undermining the data for semantic theory, this kind of strategy threatens to undermine the semantic project." (1999, p. 198)[17]

The essence of what Derose calls a 'WAM' is an appeal to the distinction between, on the one hand, *being warranted in asserting p* (even though p isn't true) and on the other hand, *truly asserting that p*. It should be clear by now that PS does not appeal to any such maneuver: according to PS something true has been said and asserted, for example, in the low standard context of utterance (from the point of view of a low standard context of interpertation.) Something false has been saliently asserted in the high standard context (from the point of view of a high standard context). Our intuitions to the effect that something true has been (literally) said and asserted are correct. PS does not explain away these intuitions as somehow erroneous (that is, as confusing warranted assertability with true assertions).

As a result, none of the objections contextualists and non-skeptical invariantists run against WAMs apply to PS. In order to respond to PS, one would have to refute SPAP as a general account of the relationship between speech act content and semantic content, not just as applied to knowledge ascriptions.

From the point of view of someone who accepts SPAP, the threat to semantic theory comes from the other direction: if you think of your task as that of accounting for our intuitions about what's asserted/said within a semantic theory, semantics will be impossible. You will, for example, find we have intuitions about what is said by utterances of sentences containing "know" that can't be part of the stable semantic content of "know", and isn't an implicature (since it is part of what was strictly, literally said); you're left trying out various tortured strategies for creating semantics that can accommodate these variable intuitions (hence the attempt to make "know" context sensitive or subject sensitive).

Context Sensitivity Only PS can Account For

Not only can PS account for all of our context shifting intuitions, but it can do so better than any of the competing theories. PS predict that there is more contextual variability in our intuitions about what is said than contextualism or non-skeptical invariantists predict. Here is the kind of case I have in mind: Consider an utterance, u, of "I know that p" by A in a context of utterance, C.

PS predicts that there could be a context of interpretation C′ in which an utterance u′ of "That's true" is true (where 'that' demonstrates u), and another utterance u″, in another context of interpretation C″, in which "That's true" is false. This would happen if what u saliently said/asserted relative to C′ is different from what u saliently asserted relative to C′. Intuitively, there are such cases. Let, for example, C be a LS-context of utterance, let C′ be LS-context of interpretation and let C′ be a SHS-context of interpretation. In such a case, our intuitions tell us that u′ is true and u″ is false.

Notice that these are cases where the speakers in C′ and C″ don't even utter the verb "know". The speakers simply demonstrate what was said by the utterance of S in C. As a result, no fancy semantic footwork of the kind contextualists and non-skeptical invariantists like to engage in will do any explanatory work (because that is all about the semantics for "know"). Theories that do not endorse SPAP will have to develop some kind of error theory for these cases. I take it to be an advantage of PS that it provides an explanation without appeal to error.[18]

Summary: PS and The Explanation of Intuitions about Content

I conclude that PS can explain the intuitions about content that motivate some non-skeptical theories. It is, contrary to what's often assumed, the non-skeptical theories that are in need of an error theory about speakers' intuitions and this is so for two reasons:

1. Non-skeptical theories have a hard time explaining the reaction that speakers have to skeptical arguments. In particular, they have a hard time accounting for how such arguments generalize (see section 1.1 above) and how they give rise to a sense of discovery.
2. Non-skeptical theories can't account for the context sensitivity that arises as a result of relativization to contexts of interpretation. They try to explain our intuitions about variability in what is said within the semantics (that, after all, is the motivation for these theories). Semantic values are not relativized to contexts of interpretation. So the alternatives to PS will have to find some way to explain why the intuitions that indicate variability from one context of interpretation to another are wrong.

2.2. Some Follow up Questions to the Reply

In the light of this reply, some additional questions naturally arise. I address three of these below—the replies also serve to elaborate on how PS explains linguistic usage.

Follow up Question #1: How is Speech Act Content Generated?

It is easy to say that speech act contents are generated in context and relativized to contexts of interpretation—but does PS come with an account of *how* they are generated in context and how one part of the speech act content becomes salient in a context of interpretation?

Reply

In short, the answer is "No". SPAP doesn't come with a general theory of how speech act content is generated and how it varies between contexts of interpretations and contexts of utterance. I'm inclined towards the view that there might not be a theory that for every context, C and context of interpretation C′ predicts what an utterance of an arbitrary sentence S in C will say (or assert or claim) relative to C′ (see chapter 13 Cappelen and Lepore (2005).)

Even if that turns out to be wrong, I don't think it cuts either way with respect to defending PS. To see why, distinguish between *foundational* and *descriptive* theories concerning speech act content. Suppose that we agree that certain propositions intuitively are said or asserted by an utterance relative to a context of interpretation. We can then go on to use this data to explain various other features of communication. To do so does not require that we solve the *foundational* question of *why* (or *how*) that proposition became part of the speech act content; it does not require that we specify the mechanism by means of which this proposition was said or asserted. Note that *none* of the participants in this debate has a solution to these foundational questions. Contextualists constantly talk about the standards for knowledge that "govern the truth-conditions of my use of 'knows' and its cognates", or "are in use" or are "in play" in a context.[19] So, a contextualist must come up with an account of *how* and *why* certain standards are "in play" in a certain context. As it happens, no contextualist has even attempted to present a full-fledged theory of this. They just take the idea of a standard being "in play" for granted—just as I suggest a PS'ist should do with respect to speech act content.

Suppose, however, that some genius came up with a solution to the foundational question. The contextualist would use that as an account of how a context sensitive term gets its semantic value (how an epistemic standard is contextually fixed); the proponents of non-skeptical invariantism will use it as an account of how their fancy semantic values are fixed (how the relevant practical interests are determined), and the PS proponent will use it as an account of how speech act content is generated and becomes salient. So at this stage at least, the lack of a foundational theory doesn't cut either way with respect to the debate between these competing theories.

These remarks will seem alien to those who think that semantics is in the business of explaining or accounting for speech act content. Semantics is a systematic enterprise, and if one task of semantics is to fix speech act content, there must be a systematic theory of speech act content. However, that is exactly the view you'll have to give up if you accept SPAP. Semantics is not in the business of explaining (or predicting or accounting for) speech act content of utterances (or of sentences relative to contexts[20]).

Follow-Up Question #2: Why Assert the Semantic Content?

The proposition semantically expressed by positive knowledge attributions is always false. Why do speakers assert it? Why keep it as part of the speech act content?

Reply

In some sense the reply is trivial: speakers assert the proposition semantically expressed because they can't help doing so: they are using an English sentence and they are stuck with its semantic value. In the case of positive knowledge attributions, that happens to be a proposition that is false.

At first glance, this reply will seem unsatisfactory. After all, if PS is true, speakers go around making false claims constantly—every time they utter a sentence of the form "A knows that p" one of the propositions they assert is false. This grand, collective illusion requires an explanation. How did they end up semantically expressing a proposition that's false?

But that's a peculiar question—in general we have very little idea of how a term ended up with the semantic value that it has. It is certainly not a question that semanticists have any good basis for answering. We have things to say about why the proposition is false (appeal to closure principles combined with skeptical possibilities), but that is not what's being asked for. So my sense is that this is a question a PS proponent doesn't have to answer (after all, no other semantics for "know" comes with a story about how "know" ended up having the semantic value that it has.)

Follow-Up Question #3: What's the Evidence for Semantic Content?

How do we know that "know" has such a "demanding" semantic value? What's the evidence for that?

Reply

It is important to point out that PS itself doesn't have anything particularly original or interesting to say in reply. The evidence is the reaction we have to skeptical arguments—or rather the skeptical arguments themselves. They make me think I don't know, didn't know, and that other don't know what we typically take ourselves to know. That reaction requires an explanation. The one provided by PS is that the proposition semantically expressed by PS is false. In a sense, you can take the defense of PS in this paper to be conditional: If that's how you explain our reaction to the skeptical arguments, then here's how to develop that view in such a way that it avoids some of the main reasons philosophers have for trying to avoid skepticism.

To show that the skeptical arguments are *sufficient* to establish that the semantic content of utterances of "S knows that p" are described by PS, would require a separate paper. In particular, it would require a general theory of what semantic content is and how we distinguish semantic content from other parts of speech act content. None of the main alternative to PS comes with that kind of elaborate theoretical background (contextualists, for example, do not present us with a general theory of semantic content, nor do non-skeptical invariantists). So, again, it wouldn't be fair to ask this of the skeptic.

That said, the version of SPAP I have argued for elsewhere comes with an account of semantic content that does fit skepticism particularly well. The versions of SPAP proposed in Cappelen and Lepore (1997), (2005), and Soames (2002) construes the semantic content of S as that which is asserted by all (sincere) utterances of S. It's the stable content that does not vary between contexts of utterance. This sits well with one important feature of the skeptical arguments. These arguments have *inter-contextual effects*; they make us inclined towards the view that *all* utterances of "S knows that p" say something false. It doesn't matter which context it is uttered in, who uttered it or when. If semantic content is that which is stable between contexts, it is ideally suited to provide an explanation for these inter-contextual effects.[21]

3. Knowledge and Assertion

I turn now to two arguments to the effect that there is a tension between skepticism and the *Knowledge Account of Assertion* (KA). In response, I show how KA must be modified in light of SPAP, and how, when properly formulated, there's no such tension.

3.1. Hawthorne and Derose on KA and Skepticism

According to John Hawthorne, if the knowledge account of assertion is true, skepticism ends up being weakly self-defeating. A theory is *weakly self-defeating* it if follows from that theory that the theory itself should not be asserted. According to the *knowledge account of assertion*, knowledge is the norm of assertion. On Williamson's formulation[22]:

KA: You must: assert p only if you know p

If skepticism is true, we know nothing, so should assert nothing. In particular, we should not assert PS (PS is weakly self-defeating).

Keith Derose has argued, from a different direction, that the Knowledge Account of Assertion yields contextualism about "know", i.e. that it is incompatible with invariantism. He says:

> "The knowledge account of assertion provides a powerful argument for contextualism: If the standards for when one is in a position to warrantedly assert that P are the same as those that comprise a truth-condition for "I know that P," then if the former vary with context, so do the latter. In short: The knowledge account of assertion together with the context-sensitivity of assertability yields contextualism about knowledge. (Derose (2002), p. 175)

According to Derose, the standards for when you are in a position to warrantedly assert that P vary with context. Assume that the conditions under which you are warranted in asserting that p are identical to the truth-conditions for "I know that p" (this is how Derose understands KA). It follows, according to Derose, that the truth conditions for "I know that p" are contextually variable, i.e. some version of contextualism follows.

3.2. Skepticism, SPAP and the Knowledge Account of Assertion

Both Hawthorne's and Derose's arguments are considerably more subtle than the outline above might give the impression of, but those subtleties won't matter in what follows. The goal here is not to evaluate the soundness of these arguments as they stand. What I do instead is develop a version of KA that's compatible with SPAP and show that this reformulated version of KA is compatible with PS (this new version of KA does not make PS weakly self-defeating nor does it provide support for contextualism).

*SPAP, KA and KA**

For a proponent of SPAP, KA raises a number of interesting questions—among them Q1-Q3. The answers I provide to these questions will supply the resources for a SPAP adjusted version of KA (and, I'll argue, this new version of KA is immune to the kinds of objections run by Hawthorne and Derose.)

> **Q1**. According to SPAP, in uttering a sentence, S, you typically assert many propositions. Suppose that in uttering S, you assert p and q and that the speaker knows that p, but doesn't know that q. What to do if you're sympathetic to something like KA? Three options spring to mind

i. KA requires that we know the proposition *saliently* asserted.
ii. KA requires that we know *all* the propositions we assert in assertively uttering a sentence.
iii. KA requires that we know only the proposition *semantically* expressed (this is always asserted).

The version of KA formulated below incorporates (i). If I'm asserting S in order to saliently assert p, and at the same time assert some other propositions $q_1 \ldots q_n$, it is sufficient that I know that p. The only argument I'll give for that here is that when combined with some other modifications to KA, it leads to an explanatorily powerful version of KA.

Q2. According to SPAP, what you saliently assert by uttering a sentence S in a context C is relativized to a context of interpretation. So the assertion of p that's mentioned in the formulation of KA must be relative to some context of interpretation. Which? Two options spring to mind:

i. KA requires that when uttering a sentence the speaker should know that which is saliently asserted by that utterance relative to the context of utterance (let the relevant context of interpretation be the context of utterance.)
ii. KA requires that when uttering a sentence the speaker should know that which is saliently asserted by the utterance relative to *all* contexts of interpretation[23].

(i) seems the more reasonable option. If in some context of interpretation other than the one I'm in (say, a context I'm completely unaware of), I saliently assert q, it would seem peculiar to require of me that I know q if the goal of my utterance is to saliently assert p (i.e. if p is what's salient in the context of utterance).
Note that if we combine this reply to Q2 with the reply I suggested to Q1, what we have so far is that KA should say something to the effect *that you should: saliently assert p in C (relative to C) only if you know that p*. We need, however, to address one more issue before we get a satisfactory version of KA.

Q3. If SPAP is correct, sentences containing "know" express many propositions in addition to the proposition semantically expressed. So when we think about knowledge attributions, we have to decide whether we're interested in what's semantically expressed by such attributions or what's saliently asserted (which might not be the semantic content.) I suggest that when we formulate KA we should focus on what's saliently asserted by a knowledge attribution (relative to the context of that attribution). In other words, what KA should require is that when a speaker in a context C saliently asserts p (relative to C), then what's saliently asserted by an utterance of "A knows that p" in C (relative to C) should be true.

If we add these modifications, the natural result is KA*:

KA*: You must: saliently assert p in C (relative to C) just in case your utterance of "I know that p" (in C) saliently asserts something true (relative to C).

KA and The Original Motivation for KA*

Not only is KA* compatible with SPAP, but does as good a job as KA accounting for the original data that motivated the knowledge account of assertion. One central argument for KA appeals to the sense we have that something is wrong about an utterance of (2)[24]:

(2) Dogs bark, but I don't know that they do

KA can explain the infelicity: if knowledge is the norm of assertion, you would, in asserting the first conjunct in (2) present yourself as knowing that p but take that back in the second conjunct. That KA can provide such an explanation has been taken by many as an argument in its favor. This is not, however, an advantage of KA over KA*. KA* explains the infelicity of (2) as follows: an utterance u of (2) saliently asserts that p (relative to C) and then denies that what's saliently asserted by an utterance in C of "I know that p" (relative to C) is true. That's in direct conflict with KA*. That is, KA* explains the infelicity of utterances of (2).

KA and the two Objections to Skepticism*

If KA* is the correct version of the knowledge account of assertion, the two objections to skepticism loose their force. First consider Derose's claim that KA undermines the invariantist component of PS. Derose moves from KA to contextualism via the assumption that the conditions for warranted assertability for P vary from one context to another. A proponent of PS can go along with that. Derose then takes from KA the premise that the standards for when one is in a position to warrantedly assert that p are the same as those that "comprise *a truth-condition for "I know that p"* ". (Derose 2002, 175.) DeRose's interpretation of *a truth condition for "I know that p"* plays a central role in his argument. He interprets that to mean *a semantic truth condition for "I know that p"*. That is to say, he assumes that KA allows him to equate the assertability conditions of *p* with the *semantic* truth conditions of "I know that p". KA* blocks that move. According to KA*, salient assertability of p co-varies with what's saliently asserted by "I know that p", but that is not, typically, the semantic content of "I know that p". In other words, KA* licenses no move from the warranted assertability of p to the semantic content of "I know that p". All KA* does is get you to the truth conditions what's saliently asserted by "I know that p". Nothing follows about the semantic content of "know".[25]

Hawthorne's concern is that KA would prevent the skeptic from asserting skepticism. Here the issues are trickier. Let *p* be the view I defend, PS. Suppose I want to (saliently) assert that *p*. According to KA*, I can do that if what's saliently asserted by "I know that p" is true. I've argued that what's saliently asserted by knowledge claims could be true even though the semantic content isn't (because we don't always saliently assert the semantic content.) But of course, that move assumes that we are *not* in a context where we focus on the semantic content of the knowledge claim (which, according to PS, is always[26] false.) The problem is that when we assert the truth of skepticism, (*p* in our example) we're typically thinking about epistemology and so are in a super-high standard context. Hence we should be focusing on the semantic content of knowledge claims. If so, what's saliently asserted by "I know that p", in a context where p = PS, should be false, according to PS. PS still seems to be weakly self-defeating.

So KA doesn't provide a simple solution to Hawthorne's problem. But it does provide partial relief. A PS proponent should grant that there's something peculiar about asserting a blanket version of skepticism. That's just a fact (and one the Pyrrhonic skeptic quite rightly made a big point of). If you know nothing, you don't know skepticism, and so how can you assert skepticism? Note, however, that this is a problem for *the skeptic* not for *skepticism* (for the person asserting the position, not for the position). The skeptic will, in asserting skepticism, engage in behavior that, at a certain level, breaks with the norms of assertion (in some sense she's doing something she should not do.)[27]

There is, however, a trick that could be used by the skeptic to get around this problem (one I've made use of through out this paper.) Some skeptics (me for example), don't *always* do epistemology—we don't always think about skeptical possibilities. Sometimes (in my case, most of the time) skeptics think about semantics and theories of speech act content. When we think about speech act content our epistemic standards aren't very high—at least not as high as when we think about skepticism and skeptical possibilities (we semanticists are not, for example, too worried about whether we are brains in vats or deceived by evil demons). When, qua semanticist, I describe the semantic content of "know" and the relationship between the semantic content of "know" and the speech act content, what's saliently asserted by an utterance of "I know that p" (where p = PS) need not be the semantic content, and hence could be true. In this sense, Lewis is right: epistemology destroys knowledge, but only temporarily—by doing some philosophy of language we can recover it again.[28]

Conclusion and Qualifications

I have argued that PS can be defended against certain kinds of objections—objections that have to do with the compatibility of PS with various aspects of our linguistic practices. Those, of course, are not the only kinds of reason one might have for worrying about skepticism. There are other objections—objections that are of an epistemological nature. Adding SPAP to skepticism won't alleviate those objections. Here's an example, from Williamson and Hawthorne, of the kind of objection that SPAP provides no response to: Skepticism, as construed here, demands that we be able to articulate a super-high epistemic standard. I have said nothing about how to do that. The natural way to do it appeals to the kind of evidence we need to have for a claim in order to know it (for the skeptic, the evidence must be *very strong*. It must entail what we claim to know). That seems to assume that our concept of evidence can be understood independently of our concept of knowledge. If Williamson (2000) is right, this assumption fails. So it becomes very hard to see how the skeptic can articulate the super-high standard required to get the skeptical arguments off the ground. This kind of objection requires an entirely different kind of reply from the skeptic, one I won't attempt here. What this indicates is that in order to refute skepticism, you have to do epistemology, not philosophy of language.[29]

Notes

1. For the kinds of reasons why I think contextualism fails, see Cappelen and Lepore (2004) and (2005).
2. I have in mind the kind of view developed by Barry Stroud in Chapter Two of Stroud (1984)
3. See for example Lewis (1996); Cohen (1991), (1999), and (2000); DeRose (1995), (1999), (2000) and (2002).
4. See for example Hawthorne (2004), Stanley (forthcoming).
5. On this view, knowledge attributions are sensitive to the non-epistemic features of the situation in which the subject of the attribution finds herself (whether S knows that p, depends, in part, on practical facts about S's situation).
6. The scope of this "every" is not all that important in what follows: there might be some exceptions. I remain neutral about the exact scope of skeptical arguments.
7. See also Vogel (1990) for earlier elaboration on the importance of co-called lottery propositions.
8. For further illustrations of this important point, see Hawthorne (2004) Chapter Three. Hawthorne uses vague terms and moral terms to illustrate the point.
9. John Hawthorne characterizes this as the view that speakers are *wrong* about the semantic value of the term "know", hence he calls it an 'error theory' (Hawthorne (2004), pp. 114–5).To the extent that this gives the impression that these speakers have made some kind of semantic mistake, it's an unfortunate characterization. They are no more mistaken in their understanding of "knows" than those who are mistaken about (or have in complete knowledge of) love, power, money, or nuclear waste are mistaken about the semantics for "love", "power", "money" or "nuclear waste". They are just mistaken or not fully informed about that which these terms refer to.
10. See for example Cappelen and Lepore (1997), (1998), (2004) and (2005), Richard (1998), Salmon (2004), (2005), Soames (2002)).
11. For many other examples of this kind see Cappelen and Lepore (1997), (1998), (2000), (2004), (2005). For very similar examples, see Chapter Three of Soames 2002.

12. Similarly, Nathan Salmon says:
    "Frequently, routinely in fact, what we represent by means of a symbol deviates from the symbol's semantics. Most obviously this occurs with the sentences we utter, whereby we routinely assert something beyond what the sentence itself semantically expresses." (Salmon (2005), p. 224.)
13. Imagine the sentence uttered by a terrorist who has placed his nuclear device in the desert and intends to use it to destroy the habitat of an endangered bird species.
14. In what follows I assume, for the sake of argument, that the contextualists' description of these examples is correct, i.e. that epistemic standards enter into the propositions expressed by knowledge attributions. That doesn't mean I endorse this view. The reply I give to the contextualist is not dependent on any detail of how these propositions are construed. It's a general strategy for dealing with contextual variability, no matter how exactly one thinks that variability affects the propositions expressed. The point made below could, with minor modifications, be applied to other ways of making knowledge attributions context sensitive—for example Lewis (1996), Ludlow (2005) and Schaffer (2004).
15. See note 14 above.
16. See DeRose (1999) and Stanley (forthcoming)
17. See Stanley and King (2005) and Stanley (forthcoming) for an endorsement of the concern DeRose expresses in this passage.
18. Hawthorne (2004) and Stanley (forthcoming) try to explain our intuitions about uses of "know" by appealing to the idea that the propositions that we express include references to the interests or practical concerns of the agent to whom the knowledge is attributed. PS could incorporate parts of that view: PS can accommodate the conviction that the propositions expressed by knowledge attributions include references to the subject's practical interests or stakes. PS leaves open the possibility that such propositions are part of the speech act content and that they are salient. In other words, a PS proponent need not take a stand on aspects of the debate between contextualists and so-called 'subject sensitive invariantists'. It's possible that both kinds of propositions enter into the speech act content. It is also possible that one kind of proposition is salient from one context of interpretation while the other kind is salient from another. So in a sense, PS can incorporate both sets of intuitions (both sets of data). Of course, what PS cannot incorporate is the idea that either of these constitutes the semantic content.
19. These examples are taken from DeRose (forthcoming), and similar locutions can be found in all the contextualist literature.
20. See Cappelen and Lepore (1997), (2005) and Nathan Salmon's (2004) and (2005) for elaboration on these points.
21. That said, I should emphasize again that the goal here is not to give a full-fledged semantic theory, but rather to show that *if* you take skeptical arguments at face value and as arguments to show that the semantic content of utterances of positive knowledge attributions require that extraordinary standards be met, *then* you can respond to many of the standard objections to skepticism by endorsing SPAP.
22. See Williamson (2000), Chapter 11.

23. A third possibility is this: call the context from which we evaluate whether an utterance is in accordance with the norm of assertion, *the normative context.* One possible view is this: in order to saliently assert p in context of utterance C, the speaker should know that which is asserted by “I know that p” relative to the normative context. On this view, a speaker might have acted in accordance with the norm of assertion relative to one normative context, but not another.
24. See Moore (1962), p. 277
25. DeRose (2002, pp. 182–4) objects to the ‘warranted assertability’ version of KA. The central part of that criticism relies on the assumption that warranted assertability conditions for “A knows that p” are stricter than warranted assertability conditions for “p”. Even if that’s true (I’m not convinced that it is), nothing follows about KA*. KA* is not about the conditions under which it is warranted to assert “p” or “A knows that p”; it is about the truth of what’s (saliently) asserted by these utterances. This, again, illustrates how combining SPAP with skepticism undermines the strategies developed for dealing with traditional versions of skepticism.
26. As mentioned in note six above, I take no stand on the exact scope of skepticism, so it’s compatible with the view defended here that PS doesn’t fall in under it—but I’ll leave that possibility unexplored.
27. I won’t discuss here how bad this is for the skeptic. One might wonder: How bad is it to break the norm of assertion, if one is doing so in the interest of truth?
28. This removes another concern that Hawthorne has about skepticism—that it undermines what he calls *the practical reasoning constraint* (see Hawthorne (2004), p. 30 and pp. 132–35) The practical reasoning constraint says *that one ought only to use that which one knows as a premise in ones practical reasoning*. It looks like the skeptic will either be unable to engage in practical reasoning or fail to respect this constraint. PS can here appeal to KA* as the basis for an alternative version of the practical reasoning constraint: *an agent A should only use p as a premise in practical reasoning in a context C, if an utterance of “A knows that p” in C saliently asserts something true.* If this is the constraint, there’s no barrier to the skeptic engaging in practical reasoning.
29. This paper was presented at workshops at the University of Oslo, the University of Stockholm, and the New University, Lisbon. Thanks to the audience on these occasions for helpful comments and suggestions. Particular thanks to Olav Gjelsvik, John Hawthorne, Jeff King, Peter Pagin, Katrina Przyjemski, Barry Smith, Jason Stanley, and Tim Williamson. My greatest debt is to Ernie Lepore—many of the ideas presented here are applications of views Ernie and I have developed jointly over the last few years. As always, his input and encouragement have been invaluable.

References

Bezuidenhout, Anne and Reimer, Marga (eds) *Descriptions and Beyond: An Interdisciplinary Collection of Essays on Definite and Indefinite Descriptions and other Related Phenomena*, Oxford University Press, 2004.

Cappelen, Herman and Lepore, Ernie ‘On an Alleged Connection between Indirect Quotation and Semantic Theory’ *Mind and Language*, 1997, pp. 278–296.

Cappelen, Herman and Lepore, Ernie 'Reply to Richard and Reimer' *Mind and Language*, 1998, pp. 117–621.
Cappelen, Herman and Lepore, Ernie 'Context-Shifting Arguments' *Philosophical Perspectives*, 2003.
Cappelen, Herman and Lepore, Ernie *Insensitive Semantics*, Blackwell, 2005.
Cohen, Stewart 'How to be a Fallibilist', *Philosophical Perspectives*, 1988, pp. 91–123.
———'Contextualism, Skepticism, and the Structure of Reasons', *Philosophical Perspectives*, 1999, pp. 57–89.
———'Contextualism Defended: Comments on Richard Feldman's 'Skeptical Problems, Contextualist Solutions'', *Philosophical Studies*, 2001, 87–98.
DeRose, Keith 'Solving the Skeptical Problem', *Philosophical Review*, 1995, pp. 1–52.
———'Contextualism: An Explanation and Defense', in J. Greco and E. Sosa (eds.), *The Blackwell Guide to Epistemology*, Blackwell, 1999, pp. 187–205.
———'Assertion, Knowledge and Context', *Philosophical Review*, 2002, pp. 167–203.
———'The Ordinary Language Basis of Contextualism and the New Invariantism'', *The Philosophical Quarterly* (forthcoming).
Hawthorne, John *Knowledge and Lotteries*, Oxford University Press, 2004.
Lewis, David 'Elusive Knowledge', *Australasian Journal of Philosophy*, 1996, pp. 549–67.
Ludlow, Peter 'Contextualism and the New Linguistic Turn in Epistemology' in *Contextualism in Philosophy*, Preyer, G. and Peters, G. (eds), Oxford University Press, 2005.
Moore, G.E *Commonplace Book: 1919–1953*, Allen & Unwin (eds.), London, 1962.
Richard, Mark 'Semantic Theory and Indirect Speech', *Mind and Language*, 1998, pp. 605–616.
Salmon, Nathan 'The Good, the Bad, and the Ugly', in Bezuidenhout, Anne and Reimer, Marga (eds) *Descriptions and Beyond: An Interdisciplinary Collection of Essays on Definite and Indefinite Descriptions and other Related Phenomena*, Oxford University Press, 2004.
Salmon, Nathan 'Two Conceptions of Semantics', in Szabo, Z (ed) *Semantics versus Pragmatics*, Oxford University Press, 2005.
Schaffer, Jonathan 'From Contextualism to Contrastivism', *Philosophical Studies* 1994, pp. 73–103.
Soames, Scott *Beyond Rigidity: The Unfinished Semantic Agenda of Naming and Necessity*, Oxford University Press, 2002.
Stanley, Jason *Knowledge and Practical Interest* (forthcoming), Oxford University Press.
Stanley, J. and King, J 'Semantics, Pragmatics, and the Role of Semantic Content,' in *Semantics vs. Pragmatics*, Szabo, Z (ed.), Oxford University Press, 2005.
Stroud, Barry *The Significance of Philosophical Skepticism*. Oxford University Press, 1984.
Vogel, J. "Are there counter-examples to the closure principles?" in *Doubting: Contemporary Perspectives on Skepticism*, Roth, M and Ross, G (eds), Kluwer, 1990.
Williamson, Timothy *Knowledge and Its Limits*. Oxford University Press, 2001.

Philosophical Perspectives, 19, Epistemology, 2005

EPISTEMIC OVERDETERMINATION AND A PRIORI JUSTIFICATION

Albert Casullo
University of Nebraska-Lincoln

Radical empiricism is the view that experience is the only source of knowledge. Hence, radical empiricism denies the existence of a priori knowledge. Its most famous proponents are John Stuart Mill and W. V. Quine. Although both reject a priori knowledge, they offer different empiricist accounts of the knowledge alleged by their opponents to be a priori. My primary concern in this paper is not with the cogency of their positive accounts. My focus is their arguments against a priori knowledge. My goal is to establish that although they offer very different arguments against the existence of a priori knowledge, each of their arguments suffers from a common defect. They both fail to appreciate the phenomenon of epistemic overdetermination and its role in the theory of knowledge.

In section 1 of the paper, I articulate Mill's position and maintain that the key premise in his argument against the existence of a priori knowledge is a version of the Explanatory Simplicity Principle. In section 2, I elaborate the role of epistemic overdetermination in a theory of knowledge, and argue that the Explanatory Simplicity Principle is incompatible with a form of epistemic overdetermination. In section 3, I turn to a version of Quine's argument against the a priori, which has been forcefully advanced by both Hilary Putnam and Philip Kitcher, and show that the key premise of the argument is the Weak Unrevisability Condition. Finally, in section 4, I examine the relationship between epistemic overdetermination and defeasible justification, and argue that the Weak Unrevisability Condition is incompatible with a form of epistemic overdetermination.

I. Mill

Mill's argument against the existence of a priori knowledge is presented within the context of offering an empiricist account of our knowledge of geometry and arithmetic. The stage for Mill's account is set by Kant. Kant characterizes a priori knowledge as "independent of experience," contrasting it with a posteriori knowledge, which has its "sources" in experience.[1] Presumably, when Kant speaks of the "source" of knowledge, he does not mean the source of the belief in question, but the source of its justification. Hence, according to Kant,

> (K) S knows a priori that p just in case S's belief that p is justified by some nonexperiential source and the other conditions for knowledge are satisfied.

Kant argues that necessity is a criterion of a priori knowledge, and maintains that "if we have a proposition which in being thought is thought as *necessary*, it is an *a priori* judgment."[2] He goes on to argue that "mathematical propositions, strictly so-called, are always judgments *a priori*, not empirical; because they carry with them necessity, which cannot be derived from experience."[3] Since Kant maintains that we know some mathematical propositions, he concludes that such knowledge is a priori.

Mill begs to differ. He agrees that we know some mathematical propositions, but denies that such knowledge is a priori. His account of mathematical knowledge is a version of inductive empiricism. Inductive empiricism with respect to a domain of knowledge involves two theses. First, some propositions within that domain are epistemically more basic than the others, in the sense that the non-basic propositions derive their justification from the basic propositions via inference. Second, the basic propositions are known by a process of inductive inference from observed cases. Mill's focus is on the basic propositions of arithmetic and geometry: the axioms and definitions of each domain. His primary goal is to establish that they are known by induction from observed cases.

The details of Mill's account are strained. He advances four primary theses regarding the definitions of geometry. First, they are not stipulations regarding the meanings of terms, but involve "an implied assumption that there exists a real thing conformable thereto."[4] Second, no real things—i.e., real points, real lines, real circles, real squares, etc.—conform exactly to the definitions. Third, they are generalizations about the points, lines, circles, and squares of our experience, and sufficiently approximate the truth regarding those things that no significant error occurs if we assume that they are exactly true. Fourth, since the definitions are not true, they are not necessarily true.

Mill advances three primary theses regarding the axioms of geometry. First, they are exactly true of the objects of our experience. Second, they are inductive generalizations based on our experience of those objects. Third, the contention that they are necessary truths is dubious since (a) it is based on the claim that their falsehood is inconceivable, but (b) the inconceivability of their falsehood is explained by the laws of associationist psychology—i.e., by the fact that we have experienced many confirming instances of them but no disconfirming instances.

Mill's account, taken in the crude form in which he presents it, is untenable, and my goal here is not to attempt to rehabilitate it. Instead, I propose to concede that Mill offers a defensible inductive empiricist account of mathematical knowledge. The question I wish to address is: How does this concession bear on the existence of a priori knowledge? The concession entails that Kant's contention that mathematical knowledge *cannot* be derived from experience is incorrect. It does not, however, entail that his contention that mathematical knowledge *is* a priori is also incorrect. The fact that mathematical knowledge is or can be derived from experience does not immediately entail that it is not or cannot be derived from some nonexperiential source. Mill recognizes that more needs to be said at this juncture. In particular, he recognizes that his opponents can maintain that experience is not necessary to justify the axioms of geometry.

Mill attempts to close the gap in his argument with the following observations:

> They cannot, however, but allow that the truth of the axiom, "Two straight lines cannot inclose a space," even if evident independently of experience, is also evident from experience. Whether the axiom needs confirmation or not, it receives confirmation in almost every instant of our lives, since we cannot look at any two straight lines which intersect one another without seeing that from that point they continue to diverge more and more. . . . Where, then, is the necessity for assuming that our recognition of these truths has a different origin from the rest of our knowledge when its existence is perfectly accounted for by supposing its origin to be the same? . . . The burden of proof lies on the advocates of the contrary opinion; it is for them to point out some fact inconsistent with the supposition that this part of our knowledge of nature is derived from the same sources as every other part.[5]

Mill moves from the premise that inductive empiricism provides an account of knowledge of geometrical axioms to the stronger conclusion that knowledge of those axioms is not a priori. The key premise in his argument appeals to a version of the *Explanatory Simplicity Principle* (ES): If a putative source of knowledge is not necessary to explain knowledge of the axioms of geometry, then it is not a source of knowledge of the axioms of geometry. Since Mill provides an account of knowledge of the axioms of geometry based on inductive generalization from observed cases, the Explanatory Simplicity Principle yields the conclusion that such knowledge is not a priori. There is no need to introduce a nonexperiential source in order to explain knowledge of the axioms of geometry. The general form of Mill's argument against the existence of a priori knowledge can be articulated as follows:

(M1) Inductive empiricism provides an account of mathematical knowledge based on inductive generalization from observed cases.

(ES) Φ is a source of knowledge for some domain D of knowledge only if Φ is necessary to explain knowledge of some propositions within D.

(M2) Therefore, mathematical knowledge is not a priori.

Clearly, the burden of the argument is carried by (ES), the Explanatory Simplicity Principle. We now turn to understanding the principle and its consequences.

II. Epistemic Overdetermination

(ES) is ambiguous. In order to bring out the ambiguity, consider the *Single Source Principle* (SS):

(SS) For each domain D of knowledge, there is only a single source of justification for the propositions within that domain.[6]

(ES) does not entail (SS) since it leaves open the possibility that a domain of knowledge is *epistemically segregated*—i.e., some propositions within D are justified only by source A, and some other propositions within D are justified only by a different source B. In such a situation, since both A and B are necessary to justify some propositions within D, (ES) allows that both are sources of justification for the propositions within D.

(ES), however, does entail the following weaker version of (SS):

(SS0) For *some* propositions within D, there is only a single source of justification.

Consider again our epistemically segregated domain of knowledge. If source A justifies every proposition justified by source B, then source B would be unnecessary to explain knowledge of domain D. Similarly, if source B justifies every proposition justified by source A, then source A would be unnecessary to explain knowledge of domain D. So, in order for both A and B to be necessary to explain knowledge of domain D, there must be at least one proposition within D justified by A but not B, and at least one proposition within D justified by B but not A.

An interesting question arises at this juncture. Does (ES) also entail

(SS1) For *each* proposition within D, there is only a single source of justification?

If we again consider our epistemically segregated domain of knowledge, (SS1) entails that for each proposition p within domain D, p is justified by either source A or source B but not both. In order to simplify matters, let us assume that domain D consists solely of four propositions: P_1, P_2, P_3, and P_4. Let us also assume that source A justifies P_1, P_2, P_3, but not P_4. Hence, source B is necessary to explain only the justification of P_4. Does (ES) leave open the possibility that source B justifies P_1, P_2, or P_3 as well?

There are two readings of (ES):

(ES1) Φ is a source of knowledge for proposition P_i of domain D only if Φ is necessary to explain the justification of P_i.

(ES2) Φ is a source of knowledge for proposition P_i of domain D only if Φ is necessary to explain the justification of some proposition, but not necessarily P_i, within D.

The first, more stringent, reading of (ES) does entail (SS1). According to (ES1), source B justifies only those propositions within D that are not justified by source A. The second, more liberal, reading of (ES) does not entail (SS1). According to (ES2), if source B is necessary explain the justification of some proposition of D, such as P_4, it can also justify other propositions within D, such as P_1, that are also justified by source A. Although (ES2) does not entail (SS1), it does entail

(SS2) If some source Φ explains the justification of *all* propositions within domain D, then for *each* proposition within D, there is only a single source of justification.

We now have two versions of (ES), each of which had different implications regarding the possibility of multiple sources of justification within a certain domain of knowledge. Is there some reason to prefer one over the other?

(ES1) strikes me as more the more plausible reading of (ES). Consider again our example. Let P_1 be Euclid's first postulate: A straight line can be drawn from any point to any other point. Let P_4 be Euclid's second postulate: Any straight line can be extended continuously in a straight line. Assume that reason is necessary to explain only the justification of P_4. Moreover, assume that reason also justifies P_1. If P_1 is indeed justified by reason, then it is in virtue of some relationship between the evidence produced by reason and the content of P_1. One familiar account is that reason produces an intuition that P_1, and the intuition that P_1 justifies the belief that P_1. Presumably, neither the fact that reason produces the intuition that P_1 nor the fact that the intuition justifies P_1 depends on whether reason also justifies P_4, let alone on whether it is necessary to justify P_4. (ES2), however, entails the following puzzling counterfactual:

(PC) If reason were not necessary to justify P_4, then reason would not justify P_1.

(PC) is puzzling because there is no apparent explanation for why P_1's being justified by reason depends on P_4's being justified by reason. Since this argument against (ES2) is not conclusive, I address both versions of (ES) in the subsequent discussion.

Both (ES1) and (ES2) should be rejected. (ES1) entails (SS1), and (ES2) entails (SS2). But (SS1) and (SS2) should be rejected for two reasons. The first is methodological. Both (SS1) and (SS2) settle by fiat substantive epistemological issues. Epistemology is concerned with the sources and extent of human knowledge. Addressing these concerns requires identifying the most general domains of human knowledge and the putative sources of knowledge for each domain. A source of knowledge for a particular domain is a cognitive capacity that, under certain conditions, generates justification for propositions within that domain. The question of how many cognitive capacities humans possess that have the requisite properties for justifying propositions within a certain domain of knowledge is substantive. In some cases, say visual perception, the evidence that humans possess such a capacity and that it justifies a certain domain of propositions about the external world may be so readily available that no further investigation is necessary in order to answer them. But epistemologists have proposed more controversial putative sources of knowledge. Roderick Chisholm offers two examples. Some maintain that, in order to explain our knowledge of other minds, "there must be another source—possibly the *Verstehen*, or 'intuitive understanding', of German philosophy and psychology."[7] The second example pertains to knowledge of religious truths: "Hugh of St. Victor held, in the twelfth century, that in addition to the *oculis canis*, by means of which we know the physical world, and the *oculis rationis*, by means of which we know our own states of mind, there is an *oculis contemplationis*, by means of which we know the truths of religion."[8]

Whether such cognitive capacities exist and, if they do, whether they have the requisite properties to justify propositions within a certain domain are substantive epistemological questions. Providing an answer to them requires both empirical and philosophical investigation. Moreover, in the absence of compelling independent evidence, there is no basis for assuming that if humans possess some cognitive capacity that explains the justification of all propositions within some particular domain of knowledge, they have no other cognitive capacity that justifies any beliefs within that domain. Both (SS1) and (SS2) make such an assumption in the absence of any independent evidence. For example, suppose that the observation of the behavior of others together with some legitimate process of inductive inference explains the justification of all propositions about other minds within a certain domain. It follows from both (SS1) and (SS2) that either humans lack intuitive understanding or it is not a source of justification of beliefs about other minds. Hence, (ES1) and (ES2) settle by fiat substantive epistemological questions. The questions of whether the cognitive capacity of intuitive understanding exists and, if it does, whether it has the requisite properties to justify beliefs about other minds should not be settled by a methodological assumption that has no independent support. Similarly, if we suppose that rational theology explains the justification of all propositions within some domain of religious knowledge, (SS1) and (SS2) entail that either humans lack an *oculis contemplationis* or that it is not a source of justification of religious beliefs. Once again, such substantive epistemological issues should not be settled by a methodological assumption that has no independent support.

There is a second reason for rejecting (SS1) and (SS2). They conflict with a familiar feature of our epistemic lives: epistemic overdetermination. The justification of some of our beliefs is overdetermined—i.e., for some of our beliefs, we have more than one justification, each of which is sufficient to justify the belief in question in the absence of the others. For example, you attended a party last night and someone asks you if Jill also attended. You didn't interact with her at the party, so you have to stop and think about it. You suddenly recall that you saw her talking to Jack, and that recollection triggers a host of additional recollections of Jill's being at the party. Presumably, your original recollection justifies your belief that Jill was at the party. But each of the other recollections that came in its wake also justifies your belief. So you have many different recollections, each of which is sufficient to justify your belief that Jill was at the party. Your justification for that belief is overdetermined.

There are two different types of epistemic overdetermination: epistemic overdetermination by the *same* source, and epistemic overdetermination by *different* sources. The first type of epistemic overdetermination occurs when we have more than one justification for a particular belief, each of which is sufficient to justify the belief in question in the absence of the others, and they come from the same source. The example in the previous paragraph is of the first type. The second type of epistemic overdetermination occurs when we have more than one justification for a particular belief, each of which is sufficient to justify the belief in question in the absence of the others, and they come from different sources. Here's an example. I've misplaced my wallet again. I wonder where I might have left it. I suddenly recall having left it on the kitchen counter when I came in from the garage last night. Presumably, my recollection justifies me in believing that my wallet is on the kitchen counter. But, just to be sure, I walk out to the kitchen to check. To my relief, I see my wallet on the counter. Presumably, my seeing my wallet on the counter also justifies me in believing that my wallet is on the counter. So here my justification is overdetermined by different sources. Both my recollection and my visual experience justify my belief about my wallet, and each is sufficient to justify that belief in the absence of the other.

Both (SS1) and (SS2) have significant consequences regarding the possibility of epistemic overdetermination. Assume that

(EO) S's belief that p is epistemically overdetermined by two different sources.

It follows that

(EO1) S's belief that p is justified by two different sources.

But (EO1) is incompatible with

> (SS1) For *each* proposition within D, there is only a single source of justification.

Since (SS1) is incompatible with epistemic overdetermination by different sources, which is a familiar fact of our epistemic lives, (SS1) and, *a fortiori*, (ES1) should be rejected.

The relationship between (SS2) and epistemic overdetermination is more complicated. Although

> (SS2) If some source Φ explains the justification of all propositions within domain D, then for *each* proposition within D, there is only a single source of justification

is compatible with (EO1), it is incompatible with

> (EO2) S's belief that p is justified by some source A, where p is a member of domain D and A explains the justification of all propositions within domain D, and S's belief that p is justified by source B.

Providing an uncontroversial example of epistemic overdetermination that satisfies (EO2) is more difficult since Mill provides little information about how to individuate domains and sources of knowledge. Hence, we must rely on the intuitive principles of individuation that epistemologists typically employ. Consider the problem of perception and knowledge of the external world. The traditional view is that perception explains the justification of propositions about the present existence and certain properties, such as shape, color, and location, of medium-sized physical objects in our immediate vicinity. Let D be the domain of all such propositions, and let us assume that perception explains the justification of all propositions within D. Now consider the following example. I'm at my desk working on a paper. I jot down some ideas with my pencil and stop to think. A new idea occurs to me, which I want to jot down quickly before I forget it. But I can't find my pencil. I suddenly recall having seen it roll off the desk a few minutes ago. I look down and see it. My belief that my pencil is on the floor is justified both by my seeing it there and by my recollection of having seen it roll off the desk. Since the proposition that the pencil is on the floor is a member of domain D and perception explains the justification of all propositions in that domain, we have a familiar case of epistemic overdetermination that satisfies (EO2). Moreover, since (SS2) is incompatible with such familiar cases of epistemic overdetermination, (SS2) and, *a fortiori*, (ES2) should be rejected.

III. Quine

Although both Mill and Quine reject a priori knowledge, they offer very different accounts of mathematical knowledge. Quine rejects inductive empiricism in favor of a version of holistic empiricism, which views all mathematical propositions as components of scientific theories and maintains that their epistemic properties are analogous to those of the more theoretical propositions of such theories. The theoretical propositions of scientific theories have two important epistemic properties. First, they are not tested directly against observation, but only indirectly via their observational consequences. Second, they don't have observational consequences in isolation, but only in conjunction with the other propositions of the theory. Hence, according to holistic empiricism, mathematical propositions are theoretical components of scientific theories, and entire scientific theories, including their mathematical components, are indirectly confirmed by experience via their observational consequences.

Our main concern, however, is not with Quine's positive account of mathematical knowledge, but with his case against a priori knowledge. Here we find a second contrast with Mill. Mill is straightforward in presenting his case against a priori knowledge; Quine's case is more elusive. Some take Quine's program of naturalized epistemology to be the primary challenge to the existence of a priori knowledge.[9] Others locate the primary challenge in his classic paper, "Two Dogmas of Empiricism."[10] But even if we focus exclusively on the latter, as I propose to do, the argument remains difficult to articulate.

In "Two Dogmas," Quine attacks a conception of analyticity inspired by Frege: a statement is analytic if it can be turned into a logical truth by replacing synonyms with synonyms. The primary points of the attack can be summarized as follows:

(1) Definition presupposes synonymy rather than explaining it.
(2) Interchangeability *salva veritate* is a sufficient condition of cognitive synonymy only in relation to a language containing an intensional adverb 'necessarily'.
(3) Semantic rules do not explain 'Statement S is analytic for language L', with variable 'S' and 'L', even if 'L' is limited to artificial languages.
(4) The verification theory of meaning provides an account of statement synonymy that presupposes reductionism. Reductionism fails but survives as the view that individual statements admit of confirmation or infirmation.
(5) Any statement can be held to be true come what may. No statement is immune to revision.

There are two striking aspects of the attack. First, it is directed at two different targets. Points (1), (2) and (3) target the notion of synonymy; points (4) and (5) target the doctrine of reductionism. Second, none of the points is explicitly directed at a priori knowledge. Hence, if "Two Dogmas" does indeed present a challenge to the existence of a priori knowledge, as many of its champions claim, then some additional premise is necessary that connects one of the two targets to the a priori. What is the additional premise?

One common response is that Quine is attacking the logical empiricist account of a priori knowledge, whose central claim is

(LE) All a priori knowledge is of analytic truths,

and that his argument purports to show that the concept of analytic truth is incoherent. Let us grant that Quine's goal is to undermine (LE), and that he succeeds in establishing that the analytic/synthetic distinction is incoherent. Does it follow that there is no a priori knowledge? No. (LE) is a thesis about the nature of the propositions alleged to be known a priori. According to logical empiricism, the truths traditionally claimed to be known a priori, such as mathematical and logical truths, are analytically equivalent to logical truths. If Quine is right, then this claim is incoherent. But from the fact that the claim that mathematical and logical truths are analytic is incoherent, it does not follow that those truths are not known a priori.

An alternative response is to take (LE) as a conceptual claim—i.e., to take it as claiming that the concept of a priori knowledge involves, either implicitly or explicitly, the concept of analytic truth. On this reading, the incoherence of the concept of analytic truth entails the incoherence of the concept of a priori knowledge. This response, however, rests on a false conceptual claim. Since I have argued this point in detail elsewhere, I will be brief here.[11] First, the concept of analytic truth is not explicitly part of the concept of a priori knowledge. As we saw earlier, the traditional concept of a priori knowledge is the concept of knowledge whose justification is nonexperiential. That concept, taken alone, neither states nor immediately entails anything about the nature of the propositions so justified. Second, the most promising route to maintaining that the concept of analytic truth is implicitly part of the concept of a priori knowledge is to endorse two theses: (a) the concept of a priori knowledge involves the concept of necessary truth; and (b) some version of the so-called "linguistic theory" of necessary truth, which maintains that the concept of necessary truth is analyzable in terms of the concept of analytic truth. There are, however, two problems with this route. First, the concept of a priori knowledge does not involve, either explicitly or implicitly, the concept of necessary truth. Second, no one has ever offered an even remotely plausible analysis of the concept of necessary truth in terms of the concept of analytic truth.

Some recent champions of "Two Dogmas" propose a different reading of its main argument that explicitly articulates the additional premise necessary to establish the conclusion that there is no a priori knowledge. Hilary Putnam rejects the orthodox reading of Quine's argument, which takes it to be an attack on the analytic/synthetic distinction based on the contention that all attempts to define 'analytic' are ultimately circular.[12] Putnam views this reading as too simplistic because Quine's arguments are not all directed toward the same target. In particular, point (5) attacks the concept of a statement that is confirmed no matter what. But, according to Putnam, that concept, unlike the concept of analyticity, is epistemic and not semantic:

> But why should this concept, the concept of a statement which is confirmed no matter what, be considered a concept of *analyticity*? Confirmation, in the positivist sense, has something to do with rational belief. A statement which is highly confirmed is a statement which it is rational to believe, or rational to believe to a high degree. If there are indeed statements which have the maximum degree of confirmation in all circumstances, then these are simply truths which it is *always rational to believe*, nay, more, truths which it is never rational to even begin to doubt. ... On the face of it, then, the concept of a truth which is confirmed no matter what is not a concept of *analyticity* but a concept of *apriority*.[13]

Moreover, Quine's argument against the concept of a truth that is confirmed no matter what is not based on some alleged circularity. Instead, according to Putnam, it is "an argument from what is clearly a normative description of the history of modern science," which Putnam locates in the following celebrated passage:

> Any statement can be held true come what may, if we make drastic enough adjustments elsewhere in the system. Even a statement very close to the periphery can be held true in the face of recalcitrant experience by pleading hallucination or by amending certain statements of the kind called logical laws. Conversely, by the same token, no statement is immune to revision. Revision even of the logical law of the excluded middle has been proposed as a means of simplifying quantum mechanics; and what difference is there in principle between such a shift and the shift whereby Kepler superseded Ptolemy, or Einstein Newton, or Darwin Aristotle?[14]

Putnam goes on to endorse Quine's argument and to maintain that the importance of "Two Dogmas" lies not in its rejection of the analytic/synthetic distinction but in its rejection of a priori knowledge.

Philip Kitcher agrees that the importance of "Two Dogmas" lies in its rejection of a priori knowledge:

> Defenders of analyticity have often construed the main thrust of Quine's most famous attack, "Two Dogmas of Empiricism," as arguing that the concept of analyticity is undefinable in notions Quine takes to be unproblematic. ... I locate Quine's central point elsewhere. The importance of the article stems from its final section, a section which challenges not the existence of analytic truths but the claim that analytic truths are knowable a priori.[15]

Kitcher goes on to maintain that Quine's central argument is located in the very same passage that Putnam quotes, and reconstructs it the following manner:

> Quine connects analyticity to apriority *via* the notion of unrevisability. If we can know a priori that *p* then no experience could deprive us of our warrant to believe that *p*. ... But "no statement is immune from revision." It follows that analytic statements, hailed by Quine's empiricist predecessors and contemporaries as a priori, cannot be a priori; ...[16]

Hence, Putnam and Kitcher agree on three points. First, the most important argument in "Two Dogmas" targets the existence of a priori knowledge. Second, the argument is located in the passage in which Quine claims that no statement is immune to revision. Finally, and most importantly, the argument involves an implicit premise that connects the concept of apriority with the concept of rational unrevisability.

Both Putnam and Kitcher endorse a version of the Unrevisability Condition, which states that rational unrevisability is a necessary condition for a priori knowledge. But the conditions that they propose are different. Putnam maintains that the concept of a statement that is confirmed no matter what is a concept of apriority. A statement that is confirmed no matter what is, according to Putnam, one that it is always rational to believe, one that it is never rational to doubt. But a statement that is *always* rational to believe is one that is rational to believe in the face of *any* evidence to the contrary. Hence, Putnam endorses a *Strong Unrevisability Condition*:

(SU) If S's belief that p is justified a priori, then S's belief that p is not rationally revisable in light of *any* evidence.

Kitcher's proposal is more modest. He maintains that if S knows that p a priori then "no experience could deprive us of our warrant to believe that p." Hence, Kitcher endorses a *Weak Unrevisability Condition*:

(WU) If S's belief that p is justified a priori, then S's belief that p is not rationally revisable in light of any *experiential* evidence.

We will focus on (WU) for two reasons. First, it is more plausible than (SU). (SU) entails that if S's justified belief that p is rationally revisable, then S's belief that p is justified a posteriori. But consider a competent mathematician who, working within her field of research expertise, carefully constructs a proof that A entails B and believes, on that basis, that A entails B. Presumably, such a belief is justified. Suppose, however, that upon later reviewing the proof, she discovers a subtle flaw and, as a consequence, withholds the belief that A entails B. (SU) has the implausible consequence that the mathematician's belief that A entails B is justified a posteriori even if both her original justification for that belief and her subsequent justification for the belief that her proof is flawed are exclusively nonexperiential. Second, even if (SU) is defensible, it is not necessary to secure the validity of Quine's argument; (WU) is sufficient. Hence, the Putnam-Kitcher version of Quine's argument can be stated as follows:

(Q1) No statement is immune to revision in light of recalcitrant experience.
(WU) If S's belief that p is justified a priori, then S's belief that p is not rationally revisable in light of any *experiential* evidence.
(Q2) Therefore, no knowledge is a priori.

Although (Q1) is open to dispute, I propose to grant it in order to assess its bearing on the existence of a priori knowledge. My focus will be on (WU).

IV. Defeasible Justification

We rejected Mill's argument against the existence of a priori knowledge on the grounds that it is incompatible with a familiar form of epistemic overdetermination. Quine's argument, as reconstructed by Putnam and Kitcher, does not appear to make any commitments with respect to the possibility of epistemic overdetermination. The appearances, however, are misleading. To show why they are misleading, we need to explore more carefully the relationship between defeasible justification and epistemic overdetermination.

We begin by introducing some additional conceptual resources. Experiential sources of justification, such as visual perception, are fallible. Some beliefs justified by visual perception are false. For example, if I carefully visually examine a sheet of paper that is on the table before me in ordinary lighting conditions and, on that basis, conclude that it is square, but fail to notice that two sides of the sheet are slightly longer than the other two sides, I have a false belief that is justified by visual perception. Fortunately, however, experiential sources also have the capacity to correct errors. Returning to our example, if I were to visually inspect the sheet of paper a second time and notice that two of its sides are slightly longer than the other two, I would have a belief, justified by visual perception, that the sheet is not square but rectangular. So, in such a situation, a single source justifies both the belief that p and the belief that not-p. Let us say that a *self-revising source of justification* is one that satisfies the following condition:

(SR) Source Φ can justify S's belief that p just in case Φ can justify S's belief that not-p.[17]

We now turn to the concept of defeasibility and distinguish two types of defeaters for a justified belief. Let us assume that S's belief that p is justified by source A. (Call a belief justified by source A an *A-justified belief.*) There are two types of defeaters for S's A-justified belief that p. An overriding defeater for S's A-justified belief that p is

(OD) S's justified belief that not-p.

An undermining defeater for S's A-justified belief that p is

(UD) S's justified belief that S's A-justification for the belief that p is inadequate or defective.

Finally, recall our distinction between epistemic overdetermination by a single source and epistemic overdetermination by different sources. My goal is to show that, in the case of self-revising sources of justification, there is an important connection between epistemic overdetermination by different sources and defeasibility by overriding defeaters.

Let us begin by assuming that S's belief that p is epistemically overdetermined by two different sources, one of which is self-revising:

(1) S's belief that p is justified by source A and by self-revising source B.

(1) entails

(2) Source B can justify S's belief that p.

Since B is a self-revising source of justified beliefs, it follows that

(3) Source B can justify S's belief that not-p.

Since S's justified belief that not-p is an overriding defeater for S's justified belief that p, it follows that

(4) S's A-justified belief that p is defeasible by an overriding defeater justified by source B.

Since (1) entails (4),

not-(4) S's A-justified belief that p is not defeasible by an overriding defeater justified by source B

entails

not-(1) It is not the case that S's belief that p is justified by source A and by self-revising source B.

In short, where B is a self-revising source, the indefeasibility of A-justified beliefs by overriding defeaters justified by source B is incompatible with epistemic overdetermination by sources A and B.

We now turn to the implications of this connection for the Putnam-Kitcher version of Quine's argument. Here we are faced with an immediate problem. Quine's argument focuses exclusively on the conditions for rational belief revision, but it does not explicitly address the conditions under which beliefs are justified. Since the case of Euclidean geometry provides the most striking putative example of experiential disconfirmation of a mathematical proposition, and since it is alleged to exemplify the holistic empiricist's account of how such propositions are disconfirmed by experience, we will focus on it. Moreover, we will assume that the very same empirical evidence that disconfirms the principles of Euclidean geometry also confirms the principles of the alternative non-Euclidean geometry. In short, we will assume that the Quinean story about the rational revision of the principles of Euclidean geometry is also the Quinean story about the rational adoption of the principles of non-Euclidean geometry. This assumption is controversial since, when generalized, it leads to a potentially problematic consequence for Quine's account. We will return to that issue later since it does not impact my case against the Putnam-Kitcher version of Quine's argument.

The Quinean story about the rational revision of the principles of Euclidean geometry is familiar. The principles of Euclidean geometry are part of an overall scientific theory describing the structure of physical space, which includes, in addition to the geometrical theory, a physical theory. Scientific theories are accepted or rejected on the basis of standard criteria such as conformity to observational data, explanatory power, conservatism, and simplicity. The principles of Euclidean geometry were rejected in favor of the principles of non-Euclidean geometry because the conjunction of Euclidean geometry with physical theory yielded an overall theory inferior, when measured by the standard criteria, to the overall theory yielded by the conjunction of non-Euclidean geometry with physical theory.

It is critical to note here that Quine's claim that no statement is immune to revision by recalcitrant experience applies to the newly adopted principles of non-Euclidean geometry. Hence, more generally, the claim that no statement is immune to revision in light of recalcitrant experience entails that the empirical evidence relevant to the justification of mathematical beliefs is self-revising in the sense defined earlier. If there is some set of experiences that can justify the principles of some geometry, then there is also some alternative set of experiences that can justify the denial of those principles, and vice versa.

How does this bear on (WU)? Let us assume the basic thesis of radical empiricism:

(RE) If p is a mathematical statement and S's belief that p is justified, then S's belief that p is justified by experiential evidence.

Since Quine maintains that all mathematical statements are subject to revision in light of recalcitrant experience, it follows that

(SR*) Experiential evidence can justify S's belief that p, where p is a mathematical statement, just in case experiential evidence can justify S's belief that not-p.

The conjunction of (RE) and (SR*) entails

(5) If S's belief that p, where p is some mathematical statement, is justified by experiential evidence, then S's belief that not-p can be justified by experiential evidence.

Since S's justified belief that not-p is a defeater for S's justified belief that p, (5) entails

(6) If S's belief that p, where p is some mathematical statement, is justified by experiential evidence, then S's belief that p is defeasible by an experientially justified belief that not-p.

(WU), however, entails

(WU*) If S's belief that p is justified a priori, then S's belief that p is not defeasible by an experientially justified belief that not-p.

The conjunction of (6) and (WU*) entails

(7) If S's belief that p, where p is some mathematical statement, is justified by experiential evidence, then S's belief that p is not justified a priori.[18]

(7) is incompatible with the following form of epistemic overdetermination:

(8) S's belief that p, where p is some mathematical statement, is justified both a priori and by experiential evidence.

But it is a substantive epistemological question whether mathematical statements are justified both a priori and by experience. Hence, (WU) settles by fiat a substantive epistemological question.

Let me briefly summarize. Quine's remarks in "Two Dogmas" can be parlayed into an argument against a priori knowledge only by introducing a substantive necessary condition on a priori justification: (WU). (WU), however, has the consequence of ruling out the possibility that mathematical statements are justified both a priori and by experience. But since it is a substantive epistemological question whether there are statements that are justified both a priori and by experience, any conception of the a priori that settles it by fiat should be rejected. Hence, Quine's argument, like Mill's, ultimately fails because it fails to take into account the possibility of epistemic overdetermination.

My argument against the Quinean account is based on the assumption that mathematical statements are justified by being embedded in an overall scientific theory that is justified by experience. That assumption, however, leads to the consequence that, in the absence of a good deal of scientific knowledge, one cannot be justified in believing elementary mathematical statements. But it is implausible to deny that skilled craftsmen, who build cabinets or musical instruments but know little physics, and educated adults, who have studied geometry and calculus but not physics, are not justified in believing any mathematical statements. Hence, some theorists who are sympathetic to both Quine's radical empiricism and his account of rational belief revision offer alternative accounts of the justification of elementary mathematical statements. Philip Kitcher, for example, stresses the authority of textbooks and teachers in accounting for one's rudimentary mathematical knowledge.[19] An alternative strategy employed by some neo-Quineans is to endorse a version of epistemic conservatism, which maintains that a belief is prima facie justified to some degree merely in virtue of being held. William Lycan, for example, endorses the Principle of Credulity: "Accept at the outset each of those things that seems to be true."[20] Gilbert Harman endorses General Foundationalism: "A general foundations theory holds that all of one's beliefs and inferential procedures at a given time are foundational at that time."[21] A belief or inferential procedure is foundational for a person at a time just in case it is non-inferentially prima facie justified for that person at that time.

Neither of these alternative accounts of the justification of mathematical statements escapes my argument against (WU) because the sources of justification they invoke, like the one that we previously considered, are self-revising. If I can be justified in believing that p on the basis of reading that p in a textbook or hearing a teacher assert that p, then I can also be justified in believing that not-p on the basis of reading that not-p in a textbook or hearing a teacher assert that not-p, and vice-versa. If I can be justified in believing some statement that p solely on the basis of believing that p (or p's seeming true to me), then I can also be justified in believing that not-p solely on the basis of believing that not-p (or not-p's seeming true to me), and vice-versa. Hence, the alternative accounts, when conjoined with (WU), also rule out the possibility that S's belief that p, where p is a mathematical statement, is justified both a priori and by experiential evidence.[22]

Notes

1. Immanuel Kant, *Critique of Pure Reason*, trans. Norman Kemp Smith (New York: St Martin's Press, 1965), 43.
2. Ibid.
3. Ibid., 52.

4. John Stuart Mill, *A System of Logic*, ed. J. M. Robson (Toronto: University of Toronto Press, 1973), 224.
5. Ibid., 231–232.
6. For Mill, the source of one's knowledge that p is the source of one's justification for the belief that p. Accordingly, he maintains that it is not necessary to assume that our knowledge of the axioms of geometry is a priori because experience confirms them in almost every instance of our lives. I frame my discussion in terms of justification, rather than knowledge, since the focus on justification locates more precisely the basis of Mill's argument.
7. R. M. Chisholm, *Theory of Knowledge*, 1st ed (Englewood Cliffs: Prentice-Hall, Inc., 1966), 65.
8. Ibid., 67.
9. W. V. Quine, "Epistemology Naturalized," in *Ontological Relativity and Other Essays* (New York: Columbia University Press, 1969).
10. W. V. Quine, "Two Dogmas of Empiricism," in *From a Logical Point of View*, 2nd ed revised (New York: Harper and Row, 1963).
11. See Albert Casullo, *A Priori Justification* (New York: Oxford University Press, 2003), chapters 1 and 8.
12. Hilary Putnam, " 'Two Dogmas' Revisited," in *Realism and Reason: Philosophical Papers, Vol. 3* (Cambridge: Cambridge University Press, 1983).
13. Ibid., 90.
14. Quine, 43; quoted by Putnam, ibid.
15. Philip Kitcher, *The Nature of Mathematical Knowledge* (New York: Oxford University Press, 1983), 80.
16. Ibid.
17. Self-revision comes in degrees since a source may be able to justify the falsehood of all or only some of the propositions that it can justify.
18. The transition from (6) and (WU*) to (7) presupposes the Equality of Strength Thesis:

    (ES) The degree of justification minimally sufficient for a priori knowledge equals the degree of justification minimally sufficient for knowledge in general.

    For a discussion of (ES) and the implications of denying it, see Casullo, chapter 2.
19. Kitcher, 91–95.
20. William Lycan, "Bealer on the Possibility of Philosophical Knowledge," *Philosophical Studies* 81(1996), 145.
21. Gilbert Harman, "General Foundations versus Rational Insight," *Philosophy and Phenomenological Research* 63 (2001), 657.
22. An earlier version of this paper was presented as the keynote address at the Canadian Society for Epistemology International Symposium on A Priori Knowledge, University of Sherbrooke, October 1–2, 2004. I would like to thank the conference participants and my colleagues at the University of Nebraska-Lincoln for their insightful comments.

Philosophical Perspectives, 19, Epistemology, 2005

WE ARE (ALMOST) ALL EXTERNALISTS NOW*

Juan Comesaña
University of Wisconsin – Madison

I. Introduction

One of the central debates in contemporary epistemology is the debate between internalism and externalism about justification. As with many other interesting philosophical issues, it is not always clear what the dispute is about, and this is, in part at least, because there are a number of *different* internalism/externalism distinctions in epistemology. Some internalists hold that whether a given belief is justified is something that can be discovered *a priori*, or at least from the armchair.[1] Some externalists deny this—for instance, according to some externalists whether a given belief is justified depends on whether it was produced by a reliable belief process, and this is understood to be a paradigmatic case of something that *cannot* be discovered *a priori*.[2] But still some other epistemologists think that the best way to characterize internalism is by appeal not to what can be known a priori or from the armchair, but to what is internal to the mind of the subject having the belief.[3]

In this paper I argue against this latter kind of internalism, which I will call, following Conee and Feldman, "mentalism." More precisely, I will understand mentalism as follows:

> **Mentalism:** All the factors that contribute to the epistemic justification of a doxastic attitude towards a proposition by a subject S are mental states of S.[4]

My objection to mentalism is that there is a special kind of fact (what I call a "support fact") that contributes to the justification of any belief, and that is not mental. My argument against mentalism, then, is the following:

Anti-mentalism argument

1. If mentalism is true, then support facts are mental.
2. Support facts are not mental.

Therefore,
3. Mentalism is not true.

In what follows I explain what support facts are, and then defend each of the premises of my argument. I conclude with some remarks regarding the relevance of my argument for the larger internalism/externalism debate(s) in epistemology.

II. What are support facts?

Let's consider two typical cases of justified belief. In the first case, Sally believes that the streets are wet (let's call this proposition *q*) because she justifiably believes that it is raining and that if it is raining then the streets are wet (let's call the conjunction of these propositions *p*). In the second case, Steve believes that the streets are wet because he is looking at them.[5]

What are the factors that contribute to the justification of the belief that *q* for Sally? It seems clear that these factors must include Sally's being justified in believing that *p*. We might say that Sally's being justified in believing that *p* constitutes her *evidence* for believing that *q*.[6] And what are the factors that justify the belief that *q* for Steve? Here matters are not as clear, but an influential epistemological tradition has it that those factors must include Steve's having a certain visual experience *e* as of the street's being wet.[7] We might say that Steve's having this experience constitutes his evidence for believing that *q*. I want to leave this term, 'evidence,' at an intuitive level. Everything I want to say can be said without appealing to it, although in more tortuous ways.[8]

The evidence that Sally and Steve have for their belief that *q* is part of what justifies each of them in having that belief. Therefore, mentalism entails that the evidence that they have is composed entirely of factors that are mental states of Sally and Steve. I will here grant that mentalism is right as far as evidence is concerned—that is, I will grant that the evidence that Steve and Sally have is composed entirely of mental states of Steve and Sally, respectively.[9]

But the evidence that Steve and Sally have for *q* doesn't exhaust all the factors that contribute to their justification for believing that *q*. In Sally's case, there is also the fact that *p supports q* (in other words, the fact that *p* is a good reason for thinking that *q*), and in Steve's case there is also the fact that *e supports q* (in other words, the fact that if someone has an experience with the same content as *e*, then that provides the subject with a good reason to think that *p*). Call facts of this kind, *support facts*. More generally, whenever a subject is justified in having a belief, there will be some facts in virtue of which the subject is so justified (we can think of these facts as the truth-makers for the claim that the subject is justified in having the belief). We can then distinguish, among those facts, between those that are of the form *the subject is justified in having some other belief(s)*, or *the subject has a certain experience*,[10] which we can call *evidence facts*, and those that are of the form *the subject's belief(s) is (are) a good reason for thinking that r* or *the subject's undergoing a certain experience e is a good reason for thinking that r* (support facts).

Could someone doubt that there are support facts so conceived? Hardly so. Surely, if *p* were not a good reason to believe that *q*, then Sally's being justified in believing that *p* would not justify her in believing that *q*.[11] And all that we are committed to when we commit ourselves to the existence of support facts are facts of that form: *p* supports *q* just in case *p* is a good reason to believe that *q*. So understood, the intuitive position is that there are support facts, and we need an argument to abandon this position.

I turn now to the defense of my anti-mentalism argument. I start with premise 2.

III. Support facts are not mental

On the face of it, the claim that support facts are mental is false. Take Sally's case: which mental state (or condition) of Sally's is the fact that her being justified in believing *p* is a good reason for her to believe that *q*? It cannot be either her believing that *p* or her believing that *q*—the support fact in question is a relation between those mental states of Sally's, and this relation doesn't seem to be reducible to either of its *relata*. But what other mental states of Sally's could possibly be relevant to her being justified in believing *q*, let alone *be* the fact that her believing that *p* is a good reason for believing that *q*? In this section I first generalize these considerations, and then I apply them to two attempts at "mentalizing" support factors, those of Richard Foley and Matthias Steup.

Any mentalist theory will say that there are mental factors M_S of a subject S such that the justificatory status of S's doxastic attitudes is determined by elements of M_S. A mentalist who wishes to claim that support facts are mental, then, will say that they are already included in M_S. But now consider the fact that, with respect to any such theory, we can ask the following question: is it the case that the obtaining of the facts mentioned in M_S is a good reason for holding the doxastic attitude in question? For instance, we can ask, with respect to Sally's case, "Is it the case that the obtaining of Sally's mental facts identified by the specific mentalist theory is a good reason for thinking that *q*?" And here a dilemma ensues. If the answer is "No," then it seems that Sally is not justified in believing that *q*, and so the theory has a counterexample (because it says that Sally is justified in believing that *q*). And if the answer is "Yes," then the theory fails to recognize a factor that is epistemically relevant, because the fact that the obtaining of *all* the epistemically relevant mental factors is a good reason for believing that *q* cannot itself be a mental factor.[12] Therefore, all epistemic theories according to which support factors are mental are either going to have counterexamples or fail to recognize relevant epistemic factors.

But doesn't this objection show too much? Suppose that I am right and Sally is justified in believing that *q* because (i) she is justified in believing that *p* and (ii) *p* is a good reason to think that *q*. Couldn't we then ask: is it the case that the obtaining of the facts mentioned in (i) and (ii) is a good reason for Sally to believe that *q*? And wouldn't then a dilemma similar to the one above arise?

It is true that we can ask, about the factors identified by *any* theory as necessary and sufficient for justification, the same question that we asked above about mentalist theories. But it doesn't follow that we will be able to reconstruct the same dilemma over the possible answers. In particular, the problem identified above with the "No" answer is peculiar to mentalist theories. The facts identified by the non-mentalist epistemologist as necessary for Sally's being justified in believing that *q* include, crucially, the support fact that *p* is a good reason to believe that *q*; and this fact *doesn't* itself support *q*: *that p is a good reason to believe that q* is not itself a good reason to believe that *q*. And this is not because the fact that *p* is a *bad* reason to believe that *q*, but because something's being a good reason to believe that *q* is itself neither a good nor a bad reason to believe that *q*. The obtaining of a support fact between some evidence and the proposition that *q* is not itself a reason to think that *q*, but this doesn't mean that, therefore, there is no good reason to believe that *q*, but simply that support facts themselves are not the right category of things to stand as *relata* of the support relation.[13]

There is an asymmetry, then, between theories according to which support facts are mental and theories according to which they are external: there is an objection to the effect that the conditions posited by the former are not sufficient for justification, whereas there is no parallel objection to the latter. The explanation for this asymmetry is, I believe, that support facts are *stubbornly external*. What I mean by this is the following: a belief that *p* will not be justified unless all of the mental factors that would contribute to its justification offer good reasons to believe that *p*. If this is so, then any attempt to internalize support factors will fail—for, if the theory is right that the internalized version of the old support factor is a necessary condition on justification, then it will be wrong in the identification of the sufficient conditions.

An analogy with Lewis Carroll's tortoise might help explain the predicament that the mentalist finds himself in with respect to support facts, and the asymmetry between the mentalist and the externalist in this respect.[14] Remember that, in Carroll's story, the Tortoise accepts (A) and (B), and yet refuses to accept (Z):

(A) Things that are equal to the same are equal to each other.
(B) The two sides of this Triangle are things that are equal to the same.
(Z) The two sides of this Triangle are equal to each other.

The Tortoise then challenges Achilles to convince him to accept (Z). Achilles tries to get the tortoise to accept:

(C) If (A) and (B) are true, then (Z) must be true.

But by now Achilles is doomed, because the Tortoise will accept (C) as well, and still refuse to accept (Z). The moral that is generally extracted from this story is that there is a crucial difference between premises and rules of inference. Rules of inference have as counterparts statements that can be added as premises to any argument, but any argument is going to use *some* rule of inference or other, and trying to do without them by adding their counterparts as premises leads to an infinite regress. That is why axiomatic systems need rules as well as axioms.

The mentalist finds himself in a position analogous to the one the Tortoise puts Achilles in. Support facts are the analogous of rules of inference, and just as the Tortoise forces Achilles to try to replace rules of inference with their counterparts incorporated as premises, the mentalist tries to replace support facts with mental counterparts. And, just as Achilles fails because any argument needs real rules of inference, and not just premises that mirror rules of inference, the mentalist fails as well because, whenever a subject is justified in believing a proposition, that is partly so because of the existence of support facts, and not just mental facts that mirror them.

The externalist, by contrast, doesn't play the Tortoise's game. The externalist recognizes that support facts are needed, and that they belong to a different category from evidence facts, and refuses to try to incorporate support facts as (mental) evidence. Thus, the externalist avoids the regress that dooms the mentalist.

I have argued that if support facts are conceived of in mentalist terms, then they will not be up to the task of providing the necessary link between evidence and the proposition justified. The argument will obviously need to be tested against particular mentalist proposals regarding support facts. In the remainder of this section I discuss the two main mentalist characterizations of support facts that I am aware of, those of Richard Foley and Matthias Steup.[15]

For Foley, what justifies, for instance, Sally's belief that *q* are: (i) her justified belief that *p*, and (ii) the fact that, if she were to reflect deeply upon the matter, she would believe that the fact that *p* is a good reason for her to believe that *q*. The inclusion of (ii) as a factor relevant to the justification of Sally's belief that *q* is Foley's attempt to incorporate support facts in a mentalistic framework (although Foley himself does not express the point in this terminology). But now consider the following question: is it the case that the obtaining of the facts mentioned in (i) and (ii) is a good reason for Sally to believe that *q*? If the answer to this question is "No," then it seems that Sally is not justified in believing that *q* after all, and so the theory has a counterexample. If the combination of the two mental facts mentioned in (i) and (ii) is not a good reason to believe that *q*, then why would Sally be justified in believing that *p* in virtue of (i) and (ii)? If, on the other hand, the answer is "Yes," then *that* fact (the fact that the obtaining of (i) and (ii) is a good reason for Sally to believe that *q*) is also something the obtaining of which justifies Sally's belief that *q*. But this shows that Foley's theory is inadequate, because it fails to recognize a factor that is epistemically relevant.

The problem runs deep: similar remarks would apply to any theory that tries to mentalize support facts by identifying them with some mental attitude towards the proposition that the evidence offers good reason for the belief in question. To do that is, in effect, to identify a support fact with the fact that the subject has a mental attitude towards that support fact itself. Unless support facts are much stranger beasts than we have reason to believe, they do not behave that way.[16]

But there are ways of attempting to mentalize support facts that do not identify them with any propositional attitude. For Steup, what justifies, for instance, Steve's belief that *q* are: (i) his undergoing experience *e*, and (ii) the fact that he has a memory impression of a track record of both perceptual and memorial success. The inclusion of (ii) as a factor relevant to the justification of Steve's belief that *q* is Steup's attempt to incorporate support facts in a mentalistic framework (although Steup himself does not express the point in this terminology). But now consider the following question: is it the case that the obtaining of the facts mentioned in (i) and (ii) is a good reason for Steve to believe that *q*? If the answer to this question is "No," then it seems that Steve is not justified in believing that *q* after all, and so the theory has a counterexample. If the combination of the two mental facts mentioned in (i) and (ii) is not a good reason to believe that *q*, then why would Steve be justified in believing that *q* in virtue of (i) and (ii)? If, on the other hand, the answer is "Yes," then *that* fact (the fact that the obtaining of (i) and (ii) is a good reason for Steve to believe that *q*) is also something the obtaining of which justifies Steve's belief that *q*. But this shows that Steup's theory is inadequate, because it fails to recognize a factor that is epistemically relevant.

There is another problem with mentalists theories that arises, too, because of their attempt to make support facts mental. In the case of Foley, the problem has been seen by many commentators,[17] but (although I won't develop them here) I believe that similar remarks would apply to Steup's theory.[18] According to Foley, the relevant perspective in evaluating the rationality of a belief is constituted by the subject's deepest epistemic standards—or, what Foley believes to be equivalent, the epistemic standards that the subject would have if she were to reflect deeply.[19] But consider someone who has totally misguided epistemic standards, like the standard that only necessarily true propositions are likely to be true, or perhaps the standard that only necessarily false propositions are likely to be true, or the standard that no proposition whatsoever is likely to be true.[20] All of these are either too narrow or too broad to capture as justified precisely those beliefs that we would intuitively count as justified. So, for instance, if a subject facing a snowball in optimal snowball-viewing conditions and with no defeaters available were to suspend judgment regarding the proposition that there is a snowball in front of him, then that attitude of his would be justified according to Foley provided only that he has a deep epistemic standard that licenses that attitude—for example, if he has the standard that only necessarily false propositions are likely to be true. But even if the subject has that standard, he would be irrational. Let's say that if a belief satisfies Foley's definition for being justified, then it is Foley-rational. The objection, then, is that Foley-rationality gives the correct results for a subject only when the subject holds the correct epistemic principles.

Foley has addressed this objection.[21] His project, he reminds us, arises from what is essentially a Cartesian standpoint: the standpoint of the believer who has nothing but his own cognitive resources in order to make sense of the world. If that is the question, Foley says, then

> it is unhelpful for you to be told to believe some claim only if it is true, and it is equally unhelpful for you to be told to use only reliable methods. Part of your predicament is to determine from your perspective what methods are reliable. In exactly the same way, it is unhelpful for Alston, Feldman and Swain to suggest to you, as each does, that you are to believe only that for which you have objectively adequate grounds, grounds that in fact make probable what you believe. For once again, part of your predicament is that of determining from your perspective what grounds are objectively adequate. And this is something that you can do more or less reasonably.[22]

Indeed, Foley could have added, it is unhelpful for you to be told *anything at all*, for part of your predicament is that of determining under what conditions to believe what you are told.[23]

Maybe Foley has a point here. If there is indeed such a predicament as the one pictured in the Cartesian standpoint, the predicament of figuring out what to believe on the basis of only your own cognitive resources at that moment, then maybe the most reasonable answer to that predicament is to believe all and only those propositions that are Foley-rational for you. But I doubt that there is any such predicament. We start to believe without trying to figure out what to believe, and thus we learn, not only facts but, crucially, new methods of belief formation (like the fundamental method of asking someone who knows). By the time that we become reflective and try to explicitly figure out what to believe—if that time ever comes—we are already in *media res*, armed with "epistemic principles" that license not only the use of glasses, but also asking other people, and appealing to science, etc. At that point, the "predicament" no longer seems that pressing.

Even if we grant Foley his Cartesian starting point, though, what is basically the same objection remains. For now Foley would be right with respect to the answer to the question, "What am I to believe if I am in the Cartesian predicament?," but he would be wrong in thinking that that question has any special epistemological significance. The most reasonable thing to do for someone in the Cartesian predicament and with the deep epistemic principle that only necessarily false propositions are likely to be true is for her to believe those propositions that she thinks are necessarily false. But results like this one show that, in effect, to be Foley-rational in your beliefs is not necessarily to be epistemically justified.

As we said before, then, the two notions (that of Foley-rationality and that of epistemic justification) would be coextensive only for those subjects with *true* deep epistemic principles. And, for those subjects, part of what justifies them is precisely the fact that their deep epistemic principles are true. For instance, if one of Steve's deep epistemic principles is that anyone that undergoes experience *e* is thereby *prima facie* justified in believing that *q*, then a crucial part of what justifies him in believing that *q* is *the fact that* anyone that undergoes experience *e* is thereby *prima facie* justified in believing that *q*, and not the fact that he has this deep epistemic principle.[24] That is, what makes Foley-rationality not even coextensive with epistemic justification is Foley's attempt to internalize support facts by making them mental. Foley's deep epistemic principles are not support facts themselves, but only the counterpart of support facts. As such, they can be epistemically effective only if they are the counterpart of *true* support facts, and in that case their effectiveness derives from the support fact itself.

In this section I have argued that it is hard to make sense of the claim that support facts are mental—in general and in the particular cases of Foley and Steup. I would like to conclude my defense of premise 2 of my argument by pointing out two things. First, some philosophers might believe that support facts are irreducible—that is, that it is not possible to understand facts of the form *p is a good reason to believe that q* in terms that do not already presuppose the language of reasons. I see no special reason for being pessimistic in this way, but what is important to note is that, even if support facts are irreducible in this way, this doesn't at all mean that they are mental. Thus, claiming that support facts are irreducible is no objection to my premise 2. Second, allowing that factive propositional attitudes (like knowing) are mental states will not help either. Of course, if we add to M_S the fact that the subject knows that the elements of M_S are good reason to think that the belief in question is true, then, given that knowledge is factive, it will be true that the elements of M_S are good reason to think that the belief in question is true. But, first, few epistemologists would be comfortable with such a strong "perspectival" requirement on justification; and second, and more importantly, the same objection to Foley's theory applies here as well: when the subject knows that a support fact obtains between his evidence and his belief, what is doing the epistemic work, so to speak, is the support fact itself, and not his knowledge of it. I turn now to the defense of premise 1.

IV. If mentalism is true, then support facts are mental

If I am right so far, then mentalists cannot deny that support facts are not mental. They can still resist the support objection, though, by claiming that mentalism doesn't entail that support facts are mental. In the rest of this paper I consider one position of that kind, suggested by work by Conee and Feldman.

In "Internalism Defended," Conee and Feldman consider and address an objection related to, but different from, the support objection.[25] After presenting their definition of mentalism, which is roughly similar to the one we started with,[26] they go on to say:

> Somewhat more precisely, internalism as we characterize it is committed to the following two theses. The first asserts the strong supervenience of epistemic justification on the mental:
>
> S The justificatory status of a person's doxastic attitudes strongly supervenes on the person's occurrent and dispositional mental states, events, and conditions.
>
> The second thesis spells out a principal implication of S:
>
> M If any two possible individuals are exactly alike mentally, then they are alike justificationally, e.g., the same beliefs are justified for them to the same extent.[27]

As I understand them, when Conee and Feldman say that internalism as they characterize it is "committed" to S and M, they mean that mentalism entails S and M—but they don't mean that the converse entailment holds. Indeed, as we shall see, I think that the converse entailment doesn't hold. But I will consider, at the end of this section, what can be said about the support objection if mentalism is taken to be equivalent to M.

Later in the paper, Conee and Feldman consider an objection that is related to the support objection. About a case like the ones used to motivate the support objection, they say

> We might then say, as a first approximation, that the justifiers for q are (i) the belief that p together with its justification, and (ii) the fact that p supports q. The fact in (ii) is not itself an internal state, and so it might be thought that internalists are faced with the difficult task of finding some internal representation of this state to serve as a justifier.

The objection would continue, then, in one of two non-exclusive ways: first, it can be pointed out that the alleged consequence is not intuitive—there are many cases of subjects that for different reasons don't believe that their evidence justifies their doxastic attitudes, and yet we count them as being justified; second, it can be pointed out that not even sophisticated epistemologists agree with each other about specific instances of justificatory relations—some philosophers think, e.g., that merely having an experience as of *p* is all the evidence one needs to be *prima facie* justified in believing that *p* (when *p* is a simple proposition about the external world), whereas other philosophers think that other beliefs are needed as well. At most one of them is right, and yet surely even those who are wrong are justified in believing some simple proposition about the external world. So, given that mentalism entails that neither the unsophisticated subjects (who don't have beliefs about justificatory relations) nor the sophisticated philosophers (who are wrong about what those relations are) are justified, mentalism is wrong.

The support objection is that mentalism entails that support facts are mental states, and this is clearly false; the objection that Conee and Feldman are considering in the passage quoted is different: it is the objection that mentalism entails that a subject is justified only if she believes that her evidence supports her beliefs, and this is clearly false. Let's call this latter objection the "higher-order requirement" objection. The support objection and the higher-order requirement objection, then, are different; nevertheless, what Conee and Feldman say about the higher-order requirement objection can be used to try to answer the support objection.[28]

In reply to the higher-order requirement objection, Conee and Feldman say the following:

> There is a sense in which p's support for q is a "justifier." It is part of an explanation of the fact that the person's belief in q is justified. But this does not imply that internalists are committed to the view that there must be some internal representation of this fact. It may be that a person's being in the state described by (i) is sufficient for the belief that q to be justified. If so, then all individuals mentally alike in that they share that state are justified in believing q. The fact in (ii) may help to account for the justification without the person making any mental use of that fact.[29]

If both (i) and (ii) are necessary for S to be justified in believing that *p*, then (i) can be sufficient by itself only if (ii) is necessarily true. This is precisely, I think, what Conee and Feldman are hinting at here: that support facts are necessary. In what follows I argue that it is by no means established that all support facts are necessary, and that, even if we grant that they are, the support objection is still fatal.

First, then, it is by no means established that all support facts are necessary. In this regard, it is interesting to note that mentalists who wish to mentalize support facts will, in general, have to think that support facts obtain contingently. This is obviously so in the cases of Foley and Steup discussed above: it is contingent whether or not Sally has a deep epistemic principle that licenses the move from *p* to *q*, and it is contingent whether or not Steve has a memory impression of a track record of both perceptual and memorial success.[30]

Conee and Feldman would likely reply "So much the worse for mentalists who want to mentalize support facts." And, indeed, in the specific cases under examination it is hard not to sympathize with Conee and Feldman on this issue. It seems that our subjects are justified in believing *q* no matter what worlds they are in, as long as they are justified in believing that *p* (in Sally's case) or as long as they are undergoing experience *e*. That is, it seems that, in this case, Conee and Feldman are right to say that (i) is sufficient for the belief that *q* to be justified for S.[31]

But take a different case. Suppose that, in this case, *q* is the belief that all swans are white, and *p* is a conjunction of beliefs of the sort *swan*$_1$ *is white, swan*$_2$ *is white, . . ., swan*$_n$ *is white*, for some fairly large number n. In fact, pick n so that the inductive argument from *p* to *q* is a very good one in our world. It seems that, in this case as well, the subject (let her be Sally again) is justified in believing that *q* because of (i) the belief that *p* together with its justification, and (ii) the fact that *p* supports *q*. But in this case it is far from clear that Sally's being in the state described by (i) is sufficient for her belief that *q* to be justified, for it is far from clear that (ii) states a necessary fact. Therefore, it is far from clear, in this case, that all individuals mentally alike in that they all satisfy (i) will be justified in believing that *q*. Take, for instance, Steve, an individual in a world where most swans are black. He is still, somehow, justified in believing *p* (for instance, the region of the world where he acquires information is a region where most swans are white)—but is he justified in believing *q*? Of course, he doesn't know *q*, if only because *q* is false. But it is plausible to hold that Steve is not even justified in believing *q*—precisely because *p* doesn't support *q* in his world, that is, precisely because (ii) doesn't obtain. In other words, the suggestion is that (even though the subject need not be aware of this) a sample must be representative if an inductive inference is going to justify belief in its conclusion, and that whether a sample is representative is a contingent matter.

Conee and Feldman could reply in one of two ways. First, they could say that Steve is justified after all. The only obvious way to do this would be to say that the inductive argument on which he relies is still a good argument in his world. But this is something hard to say if we choose the example carefully, so that the argument is, intuitively, very bad indeed.

Second, they could say that Steve is not justified in believing that *q* in a world where almost all swans are black, but this doesn't affect mentalism because Sally is not justified in believing *q* in our world either. Being justified in believing *p* is not, in this case, good evidence for a subject to believe that *q*: in addition, the subject must justifiably believe that her world is a normal one, or that the principle of uniformity of nature is true, or some other proposition to the effect that there are no obstacles to moving from *p* to *q*. If she does have such a belief, then she is justified in believing that *q*, but so will be any mental duplicate of hers.

But it seems to me that this is not a clearly good answer either. What is suggested is that even though (ii) (the fact that *p* supports *q*) might be a factor that justifies S in believing that *q*, this is not a counterexample to mentalism. It is not a counterexample, the suggestion is, because the obtaining of (i) (that S is justified in believing that *p*) is, together with a further condition (namely, that S is also justified in believing, say, that the principle of the uniformity of nature is true), sufficient for S's being justified in believing that *q*—and, so, every subject mentally like S in that she also satisfies (i) and is justified in believing in the principle of the uniformity of nature is such that she will be justified in believing that *q*. But is this last claim true? Remember Steve. He might also be justified in believing in the principle of the uniformity of nature—the belief is, to be sure, false, but, after all, the world *around him* is uniform. However, the argument from *p* plus the principle of the uniformity of nature to *q* is still very bad. In fact, all that has changed in the argument is that we have included as a premise a statement of the rule that took us from the original set of premises to the conclusion. If the original argument is bad, then any argument obtained by this transformation is also going to be bad.

I don't think that these are knockdown arguments against Conee and Feldman's claim that all support facts are necessary. Indeed, I think that some version of the first answer—the one that consists in insisting that Steve is justified—could, perhaps, be developed in a promising way. But it is important to point out that Conee and Feldman's defense against the higher-order requirement objection works only if all support facts are necessary, and this is a debatable claim that they haven't argued for.

Be that as it may, I want to grant, for the sake of argument, that all support facts are necessary. There is a much more serious problem for mentalism. The claim that support facts are necessary allows Conee and Feldman to say that, even though *(ii) is a factor that plays a role in the justification of q for S*, this is not a counterexample to M—that is, to the claim that two mental duplicates must be epistemic duplicates as well. But, as the support objection shows, acceptance of the italicized claim is already a refutation of mentalism—not of M, which is a consequence of mentalism, but of mentalism itself.[32]

Remember that (ii) is the claim that *p* supports *q*. This fact, Conee and Feldman agree, is not a mental state of S. So, given that (ii) is a factor that contributes to the fact that *q* is justified for S, then something that is not a mental state is a factor that contributes to the fact that *q* is justified for S. But mentalism is the claim that if something is a factor that is relevant to the justificatory status of a belief for a subject S, then that factor is a mental state of S. So mentalism is false. And whether M itself is shown to be false or not is completely irrelevant. Remember that, after granting that (ii) does play a role in justifying *q* for S, Conee and Feldman remark that "this does not imply that internalists are committed to the view that there must be some internal representation of this fact." Indeed it doesn't, but it surely implies that mentalists are committed to the view that *the fact itself is mental.*

V. Conclusion

Mentalism is refuted by these considerations only if I am right that mentalism entails M but is not in turn entailed by M. So Conee and Feldman could say, in reply, that I interpreted them incorrectly: when they say that mentalism is "committed" to M they mean not only that mentalism entails M, but that it is equivalent to M. There is some textual evidence that supports this alternative interpretation.[33] For instance, when considering Alston's theory that a belief is justified for a subject only if the evidence on which the subject bases that belief makes it objectively probable that the belief is true, Conee and Feldman say:

> If actual frequencies of association, or something else external to the mind and contingent, can make Alston's objective probability vary while the internal grounds remain the same, then his theory is a kind of externalism by our standards. But if it is necessary that the same grounds make the same beliefs objectively probable, then Alston's theory conforms to M and qualifies as a version of internalism. This seems exactly right: it is internalism if and only if *contingent* factors external to the mind cannot make an epistemic difference. (Conee and Feldman "Internalism Defended," p. 234, my emphasis.)

There is, of course, nothing preventing Conee and Feldman from stipulating that mentalism is to be equivalent to M—after all, they introduced the term in the epistemological literature! But there is still a substantive question in the background that cannot be dissolved by linguistic stipulation: which version of mentalism is worth arguing about, one according to which it is equivalent to M or one according to which it is stronger? To some extent, of course, it is worth getting it right with respect to both varieties of mentalism. A central issue regarding whether M is true is whether support facts obtain necessarily or not—an issue that received a preliminary discussion in the last section but that will, I believe, repay further scrutiny.[34] But mentalism is supposed to be a kind of internalism, and whether M is true or not is a tangential matter with respect to whether an interesting kind of internalism is true. No theory that allows an external factor such as (ii) to play a justificatory role is going to be internalist in any interesting sense. If internalism were simply the claim that all the factors that justify a belief are internal factors *except those that are external*, then it wouldn't be a theory worth considering. And M comes awfully close to saying exactly that, for it allows external factors to play a role in the justification of beliefs, as long as those external factors obtain necessarily.

The failure of M to capture an interesting sense of internalism is related to the general failure of supervenience theses to capture interesting dependence relations. Suppose that we want to be physicalists about mental states. If we try to capture our physicalism in terms of a supervenience thesis, we might try something like this:

> P If any two possible individuals are exactly alike physically, then they are alike mentally.

But now consider what would be the case if there were a ghostly (purely non-physical) mental state that is necessary for every subject to be in. That is a situation that no physicalist should be happy to countenance, and yet it is compatible with P. For that reason, P doesn't adequately capture physicalism.

Similarly, it is *precisely because* M is compatible with (necessarily obtaining) external factors affecting the justificatory status of a belief that M doesn't adequately capture internalism.

For those reasons, I think that the interesting internalism/externalism dispute is about whether mentalism as I have defined it is true—and not about whether M is true. I have been arguing that, with respect to this dispute at least, we should all be externalists now. But I also suspect that, once it is made clear what support facts are and why a simple supervenience thesis cannot capture an interesting sense of mentalism, we *are* (almost) all externalists now. To be sure, there might be some (Foley and Steup among them, perhaps) who will still wish to defend mentalism even in this sense. But my suspicion is that some mentalists (like Conee and Feldman) are such only in name, and that once the difference between M and mentalism is clearly made, they too will realize that externalism is true. One can only hope.

Notes

*Thanks to Manuel Comesaña, Earl Conee, Carolina Sartorio, Larry Shapiro, and Elliott Sober for helpful comments on a draft of this paper.

1. Ernest Sosa calls this kind of internalism "Chisholmian Internalism of Justification" in his "Skepticism and the Internal/External Divide," in Greco and Sosa (eds.), *The Blackwell Guide to Epistemology* (Blackwell), 1999, pp. 145–47. Richard Feldman and Earl Conee call it "Accessibilism" in their "Internalism Defended," in Hilary Kornblith (ed.), *Epistemology: Internalism and Externalism* (Blackwell), 2001, pp. 231–60. Proponents of this kind of internalism include Roderick Chisholm, *Theory of Knowledge*, 3rd. ed. (Prentice Hall), 1989 and Richard Fumerton, *Metaepistemology and Skepticism* (Rowman and Littlefield), 1996.
2. Cf. Alvin Goldman, "What is Justified Belief?," in George Pappas, ed., *Justification and Knowledge* (D. Reidel), pp. 1–23 and *Epistemology and Cognition* (Harvard University Press), 1986. Recently, John Hawthorne and Brian Weatherson have argued that maybe we should think more carefully about whether we can know *a priori* that our belief-forming methods are justified—cf. John Hawthorne, "Deeply Contingent A Priori Knowledge," *Philosophy and Phenomenological Research*, September 2002, pp. 247–69, and Brian Weatherson, "Scepticism, Rationality and Externalism," Forthcoming in *Oxford Studies in Epistemology*.
3. Sosa calls this "Cartesian Internalism of Justification," and Conee and Feldman call it "mentalism," the label that I adopt. The foremost defenders of mentalism in contemporary epistemology are Conee and Feldman themselves—cf. also Ralph Wedgwood, "Internalism Explained," *Philosophy and Phenomenological Research* 65 (2002), pp. 349–69, and Richard Foley and Matthias Steup, whose work I discuss below. As will become clear in what follows, one can be an externalist in the sense of not being a mentalist and yet be neutral regarding

accessibilism (that is why I said that only *some* externalists deny the armchair character of epistemology). See note 32.

4. I understand "mental states" broadly, so that dispositions and, more generally, mental conditions of a subject count as mental states. In what follows I limit my attention to belief, although what I said can be generalized to disbelief and suspension of judgment as well. My argument against mentalism still applies even if, with Williamson, we consider factive propositional attitudes (such as knowledge itself) as mental states—cf. Timothy Williamson, *Knowledge and Its Limits* (Oxford University Press), 2002, chapters 1–3. I deal with Conee and Feldman's official definition of mentalism below, in section IV, and in the conclusion I deal with the question whether it is (or it should be) equivalent to my definition.
5. Sally's case is a case of *non-basic justification*, because she is justified in believing a proposition only because she is justified in believing a different proposition, whereas Steve's case is a case of *basic justification*, because he is justified in believing a proposition but not because he is justified in believing a different one. It is also usual to distinguish between *doxastic* and *propositional* justification. A rough characterization of the distinction could go as follows: for the proposition that *p* to be justified for you it is enough for it to be the case that belief would be the appropriate doxastic attitude for you to have with respect to *p* if you were to consider the matter, independently of whether you believe that *p* or not (and, if you do, independently of the reasons for which you believe it); to be doxastically justified in actually believing that *p*, however, more is needed—intuitively, your belief has to be sustained for reasons which justify the proposition for you. The distinction is compatible with different accounts of doxastic and propositional justification, and with different accounts of the relations between these notions. It is also important to note that I am talking here about *prima facie* justification, which can be defeated by contrary evidence.
6. I leave it open whether what is part of Sally's evidence is the fact that her belief that *p* is justified or just her belief that *p*, but only in virtue of the fact that it is justified—deciding between these two options would be important for the issue discussed in note 9.
7. One alternative here is to say that there is nothing that justifies Steve in believing that the streets are wet that is different from the fact that he sees that the streets are wet—something like this is what some disjunctivists might have in mind. Along similar lines, Williamson has argued that beliefs can justify further beliefs only if they amount to knowledge (*Knowledge and its Limits*, chapter 9). I argue against one main motivation for disjunctivism in the case of perceptual knowledge in my "Justified vs. Warranted Perceptual Belief: A Case Against Disjunctivism," forthcoming in *Philosophy and Phenomenological Research*.
8. What I do say about evidence here is compatible with Conee and Feldman's construal of the notion in "Evidentialism," *Philosophical Studies* 48 (1985), pp. 15–34.
9. In Steve's case, it seems obvious that his evidence is mental, at least if we have identified the evidence correctly. Sally's case is complicated by the distinction mentioned in note 6. If her evidence for believing that *q* is her belief that *p* (in virtue of the fact that it is justified), then it is obvious that her evidence is mental.

But if her evidence is the fact that her belief that *p* is justified, then Sally's case is compatible with mentalism only if the fact that Sally *is justified* in believing that *p* is a mental state of Sally's. Now, of course, if mentalism is true, then the fact that Sally is justified in believing that *p is* a mental state of Sally's. But if this is all we can get from the example, we haven't advanced much. In fact, I think that we can get more from the example, but not by concentrating on Sally's evidence. So I am going to grant, for the sake of argument, that mentalism gets it right regarding both Steve's *and Sally's* evidence.

10. For simplicity's sake I talk as if only justified beliefs and experiences could be evidence, but one might also add having certain (ostensive) memories, or having certain "intellectual seemings," as belonging to this first kind of fact.
11. If support facts obtain necessarily (a possibility that I consider below), then if *p* supports *q*, it couldn't have been the case that *p* was not a good reason to believe that *q*, in which case the counterpossible "if *p* had not supported *q*, then *q* wouldn't have been justified" is, one might think, *trivially* true. But (a) it is highly debatable whether conditionals with impossible antecedents are all trivially true; and (b) we can state the fact that *p*'s being a good reason to believe that *q* is a factor that contributes to the justification of *q* in terms other than counterfactual conditionals—for instance, by saying that any explanation of why Sally is justified in believing that *q* that doesn't mention the fact that her being justified in believing that *p* is a good reason for her to believe that *q* is thereby incomplete.
12. *One* of the reasons for thinking that the support fact cannot be already included in M_S can be taken care of if support facts are partly self-referential, perhaps of the form "Evidence E plus the proposition expressed by this sentence support the proposition that *q*." But it is not clear that such sentences are even well-formed, and even if they were they certainly don't look like they refer to mental states.
13. It wouldn't help the internalist to say that the relation of epistemic support is monotonic—so that, if some evidence supports a proposition *q*, then that same evidence plus any proposition (including the proposition that that evidence supports *q*) supports *q*. Besides the fact that this just seems plain wrong, if we went along with it then the externalist would have to admit that the obtaining of evidence *e plus the obtaining of a support fact between e and the belief that q* is a good reason to believe that *q*, but the truth-maker for this claim will be the fact that *e* supports *q*, which is already included among the factors that determine the justificatory status of the belief that *q*. In other words, if the epistemic support relation is nonmonotonic (as it surely is) then the externalist will have no problem with the "No" answer, whereas if it is monotonic then he will have no problem with the "Yes" answer.
14. Cf. Lewis Carroll, "What the Tortoise Said to Achilles," *Mind* 4, No. 14 (1895), pp. 278–80.
15. Cf. Richard Foley, *The Theory of Epistemic Rationality* (Cambridge: MA, Harvard University Press), 1987, *Working Without a Net* (New York, Oxford University Press), 1993, and, for a particularly perspicuous presentation of the issue, "Chisholm's Epistemology," in L. Hahn (ed.), *The Philosophy of Roderick Chisholm* (Library of Living Philosophers), 1997, pp. 475–98; and Matthias Steup, "Internalist Reliabilism," in Ernest Sosa and Enrique Villanueva (eds.), *Philosophical Issues*, Vol. 14, pp. 403–25.

16. Maybe in some cases one can identify a proposition with the fact that some attitude is had towards that same proposition: take the case of a subject whose only belief has the content that he believes something—in this case, it could be argued that both the content of the belief and the fact that the subject believes it have the same truth-maker. As I say in the text, there is no reason to think that support facts are like this.
17. See, for example, Richard Feldman, "Foley's Subjective Foundationalism," *Philosophy and Phenomenological Research* (1989), Vol. 50, No. 1, pp. 149–58.
18. The key in applying the criticism to Steup's theory lies in noticing that the same reasons that he gives in order to require that the subject have a memory impression of a track record of both perceptual *and memorial* success for her sense experiences to be sources of justification for her also indicate that the memory impression in question should be accurate.
19. In "Foley's Subjective Foundationalism," Feldman argues convincingly that the two things are not actually the same—the counterfactual test need not give us the subject's deepest epistemic standards. As Feldman himself notes, this is not fatal to Foley's program, for he need not give us a way of knowing what our deepest epistemic standards are.
20. Or, indeed, consider Foley's own epistemic standards, which include the "no-guarantees" thesis: that, no matter what belief we form, there is no guarantee of *any* sort that the belief will be true.
21. In his "Reply to Alston, Feldman and Swain," *Philosophy and Phenomenological Research* (1989), Vol. 50, No. 1, pp. 169–188.
22. Foley, "Reply to Alston, Feldman and Swain," p. 171.
23. But then, how would what *Foley* tells us be helpful?!
24. Indeed, I would argue that this latter fact is not even necessary, but I don't need to argue this in order to make my point.
25. Earl Conee and Richard Feldman, "Internalism Defended," in Hilary Kornblith (ed.), *Epistemology: Internalism and Externalism* (Blackwell), 2001, pp. 231–260.
26. They say that mentalism "is the view that a person's beliefs are justified only by things that are internal to the person's mental life," "Internalism Defended," p. 233.
27. "Internalism Defended," p. 234.
28. One might take the higher-order objection to be a further move in the dialectic: if the internalist tries to deal with the support objection by internalizing support facts, then he must face the higher-order objection. This would be overkill, however: as I have argued in the previous section, the attempted mentalization of support facts fails in its own terms.
29. Conee and Feldman "Internalism Defended," pp. 251–2.
30. Steup explicitly recognizes that support facts are contingent—see his "Internalist Reliabilism," p. 408.
31. Remember that the justification in question is *prima facie*.
32. An externalist who grants that support facts are necessary can leave it open whether they can be known *a priori* or not, and thus externalism in this sense is perfectly compatible with accessibilism. See note 34.
33. In personal communication neither Conee nor Feldman reported any strong feelings regarding whether they meant mentalism to be equivalent to M or to merely entail it.

34. For what is worth, I think that support facts do obtain necessarily, but only in virtue of the (contingent) fact that our belief-forming practices are reliable—much like, according to some philosophers, water is necessarily H_2O, but only in virtue of contingent chemical facts about the watery stuff around us. More cautiously, I think that a necessary (but probably not sufficient) condition for the obtaining of a support fact between some evidence and the belief in question is that the obtaining of that evidence be an actually reliable indicator of the truth of the belief in question—cf. my "The Diagonal and the Demon," *Philosophical Studies* 110 (2002), pp. 249–66, and my "A Well-Founded Solution to the Generality Problem," *Philosophical Studies*, forthcoming. I do not know whether this means that support facts are knowable only *a posteriori* or not—cf. the articles by John Hawthorne and Brian Weatherson mentioned in note 2.

Philosophical Perspectives, 19, Epistemology, 2005

I CAN'T BELIEVE I'M STUPID[1]

Andy Egan
Australian National University/University of Michigan

Adam Elga
Princeton University

It is bad news to find out that one's cognitive or perceptual faculties are defective. For one thing, it's news that something bad is happening—nobody wants to have defective cognitive or perceptual faculties. For another thing, it can be hard to see what to *do* with such news. It's not always transparent how we ought to revise our beliefs in light of evidence that our mechanisms for forming beliefs (and for revising them in the light of new evidence) are defective.

We have two goals in this paper: First, we'll highlight some important distinctions between different varieties of this sort of bad news. Most importantly, we want to emphasize the following distinction: On the one hand, there is news that a faculty is *unreliable*—that it doesn't track the truth particularly well. On the other hand, there is news that a faculty is *anti-reliable*—that it tends to go positively wrong. These two sorts of news call for extremely different responses. Our second goal is to provide rigorous accounts of these responses.

I.

We begin with an easy case: ordinary, garden variety news of unreliability.

Sadly, we don't have to look far for examples. Take, for instance, the deterioration of memory with age. As you increasingly call students by the wrong names, you begin to think that your memory for names is not what it once was. How should this news of unreliability affect the strength of your beliefs about who has what names? Clearly it would be irresponsible to retain the same degree of confidence that you had before you got the bad news. On the other hand, it would be overreacting to become completely agnostic about which names people bear. What is in order is a modest reduction in confidence.

For instance, across the room is a student—you seem to remember that her name is Sarah. Your decreased trust in your memory should slightly reduce your confidence that her name is Sarah.

But in addition to reducing the strength of your beliefs about who has what names, the news should also reduce the *resiliency* of those beliefs (Skyrms 1977). In particular, the news should make it easier for additional evidence to further reduce your confidence that the student is named Sarah. To bring this out, suppose that from across the room, you hear a third party call the mystery student "Kate". Back when you thought your memory was superb, hearing this would have only slightly reduced your confidence that the student's name was Sarah. (In those days, you would have thought it likely that you'd misheard the word "Kate", or that the third party had made a mistake.) But now that you count your memory as less reliable, hearing someone refer to the mystery student as "Kate" should significantly reduce your confidence that her name is Sarah. You should think it fairly likely that you misremembered. This illustrates the way in which news of unreliability should reduce the resiliency—and not just the strength—of your beliefs about names.

How much reduction in strength and resiliency is called for? This of course depends on how compelling the news of unreliability is, and on the strength of the competing source of information. It is worth working through a simple example to see how things go.

Suppose that you're certain that the student in question is either named Sarah or Kate. Think of your memory as a channel of information with 99% reliability: it had a 99% chance of making and sustaining a correct impression of the student's name. (We're starting with the case in which you count your memory as being superb.) And think of the words that you overhear across the room as an independent channel of information, with 95% reliability.

Initially, your memory indicates that the student's name is Sarah, and so you believe this to degree .99. (Here it is assumed that, independent of your memory impressions, you count each name as equally likely.) But when you hear someone call the student "Kate", you become less confident that she is named Sarah. A quick Bayesian calculation[2] shows that your new level of confidence is .84.

So: in the "superb memory" condition, you start out very confident that the student is named Sarah (.99), and this confidence is reduced only modestly (to .84) when you overhear "Kate". How would the calculation have gone if you had counted your memory as less than 99% reliable? Suppose, for example, that you had counted your memory as being merely 90% reliable. In that case, your initial degree of belief that the student was named Sarah would have been .9—slightly lower than the corresponding degree of belief in the "superb memory" condition. Now let us consider how resilient that .9 would have been. That is, let us check how much your confidence would have been reduced upon overhearing someone call the student "Kate". Answer:[3] your new level of confidence would have been .32.

This low value of .32 brings out a striking contrast. In the "superb memory" condition, your level of confidence that the student was named Sarah was fairly *resilient*. But in the "just OK memory" condition, that level of confidence is *not at all resilient*: overhearing "Kate" in this condition *massively* reduces your confidence that the student is named Sarah. See Figure 1.

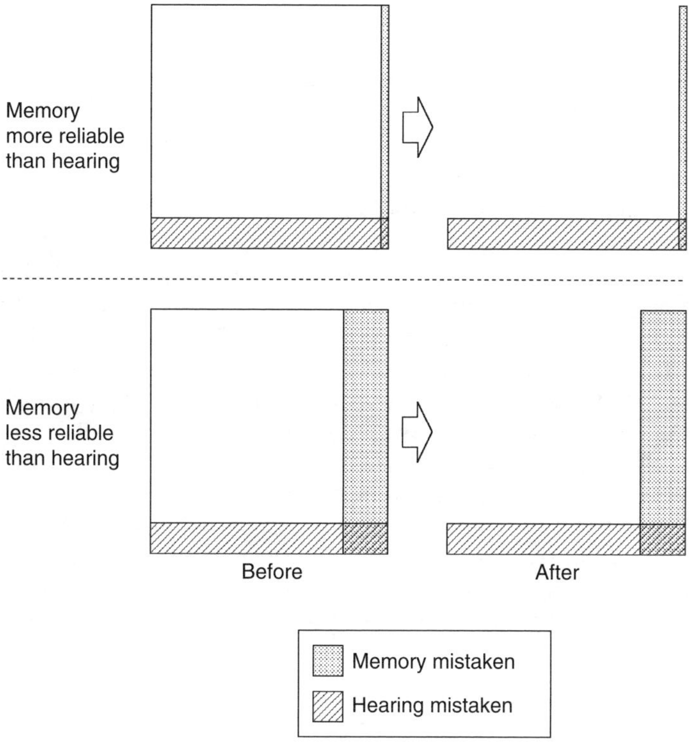

Figure 1. How reduced trust in your memory makes your memory-based beliefs much less resilient. You are attempting to determine whether a particular student is named Sarah or Kate. Initially, you seem to remember that the student is named Sarah. Each row of the figure shows how your confidence in this memory is reduced when you seem to overhear the student addressed as "Kate". In the *top row*, you are initially extremely confident in your memory—as is reflected by the extreme narrowness of the shaded region of the upper-left square (regions correspond to propositions, and each propositions has an area proportional to its probability). Seeming to hear the student addressed as "Kate" indicates that either your memory or your hearing is mistaken—which corresponds to ruling out the blank region, in which both your memory and your hearing are correct. As a result, your confidence that your memory is mistaken only increases slightly (since the shaded region only occupies a small proportion of the remaining area). In contrast, if you had started out with less initial confidence in your memory (*bottom row*), seeming to overhear "Kate" would have drastically increased your confidence that your memory was mistaken, since erasing the blank region would leave more than half of the remaining area shaded.

The above is merely a toy example, but the lesson generalizes:

> When one initially counts a channel of information as extremely reliable, a small reduction in that reliability should (a) slightly reduce your confidence in beliefs deriving from that channel, but (b) massively reduce the resiliency of those beliefs.

II.

The above is what happens in general when we get evidence that some source of information is unreliable—it wasn't important that the source of information was one of our own cognitive mechanisms. Exactly the same thing happens when our confidence in an external source of information—a newspaper, an informant, a doctrinal text—is undermined,

The case of the doctrinal text is particularly interesting: one piece of practical advice that emerges from the above discussion is that, when some faith (either religious or secular) is based on a particular revered and authoritative text, a good way to undermine that faith is to first convince the faithful that the text isn't so authoritative after all, rather than simply arguing against particular points of doctrine. So long as the flock thinks that the text is the product of divine inspiration (or of superhuman genius), they will likely count it as extremely reliable, which will make them relatively immune to corruption by other sources of evidence. But even small reductions in how much they trust the text will make the flock *much* more easily convinced that particular bits of doctrine are wrong. On the other side of the coin, it may be that the best way to protect such a text-based faith is not to defend the points of doctrine piecemeal, but to defend the infallibility (or at least the near-infallibility) of the text.

III.

The memory example above was particularly clean. In it, the news you received concerned the unreliability of only a single faculty (memory for names). Furthermore, your ability to get and respond to the news did not rely on the faculty in question.

Because the news was confined to a single faculty, it was easy to "bracket off" the outputs of that faculty, and to thereby see which of your beliefs deserved reduced strength and resiliency as a result of the news. The same would go for news of the unreliability of any perceptual system or reasoning process in a well-delineated domain. For example, one might find that one tends to misread the orders of digits in phone numbers. Or one might find that one is particularly unreliable at answering ethical questions when one is hungry. In each such case, the thing to do is to treat the outputs of the faculty in question with the same caution one might treat the display of an unreliable wristwatch.

Things aren't always so simple. Consider, for example, a case in which news of unreliability arrives by way of the very faculty whose reliability is called into question:

> Your trusted doctor delivers an unpleasant shock. "I am afraid that you have developed a poor memory for conversations," she says. "Overnight, your memories of conversations had on the previous day often get distorted." The next day, you wake up and recall the bad news. But you aren't sure how much to trust this memory. As you trust it more, you begin to think that you have a bad memory—and hence that it doesn't deserve your trust. On the other hand, as you doubt your memory, you undermine your reason for doing so. For the remembered conversation is your only reason for thinking that you have a poor memory.[4]

Neither resting place (trusting your memory, or failing to trust it) seems stable. Yet there should be some reasonable way for you to react. What is it?

The answer is that you should partially trust your memory. As an example, let us fill in some details about your prior beliefs. Suppose that you were antecedently rather confident (90%) in the reliability of your memory. Suppose that conditional on your memory being reliable, you counted it as very unlikely (1%) that you would remember your doctor reporting that your memory was unreliable. And suppose that conditional on your memory being unreliable, you thought it quite a bit more likely that you'd remember your doctor reporting that your memory was unreliable (20%). Then an easy calculation[5] shows that when you wake up the day after your doctor's visit, your confidence that your memory is reliable should be approximately .31.

The resulting state of mind is one in which you have significant doubts about the reliability of your memory. But this is not because you think that you have a reliable memory of yesterday's conversation. Rather, it is because your memory of the conversation is simultaneous evidence that (1) your memory is unreliable and (2) it has happened to get things right in this particular case. (Note that since there is a tension between (1) and (2), the reduction in trust in your memory is not as dramatic as it would have been if you had possessed, for example, a written record of your conversation with the doctor.)

The above case is analogous to the case of a self-diagnosing machine, which reports periodically on its own status. When the machine outputs "I am broken", that might be evidence that a generally unreliable self-diagnostic process has gone right on this particular occasion, so that the machine is faithfully (though not reliably) transmitting the news of its own unreliability. Alternatively, the output might have the same kind of evidential force as the output "I am a fish stick": it might be evidence that the machine is broken simply because working machines are unlikely to produce such output. Either way, we have an example of a mechanism delivering news of its own unreliability, without that news completely undermining itself.

The above is, again, only a toy example. But again, the lesson generalizes:

> News of unreliability can come by way of the very faculty whose reliability is called into question. The news need not completely undermine itself, since the reasonable response can be to become confident that the faculty is unreliable, but has happened to deliver correct news in this instance.

IV.

Now let us turn to anti-reliability.

In the simplest case, news of anti-reliability is easy to accommodate. Consider a compass, for example. When the compass is slightly unreliable, the direction it points tends to be close to North. When the compass is completely unreliable, the direction it points provides no indication at all of which direction is North. And when the compass is anti-reliable, it tends to point *away* from North. Upon finding out that one's compass is anti-reliable, one should recalibrate, by treating it as an indicator of which direction is *South*.

Similarly, one might learn that a perceptual or cognitive faculty is anti-reliable, in the sense that it delivers systematically mistaken or distorted outputs. For example, one might find that when judging whether a poker opponent is bluffing, one's initial instinct tends to be wrong. Here, too, one should recalibrate. For example, one should treat the initial hunch "Liz is bluffing" as an indication that Liz is *not* bluffing.

Other cases are trickier.

One of the authors of this paper has horrible navigational instincts. When this author—call him "AE"—has to make a close judgment call as to which of two roads to take, he tends to take the wrong road. If it were just AE's first instincts that were mistaken, this would be no handicap. Approaching an intersection, AE would simply check which way he is initially inclined to go, and then go the opposite way. Unfortunately, it is not merely AE's first instincts that go wrong: it is his all-things-considered judgments. As a result, his worse-than-chance navigational performance persists, despite his full awareness of it. For example, he tends to take the wrong road, even when he second-guesses himself by choosing against his initial inclinations.

Now: AE faces an unfamiliar intersection. What should he believe about which turn is correct, given the anti-reliability of his all-things-considered judgments? Answer: AE should suspend judgment. For that is the only stable state of belief available to him, since any other state undermines itself. For example, if AE were at all confident that he should turn left, that confidence would itself be evidence that he should not turn left. In other words, AE should realize that, were he to form strong navigational opinions, those opinions would tend to be mistaken. Realizing this, he should refrain from forming strong navigational opinions (and should outsource his navigational decision-making to someone else whenever possible).[6]

Moral: When one becomes convinced that one's all-things-considered judgments in a domain are produced by an anti-reliable process, one should suspend judgment in that domain.

V.

When AE faces an intersection, what forces AE into suspending judgment is the following: his decisive states of belief undermine themselves. For it would be unreasonable for him to both make a navigational judgment and to think that such judgments tend to go wrong. In other words, it is unreasonable for AE to count himself as an *anti-expert*—someone whose state of belief on a given subject matter is quite far from the truth (Sorensen 1988, 392). And this is no mere special case: *It is never reasonable to count oneself as an anti-expert.*[7] It follows that there are limits on the level of misleadingness one can reasonably ascribe to one's own faculties, no matter *what* evidence one gets. Let us sharpen up and defend these claims.

Start with anti-expertise. It is never rational to count oneself as an anti-expert because doing so must involve either incoherence or poor access to one's own beliefs. And rationality requires coherence and decent access to one's own beliefs.

The latter claim—that rationality requires coherence and decent access to one's own beliefs—we shall simply take for granted.[8] Our interest here is in defending the former claim: that counting oneself as an anti-expert requires either incoherence or poor access to one's own beliefs.

Start with the simplest case: the claim that one is an anti-expert with respect to a single proposition. For example, consider the claim that one is mistaken about whether it is raining:

(M) Either it is raining and I believe that it is not raining, or else it is not raining and I believe that it is raining.

No consistent agent with perfect access to her own beliefs believes M. For if such an agent believes that it is raining, she also believes that she so believes—and together these two beliefs are inconsistent with M. The same goes if she believes that it is not raining. The only other possibility is that she suspends judgment on whether it is raining, in which case she believes that she suspends judgment—which is also inconsistent with M.

The bottom line is that no consistent agent with perfect access to her own beliefs believes that she is an anti-expert with respect to a given single proposition. This is familiar news, since the relevant claim of anti-expertise is a close cousin of the famously Moore-paradoxical claim:

It is raining but I don't believe that it is. (Sorensen 1988, 15)

What is less obvious, however, is that the same Moore-paradoxicality infects claims of anti-expertise in more general settings. For example, when an entire subject-matter (not just a single proposition) is in play, the claim that one is an anti-expert with respect to that subject-matter is also Moore-paradoxical. And this result is no mere artifact of treating belief as an all-or-nothing matter: it continues to hold when degrees of belief are taken into account. Furthermore, we can be precise about the maximum degree to which one can reasonably believe that one is an anti-expert. Finally, none of these conclusions require the assumption of *perfect* access to one's own state of belief: they hold even under the assumption of *good* access to one's own state of belief.

Showing all of this will take some doing.

VI.

To be an anti-expert on a subject matter is to have beliefs on the subject matter that are inaccurate—quite far from the truth. But what exactly is it for a state of belief to be inaccurate with respect to a subject matter?

Here is one simple answer. Restrict attention to a finite list of propositions, chosen to represent a subject matter. Let us say that an agent is an anti-expert with respect to those propositions if (1) the agent is *confident* in at least one of them, in the sense that his degree of belief in it is at least 90%; and (2) at least half of the propositions (on the list) that the agent is confident in are false. For example, for AE to be an anti-expert about geography—as represented by an appropriate list of geographical propositions—is for him to be confident in at least one of those propositions, and at least half of the ones he is confident in to be false.

It turns out that the claim "I am an anti-expert about geography" is *unbelievable*, in the following sense. No coherent agent who is correct about her own beliefs believes it to degree greater than 20%.[9] For the details, we refer interested readers to Figure 2 and Appendix A, but the guiding idea can be illustrated in the special case of a subject matter that consists of exactly two propositions. Suppose that such an agent has 90% confidence in each of the two propositions. Then she must be at least 80% confident in their conjunction (for the same reason that two carpets, each of which covers 90% of the floor space of a single room, must overlap on at least 80% of the space). So she must be at least 80% confident that she is correct in both of her confident beliefs on the subject matter—and hence can be at most 20% confident that she is an anti-expert.[10]

The bottom line: no coherent agent who is correct about her own beliefs has degree of belief higher than 20% that she is an anti-expert.

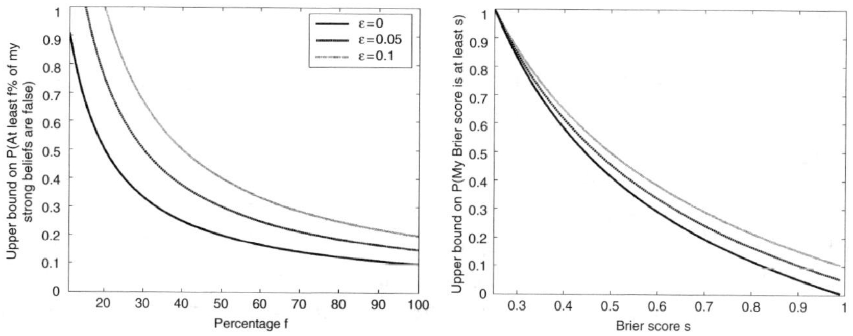

Figure 2. Upper bounds on probability of anti-expertise. Left: For each percentage *f*, graphed is an upper bound on the probability one can reasonably have that at least *f*% of one's confident (≥*90%*) beliefs are false. Right: For each score *s*, graphed is an upper bound on the probability one can reasonably have that one's Brier score is at least *s*.

In each case, it is assumed that reasonable agents are mistaken about their own degrees of belief by no more than ε, and graphs are shown for ε=0 (solid line), .05 (dashed line), and .1 (dotted line).

Now, the numerical details of the above result depend on spelling out anti-expertise in a particular way. And the way in which we've spelled it out is admittedly not very sophisticated. But fancier measures of inaccuracy change only the details: using them leads to results of the same qualitative nature. For example, one might gauge the accuracy of a state of belief by its *Brier Score*, a measure used to assess probabilistic weather predictions (Brier 1950, as cited in Joyce 1998). The Brier score measures inaccuracy on a scale of 0 (not at all inaccurate) to 1 (completely inaccurate).[10] It can be shown that every coherent agent who is correct about her own degrees of belief assigns low probability to the hypothesis that she has a high Brier score. (For instance, such an agent always has probability less than .3 that her Brier score is greater than .6. See Figure 2 and Appendix B.)

The above results concern agents who are *perfectly* correct about their own degrees of belief. Some consider this assumption too strong, even for ideally rational agents (Williamson 2000), (Williamson forthcoming). So it is worth noting that the results are perturbed only slightly if we modestly relax the assumption of perfect introspective access. For example, we might restrict attention to coherent agents who are *nearly* correct about their own degrees of belief. It remains true that every such agent assigns low probability to the proposition that she is an anti-expert. (For the details, see appendices A and B.)

The bottom line:

Given a fixed subject matter, any coherent agent who has decent access toher own beliefs assigns a low probability to the claim that she is an anti-expert about that subject matter. It follows that it can never be rational to count oneself as an anti-expert about a given subject matter.

VII.

It is unreasonable to count oneself as an anti-expert. In contrast, it can be perfectly reasonable to count someone *else* as an anti-expert. This contrast can seem puzzling. Why treat evidence about oneself so differently than evidence about others?

For example, consider Professor X. Readers of Professor X's books on geology note that her geological opinions are far from the truth. They also note that each book she publishes is as inaccurate as its predecessors, even though in each case Professor X acknowledges her past inaccuracy and tries to correct matters. Such readers may reasonably count Professor X as an incorrigible anti-expert about geology.

Now suppose that Professor X receives an anonymized version of her own track record: she is told that a certain unnamed scholar has produced a number of books, that the books have been persistently inaccurate, and so on. Couldn't Professor X reasonably conclude that the scholar in question is an anti-expert? And couldn't that judgment reasonably persist, even if she were told that the scholar in question was Professor X herself?

The alternative seems to be that rationality requires an illegitimate sort of chauvinism—that it requires Professor X to say, "When I thought that the unnamed scholar was someone else, *then* I had excellent evidence that this unfortunate soul was an incorrigible anti-expert. But not if the unnamed scholar was *me*!" That looks like pure arrogance. Yet it seems to be the response we must recommend, if we are to insist that one can never reasonably count oneself as an anti-expert. What has gone wrong?

What has gone wrong is that Professor X's response has been misrepresented. When Professor X finds out that the hapless scholar is her, she should become convinced that she has been an anti-expert. But she should do something about it: she should change her opinions about geology in such a way that she is no longer an anti-expert. For the news of her past anti-expertise is evidence that her present geological views are mistaken.

In contrast, if Professor X finds out that someone *else* has been an anti-expert about geology, that need not count at all against Professor X's present geological views. For example, it may be perfectly reasonable for Professor X to think: "Dr. Z is an incorrigible anti-expert about geology. His present geological opinions are quite far from the truth." This attitude may be reasonable because Professor X's geological opinions may be quite different from those of Dr. Z. Learning that Dr. Z's geological opinions are largely false will undermine Professor X's beliefs about geology only to the extent that Professor X, prior to receiving this news, agreed with Dr. Z.

A comparison with a simpler case is helpful here. Suppose that you are informed, "Before you received this news, you were mistaken about whether it is raining". In response, you ought to change your mind about whether it is raining. In contrast, if you are informed, "Before you received this news, *Fred* was mistaken about whether it is raining", you need be under no pressure at all to change your beliefs about the rain.

How exactly should Professor X change her geological views in the light of her dismal record? That depends on her assessment of her own abilities to recalibrate in such situations. If she trusts her ability to recalibrate, then she should do so. After doing so, she will have a state of geological opinion that she can stand behind. She will judge that she *was* an anti-expert, but that she is one no longer.

It might be that Professor X does not trust her ability to recalibrate. For example, the record might show that her past attempts to do so have been unsuccessful, and that another attempt is unlikely to do better. In that case she is in the same situation with respect to geology that AE was with respect to navigation. She should think that any confident opinions she forms about geology are liable to be mistaken. So she should suspend judgment about geological matters.

Suspending judgment guarantees that Professor X is no longer an anti-expert, since anti-expertise requires not just ignorance, but error. For example, one can only be an anti-expert about a subject matter if one holds at least one belief in the subject matter with confidence at least 90%. Similarly, one can only have a large Brier score by having many probabilities that are close to 0 or 1. More generally, one can only have a state of opinion that is extremely far from the truth by being confident in many falsehoods.

If Professor X suspends judgment, she may reasonably believe that she *was* an anti-expert (back when she had strong geological opinions). She may reasonably believe that she *would* be an anti-expert (if she were to form such opinions). She may even reasonably believe that she *will* be an anti-expert in the future (because she expects to be unable to resist forming such opinions). But this all falls short of believing that she is *presently* an anti-expert. And that she may not reasonably do.[11]

The bottom line is that one *should* treat news of someone else's past anti-expertise in a different way than one treats the corresponding news about oneself. But this is not due to chauvinism or arrogance. Rather, it is because news of one's own anti-expertise on a subject matter is inevitably evidence against one's current views on the subject matter. And no such inevitability holds in the case of news about someone else.

VIII.

On one natural way of understanding what it takes to be stupid, stupidity is productively contrasted with ignorance. The ignorant person lacks information, and so lacks strong opinions. The stupid person has strongly held *false* opinions, gotten as a result of lousy reasoning. In one sense, ignorance and stupidity are possibilities for me: other people, similar to me in relevant respects, can be both ignorant and stupid. I don't take my cognitive faculties to be constructed in some special way that precludes either ignorance or stupidity. But there is also a sense in which ignorance, but not stupidity, is a possibility for me: I can reasonably believe that I'm ignorant, but I can't believe I'm stupid.

Appendix A

The main text introduces the notion of an agent being an anti-expert about a subject matter, in the sense that at least half of the agent's confident beliefs about the subject matter are false. Here we introduce the more general notion of an agent being *f-wrong* about a subject matter (where f is some fixed fraction, not necessarily equal to one half), and give a bound for how confident a reasonable agent can be that he is f-wrong.

The bound derives from the following lemma.

Carpet lemma: Suppose that you are given n carpets, each of which occupies at least fraction x of a room with unit area. Your job is to lay all of the carpets in order to minimize A, the area that is covered by more than m layers of carpeting, where $m<n$. You may cut and overlap carpets if necessary, but no two pieces of the same carpet may overlap. *Claim*: You can do no better than $A = \text{MAX}\{0,(nx-m)/(n-m)\}$.

Proof: Consider the most favorable case, in which each carpet occupies exactly fraction x of the floor space. Then the total area of carpet to be placed is nx. Your most efficient carpet-laying strategy is as follows. First, fill the entire room uniformly to depth m. If $nx \leq m$, this task will exhaust all of the carpet, and you will have completed your task with $A = 0$. Otherwise, you will have laid area m of carpet, which leaves area nx-m of extra carpet remaining. You wish to minimize the area that this additional carpet covers, which means piling it up as high as possible over a single region. (See Figure 3 for an example.) But piling higher than n total layers is disallowed, since there are n carpets and no two pieces of the same carpet are allowed to overlap. So you must stash the extra carpet in a pile at most n-m layers high. So the extra carpet must cover an area of at least (extra carpet left/additional layers allowed), which equals (nx-m)/(n-m).

Let us use this lemma to derive our bound.

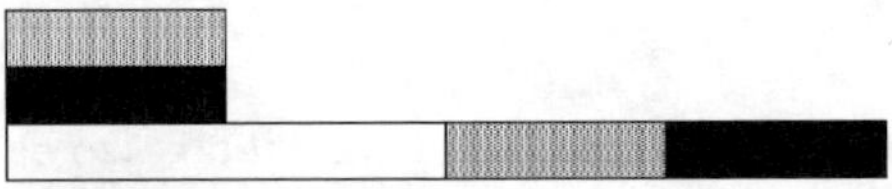

Figure 3. How to lay 3 carpets of area 1/2 in order to minimize the area covered by more than one carpet.

First some terminology and assumptions: Restrict attention to a finite set D of propositions, chosen to represent a subject matter. Let us say that an agent is *f-wrong* with respect to D if (1) the agent is *confident in* at least one member of D, in the sense that his degree of belief in it is at least x; and (2) more than fraction f of the propositions in D that the agent is confident in are false.

Assume that the agent in question has probability function P, and that he has good access to his own beliefs, in the following sense. For any proposition in D, the agent's actual degree of belief in that proposition is within ε of the degree of belief he thinks he has in it. In other words, the agent is certain that he has probability function Q, where for any X_i in S, $|Q(X_i) - P(X_i)| \leq \varepsilon$.

Claim. The agent's probability that he is f-wrong about D is no greater than $(1 - x + \varepsilon)/f$.

Proof. Let S be the set of propositions in the subject matter that the agent believes she is confident in. If S is empty, then the agent has probability zero that he is f-wrong, and we are done. Otherwise, let n be the cardinality of S. Then the agent's probability that he is f-wrong is

$$\begin{aligned} \text{P(I am f-wrong about S)} &= \text{P(fraction of propositions in S that are false} > \text{f)} \\ &= 1 - \text{P(fraction of propositions in S that are false} \leq \text{f)} \\ &= 1 - \text{P(fraction of propositions in S that are true} > 1 - \text{f)} \\ &= 1 - \text{P(number of propositions in S that are true} > \text{m)}, \end{aligned}$$

where $m = (1 - f)n$. We will get an upper bound on P(I am f-wrong about S) by getting a lower bound on P(number of propositions in S that are true > m). Without loss of generality, assume that m is an integer.

Think of logical space as a room with unit area, and think of each member of S as a carpet. In the analogy, minimizing the probability that more than m of the members of S are true corresponds to minimizing the area that is covered by more than m layers of carpet, under the conditions of the carpet lemma. Since the agent *thinks* she has at least probability x in each member of S, she *really* has probability of at least $x - \varepsilon$ in each member of S (by the assumption of good access). So we can apply the carpet lemma, assuming that each carpet has an area of at least $x - \varepsilon$. The result is that P(number of true propositions in S > m) $\leq (n(x - \varepsilon) - m)/(n - m)$, which equals $1 + (x - 1 - \varepsilon)/f$. So we have that

$$\begin{aligned} \text{P(I am f-wrong about S)} &= 1 - \text{P(fraction of propositions in S that are true} > 1 - \text{f)} \\ &\leq 1 - (1 + (x - 1 - \varepsilon)/f) \\ &= (1 - x + \varepsilon)/f. \end{aligned}$$

Q.E.D.

Appendix B

The Brier score B(P, D) of a probability function P measures the inaccuracy of P with respect to a finite set $D = \{X_1, X_2, \ldots, X_n\}$ of propositions. It is defined by

$$B(P, D) = df\ 1/n\ \Sigma_i(P(X_i) - T(X_i))^2,$$

where $T(X_i)$ is the truth value of X_i: 0 for falsity, 1 for truth.

Let P be the probability function of an agent who has good access to her own beliefs, in the same sense as described in Appendix A: the agent is certain that she has probability function Q, where for any X_i in D, $|Q(X_i) - P(X_i)| \leq \varepsilon$.

For a given value s, we seek an upper bound on how likely the agent can think it is that her Brier score is at least s. When $Q(X_i) = 1/2$ for all i, the agent will be sure that her Brier score is exactly 1/4. So we can only hope to get a substantive bound by assuming that $s > 1/4$. Without loss of generality, assume that $Q(X_i) \geq 1/2$ for all i. (No generality is lost because we can always replace X_i with not-X_i whenever $Q(X_i) < 1/2$.)

Claim. $P(B \geq s) \leq (1 - \sqrt{s})/\sqrt{s} + 2rm\varepsilon(\sqrt{s} - 1/2)/s$.
Proof. Notation: we write B for B(P, D), P_i for $P(X_i)$, and Q_i for $Q(X_i)$. We proceed by computing an upper bound on the agent's expectation for her Brier score, and then applying Markov's inequality.

The agent's expectation for her Brier score is given by

$$\begin{aligned} E[B] &= E[1/n\,\Sigma_i(P_i - T(X_i))^2] \\ &= 1/n\ \Sigma_i E[T(X_i)^2 + Q_i^2 - 2T(X_i)Q_i] \\ &= 1/n\ \Sigma_i P_i + Q_i^2 - 2P_iQ_i, \end{aligned}$$

where the third equality follows because $E[T(X_i)^2] = E[T(X_i)] = P_i$, and because $E[Q_i] = Q_i$.

Give the agent's good access to her beliefs, this expectation can never be greater than when $Q_i = P_i + \varepsilon$ for all X_i. So let us assume this. Then we may continue simplifying as follows

$$\begin{aligned} E[B] &= 1/n\ \Sigma_i P_i + (P_i + rm\varepsilon)^2 - 2P_i(P_i + rm\varepsilon) \\ &= 1/n\ \Sigma_i P_i(1 - P_i)) + rm\varepsilon^2. \end{aligned}$$

Now, in order for the Brier score to be at least s, it must be at least s in the "worst case"—the case in which all X_i are false. The agent is certain that in that case her Brier score is $1/n\Sigma Q_i^2$. So in order for the agent to have any credence that her Brier score is at least s, it must be that $1/n\Sigma Q_i^2 \geq s$. Subject to that constraint, the agent's expectation for her Brier score is maximized when $P_i = \sqrt{s} - \varepsilon$ for all i, as can be shown by using the method of Lagrange multipliers.[12]

When P takes the above values,

$$\begin{aligned} E[B] &= 1/n\ \Sigma_i P_i(1 - P_i)) + \varepsilon^2 \\ &= 1/n\ \Sigma_i(\sqrt{s} - \varepsilon)(1 - \sqrt{s} - \varepsilon) \\ &= \sqrt{s}(1 - \sqrt{s}) + 2\varepsilon(\sqrt{s} - 1/2). \end{aligned}$$

In other words, whenever $P(B \geq s) > 0$, E[B] can never exceed the above value.

Assuming that E[B] achieves the above value, set $K = s/E[B]$, so that $s = KE[B]$. Then $P(B \geq s) = P(B \geq KE[B])$, which is no greater than 1/K, by Markov's inequality (Motwani 1995, 46). So we have that

$$\begin{aligned} P(B \geq s) &\leq 1/K \\ &= E[B]/s \\ &= (\sqrt{s}(1 - \sqrt{s}) + 2\varepsilon(\sqrt{s} - 1/2))/s \\ &= (1 - \sqrt{s})/\sqrt{s} + 2\varepsilon(\sqrt{s} - 1/2)/s. \end{aligned}$$

Q.E.D.

Notes

1. Thanks to Martin Davies, Campbell Brown, Ben Blumson, Ralph Wedgwood.
2. P (student is named Sarah | overheard someone call her "Kate")

$$\begin{aligned} &= P(S|K) \\ &= P(K|S)P(S)/P(K) \\ &= P(K|S)P(S)/(P(K|S)P(S) + P(K| \sim S)P(\sim S)). \\ &= .05^*.99/(.05^*.99 + .95^*.01) \\ &\approx .84 \end{aligned}$$

3. P (student is named Sarah | overheard someone call her "Kate")=

$$\begin{aligned} &= P(K|S)P(S)/(P(K|S)P(S) + P(K| \sim S)P(\sim S)) \\ &= .05^*.90/(.05^*.90 + .95^*.10) \\ &\approx .32 \end{aligned}$$

4. Cf. example 3 ("The Antidote") from Talbott (2002), 160–1.

5. P(memory is reliable | seem to remember doctor saying "your memory is unreliable")

$$= P(R|C)$$
$$= P(C|R)P(R)/(P(C|R)P(R) + P(C|\sim R)P(\sim R))$$
$$= .01^*.9/(.01^*.9 + .2^*.1)$$
$$\approx .31$$

6. In an even worse case, AE believes not just that his confident navigational judgments tend to be wrong, but also that he only suspends judgment in cases in which the thing to do is turn left. Here AE's beliefs are unstable even if he suspends judgment.
7. For a discussion and defense of this claim in the case of all-or-nothing belief in a single proposition, see Sorensen (1988), 392–396.
8. We note that this claim is disputed. See, for example, Harman (1986).
9. Compare the discussion of "Most of my beliefs are false" in Sorensen (1988), 48–49.
10. The Brier score of a probability function P on a list of n propositions $\{X_i\}$ is defined to be: $1/n\Sigma_i(P(X_i) - T(X_i))^2$, where $T(X_i)$ is the truth value of X_i: 0 for falsity, 1 for truth.
11. Compare Sorensen (1988), 391–2.
12. We wish to find $P_1,\ldots,P_n$ which maximize $f(P_1,\ldots,P_n)$ subject to the constraint that $g(P_1,\ldots, P_n) \geq 0$, where $f(P_1,\ldots,P_n) = E[B] = (1/n\Sigma_i P_i(1 - P_i)) + \varepsilon^2)$, and $g(P_1,\ldots,P_n) = (1/n\Sigma_i Q_i^2) - s = (1/n\Sigma_i(P_i + \varepsilon)^2) - s$. We may instead use the constraint $g(P) = 0$, since increasing $g(P_1,\ldots,P_n)$ can only done by increasing some P_i, which reduces f(P). Extrema of f(P) occur when $\nabla f = \lambda \nabla g$, i.e., when for all i, $\partial f/\partial P_i = \lambda \partial g/\partial P_i$. Substituting, we have $1/n(1\text{–}2P_i) = \lambda/n\ (2P_i + 2\varepsilon)$, from which it follows that $P_i = P_j$ for all i, j. So we have that $0 = g(P) = (1/n\Sigma_i(P_i + \varepsilon)^2) - s = (P_i + \varepsilon)^2$. It follows that $P_i = \sqrt{s} - \varepsilon$ for all i. A check shows that this is indeed the solution that maximizes E[B] subject to our constraint.

References

Brier, G. W. (1950), "Verification of forecasts expressed in terms of probability," *Monthly Weather Review*, 75, 1–3.

Gilbert Harman, *Change in View* (Cambridge, Mass: MIT Press, 1986).

Joyce, J. (1998) *A Nonpragmatic Vindication of Probabilism, Philosophy of Science* 65, pp. 597–603.

Motwani, Rajeev and Prabhakar Raghavan. *Randomized Algorithms*. Cambridge; Cambridge University Press, 1995.

Roy A. Sorensen, *Blindspots* (Oxford: Clarendon Press, 1988)

Skyrms, B. "Resiliency, Propensity, and Causal Necessity." *Journal of Philosophy* 74 (1977), 704–713.

B. Skyrms. *Causal Necessity*. Yale Univ. Press, New Haven, 1980.

Talbott, William. "The illusion of defeat". In *Naturalism Defeated?: Essays on Plantinga's Evolutionary Argument Against Naturalism* by James K. Beilby (Editor) Cornell University Press (April 1, 2002).

Williamson, Timothy. *Knowledge and Its Limits*. Oxford: Oxford University Press, 2000.

Williamson, Timothy. "Probabilistic anti-luminosity," in Q. Smith, ed., *Epistemology: New Philosophical Essays*, Oxford: Oxford University Press, forthcoming.

Philosophical Perspectives, 19, Epistemology, 2005

RESPECTING THE EVIDENCE

Richard Feldman
University of Rochester

It is widely thought that people do not in general need evidence about the reliability or evidential value of perception, memory, or other basic faculties in order to have knowledge or reasonable belief on their basis. William Alston's essay, "Level Confusions in Epistemology," is often cited in defense of this view. Alston (2005) defends a similar thesis, claiming, "Again, it is crucial not to confuse the epistemic status of a non-epistemic belief and the epistemic status of the belief about the epistemic status of that first belief, or to confuse the sorts of grounding for the beliefs on the two levels"(179). Although there are those (Fumerton (1995) and Bonjour (1985)) who have raised doubts about this, I think that there is widespread support for Alston's view that you do not need higher level knowledge about epistemic connections to know ordinary facts about the world.

However, even if Alston and his supporters are right, there remain puzzling questions about the significance of second order information about the reliability of our faculties or the merits of our evidence. From the (alleged) fact that you do not need information about these matters in order to have knowledge about the world, it does not follow that the acquisition of such information cannot affect what you know or reasonably believe about the world. Alston's point leaves open what would follow from learning, or getting reason to believe, that we are not reliable with respect to certain matters or that our ordinary evidence is not so good. Since we can get, and often do have, information relevant to the epistemic status of our ordinary beliefs, it is of some interest to assess its significance.

Consider a person who has some evidence, E, concerning a proposition, P, and also has some evidence about whether E is good evidence for P. I will say that the person is *respecting the evidence* about E and P when the person's belief concerning P corresponds to what is indicated by the person's evidence about E's support for P. That is, a person respects the evidence about E and P by believing P when his or her evidence indicates that this evidence supports P or by not believing P when the evidence indicates that this evidence does not support P. Cases in which people are confronted with the possibility of respecting or not respecting their evidence present instructive epistemological puzzles about knowledge and justified (or reasonable) belief. In this paper I will first present some of these examples. I will then describe and assess possible responses to the cases. Along the way, I will argue that the puzzles arise just as clearly for theories about justification that do not make evidence the central concept.

I. The Skeptic's Student

Consider a typical undergraduate student who finds herself enrolled in an epistemology class. Prior to the class, she knew a great deal about the world around her. She knew that she had hands, she knew that there were trees on the quad, she knew that her class met at 11AM, and so on. In this respect, she was not at all unusual. Her epistemology class focused on arguments for skepticism. She found the arguments impressive, as did her teacher. Since it will matter for the points to be discussed later, I stipulate that the arguments in question generate skeptical conclusions not by claiming that knowledge requires some unobtainably demanding level of justification but rather by questioning whether ordinary beliefs satisfy a more relaxed standard. For example, the arguments rely on such claims as that she has no better reason to think that her perceptual experiences are caused by ordinary physical objects than by a computer directly hooked up to her brain.[1] Given the teacher's clear expertise and the apparent plausibility of the arguments, she has at least some decent basis for thinking that her perceptual evidence is not good evidence for the external world propositions she ordinarily believes.

In order to simplify discussion, I will consider a typical belief and the relevant evidence concerning it. Suppose that, on the way to class, the student (thought she) saw a beautiful oak tree on the quad, and she formed the belief that there is an oak tree on the quad. She then went into the class, still thinking that there is an oak tree on the quad. She then got her first exposure to the carefully formulated and ably defended skeptical arguments. At this time, she acquired reason to think that her evidence for this belief is inadequate.

It will be helpful to segregate the evidence obtained in the epistemology class from the ordinary perceptual and experiential evidence the student had prior to the class. Thus, prior to the class the student, S, had evidence E, which consists in her perceptual experiences when looking at the quad, plus any relevant background evidence that bears on the case. Assume that T is the proposition that there is a tree in the quad. Then, any fallibilist epistemological theory that holds that people can have knowledge in this sort of case, that knowledge depends upon having good enough evidence, and that the perceptual evidence included in E is the relevant evidence in this case, will endorse the following two propositions:

1. Prior to the class, S is justified in believing T
2. Evidence E provides good support for T.

What attitude S is justified in having toward (2) is left open. Alston's position implies that she need not be justified in believing (2) for (1) to be true. After learning, if that is the right word, everything she does in the epistemology course, S has acquired some new evidence concerning (2). Specifically, this is evidence suggesting that (2) is false. Call this new evidence "D". D is fairly powerful evidence, given that it includes the testimony of her teacher as well as her own impression of the arguments. Thus, it seems that:

3. Evidence D provides good support for ~(2).

It is now rather easy to pose the questions I want to raise about the example: what does an evidentialist view about knowledge and justification imply with respect to the student's belief in T after she has acquired evidence D? What does the combined evidence, E+D, support? Using the terminology introduced in the introductory paragraphs, the question can also be formulated by asking whether it is reasonable for her to respect her evidence about E and T. I will take questions about whether it is reasonable for her to believe to be equivalent to questions about what she "epistemically should" believe in the circumstances. Thus, the central question is what she should believe after getting evidence D. It is worth noting that I am not assuming that E includes no evidence relevant to (2). It may be that her background and experiential evidence does provide some support for (2).

I will sometimes describe questions about T, or the reasonableness of her believing T, as "first-order" questions or "object-level" questions. A set of second-order questions also arises. What is it reasonable for her to believe about her (potential) belief in T? Is she justified in believing that this belief is justified? that she has good reasons to believe T? These are "second-order" or "meta-level" questions.

II. Clarifications

A few points will help to clarify the questions and to identify some alternative ways to pose them.

As I understand epistemic evaluations, a person can be justified in believing a proposition that the person does not in fact believe. Having good enough overall evidence suffices for that. When a person does believe a proposition on the basis of good evidence, then that belief is *well-founded*. We could also say that the person *justifiably believes* the proposition. Our questions about the skeptic's student can be formulated as questions about what she is justified in believing or as questions about whether her beliefs are well-founded. The latter questions arise only in versions of the example in which she does continue to believe T and continues to believe that she is justified in believing T.

It is also possible to formulate the questions as questions about knowledge. If the student does continue to believe T, then we can ask whether she knows T. Assuming that T is true, then setting aside the possibility that this is a Gettier case, she knows T if and only if she justifiably believes T. Analogously, if she continues to believe that she has knowledge, then the second-order question can be formulated as a question about whether she knows that she knows T.

Discussion of these issues cannot proceed productively without first resolving some confusing terminological matters. These points can be brought into focus by thinking about a different example. People have thought, apparently mistakenly, that there was a strong correlation between going out in cold weather without wearing warm clothing and getting a cold. Assume for the sake of discussion that they thought that the correlation was very strong and that most people who went out without coats and hats got colds. They might be inclined to state their claim this way:

A. Going outside without a hat and coat in cold weather is good evidence that one will soon get a cold.

Given that (A) expresses what was a kind of folk wisdom, it might have been quite reasonable for people to make predictions about future colds on the basis of the relevant behavior. Thus, we might also say that

B. Knowing that Junior went out without a hat and coat in cold weather was a good reason for Grandma to believe that Junior would get a cold.

One might also put the point suggested by (B) by saying:

C. It was reasonable for Grandma to believe that Junior would soon get a cold on the basis of the fact that he went outside in cold weather without a hat and coat.

Assume that it is now known that there is no connection between going outside in cold weather without a hat and coat and getting a cold. What does this imply with respect to (A), (B), and (C)? My guess is that people will disagree about this, and that there is no fixed usage of the key terms. Some people might introduce "objective" and "subjective" readings of the key terms. Others might say that (B) and (C) are true, but that the recent information shows that (A) is false. On this usage, evidential relations are contingent matters, depending in part upon what correlations obtain in the world. Where we have mistaken information about those correlations, we are willing to grant that a person can be reasonable in believing something on the basis of the observed presence of the (allegedly) correlated factor. In other words, the presence of that factor provides a good reason to believe that the other factor is there, but it is not "really" evidence for its presence. Still others might think that the recent information undermines (A) and (B) but not (C). One issue that needs to be resolved, then, has to do with the way the words "evidence" and "reasons" apply in cases such as this.

There is a further complication that can make evaluating (A), (B), and (C) difficult. One might argue that, strictly speaking, (A), (B), and (C) are false regardless of the recent findings. The real reason for believing that someone will get a cold is not the mere fact that the person has gone out without a hat and coat (or that one knows that the person has done this) but rather a more complex reason of which this is a part. That more complex reason might be the conjunction: he's gone out in cold weather without a hat and coat *and* most people who do this get colds. If we say that the actual reason is this more complex one, then we can also say that this more complex reason really is evidence that the person will get a cold. Perhaps it is false evidence, since the second conjunct is false. But, nevertheless, it is evidence. Of course, there is a further complication here, in that there might be some resistance to saying that false propositions can be evidence, even though they can be reasons. (See, for example, Williamson (2000), Ch. 9.)

I do not believe that there is a unique correct way to steer through this terminological minefield. In addition, I think that the central issues of this paper, about how evidence about evidence affects justification and knowledge, will emerge no matter how we systematize our vocabulary. I will simply stipulate how I will (try to) consistently use these terms. I will use "good reason" and "evidence" interchangeably and I will say that something is evidence for something else only if that thing is all by itself evidence for that thing. If you learned only that Junior had gone out without a hat and coat, you would have no evidence at all for the proposition that he will get a cold. Thus, in my view, (A), (B) and (C) are all false, independently of the recent information about the lack of a connection between going out without a hat and coat and getting a cold. However, given the testimonial and other information people used to have, it is likely that revised versions of (A), (B), and (C), making reference to the more complex evidence they had would be true.[2]

Returning, then, to the example about the student of the skeptic, I will be understanding claim (2) to imply that the student's perceptual evidence, plus her relevant background evidence, is by itself good reason to believe T. And I take the skeptical arguments to be designed to contest that claim: they are supposed to show that, contrary to the common assumption, this ordinary evidence is not good evidence.

Finally, I have formulated the questions in terms of evidence about evidence. However, similar questions arise if what the student learns casts doubt on the reliability of her belief-forming methods. For example, if skeptical arguments lead her to have reason to deny or suspend judgment about the reliability of various belief-forming processes, she will then be in a similar situation to the one I have described.

III. Another Example – Informed Disagreements

The example concerning the student of the skeptic is similar in structure to a variety of other cases. In some of these other cases seemingly reasonable people examine a body of evidence and come to radically different conclusions about what that evidence supports. Philosophical disputes are paradigm examples of this phenomenon, but they are by no means the only examples. Very similar things also happen in political, scientific, and religious examples. A philosophical example that nicely illustrates the point is provided by Peter van Inwagen (1996), who describes his disagreement with David Lewis about freedom and determinism.

> How can I believe (as I do) that free will is incompatible with determinism or that unrealized possibilities are not physical objects or that human beings are not four-dimensional things extended in time as well as in space, when David Lewis—a philosopher of truly formidable intelligence and insight and ability—rejects these things I believe and is already aware of and understands perfectly every argument that I could produce in their defense? (138)

There are a number of issues raised by this passage, but here I will focus on just one of them. Suppose one thinks that there is a fact about which side of the dispute is better supported by what we might call the "objective evidence" provided by the arguments. That is, one might think that the collection of arguments and considerations about the freedom and determinism problem with which van Inwagen and Lewis are both familiar in fact supports one position. For the sake of discussion, suppose that the evidence supports van Inwagen's incompatibilist view. However, van Inwagen is aware of the fact that Lewis, whom van Inwagen acknowledges to be an intelligent and highly competent judge of such things, contends that the evidence does not support that conclusion. Suppose that van Inwagen continues to believe that incompatibilism is correct.

Cases of seemingly reasonable disagreement of the sort just described run parallel to the case of the skeptic's student in salient ways. There is a body of evidence which in fact (we are supposing) supports a particular conclusion. A person believes that conclusion on the basis of that evidence. The person then gets reason to think that this evidence does not support that conclusion. In this case, that reasons come in the form of the claims of a highly competent thinker on the same topic. The question that then arises is whether it is reasonable to maintain one's view in the light of this evidence about the evidence. If one's second order evidence indicates that the first order evidence does not support a conclusion, then if one should respect the evidence, one should not maintain belief in that conclusion. In effect, in this example van Inwagen is in a position analogous to that of the student of the skeptic.

There is this difference between the two cases: whereas the student and teacher stand in relation of novice and expert, the participants in the disagreement are peers. Perhaps this makes the significance of the evidence about the evidence greater in the former case than in the latter.

IV. The Possibilities

A. Three Views

Possible views about the examples I have described fall into a few categories. I will initially state them as views about whether the subject knows the propositions in question to be true, and then restate them as questions about justification. In each case, there are (at least) two propositions that are potential objects of knowledge: an object level proposition and a proposition about whether the person knows that proposition. Thus, for example, there is a question about whether the student knows T and there is a question about whether she knows that she knows T. Analogous questions can be framed in terms of justification. And analogous questions can be raised in cases of seemingly reasonable disagreement. There are four possible views about each pair of questions. In the case of the student's knowledge, the four possibilities are:

i) S knows T but does not know that she knows T;
ii) S knows T and knows that she knows it;
iii) S knows neither T nor that she knows T; and,
iv) S does not know T, but does know that she knows T.

Obviously, since knowledge implies truth, (iv) is not a viable option. I will now describe the three live options in more detail.

View 1: Disrespecting the Evidence

One possible view holds that the epistemic status of the belief in the object level proposition is unaffected by the meta-level information about what supports what, but this information does affect the epistemic status of the meta-level belief about what supports what. Applied to the student of the skeptic, this view implies that the student continues to know T but does not know that she knows T. It accepts (i) above. The idea, presumably, is that what she learns in class undermines her belief (assuming it is maintained) that she has knowledge about what is in the quad, but it does not undermine her belief about what is in the quad. As a view about justification, View 1 implies that she remains justified in believing T, but not justified in believing that she knows (or is justified in believing) T.

View 1 analyzes the case of disagreements similarly. It holds that the participant in the dispute who was properly interpreting the evidence remains as well justified in the object level proposition as he was before encountering the dissenting view, but loses justification for beliefs about the merits of the evidence. Thus, since the arguments do in fact support incompatibilism, and van Inwagen believes on their basis that incompatibilism is correct, his belief is still well-justified (though perhaps not well enough justified for knowledge). However, learning that Lewis denies that the arguments support that position renders him not justified in believing that his own take on the merits of the evidence is correct. Thus, van Inwagen should not respect his evidence about the arguments. He should maintain his belief, but should not believe that his evidence supports it.

View 2: Respecting the Evidence and Continuing to Know

A second possible view is that the mistaken claims about the evidence do not change the answers to our questions: The student continues to know T and continues to know that she knows T. (This assumes that she had the meta-level knowledge previously.) On this option, (ii) above is true. Of course, this is true only if she continues to believe that she has knowledge in spite of the worries induced by the skeptical arguments. Let us assume that she continues to believe T, and she continues to believe that she knows T, even though she sees some merit in the considerations in favor of skepticism.[3] Applied to reasonable disagreements, this second view implies that the party to the dispute who got things right in the first place continues to be well justified in thinking he got it right. Thus, van Inwagen is justified in believing not only that incompatiblism is correct, but also that the evidence supports this conclusion. The fact that Lewis sincerely asserts what he does simply makes no difference, even though Lewis is acknowledged to be an extremely thoughtful and intelligent judge of these matters. On this view, van Inwagen should respect his evidence about the arguments, but this is because, contrary to the intended account of the example, his evidence indicates that the arguments do support his view.

This second view is somewhat easier to spell out in terms of justification. According to it, the student is justified in believing both that T is true and that she is justified in believing T. It may be that the teacher shakes her confidence. It may even be that she will stop believing T, or stop believing that her evidence supports T. Nevertheless, according to View 2, continued belief is in fact justified. She "should not" be swayed by the teacher's arguments for skepticism. No philosophical arguments can undermine plain common sense about this matter. Similarly, van Inwagen is justified in thinking (correctly) that the arguments support his view, and the evidence from Lewis does not change this.

This view implies that people should respect their evidence about their evidence, but it implies that this is true in part because, contrary to the suggestion of the example, the claims of those who disagree do not provide good reason to think that their evidence fails to support the conclusions they initially thought it supported.

View 3: Respecting the Evidence and Losing Knowledge

A third possible view is that the evidence about the merits of one's evidence does undermine one's knowledge and justification for the first order propositions. When the student is authoritatively presented with the arguments for skepticism and she finds nothing wrong with them, she loses her knowledge of the world. In the light of the arguments, she no longer knows that there is a tree in the quad. Learning D undermines the justification E provides for T. Similarly, according to this view, the evidence of disagreement about the significance of one's evidence from a respected peer undermines the justification one has for forming a belief on the basis of that evidence. Thus, learning about Lewis's views undermines the justification van Inwagen initially had. This view accepts the intended implication of the example about the evidential significance of Lewis's claims for van Inwagen's beliefs about the evidence, and it holds that van Inwagen should respect that evidence about his evidence.

View 3 implies that we should respect our evidence and it upholds the suggestion of the examples that the second order evidence undermines justification for both the original object level conclusion and for the proposition that the first order evidence supports that conclusion.

B. Defeaters

The three views just described can be distinguished by characterizing their implications concerning *defeaters* for the justification the initial evidence provides. In the case of the skeptic's student, we are assuming that prior to entering the classroom the student believes the proposition, T, that there is a tree in the quad, on the basis of her perceptual and background evidence, E. Upon hearing the arguments for skepticism, she acquires evidence D. I am assuming that the following propositions are true:

1. Prior to class, S is justified in believing T.
2. Evidence E provides good support for T.

The example is designed to support the idea that it is also true that

3. Evidence D provides good support for ~(2).

The student's total relevant evidence after the class is E + D (or her recollection of this evidence). The key questions I have raised are about what this evidence supports. The issue thus concerns

4. (E&D) does not provide good support for T.

One use for the word "defeater" in epistemology applies here. Roughly, a proposition X is a justification defeater for proposition P for a person provided the person was justified in believing P prior to becoming justified in believing X but as a result of becoming justified in believing X, the person is no longer justified in believing P.[4] Where Y is the person's original evidence for P, and Y adequately supports P, the conjunction of X and Y fails to support P. Thus, another way to express what is at issue here is:

5. D defeats S's justification, E, for T.

View 1 denies (4) and (5). It grants that (3) is true, since the evidence from class undermines the proposition that E provides good support for T. But this, it says, does not defeat the student's justification for believing T. She remains justified in that belief. View 2 also says that she remains justified in believing T, but it denies that the evidence from the class undermines (2). Thus, it denies both (3), as well as (4) and (5).[5] View 3 accepts all of (3)-(5).

Analogous points apply to the example about disagreements. We are assuming that the arguments in fact best support one side of the debate. The issue raised by the example concerns whether the evidence from the other trustworthy inquirer constitutes a defeater for the justification initially provided by those arguments.

C. Odd Implications

Each of these three views has an odd implication. View 3, according to which we should respect the evidence and we thereby lose knowledge, has the surprising implication that the skeptical arguments succeed, in a certain sense, even if they are unsound. That is, on this view, by effectively defending the skeptical arguments, the instructor can make it the case that his students are not justified in their ordinary beliefs. This makes the conclusions of the skeptical arguments true, at least as they apply to the students, even though the arguments themselves are unsound. This is reminiscent of David Lewis's (1996) remark that if certain versions of contextualism are true, then "epistemology robs us of our knowledge"(550). But on Lewis's version, the truth in this remark is that studying epistemology can raise the standards for knowledge to a level that we do not ordinarily meet. This generates a context in which it is not correct to apply the word "knowledge" to ordinary beliefs. The beliefs are, nevertheless, as well supported as they ever were. In contrast, View 3 implies that being presented with skeptical arguments, even if they are unsound, can undermine one's justification for ordinary propositions. View 3 implies something more striking than the familiar fact that presenting people with arguments for skepticism can eliminate knowledge by eliminating belief. It holds that being presented with the (unsound) skeptical arguments, perhaps together with the appropriate commentary, can undermine justification for ordinary propositions.

View 2, according to which we should respect the evidence but we do not thereby lose knowledge, has the remarkable implication that authoritative and reliable testimony from an apparent expert epistemologist about an epistemological topic cannot undermine one's justification for a proposition inconsistent with that testimony. Following the reflection brought about by the class, the student remains (or becomes!) justified in believing that E supports P, in spite of the teacher's claims to the contrary. It is difficult to understand why the justification for a proposition would be immune to undermining in this way.

View 1, according to which we should not respect the evidence about the evidence, has the implication that a person could be in a situation in which she justifiably denies or suspends judgment about whether her basis for believing a proposition is a good one, but nevertheless justifiably believes the proposition. Imagine such a person reporting her situation: "P, but of course I have no idea whether my evidence for P is any good." At the very least, this sounds odd.

V. Externalism

In the preceding sections of this paper I have presented the puzzle about how information about the significance of one's evidence affects the epistemic status of one's beliefs in purely evidentialist terms. That is, I have described the puzzle as it affects views according to which knowledge and justification are matters of evidential support. However, I think that the examples also raise difficult questions for non-evidentialist views.

Consider a crude version of reliabilism. Although it is possible that details in the way a reliabilist theory is developed would affect the points I want to make, I believe that this is not the case. A crude reliabilist theory about knowledge holds that a person has knowledge when the person has a true belief resulting from a reliable belief-forming process. A crude reliabilist theory about justification drops the truth condition, holding that a justified belief is a belief resulting from a reliable process. An apparent attraction of reliabilism (and of externalism more generally) is supposed to be that it implies that people can have knowledge (or justified beliefs) without having to know about the reliability of the processes that produce the beliefs. First-order knowledge about the world is not dependent upon second-order knowledge about the sources of our first-order beliefs. Children and animals, as well as most adults, can thus have knowledge without having difficult to obtain knowledge about what justifies what or about where their beliefs come from. This seems to many to be a virtue.

Applied to our puzzle cases, it might seem that reliabilism is well-suited to defending a version of the view that we should not respect our evidence (View 1). Consider first its implications for the skeptic's student. Since her perceptual processes are, we may assume, reliable, her belief that there is a tree in the quad can be justified, and this can be a case of knowledge. The status of any beliefs she has about her evidence or her reliability is irrelevant. Thus, she can know that there is a tree in the quad without knowing that she knows this. Similarly, it may be that in their dispute about freedom and determinism, van Inwagen but not Lewis is responding to the arguments via a reliable process, and thus van Inwagen but not Lewis has knowledge (or justified belief). This leaves entirely open whether the process leading to the meta-level beliefs about the evidence arise via reliable processes. Since these are different beliefs, arising via different processes, it can be that some result from reliable processes and the others do not. The object level beliefs and the second level beliefs are simply independent of one another.

These claims about the implications of reliabilism are not well supported, however. It is extremely difficult to tell what the crude reliabilist theory implies concerning these cases. Consider the student's belief in T once she has heard the skeptical arguments. One might say that this belief is caused by a reliable perceptual process. However, another possibility is that the belief is maintained by a more complex process that involves continuing to trust a source one has good reason not to trust. Perhaps this latter process is not reliable. This leaves it unclear what the theory implies about the status of the object level belief. Similar considerations apply to van Inwagen's continued belief in incompatibilism in the face of Lewis's claims. This may be a reliable response to evidence or it may be an unreliable dismissal of worthy testimony.

The questions about the implications of reliabilism for the meta-level beliefs are equally obscure. Assume that, prior to the complications arising from being presented with the skeptical arguments, the student's perceptual beliefs are reliably formed. If she frequently thinks about such beliefs and regularly thinks that they are cases of knowledge, then perhaps the process leading to this conclusion is a reliable one. So perhaps she knows that she knows. (See Cohen, (2002) for discussion of this possibility.) On the other hand, perhaps the belief that she has knowledge is not reliably maintained after the class, since it involves discounting the claims of her teacher. On yet another hand, the teacher is in fact mistaken on this topic, so perhaps ignoring his testimony does not undermine reliability. Of course, accepting other things on the basis of his and other people's testimony is, presumably, reliable (and justified). It is, therefore, extremely difficult to know what crude reliabilism implies about the meta-level beliefs.

The fact is, I believe, we have no idea what crude reliabilism implies about this case. It is not at all obvious that it does support View 1. Approximately equally good cases can be made for the conclusion that it supports either of the other views. A more well-developed reliabilist theory is needed before any such conclusion can be rationally defended. Whether the more well-developed reliabilist view will have generally plausible implications remains to be seen.

It is worth noting that reliabilism has been developed with a "no defeaters" clause. That is exactly the view Alvin Goldman (1979) defended in one of his earliest statements of reliabilism. He tentatively proposed adding to the core reliability conditions on justification the following:

> If *S*'s belief in *p* at *t* results from a reliable cognitive process, and there is no reliable or conditionally reliable process available to *S* which, had it been used by *S* in addition to the process actually used, would have resulted in *S*'s not believing *p* at *t*, then *S*'s belief in *p* at *t* is justified.(20)

The second conjunct is designed to accommodate defeaters. Goldman acknowledges that there are matters of detail in this condition that require elaboration or refinement. Those details need not concern us here. The key point is that Goldman himself saw the need for a "no-defeaters" condition on justification. Given that he is right about this, questions about how information indicating that one's reasons are not good ones should affect one's first order beliefs arise just as much for reliabilism as for evidentialist theories. Reliabilists do not escape questions about whether we should respect our evidence.

Although this "no defeaters" condition has been ignored in a great deal of the subsequent literature on reliabilism, there is strong intuitive support for its inclusion in a developed reliabilist theory. What implications the no-defeaters clause has in the cases presently under consideration remains to be seen. In my view, a key question about these cases is whether the meta-evidence constitutes a defeater for the support E provides for T. The no-defeaters version of reliabilism faces exactly the same question.

Although I will not develop the point here, I think that other externalist theories face perfectly analogous questions. For example, it is unclear just how a proper function theory (see Plantinga (1993)) will accommodate points about defeaters. In my view, the theory should be developed in a way that properly deals with defeaters. A properly functioning system does not simply ignore defeaters. If evidence about evidence can be a defeater, the theory will include this fact. Thus, if the evidence provided to the student by her skeptical teacher constitutes a defeater for beliefs about what she sees, then the theory should reflect that fact. Similarly, in reasoned disputes such as the one between van Inwagen and Lewis, if the fact that a thinker every bit as responsible and intelligent as oneself appraises the arguments differently constitutes a defeater for the initial justification or warrant one has, then the theory should reflect that fact. In that case, it should have the same implications as an evidentialist theory.

There is no argument for or against externalism intended here. Rather, the point is that externalists, no less than evidentialists, must face the fact that there are puzzles about how to deal with cases in which one is faced with the prospect of respecting the evidence about the evidence. If there is a proper answer to these questions, and some or all externalist theories get them wrong, so much the worse for those theories. If they get them right, so much the better. In any case, it is one thing to say that we can have knowledge or justified belief without having information about the sources of our beliefs. It is quite another to say that our knowledge survives the acquisition of evidence that our reasons are not so good or that our processes are not so reliable. The implications of externalism for these examples, as well as the truth about the examples, remain elusive.

VI. Against Disrespecting the Evidence

I have described some situations in which people have evidence about their evidence concerning a topic, and raised a question about what it is reasonable for them to believe in such situations. I described three possible views. View 1 holds that there is a fact about what the evidence supports and the addition of evidence about the significance of that evidence does not undermine the reasonableness of the object level belief. Thus, it is reasonable to stick with ordinary beliefs in the face of good reasons to think our reasons for those beliefs are not adequate. The meta-level evidence does not defeat the justification provided by the initial evidence. In the terminology described earlier, View 1 implies that in these cases we need not respect the evidence.

The other two views imply that we should respect the evidence. One of these, View 2, implies that our correct judgments about the merits of the evidence are not undermined by what we are told by others. Thus, the student remains justified in believing that her ordinary evidence is good evidence even though the skeptical instructor is a seemingly trustworthy source who has presented her with plausible sounding arguments to the contrary. Similarly, a person who has properly assessed the evidence about some controversial topic remains justified in thinking that the evidence does support the conclusion he thinks it does, even though a reliable, intelligent, sincere, and otherwise trustworthy person has argued otherwise. View 3 also implies that we should respect the evidence, but it allows that the assertions of the skeptical instructor and the trustworthy advocate of a competing view can undermine the justification people have for the initial (and correct) assessments of the evidence. This view implies that the meta-level evidence defeats the justification the object level beliefs initially had.

In this section I will argue against View 1. View 1 leads to the conclusion that our student can correctly believe things such as

6. T, but my overall evidence does not support T.

This is extremely odd.[6] In a recent discussion of similar issues, Michael Bergman (2005) describes someone who believed something along of the lines of (6) as being "in an epistemically bad state of affairs."(424) I will consider two points, each designed to provide some support for this conclusion.

A. An Unknowable Conjunction

As noted, (6) seems odd. No doubt things like (6) can be true. And it may be that (6) does not have quite the paradoxical air that "T, but I don't believe T" has. Still, when the student acknowledges in the second conjunct that her evidence does not support T, she says that she does not have good reason to assert the first conjunct. So, if she is right about the second conjunct, her evidence does not support the first conjunct. Thus, if reasonable belief requires evidential support, it is impossible for the student's belief in (6) to be both true and reasonable. And, if knowledge requires truth and reasonable belief, it also follows that she cannot know (6). While it does not follow that belief in (6) cannot be reasonable, it does make it peculiar. One wonders what circumstances could make belief in it reasonable. And if our student is aware of this argument, then it is even harder to see how believing (6) could be reasonable. For then she would be believing something she knows is not reasonable if it is true.

Notice that there are times when there is nothing wrong with *saying* things that take the form of (6), but such examples do not undermine the point here. For example, if I ask you to guess which hand I am hiding a coin in, you might say, "It's in your left hand, but my evidence does not support that claim." You are not to be criticized for saying this. There was nothing wrong with saying what you did, since you were required in the circumstances to say something. However, what's puzzling about View 1 is that it implies that things of this form are reasonable to believe. I take it to be obvious that it is not reasonable for you to believe that the coin is in my left hand, even if saying that it is in my left hand is unobjectionable.

There may be some unusual circumstances in which believing things such as (6) is reasonable. For example, mistaken views about the general nature of evidential support might make it possible. I think that it is possible for someone to believe such things as that some evidence supports a proposition only if necessarily, everyone who had that evidence would believe that proposition. Noting that your evidence does not meet this condition, you might believe that your evidence does not support the proposition. If all of this could be justified, then, perhaps, things like (6) could be justified as well.

The central examples under discussion here do not involve this sort of gross error about the nature of evidential support. Thus, propositions such as (6) are peculiar, and it is plausible to think that they are not justified in the circumstances of these examples. It is true that the examples do involve erroneous information about what supports what. But such information, when it is justified, can affect what else is justified. I develop this point next.

B. Second order evidence can affect first order beliefs

We clearly can sometimes reason to object-level conclusions from information about evidence. Suppose a person has some evidence, E1, and is told by a reliable authority that this is good evidence for conclusion C. The person might formulate what he has been told as "If E1, then C." The person can then reason along the following lines: E1, if E1 then C, so C. This seems to be sensible reasoning. It would be absurd for the person to admit that E1 is true, and that E1 is good evidence for C, but to suspend judgment about C on the grounds that he has evidence only about the evidence, not about C.[7] But it is very difficult to see why something similar would not be suitable when the information is that the evidence does not support the conclusion. That is, the thinking would be: E1 is the only evidence I have concerning C, E1 is not good evidence for C, so I suspend judgment about ~C.[8] The conclusion drawn, clearly, should not be ~C, since the premise is not that E1 is good evidence for ~C. But if reasoning to the belief in C is reasonable in the first case, it is hard to see why reasoning to suspension of judgment about C in the second case is not also reasonable. And if that is the case, then similar reasoning can apply in the examples of the student of the skeptic and in reasonable disagreements. Since it cannot be that both believing the original conclusions and suspending judgment about them are reasonable, if the reasoning about the evidence is good reasoning, it must be that continuing to believe the conclusions is not reasonable. And that is to say that if the reasons for thinking that E1 does not support C are good ones, then the added evidence defeats the original evidence. This is contrary to View 1.

VII. Some Attempts to Defend Disrespecting the Evidence

In this section I will discuss three points that might be used to support the idea that it is reasonable to disrespect one's evidence.

A. Levels

As I noted at the outset, William Alston (1980) has rightly warned us of the dangers of levels confusions in epistemology. One line of thought in support of not respecting the evidence relies on the idea that only those guilty of levels confusions would think that there is a problem with disrespecting one's evidence about evidence. On this view, there is an independence of object level and meta-level evidence. Applied to the example of the student of the skeptic, the claim is that the teacher did not provide any direct evidence against T. The (possibly misleading) evidence from the epistemology class is evidence about her evidence and perhaps about her knowledge, but not evidence about first order propositions about the world. It therefore can make it the case that she lacks second order knowledge—she does not know that she knows. But she still knows that there are trees on the quad, just like her friends who are enrolled in an economics course.

I believe that this response makes too much of the distinction between levels. Information about whether the evidence supports a conclusion is evidence relevant to the rationality of belief in that conclusion. It is absurd to think that information about the significance of some evidence concerning a proposition has no bearing on the epistemic status of that proposition. Suppose that I have no direct evidence about a proposition at all, but I then learn that the available evidence on balance supports it. (This is my actual situation with regard to a large portion of my beliefs about contemporary science.) Surely this does provide me with good reason to believe the propositions I know to be supported. But if the independence between levels appealed to in support of View 1 were correct, it would follow that in such cases I have reason to believe that the evidence supports these propositions, but lack reason to believe the propositions themselves. I take that to be a reductio of the more general line of thought.

It is important to distinguish View 1 from a considerably more plausible related view. The related view is that people do not need to have evidence about the merits of their evidence to have justified beliefs about the world. This helps to explain how non-human animals and unsophisticated people can have knowledge. They are not precluded from having knowledge of the world even though they lack justification for propositions about the merits of their evidence. It is worth mentioning that both evidentialists and externalists about knowledge and justification can agree to this point. Externalists, obviously, will say that such individuals can form beliefs in reliable or proper ways, and thus have knowledge or justification. But evidentialists can argue that what gives them knowledge or justification in the cases in which they have it is in part the sensory experience that constitutes their evidence. They need not saddle their theory with the additional requirement that people always know that their evidence supports their conclusion.

There is a detail about the point just made that deserves elaboration. I take it to be uncontroversial that the unsophisticated knowers just discussed lack beliefs about whether their beliefs are justified or whether their evidence is good evidence. It is less clear that they lack justification for propositions about these matters. Perhaps the course of their experiences has provided them with some evidence for this, and perhaps there is something they can know a priori that provides such support. Against this, however, it should be noted that they need not have the conceptual sophistication required to put all this together. They may not even have the concepts of knowledge and justification. That, I take it, is sufficient to make it true that they are not justified in believing these propositions. The situation may well be different for more sophisticated believers.

View 1, which allows for disrespecting one's evidence, implies something much more contentious than that one can have knowledge and justification without justifiably thinking that one does or without even having the sophistication for such thoughts. It implies that one can have knowledge and justification when one has good reason to think that one does not. Whatever is true of those lacking information about their evidence, it remains open what is true of those who do have that information. The truth behind the levels confusions arguments does not provide support for disrespecting one's evidence.

B. Kinds of Defeaters

A second response to the considerations advanced in section VI has to do with defeaters. I have argued that the evidence provided by the teacher or by a person with whom one converses (or argues) can provide a defeater for the justification provided by one's original evidence. But these defeaters, if that is what they are, differ in an important way from other defeaters. Much of the discussion of defeaters traces to the work of John Pollock (1986). Pollock identifies two kinds of defeaters: undercutting defeaters and rebutting defeaters. When one has evidence that a proposition is true, and then gets stronger evidence indicating that the proposition is in fact false, one has a rebutting defeater. Rebutting defeaters are simply counter-evidence, evidence against the proposition supported by one's original evidence. Undercutting defeaters are not evidence that the proposition is false. Instead, Pollock explains, they "attack the connection between the evidence and the conclusion" (39). Here is an example, not from Pollock. Suppose I am told that some website reliably reports the previous day's baseball scores. I check out the site and see its report that the Mets beat the Dodgers 4–2, and I believe this to be correct. Assume that no background information gets in the way, and that is a well-justified belief. Suppose I then am told by a very trustworthy source that there is a peculiar problem with this website today. Although it invariably gets the right score for the game, it is as likely as not to assign the scores to the wrong teams. Thus, I can be sure that the score of the game was 4–2, but I have no idea which team got which score. The information about the unreliability of the website defeats the justification I had gotten by reading its reports. But this is not counter-evidence; it is not evidence that the Mets did not win. Rather, it is evidence showing that it is not reasonable to trust the report on this occasion.

The website example shares some features with the example about the student of the skeptic. In each case, there is some initial evidence that supports a conclusion and then some additional evidence is obtained that (seemingly) attacks the connection between that initial evidence and the conclusion believed on its basis. In both cases, the additional evidence is not a rebutting defeater because it is not evidence that the original conclusion is false.

However, there is a notable difference between the cases. This difference could be exploited in an effort to argue that the skeptic's claims are not defeaters for the student's justification for her ordinary beliefs. In the website example, the defeater attacks "the connection between the evidence and the conclusion" by providing a reason in a specific case not to rely on an otherwise generally reliable connection. The same thing happens in what may be the paradigm example of an undercutting defeater: Evidence that a red light is shining on an object can be an undercutting defeater for the perceptual evidence the red appearance provides for the proposition that the thing is red. In such a situation, it is not reasonable to rely on the generally reliable connection between apparent color and actual color. It remains true, however, that a thing's looking red is a good reason for believing that it is red. The defeater does not deny the general connection. Even in this case, that it looks red is still a reason to believe that it is red. The defeater just shows that this evidence should not be relied upon in the present case. Similarly, in the website example, seeing the score reported on the website is a good reason to believe that the score is as reported, but the specific evidence about the defect in the site provides reason not to rely on that connection in this case.

The central examples under consideration in this paper do not work in the same way. The skeptic, for example, does not argue that generally good perceptual evidence ought not be trusted in a particular case, but rather that perceptual evidence is not good evidence at all. The evidence provided by the teacher contends that no one is justified in believing external world propositions on the basis of the perceptual evidence. In contrast, in analyzing the website example (or the red light example) it is not claimed the defeater shows that people are not justified in believing on the basis of the ordinary evidence. Thus, the evidence provided by the teacher, or by the person with whom one disagrees, is not a rebutting defeater and is not a familiar kind of undercutting defeater. Perhaps it can plausibly be maintained that this evidence is not a defeater at all.

I grant that the central examples discussed here rely on defeaters that differ from the other defeaters. The evidence about the evidence is not a familiar kind of defeater. But I think that it is still a defeater. Whether it is a different sort of undercutting defeater or a new kind of defeater is a terminological issue not worth worrying about. The new evidence does "attack the connection between the evidence and the conclusion." But it does this not by claiming that a commonly present connection fails to hold in a particular case, but rather by denying that there is an evidential connection at all. Since second order evidence can have first order evidential implications, I do not see why this sort of attack cannot be effective. (See Bergmann (2005) for defense of a similar claim.)

C. Quiz Show Knowledge

A third point that can be used to support the view that we need not respect our evidence turns on the existence of what we might call "quiz show knowledge." We say of a person who gives the right answer to a question on a quiz show that she knew the answer. But such a person might justifiably believe that she lacks knowledge and that her evidence does not support her answer. For example, if the question is, "What is the capital of South Carolina?" and the contestant comes up with the answer "Columbia," we might credit her with first-order knowledge but deny second-order knowledge or justification. Thus, the contestant might say

7. The capital is Columbia, but I do not have any good reason to believe this.

If her answer is correct, she has "quiz show knowledge."[9] If she is also justified in her claim about her lack of reasons, then this is an instance of the kind of claim that I earlier said was nearly paradoxical. Similarly, then, perhaps the student of the skeptic can know that there is a tree in the quad while thinking that she has no good reason to believe this.

I concede that we will say of the person who gets the right answer that she "knew" it. But this sort of talk is puzzling. For one thing, the person who blurts out the correct answer to a quiz show question may not even believe that it was correct. She had a motive to give some answer, and this one came to mind. She may have had no stable belief-like disposition concerning the topic. So if we take it that she knew that Columbia is the capital just because she gave the right answer, then we are left with the idea that knowledge does not even require belief. This strikes me as wildly implausible.

Moreover, the judgment that the contestant had knowledge seems to me to be quite fragile. If someone who asserted that the contestant knew found out that she was just guessing, the person would almost surely retract the attribution. Perhaps the reason we often assume that the person who does get the right answer has knowledge is that the likelihood of getting the right answer without knowing it is low. That is, it is not likely that a person will guess correctly.[10] Alternatively, one might argue that the contestant does have reasons to think that she has evidence for her belief, so that the second conjunct of (7) is not justified. The reason comes from the fact that this answer came to mind. She has good reason to think (whether she actually thinks it or not) that such answers come to mind because of some past association, even if she is unable to recall it. Arguably, then, either it is not a case of knowledge or she does have reason to think that it is supported. In that case, View 1 finds no support here.

Before turning to some final comments on quiz show knowledge, it will be helpful to consider briefly one additional example. Suppose I have read a novel in which Richard Nixon appears. My current beliefs about Nixon are a blend of facts remembered from news reports during his life and propositions drawn from the novel. One such belief comes to mind. I might say that I do not know whether this is an item of knowledge or something drawn from the novel. Suppose in fact that it is a truth that I learned and remembered. If it is, and if this makes it a piece of current knowledge, then this may be another case in which one knows but has reason to deny (or doubt) that one knows.

I find the example unconvincing. I think that the remembered facts are not items of knowledge in these circumstances. Even though from one perspective it is not an accident that the beliefs are true, I think that they do not count as knowledge. Testifying to such matters under oath would, I think, be improper, and that's because one would not know what one was talking about. Along these lines, given that even externalist theories must recognize defeaters, it is not clear what view about knowledge even has the result that such items are knowledge. The same is true of alleged quiz show knowledge.

No doubt, some readers will not be convinced. For them, I retreat to the following point. If quiz show knowledge is knowledge, and if the remembered fact in the Nixon example is knowledge, then knowledge and reasonable belief differ crucially. I raised my questions initially as questions about reasonable belief, but slid into talk about knowledge on the grounds that knowledge required reasonable belief. I think that it is clear that the beliefs in these examples are not reasonable beliefs. If they are knowledge, then my thesis about respecting the evidence applies only to reasonable belief.

VIII. How to Respect the Evidence

If the considerations of the previous sections are right, then we should respect our evidence. In the examples under consideration here, upon getting evidence about the merits of one's evidence, either one should stick to one's initial, and correct, view about what that evidence supports or one should give up one's original object level belief. View 2 favors the former option and View 3 favors the latter. There is no decisive reason to think that all cases must be treated alike. It is possible the evidence about the evidence is a defeater in some cases and not in others.

View 2 has some similarity to what is sometimes described as a Moorean view about related issues. The idea is that we have more reason to think that the perceptual evidence supports the ordinary conclusion than to accept any philosophical argument, no matter how plausible it seems and how trustworthy and convincing its proponent may be. One way to defend this view is to argue that facts about epistemic support relations are knowable a priori, and cannot be defeated by arguments against them. Thus, the student's belief that E supports T is known a priori, and nothing can undermine this knowledge. This is not to say that everyone knows this sort of fact about epistemic support. It may be that people need some kind of training to get their minds focused on the relevant fact. But once they have latched on to that fact, no testimony and no skeptical arguments undermine their knowledge. Defenses of View 2 need not rely on claims about a priori justification. It can be argued that for typical people, the course of their experiences provides them with strong evidence in support of the reliability of, or evidential value of, perception, memory, and other sources of justification. On this view, then, the skeptic's student should reject her teacher's arguments, even if she unsure how to articulate responses to the details of those arguments.

The example of the skeptic's student involved skepticism concerning perceptual evidence. My own view (2003, Chapter 7) is that this sort of skepticism raises an extremely difficult issue and that considerations of inference to the best explanation constitute the best line of response. I think that one could reasonably, but mistakenly, come to the conclusion that this response does not work and that the skeptical arguments succeed. That one could not reasonably come to this conclusion, as would be the case if View 2 is the right approach to all versions of this example, strikes me as unbelievable.

The issue is rendered more complicated if we try to be more careful about exactly what the relevant evidence is. One might think that the perceptual evidence is simply the relevant perceptual experience. Alternatively, one might think that the evidence is more complex, including support for some general principle having to do with best explanations of perceptual experiences. This, in effect, seems to reintroduce some sort of higher-level requirement on justification. If the evidence does include some connecting principle, the Moore-like view becomes easier to swallow since it becomes harder to see what could legitimately introduce a question about what the more complex body of evidence supports. Of course, at the same time, it becomes harder to see that people generally have the required evidence, since it seems to require greater intellectual insight. It may be that examples differ in this regard, in that some evidence requires linking principles and some does not. Thus, a general defense of View 2 seems to have the cost of suggesting that we have good reasons for our beliefs less often than we might otherwise think.

View 3, I think, is more plausible, at least in many cases. It holds that the second-level information does defeat the initial object-level belief. Considerations of symmetry support this result. This is most readily seen in the case of seemingly reasonable disagreements. It can then be extended to the case of the skeptic's student on the basis of the similarity of the cases. A striking thing about the cases of seemingly reasonable disagreement is the symmetry of the situation. Even if it is true that the arguments in fact favor one side in the debate, the outcome of the discussion includes the participants' realization that for each thing one of them can say in support of his view, the other can say something analogous in support of the other view. To stick to one's guns in such a situation is to fail to treat like cases alike. It is a violation of what I take to be a clear condition of rational belief.

The exact violation of the requirement to treat like cases alike may require some clarification. It can be brought out by considering the perspective a neutral third person should have about the dispute. That person might see it as a draw, with considerations on each side that balance one another out. It is hard to see why what is justified for a participant differs at all from what is justified for this observer. Compare a case in which in you have competing testimony from two experts and reasonably suspend judgment about a topic. It is difficult to see why one of the experts would be justified in sticking to his view simply because it is his view. (I discuss similar issues in Feldman (forthcoming).)

Something similar can be said of the skeptic's student. For one thing, she would be in a situation very much like the disagreement just described if she engaged in a conversation with a fellow student who responded to the arguments by giving up the belief in T. Moreover, if the student rejects some bad reasoning—say an instance of the gambler's fallacy—on the basis of her teacher's arguments but retains other beliefs in the face of seemingly equally compelling objections, she is also failing to treat like cases alike.

As noted earlier, View 3 is not without its own odd implication. If the skeptical arguments are mistaken but can lead to reasonable doubt about the merits of one's evidence and thus about the truth of ordinary propositions, then the arguments are perversely effective. In the course of mistakenly arguing that ordinary beliefs are not justified, they render unjustified the ordinary beliefs of those who hear the arguments effectively presented. While this may be odd, it is not a basis for a good objection to View 3. Unsound arguments can be rationally compelling, perhaps because they have false but justified premises. Moreover, what is doing some of the work in these cases is not the arguments themselves, but rather the testimony of an authority. The testimonial arguments need not be unsound. So, accepting View 3 does not lead to the puzzling result described.

View 3 does have the implication that we may have less knowledge, or fewer justified beliefs, than we might have otherwise thought. It seems to have the discouraging implication that thinking about epistemology, and conversing with intelligent people who disagree with us, can undermine the justification we have for our beliefs. On reflection, however, that result strikes me as being exactly right.

IX. Conclusion

I conclude that we should respect our evidence. It is less clear whether we should do this by giving up beliefs when confronted with seemingly good reasons to think our evidence is not good or by rejecting those reasons for thinking our reasons are not good. There need not be a single answer that covers all cases. However, I think that, in at least some notable cases, the reasonable thing to do is give up beliefs that are otherwise well-supported. This implies that skeptics, and those generally reasonable agents with whom we disagree, can undermine our ordinary knowledge and justification.[11]

Notes

1. Using some helpful terminology introduced in Vogel (2004), the arguments defend *domestic skepticism* rather than *exotic skepticism*.
2. Elizabeth Fricker has pointed out (in discussion at the Rutgers Epistemology Conference, May 2005) that there is a use of the word "evidence" that is more restrictive than the one I advocate here. She notes that there are settings in which a request for evidence demands something other than a reason constituted by the testimony of someone else. If you are asked what the evidence is that Lee Harvey Oswald was the lone assassin of President Kennedy, there is something odd about appealing to testimony. Something more fundamental than that is desired. Still, testimonial evidence is evidence.
3. Advocates of View 2 need not say that the second-level evidence makes *no* difference. They can say that the student remains justified in believing both T and that she knows T, but that her degree of justification is reduced slightly.
4. A complication in this general area concerns the role of doubt. Suppose the skeptic induces in the student the belief that her evidence lacks merit. Bergmann

(2005) and Lackey (forthcoming) suggest that this doubt itself serves as a defeater. My own view is that the doubt itself is not a defeater. Rather, any reasons that make such doubt suitable would be defeaters, not the fact of doubting itself. However, if the feeling of doubt induced by consideration of the skeptical arguments is itself a defeater, then it is rather easy to see that there can be a defeater in these cases.

5. Variations on View 2 are possible. Instead of saying that (3) is false, one might say that although (3) is true, S has some further evidence, in addition to D and E, and that her total evidence supports (2).
6. Equally odd is the similar claim "T, but I suspend judgment about whether my evidence supports T." I will focus on (6), but similar remarks apply to this variation.
7. If this point is correct, then a variation on the example of the student of the skeptic leads to a surprising result. Suppose the student is taught by a convincing non-skeptic who leads her to justifiably but falsely believe that some body of evidence E* is good evidence for some conclusion C*. If the student really is justified in believing this, then she is justified in believing C* on the basis of the combination of E* and what she has learned from her teacher. Thus, even though E* is not itself good evidence for C*, E* plus the teacher's testimony can be good evidence for C*. Therefore, the student can in this way become justified in believing the conclusion. This is a surprising result. But, on reflection, it seems to me to be exactly right. The teacher does enable the student to become justified in this belief. I thank Earl Conee for raising this issue.
8. The reasoning presented here suggests that the conclusion is a conclusion about what I will (or, perhaps, should) do. That's not what I intend. Reasoning can have the result that one does suspend judgment, and that's what I have in mind here.
9. An assumption here is worth making explicit. It is one thing to say that she knew the answer, it is another to say that she knew that Columbia is the capital. Possibly, something could be made of this distinction. I will not attempt that here. I concede that people will say that she knew that Columbia is the capital.
10. This is also true in the case of multiple choice questions. But it is also clear that we will withhold an attribution of knowledge to a person who we thought was guessing.
11. I am grateful to John Bennett, Stewart Cohen, Earl Conee, Jon Kvanvig, Greg Wheeler, and Edward Wierenga for helpful comments on drafts of this paper.

References

Alston, William. 1980. "Level Confusions in Epistemology." *Midwest Studies in Philosophy* 5: 135–150.

———. 2005. *Beyond "Justification": Dimensions of Epistemic Evaluation*. Ithaca: Cornell University Press.

Bergmann, Michael. 2005. "Defeaters and Higher-Level Requirements," *The Philosophical Quarterly* 55: 419–436.

BonJour, Laurence. 1985. *The Structure of Empirical Knowledge*. Cambridge: Harvard University Press.

Cohen, Stewart. 2002. "Basic Beliefs and the Problem of Easy Knowledge," *Philosophy and Phenomenological Research* 65: 309–29.
Feldman, Richard. 2003. *Epistemology*. Upper Saddle River, NJ: Prentice Hall.
———. Forthcoming. "Epistemological Puzzles About Disagreement," *Epistemology Futures*, edited by Stephen Hetherington. Oxford: Oxford University Press.
Fumerton, Richard. 1995. *Metaepistemology and Skepticism*. Lanham, Md.: Rowman & Littlefield.
Goldman, Alvin. 1979. "What is Justified Belief?" George S. Pappas, ed. *Justification and Knowledge* (Dordrecht: D. Reidel) pp.: 1–24.
Lackey, Jennifer. Forthcoming. "Learning from Words," *Philosophy and Phenomenological Research*.
Lewis, David. 1996. "Elusive Knowledge," *Australasian Journal of Philosophy* 74: 549–67.
Plantinga, Alvin. 1993. *Warrant and Proper Function*. Oxford: Oxford University Press, 1993.
Pollock, John. 1986. *Contemporary Theories of Knowledge*. Totawa, NJ: Rowman & Littlefield.
van Inwagen, Peter. 1996. "It is Wrong, Always, Everywhere, and for Anyone, to Believe Anything, Upon Insufficient Evidence" in J. and D. Howard-Snyder eds., *Faith, Freedom and Rationality*. MD: Rowman and Littlefield, pp. 137–154.
Vogel, Jonathan. 2004. "Skeptical Arguments," *Philosophical Issues* 14: 426–55
Williamson, Timothy. 2000. *Knowledge and Its Limits*. Oxford: Oxford University Press.

Philosophical Perspectives, 19, Epistemology, 2005

SPECKLED HENS AND OBJECTS OF ACQUAINTANCE

Richard Fumerton
University of Iowa

The speckled hen has been pecking away at various versions of classical foundationalism for well over sixty years.[1] It has been raised again recently by Ernest Sosa (2003a and b) to criticize the kind of acquaintance theory of noninferential justification that I have defended in a number of articles and books.[2] In this paper I want to re-examine the problem(s) Sosa raises and to canvas a number of solutions available to those who are interested in defending an acquaintance theory of noninferential justification.

Classical Foundationalism and Direct Acquaintance:

Classical foundationalists claim that all knowledge and justified beliefs owe their justification ultimately to noninferentially justified knowledge/belief. The most obvious and most critical question for all foundationalists concerns what could render a belief noninferentially justified. And it is an understatement to suggest that classical foundationalists have differed amongst themselves concerning the answer to that question. Some of the most hard-core foundationalists, however, have sought to identify plausible candidates for foundations with infallibility. The foundations for knowledge and justified belief are found by following a Cartesian method of doubt. We strip away from our beliefs all that can be in error and what is left will be the foundations upon which we can build through legitimate inference the rest of what we know and justifiably believe.

It is important when thinking about infallibility to make distinctions. So one might take the above view to amount to the suggestion that foundations consist of infallible belief, where a belief is infallible if the mere having of the belief entails that it is true.[3] Descartes, for example, was confident that he had found at least one building block of the foundations of knowledge when he reflected on the fact that he couldn't believe that he existed without his existing. The mere contemplation of the question by *him* requires that he exist.

But as many have argued, it is not clear that we are getting at the heart of an interesting *epistemic* concept with the notion of an infallible belief. Trivially, if one finds oneself believing a necessary truth, for example, one's belief will entail the truth of what one believes. But one can believe a necessary truth for a bad epistemic reason that renders unjustified the belief. Similarly, I might believe an enormously complex contingent truth that is entailed by the proposition that I exist, but where the proposition entailed is far too complex for me to "see" the entailment. Again while the truth of that proposition will be entailed by my believing it, it is implausible to suppose that my belief is justified.

If one is determined to locate foundations relying on something like Descartes's method of doubt, it is more plausible to turn one's attention from infallible belief to infallible justification. One's justification renders a belief infallible when one's *justification* guarantees the truth of what one believes. One still, of course, faces the problem of necessary truth. Even if one believes a necessary truth based on the testimony of someone one takes to be an authority, the justification for one's belief will (trivially) entail the truth of what one believes. Yet there is a clear sense in which the *epistemic* probability of what one believes is less than 1. Furthermore, there are externalist proposals for noninferential justification that would render noninferential justification infallible even though it would hardly satisfy a Descartes searching for secure foundations. If one takes one's paradigm of foundationally justified belief, for example, to be belief directly caused by the truth maker for that belief, then such justification will (again, trivially) entail the truth of what is believed. But the internalist is concerned that the causal connection that guarantees the truth of the belief might be "hidden" from the believer in a way that renders the guarantee epistemically impotent—at least if epistemic guarantees are supposed to give one the kind of assurance that Descartes sought.

Intuitively, one wants the relevant sort of infallible justification to include as a constituent the truth-maker of the belief and to include it in a way that renders the belief based on that justification *transparently* true. One wants the truth-maker "before" consciousness in a way that provides complete intellectual assurance concerning the truth of what one believes. But all this is highly metaphorical. Critics of the idea are often convinced that the search for such epistemic assurance is the search for an illusion. But some proponents of the idea turn to the technical concept of direct acquaintance to capture the relevant relation to truth-makers that ends regresses of justification. When one is in pain and one is directly acquainted with the pain, the thought that one is in pain and the correspondence between the thought and the pain, one has all that one needs, all one could possibly want, by way of epistemic assurance that what one believes is true.

One would, no doubt, like an analysis of the relation of direct acquaintance before accepting a foundationalism that relies critically on the concept. Unfortunately, proponents of the view are likely to take the relation to be unanalyzable. Still, one can try to "ostend" the relation through thought experiments. Consider again a prime candidate for direct acquaintance, one's introspective awareness of one's own pain as one feels it. To be sure, externalists have their own accounts of introspection. A reliablist, for example, might argue that so-called introspective awareness of one's pain just is one's belief that one is in pain produced by the pain itself without the causal mediation of other beliefs. But there seems to me to be a world of difference between merely believing that one is in pain and one's being directly aware of one's pain. Suppose, for example, that one becomes convinced (perhaps through philosophical argument) that one can be in pain without being aware of that pain. One is further convinced by a neurophysiologist scanning one's brain that one is in severe pain right this moment, even though one isn't aware of it. Though one believes that one is pain, one's situation is quite different from that of the person whose belief is based on direct awareness of the pain itself "present" before consciousness.

Of course, many would reject the intelligibility of a pain distinct from our awareness of it. One might suppose that it is the mark of a genuinely mental state that it cannot occur without one's being conscious of it. But this supposition is highly problematic. Most of us are familiar with pains that "recede" from consciousness as we become interested in something else. I have a bad backache, but as I become engaged in a heated political debate, I don't notice the pain for a period of time. As soon as the conversation ends, I am again distinctly aware of the pain. There are two alternative descriptions of the familiar phenomenon I just described. On the first, one says that for a period of time the pain itself ceased. On the second, one supposes that while the pain continued, I was temporarily unaware of it. I'm not sure that any evidence will render conclusive one hypothesis over the other, but one can imagine that neural evidence correlating certain brain states with pain might corroborate the view that the pain was there all along while I lost introspective "sight" of it for a period of time. If one finds persuasive this characterization of the situation one will have a definite description that succeeds in denoting acquaintance. Acquaintance is that relation I had to my pain (something other than belief) that was present, temporarily ceased during my conversation, and began again when the conversation ended.

The Problem of the Speckled Hen:

What do speckled hens have to do with classical foundationalism built on the idea of direct acquaintance? Well, as we saw, many classical foundationalists sought to identify the objects of direct acquaintance by stripping from experience all that is clearly not before consciousness. One does this through something resembling a Cartesian method of doubt. So suppose, for example, that someone thinks that one is directly acquainted with physical objects and their properties. The classical foundationalist asks such a person to compare the justification one has for believing that there is something physical that is brown and rectangular before one with the justification one would have for believing that same proposition were one vividly dreaming or hallucinating while one is unaware of the nonveridical character of that experience. The claim (controversial to be sure) is that the justification in the two situations is the same. Since direct acquaintance is supposed to involve a real relation that requires the existence of its relata, and since by hypothesis there is nothing physical that is brown and rectangular before one in the nonveridical experience, one cannot take oneself to be directly aware of a brown rectangular physical object in the veridical case. So far, so good. But the next move is to take subjective experience with its phenomenal character to be a plausible object of acquaintance, an acquaintance that allows noninferentially justified beliefs about the phenomenal character of that experience.

Enter the speckled hen. Or, more precisely, enter the sort of appearance that a speckled hen might produce in one's visual field. For the moment, let's characterize that appearance as a sense datum. If one is conscious of one's experience one is supposed to be directly acquainted with its phenomenal character. But the visual field is occupied by a shape with many speckles. For the sake of argument, suppose that there are, in fact, 48 speckles present in the visual field. Unless one has "Rainman" like abilities,[4] one will have no idea precisely how many speckles are present in the visual field. Despite one's acquaintance with one's experience there are truths about the experience that remain epistemically problematic. Clearly direct acquaintance with an experience cannot yield the epistemic results the acquaintance foundationalist wants. In Sosa's (2003a and b) version of the problem, the kind of experience that we have of our own conscious mental state can be described as experiential awareness (henceforth e-awareness). It just is whatever renders an experience conscious. There is e-awareness of the many-speckled visual field. Experiential awareness is contrasted with noticing-awareness (henceforth n-awareness). N-awareness is whatever is involved in realizing that, becoming aware of, noticing that the appearance has some feature, for example 48 speckles. N-awareness, Sosa suggests, looks more like justified belief or propositional knowledge. So we have a dilemma. If we appeal to e-awareness to ground foundational knowledge of the phenomenal character of experience, it apparently isn't up to the job, at least with respect to certain characteristics of the experience. If we appeal to n-awareness, we are surreptitiously appealing to the very concept of propositional knowledge we were trying to explicate—our account has become viciously circular.

Moving More Carefully—The Nature of Sensation:

We have been painting with a very broad stroke. It's time to make distinctions. As we shall see, epistemology quickly meets metaphysics. First, as I have already suggested, it seems to me that we need to distinguish experience (sense experience, belief, imagination, desire, fear, and so on) from our awareness of that experience. We don't want to assume that every time we have an experience we are aware of that experience or any feature of that experience. I argued earlier, that it might make perfectly good sense to allow that one could be in pain even when one is momentarily not aware *in any sense* of the pain that one feels. The issue is complicated by the fact that when we describe ourselves as *feeling* pain, we often run together the pain and the awareness of the pain. If the so-called adverbial theorist is correct, pain just is a certain property, a certain kind of feeling. But from the fact that one exemplifies the feeling it doesn't follow that one is aware of the feeling. Still less does it follow that one has any *beliefs* about the feeling. It seems to me that we ought to say the same thing about *all* mental states. At one time I thought that the Freudian idea of an unconscious desire, belief, or fear, made no sense unless it was defined in terms of some set of dispositions to behave in certain ways—I was in the grips of the familiar idea that all experience is conscious experience. But there now seems to me no good argument for that view. We ought to allow at least the possibility that the very same sorts of fears and desires that we are typically conscious of sometimes exist but lie beneath the reach of consciousness. And to reach this conclusion we don't need to give externalist analyses of these unconscious mental states. We can identify them as states having the very same intrinsic character of which we are aware when we are conscious of them. So for any experience E, it seems to me that one should distinguish ontologically 1) E, 2) one's awareness of E and its various characteristics, and 3) one's beliefs about the various characteristics exemplified by E.

The next set of ontological issues one should ideally address before trying to come to grips with puzzles posed by the experience of a speckled hen concerns the ontological status of sense experience. I have already implied that the *classical* foundationalist (unlike his externalist counterpart) wants to think of the experience with which one is directly acquainted as experience stripped of everything external, everything the absence of which would leave the resulting experience phenomenologically indistinguishable from the experience with its typical external cause. But how shall we conceptualize sense experience stripped of everything external? The classical foundationalists were split between the earlier sense-datum theory and the more recent adverbial theory.[5] The sense-datum theorist finds in all sense experience an *object*, a sense datum, of which one is aware. When one hallucinates something red and round, there may be no physical object present, but there is *something* present to consciousness and that thing really is phenomenally red and round.[6]

The adverbial theorist, by contrast, wants to characterize the subjective experience in terms of the *way* someone is sensing. The adverbial theorists typically try to introduce their view with analogies. When we describe Jones as dancing a waltz, we might be seduced by the "surface grammar" of our description into thinking that there is some "act," dancing, performed upon some "object" the waltz. But it isn't hard to convince oneself that there is really just the dancing. The waltz that is danced is just a certain *way* of dancing. Similarly, one might suppose that when we feel pain we stand in the relation of feeling to some object, the pain. But, the adverbial theorist suggests, we ought to take seriously the suggestion that there is no more to the pain than a certain kind of feeling. The grammatical object "pain" in the sentence "S feels pain" should be thought of as a kind of "disguised" adverb modifying the way in which the person feels. Feeling pain, feeling anxious, feeling happy, are all just different ways of feeling. By recognizing that there is no more to the pain that the feeling, one understands why it is absurd to suppose that the world might contain pain without minds. Feeling pain just is a property of a mind. By definition, nothing could exemplify this property but a mind.

While the adverbial theorists explain their theory starting with kinds of experience that lend themselves most naturally to their analysis, their ultimate goal was to approach all experience the same way. So while the sense-datum theorists thinks that when one hallucinates a speckled hen one is aware of a many-speckled object, the appearing theorist suggests that we should characterize the relevant visual experience as one's sensing in a speckled-hen-like way, or, to invent a decidedly ugly adverb—sensing speckled-hen-ly.

Now we are not about to settle the debate between sense-datum theorists and adverbial theorists here. But it is important to realize that the acquaintance theorist dealing with the problem of the speckled hen may have room to maneuver that is not as obviously available to the sense-datum theory. So, for example, as Chisholm pointed out long ago, it is difficult to take seriously the idea that there is some *object* occupying visual space that has *many* speckles but has no determinate number of speckles.[7] On the other hand, the adverbial theory is already a bit mysterious—experience, after all, is identified with the exemplification of properties for which we have no non-artificial predicate expressions. It might not be that hard to convince oneself that even though one is appeared to many-speckled-ly, one is not appeared to 48-speckled-ly, 47-speckled-ly or any other determinate number n-speckled-ly. One might, then, attempt to block the problem posed by the speckled hen by simply denying that there is the relevant feature of experience of which one is supposed to remain ignorant. One is aware of being appeared to speckled-ly, but one is not aware of being appeared to 48-speckledly, but only because one *isn't* being appeared to 48-speckledly.

While the gambit is formally available it is, nevertheless, a bit hard to convince oneself that one will be unable to translate the problem from a sense-datum language to an appearing language. Just as the sense datum presumably exemplifies not just having many speckles but also having some specific number of speckles, so also the adverbial theorist's property of being appeared to is plausibly thought of as perfectly determinate in character even if there is a more generic property of being appeared to many-speckled-ly that supervenes on the determinate property. Still, this distinction between determinate properties and the determinables that supervene upon them might be useful for the acquaintance theorist trying to understand more clearly the way in which acquaintance yields noninferential justification. We'll return to this suggestion later.

While the sense-datum theory and the adverbial theory were the two main competing accounts of sense experience for the classical foundationalists, many contemporary philosophers are convinced that sensation is fundamentally representational or intentional in character. Just as belief represents the world being a certain way, so sense-experience represents the world being a certain way. A veridical sense experience, like a true belief, represents the world accurately. A non-veridical experience, like a false belief, fails to represent the world accurately. For the purposes of discussing the problem of the speckled hen, I'm going to presuppose such views are false. If sensation, like belief, really were a kind of intentional state then I'm not sure how the problem of the speckled hen even arises for the foundationalist who claims noninferential knowledge of appearance grounded in acquaintance with that appearance. The problematic strategy discussed above for the appearing theorist clearly will work for the representationalist. One can obviously *believe* that the surface of an object contains many speckles without believing that it has some particular determinate number of speckles. If sensation/appearance is a kind of intentional state, then it too can represent the surface of a physical object has having many speckles without representing it has having some determinate number of speckles. On such a view, the acquaintance theorist can straightforwardly explain our lack of knowledge concerning the determinate number of speckles represented in sense experience. One is directly acquainted with one's sense experience. The sense experience is an intentional state whose intentional object is a many-speckled surface, but whose intentional object does not involve the exemplification of any determinate number of speckles. One has propositional knowledge that one has a sensation with the generic content. One lacks propositional knowledge that one has a sensation with the determinate content—but only because one doesn't have a sensation with the determinate content. If I thought that sensation was a species of intentional state, I'd end this paper here. I don't, however,[8] and so I'm interested in pursuing the alternative strategies for dealing with Sosa's objection.

With What Ontological Categories is One Acquainted?

Even if an acquaintance theorist isn't exactly forthcoming when it comes to defining the critical relation of acquaintance upon which the theory relies, one might expect the theorist to at least identify the relata of the relation. We have already said something about what the classical acquaintance theorist thought we could be acquainted with, but I'm more interested here in the ontological *categories* of entities which might constitute the objects of acquaintance. So we might claim to be directly acquainted with particulars, properties, or facts (particulars' exemplifying properties). Trivially, what one says on this score will not be independent of one's other ontological commitments. So if one embraces a bundle theory of objects, one is likely to reject acquaintance with particulars as something distinct from acquaintance with properties. And this is so whether one is a sense-datum theorist or an adverbial theorist. The bundle theorist who is a sense-datum theorist will take the sense datum to be a bundle of properties while the bundle theorist who is an appearing theorist will take the self to be constituted at least in part by ways of being appeared to. One's acquaintance with one's self, on such a view, just will be the Humean awareness of various experiential states. On either view, though, acquaintance with objects will just be acquaintance with all or some of the properties that constitute those objects. Alternatively, one might have either phenomenological or dialectical reasons for thinking that an object is something over and above the properties it has and, one might affirm or deny that one can be directly acquainted with such things.[9]

An acquaintance theorist seeking to ground noninferential justification in direct acquaintance is likely to be most interested in the possibility of being directly acquainted with *a fact*. As Sellars (1963, 130–32) pointed out, the goal of foundationalism is to discover a kind of *truth* that can be known directly and without inference. Facts are not truths, but they are, arguably, truth-makers. On the kind of acquaintance theory I defend, one has no epistemic access to truth until one combines one's direct acquaintance with a truth-maker with direct acquaintance to both a truth-bearer and the relevant relation of correspondence that holds between a truth-bearer and its truth-maker. If facts are partially constituted by properties, direct acquaintance with facts may essentially involve acquaintance with the properties that are at least partially constitutive of those facts.

It is an understatement to observe that the ontological commitments in the above account of noninferential justification are controversial. The account commits itself to a correspondence theory of truth replete with an ontology of facts that serve as truth-makers. I fully concede that a full defense of this version of foundationalism requires a defense of these ontological positions, a defense I have offered elsewhere (2002). The question I am interested in here is how one might deal with the problem of the speckled hen within the broad framework defined by these ontological commitments.

If one endorses a sense-datum theory and allows that one can be directly acquainted with sense data, one will, of course, need to be very careful in reaching conclusions about direct acquaintance with *facts* involving those sense data. Sense data are objects that exemplify properties. We can be either liberal or conservative in our commitment to the existence of properties. The most liberal approach allows that there is a property picked out by any well-formed predicate expression. Some of these properties will be non-relational; others, relational. If we allow both non-relational and relational properties in our ontology and adopt fairly loose criteria for recognizing the existence of relational properties, then sense data, like all other objects, will exemplify infinitely many properties. No acquaintance theorist will allow that our direct acquaintance with subjective sense data translates into direct acquaintance with infinitely many facts involving those sense data. That a given sense datum comes into existence two and a half thousand years after the assassination of Julius Caesar is not a fact with which any traditional foundationalist thinks one is directly acquainted. So, if one allows that one can be both directly acquainted with sense-data and facts about sense data, one must carefully restrict one's claims about the nature of the facts about sense data with which one can be acquainted. At most one will claim that in experience one's acquaintance with sense data always involves acquaintance with the intrinsic or non-relational character of sense data. One may also allow that one can be directly acquainted with relations that obtain between the sense data with which one is acquainted.

So what is the structure of the critical experiential fact that is causing the difficulty in the case of the speckled hen? Do sense data have the property of containing 48 speckles? Is that a relational property? If it is, does it involve relations that hold between sense data—perhaps a relation between a given whole and some of its distinct shaped parts? Either way, is this a property with which one can be directly acquainted?

If one embraces some version of the appearing theory, the relevant fact involves the exemplification of non-relational appearing properties. When one is conscious of some experience, the acquaintance theorist will claim that one is directly acquainted with the self's exemplifying a property. In the case of the visual experience produced by the speckled hen, one is directly acquainted with one (or, as we shall see, more) non-relational properties exemplified by the self.

With this as background, let's look at what one might say about direct acquaintance with the experience produced by our encounter with the speckled hen and how the acquaintance theorist might explain our failure to know truths about that experience.

Acquaintance with Correspondence:

In a forthcoming article, "Acquaintance and the Problem of the Speckled Hen," Ted Poston suggests that we should concede Sosa's distinction between e-awareness and n-awareness, argue that that we have e-awareness of the 48 speckled datum in our visual field, but also concede that we don't know that the datum contains 48 speckles. He goes on to suggest that we explain our lack of propositional knowledge by denying that we have e-awareness of the relevant relation of *correspondence* holding between the thought that the datum contains 48 speckles and the fact that would make that thought true. It is certainly true that even if there is an internal relation[10] of correspondence between the thought that P and the fact that P, and even if we are directly acquainted with both the thought that P and the fact that P, it simply doesn't follow that we are directly acquainted with every internal relation holding between the thought and the fact. Consider, for example, entailment. If P entails Q then that entailment holds in all worlds in which P and Q exist—entailment is an internal relation. But it just isn't true that we will be aware of the entailment whenever we hold before our minds P and Q. If it were, logic exams would be much easier than they are.

Poston succeeds, I think, in identifying a coherent response for the proponent of an acquaintance theory of noninferential justification. Certainly, on the theory I defend, direct acquaintance with a potential truth-maker is not sufficient for having a noninferentially justified belief. One must also have the relevant thought which corresponds to the truth-maker, and one must be directly aware of the correspondence between the thought and the truth-maker. On some versions of a correspondence theory, for example Russell's view of belief as a polyadic relation, at least some of the constituents of a belief state are identical with constituents of the fact that makes true the belief. But however one understands the relata of the correspondence relation, it will be critical to have direct acquaintance with the relation in order to have the kind of direct acquaintance that yields direct knowledge. And the more complex the relata, the less obvious it is that one will automatically become acquainted with the relation in becoming acquainted with its relata.

While there are no formal difficulties with Poston's defense of the acquaintance theory against Sosa's objection, and while I always appreciate any help I can get, I'm not sure that the reply is phenomenologically plausible—I'm not sure that we have direct acquaintance with the relevant relata of the correspondence relation in the kind of case that Sosa envisions. It seems to me that there are, at the very least, alternative explanations of what we are and are not acquainted with in the experience of the speckled hen that might give an equally satisfying explanation of why we lack knowledge of the proposition to which Sosa points.

Feldman and Phenomenal Concepts:

Richard Feldman (2003) also tries to help the radical foundationalist formulate a response to Sosa's objection. Feldman's response focuses on a distinction that Sosa himself seems to acknowledge between two kinds of *concepts*—those that are indexical or phenomenal, and those that are not. Indexical concepts have relatively little content. As the term implies, we might express such concepts using indexicals. When presented with the appearance of the speckled hen, one might characterize the experience by applying the concept: being appeared to this way. What way? THIS way, and one gestures towards the experience. I'm not sure that Feldman defines a phenomenal concept, but he characterizes it as one that allows one to categorize an experience as being of a certain kind, where the justified application of the concept involves nothing other than one's awareness of the relevant phenomenal character of the experience. In what follows I'll focus on phenomenal concepts—I agree with Sosa that indexical concepts aren't rich enough to secure the propositional knowledge that the acquaintance theorist seeks.

Feldman argues that if we employ our understanding of a phenomenal concept, and we also recognize a distinction within e-awareness between properties with which we are acquainted but upon which we are not directing our attention and those upon which we are directing our attention, we have the resources to respond to Sosa's objection. In this section I will focus on the distinctions between kinds of concepts. In the next, I'll discuss the idea of focused awareness.

So what precisely is the distinction between concepts that are phenomenal and those that are not? I think Sosa would like to define the distinction in terms of how we would or could go about justifiably applying the concept. Intuitively, we can distinguish the way in which one can tell "at a glance" that a given figure in one's visual field is three-sided, for example, from the way in which most of us would need to go about discovering that an object has twenty-seven sides. As I understand him, Sosa wants to suggest that the difference in the nature of the concepts is best understood in terms of a distinction between capacities. Upon having e-awareness of the 27-sided sense datum, most of us cannot reliably reach the conclusion that the figure has 27 sides. When e-aware of a 3-sided figure, we can reliably form the judgment that the figure has three sides.

The acquaintance theorist will surely not want to understand the distinction between concepts that are phenomenal and those are not this way. So-called concept possession is identified with the ability to respond reliably to characteristics of one's experience with the judgment that the experience has those characteristics. The suggestion, presumably, is that the justified character of the judgment so formed is a function of its reliability. Acquaintance is dropping out of the picture as that which is epistemically relevant. But there is a deeper concern. It is not clear to me that we can get an account of the essential distinction between two thoughts or concepts by talking about the way in which one can reach conclusions that employ the concepts. The thought that the figure is 48-sided is different in important respects from the thought that a figure is three-sided, and that is true regardless of considerations concerning the epistemic status of that thought.

Feldman and Sosa do seem to be on to an important distinction. For most of us, the thought of being 27-sided, or the thought of containing 48 speckles is perhaps more like the thought of a given *process*—specifically the process of counting sides or speckles. If we model thoughts on pictures, these "process" thoughts are more like motion pictures. The process pictured is one that takes time and it is unlikely that a classical foundationalist will allow that one can be directly acquainted with the kind of "process" fact to which our "process" thought would correspond. By contrast, one might suggest, one can form a thought about something's being three-sided, or containing three speckles, that is more like a "still" picture with the capacity to correspond to a "still-life" fact. I have warned elsewhere that the picturing metaphor is dangerous. Thoughts are not literally pictures or images in the mind (though such pictures or images may accompany them). Nevertheless, metaphors are useful, and the above metaphors might still help us gesture towards the relevant differences between kinds of thoughts.

In general, it seems to me that one must be very careful in trying to uncover the nature of mathematical/geometrical thought. For one thing, I'm not sure that we easily leave the level of language when forming mathematical thoughts. Typically, when I think about summing 379 and 524, for example, I suspect I'm doing nothing more than thinking about the manipulation of symbols. To be sure, I know that these symbols have a meaning and I use them meaningfully. It is, of course, a matter of great controversy as to what constitute the meanings of numerals as they occur in a given sentence. Grammatically, they seem to function most comfortably as adjectives and that suggests they may refer to properties. If we reach this conclusion we need to figure out what exemplifies the properties—collections, classes, sets, and so on. Others are more comfortable thinking of numerals as functioning in language the way quantifiers function. We have the existential quantifier, "there exists", the "one" quantifier "there exists just one" and so on. However we understand these fundamental questions in the ontology of mathematics, however, I'm suggesting that we don't have an easy time leaving the level of language to think independently of that which the language represents. In fact, I'm inclined to think that this phenomenon is not restricted to complex mathematical/geometrical thought. I suspect that the reason linguistic nominalism has been attractive to so many over the years is the phenomenological fact that when we form highly abstract thoughts, there often is nothing but sentences and words running through our minds. When I form the thought that democracy is on the rise in the Middle East, I'm not sure that anything much happens other than my saying to myself "Democracy is on the rise in the Middle East" as a competent speaker of the English language.

The above is obviously but the barest sketch of a view that would need to be worked out and defended in much more detail. But even if some version of the view were true, it would be a terrible mistake to suppose that thought cannot have as its object anything other than language. The kind of thought that does have as its content something non-linguistic is just the kind of thought that has the potential to "transparently" correspond to its truth-maker, where the correspondence is transparent just because we can hold before our mind both the thought, its truth-maker, and the correspondence that holds between them.

So I agree with Feldman that there is an important difference between having the phenomenal thought that the sense datum contains 48 speckles (or that I'm appeared to 48-speckledly) and something that we might call the process thought that involves something like sequentially counting aspects of items in that exrperience. Armed with this distinction, it seems to me that Feldman is right to suggest that the acquaintance theorist should restrict foundational justification to thought that is phenomenal. It is only when one has the capacity to form such thoughts that one can be directly acquainted with the thought and its correspondence to its truth-maker.

As Feldman notes, Sosa worries that the acquaintance theorist who relies exclusively on phenomenal thought is in danger of reducing the foundations of knowledge and justified belief to a structure too flimsy upon which to build. The concern that classical foundationalism leads inevitably to a fairly extreme skepticism is one that many have raised. It is one of the main reasons Quine recommended naturalizing epistemology. Feldman is much more optimistic than I am that we can reconstruct commonsense knowledge and justified belief relying on the foundations provided by direct acquaintance, but I have argued elsewhere that one shouldn't require of a plausible epistemology that it cater to the ambitions of philosophers.

Determinates and Determinables:

Earlier we noted that the object of acquaintance that will be of most interest to an acquaintance theorist is a fact. Again, for our present purposes we can understand a fact in terms of the exemplification of properties. We also noted that if there are sense data and if we can become acquainted with them, it will not follow that we are acquainted with the sense data's exemplifying all of the properties they exemplify. At the very least, we will make a distinction between relational and nonrelational properties. If we embrace the appearing theory, we need to be a bit more careful in how we state the point. On the appearing theory the experiences with which we are acquainted just are the self's exemplifying various properties. But again no careful acquaintance theorist will allow that we are always directly acquainted with all of the properties, not even all of the experiential properties, exemplified by the self. I may exemplify the property of feeling pain two hours after thinking about the problem of the speckled hen, but the fact that I exemplify this complex property is not one with which I am acquainted.

In the previous section we discussed the nature of our thought about the relevant property of the experience presented by the speckled hen. But what shall we say about either the sense datum's exemplifying the property of containing 48 speckles, or the self's exemplifying the property of being appeared to 48-speckledly (assuming that there is such a property)? Well, the sense datum's property is probably best construed as relational. We have, so to speak, sense data occupying a place within a larger sense data. Still, the relata of the sense-data are all themselves sense-data and one might suppose that that should pose no obstacle to our becoming directly aware of the relevant truth-maker for the thought that the "larger" sense datum contains 48 speckles (48 smaller sense data). On the appearing theory it is at least tempting to think that the property of being appeared to can be broken down into simpler constituent properties. For ease of exposition I'll discuss the relevant issues presupposing the language of a sense-datum theory. I suspect one can find ways of translating the relevant points into the language favored by the appearing theorist.

As we saw, Sosa wants to suggest that we have some kind of awareness of all experience just in virtue of its occurrence. As we also saw, we surely don't want to allow that we have awareness in any sense of many of the properties exemplified by an experience. An acquaintance theorist will insist on restricting the properties to non-relational properties or relations where the relata are themselves objects of acquaintance. Earlier, I argued that it is a mistake to suppose that it is an essential feature of experience that we have any kind of awareness of it. Of course we can make it trivially true that *conscious* experience, that is experience of which we are conscious/aware, is always experience of which we are aware. But then the relevant question becomes which experiences, or which aspects of experience, are conscious, i.e. objects of direct acquaintance.

Feldman suggests that even when we are directly aware of features of our experience we can profitably distinguish those features of our experience to which we attend, or upon which we focus, and those which lie at the periphery of consciousness. And Feldman rejects the suggestion that this focused awareness is nothing other than Sosa's n-awareness, i.e. judgments we make about our experience. Feldman's idea is attractive. Indeed, I once suggested a version of it myself.[11] It is tempting to think, for example, that if we do our "phenomenal" counting of the speckles in our visual field we are sequentially focusing on, or attending to, the various speckles. If we accept the idea that there is this focused mode of direct acquaintance, we have yet another possible response to Sosa's questions concerning the way in which acquaintance can yield noninferential justification or knowledge. We have noninferential knowledge that a visual sense datum contains the 48 speckles only if we are directly acquainted in the relevant focused way with the property of containing 48 speckles. Because we are not capable of focusing on such a property (even when it is in some sense before consciousness) we can't get the right sort of acquaintance with the fact that is the truth-maker for the relevant proposition.

I'm not as confident as I once was that there are species of direct acquaintance—that the light of direct acquaintance can shine more brightly on certain aspects of experience. One must ultimately rely on the phenomenological evidence, and I'm just not sure that the attention to which Feldman appeals, or the focusing to which I appealed, doesn't actually change the experience itself. In any event, I want to suggest that there may be another ontological distinction to which one might appeal that will achieve the same end, and that will enable us to explain why we lack propositional knowledge concerning the number of speckles present in the visual field.

Thinking about the nature of properties, it seems to many that we can make a distinction between perfectly determinate properties and the many determinable generic properties that supervene upon those determinate properties. So, for example, a visual sense-datum may be a particularly bright shade of cherry red. It is also cherry red, red, dark-colored, and colored. We need to reach difficult ontological conclusions concerning the nature of the generic or determinable properties—being cherry red, red, dark-colored, colored, and so on. The radical British empiricists were, for the most part, convinced that all properties were perfectly determinate. They realized they needed to give some sort of account of what we are doing when we think abstractly, when we think of triangularity, or redness in general, but the account usually involved commitment to nothing other than particular triangular shapes and particular shades of redness. It is, however, an understatement to suggest that such attempts to explain abstract thought did not meet universal acceptance.

Again, we are not about to settle here the question of whether there are determinable properties whose exemplification is distinct from, but supervenes upon, the exemplification of perfectly determinate properties. One of the more persuasive arguments for the existence of such properties, though, is phenomenological.[12] A witness sees a car speed away from the scene of an accident. When interviewed by the police the witness is absolutely sure that the car was a dark color, but has no idea whether it was blue, black, maroon, dark red, or any other particular dark color. The example isn't quite what we want—the acquaintance theorist under discussion is unlikely to suppose that one can be directly acquainted with any facts about the colors of physical objects. But we need only imagine a philosophically sophisticated policeman who starts asking about the apparent color of the car. When asked if the car looked blue, red, maroon, and so on, the witness responds only that it just looked dark. It is at least tempting to suppose that the problem the witness has is not epistemological. In the language of determinates and determinables, it is tempting to suppose that the witness was aware of the exemplification a generic property, being dark colored, even though the witness had no awareness of the determinate property upon which the determinable supervenes. If we can convince ourselves that there are these many different "levels" of properties standing in the determinate/determinable relation, it should be obvious how we might appeal to this ontology of properties in deciding what to say about the appearance presented by the speckled hen.

On the sense datum theory, we are directly acquainted with the datum's exemplifying the property of being many speckled. On the appearing theory, we are directly acquainted with our being appeared to many-speckled-ly. We are not, however, directly acquainted with the datum's containing exactly 48 speckles, nor are we acquainted with our being appeared to 48-speckled-ly. It is not that the more determinate properties aren't exemplified—it's just that we are not directly aware of them. Again, if there are determinable properties, it may not be particularly surprising that our awareness is often directed at them and not their finely-grained subvenient base. Evolution may have programmed us to notice only properties of a certain level of generality. It might help us deal with what would otherwise be an overwhelmingly chaotic world of property exemplification. Just as we sometimes really do fail to see the forest for the trees, so we can imagine that our epistemic situation is better for our ability to notice generic properties (the forest) without getting bogged down with awareness of their determinate base (the trees).

Conclusion:

In trying to figure out how the acquaintance theorists can reconcile their account of noninferential justification with the failure to know propositions describing certain features of experience of the sort Sosa directs our attention to, we have found that there are a number of plausible positions available. Each has its own ontological commitments that must be independently defended. 1) We might embrace an appearing theory and claim that the hen that has a determinate number of speckles produces in us only a way of being appeared to many-speckled-ly. There isn't the relevant truth of which Sosa claims we lack knowledge. 2) We might embrace the view that sensation is a species of intentional state and again simply assert that there isn't the relevant problematic truth of which Sosa claims we lack knowledge. 3) We might argue, with Poston, that though we have direct acquaintance with thoughts and facts about experience, the complexity of the thoughts and facts with which we are acquainted sometimes preclude (causally) our direct acquaintance with the correspondence between the thought and its truth-maker. We lack noninferential knowledge of the 48 speckled character of our visual experience because we lack acquaintance with the correspondence between the relevant thought and its truth-maker. 4) We might argue, with Feldman, that noninferential knowledge requires that the concepts applied be of a special "phenomenal" kind that makes them accessible to acquaintance (and makes accessible a relation of correspondence that holds between those concepts and the exemplification of properties). The concepts to which we are limited in making judgments about the properties of the visual data presented by the speckled hen are not of the right sort to allow the relevant access to the properties to which those concepts correspond. 5) We might argue that there is a special kind of acquaintance—focused acquaintance—that we simply lack when it comes to the property, exemplification of which is the truth-maker for the claim about the specific "speckled character" of the appearance presented by the speckled hen. And lastly, 6) we might argue that in at least some experience we are directly acquainted with determinable properties and not with the determinate properties upon which those generic properties supervene. That explains why we can know noninferentially that the hen presents a many-speckled appearance without knowing the more detailed truths about the n-speckled character of the experience. I suspect that somewhere in this menu the classical foundationalist can find an appetizing solution to Sosa's concerns.

Notes

1. Chisholm's classic article (1942) presents the problem as one raised by Gilbert Ryle in a discussion with A. J. Ayer. Paul Ushenko (1946, p. 103) claims that the example of the speckled hen was first given by H.H. Price, but that he (Ushenko)

raised a variation of the same problem in *The Philosophy of Relativity* (p. 90) in 1937 Ushenko also claims that he discussed the problem with Ayer. I thank Steven Bayne for pointing out to me Ushenko's contribution to the debate (in his history of analytic philosophy electronic mailing).

2. See among others Fumerton (1985, 1996, 2001).
3. It is not unproblematic to talk of one state of affairs or fact entailing another. The most natural definition of entailment requires that the relation holds between the bearers of truth values. While one might take a state of affairs to be a proposition (where a state of affairs is true when it obtains; false, when it fails to obtain), one might instead take states of affairs to be truth makers (where false propositions fail to correspond to any state of affairs). If states of affairs or facts are truth makers we can say that one fact entails another when the proposition the former makes true entails the proposition the latter makes true.
4. The reference is to the character in a movie of the same name who has uncanny abilities to "see" at a glance complex truths involving large numbers—including truths about the number of things standing in spatial relations to one another.
5. Though figuring out which view came first is complicated by the fact that important historical figures used neither the terminology of the sense-datum theory or the adverbial theory. Berkeley might have been implicitly committed to the adverbial theory, for example. One can certainly find passages in which he seemed to identify the idea perceived with the perceiving. Interpreting Berkeley in this way would certainly help him justify his insistence that it makes no sense to suppose that the idea perceived could exist independently of its being perceived. More recent foundationalists might take sensation to be an intentional or representational state. Such views complicate the following discussion in a host of ways.
6. We need to add the adverb "phenomenally" to stress that the redness and roundness exemplified by a sense datum may not be the same redness and roundness exemplified by a physical object. On one famous view, for example, a physical object's being red is to be identified with the object's possessing the power to affect conscious beings under certain conditions with red sense data. To avoid circularity, such views need to distinguish the meaning of the first "red" and the meaning of the second "red" in the preceding sentence.
7. A suggestion Ayer (1953, 124–25) nevertheless made.
8. While sensation is not an intentional state it is interpreted by us so seamlessly that we can easily be misled into think that it is. The intentional states are the familiar expectations produced by sensation.
9. For an argument that presupposes an ontology of particulars but denies that we can be directly acquainted with them, see Addis (1967).
10. A relation that holds between an X and a Y is internal if it is necessary that the relation holds given the existence of X and Y.
11. In Fumerton (1985), pp. 59–61, I argued that one might find room within an acquaintance theory for false noninferentially justified belief. Part of what I allowed is that one can be acquainted with an experience but fail to notice or focus upon some element of it. Laird Addis (1986) also suggests that we might

allow that there is a "heightened form" of awareness involved in attending to some feature of experience—he calls it a *supermode* of awareness.

12. For a more detailed phenomenological defense of generic properties along the lines I'm about to sketch see Fales (1990, Part Two, Chapter 9).

References

Addis. Laird. 1967. "Particulars and Acquaintance." *Philosophy of Science* 34, 251–59.

———. 1986. "Pain and Other Secondary Mental Entities." Philosophy and Phenomenological Research 47, 59–74.

Ayer, A. J. 1953. *The Foundations of Empirical Knowledge*. Macmillan.

Chisholm, Roderick. 1942. "The Problem of the Speckled Hen." *Mind*, October, 368–73.

Fales, Evan. 1990. *Causation and Universals*. Routledge

Feldman, 2003. "The Justification of Introspective Belief." In Conee and Feldman, *Evidentialism*, 199–218. Oxford University Press.

Fumerton, Richard. 1985. *Metaphysical and Epistemological Problems of Perception*. University of Nebraska Press.

———. 1996. *Metaepistemology and Skepticism*. Rowman and Littlefield.

———. 2001. "Classical Foundationalism." In *Resurrecting Old-Fashioned Foundationalism*, ed. Michael DePaul. Rowman and Littlefield.

———. 2002. *Realism and the Correspondence Theory of Truth*. Rowman and Littlefield.

Poston, Ted. Forthcoming. "Acquaintance and the Problem of the Speckled Hen." *Philosophical Studies*.

Sellars, Wilfred. 1963. *Science, Perception and Reality*. Routledge and Kegan Paul.

Sosa, Ernest. 2003a. "Privileged Access." In *Consciousness: New Philosophical Essays*, ed. Quentin Smith, 273–92. Oxford University Press.

Sosa, Ernest, and Bonjour Laurence. 2003b. *Foundations vs Virtues*. Blackwell.

Ushenko, Andrew Paul. 1937. *The Philosophy of Relativity*. Allen and Unwin.

———. 1946. *Power and Events: An Essay on Dynamics in Philosophy*. Princeton University Press.

Philosophical Perspectives, 19, Epistemology, 2005

SCOTCHING DUTCH BOOKS?

Alan Hájek
Australian National University

1. Introduction

The Dutch Book argument, like Route 66, is about to turn 80. It is arguably the most celebrated argument for subjective Bayesianism. Start by rejecting the Cartesian idea that doxastic attitudes are 'all-or-nothing'; rather, they are far more nuanced *degrees of belief*, for short *credences*, susceptible to fine-grained numerical measurement. Add a coherentist assumption that the rationality of a doxastic state consists in its internal consistency. The remaining problem is to determine what consistency amounts to for credences. The Dutch Book argument, in a nutshell, says that if your credences do not obey the probability calculus, you are 'incoherent'—susceptible to sure losses at the hands of a 'Dutch Bookie'—and thus irrational. Conclusion: rationality requires your credences to obey the probability calculus.

And like Route 66, the fortunes of the Dutch Book argument have been mixed. Opinions on the argument are sharply divided. The list of its proponents is quite a 'who's who' of philosophers of probability; they include de Finetti (1937, 1980), Carnap (1950, 1962, and more fully, 1955), Kemeny (1955), Lehman (1955), Shimony (1955), Adams (1962), Mellor (1971), Rosenkrantz (1981), van Fraassen (1989), Jeffrey (1983, 1992), and Gillies (2000).[1] Ramsey (1926—hence the imminent 80th birthday) belongs at the head of the list, although we will see that the full story about him is more interesting than has been previously recognized. The argument has found some notable opponents too, including Kyburg (1978), Kennedy and Chihara (1979), Schick (1986), and Maher (1993, 1997); however, they are surely in the minority. In this paper I will begin by joining their ranks. The Dutch Book argument, in the form that has become a philosophical staple, is simply invalid, and to the extent that we have bought it for so many years we have, as it were, been Dutch Booked ourselves; indeed, in endorsing it we have been guilty of a certain form of incoherence. However, like Route 66, the argument can be reconstructed, or better still, restored. I will favor a version of the argument that avoids the defects of the staple version—thus, I hope, a better argument for Bayesianism. I will conclude by arguing that it was implicit in Ramsey's original presentation all along, and that it was subsequent expositors of the argument who got it wrong.

2. The Dutch Book argument

Let me make clear what I take the Dutch Book argument—the philosophical staple—to be, and thus, which argument it is that I claim is invalid. (In the final section I will consider a variant of the argument whose emphasis is rather different.) What follows should look completely familiar to any student of the argument. I begin with some background.

You are a rational agent who assigns credences to a non-empty set of sentences assumed to be closed under negation and disjunction—although nothing in the Dutch Book argument justifies these closure assumptions. We assume that your credences are sharp—as opposed to indeterminate, or vague—although again nothing in the argument justifies this assumption. (Levi 1974 and 1980 relaxes this assumption.) It is further assumed that your credences can be identified with your betting dispositions concerning the sentences. Your credence in X is p iff you are prepared to buy or to sell a bet that pays S units of utility (the 'stake') for pS ('the price your consider fair', for short 'your fair price' for the bet); equivalently, you are prepared to bet on or against X at odds $p: 1 - p$, at any stake. For example, if you assign a credence of 1/2 to this coin toss landing heads, and if for you utility is linear in money, then you are prepared to buy or to sell the bet

$1 if heads
0 otherwise

for 50 cents. (If for you utility is not linear in money, read the '$' sign as representing one unit of utility, and 'cents' as hundredths of a unit.) So construed, a betting transaction involves four things: the proposition X, the stake S, your fair price pS for the bet—equivalently, your odds $p: 1 - p$—and the side of the bet that you take (buying or selling, betting on or against X). We can reduce this to three by allowing negative stakes, identifying positive stakes with your betting on the proposition, negative stakes with your betting against it.

The Dutch Book argument purports to show that rationality requires your credences to obey the probability calculus. That is, it requires that your credences can be represented as a probability function, P, over a non-empty set of sentences **S** closed under negation and disjunction, where P satisfies the usual axioms:

1. Non-negativity: $P(X) \geq 0$ for all X in **S**.
2. Normalization: $P(T) = 1$ for any tautology T in **S**.
3. Additivity: $P(X \vee Y) = P(X) + P(Y)$ for all X, Y in **S** such that X is incompatible with Y.

It is important now to distinguish three things: the *definition* of a Dutch Book, the Dutch Book *theorem (and its converse)*, and the Dutch Book *argument*. First, the definition. A Dutch Book is a set of bets, each of which you consider fair, that collectively guarantee your loss.[2]

Next, the theorem. *If your credences violate the probability calculus, then there exists a Dutch Book against you.* That is, if your credences disobey any of the above axioms, then there exists a set of bets, each of which you consider fair, that will result in a net loss for you however the world turns out. Said another way, if your credences violate the probability calculus, then there exists a set of propositions and stakes (positive or negative) such that betting at your odds at those stakes on those propositions, you will lose, whatever transpires.

I will not present the full proof of the theorem here, but I can easily convey how it works. We really have three sub-theorems, one for each axiom, with a separate proof of each (see Skyrms 1986). The most interesting one concerns the additivity axiom. Suppose, for example, that you violate additivity by assigning $P(A \vee B) > P(A) + P(B)$ for incompatible A and B. Then you effectively overprice a bet on $A \vee B$ relative to bets on A and on B, and you will suffer a sure loss if you buy the first bet (at a comparatively high price) and sell the second and third bets (at comparatively low prices). Specifically, you are prepared to buy—from the dreaded 'Dutch Bookie'—a \$1 bet on $A \vee B$ for \$$P(A \vee B)$ and to sell bets on A and on B for \$$P(A)$ and \$$P(B)$ respectively, for an initial loss of

$$\$[P(A \vee B) - (P(A) + P(B))] > 0.$$

But from then on your net wealth remains the same, whatever happens. If neither A nor B occurs, all bets lose; if exactly one of A and B occurs, the \$1 that you pay out on that bet is offset by the \$1 that you gain on the $A \vee B$ bet. This exhausts the cases (since A and B cannot both occur). And so it goes for all of the other ways in which you could violate the probability calculus: in each case you are susceptible to a Dutch Book.

Moreover, the converse theorem also holds: *if your credences do not violate the probability calculus, then there does not exist a Dutch Book against you* (Kemeny 1955, Lehman 1955). Thus, what I will call *the complete Dutch Book theorem*, which combines the Dutch Book theorem and its converse, asserts a biconditional between your violating the probability calculus and your receptivity to a Dutch Book. This is simply a piece of mathematics, and there is no disputing it.

Finally, the argument. It is thought by many to follow from the Dutch Book theorem that rationality requires you to obey the probability calculus. After all, it is said, your state of opinion would be an unhappy one if, in virtue of its purely intrinsic characteristics, it exposed you to sure losses at the hands of a Dutch Bookie. This inference is clearly too quick: for all the Dutch Book theorem says, you may be exposed to the sure losses of a Dutch Book whether or not you obey the probability calculus; indeed, for all the theorem says, your losses may be even greater if you obey it. But the Converse Dutch Book theorem rules out these possibilities: adherence to the probability calculus shields you from the losses inherent in a Dutch Book. So it is supposed to follow from the complete Dutch Book theorem that you would be irrational to violate the probability calculus.

It is supposed to follow, but it does not.

3. The Good Book argument

I will show that the Dutch Book argument is invalid first by parodying it, then by identifying the flaw in both the parody and the argument itself. I call my parody the *Good Book argument*. It is rather younger than Route 66; in fact, I have not seen it before.

It is important now to distinguish three things: the *definition* of a Good Book, the Good Book *theorem (and its converse)*, and the Good Book *argument*. First, the definition. A Good Book is a set of bets, each of which you consider fair, that collectively guarantee your *gain*.[3]

Next, the theorem. *If your credences violate the probability calculus, then there exists a Good Book for you.* That is, if your credences disobey any of the above axioms, then there exists a set of bets, each of which you consider fair, that will result in a net gain for you however the world turns out. Said another way, if your credences violate the probability calculus, then there exists a set of propositions and stakes (positive or negative) such that betting at your odds at those stakes on those propositions, you will win, whatever transpires.

Moreover, the converse theorem also holds: *if your credences do not violate the probability calculus, then there does not exist a Good Book for you.* The proofs are straightforward: simply replace 'buy' by 'sell' and vice versa throughout the proofs of the Dutch Book theorem and its converse. You just swap sides with the Dutch Bookie in the original proofs, turning him into a Good Bookie. Thus, what I will call *the complete Good Book theorem*, which combines the Good Book theorem and its converse, asserts a biconditional between a violation of the probability calculus and receptivity to a Good Book. This is simply a piece of mathematics, and there is no disputing it.

Finally, the argument. It might be said to follow from the Good Book theorem that rationality requires you to violate the probability calculus. After all, it might be said, your state of opinion would be a happy one if, in virtue of its purely intrinsic characteristics, it exposed you to sure gains at the hands of a Good Bookie. This inference is clearly too quick: for all the Good Book theorem says, you may be exposed to the sure gains of a Good Book whether or not you disobey the probability calculus; indeed, for all the theorem says, your gains may be even greater if you obey it. But the Converse Good Book theorem rules out these possibilities: adherence to the probability calculus shields you from the gains inherent in a Good Book. So it follows from the complete Good Book theorem that you would be irrational to obey the probability calculus.

4. Diagnosis

What is wrong with the Good Book argument, and with it, the Dutch Book argument? We have before us a pair of biconditionals with existentially quantified consequents:

Iff you violate the probability calculus, there exists a SPECIFIC BAD THING (a Dutch Book against you).

Iff you violate the probability calculus, there exists a SPECIFIC GOOD THING (a Good Book for you).

Each argument focuses on one of the conditionals while ignoring the other. But we apparently have perfect symmetry here, the yin of the one mirrored by the yang of the other. The Dutch Book argument sees the incoherent agent's glass as half empty, while the Good Book argument sees it as half full. Advocates of the Dutch Book argument seem to regard the possibility of sure losses as more compelling than the possibility of sure gains. It's as if they are employing some sort of maximin reasoning, more concerned as they are by the prospect of loss than by the prospect of gain. But this should seem quite out of place coming from the mouth, or pen, of a *Bayesian*—someone who seeks to supplant a theory of decision under uncertainty, in which probabilities for outcomes are not assigned (thus requiring decision rules such as maximin), with a theory of decision under risk, in which they are assigned. An advocate of the Good Book argument, in turn, could regard the possibility of sure gains as more compelling than the possibility of sure losses, perhaps employing some sort of maximax reasoning. Like a particle and its antiparticle, the two arguments annihilate each other.

It is said that the Dutch Book argument exposes the incoherent agent as guilty of an evaluative inconsistency, valuing the same state of affairs in two different ways depending on how it is presented.[4] Someone who propounds the Dutch Book argument while baulking at the Good Book argument is not quite guilty of that sin, since they are of course not the same argument. Still, given the symmetry between them, these opposed evaluations seem to evince a kind of double-think, if not quite double-Dutch.

You might try to break the symmetry with an assumed *asymmetry* in the world. You might contend that it is easier to find Dutch Bookies than it is to find Good Bookies: the incoherent agents will have no trouble finding Dutch Bookies eager to exploit their incoherence, but they will not find Good Bookies for their incoherence to exploit. I will call this the *bad neighborhood defence*, because it assumes that agents are more likely to run into bookies of the 'bad' kind than of the 'good' kind.

I have often heard this line of argument but I find it puzzling, several times over. Firstly, the Dutch Book theorem is a mathematical result that concerns the existence of abstract objects of a certain sort: sequences of bets with certain properties. Susceptibility to a Dutch Book is a dispositional property of an agent, one that he or she has independently of what other people are out there, and what they are like—in fact there need not be other people out there at all. (Compare: solubility is a property that salt has independently of whether or not water is out there.) No surprise, then, that the theorem makes no mention of bookies, Dutch or Chinese, bad or otherwise. Yet now the argument brings on such dramatis personae, and moreover attributes to them self-interested or nefarious motives, getting their kicks at the agent's expense. No piece of mathematics can derive the existence of such characters, let alone their preponderance in this neighborhood or that.

On the other hand, the argument surely does not turn on the empirical claim that our world has more would-be Dutch Bookies than would-be Good Bookies. If you want to conduct a survey of just how mean the streets are out there, be my guest. For what it's worth, the findings of experimental economists on the surprisingly 'fair' behavior of actual subjects in 'dictator' and 'ultimatum' games suggest to me that they may not be so mean after all; and recent work in comparative anthropology suggests that how mean they are will vary from one part of the world to another. But it's worth little here, because of course the Dutch Book argument is intended as a piece of philosophy, not sociology. Indeed, it is premised on the highly idealized assumption of perfect rationality of the agent concerned. (No respect for the empirical facts *there!*) The imaginary Dutch Bookies, in their turn, are supposed to be perfectly rational, logically omniscient, and more besides: they must know the agent's betting odds in order to exploit them, and they must be willing to do so. All the more dubious, then, is the apparently empirical claim that such characters predominate. But if this claim is another idealization (which is to say, a fiction), why should we accept it? In particular, why should we prefer it to the idealization (fiction) that Good Bookies predominate? Again, we seem to have a perfect symmetry here.

However, let us grant for the sake of the argument that Dutch Bookies prowl the agent's 'hood, and that Good Bookies are nowhere to be found. Still, it does not follow that the incoherent agent cannot enjoy the benefits of a Good Book. All he or she needs to do is spread the bets around: as it might be, selling a bet on $A \vee B$ to Bookie 1, while buying bets on A and on B to Bookies 2 and 3. No single bookie, then, need be incoherent; no single bookie need be milked. The Dutch Book theorem did not assume that there actually are bookies at the other ends of the imagined transactions; still less did it assume that there is exactly one, involved with them all.

However, all this concedes far too much to the bad neighborhood defence; indeed, the whole tenor of the defence is quite misguided. It turns on certain contingent putative 'facts'—rather dubious ones, as I have noted. But according to the Bayesian account of rationality, what matters are not the facts, but rather *what the agent takes the facts to be*. More precisely, what matters in determining what the agent should do are the agent's own probability assignments. Your neighborhood could be bad without you realizing it—for example, because you have no evidence that it is. So the bad neighborhood defence needs to make an assumption to the effect that *the agent assigns sufficiently high probability to his or her neighborhood being bad.* When fully spelled out, the assumption will be rather more complicated than this, involving the agent's probability assignments to various hypotheses about just how bad the neighborhood is, and what the expected utilities will look like in each case. But let us not waste time trying to articulate this assumption, because it is all beside the point. *Rationality* does not require the agent to have particular opinions about any contingent matter, and that includes the local demographics. *Coherence* is not answerable to the world (the way that truth is), and coherence is all that the Dutch Book argument claimed to address.

I conclude that the standard Dutch Book argument fails. Like Route 66, it needs some repairing.[5]

5. Reconstructing/restoring the argument[6]

For some reason, most of the presenters, both sympathetic and unsympathetic, of the Dutch Book argument that I am aware of focus solely on bets bought or sold at *exactly* your fair prices, bets that you consider fair. The list, containing many a luminary in the philosophy of probability, includes: Adams (1962), Adams and Rosenkrantz (1980), Armendt (1992), Baillie (1973), Carnap (1950, 1955), Christensen (1991, 1996, 2001), de Finetti (1980), Döring (2000), Earman (1992), Gillies (2000), Howson and Urbach (1993), Jackson and Pargetter (1976), Jeffrey (1983, 1992), Kaplan (1996), Kemeny (1955), Kennedy and Chihara (1979), Lange (1999), Lehman (1955), Maher (1993), Mellor (1971), Milne (1990), Rosenkrantz (1981), Seidenfeld and Schervish (1983), Skyrms (1986), van Fraassen (1989), Weatherson (1999), Waidacher (1997), and Williamson (1999). But bets that you consider fair are not the only ones that you accept; you also accept bets that you consider *favorable*—that is, better than fair. You are prepared to sell a given bet at higher prices, and to buy it at lower prices, than your fair price. This observation is just what we need to break the symmetry that deadlocked the Dutch Book argument and the Good Book argument.

Let us rewrite the theorems, replacing 'fair' with 'fair-or-favorable' throughout, and see what happens:

Dutch Book theorem, revised:

If you violate the probability calculus, there exists a set of bets, each of which you consider fair-or-favorable, that collectively guarantee your loss.

Converse Dutch Book theorem, revised:

If you obey the probability calculus, there does not exist a set of bets, each of which you consider fair-or-favorable, that collectively guarantee your loss.

Good Book theorem, revised:

If you violate the probability calculus, there exists a set of bets, each of which you consider fair-or-favorable, that collectively guarantee your gain.

Converse Good Book theorem, revised:

If you obey the probability calculus, there does not exist a set of bets, each of which you consider fair-or-favorable, that collectively guarantee your gain.

The first three of these revisions are true, obvious corollaries of the original theorems. Indeed, the revised versions of the Dutch Book theorem and the Good Book theorem follow immediately, because any bet that you consider fair you *ipso facto* consider fair-or-favorable. The revised version of the Converse Dutch Book theorem also follows straightforwardly from the original version: Suppose you obey the probability calculus. Suppose for reductio that there *does* exist a set of bets, each of which you consider fair-or-favorable, that collectively guarantee a loss; let this loss be $L > 0$. Then you must regard at least one of these bets as favorable (for the Converse Dutch Book theorem assures us that if you regarded them all as fair, then there could not be such guaranteed loss). That is, at least one of these bets is sold at a higher price, or bought at a cheaper price, than your fair price for it. For each such bet, replacing its price by your fair price would increase your loss. Thus, making all such replacements, so that you regard all the bets as fair, your guaranteed loss is even greater than L, and thus greater than 0. This contradicts the Converse Dutch Book theorem. Hence, we must reject our initial supposition, completing the reductio. We have proved the revised version of the Converse Dutch Book theorem.

But the revised version of the Converse Good Book theorem is *not* true: if you obey the probability calculus, there *does* exist a set of bets, each of which you consider fair-or-favorable, that collectively guarantee your gain. The proof is trivial. Suppose you obey the probability calculus; then if T is a tautology, you assign $P(T) = 1$. You consider fair-or-favorable paying less than \$1—e.g, 80 cents—for a bet on T at a \$1 stake, simply because you regard it as favorable; and this bet guarantees your gain. The revision from 'fair' to 'fair-or-favorable' makes all the difference. And with the failure of the revised version of the Converse Good Book theorem, there can be no revised version of the complete Good Book theorem, and thus no revised version of the Good Book argument. There were no Good Books for a coherent agent, because Good Books were defined in terms of *fair* bets. But there are other profitable books besides Good Books, and incoherence is not required in order to enjoy those. Opening the door to fair-or-favorable bets opens the door to sure profits for the coherent agent. So my parody no longer goes through when the Dutch Book argument is cast in terms of fair-or-favorable bets, as it always should have been.

I began this section by observing that *most* of the presenters of the Dutch Book argument formulate it in terms of your fair prices. You may have noticed that I left Ramsey off the list of authors.[7] His relevant remarks are confined to "Truth and Probability", and what he says is somewhat telegraphic: "If anyone's mental condition violated these laws [of probability], his choice would depend on the precise form in which the options were offered him, which would be absurd. He could have a book made against him by a cunning bettor and would then stand to lose in any event" (1980, 41). "Having degrees of belief obeying the laws of probability implies a further measure of consistency, namely such a consistency between the odds acceptable on different propositions as shall prevent a book being made against you" (1980, 42). Note that Ramsey does *not* say that all of the bets in the book are individually considered fair by the agent. He leaves open the possibility that some or all of them are considered better than fair; indeed "acceptable" odds sounds *synonymous* with "fair-or-favorable" odds. After all, one would *accept* bets not only at one's fair odds, but also at better odds. Ramsey again:

> By proposing a bet on *p* we give the subject a possible course of action from which so much extra good will result to him if *p* is true and so much extra bad if *p* is false. Supposing the bet to be in goods and bads instead of in money, he will take a bet at any better odds than those corresponding to his state of belief; in fact his state of belief is measured by the odds he will just take; ... (1980, 37).

It was the subsequent authors who restricted the Dutch Book argument solely to fair odds.

Ramsey's formulation of the argument in terms of *consistency* has proved to be very influential. De Finetti also speaks of invulnerability to Dutch Books as a "condition of consistency" (1980, 213). The view has been forcefully advocated more recently by Skyrms, who writes: "... what is basic is the consistency condition that you evaluate a betting arrangement independently of how it is described (e.g., as a bet on *p or q* or as a system of bets consisting of a bet on *p* and a bet on *q*)" (1984, 22). On this view, Dutch Books merely dramatize a deeper defect of an incoherent agent. Armendt (1993) endorses this interpretation and calls giving two or more different evaluations to the same option "divided mind inconsistency".[8]

Put this way, the argument has nothing especially to do with sure *losses* per se. The sure *gains* inherent in Good Books presumably dramatize the same defect. The only difference is that your sure losses are more *dramatic* than your sure gains; an incoherent state of opinion somehow seems more *defective* when it results in sure losses rather than in sure gains. But as far as the point about inconsistency goes, the Dutch Book and the Good Book are on a par. That point is free-standing, and it is no *more* 'Dutch' than 'Good'.

Skyrms describes the Dutch Book theorem as "a striking corollary" of an underlying inconsistency inherent in violating the probability axioms (1984, 22).

But either the striking corollary does no real work, or it does real work: either the prospect of sure losses is not taken seriously, or it is. In the former case, the *argument* does not especially concern Dutch Books at all, and 'Dutch Book argument' does not fully capture the essence of the argument; indeed, 'Good Book argument' would be just as good a name for it (although for historical reasons I doubt that it will catch on!). In the latter case, the symmetric prospect of sure gains should be taken *exactly as seriously*. The Good Book theorem is another corollary—equally striking—of an underlying inconsistency. But then the prospect of sure losses loses its sting; it is neutralized by the symmetric prospect of sure gains. In any case, it is the original corollary that has received all the limelight in the literature, so much so that one could easily get the impression that it was the heart of the argument itself.

I am suggesting that there is a simple way to restore the full force of the corollary, and that Ramsey saw it all along. He did not live to finish "Truth and Probability", and his version of the Dutch Book argument will forever remain telegraphic. But there is enough in what he *did* say to convince me that subsequent expositors did him a disservice in recasting the argument in terms of 'fair' bets. Once we return to Ramsey's notion of "acceptable" bets, replacing 'fair' bets by 'fair-or-favorable' bets throughout the Dutch Book argument, there is no Good Book-style neutralization. An important route to Bayesianism is clear again.[9]

Notes

1. On a liberal understanding of 'Dutch Book arguments', the list would also include Skyrms (1980, 1984, 1986, 1987), Armendt (1992), and Lewis (1999). They downplay pragmatic talk of sure losses, bookies and so on, taking all of this to be a dramatization of a deeper defect of an incoherent agent: evaluating a single betting situation in conflicting ways, depending on how it is described. We will return to these authors in the final section, where I will be less liberal in my understanding.
2. Note that we should really make explicit the relativization *to you*: a Dutch Book is really a two-place *relation* that a set of bets bears (or not) to an agent, so there is no such thing as a Dutch Book *per se*. Nevertheless, I will sometimes follow the usual practice of gliding over this relativization, since the agent will be *you* in what follows.
3. Note that we should really make explicit the relativization *to you*: a Good Book is really a two-place *relation* that a set of bets bears (or not) to an agent, so there is no such thing as a Good Book *per se*. Nevertheless, I will sometimes glide over this relativization, since the agent will be *you* in what follows.
4. See footnote 1, and Section 5.
5. We could similarly parody, and offer similar diagnoses for, other Dutch Book arguments: for countable additivity (Adams 1962); for updating by conditionalization (Lewis 1999); for updating by Jeffrey conditionalization (Armendt 1992); and for the 'Reflection Principle' (van Fraassen 1984). We could even parody the

so-called 'semi Dutch Book' argument for strict coherence (Shimony 1955) with a 'semi Good Book' against it, with a similar diagnosis again. In this paper I am happy to confine myself to that part of Bayesianism that is most entrenched: the demand for synchronic conformity to the probability calculus, as presented in §2,

6. In commenting on an earlier version of this paper, Tom Cunningham and Brad Monton independently came up with versions of this formulation of the argument.
7. Skyrms (1986) was on the list, but not Skyrms (1980, 1984, or 1987). For example, in his (1987) he notes that an agent will buy or sell contracts "at what he considers the fair price or better" (p. 225), and in his (1980), he explicitly states the Dutch Book theorem in terms of "fair or favorable" bets (p. 118). Shimony (1955), Levi (1974), Kyburg (1978), Armendt (1993), Douven (1999), and Vineberg (2001) also leave open that the bets concerned are regarded as favorable. It is hard to tell whether certain other writers on the Dutch Book argument belong on the list or not (e.g., Ryder 1981, Moore 1983).
8. This interpretation also has its share of critics, including Maher (1993) and Vineberg (2001).
9. I am grateful to Erik Angner, Fiona Cowie, Tom Cunningham, Peter Gerdes, Matthias Hild, Andrea Scarantino, Neil Thomason, Brian Weatherson, Jim Woodward, Lyle Zynda, and especially Brad Armendt, Mark Colyvan, Adam Elga, Chris Hitchcock, Brad Monton, Paul Updike, Susan Vineberg, and James Worcester for very helpful discussion. Thanks also to audiences at Universidade Federale de Santa Caterina the Catholic University of Rio de Janeiro, Monash University, and Melbourne University. Some of this paper was written at the Center for Philosophy of Science at the University of Pittsburgh, which I thank for its financial and intellectual support. Special thanks to Branden Fitelson, who gave me very incisive feedback on several time-slices of this paper.

References

Adams, Ernest (1962), "On Rational Betting Systems", *Archive für Mathematische Logik und Grundlagenforschung* 6, 7–29, 112–128.

Adams, Ernest W. and Roger D. Rosenkrantz (1980), "Applying the Jeffrey Decision Model to Rational Betting and Information Acquisition", *Theory and Decision* 12, 1–20.

Armendt, Brad (1992), "Dutch Strategies for Diachronic Rules: When Believers See the Sure Loss Coming", *PSA 1992*, vol. 1, eds. D. Hull, M. Forbes, K. Okruhlik, East Lansing: Philosophy of Science Association, 217–29.

Armendt, Brad (1993), "Dutch Books, Additivity and Utility Theory", *Philosophical Topics* 21, No. 1, 1–20.

Baillie, Patricia (1973), "Confirmation and the Dutch Book Argument", *The British Journal for the Philosophy of Science* 24, 393–397.

Carnap, Rudolf (1950), *Logical Foundations of Probability*, University of Chicago Press.

Carnap, Rudolf (1955), *Notes on Probability and Induction* (UCLA, Philosophy 249, Fall Semester 1955), Unpublished Manuscript, Carnap Archive, University of Pittsburgh, RC-107-23-01.

Carnap, Rudolf (1962), "The Aim of Inductive Logic", in *Logic, Methodology and Philosophy of Science*, eds. Ernest Nagel, Patrick Suppes and Alfred Tarski.

Christensen, David (1991), "Clever Bookies and Coherent Beliefs." *The Philosophical Review C*, No. 2, 229–247.

Christensen, David (1996), "Dutch-Book Arguments Depragmatized: Epistemic Consistency for Partial Believers", *The Journal of Philosophy*, 450–479.

Christensen, David (2001), "Preference-Based Arguments for Probabilism." *Philosophy of Science* 68 (3): 356–376.

De Finetti, B. (1937), "La Prévision: Ses Lois Logiques, Ses Sources Subjectives", *Annales de l'Institut Henri Poincaré*, 7: 1–68; translated as 'Foresight. Its Logical Laws, Its Subjective Sources', in *Studies in Subjective Probability*, H. E. Kyburg, Jr. and H. E. Smokler (eds.), Robert E. Krieger Publishing Company, 1980.

De Finetti, B. (1980), "Probability: Beware of Falsifications", in *Studies in Subjective Probability*, eds. H. E. Kyburg, Jr. and H. E. Smokler, Robert E. Krieger Publishing Company.

Döring, Frank (2000), "Conditional Probability and Dutch Books", *Philosophy of Science* 67 (September), 39, 1–409.

Douven, Igor (1999), "Inference to the Best Explanation Made Coherent", *Philosophy of Science* 66 (Proceedings), S424–S435.

Earman, John (1992), *Bayes or Bust?*, Cambridge, MA: MIT Press.

Gillies, Donald (2000), *Philosophical Theories of Probability*, Routledge.

Howson, C. and P. Urbach (1993), *Scientific Reasoning: The Bayesian Approach.* La Salle, Illinois, Open Court.

Jackson, F. and R. Pargetter (1976), "A Modified Dutch Book Argument", *Philosophical Studies* 29, 403–407.

Jeffrey, R. (1983), *The Logic of Decision*, University of Chicago Press, 2nd ed.

Jeffrey, R. (1992), *Probability and the Art of Judgment*, Cambridge: Cambridge University Press.

Kaplan, Mark (1996), *Decision Theory as Philosophy*, Cambridge: Cambridge University Press.

Kennedy, Ralph and Charles Chihara (1979), "The Dutch Book Argument: Its Logical Flaws, Its Subjective Sources", *Philosophical Studies* 36, 19–33.

Kemeny, J. (1955), "Fair Bets and Inductive Probabilities", *Journal of Symbolic Logic*, 20: 263–273

Kyburg, Henry (1978), "Subjective Probability: Criticisms, Reflections and Problems", *Journal of Philosophical Logic* 7, 157–180.

Lange, Marc (1999), "Calibration and the Epistemological Role of Bayesian Conditionalization", *The Journal of Philosophy*, 294–324.

Lehman, R. (1955), "On Confirmation and Rational Betting", *Journal of Symbolic Logic* 20, 251–262.

Levi, Isaac (1974), "On Indeterminate Probabilities", *Journal of Philosophy* 71, 391–418.

Levi, Isaac (1980), *The Enterprise of Knowledge: An Essay on Knowledge, Credal Probability and Chance*, Cambridge MA: MIT Press.

Lewis, David (1999), *Papers in Metaphysics and Epistemology*, Cambridge: Cambridge University Press.

Maher, Patrick (1993), *Betting on Theories*, Cambridge: Cambridge University Press.

Maher, Patrick (1997), "Depragmatized Dutch Book Arguments", *Philosophy of Science* 64, 291–305.

Mellor, D. H. (1971), *The Matter of Chance*, Cambridge: Cambridge University Press.

Milne, Peter (1990), "Scotching the Dutch Book Argument", *Erkenntnis* 32, 105–126.

Moore, P. G. (1983), "A Dutch Book and Subjective Probabilities", *The British Journal for the Philosophy of Science* 34, 263–266.

Ramsey, F. P., (1926), "Truth and Probability", in *Foundations of Mathematics and other Essays*, R. B. Braithwaite (ed.), Routledge & P. Kegan , 1931, 156–198; reprinted in *Studies in Subjective Probability*, H. E. Kyburg, Jr. and H. E. Smokler (eds.), 2nd ed.,

R. E. Krieger Publishing Company, 1980, 23–52; reprinted in *Philosophical Papers*, D. H. Mellor (ed.) Cambridge: University Press, Cambridge, 1990.

Rosenkrantz, R.D. (1981), *Foundations and Applications of Inductive Probability*, Ridgeview Publishing Company.

Ryder, J. M. (1981), "Consequences of a Simple Extension of the Dutch Book Argument", *The British Journal for the Philosophy of Science* 32, 164–167.

Schick, Frederic (1986), "Dutch Bookies and Money Pumps", *Journal of Philosophy* 83, 112–119.

Seidenfeld, Teddy and Mark J. Schervish (1983), "A Conflict Between Finite Additivity and Avoiding Dutch Book", *Philosophy of Science* 50, 398–412.

Shimony, A. (1955), "Coherence and the Axioms of Confirmation", *Journal of Symbolic Logic* 20, 1–28.

Skyrms, Brian (1980), "Higher Order Degrees of Belief", in *Prospects for Pragmatism*, ed. D.H. Mellor, Cambridge: Cambridge University Press, 109–37.

Skyrms, Brian (1984), *Pragmatics and Empiricism*, Yale University.

Skyrms, Brian (1986), *Choice and Chance*, Wadsworth, 3rd ed.

Skyrms, Brian (1987), "Coherence", in N. Rescher (ed.), *Scientific Inquiry in Philosophical Perspective*, Pittsburgh: University of Pittsburgh Press, 225–242.

van Fraassen, Bas (1984), "Belief and the Will", *Journal of Philosophy* 81, 235–256.

van Fraassen, B. (1989), *Laws and Symmetry*, Oxford: Clarendon Press.

Vineberg, Susan (2001), "The Notion of Consistency for Partial Belief", *Philosophical Studies* 102 (February), 281–296.

Waidacher, C. (1997), "Hidden Assumptions in the Dutch Book Argument", *Theory and Decision* 43 (November), 293–312.

Weatherson, Brian (1999), "Begging the Question and Bayesians", *Studies in History and Philosophy of Science* 30A, 687–697.

Williamson, Jon (1999), "Countable Additivity and Subjective Probability", *The British Journal for the Philosophy of Science* 50, No. 3, 401–416.

Philosophical Perspectives, 19, Epistemology, 2005

HOW PROBABILITIES REFLECT EVIDENCE

James M. Joyce
The University of Michigan

Many philosophers think of Bayesianism as a theory of practical rationality. This is not at all surprising given that the view's most striking successes have come in decision theory. Ramsey (1931), Savage (1972), and De Finetti (1964) showed how to interpret subjective degrees of belief in terms of betting behavior, and how to derive the central probabilistic requirement of coherence from reflections on the nature of rational choice. This focus on decision-making can obscure the fact that Bayesianism is also an epistemology. Indeed, the great statistician Harold Jeffries (1939), who did more than anyone else to further Bayesian methods, paid rather little heed to the work of Ramsey, de Finetti, and Savage. Jeffries, and those who followed him, saw Bayesianism as a theory of inductive evidence, whose primary role was not to help people make wise choices, but to facilitate sound scientific reasoning.[1] This paper seeks to promote a broadly Bayesian approach to epistemology by showing how certain central questions about the nature of evidence can be addressed using the apparatus of subjective probability theory.

Epistemic Bayesianism, as understood here, is the view that evidential relationships are best represented probabilistically. It has three central components:

> *Evidential Probability.* At any time t, a rational believer's opinions can be faithfully modeled by a family of probability functions $\boldsymbol{c}_t$, hereafter called her *credal state*,[2] the members of which accurately reflect her *total evidence* at t.
>
> *Learning as Bayesian Updating.* Learning experiences can be modeled as shifts from one credal state to another that proceed in accordance with Bayes's Rule.
>
> *Confirmational Relativity.* A wide range of questions about evidential relationships can be answered on the basis of information about structural features credal states.

The first of these three theses is most fundamental. Much of what Bayesians say about learning and confirmation only makes sense if probabilities in credal states reflect states of total evidence. It is often said, for instance, that learning one proposition E increases a person's evidence for another X just in case X's probability conditional on E exceeds X's unconditional probability. Clearly, this assumes that the unconditional and conditional probabilities in a person's credal state somehow reflect her total evidence.

The aim of this essay is to clarify the thesis of Evidential Probability by explaining how a person's subjective probabilities reflect her total evidence. After a brief discussion of the Bayesian formalism and its epistemological significance, it will be argued that a person's total evidence in favor of any proposition can be decomposed along three dimensions that have rather different probabilistic profiles. The overall *balance* of the evidence is a matter of how decisively the data tells in favor of the proposition. This is what individual probability values reflect. The *weight* of the evidence is a matter of the gross amount of relevant data available. It is reflected in the concentration and stability of probabilities in the face of changing information. The *specificity* of the evidence is a matter of the degree to which the data discriminates the truth of the proposition from that of alternatives. It is reflected in the spread of probability values across a credal state. By appreciating these disparate ways in which probabilities can reflect total evidence we shall come appreciate the richness of the Bayesian formalism, and its importance for epistemology. The central theses of the paper are (i) that any adequate epistemology must be capable of accurately representing the distinctions between the balance, weight and specificity of evidence, and (ii) that only a probabilistic theory is capable of doing this properly.

Many of the points made here have been made by others. Indeed, the distinctions between balance, weight and specificity have all been made before, albeit often in an incomplete or piecemeal way. The novelty here is the integration of these insights into an appealing and coherent probabilistic theory of evidence. We begin with a brief sketch of Bayesianism.

1. Credences as Estimates of Truth-Value.

Any adequate epistemology must recognize that beliefs come in varying *gradations of strength*. Instead of asking whether a person accepts or rejects a proposition outright, we must inquire into her level of confidence in its truth. These confidence levels go by a variety of names—degrees of belief, subjective probabilities, grades of uncertainty—but 'credences' will be the preferred term here. By any name, a person's credence in X is a measure of the extent to which she is disposed to presuppose X in her theoretical and practical reasoning.[3]

People also have graded *conditional* beliefs that express their degrees of confidence in the truth of some propositions on the supposition that other propositions obtain. It is often said that a believer's credence for X conditional on Y is the credence she would invest in X if she were to *learn* Y. While there is something right in this idea, it must be handled delicately. A person's credence for X conditional on Y will only coincide with her unconditional credence for X after learning Y when the learning induced belief change is not driven by any arational processes that ignore Y's content, and when Y encompasses literally everything that the person learns (even the fact that she has learned Y). For current purposes, it is not crucial to get clear about the precise relationship between conditional belief and learning. The essential point is that conditional credences have a clear epistemic interpretation: the epistemic effect of conditioning on Y is to provisionally augment the believer's total evidence by the addition of Y and nothing else.

Graded beliefs help us *estimate* quantities of interest. These can be almost anything: the fair price of a bet, the proportion of balls in an urn, the average velocity of stars in a distant galaxy, the truth-value of a proposition, the frequency of a disease in a population, and so on. Since the values of such quantities often depend on unknown factors, we imagine the believer being uncertain about which member of a given set $\mathbf{w}$ of total contingencies (= possible worlds) actually obtains, and we think of the quantity of interest as a function, or 'random variable', f that assigns each world W in $\mathbf{w}$ a unique real number $f(W)$. The objective in estimation is to come up with an anticipated value f^* for f that is, in some sense, the best possible given the information at hand.

The accuracy of such estimates can be evaluated in a variety of ways. One can employ a *categorical* scale that recognizes only two ways of fitting the facts: getting things exactly right, so that $f^* = f$, or having them wrong. This approach makes no distinctions among different ways of being wrong, so that "a miss is as good as a mile." Alternately, one can use a *gradational*, or "closeness counts," scale that assigns estimates higher *degrees of accuracy* the closer they are to the actual value of quantity being estimated. In (Joyce 1998) it is argued that degrees of belief are principally used to make estimates that are judged on a gradational scale. One can assess the overall quality of a person's credences by considering the accuracy of the estimates they sanction. It is, for example, a flaw in a credence function if it sanctions estimates $f^* > g^*$ when g *dominates* f in the sense that $g(W) \geq f(W)$ for all W in $\mathbf{w}$.

Different Bayesians construe credences differently depending on the sorts of estimates they tend to consider. The role of credences in estimating utilities of actions is often highlighted. This engenders a Bayesianism that emphasizes the practical virtues of having certain kinds of credences. For example, synchronic "Dutch book" arguments purport to show that one can only avoid choosing strictly dominated acts by having credences that obey the laws of probability. Diachronic Dutch books seek to show, in addition, that one will also be subject to dominance unless one updates by conditioning on the information one receives. In each case the take-home lesson is that defective beliefs spawn defective desires. While it is perfectly legitimate to think in this practical vein, it is crucial to appreciate that (a) credences are used to estimate all sorts of quantities, (b) they play the same formal role in estimating these quantities as in the estimation of utilities, and (c) for certain purposes it can be illuminating to emphasize their role in estimating quantities that are not so directly tied to actions. With respect to this last point, it is worth noting that (van Fraassen 1983) and (Shimony 1988) have focused on the role of credences in estimating relative frequencies, while (Joyce 1998) emphasizes their role in estimating truth-values (with true = 1 and false = 0). This last approach is best for bringing out epistemologically salient aspects of degrees of belief. We shall, therefore, think of a person's credence in *X* as being linked to her best estimate of *X*'s truth-value, where it is understood that such estimates are evaluated on a gradational scale that rewards those who believe truths strongly.[4]

2. Representation of Credences.

Bayesians are often accused of being committed to the existence of sharp numerical degrees of belief. This is not true. The idea that people have sharp degrees of belief is both psychologically implausible and epistemologically calamitous. Sophisticated versions of Bayesianism, as found in, e.g., (Levi 1980, 85–91) and (Kaplan 1996, 27–31), have long recognized that few of our credences are anywhere near definite enough to be precisely quantified. A person's beliefs at a time *t* are not best represented by any one credence function, but by a *set* of such functions c_t, what we are calling her *credal state*. Each element of c_t is a sharp credence function that assigns a unique real number $0 \leq \mathbf{c}(X|Y) \leq 1$ to each proposition *X* and condition *Y*.[5] Each such function defines unconditional credences via the rule $\mathbf{c}(X) = \mathbf{c}(X|\mathrm{T})$, for T is any logical truth.

Without further ado, we shall assume that all credences in an epistemically rational believer's credal state satisfy the laws of (finitely additive) probability, so that (i) $\mathbf{c}(\mathrm{T}) = 1$ for T any logical truth, (ii) $\mathbf{c}(Y) \geq 0$, (iii) $\mathbf{c}(X) + \mathbf{c}(Y) = \mathbf{c}(X \vee Y) + \mathbf{c}(X \,\&\, Y)$ for any propositions *X* and *Y*, and (iv) $\mathbf{c}(X|Y) = \mathbf{c}(X \,\&\, Y)/\mathbf{c}(Y)$ whenever $\mathbf{c}(Y) > 0$. Many arguments have been offered for thinking that credences must be probabilistically coherent, but considering them would take us off track. Our question is this: given that credences obey the laws of probability, how do they reflect evidence?

Determinate facts about the person's beliefs correspond to properties that are invariant across all elements of c_t. For example, the person can only be said to determinately believe *X* to degree *x* when $\mathbf{c}(X) = x$ for every $\mathbf{c} \in c_t$, and she is only more confident in *X* than in *Y* if $\mathbf{c}(X) > \mathbf{c}(Y)$ for every $\mathbf{c} \in c_t$. Such invariant facts can come in a wide variety of forms. It might be invariant across c_t that a certain quantity has a specific expected value, or that a particular distribution of probabilities has a uniform, binomial, normal, or Poisson form, and so on.

For purposes of epistemology, it is useful to divide the c_t-invariant facts into three classes. Some can be interpreted as *evidential constraints* that are imposed upon the believer by her overall epistemic situation. These will sometimes be 'deliverances of experience' that directly fix facts about credences. To borrow a famous example from Richard Jeffrey (1983, p. 165), looking at a piece of cloth under dim light might lead a believer to assign a credence of 0.7 to the proposition G that it is green, in which case the evidence requires $\mathbf{c}(G) = 0.7$ to be satisfied throughout her credal state. Or, it might be that seeing two pieces of cloth under yellow light leads the person to judge that the first is more likely than the second to be green, so that every $\mathbf{c}$ in c_t satisfies $\mathbf{c}(G_1) > \mathbf{c}(G_2)$. One can also imagine higher-level evidential constraints. At a given time it might be part of a person's evidence that a certain test for heroin use has a fifteen percent false positive rate, in which case $\mathbf{c}(+\text{test}|\text{no heroin}) = 0.15$ everywhere in c_t. In contrast to the constraints that are imposed by the evidence, other c_t-invariant facts are best interpreted as subjective biases or prejudices. It might, for instance, simply strike the agent as more plausible than not that eight-graders in Cleveland have about eight unmatched socks under their beds. Evidence and prejudice can combine to produce additional c_t-invariants.

While no attempt will be made here to explain how the invariant features of credal states are divided up into evidential constraints or subjective biases, a few sketchy remarks might allay confusion. Bayesians are often portrayed as radical subjectivists who reject any meaningful epistemic distinction between evidence and biases. On a subjectivist picture, a person's biases merely reflect her 'prior' judgments of credibility about various propositions, while her evidence is the 'posterior' information she gains from experience. This suggests a model in which a person starts off with a prior probability $\mathbf{c}_0$ that reflects her initial judgments of credibility (sophisticated treatments make this a set of priors), and learning proceeds by updating the prior in light of data. In the simplest case where the data specifies that each of the propositions $E_1, E_2, \ldots, E_n$ is true, the posterior $\mathbf{c}_1$ arises from the prior by simple conditioning, so that $\mathbf{c}_1(-) = \mathbf{c}_0(-|E_1 \,\&\, E_2 \,\&\, \ldots \,\&\, E_n)$. Priors are required in this process, it is claimed, in order to get inductive reasoning off the ground. So, according to subjectivist Bayesians, a person's total evidence in favor of a proposition X will encompass both the 'posterior' beliefs that she comes to have as the result of learning experiences as well as her 'prior' opinions about the intrinsic credibility of various propositions, including X itself.

While this fairly characterizes the views of some Bayesians, the probabilistic approach to epistemology is compatible with the existence of an objective distinction between evidence and bias. Different Bayesians will surely draw the line differently. Some might restrict the class of evidential beliefs to those that reflect observed relative frequencies or known objective chances. Others might go reliabilist and argue that a person's evidence is found in those invariant features of her credal state that were produced by belief-forming mechanisms that assign high credences to truths and low credences to falsehoods. Others might claim that some constraints are just 'given' in experience. There are other options as well: indeed, almost everything epistemologists have had to say about the nature of evidence and be imported into the Bayesian framework.

For present purposes, it does not much matter how one draws the line between evidence and bias, or on which side subjective judgments of credibility lie. What is important is that at any time there should be some set of constraints $\mathcal{E}_t$ that specify those invariant features of a person's credal state that are directly imposed by her evidence. In the examples we consider $\mathcal{E}_t$ will never be anything fancy: it will consist in information about the distribution of objective probabilities over some set of hypotheses about objective chances, and a specification of truth values for data propositions. The goal is to use such simple cases to come to understand how the evidence in $\mathcal{E}_t$ is reflected elsewhere in the believer's credal state. To help us focus on essentials, we shall confine our attention to the ideal case of a person with no biases, so that every invariant feature of $\mathcal{C}_t$ is either an evidential constraint or a consequence of such constraints. This will seem like no restriction to subjectivists, but the more objectively minded will view it as an idealization. Either way, the supposition is needed if we are to isolate those aspects of the believer's credal state that reflect her overall evidential situation.

3. The Distinction Between Balance and Weight.

At an intuitive level, the total evidence for a proposition X is the sum of all those considerations that tell in favor of its truth. Bayesians, and their opponents, have often proceeded as if the total *amount* of evidence for X is directly reflected in X's credence. When $\mathbf{c}(X) = x$ holds all across $\mathcal{C}_t$, this amounts to the claim that the number x is a meaningful measure of the total amount of evidence for X. More generally, the view is that (a) the person has more evidence for X than for Y iff $\mathbf{c}(X) > \mathbf{c}(Y)$ over $\mathcal{C}_t$, (b) she has strong evidence for X iff $\mathbf{c}(X) \approx 1$ over $\mathcal{C}_t$, (c) E provides the person with incremental evidence for X iff $\mathbf{c}(X|E) > \mathbf{c}(X)$ over $\mathcal{C}_t$, and so on. This picture of the relationship between credences and evidence is seriously misleading. As we shall see, the total evidence in favor of a hypothesis can be separated into at least three components—balance, weight, and specificity—only one of which is directly reflected in credences.

Let us first distinguish between the *balance* of the evidence, which is a matter of how decisively the data tells for or against the hypothesis, and what J.M. Keynes (1921) called the *weight* of the evidence, which is a matter of the gross amount of data available. Here is Keynes:

> As the relevant evidence [for a hypothesis] at our disposal increases, the magnitude of [its] probability may either decrease or increase, according as the new knowledge strengthens the unfavorable or favorable evidence; but *something* seems to have increased in either case—we have a more substantial basis on which to rest our conclusion... New evidence will sometimes decrease the probability of [the hypothesis] but will always increase its 'weight'. (1921, p. 77)

The intuition here is that any body of evidence has both a kind of valence and a size. Its valence is a matter of which way, and how decisively, the relevant data 'points.' A body of evidence will often be composed of items of data with different valances that need to be compared. It is this 'balance of the evidence' that credences reflect. The size or 'weight' of the evidence has to do with how much relevant information the data contains, irrespective of which way it points. As Keynes emphasized, we should not expect the weight of a body of evidence to be reflected in individual credence values. From the fact two hypotheses have the same credence we can infer that the balance of the evidence for each is the same, but we cannot infer anything at all about the relative weights of the evidence in their favor.

To clarify the distinction, it will be useful to consider a simple sampling case.

> *Four Urns*: Jacob and Emily both start out knowing that the urn U was randomly chosen from a set of four urns $\{\text{urn}_0, \text{urn}_1, \text{urn}_2, \text{urn}_3\}$ where urn_i contains three balls, i of which are blue and $3 - i$ of which are green. Since the choice of U was random both subjects assign *equal* credence to the four hypotheses about its contents: $\mathbf{c}(U = \text{urn}_i) = 1/4$. Moreover, both treat these hypotheses as statements about the *objective chance* of drawing a blue ball from U, so that knowledge of $U = \text{urn}_i$ 'screen offs' any sampling data in the sense that $\mathbf{c}(B_{next}|E \;\&\; U = \text{urn}_i) = \mathbf{c}(B_{next}|U = \text{urn}_i)$, where B_{next} says that the next ball drawn from the urn will be blue and E is a proposition that describes any prior series of random draws with replacement from U. Finally, Jacob and Emily regard random drawing with replacement as an *exchangeable* process, so that any series of draws that produces m blue balls and n green balls is as likely as any other such series, irrespective of order. Use B^mG^n to denote the generic event in which m blue balls and n green balls are drawn at random and with replacement form U. Against this backdrop of shared evidence, suppose Jacob sees five balls drawn at random and with replacement from U and observes that all are blue, so his evidence is B^5G^0. Emily, who sees Jacob's evidence, looks at fifteen additional draws of which twelve come up blue, so her evidence is $B^{17}G^3$. What should Emily and Jacob think about B_{next}?

It would be clear what each should think if the true chance hypothesis were known with certainty: since credences should reflect known objective chances,[6] $\mathbf{c}(B_{next}|U = \text{urn}_i) = i/3$ should hold throughout Emily and Jacob's credal states. Unfortunately, neither Emily nor Jacob knows the true chance hypothesis, and so each has to rely on sampling data to form opinions about the various $U = \text{urn}_i$ possibilities.

Intuitively, Jacob's total evidence points more decisively than Emily's does toward B_{next}: all the balls he observed were blue, whereas three of the balls she saw were green. On the other hand, Emily has a greater volume of relevant evidence than Jacob does in virtue of having seen more draws. Both these facts are reflected in their credal states. After seeing five blue balls Jacob's degrees of belief will have shifted from an even distribution over the chance hypotheses to a distribution in which the urn_3 hypothesis is judged to be very probable, so that every function in his credal state looks like this:

Jacob: $\mathbf{c}(U = \text{urn}_0 | B^5G^0) = 0$
$\mathbf{c}(U = \text{urn}_1 | B^5G^0) = 0.0036$
$\mathbf{c}(U = \text{urn}_2 | B^5G^0) = 0.1159$
$\mathbf{c}(U = \text{urn}_3 | B^5G^0) = 0.8804$

The probability of the next ball draw being blue is then $\mathbf{c}(B_{next} | B^5G^0) = 0.959$. Emily, in contrast, has credences that make her almost certain that there are precisely two blue balls in the urn. All the functions in her credal state look like this:

Emily: $\mathbf{c}(U = \text{urn}_0 | B^{17}G^3) = 0$
$\mathbf{c}(U = \text{urn}_1 | B^{17}G^3) = 0.00006$
$\mathbf{c}(U = \text{urn}_2 | B^{17}G^3) = 0.99994$
$\mathbf{c}(U = \text{urn}_3 | B^{17}G^3) = 0$

When Emily estimates the probability of B_{next} she comes up with a number indistinguishable from 2/3 out to the fourth decimal: $\mathbf{c}(B_{next} | B^{17}G^3) = 0.666626$.

This difference in subjective probability reflects a disparity in the respective balances in the total evidence that Jacob and Emily have for B_{next}. The idea of a balance of evidence is fairly clear in cases where subjective credences are mediated by beliefs about objective chances. Chance hypotheses function as evidential funnels: data can only affect a person's beliefs about the proposition of interest by altering his or her opinions about its chance. It is then reasonable to interpret the chances $i/3$ and $(3 - i)/3$ as gauging the strength of the evidence for and against B_{next} *when* $U = \text{urn}_i$ *is know for certain.*[7] Thus, someone with enough evidence to justify unreserved confidence in $U = \text{urn}_i$ has $i/(3 - i)$ times the evidence for B_{next} as for $\sim B_{next}$. More generally, whatever the value of $\mathbf{c}(U = \text{urn}_i)$, the conditional credence $\mathbf{c}(B_{\text{next}} | U = \text{urn}_i)$ can be interpreted as that proportion of the balance of total evidence for $U = \text{urn}_i$ that also contributes toward the balance of total evidence for B_{next}. Given this, a rational believer should use the quantity $\mathbf{c}(B_{next}) = \Sigma_i\ \mathbf{c}(U = \text{urn}_i) \times \mathbf{c}(B_{next} | U = \text{urn}_i) = \Sigma_i\ \mathbf{c}(U = \text{urn}_i) \times i/3$ as her estimate of the balance of her evidence for B_{next}. That is, she should proportion her beliefs to the evidence by having her credence reflect the expected balance of her evidence for the proposition believed.

This explains why Jacob's credence for B_{next} increases more dramatically than Emily's does. Since both initially know that U was randomly selected from $\{\text{urn}_0, \text{urn}_1, \text{urn}_2, \text{urn}_3\}$, each starts out with determinate, perfectly symmetrical evidence for and against the claim that the next ball will be blue. After seeing five blue balls Jacob's evidence requires him to regard the two chance hypotheses that favor B_{next}, $U = \text{urn}_3$ and $U = \text{urn}_2$, as much more likely than their symmetrical counterparts, $U = \text{urn}_0$ and $U = \text{urn}_1$. In particular, he assigns $U = \text{urn}_3$, the hypothesis whose truth would conclusively justify B_{next}, a credence of 0.8804, while he assigns $U = \text{urn}_0$, whose truth would conclusively justify $\sim B_{next}$, a credence of 0. As a result, Jacob's estimated total evidence for B_{next} exceeds his estimated total evidence against B_{next} by a factor of $\mathbf{c}(B_{next}|B^5G^0)/\mathbf{c}(\sim B_{next}|B^5G^0) \approx 24$. Emily's evidence, on the other hand, forces her to regard both $U = \text{urn}_3$ and $U = \text{urn}_0$ as certainly false, and to concentrate almost all her credence on $U = \text{urn}_2$. As a result, her estimate of the total evidence for B_{next} exceeds her estimate of the total evidence against B_{next} only by a factor of $\mathbf{c}(B_{next}|B^{17}G^3)/\mathbf{c}(\sim B_{next}|B^{17}G^3) \approx 2$. There is thus a clear sense in which Jacob has better evidence than Emily does: on balance, his evidence tells more decisively in favor of B_{next} than hers does.

Emily's evidence is better along another dimension. Since she has seen a greater number of draws, her evidence, though slightly less decisive, provides her with a more settled picture of the situation. Indeed, if both subjects received evidence that tells against B_{next}, then Jacob's beliefs are likely to change more than Emily's will. Suppose that both see five more balls drawn, and all are green. Jacob's credence will fall from near 0.96 to 0.5. Emily's will move hardly at all, dropping from 0.666626 to 0.666016. This illustrates the point, made persuasively by Brian Skyrms (1980), that the weight of the evidence for a proposition X often manifests itself not in X's unconditional credence, but in the *resilience* of this credence conditional on various potential data sequences. A person's credence for X is resilient with respect to datum E to the extent that her credence for X given E remains close to her unconditional credence for X. Note that resilience is defined relative to a specific item of data: a person's belief about X may be resilient relative to one kind of data, but unstable with respect to another. That said, it is usually the case that the greater volume of data a person has for a hypothesis the more resilient her credence tends to be across a wide range of additional data. Our example illustrates this nicely. Even though Jacob's evidence points more definitively toward a blue ball on the next draw, his credence is less resilient than Emily's with respect to almost every potential data sequence, the sole exceptions being those sequences in which *only* blue balls are drawn. In this regard Emily's evidence is better than Jacob's: even though she is not so sure as he is that a blue ball will be drawn, her level of confidence is better informed that his, and so is less susceptible to change in the face of new data.[8]

This example suggests the following provisional conclusions: (i) As Keynes argued, there is intuitive distinction between the balance of the total evidence in favor of a hypothesis and the weight of this evidence. (ii) Balances of evidence are reflected in credences in two ways: a rational believer's credence for X reflects the balance of her total evidence in favor of X; her credence for X conditional on Y reflects that proportion of the balance of her total evidence for Y that contributes toward the balance of evidence for X. (iii) Weights of evidence are, at least in some cases, reflected in the resilience of credences in the face of additional data.

These conclusions raise as many questions as they answer. Even if it is plausible to think that probabilities express balances of total evidence in our toy example, why think this is true in general? Indeed, why think that balances of evidence can be expressed in terms of numbers at all? (Keynes himself doubted they could!) Even if they can be quantified, why think balances of evidence are probabilities? Is there any way to make the concept of "weight" formally precise, say by specifying some way of measuring it? Partial answers to these and other questions will be provided in the next two sections.

4. Measuring Balances of Evidence.

Let's begin by focusing on what it means to say that a body of data provides *some* evidence in favor of a hypothesis. If we recall that a believer's total evidence is a set ε_t of constraints on credence functions allowed into her credal state, then it is natural to say that ε_t provides *some* evidence for X just in case the joint satisfaction of the constraints in ε_t requires X to have a positive credence throughout c_t. Consider, for example,

$$\varepsilon_1 = \{\mathbf{c}(E) = 0.99,\ \mathbf{c}(X|E) > \mathbf{c}(X|{\sim}E)\}$$
$$\varepsilon_2 = \{\mathbf{c}(E) = 0.99,\ \mathbf{c}(X|{\sim}E) > \mathbf{c}(X|E) = 0\}$$
$$\varepsilon_3 = \{\mathbf{c}(X \vee Y) = 1,\ \mathbf{c}(Y|E) = 0,\ \mathbf{c}(E) = 1\}$$

In all these cases the believer has some evidence in favor of X. The first constraint does not specify any particular credence for X, but it does require it to be positive. The second highlights the fact a person can have some evidence for X even though the data makes X incredible (ε_2 requires $0 < \mathbf{c}(X) < 0.01$). If this seems odd, keep in mind that a single body of data can provide evidence both for and against X. ε_3 provides *conclusive* evidence for X since, in addition to forcing her to recognize that X has some chance of being true, it also requires her to recognize that X has no chance of being false.

Our next step is to understand how the evidence for and against a proposition can be 'balanced'. It is useful to investigate this matter by considering a more general problem. Given that ε_t provides some evidence in favor of each of $X_1, X_2, \ldots, X_N$, how might this evidence be pooled to yield an overall measure of the amount of total evidence that ε_t provides for the combination of the propositions? More specifically, under what conditions will it make sense to say that ε_t provides a greater overall balance of total evidence for the propositions in $\{X_1, X_2, \ldots, X_N\}$ than for those in $\{Y_1, Y_2, \ldots, Y_N\}$? One tempting answer invokes a kind of dominance principle:

Combination Principle. If ε_t provides at least as great a balance of total evidence for X_i as for Y_i for each $i \leq N$, then ε_t provides at least as great a balance of total evidence for the combination of the X_i as for the combination of the Y_i.

Unfortunately, if "combination" means "conjunction" or "disjunction," this is mistaken. For conjunction, note that on a July day we have more evidence for thinking that a fair coin will come up heads on its next toss, X_1, than for thinking that it will rain in Los Angeles at noon, Y_1, and we also have more evidence for thinking that the coin will not come up heads, X_2, than for thinking that Los Angeles will be struck by an major earthquake at noon, Y_2. Even so, it in no way follows that the balance of the evidence favors X_1 & X_2, which is impossible, over Y_1 & Y_2, which is merely improbable. (Readers may figure out the dual argument for disjunction.)

There is, however, another sense of "combination" in which we do have more evidence for the combination of X_1 and X_2 than for the combination Y_1 and Y_2: we have more evidence *on average* for the X_is than for the Y_is. This disparity in average evidence becomes clear when we try to estimate the number of truths in the two sets. Even thought we have more evidence for Y_1 & Y_2 than for X_1 & X_2 we also think it unlikely that either Y_1 or Y_2 is true, whereas we know that exactly one of X_1 or X_2 is true. So, if we had to come up with estimates for the number of truths in $\{X_1, X_2\}$ and $\{Y_1, Y_2\}$, we would settle on a value 1 for the first and a value only marginally above 0 for the second. This difference in estimates reflects the different balances of total evidence we have in favor of the X_i and the Y_i. The general principles at work here are these:

- The balances of a person's total evidence for the propositions in $\{X_1, X_2, \ldots X_N\}$ is reflected in her estimate of the number of truths the set contains.[9]
- If the balance of total evidence in favor of X_i is increased, and if no other X_j experiences a decrease in the balance of total evidence in its favor, then the person's estimate for the number of truths in $\{X_1, X_2, \ldots X_N\}$ should also increase.

A first stab at the combination principle we seek would require all such estimates to reflect the balances of total evidence in favor of individual hypotheses.

> *Combination* (first approximation). If ε_t provides at least as great (a greater) balance of total evidence in favor of X_i as it does in favor of Y_i for each $i \leq N$, then ε_t constrains a person's credal state in such a way that her estimate of the number of truths among the X_i is at least as great as (greater than) her estimate of the number of truths among the Y_i.[10]

This is only a first approximation because it applies only to sets of the same cardinality. We often want to compare the evidence for the propositions in one set with the evidence for propositions in another set with more or fewer elements. For example, if the geologists are right, we have significantly more evidence for thinking that California will suffer a major earthquake sometime in the next century, X, than we do for thinking either that a roll of a fair die will produce a number strictly greater than 2, Y_1, or that it will produce an odd number, Y_2. Our estimate of the number of truths in $\{X\}$ is just our credence for X, let's say 9/10, whereas our estimate of the number of truths in $\{Y_1, Y_2\}$ is $2 \times 1/3 + 1 \times (1/6 + 1/3) = 7/6$. In an aggregate sense, then, we have more evidence for the Y_is than we have for X, but this is only because there are more Y_is. To factor out the effect of this difference in cardinality, we can focus on the *average* amount of evidence for X and for the Y_is by replacing sets of propositions, which, by definition, have no repeated elements, by ordered sequences of propositions, whose elements can repeat. If we compare our estimates of the average number of truths in the sequences $<X, X>$ and $<Y_1, Y_2>$ we get 9/10 and 7/12. This reflects the fact that, on average, the balance of evidence in favor of X exceeds the balances of evidence in favor of Y_1 and Y_2.

Generalizing on this idea leads to the correct version of the combination principle,

> *Combination.* Let $<X_1, X_2, \ldots, X_N>$ and $<Y_1, Y_2, \ldots, Y_N>$ be ordered sequences of propositions, which may contain repeated elements. If ε_t provides at least as great (a greater) balance of total evidence in favor of X_i as in favor of Y_i for each $i < N$, then ε_t constrains a person's credal state in such a way that her estimate of the number of truths among the X_i is at least as great as (greater than) her estimate of the number of truths among the Y_i.

Combination supplies the crucial link between balances of evidence and probabilities. The connection is forged with the help of a simple consistency condition that was first explored in (Kraft, et. al, 1959) and was put in a particularly elegant form in (Scott 1964). It says, simply, that if two sequences of propositions have the same number of truths as a matter of logic, then no body of evidence can require a person's estimate of the number of truths in the first sequence to exceed her estimate of the number of truths in the second. More formally, the requirement is this

> *Isovalence.* Suppose two ordered sequences of propositions $<X_1, X_2, \ldots, X_N>$ and $<Y_1, Y_2, \ldots, Y_N>$ are *isovalent* in the sense that, as a matter of logic, they contain the same number of truths. If the balance of total evidence in favor of X_i is at least as great as (greater than) the balance of total evidence in favor of Y_i for all $i < N$, then the balance of total evidence in favor of Y_N is at least as great as (greater than) the balance of total evidence in favor of X_N.

Isovalence has the following intuitively appealing consequences:

> *Normality.* The balance total evidence in favor of any proposition never exceeds the balance of total evidence in favor of any logical truth.
>
> *Consequence.* The balance of total evidence in favor of X never exceeds the balance of total evidence in favor of any proposition that X entails.

Partition. If the balance of balance of total evidence in favor of X & Y exceeds the balance of total evidence in favor of X & Z, then the balance of total evidence in favor of X & $\sim Z$ exceeds the balance of total evidence in favor of X & $\sim Y$.

Each of these brings out a different aspect of the concept of a balance of evidence. The first two principles make it clear that the 'evidence' includes not only empirical information, like the colors of balls drawn from urns, but also *logical* information, like the fact that a blue ball is also a blue or green ball. This makes perfect sense as long as we keep in mind that we are interested in balances of *total* evidence. As noted by Carnap (1962), total evidence (which he referred as 'firmness') satisfies both Normality and Consequence. While not every notion of evidence has this property (e.g., incremental evidence lacks it), total evidence clearly does. If a body of evidence provides any reason to think that a proposition is true, then it provides at least as much reason to think that any logically weaker proposition is true. The partition condition requires the balance of evidence for a proposition to remain the same no matter how the proposition happens to be partitioned. It says that if the total evidence, on balance, favors one way for X to be true over another, then it must also favor X being true in something other than the second way over its being true in something other than the first way.

As show in (Kraft, et. al., 1959), Isovalence ensures that balances of total evidence can be represented as probabilities. When Isovalence holds there will always be at least one (usually many) finitely additive probability functions $\mathbf{c}$ such that $\mathbf{c}(X) \geq \mathbf{c}(Y)$ whenever ε_t provides at least as great a balance of total evidence in favor of X as in favor of Y. Moreover, for any sequences of hypotheses $<X_1, X_2, \ldots, X_N>$ and $<Y_1, Y_2, \ldots, Y_N>$, each such function will satisfy $\mathbf{c}(X_1 + \ldots + X_N) \geq \mathbf{c}(Y_1 + \ldots + Y_N)$ whenever ε_t provides at least as great a balance of total evidence in favor of X_i as in favor of Y_i for each $i \leq N$. Clearly, this can only happen if balances of total evidence correspond to probabilistically coherent truth-value estimates. Since a rational believer's truth-value estimates coincide with her credences, it follows that her credences reflect the balances of her total evidence. Though we will not make the case in detail, it also follows that the believer's credence for X given Y reflects that portion of the balance of her evidence for Y that counts in favor of X.

5. Measuring Weight.

No satisfactory measure of the weight of evidence has yet been devised. Most of the functions that have been suggested for the task—e.g., the log-likelihood ratio $\log(\mathbf{c}(E|X)/\mathbf{c}(E|\sim X))$ of (Good 1984)—are really measures of *evidential relevance* that compare balances of total evidence irrespective of weight. Since the values of these measures can remain fixed even as the volume of data increases, they do not capture the weight of evidence in the sense Keynes had in mind. The difficulties of formulating a general measure of weight are not to be underestimated. Indeed, Keynes argued that it is impossible to capture the weight of a body of evidence using a single number. This may or may not be so, but it turns out that we can make some headway in the special case where a subject's credence for H depends on her credences for hypotheses about objective chances.

It was suggested above that the weight of evidence manifests itself in the resilience of credences in the face of new data. This is only partly right. While resilience is often a reliable symptom of weight, it is not the heart of the matter. Consider a believer whose credence for X is her estimate of its objective chance, so that $\mathbf{c}(X) = \Sigma_x\, \mathbf{c}(\mathrm{Ch}(X) = x)\cdot x$ all across c_t for some fixed partition of chance hypotheses $\{\mathrm{Ch}(X) = x\}$, and where $\mathbf{c}(X|\mathrm{Ch}(X) = x) = \mathbf{c}(X|E\ \&\ \mathrm{Ch}(X) = x)$ for any potential item of data E. Here, the weight of evidence tends to stabilize X's credence in a particular way: it stabilizes credences of chance hypotheses, while concentrating most of the credence on a small set of these hypotheses. Since acquiring the datum E will not alter X's probability conditional on any chance hypothesis, the disparity between $\mathbf{c}(X|E)$ and $\mathbf{c}(X)$ will, other things equal, tend to be small when the disparity between $\mathbf{c}(\mathrm{Ch}(X) = x|E)$ and $\mathbf{c}(\mathrm{Ch}(X) = x)$ is small for most x. That said, data that alters the credence of $\mathrm{Ch}(X) = x$ will also, other things equal, induce a smaller change in X's credence when x is close to $\mathbf{c}(X)$ than when x is far from $\mathbf{c}(X)$. Consequently, even if E does not alter the probability of a given chance hypothesis at all, so that $\mathbf{c}(\mathrm{Ch}(X) = x|E) = \mathbf{c}(\mathrm{Ch}(X) = x)$, this promotes *in*stability in the subject's beliefs if E affects other chance hypotheses in such a way that the distance between x and $\mathbf{c}(X|E)$ is greater than the distance between x and $\mathbf{c}(X)$. The real effect of the weight of evidence is to ensure that such increases in the disparity between chance and credence are compensated by proportional decreases in the probabilities of the offending chance hypotheses. Weight really stabilizes not the probabilities of the chance hypotheses themselves, but their probabilities discounted by the distance between X's chance and its credence. So, the most basic resilient quantity is not $\mathbf{c}(X)$ or even $\mathbf{c}(\mathrm{Ch}(X) = x)$; it is $\mathbf{c}(\mathrm{Ch}(X) = x)\cdot|x - \mathbf{c}(X)|$ or, what is better for technical reasons, $w(x) = \mathbf{c}(\mathrm{Ch}(X) = x)\cdot(x - \mathbf{c}(X))^2$.

The proposal is this: When a subject's credence for X is mediated by chance hypotheses, the weight of her evidence for X tends to make $w(x)$ resilient, so that the difference between $\mathbf{c}(\mathrm{Ch}(X) = x|E)(x - \mathbf{c}(X|E))^2$ and $\mathbf{c}(\mathrm{Ch}(X) = x)(x - \mathbf{c}(X))^2$ is small for most data propositions E. We can then evaluate the overall weight of the evidence for X relative to E by summing these quantities

$$w(X, E) = \Sigma_x|\mathbf{c}(\mathrm{Ch}(X) = x|E)\cdot(x - \mathbf{c}(X|E))^2 - \mathbf{c}(\mathrm{Ch}(X) = x)\cdot(x - \mathbf{c}(X))^2|$$

The weightier the evidence for X is, the smaller $w(X, E)$ will tend to be.

w is not a perfect measure of weight. Its applicability is limited since it assumes that X's credence is mediated by credences for chance hypotheses. Moreover, its value depends on the choice of E (though weighty evidence will tend to make $w(X, E)$ it small for a wide range of E). Even so, w has some properties that any measure of weight should have. First, it has no evidential valence, i.e., its value is the same for X as for $\sim X$. Second, when $w(X, E)$ is small, X's credence will tend to be resilient, and when $w(X, E)$ is large X's credence will tend not to be resilient (except for accidental reasons). Third, w relates the weight of evidence to the stable concentration of credences. It is easy to show that $w(X, E)$ is never less than the absolute difference between X's variance conditional on E and its unconditional variance: $w(X, E) \geq |\sigma^2(X|E) - \sigma^2(X)|$.[11] Consequently, when the evidence for X is weighty $w(X, E)$ places a low upper bound on the amount by which the spread in probabilities for chance hypotheses can change when E is learned. This highlights what is perhaps the most important fact about the weight of evidence. Increasing the gross amount of relevant evidence for X tends to cause credences to concentrate more and more heavily on increasingly smaller subsets of chance hypotheses, and this concentration tends to become more resilient. As a result, the expected chance of X comes to depend more and more heavily on the distribution of credence over a smaller and smaller set of chance hypotheses. This is what weight does, and what w measures.

6. Specificity of Evidence.

Another subtlety in the way credences reflect evidence concerns the handling of *unspecific* data. In the terminology to be used here, data is less than fully specific with respect to X when it is either *incomplete* in the sense that it fails to discriminate X from incompatible alternatives, or when it is *ambiguous* in the sense of being subject to different readings that alter its evidential significance for X.[12] Both incompleteness and ambiguity are defined relative to a given hypothesis, and both are matters of degree. When you are told that Ed is either a professional basketball player or a professional jockey you are given very specific information about the hypothesis that he is an athlete, but somewhat less specific information about the hypothesis that he is a jockey. Likewise, if you draw a ball at random from an urn and examine it under yellow light that makes it hard to distinguish blue from green, then finding that the ball looks blue gives you specific information about how it appears in yellow light, but the data is ambiguous with respect to the hypothesis that the ball is actually blue.

The treatment of unspecific evidence has always posed a challenge for Bayesians. One approach to the problem has been to invoke some version of Laplace's infamous *Principle of Insufficient Reason.* The Principle states that "equipossible" hypotheses, those for which there is symmetrical evidence, should always be assigned equal probabilities. The idea that credences should reflect evidence might seem to require us to endorse Laplace's Principle, and the fact that unspecific evidence tends to be symmetric among possibilities would seem to show that it is applicable. To see why not, consider the following series of examples:

> *Four Urns-II*: Joshua knows that each of four urns – U_1, U_2, U_3, U_4 – was selected from a (different) population of urns {urn_0, urn_1, urn_2, ..., urn_{10}} where urn_i contain exactly i blue balls and $10 - i$ green balls. A ball will be randomly chosen from each urn U_i, and B_i is the proposition that it will be blue. Here is Joshua's evidence:
>
> U_1: Joshua has been allowed to look into the first urn and has seen that it contains exactly five blue balls and five green balls, so he knows that $U_1 = \text{urn}_5$.
>
> U_2: Joshua knows that the second urn was selected in such a way that each urn_i had an equal probability of being chosen.
>
> U_3[13]: Joshua knows that the third urn was selected in such a way that urn_i was chosen with probability $({}^{10}{}_i)/2^{10}$ where $({}^{10}{}_i) = 10!/i!(10 - i)!$
>
> U_4: Joshua has no information whatever concerning the process by which the fourth urn was selected.
>
> What credences should Joshua assign to the various B_i?

There is perfect symmetry in both the balance and weight of evidence for and against each B_i. So, if rational credences must reflect total evidence, it looks as if Joshua should treat each B_i and its negation equally by assigning each credence 1/2, just as the Principle of Insufficient Reason suggests. While this seems like a fine idea in the first three cases, it is clearly wrong in the fourth. Let's consider each case in turn.

Because Joshua knows $U_1 = \text{urn}_5$, he has specific and precise evidence that is entirely symmetrical for and against B_1. This clearly justifies setting $\mathbf{c}(B_i) = 1/2$. Joshua's evidence about U_2 is not quite so definitive, but it is still specific enough to determine a distribution of credences over chance hypotheses: $\mathbf{c}(U_2 = \text{urn}_i) = 1/11$. Since this distribution is uniform, the balance of Joshua's evidence is again captured by $\mathbf{c}(B_2) = 1/2$. The third case is like the second, except that the distribution is binomial rather than uniform. It is still symmetrical about 1/2, i.e., $\mathbf{c}(U_4 = \text{urn}_i) = \mathbf{c}(U_4 = \text{urn}_{10-i})$ for each i, so $\mathbf{c}(B_2) = 1/2$ again captures the balance of Joshua's evidence.

Things get dicey in the last case. Since Joshua is in a state of complete ignorance with respect to the fourth urn, his evidence does not pick out any single distribution of credences over the chance hypotheses $U_4 = \text{urn}_i$. This is precisely the point at which some Bayesians tend to overreach by trotting out the Principle of Insufficient Reason and proposing that there is a *single* probability function—an "ignorance prior," "uninformative prior," or "objective Bayes" prior—that captures Joshua's evidential state. The siren song sounds like this: Since Joshua has no evidence either for or against any chance hypothesis, he no grounds for thinking that any one of them is more or less likely than any other. Given this perfect symmetry in his reasons, Joshua should not play favorites. The only way for him to avoid playing favorites is by investing equal credence in each chance hypothesis, so that $\mathbf{c}(U_4 = \text{urn}_i) = 1/11$.

Many philosophers and statisticians object to this sort of reasoning on the grounds that it yields inconsistent results depending upon how the possibilities happen to be partitioned. This objection was first raised by John Venn in the 1800s and has been recapitulated many times since. Here is a version: Suppose you have inherited a large plot of land. You know the parcel is a square that is between one and two kilometers on a side, but this is *all* you know. How many square kilometers of land would you estimate that you own? On one hand, you might partition the possibilities by side-length in kilometers. If so, the Principle of Insufficient Reason seems to require each hypothesis L_x = "Each side has length x km^2," for $1 \leq x \leq 2$, to be accorded the same credence. The expected side length of your parcel is then 3/2 km and its expected area is 9/4 km^2. On the other hand, if you partition the possibilities by area in square kilometers, the Principle tells you to distribute your credence evenly over A_y = "The area of the parcel is y km^2," where $1 \leq y \leq 4$. The expected length and area are then $\sqrt{5}/2$ km and 5/2 km^2. So, applying the Principle jointly to length and area produces a contradiction.

While opponents of the Principle of Insufficient Reason often regard this objection as fatal, few of its defenders are troubled by it. It is clear, they argue, that your "prior" should not be uniform over *either* length in meters or area in square kilometers. After all, these distributions are tied to specific units for measuring distance, and it is clear *a priori* that your credences should not depend on the (arbitrary) choice of a distance scale. Specifically, if your credences over the side-lengths have the functional form $\mathbf{c}(L_x) = \mathbf{f}(x)$, and if $\mathbf{t}(x) = u{\cdot}x$, with $u > 0$, is a transformation that alters the unit of distance ($u = 0.6214$ to switch kilometers to miles), then your credences for the rescaled side-lengths $L^*_{\mathbf{t}(x)}$ = "Each side has length $\mathbf{t}(x)$ in units u," should have the form $\mathbf{c}(L^*_{\mathbf{t}(x)}) = \mathbf{f}(\mathbf{t}(x))$. This guarantees, for example, that the probability of finding the side length between 1.2 and 1.3 kilometers is the same as that of finding it between 0.6214 and 0.8078 miles. It is easy to show, (Lee 1997, 101–103), that any $\mathbf{f}$ that has this property for all u produces credences of the form $\mathbf{c}(x) = k_x/x$ where k_x is the normalizing constant $k_x = \int_1^2 dx/x = ln(2)$. Similar reasoning shows that your credences for area hypotheses must have the form $\mathbf{c}(A_y) = k_y/y$ where $k_y = \int_1^4 dy/y = ln(4)$. With these priors the contradiction vanishes. Computing expected area by averaging over side-length yields $\int_1^2 x^2 dx/x = 3/2ln(2)$, while computing it by averaging over area also yields $\int_1^4 y\,dy/y = 3/ln(4) = 3/2ln(2)$. As shown in (Jeffries 1939), this sort of maneuver can be used in a wide variety of situations.

Adjudicating this dispute is too large a task to be undertaken here, but it is worth noting that, while the k/x prior has some nice features, it has some odd ones as well. Since it probabilifies values of x in inverse proportion to their size, the function blows up to infinity as x approaches zero. This makes k/x an "improper prior" in the sense that $\int_0^b dx/x = \infty$ for any $b > 0$. Clearly, no such function can represent the credences of a rational believer over any interval containing zero. Likewise, since $\int_a^\infty 1/x \, dx = \infty$ for any $a > 0$ the k/x prior cannot represent the credences of a believer who is unable to impose an upper bound on the size of x. There are ways to finesse these difficulties. In some situations one can plausibly argue that uncertainty can be confined to an interval $[a, b]$ with $0 < a < b < \infty$. It is also possible to show that many improper priors generate *proper* posterior probabilities when updated using Bayes' Theorem. So, even though they cannot represent coherent beliefs, some improper priors (e.g., k/x) can be used as starting points for learning from experience. Whether or not these gambits actually succeed is a matter of controversy.[14]

Whatever the ultimate verdict on the k/x prior and its brethren, there is a deeper problem with "uninformative priors." The real difficulty is not that the Principle of Insufficient Reason might be incoherent; it is that the Principle, even if it can be made coherent, is defective epistemology. It is wrong-headed to try to capture states of ambiguous or incomplete evidence using a *single* credence function. Those who advocate this approach play on the intuition that someone who lacks evidence that distinguishes among possibilities should not "play favorites," and so should treat the possibilities equally by investing equal credence in them. The fallacious step is the last one: equal treatment does not require equal credence. When Joshua, who knows nothing about the contents of U_4, assigns each hypothesis $U_4 = \text{urn}_i$ an equal probability he is pretending to have information he does not possess. His evidence is compatible with *any* distribution of objective probability over the hypotheses, so by distributing his credences uniformly over them Joshua ignores a vast number of possibilities that are consistent with his evidence. Specifically, if we let p range over all probability distributions on $\{U_4 = \text{urn}_i\}$, and if we consider all hypotheses of the form O_p = "U_4 was chosen by a probabilistic process governed by distribution p," then Joshua is ignoring all those O_p in which $p(U_4 = \text{urn}_i) \neq 1/11$.

Proponents of Insufficient Reason might respond that Joshua need not ignore any O_p. With no evidence that favors any one of them over any other, they will say, Joshua should distribute his credences uniformly over the O_p. If he does this he is not ignoring any O_p: in fact, he is treating them equally. Moreover, when he computes expected truth-values relative to the uniform distribution over O_p he arrives at a credence function in which $\mathbf{c}(U_4 = \text{urn}_i) = 1/11$. We should not be mollified by this response since it only pushes the problem up a level. Instead of ignoring potential distributions of objective probability over $\{U_4 = \text{urn}_i\}$, Joshua is now ignoring distributions of objective probability over the O_p. He is acting as if he has some reason to rule out those possibilities in which the O_p have different chances of being realized, even though none of his evidence speaks to the issue. One could, of course, move up yet another level, but the same difficulties would rearise. In the end, there is no getting around the fact that the Principle of Insufficient Reason (even if coherent) is bad epistemology because it requires believers to ignore possibilities that are consistent with their evidence.

As sophisticated Bayesians like Isaac Levi (1980), Richard Jeffrey (1983), Mark Kaplan (1996), have long recognized, the proper response to symmetrically ambiguous or incomplete evidence is not to assign probabilities symmetrically, but to refrain from assigning precise probabilities at all. Indefiniteness in the evidence is reflected not in the values of any single credence function, but in the spread of values across the *family* of all credence functions that the evidence does not exclude. This is why modern Bayesians represent credal states using sets of credence functions. It is not just that sharp degrees of belief are psychologically unrealistic (though they are). Imprecise credences have a clear epistemological motivation: they are the proper response to unspecific evidence.

Joshua's case illustrates this nicely. Given his complete lack of evidence regarding U_4, Joshua is being epistemically irresponsible unless, for each i and for each x between 0 and 1, his credal state $\mathcal{C}_t$ contains at least one credence function such that $\mathbf{c}(U_4 = \text{urn}_i) = x$. If his opinions are any more restrictive than this, then he is pretending to have evidence that he does not have. Moreover, if Joshua's credal state is as described, then he treats each chance hypothesis $U_4 = \text{urn}_i$ exactly the same way. For every assignment $\mathbf{c}(U_4 = \text{urn}_i) = x_i$ that appears in Joshua's credal state, and for every way s of permuting the eleven indices, the assignment $\mathbf{c}_s(U_4 = \text{urn}_i) = x_{s(i)}$ also appears in Joshua's credal state. This is all that good epistemology demands. Symmetrical evidence only mandates equal credences when the data is entirely unequivocal and sufficiently definitive to justify the assignment of sharp numerical probabilities. When the evidence lacks specificity, propositions that are equally well supported by the evidence should receive equal treatment in the probabilistic representation. Proponents of the Principle of Insufficient Reason were right to think that good epistemology requires us to treat hypotheses for which we have symmetrical evidence in the same way; they went wrong in thinking that equal treatment requires equal investments of confidence.

7. The Contrast Between Balance and Specificity.

In general, a body of evidence $\mathcal{E}_t$ is specific to the extent that it requires probabilistic facts to hold across all credence functions in a credal state. If $\mathcal{E}_t$ entirely specific with respect to X, then it requires $\mathbf{c}(X)$ to have a single value all across $\mathcal{C}_t$. So, perfectly specific evidence produces a determinate balance of evidence for X. Less specific evidence leaves the balance indeterminate. When the evidence for X is unspecific its credence will usually be "interval-valued," i.e., the values of $\mathbf{c}(X)$ represented in C_t cover an interval $[x^-, x^+]$.[15] It is then only determinate that the balance of evidence for X is at least x^- and at most x^+. The difference between the 'upper probability' x^+ and the 'lower probability' x^- provides a rough gauge of the specificity of the evidence with respect to X (where smaller = more specific). Even if the evidence for X is less that entirely specific, certain facts about balances of evidence can still be determinate. For example, even though one or both of $\mathbf{c}(X)$ and $\mathbf{c}(Y)$ might be interval-valued, the evidence can still dictate that $\mathbf{c}(X) > \mathbf{c}(Y)$ should hold across c_t, in which case it is determinate that there is a greater balance of evidence for X than for Y.

One thing that might seem to put pressure on the balance/specificity distinction is the fascinating phenomenon of probabilistic *dilation* discussed in (Seidenfeld and Wasserman 1993). Here is a motivating example:

> **Trick Coins**. The Acme Trick Coin Company makes coins in pairs: one silver, one gold. The silver coin in each pair is unremarkable, but always fair. The gold coin is quite remarkable. It contains a tiny device that can detect the result of the most recent toss of the silver coin. The device then determines a bias$(G|S) \in [0, 1]$ for a gold head in the event of a silver head, and a bias$({\sim}G|{\sim}S) \in [0, 1]$ for a gold tail in the event of a silver tail. The device can be set at the factory so that the first bias is any real number between 0 and 1, but the second bias is always the same as the first. A gold coin set at bias$(G|S) = 2/3$ will come up heads two times in three after the silver coin lands heads, but it will come up heads only one time in three after the silver coin lands tails. You have a pair of Acme coins in front of you, which are about to be tossed in sequence (silver, then gold). How confident should you be that the gold coin will come up heads?

Interestingly, there is a determinate answer to this question even though your evidence is quite unspecific. Since you are completely ignorant about the gold coin's bias, your credal state contains functions whose values for $\mathbf{c}(G|S)$ and $\mathbf{c}({\sim}G|{\sim}S)$ span the whole of [0,1]. Despite this, your credence for G is fully determinate. Every function in your credal state will satisfy $\mathbf{c}(G|S) = \mathbf{c}({\sim}G|{\sim}S)$. Since the silver coin is fair, it follows that $\mathbf{c}(G) = \mathbf{c}(S)\mathbf{c}(G|S) + \mathbf{c}({\sim}S)\mathbf{c}(G|{\sim}S) = 1/2$. Thus, your evidence for G and ${\sim}G$ is determinately and perfectly balanced even though your evidence about the bias of the coin is highly unspecific.

So far there is nothing to worry about: evidence that is unspecific in one respect can be specific in another. Things get hairy when we imagine that the silver coin is tossed. Suppose it comes up heads. Intuitively, it would seem that adding this very specific item of data to your evidence should increase its overall specificity, and the general effect should be a narrowing of ranges of permissible credences. Precisely the opposite happens. Once you learn S your new set of credences for G corresponds to your old set of credences conditioned on S. Since $\mathbf{c}(G|S)$ ranges over the whole of [0,1], $\mathbf{c}_{\text{new}}(G)$ ranges over the whole of [0,1] as well. Obviously, the same will happen if the silver coin comes up tails. This looks like a problem. If the addition of a completely precise and specific item of data can make a body of evidence so much less specific that the balance of evidence in favor of a hypothesis goes from completely determinate to entirely indeterminate, then one wonders whether any cogent distinction between specificity and balance can be maintained.

Things are not as dire as they seem. Even though you start out knowing that bias($G|S$) = bias($\sim G|\sim S$), the evidential relevance of this information for questions about G's truth-value is rather vexed. Clearly, the information can only be relevant the extent that it allows you to use evidence about S and $\sim S$ to draw conclusions about G. Oddly, in this case your ability to do this turns on the amount of total evidence you have for S. To see this, suppose for a moment that you do not know the bias of the silver coin. Then $\mathbf{c}(G) = \mathbf{c}(\sim S) + [\mathbf{c}(S) - \mathbf{c}(\sim S)]\mathbf{c}(G|S)$ will hold all across your credal state. You will then be able to draw reasonably determinate conclusions about G if your credences for S and $\sim S$ are close together, but not if they are far apart. For if $\mathbf{c}(S) - \mathbf{c}(\sim S)$ is small then the imprecise term $\mathbf{c}(G|S)$ will not matter much to your views about G, but it will matter if $\mathbf{c}(S) - \mathbf{c}(\sim S)$ is large. The moral is that the relevance of the information bias($G|S$) = bias($\sim G|\sim S$) to your opinions about G declines with the distance between $\mathbf{c}(S)$ to $\mathbf{c}(\sim S)$. It is only when $\mathbf{c}(S) = \mathbf{c}(\sim S)$ that it is completely relevant, and its degree of relevance shrinks to nothing when $\mathbf{c}(S)$ or $\mathbf{c}(\sim S)$ is 1. So, while learning S or $\sim S$ does make your evidence more specific overall, it also decreases the amount of specific evidence that is relevant to G. It does this not by making the evidence any less specific, but by making it less relevant.

8. The Contrast Between Weight and Specificity.

It is particularly difficult to disentangle weight and specificity because increases in one are often accompanied by increases in the other. This is no accident: it follows from the well-known "washing out" theorems,[16] which show that subjective probabilities, as long as they are not too much at odds with one another, tend to converge toward a consensus as more and more data accumulates. Here is a simple case: Imagine that a subject's credal state contains only two functions $\mathbf{c}$ and $\mathbf{c}^*$, which assign X different probabilities strictly between 0 and 1. Suppose also that there is an infinite sequence of evidence propositions $\{E_1, E_2, E_3, \ldots\}$ such that:

- $\mathbf{c}$ and $\mathbf{c}^*$ assign each finite data sequence $D_j = \pm E_1 \& \ldots \& \pm E_j$ a probability strictly between 0 and 1 (where $\pm E$ is either E or $\sim E$).
- X and $\sim X$ function like a chance hypotheses with respect to the E_js, so that $\mathbf{c}(E_k/X) = \mathbf{c}(E_k/\pm X \& E_j) = \mathbf{c}^*(E_k/X) = \mathbf{c}^*(E_k/\pm X \& E_j)$.
- At each time j the subject acquires (perfectly specific) evidence that makes her certain of either E_j or $\sim E_j$, so that her credal state at j is $\{\mathbf{c}(X/D_j), \mathbf{c}^*(X/D_j)\}$ where D_j is the data she has received up to j.

Under these circumstances the subject's credences for X at successive times form a *martingale sequence* in which each term is the expected value of its successor. The Martingale Convergence Theorem of (Doob 1971) entails that, except for a set of data sequences to which the subject assigns probability zero, $\mathbf{c}_j(X)$ and

$\mathbf{c}_j^*(X)$ each converge to a definite limit. Moreover, since X and $\sim X$ function like chance hypotheses these limits coincide.

Results of this sort show that, in a wide variety of circumstances, increasing the amount of specific, relevant data that a subject has for a proposition will tend to shrink the range of its admissible credence values. Of course, increasing the amount of specific, relevant data for X increases the weight of the evidence for X, and this causes the values of $\mathbf{c}(X)$ and $\mathbf{c}^*(X)$ to be increasingly stable. So, there is a natural convergence of opinion, and an attendant reduction of imprecision, that tends to occur as increasingly weighty evidence is acquired. This makes it difficult to separate the effects of weight from those of specificity, and many who have written on the topic have run the two together. Indeed, in an excellent recent paper Brian Weatherson (2002, 52) has argued than many of Keynes's remarks are best interpreted as supposing that the weight of the evidence for a hypothesis is reflected in the spread of its credence values. Weatherson proposes, on behalf of Keynes, that the weight of a person's evidence for X can be measured as $1 - (x^+ - x^-)$. While this is a very plausible reading of Keynes, it also shows that he conflated weight with specificity. It is a natural conflation to make, given that two quantities typically increase together as data accumulates, but it does run together quite different things. As we have seen, the overall volume of relevant evidence for X is tied not to the spread of values for X's credence across a credal state, but to the stability and concentration of these values in the face of potential future data. The spread in credence values is a matter of the level of incompleteness or ambiguity in the data.

To illustrate this point we need an example in which the weight evidence for X increases, but its specificity with respect to X does not. It not easy to find such an example that is both simple and uncontrived, so contrived will have to do.

> *Guess the Weight*. You are a contestant on a rather odd game show. The host holds up an opaque bag and tells you that it contains either an iron or an aluminum ingot that was chosen at random from among ingots produced yesterday at the Acme Foundry. Your job is to guess whether the ingot is iron or aluminum. You know that the iron ingots produced at Acme tend to heavier than the aluminum ones, but neither have a uniform weight. The weights of iron ingots are normally distributed about a mean of 500 oz with a variance 200 oz, whereas the aluminum ingots are normally distributed about a mean of 300 oz, again with a variance of 200 oz. You have no specific information about the proportions of iron and aluminum ingots that Acme produces, and so your credence for the proposition I that the ingot in the bag is iron covers all of [0, 1]. The host tells you that you may weight the bag ten times on a special scale before guessing. Unfortunately, the scale is not a terribly accurate: its results tend to be normally distributed around the true weight with a variance of 100 oz. Moreover, the scale does not report weights as such. Rather, it contains a detector that determines whether the ingot in the bag is iron or aluminum, and then it reports the difference between the ingot's true weight and the mean weight of ingots of its type. So, if the scale reads 10 oz this might mean that the ingot is iron and the scale determines it to be 510 oz, or that the ingot is

aluminum and the scale determines it to be 310 oz. You place the bag on the scale ten times and get readings of 10, −15, −8, 4, −4, 16, 12, −7, −11, 3. Call this data *D*, and note that the mean of the data is 0 and that it variance is 100. How does the evidence you have for *I* before the weighing compare with the evidence you have after you learn *D*?

The contrived nature of the example ensures that there is no difference at all in the specificity of your evidence for *I* before and after the weighing. The information you glean from each individual weighing does nothing to distinguish *I* from $\sim I$ since each report is symmetrically ambiguous between the two. Moreover, the spread of reported values also provides no grounds for distinguishing *I* from $\sim I$ since the standard deviation in the weights of iron and aluminum ingots is identical. So, both before and after you learn *D* your credence for *I* is spread over all of [0, 1].

Though you gain nothing in specificity, you do gain in weight. After you condition on *D* your credal state sets probabilities for ingot weights conditional on both *I* and $\sim I$ that are normally distributed about the same means of 500 oz and 300 oz, but with a common, smaller variance of 9.52. The smaller variance indicates that you are now more certain than you were that the ingot is close to average for its type. Moreover, these conditional means and variances are much more stable in the face of information about the ingot's weight than they were before you learned *D*. It is easy to see that they will be more stable in the face of more measurements on the host's unspecific scale. What might not be so obvious is that they also tend to be more stable under specific information about the ingot's actual weight (not just it weight relative to the mean in its class). Suppose, for example, that the ingot weighs in at 450 oz on a (real) scale that returns a value that is normally distributed about the true weight with a variance of 50 oz. Then the variance of both conditional distributions will shrink from 9.52 to 9.34 oz, and their means will become, respectively, about 475 oz and 375 oz. Contrast this with what happens if you learned this same fact about the ingot's weight before knowing *D*. In this case, the variances of both conditional distributions shrink to 40 oz., but their means become 458 oz and 425 oz, respectively. This sort of thing happens across the board. For any value the scale might read (except the midpoint 400 oz), both the changes in variances and the changes in the mean values for weights conditional on *I* and $\sim I$ will be smaller after *D* is learned than before. As we saw above, this kind of stable concentration of probability is precisely what one expects when the weight of evidence increases. Again, the weight of a body of evidence and its specificity are different things. While the first is plausibly measured by the spread in credence values over a credal state the second is not.

9. Conclusion.

Subjective probabilities reflect three aspects of a believer's total evidence—balance, weight, and specificity—in significantly different ways. The unconditional credence of a proposition reflects the balance of total evidence in its favor. The weight of this evidence is reflected in the tendency for credences to stably concentrate on a small set of hypotheses about the proposition's objective chance. The specificity of the evidence is reflected in the spread of credence values for the proposition across the believer's credal state. Any satisfactory epistemology must recognize these three aspects of evidence, and must be attuned to the different ways in which they affect credences. It is a great strength of the Bayesian approach to epistemology that it can characterize the differences between the balance, weight and specificity of evidence in such perspicuous and fruitful ways.[17]

Notes

1. For a splendid discussion of Jeffries's work see (Howie 2002).
2. The terminology here is from (Levi 1980).
3. As noted in (Ramsey 1932, p. 169), it is a mistake to equate the strength of an opinion with the intensity of any feeling of conviction the believer might have since the beliefs we hold most strongly are often associated with no feelings at all.
4. It is a matter of some subtlety to say how the accuracy of truth-value estimates should be evaluated. One natural measure is the *Brier score* (Brier 1950), which was developed as a way of judging the accuracy of weather forecasts. For discussion see (Joyce 1998) and (Joyce forthcoming).
5. The proposition X is chosen from some underlying Boolean of algebra of propositions, and the condition Y is taken from some distinguished set within this algebra.
6. David Lewis (1980) dubs this the 'Principal Principle'. As Lewis observes, it can come undone in circumstances where 'undermining' evidence is possible, but no such situation will be entertained here.
7. This assumes a measurement scale on which a value of 1 indicates the existence of conclusive evidence for the truth of the proposition, 0 signifies conclusive evidence against its truth, and 1/2 means that the evidence (determinately) tells for and against the proposition in equal measure. The merits of such a measurement scheme will be discussed below.
8. Failure to keep straight the distinction between balances and weights of evidence can lead to confusion. See, for example, Popper's infamous "paradox of ideal evidence" (1959, 406), and Jeffrey's (1983, 196) decisive refutation of it.
9. Formally, a person's estimate of the number of truths in $\{X_1, X_2, \ldots X_N\}$ is her estimated value of the sum $X_1 + X_2 + \ldots + X_N$, where each proposition is an indicator functions that has value 1 when true and 0 when false.
10. A person's *estimate* of the number of truths in one set may exceed her estimate of the number of truths in another set even though she invests a *low* credence is the *proposition* that the first set contains more truths than the second. This will happen, for example, when $\mathbf{c}(H_1 \mathbin{\&} H_2) = 1/3$, $\mathbf{c}((H_1 \mathbin{\&} {\sim}H_2) \vee ({\sim}H_1 \mathbin{\&} H_2)) = 0$, $\mathbf{c}({\sim}H_1 \mathbin{\&} {\sim}H_2) = 2/3$, and $\mathbf{c}(G_1 \mathbin{\&} G_2) = 0$, $\mathbf{c}((G_1 \mathbin{\&} {\sim}G_2) \vee ({\sim}G_1 \mathbin{\&} G_2)) = 1/2$, $\mathbf{c}({\sim}G_1 \mathbin{\&} {\sim}G_2) = 1/2$.

11. $\sigma^2(X|E) = \Sigma_x \mathbf{c}(\mathrm{Ch}(X) = x|E)\cdot(x - \mathbf{c}(X|E))^2$ and $\sigma^2(X) = \Sigma_x\ \mathbf{c}(\mathrm{Ch}(X) = x)\cdot(x - \mathbf{c}(X))^2$.
12. Readers should be cautioned that unspecificity is different from vagueness. When the evidence for X is vague it is impossible even to assign determinate upper and lower credences to X. The treatment of vague evidence is a difficult problem that goes far beyond the scope of this paper.
13. This distribution is obtained by first randomly choosing from all the 2^{10} possible ordered sequences of blue and green balls, and then selecting the urn$_i$ that has the same number of balls as the chosen sequence.
14. Interested readers are encouraged to consult (Howson 2002, 53–56).
15. This is only "usually" because C_t need not be convex. This can happen, in particular, when E_t only determinately specifies facts about probabilistic dependence and independence.
16. For an especially lucid discussion of the convergence results see (Hawthorne 2005).
17. I am grateful to Aaron Bronfman, Branden Fitelson, Dustin Locke, Louis Loeb, Eric Lormand, Jason Stanley and Michael Woodroofe for their insightful comments on the issues discussed in this paper. This research was supported by a Rackham Interdisciplinary Research Grant from the Rackham School of Graduate Studies at the University of Michigan

References

Carnap, Rudolf. 1962. *Logical Foundations of Probability*, 2nd. edition. Chicago: University of Chicago Press.

de Finetti, Bruno. 1964. "Foresight: Its Logical Laws, Its Subjective Sources", in H. Kyburg and H. Smokler, eds., *Studies in Subjective Probability*. New York: John Wiley and Sons: 93–158; all page references are to the later edition.

Doob, J. 1971. What is a Martingale," *American Mathematical Monthly* **78**: 451–462.

Good, I. J. 1984 "The Best Explicatum for Weight of Evidence," *Journal of Statistical Computation and Simulation* **19**: 294–299.

Hawthorne, James. 2005. "Inductive Logic", *The Stanford Encyclopedia of Philosophy (Summer 2005 Edition)*, Edward N. Zalta (ed.), URL=<http://www.plato.stanford.edu/archives/sum2005/entries/logic-inductive/>.

Howie, David. 2002. *Interpreting Probability: Controversies and Developments in the Early Twentieth Century*. Cambridge: Cambridge University Press.

Howson, Colin. 2002. "Bayesianism in Statistics," in R. Swinburne, e.d., *Bayes's Theorem*. Oxford: British Academy/Oxford University Press.

Jeffries, Harold. 1939. *Theory of Probability*. Oxford: Oxford University Press.

Joyce, James M. 1998. "A Nonpragmatic Vindication of Probabilism," *Philosophy of Science* **65**: 575–603.

——— 1999. *The Foundations of Causal Decision Theory*. Cambridge: Cambridge University Press.

——— forthcoming. "Accuracy and Coherence: Prospects for an Alethic Epistemology of Partial Belief," to appear in F. Huber and C. Shmidt-Petri, eds., *Degrees of Belief*. Oxford: Oxford University Press.

Kaplan, Mark (1996). *Decision Theory as Philosophy*. Cambridge: Cambridge University Press.

Keynes, John Maynard. 1921. *A Treatise on Probability*. London: Macmillan.

Kraft, C., Pratt, J., and Seidenberg, A. 1959. "Intuitive Probability on Finite Sets," *Annals of Mathematical Statistics* **30**, pp. 408–419.

Lee, Peter M. 1997. *Bayesian Statistics: An Introduction*, 2nd edition. London: Arnold.

Levi, Isaac. 1980. *The Enterprise of Knowledge*. Cambridge, MA: MIT Press.

Lewis, David. 1980. "A Subjectivist's Guide to Objective Chance," in R. Jeffrey, ed., *Studies in Logic and Inductive Probability*, Vol. 2. Berkeley: University of California Press.

Popper, Karl. 1959. *The Logic of Scientific Discovery*. London:Hutchinson.

Ramsey, Frank. 1931. "Truth and Probability," in R. Braithwaite (ed.), *The Foundations of Mathematics and Other Logical Essays*. London: Kegan Paul: 156–98.

Savage, Leonard. 1972. *The Foundations of Statistics*, 2nd edition. New York: Dover.

Scott, Dana. 1964. "Measurement Structures and Linear Inequalities," *Journal of Mathematical Psychology* **1**: 233–47.

Seidenfeld, T. and L. Wasserman. 1993. "Dilation for convex sets of probabilities," *Annals of Statistics* **21**: 1139–1154.

Shimony, Abner. 1988. "An Adamite Derivation of the Calculus of Probability," in J. H. Fetzer, ed., *Probability and Causality*. Dordrecht: D. Reidel: 151–161.

Skyrms, Brian. 1980. *Causal Necessity*. London, Yale University Press

van Fraassen, Bas. 1983. "Calibration: A Frequency Justification for Personal Probability," in R. Cohen and L. Laudan, eds., *Physics Philosophy and Psychoanalysis*. Dordrecht: D. Reidel: 295–319.

Weatherson, Brian. 2002. "Keynes, Uncertainty and Interests Rates," *Cambridge Journal of Economics*: 47–62.

Philosophical Perspectives, 19, Epistemology, 2005

MOOREAN FACTS AND BELIEF REVISION, OR CAN THE SKEPTIC WIN?

Thomas Kelly
Princeton University

I. Introduction

A **Moorean fact**, in the words of the late David Lewis, is 'one of those things that we know better than we know the premises of any philosophical argument to the contrary'. Lewis opens his seminal paper 'Elusive Knowledge' with the following declaration:

> We know a lot ... We have all sorts of everyday knowledge, and we have it in abundance. To doubt that would be absurd ... It is a Moorean fact that we know a lot. It is one of those things that we know better than we know the premises of any philosophical argument to the contrary (1999: 418).

I take it that these remarks are put forth in a methodological spirit. 'Elusive Knowledge' stands as Lewis' fullest statement of his own positive views on knowledge and skepticism. It is here that he lays out the details of his own contextualist epistemology. In beginning the paper in this way, I take Lewis to be endorsing a thought along the following lines: Before we commence with the Hard Epistemology, here is something that we can lay down at the outset: We know a lot. The proposition that *We know a lot* can serve as a fixed point in our inquiry, and we should make adjustments elsewhere as needed in order to hold on to this fundamental commitment. Simply put, we should build the rest of our theory around this fixed point.[1]

In proceeding in this way, Lewis is far from alone among prominent contemporary philosophers. Compare David Armstrong on the proposition that *Things move*:

> It is a very fundamental part of the Moorean corpus that there is motion. Things move. Perhaps we have still not, after two and a half thousand years, got to the full bottom of Zeno's brilliant arguments against the existence of

> motion ... But certainly Zeno should not persuade us that things do not move. Neither should anybody else (1999: 79).

Elsewhere, Armstrong suggests that since the belief that *inductive inference is rational* similarly enjoys the status of 'Moorean knowledge', Hume's formidable argument to the contrary is powerless to show otherwise. Indeed, Armstrong insists that the fundamental rationality of inductive inference can legitimately be taken as a *datum* for philosophy and used as a premise for theorizing in metaphysics (1983: 53–54).

According to the conception advanced by Lewis and Armstrong, belief in a Moorean fact has a kind of epistemic standing which renders it peculiarly resistant to being rationally undermined. Indeed, it is occasionally suggested that belief in a Moorean fact cannot be rationally undermined at all. According to a more common conception—and the one to be explored here—belief in a Moorean fact is invulnerable to being undermined *by means of philosophical argument*. This leaves open the possibility that such a belief could be rationally undermined by particular courses of experience or by the right sorts of scientific discoveries. This invulnerability to being undermined by philosophical argument then, is a reflection not only of the epistemic standing that is claimed for such beliefs but also of the perceived impotence of philosophy itself.

This line of thought is made explicit by Kit Fine:

> In this age of post-Moorean modesty, many of us are inclined to doubt that philosophy is in possession of arguments that might genuinely serve to undermine what we ordinarily believe. It may perhaps be conceded that the arguments of the skeptic appear to be utterly compelling; but the Mooreans among us will hold that the very plausibility of our ordinary beliefs is reason enough for supposing that there *must* be something wrong in the skeptic's arguments, even if we are unable to say what it is. In so far then, as, the pretensions of philosophy to provide a world view rest upon its claim to be in possession of the epistemological high ground, those pretensions had better be given up (2001: 2).

The strategy of attempting to defuse skeptical challenges by appeal to the alleged sanctity of Moorean facts is not without its detractors.[2] Nevertheless, the popularity of the strategy runs high.[3] Moreover, it is not simply the sheer number of prominent philosophers who follow Moore in relevant respects which is noteworthy but also the philosophical orientations of those who do. After all, Lewis, Armstrong, and Fine hardly resemble common sense philosophers of yore: they are not, for example, purveyors of paradigm case arguments or even practitioners of an essentially conservative Strawsonian descriptive metaphysics. Rather, all three stand squarely in the venerable tradition of speculative metaphysics. The fact that philosophers of their general orientation nevertheless pay homage to Moore does as much as anything to bolster the credibility of Fine's claim that ours is an age of 'post-Moorean modesty'.[4]

I believe that the topic of Moorean facts raises deep questions of both philosophical method and first order epistemology. How should we respond to arguments that challenge beliefs of which we are extremely confident? To what extent can such arguments—or rather, those who put them forth—hope to get some rational grip or traction on us? To what extent, if at all, does one's starting point constrain the kinds of revisions in one's views that philosophy might legitimately inspire? When (if ever) is one justified in refusing to be swayed by an argument which is flawless as far as one can tell, and when is such refusal simply dogmatism? These are large questions, and ones which I will not attempt to fully answer here. My more modest ambition is to attempt to make progress with respect to these and related issues by way of examining the notion of a Moorean fact that I find in Lewis and others.

My own sympathies lie with the Moorean. I believe that there are very substantial limits on how radical a change in our views philosophy might legitimately inspire. For example, in epistemology—the domain on which I'll focus in what follows—I suspect that, ultimately, the skeptic[5] simply cannot win. The sense in which the skeptic cannot win is not that he will inevitably fail to persuade us of his conclusion—that, after all, might be a matter of mere psychological stubbornness on our part, which would, I think, be of rather limited philosophical interest. Rather, the sense in which the skeptic cannot win is that it would never be reasonable to be persuaded by the skeptic's argument. Moreover, I think that this is something that we can know even in advance of attending to the specifics of the skeptic's argument: in a sense, the skeptic has lost before the game begins. I concede that it is not easy to see what distinguishes this stance from simple dogmatism (if anything does). Indeed, much of what follows is devoted to criticizing various ways of developing the Moorean response to skepticism that I believe are unsuccessful. Towards the end of the paper, I sketch a way of understanding that response on which it has, I believe, a great deal of force.

Of late, there has been a strong resurgence of interest in Moore's response to the skeptic. In particular, the status of his famed 'proof of an external world'—'Here is one hand; Here is another; Therefore, the external world exists'—has been vigorously debated.[6] This focus on the virtues and vices of Moore's proof naturally encourages a certain picture of the dialectic between Moore and his opponents. According to the picture in question, Moore is essentially *playing offense* against the skeptic. That is, Moore has taken up the burden of proof, a burden that he can discharge only by providing a successful argument for an anti-skeptical conclusion. On this reading of Moore, he is primarily of interest to the philosopher concerned with skepticism as one among countless others who has taken the bait and risen to meet the challenge of providing an anti-skeptical argument that fulfills the criteria of argumentative goodness (whatever exactly those criteria are). In aim and ambition, Moore is comparable, perhaps, to one who offers an inference to the best explanation argument against the skeptic.

I think that this debate over the status of Moore's proof has proven illuminating and worthwhile. However, there is a danger that a fixation on Moore's proof will lead us to neglect what is arguably the deepest and most distinctive aspect of his critique of radical skepticism. For there is an alternative reading of Moore available, according to which Moore is ultimately not playing offense against the skeptic but rather *playing defense*. On this reading of Moore, the onus is on the skeptic to provide a compelling argument for *his* conclusion, and Moore is providing reasons for thinking that such a project will inevitably end in failure. Thus, even when Moore is presenting his own proof, that presentation is, in the vocabulary of Scott Soames (2003a: 23), 'ironic': Moore is really calling attention to the relative weakness of the skeptic's own premises compared to those which he himself employs. Whether or not this is ultimately correct as a matter of textual exegesis, I believe that much of Moore's influence on contemporary philosophy consists in the belief that he succeeded in providing an effective recipe for playing defense against the skeptic. (Notice, for example, that in each of the passages from Lewis, Armstrong, and Fine quoted above, the focus is on the alleged impotence of the *skeptic's* argument.) Among contemporary expositors and defenders of Moore, this perspective is most well-developed by William Lycan (2001) and Soames (2003a). Although I criticize both Lycan and Soames below, the general approach adopted here is most akin to theirs.

II. Predictions and Policies

The skeptic presents us with an argument for a conclusion radically at odds with common sense. How should we respond? Best of all, of course, would be to identify some false premise or fallacious step in the argument. But suppose that we find that we can do neither. What then? As we have seen, Fine suggests that, in such circumstances, we should conclude that *something* must be wrong with the skeptic's argument and simply retain our original beliefs. But how can a stubborn refusal to be moved by an argument for which one can admittedly find no flaw be anything other than dogmatic?

Perhaps the picture is something like this. In any case in which one scrutinizes an argument and fails to find any flaw in that argument, there are two competing potential explanations of one's failure. First, one's failure might be due to the flawlessness of the argument. Alternatively, it might be that the argument is in fact flawed, and one's failure is due to one's own cognitive limitations. (If one were better informed, one would recognize one of the premises as false; if one were more sophisticated or insightful, one would detect some subtle fallacy.) In deciding how to respond to any argument which appears to be flawless, one is thus in the position of performing an inference to the best explanation, where the *explanandum* is one's inability to identify any flaw despite having attempted to do so. If the better explanation of this fact is the flawlessness of the argument, then one should come to believe its conclusion and revise one's other beliefs accordingly. If, on the other hand, the better explanation of one's failure is one's own cognitive limitations, then one should remain unmoved in the face of the argument. We can view the Moorean as someone who holds that, for arguments aimed at overturning Moorean facts, 'hidden flaw' explanations will inevitably trump 'no flaw' explanations.

Notice that, if this is dogmatism, there is a respect in which it is an unusually modest variety. For when one reasons in this way, one's refusal to change one's beliefs is due to the weight that one gives to one's own cognitive limitations. In marked contrast, the skeptic will insist that one treat the fact that his argument *seems* or *appears* to be flawless as a reliable indication that it *is* flawless. Here—but not elsewhere—the skeptic will insist that one treat appearances as a reliable guide to reality.

Still, this does nothing to answer the question of why Moorean facts might have the relevant status. I'll consider some answers to this question in the next section. But first, I want to further explore some related Moorean themes.

Recall Lewis' informal gloss of a Moorean fact as 'one of those things that we know better than we know the premises of any philosophical argument to the contrary'. This gloss admits of weaker and stronger readings. A relatively weak reading is the following: a Moorean fact is one of those things that we know better than we know the premises of any philosophical argument to the contrary *which has yet been offered*. On this reading, to declare that F is a Moorean fact is to declare that none of the known philosophical arguments for not-F is rationally compelling. It is to say nothing about the possibility, or even the likelihood, that there is some compelling argument which we have yet to encounter. (One might, after all, hold that while as a matter of fact none of the known arguments for not-F is strong enough to undermine one's belief that F is true, this situation might very well change with the publication of the next volume of *The Philosophical Review* or *Noûs*.)

The claim that some fact is Moorean in this weak sense is not a trivial one. There are, after all, some who suspect that we *do* presently possess arguments that are sufficiently strong to undermine our confidence even in those beliefs that we ordinarily take to be among the most certain. Nevertheless, I think that to adopt this interpretation would be to seriously underestimate what those who appeal to Moorean facts often have in mind. When Armstrong declares

> ... certainly, Zeno should not persuade us that things do not move. Neither should anybody else

I don't think that he is plausibly interpreted as *noncommittal* on the question of what the next volume of *The Philosophical Review* might bring, or what our epistemic position with respect to the proposition that *Things move* will be after we've fully absorbed its contents.

One who declares that F is a Moorean fact is not simply making a claim about the relationship between F and those arguments for not-F that have been offered thus far, I think. Rather, he or she is also making a claim about the relationship between F and all of those arguments for not-F that might be offered in the future. But what, exactly, is the relevant relationship? In declaring something a Moorean fact, what is one doing?

Here there are at least two possibilities worth considering:

(i) *To declare something a Moorean fact is to make a prediction.* In particular, to declare that F is a Moorean fact is to claim not only that none of the presently known arguments suffices to rationally undermine one's belief that F is true, but that we will not encounter such an argument in the future, either.

Perhaps one simply takes the epistemic standing of a particular proposition to be such as to license the relevant prediction straightaway. On the other hand, the prediction might also be construed as the conclusion of an inductive inference. Consider the claim that *We know a lot.* For thousands of years, philosophers have been offering skeptical arguments for the denial of this claim. Suppose that one judges that even the most formidable of these arguments is insufficient to undermine one's belief that *We know a lot.* Given such an estimation of the relevant inductive base, one might naturally infer that we will not encounter a sufficiently strong argument in the future, either.

Alternatively, it might be that

(ii) *To declare something a Moorean fact is to endorse a policy.* In particular, to declare that F is a Moorean fact is to endorse the following policy for evaluating arguments: any argument that has as its conclusion not-F should be judged a bad argument.

In general, one's judgement as to the probative force of a given argument is not independent of one's judgement as to the credibility of its conclusion. As we've noted, if one takes oneself to have strong reasons to believe that F is true, then one will take oneself to have strong reasons to believe that a given argument for not-F is a flawed argument, even if one finds oneself unable to identify any particular flaw that the argument contains. Given this, adoption of the following policy might seem the most reasonable course: one should conclude that any argument which has as its conclusion the denial of a Moorean fact is a flawed argument. In effect, one who adopts such a policy resolves to treat the fact that an argument has the denial of a Moorean fact as its conclusion as a *reductio ad absurdum* of (the conjunction of) that argument's premises.

Are those who appeal to Moorean facts in the context of philosophical argument better understood as making a prediction or as endorsing a policy? I believe that they are best understood as doing both. On the one hand, they are endorsing a policy of evaluating skeptical arguments negatively. On the other hand, their willingness to endorse this particular policy is presumably not independent of their confident belief that we will never encounter a skeptical argument that is sufficiently strong to make it reasonable to believe its conclusion. That such individuals mean to be endorsing a policy is seen, I believe, in the contexts in which appeals to Moorean facts are typically made. The relevant contexts are ones in which methodological advice is on offer: what is up for discussion is the proper way to respond to skeptical arguments, what one could and could not learn from skepticism, and so on.[7] On the other hand, it is not as though one's willingness to endorse such a policy is independent of one's willingness to predict that we will not encounter a compelling skeptical argument in the future. For of course, the goodness of the policy would seem to depend directly on the accuracy of the prediction: if it's in fact the case that we will never encounter a compelling skeptical argument, then consistently adhering to a policy of negatively evaluating skeptical arguments will invariably lead one to classify such arguments correctly.

Still, even if one is completely convinced that we will never encounter a compelling skeptical argument, it is not obvious why one would want to endorse any general policy at all. Why not judge each argument by the content of its character, rather than engaging in what would seem to be a kind of invidious group discrimination? After all, some skeptical arguments are more formidable than others: this much is not in dispute. (Presumably, even those who think that no skeptical argument is or could be compelling will admit that some skeptical arguments are *transparently bad* in a way that others are not.) Given this, why would one think it a good idea to have some general policy for classifying arguments that might have nothing in common other than their conclusion (e.g. 'We don't know a lot')?

Here is a *possible* reason why one might think that it is a good idea (I make no claim that this consideration is in fact what drives those who appeal to Moorean facts.): one thinks that one is more likely to make mistakes in particular cases if one judges each individual without recourse to a general policy. For example, it's sometimes suggested that a central intrapersonal function of adopting general policies is the role that doing so plays in enabling us to overcome particularly tempting mistakes (Ainslie 1975, 1986; Nozick 1993: 17–18). One's considered, reflective judgement is that it is best to do A1 when in circumstances C; however, one knows that when one is actually in circumstances C, one will be strongly tempted to do A2 instead. One thus decides to adopt a general policy of always doing A1 when in circumstances C, and one's explicit adoption of this policy makes it easier to resist the temptation to do A2 rather than A1 when one later finds oneself in circumstances C. The adoption of a policy by one who will resolutely adhere to the policy which she has adopted thus involves a certain trade-off. On the one hand, one formulates the policy without the benefit of relevant information that might become available later. On the other hand, one has a certain psychological bulwark against local temptations that ought to be ignored. Applied to the present case, the analysis yields the following result. One confidently believes that it will never be rational to abandon one's belief that *We know a lot* on the basis of a skeptical argument. However, one knows that skeptics are a crafty lot and capable of great ingenuity in the service of their cause: the skeptic will labor to construct transparently valid arguments whose premises seem intuitively beyond reproach. Faced with such a skeptical argument, and finding oneself unable to identify any particular flaw which it contains, one might be strongly tempted to conclude—incorrectly, by one's present lights—that we don't know a lot after all. By adopting a general policy of evaluating skeptical arguments negatively, one fortifies oneself against the possibility of being taken in by the skeptic. By adopting such a policy, one helps to remind oneself that, even in these circumstances, one has (what one now takes to be) a decisive reason for rejecting such an argument: its conclusion.

On this way of understanding things, the prediction is prior to the policy. One confidently predicts that one will never encounter a compelling skeptical argument; because of this, one thinks that, if one did change one's mind in response to a skeptical argument in the future, one would surely be making a mistake in doing so. One thus adopts the policy as an attempt to avoid making such a mistake.[8]

But there is, I think, an alternative way of understanding things that better captures the intent of the Moorean. On this alternative, it is the policy which is prior to the prediction. That is, the Moorean thinks that if we possess a sufficiently rich understanding of what are in fact the correct norms of belief revision, we will see that these norms effectively guarantee that it would never be reasonable to abandon one's belief in a Moorean fact in response to a skeptical argument. Thus, the relevant prediction is not some potentially precarious prediction to the effect that, say, we will never encounter a sufficiently ingenious skeptic in the future. It is, rather, a trivial consequence of the correct application of the norms of belief revision that we ought to employ.

Consider an analogy drawn from the philosophy of mathematics. In the heyday of conventionalist accounts of the *a priori*, a staple of conventionalist manifestos was the claim that we will never make any observations which will falsify (or even disconfirm) a proposition of arithmetic or geometry.[9] In the mouth of the conventionalist, of course, this claim was not some potentially precarious prediction about the future course of natural science or about the contents of the experiences that human beings will in fact undergo in the future. Rather, the conventionalist is impressed with what is, arguably, an important aspect of our mathematical practice: our adhering to a general policy of refusing to treat empirical considerations as *the kind of thing* which might count as evidence against a select class of propositions. For the conventionalist, the knowledge that no future experimental outcome will disconfirm a proposition of arithmetic is readily available to anyone with an adequate grasp of the relevant bits of epistemology. We should, I think, view the Moorean in a parallel way: as one who thinks that, according to what are in fact the correct norms of belief revision, philosophical considerations are simply not the kind of thing which could undermine another select class of propositions, 'the Moorean facts'. That we will never encounter a compelling skeptical argument is a piece of knowledge that is readily available to anyone with a sufficiently rich understanding of those norms.

But what would the norms of belief revision have to be like, in order for this picture to be correct? I turn to this question next.

III. Some Norms of Belief Revision

Suppose that I believe that F is true. Attempting to convince me otherwise, you offer a philosophical argument for the contrary conclusion. I remain unmoved. You invite me to point out some false premise or fallacious step in your argument. I decline the invitation. I assure you that there must, of course, be *something* wrong with your argument, but I insist that it is not a condition of my knowing this that I am able to identify some specific flaw. Determined, you signal your intention to offer further arguments for the same conclusion. I advise you not to bother. For F is a *Moorean fact*, and thus, the rationality of my continuing to believe F is simply not susceptible to being undermined by your arguments. Infuriated, you accuse me of dogmatism. I deny the charge—at least, if the charge of dogmatism carries with it the suggestion that the dogmatist is being unreasonable. Indeed, far from being unreasonable, I respond, my unwillingness to abandon my belief in the face of your arguments is the *uniquely* reasonable response in the circumstances.[10]

In carrying on in this way, I might have either one of two pictures in mind. First, I might think that it is simply a fundamental epistemic norm that

> MOORE One should never abandon one's belief in a Moorean fact on the basis of a philosophical argument.

One way of thinking about Moorean facts then, would be this: Moorean facts make up a class of special, privileged propositions, and it is simply a fundamental norm of belief revision that one should never stop believing a member of this class in response to a philosophical argument.

This approach involves reifying the notion of a Moorean fact in a particularly strong way. Moorean facts make up a category of epistemically special entities, things to which the normal rules do not apply. Of course, much of the history of epistemology involves such reification: Cartesian foundations, empiricist sense data reports, Kantian synthetic *a priori* principles, Carnapian linguistic rules and Wittgenstinian hinge propositions were all thought of as in some respect standing outside the rules that apply to more mundane propositions. According to this way of thinking about Moorean facts, Moorean facts are simply among the more recent additions to the epistemologist's bestiary.[11]

Perhaps some have thought of Moorean facts in this way, or along similar lines.[12] But there is an alternative—and, I think, preferable—way to attempt to make sense of the notion of a Moorean fact. On this way of thinking about Moorean facts, MOORE is not itself a fundamental norm. While it's true that one should never abandon one's belief in a Moorean fact in response to a philosophical argument, the fact that one should never do so falls out of higher-level, more fundamental norms. Again, Lewis writes of Moorean facts as things that we 'know better' than the skeptic's premises. Consider then the following norm of belief revision:

KNOWN BETTER One should never abandon a belief in response to an argument when that belief is known better than (at least one of) the premises of the argument.

The present picture then, is one according to which propositions can be ranked along some relevant dimension (perhaps: 'the known better' dimension). It is the position of a proposition along this dimension that determines which other propositions might in principle be employed to rationally undermine one's belief that it is true. A Moorean fact simply falls so far along the relevant dimension that there is simply no place to stand from which one might hope to dislodge it.

On this picture, it is not that Moorean facts differ in kind from more mundane propositions and inherit their relative immunity by dint of possessing some special property or feature which they and they alone possess. Rather, their relative immunity is a *de facto* matter, and consists in their scoring highest along that dimension—whatever it is—which determines the relative vulnerability of *any* proposition.[13]

In what follows, I'll proceed on the assumption that this is in fact the correct way to think about Moorean facts: the framework is adopted as a working hypothesis, in the hope that proceeding in this way might shed light not only the notion of a Moorean fact but also on the relevant norms of belief revision themselves. The immediate task will be to figure out exactly what the relevant dimension might be.

Why not simply settle for KNOWN BETTER? My own primary reason for dissatisfaction with this norm is not so much a conviction that it is false but rather that it is extremely obscure. What is it, exactly, for one proposition to be 'known better' than another? One difficulty, perhaps, is that the locution 'known better' or 'better known' strongly suggests knowledge by acquaintance rather than propositional knowledge. That is, the 'known better' locution seems difficult to disentangle from its strong associations with the idea of *greater familiarity*—which, presumably, is not what is at issue here. We should, I think, insist upon a less enigmatic formulation of the relevant norm.

A more popular candidate for the relevant dimension is *plausibility*. As we've seen, Fine holds that it is the plausibility of our ordinary beliefs that justifies us in supposing that skeptical arguments must be flawed. Plausibility also seems to be the central notion for Lycan (2001). Consider then, the following norm:

> MORE PLAUSIBLE: One should never abandon a belief in response to an argument when the proposition believed is more plausible than (at least one of) the premises of the argument.

One immediate attraction of MORE PLAUSIBLE for the Moorean is the following: the sorts of common sense propositions which are his stock in trade really do seem more plausible than the kinds of principles that are typically employed by the skeptic in attempting to cast doubt on them. I take this point to have been successfully established by Lycan, who drives it home with great gusto. Given this fact about comparative plausibility, the truth of MORE PLAUSIBLE would seem to deliver a quick vindication of the Moorean response to skepticism.

Unfortunately for the Moorean, MORE PLAUSIBLE is false—at least, it's false if we understand 'plausibility' in its literal sense. For strictly speaking, the plausibility of a proposition concerns, not its all-things-considered worthiness of belief, but rather its *apparent* or *seeming* worthiness of belief, or its worthiness of belief upon preliminary examination. Roughly: a proposition is plausible to the extent that it seems to be true to one who considers it. However, as Earl Conee has noted (2001: 57), plausibility in this sense is not a good candidate for being that which determines normative facts about what one ought to believe all things considered. Indeed, a given proposition's being extremely plausible is consistent with its being known to be false: Frege's Unrestricted Comprehension Principle does not cease to be plausible when one learns of its falsity. Given that plausibility is consistent with known falsity, it's clear that comparative plausibility is not the correct guide to belief revision. Thus, MORE PLAUSIBLE is itself an example of a plausible principle that turns out to be false.[14]

Perhaps the most popular candidate for the relevant dimension among Mooreans has been that of *certainty*. Moore himself employed the vocabulary of certainty throughout his corpus, and others have followed him in this. The following is a characteristic passage from Moore:

> Russell's view that I do not know that this is a pencil or that you are conscious rests, if I am right, on no less than four distinct assumptions ... And what I can't help asking myself is this: Is it, in fact, as certain that all these four assumptions are true, as that I do know that this is a pencil and that you are conscious? I cannot help answering: It seems to me *more* certain that I *do* know that this is a pencil and that you are conscious, than that any single one of these four assumptions is true, let alone all four ... of no one of these ... do I feel as

> certain as that I do know for certain that this is a pencil (2000: 29, all emphases his).

Compare Armstrong on 'the less certain' and 'the more certain':

> It is the bedrock of our beliefs that G.E. Moore defended in his vindication of common sense ... One of the problems involved in casting doubt upon such beliefs is that the doubt-casting arguments require premises, but it is not easy to see where the premises can be collected. To use premises which are not drawn from the bed-rock of our beliefs is to bring the less certain as a reason for doubting the more certain (1983: 53–54).

Consider then the following norm:

> MORE CERTAIN: One should never abandon a belief in response to an argument when one is more certain of that belief than one is of (at least one of) the premises of the argument.

How should we understand MORE CERTAIN? It is a familiar fact that talk of 'certainty' is often ambiguous. On the one hand, 'certainty' might mean *psychological certainty* or confidence. In this sense of certainty, to say that one is more certain of p than of q is to say that one is *more confident* that p is true than that q is true. It is thus to report on one's present psychological state. Alternatively, 'certainty' might mean *evidential certainty*. The notion of evidential certainty concerns, not one's actual level of confidence that some proposition is true, but rather the level of confidence that it is rational for one to have that the proposition is true given one's epistemic situation. This is the sense of certainty which is in play in statements such as 'Given what we know now, it is certain that there is no intelligent life at the center of the sun'. When used in this way, certainty concerns what it is *reasonable to believe* given the evidence and arguments with which one is acquainted.[15]

Some Mooreans suggest that it is psychological certainty which is the key notion. The idea that it is psychological certainty or confidence which is crucial seems to be the view of Pollock and Cruz:

> If we reflect upon our beliefs, we will find that we are more confident of some than of others. It is reasonable to place more reliance on those beliefs in which we have greater confidence, and when beliefs come in conflict we decide which to reject by considering which we are least certain of ... In typical skeptical arguments, we invariably find that we are more certain of the knowledge seemingly denied us than we are of some of the premises. Thus it is not reasonable to adopt the skeptical conclusion that we do not have that knowledge. The rational stance is instead to deny one or more of the premises (1999: 6–7).

Moore himself is sometimes interpreted as having held that what is crucial are psychological facts about how confident one is that various propositions are true. Consider, for example, the interpretation offered by Soames:

> As Moore saw it, conflicts between speculative philosophical principles and the most basic convictions of common sense confront one with a choice. In any such case, one must give up either one's common sense convictions or the speculative philosophical principle. Of course, one ought to give up whichever one has the least confidence in. But how, Moore wondered, could anyone have more confidence in the truth of a general philosophical principle than one has in the truth of one's most fundamental convictions—convictions such as one's belief that there are many different objects, and many different people, that exist independently of oneself? In the end, Moore came to think that one's confidence in a general principle of philosophy never could outweigh one's confidence in convictions such as these ... As a result philosophers have nothing that could be used to undermine the most central and fundamental parts of what we take ourselves to know (2003a: 8–9).

Here is a seemingly straightforward model of how we should resolve conflicts among our beliefs. Moreover, if this model is correct, it would seem to constitute a quick vindication of the Moorean response to skepticism. Consider then the following norm of belief revision:

> MORE CONFIDENT In resolving conflicts among one's beliefs, one should always favor those beliefs of which one is more confident over those beliefs of which one is less confident.

The suggestion that, in revising one's beliefs, one should resolve conflicts in favor of those beliefs of which one is more confident has an undeniable ring of plausibility to it. Indeed, the suggestion that one should favor those beliefs of which one is more confident might seem to be simply common sense. (Might one claim that this suggestion is itself a Moorean fact?) What, after all, is the alternative—favoring those beliefs of which one is *less* confident? Moreover, the idea that the Moorean facts are just those propositions in which we invest the greatest confidence is itself a plausible view about what ultimately distinguishes Moorean facts from other propositions. Finally, as we've just noted, MORE CONFIDENT is explicitly embraced by some Mooreans and is attributed to Moore himself by Soames. For these reasons, I want to consider it at some length.

Despite its plausibility, I don't believe that MORE CONFIDENT withstands scrutiny. In what follows, I'll consider what I take to be the two most natural ways of understanding this norm and argue that, on neither interpretation is it a good candidate for being the norm that we seek.

First, let's try to bring MORE CONFIDENT into sharper focus. As Pollock and Cruz emphasize, we are more confident of some of our beliefs than of others. Imagine an ordered list of all of those propositions that you believe at the present moment, time t0. The position of a given proposition on the list is determined by how confident you are that that proposition is true: the more confident you are of its truth, the higher its position on the list. Call this The List of Things You Believe. At time t1, an instant later, the skeptic will present you with an argument that you have never seen before. Of course, a formidable skeptic will choose his premises with great care—unless the skeptic finds premises that you believe—or at least, are strongly inclined to believe—he has no hope of dialectical effectiveness. Imagine that the best case scenario for the skeptic is realized: at time t1, the skeptic succeeds in producing an argument that is transparently valid, and the premises of which all appear on The List of Things You Believe. Of course, the negation of the skeptic's conclusion (e.g., 'We know a lot') will also be on the List. The skeptic has thus succeeded in at least this much: he has succeeded in identifying a genuine conflict among your beliefs. The List of Things You Believe is inconsistent. Question: How should you resolve this conflict? Here is a possible decision procedure for doing so. Locate the position of the proposition that is under attack by the skeptic on the List, and compare its position to the position of each of the skeptic's premises. Resolve the conflict by eliminating whichever proposition was lowest on the List at t0 from the new List of Things You Believe at time t1.

Notice that, if this decision procedure is in fact the one which we should employ, then, given that the Moorean facts are just the highest propositions on the List at time t0, it seems as though the Moorean will inevitably win against the skeptic. For at time t0, the Moorean will be able to reason as follows: 'No matter what happens at t1, I know now that, even if I'm forced to employ the decision procedure then, it will tell me to retain my belief in the Moorean fact and abandon my belief in one of the skeptic's premises'.

Consider then the following interpretation of MORE CONFIDENT:

MORE CONFIDENT (1): In resolving conflicts among one's beliefs, one should abandon one's belief in whichever proposition one was least confident of immediately prior to becoming aware of the conflict.

Unfortunately for the Moorean, the decision procedure in question is not correct. In order to appreciate its inadequacy, consider first the following point: it might very well be that the fact that a given proposition occupies a high position on the List of Things that You Believe at time t0 depends in part on your assuming that *there are no formidable arguments to be made against that proposition*. Indeed, I suspect that this is the usual case with respect to propositions of which we are extremely confident. Typically, when I am extremely confident that something is true, I also think that, if someone were to argue that it is *not* in fact true, he or she wouldn't get very far. For example, I am extremely confident that the next President of the United States will be either a

Democrat or a Republican. My confidence that this is so is by no means independent of my belief that if someone were to argue that this is not the case ('No, it won't be a Democrat or a Republican, a third party candidate will win') the case that he or she would be able to offer would be extremely weak. Contrast some belief that I hold with considerably greater diffidence: for example, my belief that capital punishment as presently practiced in the United States does not have a deterrent effect on crime. My relative diffidence here is not at all unrelated to my belief that, if someone were to argue for the opposite conclusion, he or she could adduce some formidable reasons in support of that view.[16] The general moral: how confident one is that something is true is not independent of one's expectations about the quality of the case that might be made against it. This fact might seem obvious. But it's enough, I think, to undermine the decision procedure on offer.

For suppose that my being extremely confident that p is true at the earlier time t0 depends on my (perhaps tacit) assumption that there are no formidable arguments for not-p. Suppose further that at time t1, I discover first-hand that this assumption is false: someone presents me with a formidable argument for not-p. The argument in question is transparently valid and each of its premises appears on the List of Things That I Believe. Perhaps one of its premises falls below p on the List. Does it follow from this that I should retain my belief that p in these circumstances? It does not follow. For the superior position of p on the original List depended in part on an assumption that I *now know* to be false: viz., that there are no formidable arguments for not-p. When I'm subsequently presented with a formidable argument for not-p, I in effect come into possession of a new piece of relevant information, viz. that there *is* such an argument. To rely solely on how confident I was that various propositions are true before I came into possession of this new piece of relevant information would be in effect to neglect part of what is now my total evidence.[17]

Of course, in response to this kind of objection, someone might offer a somewhat different model of how to resolve conflicts in one's beliefs, a model on which confidence remains the central notion. In particular, someone might propose the following: 'Look, what matters isn't how confident you *were* that various things are true back at t0, prior to being presented with the skeptic's argument. Rather, what matters is how confident you *are* at time t1, once you have seen the argument, or (better yet) at some later time t2, after you have had an opportunity to thoroughly scrutinize and digest the argument. That is, what matters is how confident you are that the relevant propositions are true *after the dust has settled*.'

Consider then

MORE CONFIDENT (2): In resolving conflicts among one's beliefs, one should abandon one's belief in whichever proposition one is least confident of once one becomes aware of the conflict.

However, unlike the previously considered interpretation of MORE CONFIDENT, the view on offer simply could not be a general recipe or decision procedure for resolving conflicts among one's beliefs. For consider again my situation, immediately after a newly-encountered argument has called my attention to an inconsistency among my beliefs. Suppose that I'm in the process of actively *deliberating* about how to resolve this inconsistency; that is, suppose that I have not yet made up my mind which of the conflicting beliefs I will abandon and which I will retain. In these circumstances, the recommendation of the previously-considered norm—'Abandon whichever belief you were least confident of, *prior* to being presented with the argument'—is at least applicable advice (although for the reasons provided above, it is not, I think, the correct view). In contrast, the present recommendation—'Abandon whichever belief you are least confident of now that you have seen the argument'—is simply not advice that is applicable in these circumstances. For, *ex hypothesi*, what I am in the process of deciding is exactly how confident I will be that the various propositions are true, now that I have seen the argument. In these circumstances, one simply cannot appeal to how confident one will be after the dust settles, for what is at issue in one's deliberations is precisely how the dust *ought* to settle.

In deliberating as to how I should resolve a newly-discovered inconsistency among my beliefs, what, exactly, am I attempting to figure out? Simply this: which of the beliefs it is more reasonable for me to retain, given the totality of relevant evidence and arguments to which I have been exposed—including the argument with which I have just been presented. That is, the true norm here, I think, is simply this:

*MORE REASONABLE In resolving conflicts among one's beliefs, one should always favor those beliefs that it is more reasonable for one to think are true given the totality of evidence and arguments to which one has been exposed.

Indeed, I suspect that *this* norm is close to trivial. Thus, the sense of 'certainty' in which it's true that we should favor beliefs that are 'more certain' over those that are 'less certain' is evidential certainty, not psychological certainty. We can view potentially more informative norms such as MORE CONFIDENT as attempts to specify *what makes it the case* that it is more reasonable to retain some beliefs rather than others in cases of conflict. However, if the arguments provided above are sound, none of the other norms that we have canvassed is even extensionally equivalent to MORE REASONABLE in its recommendations. What's the significance of this?

If I'm correct in thinking that MORE REASONABLE is the operative norm, and that this norm is not equivalent to norms such as MORE CONFIDENT or MORE PLAUSIBLE, then this is, I think, a disappointing result for the Moorean. For even if the Moorean is correct in thinking that MORE REASONABLE will in fact always favor Moorean facts over skeptical premises, it seems hopeless to *show* that this is so, or to *explain why* this is so, by appeal to MORE REASONABLE itself. Here a contrast with the discarded norm MORE CONFIDENT is instructive. On the picture suggested by MORE CONFIDENT, normative facts about how one ought to revise one's beliefs in cases of conflict are in effect constituted or determined by psychological facts about how confident one is that the propositions in question are true. Thus, if MORE CONFIDENT were true, the Moorean would have a potentially satisfying answer to the question of why, as a general rule, one should retain one's belief in a Moorean fact when it conflicts with a skeptical principle. Namely: one should retain one's belief in the Moorean fact because one is more confident that it is true than than that the skeptic's premises are true, and these are the facts which determine how one ought to respond to the conflict. This, at least, has the form of an acceptable answer to what is the most pressing question for the Moorean. In contrast, the attempt to answer the same question by appealing in a parallel way to MORE REASONABLE would yield the following: 'One should always retain one's belief in a Moorean fact rather than the skeptic's premises because this is what it is more reasonable to do'. But this, of course, is a mere restatement of the Moorean thesis.

No doubt, the Moorean is convinced that the norm MORE REASONABLE will always favor retaining our common sense beliefs when correctly applied, and that, when push comes to shove, this norm will dictate abandoning the philosophical principles on which the skeptic relies. But again: why should that be? In the last section, I want to sketch what I take to be the Moorean's most promising answer to this question.

IV. Moore and Metaphilosophy

Let's briefly recapitulate. In section 2, I suggested that we should view the Moorean as someone who both (i) confidently predicts that we will never encounter a compelling skeptical argument and (ii) endorses a policy of concluding that any particular skeptical argument must be flawed in some way (even if we are unable to identify the flaw). I also suggested that, for the Moorean, the endorsement of the policy is more fundamental than the prediction: *that* it will never be reasonable to abandon one's belief in a Moorean fact is in effect guaranteed by a correct application of what are in fact the true norms of belief revision. In section 3, I distinguished two different ways of understanding this suggestion. According to the first way, Moorean facts differ in kind from other propositions, and it is simply a fundamental epistemic norm that one should never abandon one's belief in a Moorean fact. According to the second way, while it's true that one should never abandon one's belief in a Moorean fact, this is not itself a fundamental epistemic norm; rather, this fact falls out of more fundamental norms that do not themselves make mention of Moorean facts but rather govern how one ought to revise one's beliefs more generally. I suggested that this latter way of thinking about Moorean facts is preferable. I thus canvassed a number of proposed norms of belief revision that looked initially promising for the Moorean. I provided reasons for doubting that any of these norms was correct. I ultimately endorsed the relatively trivial norm MORE REASONABLE but suggested that, in part because of its triviality, it seems not to advance the Moorean's cause. Given that MORE REASONABLE is in fact the correct norm for resolving conflicts among one's beliefs, the Moorean still needs to supply some reason for thinking that it will be more reasonable to retain our common sense beliefs when these turn out to be inconsistent with the skeptic's premises. How might the Moorean do this?

A recurrent theme among interpreters sympathetic to Moore is that his deepest point against the skeptic is a metaphilosophical one. According to this line of thought, the skeptic is ultimately undermined by a correct appreciation of philosophical method. This understanding of Moore has been embraced by interpreters both early and late. Thus, Malcolm (1942) famously interpreted Moore as offering paradigm case arguments on behalf of common sense. According to Malcolm, the reason why it would be unreasonable to adopt the skeptic's claims is that those claims 'go against ordinary language' (349) and this suffices to guarantee their falsity. However, the paradigm case argument is rightly discredited, and Moore declined to endorse Malcolm's interpretation when explicitly offered the chance to do so (Moore 1942).[18]

More recently, Soames has also suggested that Moore should be understood as making a point about philosophical method. According to Soames

> [Moore's] position regarding the propositions of common sense is that they constitute the starting point for philosophy, and, as such, are not the sorts of claims that can be overturned by philosophical argument (2003a p.5).[19]

However, it is at the very least unclear why something's being among the starting points for philosophy would render it as such immune to being subsequently overturned on the basis of philosophical argument. Perhaps on some substantive views of what makes something a proper starting point for philosophy, anything which qualifies as such will in fact enjoy the relevant kind of immunity. Thus, perhaps on a broadly Cartesian view of philosophical inquiry, the qualifications for being a proper starting point are sufficiently demanding that anything which satisfies them is *ipso facto* not susceptible to being subsequently overturned. At the other end of the spectrum, Harman (1999), following Quine, insists that the proper starting point for philosophy is simply everything that one presently believes. On such a view, the suggestion that the starting points for philosophy cannot be overturned by philosophical argument is equivalent to the suggestion that philosophical argument is powerless to overturn *any* of our pre-philosophical beliefs, no matter how tenuous or tentatively-held—a conclusion that is surely too strong. In general, to take something as a philosophical starting point is not to hold that it as such immune to being overturned by subsequent philosophical argument—any more than to take something as a starting point for inquiry more generally is to hold that it cannot be given up at some later stage of inquiry.

Nevertheless, I believe that the view that Moore's deepest point against the skeptic is a metaphilosophical one is correct. Why can't the skeptic win? The Moorean's best answer to this question, I think, runs as follows: the skeptic cannot win because the skeptic is implicitly committed to a methodology for philosophical theorizing that does not withstand scrutiny once it is forced out into the open.

In order to see why this might be so, let's begin by considering one last interpretation of Moore, an interpretation on which metaphilosophical considerations remain central: Moore as *particularist*. This interpretation is offered by Roderick Chisholm in his classic discussion of 'the Problem of the Criterion' (Chisholm 1973). There, Chisholm distinguishes between two different ways in which one might theorize about knowledge: as a particularist or as a methodist. Roughly, the particularist takes as data our considered judgements about whether knowledge is present or absent in particular cases (e.g., 'I know that I have hands', 'I know that my name is Thomas Kelly', 'George Bush knows that he is a Republican', 'I do not know the identity of the next President of the United States'). He then uses these judgements about particular cases to evaluate proposed general principles about knowledge. When a general principle conflicts with a considered judgement about a particular case—say, it suggests that I *do* know the identity of the next President of the United States or that I do *not* know that my name is Thomas Kelly—then this counts as at least some evidence against the principle. On the other hand, to the extent that the general principle accommodates our judgements about cases, this counts in its favor. Thus, for the particularist, the tenability of a general principle is ultimately determined by how well it accommodates our judgements about cases. One philosophical theory is better supported than another when it does a superior job overall of accommodating such judgements. For Chisholm, Moore is the example *par excellence* of a particularist.

In contrast to the particularist, the methodist begins with a commitment to some general philosophical principle or principles about the nature of knowledge and utilizes these principles to arrive at judgements about whether knowledge is present or absent in particular cases. Chisholm's own example of a methodist is David Hume, who begins with a firm commitment to a general philosophical theory about human knowledge, viz. empiricism, and appeals to that theory again and again in drawing conclusions about whether human beings should be credited with this or that bit of putative knowledge. For Hume, our pre-theoretical judgements about whether knowledge is present or absent in this or that particular case should be retained if and only if the judgements in question match those returned by a consistent and rigorous application of empiricism.

Strictly speaking, particularism is not inconsistent with radical forms of skepticism (Cf. Lemos 2004:110). Indeed, at least one prominent argument for radical skepticism takes as its starting point an intuitive judgement about a particular case.[20] However, as Chisholm emphasizes, it seems clear that the skeptic will find the methodology of methodism more congenial than that of particularism. For if one evaluates general principles about knowledge by reference to how well they fit with one's pre-theoretic judgements about whether knowledge is present in particular cases, then, given that at least a substantial number of such judgements are to the effect that knowledge *is* present, it seems as though the kinds of epistemic principles that would generate skeptical conclusions if true will be eliminated from consideration on this basis. To put the point in comparative terms: if the sole standard of evaluation for theories is how well they accommodate our judgements about particular cases, then surely the *best* theory will not overturn all (or almost all) of one's positive attributions of knowledge.

In contrast, suppose that one proceeds as a methodist. In that case, the purpose in seeing how a presently-accepted principle matches one's judgements about cases is to answer questions about which judgements about cases should be retained and which discarded. As a general rule, friction between judgements about principles and judgements about cases are resolved in favor of the former and at the expense of the latter. Given such a method, there seems to be nothing to preclude a rather sweeping revision of our judgements about cases. In short, methodism seems to leave the door open to skepticism—or more broadly, views that are radically revisionary with respect to our pre-theoretical judgements about particular cases—in a way that particularism does not. Indeed, I think that the point generalizes beyond epistemology and holds for philosophical revisionism in other domains as well.[21]

Chisholm ultimately embraces the particularist methodology that he finds in Moore. Should we follow him? In considering this question, the first thing that we should note is that the choice between particularism and methodism as described above is clearly not exhaustive. The particularist holds that our judgements about cases have priority over our judgements about principles; the methodist holds that our judgements about principles have priority over our judgements about cases. Once posed in these terms, it seems clear that there is a further alternative. For one might hold that neither type of judgement has such priority. Rather, our most fundamental judgements about cases and about principles should both receive substantial weight in our theorizing as we attempt to achieve a stable coherence among judgements at different levels through a process of mutual adjustment. This, in its barest essentials, is the method of *reflective equilibrium*, (Goodman 1953, Rawls 1972).

We have then three possible methods for theorizing about knowledge: particularism, methodism, and reflective equilibrium. Even this enriched picture of our options, however, is apt to make the range of possible methodologies appear more limited than it in fact is. For I've described an especially pure form of each of these views. Thus, as described above, the particularist is a theorist who gives literally no weight to the intuitive plausibility of general principles; for him, the sole determinant of the tenability of a general principle is how well it accords with our judgements about cases. On this view, if two incompatible principles matched our judgements about cases equally well, there would be nothing to choose between them, even if one of the two principles had a high degree of intuitive plausibility while the other was completely counterintuitive, hopelessly gerrymandered and *ad hoc*. This is *hyper-particularism*. Hyper-particularism is not an attractive view, and I doubt whether it can be charitably attributed to anyone. But surely there are methodologies worthy of the name 'particularism' other than hyper-particularism: methodologies which, while placing a special emphasis on preserving judgements about cases, also give some significant weight to other factors as well. In a similar way, we can distinguish between hyper-methodism—a view on which our judgements about cases are given zero or negligible weight—from more temperate, moderate versions.

Of course, the more weight a particularist is willing to give her judgements about principles in the course of her theorizing, the less her methodology will resemble hyper-particularism and the more it will begin to shade off into a version of reflective equilibrium. In a parallel way, the more weight a methodist is willing to give to his judgements about particular cases, the less his view will resemble hyper-methodism and the more it will begin to shade off into (another version of) reflective equilibrium. Undoubtedly, the boundaries in question are vague. The tripartite division between particularism, methodism, and reflective equilibrium encourages us to think of the relevant logical space as carved up into three discrete units. But we do better, perhaps, to think of a continuum of methodologies, ordered according to the relative weights that each would have us give to our judgements about cases on the one hand and our judgements about principles on the other.

Having noted this complication, let's return to the simple tripartite division between particularism, methodism, and reflective equilibrium. Above, I suggested that for the purposes of the skeptic, methodism seems to hold out more hope than particularism. How should we expect the skeptic to fare if we proceed according to the method of reflective equilibrium? Despite its considerable popularity, the method of reflective equilibrium is typically not described in much detail by either its proponents or its detractors: presently, we lack a well-worked out account. I will not attempt to rectify that state of affairs here. Nevertheless, even in the absence of such an account, we have good reason to think that the skeptic is unlikely to fare well given this methodology. For the reflective equilibrium theorist resembles the particularist in that she too wants to give substantial weight to our judgements about cases in assessing which principles it is reasonable for us to accept. Again, given that the claims of the skeptic are ex hypothesi *radically* inconsistent with our judgments about cases, the reflective equilibrium theorist will join the particularist in taking this to constitute strong reason to reject the skeptic's principles. The skeptic advocates what is in effect a revolution in our thinking: the Cartesian skeptic, for example, advocates an abandonment of all of our positive attributions of knowledge of the external world. The reflective equilibrium theorist, however, will insist that many judgements from this targeted class should be given substantial weight in our deliberations about which philosophical principles to accept and which to reject. Because of this, the method of reflective equilibrium will militate against the kind of sweeping revisionism that the skeptic envisions. In this respect, the method of reflective equilibrium seems to be an inherently conservative one. Given this conservatism, the method would not seem to be a promising one for the skeptic.

Admittedly, in the absence of a well-worked out account of reflective equilibrium, the claim that it is an inherently conservative method takes on a certain speculative air. Moreover, given that I have not attempted to spell out in detail how *I* understand the method, one might naturally worry that my claim of conservativeness is based on presupposing some perhaps idiosyncratic conception that has been left off-stage. However, it's noteworthy that reflective equilibrium has often been taken to be a fundamentally conservative method by a wide range of both its advocates and its detractors. Thus, Goodman (1953) originally proposed the method of as a way of effectively 'dissolving' Humean skepticism about the deliverances of inductive reasoning. Stitch (1983, ch.4) takes the conservative character of reflective equilibrium as a reason to reject it. Particularly in the wake of Rawls' endorsement of the method in moral and political philosophy (1972), it was widely criticized on the grounds that it is overly conservative (See, e.g., Singer 1974, Copp 1985).[22] On the other hand, the alleged conservatism of reflective equilibrium was both acknowledged and claimed as a virtue by the philosopher who has been perhaps its most persistent and epistemologically sophisticated defender (Harman 1994, 2003, 2004).[23] My present purpose is not to side either with those who see the apparent conservatism of reflective equilibrium as a virtue or with those who see it as a vice. My point is rather that, unless each of these philosophers is rather fundamentally confused about how reflective equilibrium operates, then it is a conservative method. Again, inasmuch as the skeptic advocates what is in fact a genuinely revolutionary change in our thinking, reflective equilibrium would seem to be an unpromising methodology for his purposes.

Chisholm takes Moore's rejection of skepticism to follow directly from his commitment to a particularist methodology. (Indeed, the anti-skeptical promise of particularism seems to be one of the things that recommends it in Chisholm's eyes.) The question that I would like to press, however, is not which methodology best serves the interests of the anti-skeptic, but rather which methodological options are left open to the skeptic. For as we have seen, it is not only particularism which seems inimical to skepticism—the method of reflection equilibrium also seems to be a method on which it's difficult to see how the skeptic can gain the kind of traction requisite to effect the dramatic change in our views that he advocates.

The picture that the skeptic presupposes seems to be something like the following. There are certain philosophical principles that have radically revisionary implications. The intuitive plausibility of these principles renders them worthy of belief at the outset of inquiry. Moreover, this belief worthiness is indefeasible in the following sense: it survives the realization that the principles in question are inconsistent with large numbers of our most fundamental judgements about cases. The Moorean claims that it would be unreasonable to continue to accept a philosophical principle once it has been shown that this principle is inconsistent with the judgement that *Moore knows that he has hands*. The skeptic denies this; on his view, inconsistency with *Moore knows that he has hands* is insufficient to undermine the reasonableness of continued acceptance of a philosophical principle. Moreover, it's clear that the skeptic's reaction is not a matter of dissatisfaction with Moore's specific choice of example. The skeptic would be no more impressed if Moore had chosen as his example the proposition that *Lloyd George knows that he has hands*, or that *Moore knows that he has feet*. Rather, against the Moorean, the Cartesian skeptic will maintain the following: there are no judgements attributing knowledge of the external world inconsistency with which suffices to undermine the reasonableness of continuing to accept a philosophical principle. This, of course, is a relatively strong metaphilosophical claim. Indeed, for the skeptic to insist that we endorse this claim is in effect to insist that we embrace the methodology of hyper-methodism: the view that no significant weight should be given to one's considered judgements about particular cases in evaluating principles.

At this point, the dispute between the skeptic and the Moorean seems to have devolved into a dispute about which methodology is in fact correct. How might *this* dispute be resolved? Chisholm held that, in the end, the choice between particularism and methodism could only be made by begging the question (1973: 37). Perhaps that's so. However, in the present context, the following seems to me to be a fairly telling point in favor of the Moorean: the methodology which the skeptic advocates seems utterly at variance with the methodology employed elsewhere in philosophy in the assessment of general principles.[24] Indeed, it is at variance with the generally accepted methodology for theorizing about knowledge when skepticism is not at issue. Thus, Gettier (1963) was famously taken to have refuted an extremely plausible general theory of knowledge by showing how that theory returned verdicts about particular cases that are inconsistent with our judgements about those cases. If hyper-methodism is the correct methodology, however, then this near[25] universal reaction to Gettier was simply a mistake. For if hyper-methodism is correct, then to abandon a highly plausible account of knowledge on the basis of its failure to return the intuitively correct verdict about a particular case is to give too much weight to one's judgements about cases in the assessment of principles. One who looks askance at the Moorean response to skepticism should, I think, take a similarly dim view of those who take Gettier to have shown that the traditional justified true belief account of knowledge is incorrect.

For the sake of further comparison, consider also the history of the logical positivists' attempts to formulate an acceptable version of the verifiability criterion of meaning. Successive principles were abandoned on the grounds that they classified what seemed to be clearly meaningful linguistic expressions as meaningless. Here again, inconsistency with judgements about cases was taken as a sufficient reason to abandon a general principle. Moreover, this was taken as a sufficient reason not only by those unsympathetic to the general picture of meaning in play but by the positivists themselves. Again, given a methodology of hyper-methodism, this reaction was simply a mistake.

Notice, moreover, that the positivists' willingness to abandon general principles on this basis does not mean that the positivists were particularists in Chisholm's sense. On the contrary, the positivists were prepared to be quite revisionary with respect to widely-held pre-theoretical judgements about the meaningfulness of various linguistic expressions. (Indeed, an appetite for such revisionism was a primary motivation for the development of the verifiability criterion of meaning in the first place.) Similarly, it would be unwarranted to think that all of those who took Gettier to have successfully refuted the traditional analysis of knowledge have thereby incurred a commitment to the substantive metaphilosophical view of particularism. One need not be a particularist in order to believe in counterexamples.

A traditional complaint against the skeptic is that he is guilty of importing artificially demanding standards for knowledge. According to this line of thought, the skeptic proceeds as though some condition C is necessary for knowledge (where C is a condition which human beings seldom if ever satisfy); however, in ordinary life, it is claimed, we confidently and unhesitatingly attribute knowledge even in cases in which it is clear that C is not satisfied.[26] I think that this charge is made with greater justice when it is leveled against some skeptics than when it is leveled against others. My own charge against the skeptic is a structurally-similar one, entered one level up: in insisting that we give so little weight to our judgements about cases in the evaluation of principles, the skeptic is guilty of importing artificially demanding standards for what it takes to undermine a general philosophical principle. That is, elsewhere in philosophy, we confidently and unhesitatingly take a general principle to have been adequately undermined by showing that it is inconsistent with sufficiently fundamental judgements about cases.

It is natural to interpret one who appeals to Moorean facts as a particularist. The Moorean is thus viewed as one who is committed to an extremely substantive metaphilosophical thesis. Indeed, some proceed as though showing the unsatisfactoriness of particularism would suffice to undermine the Moorean response to skepticism.[27] If the present line of thought is correct, however, then this considerably overstates the vulnerability of the Moorean. For to view the dialectic in this way is to overestimate the Moorean's methodological commitments while underestimating those of the skeptic. One who appeals to

Moorean facts does not thereby incur a commitment to particularism. Rather, the methodological commitment incurred is that there are some particular judgements inconsistency with which suffices to undermine the credibility of a general principle to the point that it is reasonable to reject that principle. And this idea is not the exclusive property of the particularist but might also be shared by methodologies that are incompatible with particularism, viz. reflective equilibrium and more moderate forms of methodism. On the contrary: it is not the Moorean but rather the skeptic who seems committed to an extremely strong metaphilosophical view, and an unattractive one at that. Indeed, on the present view of the dialectic, it is the skeptic who would seem to be guilty of the very charge that is often leveled at the Moorean: that he treats his favorite commitments as sacrosanct. For it is the skeptic who demands that we retain belief in his principles even after those principles have failed exactly the sorts of tests that are ordinarily taken to warrant rejection of general principles. In this respect, it is the skeptic, more than the Moorean, who seems to resemble the dogmatist.[28]

Notes

1. A note about the interpretation of Lewis is in order here. One who emphasizes this Moorean aspect of Lewis's thought (as I intend to do) might seem to slight other aspects of his thought which are more congenial to the skeptic. In particular, as is often noted, Lewis's own version of contextualism is in one crucial respect unusually concessive to the skeptic, inasmuch as it makes it a relatively trivial matter for the skeptic to establish extremely demanding standards for knowing in a given conversational context. The upshot of this for Lewis is that any minimally competent skeptic is more or less guaranteed to win any argument with a non-skeptic. Given this, isn't it misleading in the extreme for me to dwell on a few Moorean pronouncements?

   Considerable care is needed here, however. A primary motivation for Lewis's particular version of contextualism is his desire to reconcile infallibilism about knowledge with the truth of *We know a lot* (418–420). However, as Lewis makes explicit, his commitment to the truth of *We know a lot* is deeper than his commitment to infallibilism: if forced to choose, he would abandon the latter in order to preserve the former (419). Thus, Lewis's commitment to the truth of many of our everyday attributions of knowledge is more fundamental than his commitment to those aspects of his epistemology that are more congenial to the skeptic. And indeed, similar Moore-style appeals recur throughout the Lewisian corpus. Compare, for example, the following from Lewis (1986): 'Our knowledge of mathematics is ever so much more secure than our knowledge of the epistemology that seeks to cast doubt on mathematics' (p.109). For more on this Moorean aspect of Lewis' thought see Nolan (2005), chapter 9.
2. Prominent figures here include BonJour (1985, ch.1), Stroud (1984, ch.3), and Unger (1975).
3. In addition to Lewis, Armstrong, and Fine, I would also include Lycan (2001), Pollock and Cruz (1999, especially pages 6–7), Soames (2003a), and Hirsch (2002)

among the ranks of prominent contemporary Mooreans. Finally, the usual allures of historical revisionism notwithstanding, I believe that Moore (1993) himself was a Moorean in the relevant respects. I discuss the views of each of these figures below.

4. For the suggestion that our own philosophical era is more commonsensical than some previous ones, see also Rosen (1994: 277–278) on nineteenth versus twentieth century idealisms, and especially Soames (2003a). Indeed, Soames holds that the adoption of what is an essentially Moorean orientation towards philosophy (or perhaps, a Moorean-cum-Quinean orientation) stands as 'one of the two most important achievements that have emerged from the analytic tradition' (pp.xi-xii). He elaborates on this theme as follows:

   One of the recurring themes in the best analytic work ... has been the realization that no matter how attractive a philosophical theory might be in the abstract, it can never be more securely supported than the great mass of ordinary, pre-philosophical convictions arising from common sense, science, and other areas of inquiry about which the theory has consequences. All philosophical theories are, to some extent, tested and constrained by such convictions, and no viable theory can overturn them wholesale. Analytic philosophers are, of course, not the only philosophers to have recognized this; nor ... have they always been able to resist the seductions of unrestrained, and sometimes highly counter-intuitive, theorizing. Still, the tradition has had a way of correcting such excesses, and returning to firmer foundations (xi-xii).

   For a contrary view of the present state of philosophy, see especially the opening pages of Hirsch (2002).

5. Here and below, I use 'skepticism' generically, to refer to any sufficiently radical variety of the view (as opposed to, say, skepticism about the existence of God or about the claims of psychical research). If more specificity is wanted, one might take the claims of the Moorean as being directed at skepticism about our knowledge of the external world.
6. See, e.g., the papers by Pryor (2004), Wright (1985, 2000, 2002, 2003, 2004), and Davies (2000, 2003, 2004).
7. This is true of all of the works by Mooreans mentioned in footnote 3 above.
8. Compare Saul Kripke's 'dogmatism paradox', first presented in Harman (1973).
9. A *locus classicus* of the genre is Ayer (1952).
10. On 'reasonable dogmatism', see Pryor (2000) and (1996). We should distinguish carefully, however, between the kind of dogmatism advocated by Pryor and the kind of dogmatism the reasonableness of which is at issue here. Again, the distinction between playing offense and playing defense (Cf. section 1 above) is apposite. According to the dogmatism advocated by Pryor, one can be justified in believing p even if one cannot offer a certain kind of non-question begging argument for p. Intuitively: one can be justified in believing things even if one is not adept at playing offense. According to the kind of dogmatism presently under consideration, one can be justified in believing propositions even when one is not adept at playing defense. That is, one might be justified in believing a proposition even if one finds oneself unable to identify any objectionable premise or transition in the skeptic's attempt to provide a non-question-begging argument for the negation of that

proposition. It's natural to think that the task of constructing non-question-begging philosophical arguments is, in general, a more demanding intellectual task than that of raising doubts about someone else's attempts to do the same. At least at first pass then, the kind of dogmatism at issue here would seem to be considerably more radical than the kind of dogmatism endorsed by Pryor.

11. Although popular within the larger history of philosophy, the claim that a certain class of propositions enjoys an epistemically privileged role runs counter to one of the great trends of late twentieth century epistemology: its leveling tendency. As noted, many of the objects of traditional epistemological concern (Cartesian foundations, empiricist sense data reports, Carnapian linguistic rules) were alleged to enjoy a distinctive epistemic status. Indeed, the properties which allegedly set them off as distinctive (indubitability, incorrigibility, being 'unrevisable on the basis of experience' or 'confirmed come what may', and so on) often became objects of epistemological reflection in their own right. Much of the second half of twentieth century epistemology might be viewed as a kind of egalitarian reaction to these claims of epistemic privilege. Thus, Quine and his followers held that no statement is in principle immune to revision; their suggestive metaphor of 'the web of belief' is one according to which epistemic differences are a matter of degree as opposed to a matter of kind. Contemporary foundationalists go to great lengths to emphasize that the foundations which they posit need not possess any of the special properties (e.g., certainty, indubitability, incorrigibility) that were typically claimed for such foundations by their classical predecessors. In a similar spirit, many contemporary rationalists emphasize that, on their view, a belief's being *a priori* justified at one time does not preclude that justification from being defeated—indeed, defeated by empirical considerations—at later times. Despite their diversity, all of these trends might be viewed as part of a larger reaction against traditional claims of epistemic privilege. On the present way of thinking about Moorean facts, the friend of such facts seems to swim against this general current.
12. Notably, Wittgenstein (1972) seems to hold that the status of the propositions to which Moore calls our attention differs in kind, and not merely in degree, from more mundane propositions whose truth might be debated in non-philosophical contexts. Indeed, part of Wittgenstein's dissatisfaction with Moore seems to be his sense that Moore was insufficiently appreciative of this point. Of course, it would be completely contrary to the spirit of Wittgenstein's later philosophy to assimilate his notion of a 'hinge proposition' too closely to more traditional epistemological categories. My failure to engage with this fascinating though enigmatic text in the present paper does not reflect any doubt about its importance for the topic but rather an awareness of the inadequacy of my present understanding of it.
13. The picture adumbrated here is, of course, a Quinean one in its essentials.
14. Sometimes 'plausible' is simply used as a synonym for 'reasonable to believe, all things considered'. As a terminological matter, I think that this is best avoided. Reading 'plausible' as 'reasonable to believe all things considered' in interpreting MORE PLAUSIBLE yields a norm equivalent to the norm MORE REASONABLE, which I discuss below.
15. Notice that in the passage quoted above, Moore himself seems to waver in the way that he uses 'certainty': some appearances of the word 'certain' seem to call

out for a psychological reading while others suggest an evidential reading. Thus, the line 'of no one of these assumptions do I feel as certain ...' strongly suggests psychological certainty. On the other hand, 'Is it, in fact, as certain ...?' seems to read more naturally as concerning the evidential notion.

16. Perhaps along the lines of Cassell (2004). See especially pages 190–197.
17. Compare: at a young age, I was extremely confident—indeed, I suspect that I was psychologically certain—that the earth was stationary (in an absolute, Newtonian sense of 'stationary'). I lost this conviction as the end result of a process of reconsideration that was prompted by being told various things by others. No doubt, the things that were told to me were at least somewhat plausible—if they had struck me as ludicrous or absurd I would have dismissed them out of hand. However, given my extreme confidence that the earth is stationary, it's quite likely that I had greater confidence that the earth is stationary than in at least some of the things that were said to me (and certainly, greater confidence than in the conjunction of the relevant propositions). Nevertheless, the process by which I abandoned my belief that the earth is stationary was not an irrational or even an arational process.
18. A recent criticism of Malcolm's argument in particular is Soames (2003b, Chapter 7). An excellent overview of the paradigm case argument and the classical debate over its merits is Donellan (1967); a relatively recent attempt at its rehabilitation is Hanfling (1991).
19. Compare pages xv-xvi of Soames (2003b) where the starting point idea seems to recur.
20. Here I have in mind arguments of the following form:

    (1) I don't know that I'm not a Brain-in-a-Vat (BIV).
    (2) If I don't know that I'm not a BIV, then I don't know that I have hands.
    (3) Therefore, I don't know that I have hands.

    See, e.g., Nozick (1981: Ch.3), Cohen (1988), and DeRose (1995). Unlike some philosophers, I don't think that this is an especially strong argument compared to others which the skeptic might offer. In particular, I think that (1) is an *extremely* strong claim to take as an unargued-for premise in an argument that is supposed to establish skepticism. If the skeptic simply asserts (1), then I think that the non-skeptic is well within her rights to simply decline to accept it.

    Of course, one who puts forth such an argument might attempt to *motivate* acceptance of premise (1) in various ways ('But *how* do you know that you're not a BIV, if you do?' 'Wouldn't everything seem exactly the same to you if were a BIV?') At this point, I think that the skeptic is best understood as tacitly appealing to some general epistemic principle in order to establish (1). (Perhaps: 'if one can't reliably discriminate between H and some incompatible H', then one doesn't know that H.') In that case, I think that it's at least somewhat misleading to represent such a skeptic as taking a particular judgement about the absence of knowledge as a *starting point*. Rather, I think that the relevant claim is better represented as an intermediate lemma of a more complicated argument for skepticism. (Admittedly, these are large issues which deserve greater scrutiny than I am able to offer here.)

    In holding that the skeptic *does* require an argument for (1), I join Byrne

(2004), Feldman (1999), and Greco (2000: 52, fn.16). For a strong opinion to the contrary, see especially Nozick (1981, p.201).

21. For example, I believe that those who espouse radically revisionary views in ethics (i.e., views that depart in radical ways from 'common sense morality') are often best understood as methodists in Chisholm's sense. Here I have in mind especially those who have championed revisionary forms of consequentialism in the tradition that extends from Bentham to Kagan (1989) and Singer (1995).
22. A recent attempt to defend the use of reflective equilibrium in moral and political philosophy against the charge that the method is overly conservative is Scanlon (2002). See especially pages 145–151.
23. Harman offers the following characterization:

    We correct our considered intuitions about particular cases by making them more coherent with our considered general principles and we correct our general principles by making them more coherent with our judgements about particular cases. We make progress by adjusting our views to each other, pursuing the ideal of reaching a set of particular opinions and general views that are in complete accord with each other. The method is conservative in that we start with our present views and try to make the least change that will best promote the coherence of our whole view ("Three Trends", p.416).

24. Compare Soames (2003b:160). The second example below is borrowed from this paragraph.
25. Apparent dissenters are Weatherson (2003) and Hetherington (2001).
26. A *locus classicus* of this charge is Edwards (1951).
27. See, e.g, BonJour (1985, 2002).
28. Earlier versions of this paper were read at Princeton University, MIT, Brandeis, the University of Wisconsin at Milwaukee, and a Pacific Division meeting of the American Philosophical Association; I am grateful to the audiences present on those occasions. In addition, I would like to thank the following individuals for helpful feedback: Paul Benaceraf, Mark Johnston, Jonathan Vogel, Jim Pryor, Kelly Jolley, Shelly Goldstein, Roger White, and the participants in my Spring 2005 graduate seminar at Princeton.

References

Ainslie, George (1975). "Specious Reward: A Behavorial Theory of Impulsiveness and Impulse Control" in the *Psychological Bulletin* 82: 463–496.

Ainslie, George (1986). "Beyond Microeconomics". In *The Multiple Self*, edited by Jon Elster (Cambridge: Cambridge University Press): 133–178.

Armstrong, David (1983). *What is a Law of Nature?* (Cambridge: Cambridge University Press).

Armstrong, David (1999). "A Naturalist Program: Epistemology and Ontology". The Eleventh Annual Romanell Lecture. Reprinted in *Proceedings and Addresses of the American Philosophical Association*, vol.73, No.2.

Ayer, A.J. (1952). *Language, Truth, and Logic* (New York: Dover).

BonJour, Laurence (1986). *The Structure of Empirical Knowledge*. (Cambridge, MA: Harvard University Press).

BonJour, Laurence (2002). *Epistemology*. (Oxford, England: Rowman and Littlefield Publishers).
Byrne, Alex (2004). "How Hard Are the Sceptical Paradoxes?" *Noûs*, 38, 299–325.
Cassell, Paul (2004). "In Defense of the Death Penalty". In *Debating the Death Penalty: Should America Have Capital Punishment? The Experts on Both Sides Make Their Best Case*. Edited by Hugo Adam Bedau and Paul G. Cassell (Oxford: Oxford University Press).
Chisholm, Roderick (1973). *The Problem of the Criterion*. (Milwaukee, WI: Marquette University Press).
Cohen, Stewart (1988). "How to Be a Fallibilist" in James Tomberlin (ed.) *Philosophical Perspectives* 2 (Atascadero, CA: Ridgeview Publishing Company).
Conee, Earl (2001). "Comments on Bill Lycan's Moore Against the New Skeptics", *Philosophical Studies* 103: 55–59.
Copp, David (1985). "Considered Judgements and Justification: Conservatism in Moral Theory", in D. Copp and M. Zimmerman (eds.) *Morality, Reason, and Truth*. (Totowa, NJ: Rowman and Allenheld): 141–169.
Daniels, Norman (1996). *Justice and Justification: Reflective Equilibrium in Theory and Practice*. (Cambridge: Cambridge University Press).
Davies, Martin (1998). "Externalism, Architecturalism, and Epistemic Warrant", in Wright, Crispin, Smith, Michael, and Macdonald, Cynthia (eds.), *Knowing Our Own Minds: Essays in Self-Knowledge*, (Oxford: Oxford University Press): 321–361.
Davies, Martin (2000). "Externalism and Armchair Knowledge", in Boghossian, Paul and Peacocke, Christopher (eds.), *New Essays on the A Priori* (Oxford: Oxford University Press): 384–414.
Davies, Martin (2003). "The Problem of Armchair Knowledge", in Nuccetelli, Susana (ed.) *News Essays on Semantic Externalism and Self-Knowledge*. (Cambridge, MA: MIT Press): 23–55.
Davies, Martin (2004). "Epistemic Entitlement, Warrant Transmission, and Easy Knowledge", *Aristotelian Society Supplement*, 78, pp. 213–245.
DeRose, Keith (1995). "Solving the Skeptical Problem" *Philosophical Review* 104: 1–52.
Donellan, Keith (1967). "The Paradigm Case Argument", in Paul Edwards (ed.) *The Encyclopedia of Philosophy* (New York: MacMillan):39–44.
Edwards, Paul (1951). "Bertrand Russell's Doubts About Induction", in Antony Flew (ed.) *Essays in on Logic and Language* (Oxford: Oxford University Press).
Feldman, Richard. "Contextualism and Skepticism" in *Philosophical Perspectives* 13: 91–114.
Fine, Kit (2001). "The Question of Realism". *The Philosophers' Imprint* vol.1, no.1.
Gettier, Edmund. "Is Justified True Belief Knowledge?" *Analysis* 23: 121–123.
Goodman, Nelson (1953). *Fact, Fiction, and Forecast*. (Cambridge, MA: Harvard University Press).
Hanfling, Oswald (1991). "What is Wrong with the Paradigm Case Argument?" in *Proceedings of the Aristotelian Society* vol.91: 21–38.
Harman, Gilbert (1973). *Thought*. (Princeton, NJ: Princeton University Press).
Harman, Gilbert (1986). *Change in View*. (Cambridge, MA: The MIT Press).
Harman, Gilbert (1994). "Epistemology and the Diet Revolution", in Michaelis Michael and John O'Leary-Hawthorne (eds.), *Philosophy in Mind*. (The Netherlands: Kluwer Academic Publishers).
Harman, Gilbert (1999). *Reasoning, Meaning, and Mind*. (Oxford: Oxford University Press).
Harman, Gilbert (2003). "Skepticism and Foundations", in Steven Luper (ed.) *The Skeptics: Contemporary Essays*. (Ashgate: Aldershot): 1–11.
Harman, Gilbert (2004). "Three Trends in Moral and Political Philosophy" in *The Journal of Value Inquiry*, 37: 415–425.
Hetherington, Stephen (2001). *Good Knowledge, Bad Knowledge*. (Oxford: Oxford University Press).
Hirsch, Eli (2002). "Against Revisionary Ontology" in *Philosophical Topics* vol.30, no.1.
Kagan, Shelly (1989). *The Limits of Morality*. (Oxford: Oxford University Press).
Lemos, Noah (2004). *Common Sense*. (Cambridge: Cambridge University Press).

Lewis, David (1986). *On the Plurality of Worlds* (Blackwell Publishers: Cambridge, MA).
Lewis, David (1999) "Elusive Knowledge", reprinted in his collection *Papers in Metaphysics and Epistemology* (Cambridge: Cambridge University Press), pp. 418–445.
Lycan, William (2001). "Moore against the New Skeptics". *Philosophical Studies* 103 (1):35–53.
Malcolm, Norman (1942). "Moore and Ordinary Language", in *The Philosophy of G.E. Moore*, vol.I, ed. P.A. Schilpp (La Salle, IL: Open Court) 343–368.
Moore, G.E. (1942). "Replies" in *The Philosophy of G.E. Moore*, vol.I ed. P.A. Schilpp (La Salle, IL: Open Court).
Moore, G.E (1993). *Selected Writings*. Edited by Thomas Baldwin. (London: Routledge).
Moore, G.E. (2000). "Four Forms of Skepticism". Reprinted in Kim and Sosa (eds.) *Epistemology: An Anthology* (Oxford: Blackwell Publishers): 27–29.
Nolan, Daniel (2005). *David Lewis*. (McGill: Queen's University Press).
Nozick, Robert (1981). *Philosophical Explanations*. (Cambridge, MA: Harvard University Press).
Nozick, Robert (1993). *The Nature of Rationality*. (Princeton: Princeton University Press).
Pollock, John and Cruz, Joseph (1999). *Contemporary Theories of Knowledge* (Oxford: Rowman and Littlefield).
Pryor, James (1996). *How to be a Reasonable Dogmatist*. Unpublished doctoral dissertation. Princeton University, 1996.
Pryor, James (2000). "The Skeptic and the Dogmatist", *Noûs* 34: 517–549.
Pryor, James (2004). "What's Wrong With Moore's Argument?" in *Philosophical Issues* 14.
Rawls, John (1972). *A Theory of Justice*. (Cambridge, MA: Belnkap)
Rosen, Gideon (1994). "Objectivity and Modern Idealism: What is the Question?" in Michaelis Michael and John O'Leary-Hawthorne (eds.), *Philosophy in Mind*. (The Netherlands: Kluwer Academic Publishers): 277–319
Scanlon, Thomas (2002). "Rawls on Justification" in *The Cambridge Companion to Rawls*, edited by Samuel Freeman (Cambridge: Cambridge University Press): 139–167.
Singer, Peter (1974). "Sidgwick and Reflective Equilibrium" in the *Monist* 58: 490–517.
Singer, Peter (1995). *Rethinking Life and Death: the Collapse of our Traditional Ethics*. (New York: St. Martin's Press).
Soames, Scott (2003a). *Philosophical Analysis in the Twentieth Century. Volume 1: The Dawn of Analysis*. (Princeton, NJ: Princeton University Press).
Soames, Scott (2003b). *Philosophical Analysis in the Twentieth Century. Volume 2: The Age of Meaning*. (Princeton, NJ: Princeton University Press).
Stitch, Stephen (1983). *The Fragmentation of Reason* (Cambridge, MA: The M.I.T. Press).
Strawson, P.F. (1985). *Skepticism and Naturalism: Some Varieties*. (New York: Columbia University Press).
Stroud, Barry (1984). *The Significance of Philosophical Skepticism*. (Oxford: Oxford University Press).
Unger, Peter (1975). *Ignorance: A Case for Skepticism* (Oxford: Oxford University Press).
Weatherson, Brian (2003). "What Good Are Counterexamples?" *Philosophical Studies* 15: 1–31.
Wittgenstein, Ludwig (1972). *On Certainty*. Edited by G.E.M. Anscombe and G.H. von Wright. (New York: Harper and Row)
Wright, Crispin (1985), "Facts and Certainty", *Proceedings of the British Academy* 71: 429–472.
Wright, Crispin (2000). "Cogency and Question-begging: Some reflections on McKinsey's Paradox and Putnam's Proof" in *Philosophical Issues* 10: 140–163.
Wright, Crispin (2002). "(Anti)skeptics simple and subtle: Moore and McDowell". *Philosophy and Phenomenological Research* 65:.330–348.
Wright, Crispin (2003). "Some Reflections on the Acquisition of Warrant by Inference", in Nuccetelli, Susana (ed.) *New Essays on Semantic Externalism and Self-Knowledge* (Cambridge, MA: MIT Press): 57–77.
Wright, Crispin (2004). "Warrant for Nothing (and foundations for free)? *Aristotelian Society Supplement*.

Philosophical Perspectives, 19, Epistemology, 2005

ENOUGH IS ENOUGH: PRETENSE AND INVARIANCE IN THE SEMANTICS OF "KNOWS THAT"

Krista Lawlor
Stanford University

1. The puzzling nature of "knows that"

Our use of "knows that" can seem puzzling. On the one hand, we ascribe propositional knowledge as if it were in *some way* sensitive to context: one may claim to know something in one situation, but in a different situation, when the stakes have gone up, one hesitates over the same claim, even if one has the same evidence. On the other hand, we ascribe knowledge as if it were in *no way* sensitive to context: when one claims to know, one makes no mention of the context-sensitivity of the truth of one's claim, and one's claim to know must stand the test of subsequent challenges as though its content were absolute.

For example: Kate and Rob are taking a casual walk through the museum of modern art. Kate asks, "Is that a Diebenkorn, do you know?" and Rob replies, "yes, it is—I know it's his." Suppose Rob's claim to knowledge is supported by a good background in modern art history, and the painting is in fact by Diebenkorn. His claim to know that the painting is by Diebenkorn is true. Now imagine a different scenario, in which the museum director, John, asks Rob the same question. John is thinking of purchasing the painting for the museum. The stakes here are higher than in the first situation. Given the higher stakes, Rob's claim to know, grounded as it is in a good art history education, might not stand—in fact, Rob might understandably hesitate to make a claim to knowledge in this situation.

Such cases illustrate that we take claims of the form "S knows that p" to be true when uttered in one situation, but not when uttered in another, even though nothing about the putative knower's evidence changes (the putative knower, S, grasps the same positive considerations in favor of the proposition, p). We ascribe knowledge as if the meaning of "knows" were in some way context-sensitive. (By "context-sensitive" at this juncture we should have in mind a broad and non-technical sense, something like "varying with some to-be-specified parameter concerning the utterer, or the putative knower, or what have you.")

Now consider another example: Kate asks Rob, "Why did you hesitate? Didn't you just say you knew it was a Diebenkorn?" One thing Rob will not say in reply is "Yes, I knew it when I was talking to you, but I don't know it now the stakes have gone up." He won't say, "I was right then, to say 'I know', because it didn't matter very much." Rather, he will feel compelled to withdraw or modify his earlier claim, weakening it in some way, as in "Well, of all the painters it is likely to be, if it is genuine, it's a Diebenkorn." (Often, when the stakes go up, new defeating possibilities become salient, and so Rob might explain his reluctance to claim knowledge now, saying "I can't rule out it's not a forgery.") One thing he won't do is insist that his earlier knowledge claim should stand, since it was made in a different context.

Such cases illustrate that we treat claims of the form "S knows that p" to be true or false independently of the situation in which they are uttered. That is, one's claim to know must stand the test of subsequent challenges as though its content were absolute; if on a subsequent occasion one cannot claim knowledge, one will accordingly withdraw earlier claims to know.

Our usage then, seems to have a tension in it: we seem to use "knows" as though its meaning were context-sensitive and as though it were not. This apparent tension is the root of serious difficulties for leading accounts of the semantics of "knows." I'll canvass these accounts in the next section, so we get a good feeling for the difficulties presented by the tension.

In response to this tension, some argue that relativism is the answer—we should just accept that the self-same utterance can be both true and false, depending on who is assessing the claim; others argue that nihilism is correct—we should just give up and admit our concept of knowledge is incoherent. I think neither response is right. I argue in section 3 that relativism doesn't dispel the tension, but has its own difficulties accounting for our usage. And we should only give up making sense of how "knows" works if we are certain we have exhausted our alternatives.

I think we're not out of alternatives yet. My aim in this paper is to explore an alternative semantics for "knows"—what we can call *pretense semantics*. As we will see, a pretense semantics for "knows" does a good job making sense of the apparent tension in our linguistic practice that other accounts stumble over. Moreover, it offers a distinctive and, I think, superior treatment of certain skeptical challenges.

2. Leading attempts & problems posed by the tension

Here is a brief survey of leading accounts of the semantics of "knows", and of the difficulties each encounter with the apparent tension in our usage.[1]

(i) *contextualism.* As we have seen,

(a) we ascribe knowledge as if "knows" were in some way context-sensitive.

One explanation of this fact is that the meaning of "knows" *is* context-sensitive. This is what so-called "contextualists" claim.[2] The contextualist holds that knowledge ascriptions are sensitive to the knowledge *ascriber*. More specifically, the contextualist asserts that, as used in a given context C, "knows" expresses a relation

Knows: <S, P, R, E(C)>

between a putative knower or subject, S, and proposition P in circumstance R, that holds just in case S meets a particular contextually supplied standard, E(C), where the value of E(C) is set by facts about the knowledge ascriber. Such facts may include what is salient to the ascriber, what the interests of the ascriber are, what is at stake for the ascriber in S's being right about P, and so forth.[3]

Consequently, the contextualist will say, if it seems that "knows" is context-sensitive, that's because it is.[4] How well placed a subject needs to be to stand in the "knows" relation to a given proposition in a given circumstance depends on what is at stake and of interest to the ascriber in the subject's getting things right.

What then of the apparent insensitivity of knowledge ascriptions? Were "knows" ascriber-sensitive in the way contextualism says it is, these utterances by Rob (speaking to the curator) would seem to be licensed:

Back then, my claim "I know it is a Diebenkorn" was true

What I said, when I said "I know" back then, was that I met the standard for knowing in place when I said it

Or Kate, speaking about Rob's knowledge:

It doesn't matter much to me, so Rob knows it's a Diebenkorn.

But these utterances sound odd. In fact,

(b) we do not ascribe knowledge as if the truth of the knowledge claim depended on features that vary with the knowledge ascriber.

In this way, "knows" is unlike other context-sensitive terms. For instance, we might say "It's raining", and then two minutes later, "It's not raining." Our later statement does not force us to retract our earlier statement. And we can deny a change of mind, saying "It was raining then, but it's not raining now." We can call on the fact that the meaning of terms involved in "It's raining" have parameters fixed in the context of utterance, in order to explain our making and withholding "It's raining" on different occasions. This is not how "knows" works.

So contextualism runs into serious difficulties explaining the apparent insensitivity in our use of "knows."

(ii) *sensitive invariantism.* In an effort to circumvent the difficulties for contextualism, another explanation of apparent context-sensitivity of "knows" in terms of its actual context-sensitivity has been proposed—namely, sensitive invariantism.[5]

Sensitive invariantists hold that knowledge ascriptions are sensitive to the knowledge *ascribee*, or subject. More specifically, the sensitive invariantist asserts that, as used in any given context C, "knows" expresses a relation

Knows: <S, P, R, E(S, R)>

that holds just in case S meets a particular contextually supplied standard, E(S,R), where the value of E(S, R) is set by facts about the subject of the knowledge claim. Such facts might include what is salient to the subject, what the interests of the subject are, what is at stake for the subject in the circumstance R in which the knowledge is had.[6]

Real context-sensitivity underwrites fact (a) above, on this view, but it is not ascriber-sensitivity. The sensitive invariantist thus diagnoses the contextualist's difficulties—in settling the standards for knowing it doesn't matter what the ascriber's concerns are in the context of utterance (thus the view is "invariantist"). For this reason, a speaker won't say such things as, "It doesn't matter much to me, so Rob knows it's a Diebenkorn." According to the sensitive invariantist, how well placed a subject needs to be to stand in the "knows" relation to a given proposition in a given circumstance depends on the stakes and interests of the subject in getting things right, not the ascriber.

Although sensitive invariantism gives us a solution to the problem facing the contextualist, unfortunately, it also brings new problems. For we also routinely resist treating "knows" as subject-sensitive. Were "knows" context-sensitive in the way sensitive invariantism says it is (that is, sensitive to subject-dependent standards), these utterances would seem to be licensed:

He knew it was a Diebenkorn until he realized what might be at stake.

I know that I won't be able to afford the Safari, but you don't know that you won't. (Solely on the basis of the fact that you're being offered a lottery ticket right now, while I've already bought mine.)[7]

The reason these utterances sound odd is that the following is also a fact about our usage:

(c) we do not ascribe knowledge as if the truth of the knowledge claim depended on features that vary with the subject of the knowledge claim.

In fact, we ascribe knowledge as if "knows" did not vary with the subject. So sensitive invariantism also runs into difficulty with the apparent insensitivity of knowledge ascription.[8]

(iii) *invariantism* (moderate and skeptical)

Perhaps then the right view is that the meaning of "knows" is not sensitive to context? The strict invariantist says that knows contributes the same relation

Knows: <S, P, E>

to propositions expressed by utterances in which it figures. The standard of evidence, E, that an utterance must meet is settled once and for all. Of course, this standard need not be impossibly demanding—it might be a standard easily enough met that most or many of our ordinary knowledge claims are true.

The invariantist easily makes sense of the apparent insensitivity to context of our knowledge claims—we don't ascribe knowledge as if the truth of our knowledge claims depended on contextually provided features, because the truth of our claims does not so depend. What an invariantist has trouble explaining of course, is fact (a) above, that we ascribe knowledge as if "knows" were in some way context-sensitive, and as if the truth or falsity of our knowledge claims did so depend.

Invariantists routinely appeal to the mechanics of conversational implicature to explain apparent sensitivity.[9] It is worth noting that other views, too, may appeal to conversational implicature in order to explain recalcitrant features of our usage. For instance, one might defend contextualism by saying that (b) is better registered as a non-semantic fact about the pragmatics of ascribing knowledge. Then we might say, the fact that we do not in certain cases use "knows" in a manner consistent with its ascriber-sensitivity owes to a desire to avoid the unwanted conversational implicatures generated by doing so in those cases. So for instance, we might explain the fact that Rob resists saying

When I was talking to Kate, my claim "I know" expressed a truth

We explain Rob's resistance, claiming that there are unwanted conversational implications generated by this otherwise licensed claim. Perhaps, simply by saying "back then 'I know' expressed a truth", Rob generates expectations that he knows that he knew that p. But since knowledge is factive, he generates expectations that he knows now that p. But this is just what he doesn't want anyone to understand by his utterance. So he avoids saying what he knows to be true, namely, that he was right to say "I know" in the former context of utterance. Invoking conversational pragmatics in this way, we can try to explain why our usage is sometimes inconsistent with a sensitive semantics for "knows."

Alternatively, one could try to save any of the foregoing views by appeal to an error theory. (In fact, an error theory and implicature will in the normal course be jointly invoked, since one assumes interlocking explanatory burdens on taking either option.) For instance, we might invoke an error theory to explain (b) away, and so say that although "knows" is in fact subject-sensitive, we erroneously suppose it isn't. Alternately, we explain (c) away, if we want to cling to the idea that "knows" is ascriber-sensitive.

The possibilities here are many, and a full discussion is beyond the scope of this paper, so I won't go into these matters, except to note two points. First, it is far from clear that conversational implicatures will generate *all* the data that need explanation, for the invariantist or anyone else. For instance, conversational implicature can explain why Rob might refrain from claiming knowledge later, but cannot explain the intuition that it is outright false to claim such knowledge, and why Rob will expressly deny having known.[10] Second, other things equal it is more desirable to have a semantic theory that does not ascribe wholesale error to users of the language. This has been a sore spot for all the leading contenders thus far—as John Hawthorne notes, everyone 'til now has been forced to ascribe some sort of wholesale error to language-users. This fact doesn't mean we should give up trying for a view that avoids ascribing massive error. I believe we can explain the puzzling tension in our practice of knowledge attribution, without invoking conversational implicatures or an error theory.

Before turning to the explanation I favor, I want to consider two other important alternatives.

3. Relativism

One might claim that, in consideration of facts (a)-(c), that our usage is just plain inconsistent. Perhaps then, the concept of knowledge is incoherent, and no semantic theory of "knows" is to be had. Schiffer, for instance, suggests that our concept of knowledge is incoherent.[11] But I think most will agree that this sort of nihilism is a last resort, and one we should adopt only if we are certain we have exhausted all our options.

Recently, still others have argued that before admitting that the concept of knowledge is incoherent, we should accept relativism.[12] The relativist claims that knowledge ascription is sensitive to the knowledge *assessor*. We must be careful how we characterize relativism, however. In keeping with the foregoing characterizations, we might try to say that the relativist holds that the semantic contribution of "knows" is the relation

Knows: <S, P, R, E(A, S, R)>

where A is a parameter for the assessor. This is misleading, however, since it suggests that, as used in a given context C, "knows" expresses a single relation. But according to the relativist, as used in a given context C, "knows" does *not* express a single relation. For the relativist, a particular token use of "knows" may actually express *different* relations between a given subject and a given proposition, depending on who is assessing it. Thus a particular token utterance has its truth value determined relative to whoever assesses it, and not once and for all—the self-same utterance "S knows that P", can be true relative to one context of assessment, and false relative to another.

According to the relativist, the reason it seems right for Rob to say "I know that's a Diebenkorn" on one occasion but wrong the next is that the context of assessment changes. We assess Rob's claim initially much as Kate does, and relative to epistemic standards put in place by our assessment, his claim to know is true. Later we understand the stakes in Rob's being right have gone up, and that changes the context of our assessment. Now we think Rob's epistemic position is not strong enough in the new context of assessment, so his utterance is false. According to the relativist, Rob's utterance to Kate "I know it's a Diebenkorn" is true and false, relative to our two contexts of assessment.

The relativist thus offers the following explanation of the puzzling features of our usage. The fact (a) of apparent context-sensitivity of knowledge attribution is explained, since "knows" *is* context-sensitive, but just not in any of the standardly accepted ways. Apparent insensitivity reflected in facts (b) and (c) is explained by the fact that "knows" is neither ascriber-sensitive nor subject-sensitive.

There are problems, however, for relativism. First, here as elsewhere, relativists face the problem of accommodating genuine disagreement. Since the truth of a knowledge ascription depends on the assessor, according to the relativist, the very same utterance can be assessed by two people, and have two truth-values. So the relativist says that, while there is an understandable *appearance* of conflict in utterances by the two assessors, this is only an appearance.

The second problem with relativism is that it too stumbles over certain features of our usage. The two problems are related. Returning to our example to illustrate: Rob claims to know that the painting is by Diebenkorn. Imagine both his friend Kate and the curator, John, hear his claim. Suppose it matters very little to Kate but very much to John whether Rob is right. Then they might claim:

Kate: "what Rob said is true"
John: "what Rob said is false"

and what each says is true relative to their respective contexts of assessment. What are Kate and John to think, on hearing each other's claims? As long as their contexts of assessment are different, each need feel no pressure from the other's claim, at least if they are at all aware of the semantics of "knows." But we do feel pressured by conflicting assessments.[13] In fact, John will want to say to Kate, "No, what Rob said is *false*."

We can put a finer point on this issue by finding an embarrassing utterance that relativism licenses. Since the relativist specifically takes care to frame a kind of sensitive semantics for "knows" that avoids the aforementioned embarrassments, such an utterance can be difficult to find. According to the relativist the truth of a knowledge claim depends on its assessor, and a single assessor makes her assessment from a single epistemic viewpoint, so a person won't say "When I said 'I know' back then, I was right, but I don't know now." In claiming not to know now, the person assesses her earlier claim as false, and she will not be inclined to defend her earlier assertion. Nor will she say "He knew, until he worried" because as an assessor, she has a single viewpoint about the epistemic standards in play, and these do not depend on the subject's state of mind. If the subject's worries were enough to prevent his knowing later, according to the assessor, then they were enough to prevent his knowing earlier.

It may be harder to discern an embarrassing utterance for the relativist, but if we acknowledge that language has devices for quoting others, it is possible. One such device is "Yes," where one acknowledges what another person has said as being true in that person's mouth.For instance, Rob's mother says "I feel cold!" and Rob says "Yes—but I don't." Rob's utterance of "yes" is more than a verbal tick; it's meant to register acknowledgment of the truth of his mother's claim in her mouth. If the relativist is right about the semantics of "knows" being assessor relative, then one assessor might say, "Rob's claim to know is true" and a second assessor might say, "Yes—but it's not." And that sounds odd.

This fact about our usage is suggested by the foregoing:

(d) we do not ascribe knowledge as if the truth of the knowledge claim depended on features that vary with the assessor of the knowledge claim

Relativism, then, also runs into difficulties with the apparent tension in our usage.

To recap: We face a puzzle about our usage. Certain facts about of our talk of knowledge seem to be in tension with each other: fact (a) suggests the context-sensitivity of "knows", while (b), (c), and (d) suggest insensitivity. This tension in our usage presents a problem for all the leading views of the semantics of knowledge reports: (a) is a problem for strict invariantism, (b) is a problem for contextualism, (c) for sensitive invariantism, and (d) for relativism.

Fortunately, we are not out of alternatives yet. We can build an account of the semantics of "knows" that makes sense of the puzzling tension between sensitivity and insensitivity in our use of "knows." The alternative requires us to be more contextualist than existing views have been. Specifically, the key to resolving the tension, I will argue below, is to understand how the meaning of "knows" might be invariant, while the truth-conditions of utterances involving "knows" nonetheless depend on context.[14]

4. Pretense Semantics

Suppose the linguistic or lexical meaning of "knows that" is invariant—something like "has conclusive reasons for believing."[15] How might we nonetheless use "knows" to say true things, even as the demands on our knowledge claims change from one occasion to the next?

I want to explore a possible answer here that has found employment elsewhere—namely, a *semantic pretense* account.

Semantic pretense has been explored as a solution to puzzles about identity claims, fictional entities and metaphor.[16] In the next sections I draw on Mark Crimmins' work in order to lay out the framework of a semantics for "knows that." Then I'll show how the account allows us to resolve the puzzling tension in our usage.

Start with this observation: we sometimes make as if to say one thing, so as really to say another. We do so for a variety of reasons: to gain efficiency of expression, to emphasize one point or another, to make our talk more polite or more vivid. Here is a case where a speaker gains efficiency of expression: Wanting milk for his morning cereal, Henry asks Sarah "Is there some milk in the icebox?" "No," Sarah answers, "There's none." Hearing Sarah's answer, Henry puts the cereal away and fixes toast instead. All the while, Sarah has been studying the state of the icebox, including some dried splashes of milk on the shelves.

Is Sarah lying when she says there's no milk? Certainly not. How explain this fact? Sarah says "No, there's none" instead of "There is no quantity of milk sufficient for any purpose you might have for milk at breakfast" because saying "There's none" is easier than saying the more elaborate thing, and yet conveys the more elaborate thing to a hearer ready and able to understand. But just how does Sarah communicate the more elaborate thing by saying "There's none"?

Let's consider how a pretense-semantic account might explain this. The central idea of pretense semantics is that an utterance has its truth-conditions established in the course of a conversation, and we can understand a conversation in terms of a game of make-believe. The game needn't be a full-blown imaginative adventure. What Crimmins calls a "shallow pretense" is less like a child's game of make-believe with all the elaborate imagination and rule-following that might suggest, and more like an impromptu and tacit cooperative agreement between speaker and audience to let certain things go unsaid, and to permit certain other things to get said more easily. And the game needn't be aimed at having fun—conversational pretense is aimed at getting serious things said about the real world.

When Henry asks about the milk, he invites Sarah to join a little pretense governing what will count as the presence of milk in the icebox and what won't. Dried splashes don't count, and useable quantities do. Saying "There's none" in this shared pretense permits Sarah to more easily say that there is not enough milk for any of the usual purposes that milk serves at breakfast. There are two claims we might identify, then—the claim one makes as if to express with one's utterance in the pretense, and the claim one thereby manages to express:

Claim one makes as if to express	Claim one manages thereby to express
There is no milk whatsoever in the icebox	There is no quantity of milk in the icebox sufficient for any of the usual purposes milk serves at breakfast

Since the meaning of "none" doesn't change from game to game, and is just what we might naturally take it to be—roughly "no quantity whatsoever"—the claim Sarah makes as if to express is the claim that there is no milk whatsoever in the icebox. She makes as if to express this claim, in order thereby to express the more complicated claim.

But just how does Sarah manage to convey the one claim by making as if to express the other? The conversational pretense has some structure, in light of which these two claims are related.[17] This structure has two elements: *principles of generation* and explicit *pretense-establishing claims* shape the way the game is run. So there are two ways propositions can be true in the game, or turn out to be true in the game: by being explicitly settled on, announced as true, or by being generated from basic rules of the game, in combination with other pretense-based truths and ways the world actually is.

To illustrate, let's imagine another game of make-believe, where it is clearer to see just what is pretended, and what is real, and how the two together determine the truth of what is expressed. Imagine a game at the beach, where incoming waves of a sufficiently large size count as tsunamis, pieces of flotsam serve as ocean-going vessels and so on:

Foundational propositions	Principles of generation
These are giant tsunami (said of incoming waves) These are ocean liners (said of a floating pieces of wood)	Whatever the wave breaks over is destroyed by the tsunami

Foundational propositions say what is true in the game, period. Principles of generation are conditional principles for generating further truths in the game. So principles of generation help to determine which propositions are true in the game, given the things explicitly taken to be true, and given the way the actual world is. The proposition

My ocean liner was just destroyed

is true if a principle of generation for the game is as above, and a wave breaks over the piece of wood I happen to be pushing along.

We can say things about the real world items that figure in our pretense, about their properties being such as to make certain claims true in the game. If you say

Two ocean liners have collided

your utterance is true in the game we are playing just in case two pieces of flotsam bump into each other. When you say this, you express a commitment to the real world with its two pieces of flotsam being such as to make true the claim in our game that there has been a collision.

You might also say things in the pretense in order to convey real world truths. Suppose my back is turned to the ocean, and you want to warn me of a large wave—"there's an enormous tsunami coming!" you say. The truth-condition of your utterance is one the pretense equips it with, namely, that there is an enormous wave coming in. You speak through our pretense to tell me about the state of the real world.

Now return to Sarah's utterance,

(1) There's none

in response to Henry's question about the milk in the icebox. Is it explicitly pretended true? In asking about the milk, Henry is not asking Sarah to join him in simply pretending something one way or another about their milk supply, nor is Sarah in replying asking Henry to join her in simply pretending that there's no milk in the icebox. What good would that be? The point of engaging in pretense is to let certain claims made in a cooperative spirit tell us about how things really stand with the world. What we agree to pretend true, and the shape of our game, is tacitly agreed upon by us in view of what makes sense for communicating real world truths of interest. Thus we do better to characterize Sarah and Henry's pretense as having the following structural features:

Foundational propositions	Principles of generation
Milk is found in the icebox	Milk is a pourable liquid
Cereal is found in the cupboard	

The principle that milk is a pourable liquid tells Sarah and Henry that they can ignore dried splashes. In light of the principle, dried splashes of milk don't count as milk at all, and the possibility of some milk being in a dried-up state is one our speaker and hearer can ignore. Consequently, Sarah can simply say, "There's none" in response to Henry's question. Given the principle that milk is only ever liquid and given the real-world fact that there are only dried splashes of milk in the icebox, Sarah's utterance is true.

True, you say? Or made-believe true?

The answer to this question is, Both. The truth or falsity of Sarah's utterance is settled through the shared conversational pretense, and in the pretense, Sarah's utterance is true. The real truth-conditions for her utterance, "There's none", are the conditions established through the pretense, namely, that there is no quantity of milk in the icebox sufficient for any of the usual purposes milk serves at breakfast. Since there are only dried splashes of milk in the icebox, these conditions are met and her utterance is true.[18]

It is important to note that the proposition Sarah makes as if to express

(2) there is no milk whatsoever in the icebox

is quite a strong claim, and were (2) to capture the truth-conditions of her utterance, what she says would be false. In fact, her utterance does not have the truth-condition in (2), but rather has the truth-condition that the pretense equips it with, namely,

(3) There is no quantity of milk in the icebox sufficient for any of the usual purposes milk serves at breakfast

Sarah's utterance is really true just in case it is true within their conversational pretense. And since the conversational pretense equips her utterance with the truth-conditions given by (3), her utterance is true—really true.[19]

But really, someone might worry, really truly there is milk in the icebox, and we all know it. So what Sarah has said is really truly false, and only (granting this much to the pretense account) made-believe true.

The worry is natural. Let us remember, however, that according to the pretense semantic account, Sarah's utterance is false only if we play another game, with another principle of generation, to the effect that *milk is a stuff that comes in solid and liquid forms*. Imagine Henry were to say to Sarah, "But you're wrong—there's that dried-up spot splashed on the back." If Henry were serious, we would have to suppose that he asked about milk for a different reason than wanting some for breakfast, and consequently that Henry wants different principles in play. Whatever may be said in favor of a game run by one set of principles of generation over another, the point is that there will be some principles or other governing the conduct of speakers in conversations. On the pretense semantics account, it is incorrect to imagine that Sarah's utterance has truth-conditions independently of some such principles, in light of which it is equipped with truth conditions.

There will be philosophers who prefer to say that when Sarah utters "There's none", what she has said, in some strict sense of saying, is false, and only what she's implied is true. These philosophers will think it misguided to seek a story on which the utterance "There's none" is true. (They will go on to give an account of how Sarah's speaking as she does is appropriate, and perhaps, how what she conversationally implicates is true.) A great deal more would have to be said here, about literal meaning and related issues, in order to convince these philosophers to adopt a pretense semantics. I want to note here two points in favor of pretense semantics: first, we should ask ourselves just how misguided it is to think Sarah's utterance is true. Note how strong our ordinary and untutored judgments are about what Sarah says: has she lied? No. If Henry checks on her, will he think she is right about there being no milk? Yes. Such judgments on our part speak strongly in favor of an account of utterance truth on which utterances such as Sarah's are true.[20]

The second point in favor of adopting a pretense semantics, specifically for "knows", is its power to resolve various semantic and epistemic puzzles. My task in the next sections is to explore the power of pretense semantics for explaining away the puzzling tension in our use of "knows."

5. Pretense semantics for "knows"

Let us apply the pretense account to talk about knowledge.

Suppose Kurt and Steven are thinking about what kind of vacation they might afford. After studying their bank statement and some vacation brochures, and tallying some figures, Kurt says

(4) I know we can't afford that vacation

With a pretense semantics for knowledge, "knows" means what we might naturally expect it to mean—something like "has absolutely conclusive reasons for believing"—which meaning does not vary from conversation to conversation. Utterances involving "knows" have their truth conditions determined by conversational pretense. Kurt's utterance is really true just in case it is true within Kurt and Steven's conversational pretense.

Now, we face some choices about how to characterize conversational pretenses concerning knowledge. Let's say a proposition, q, is a *counter-possibility* to p if the truth of q implies the falsity of p. The base meaning of *knows* is something like "has absolutely conclusive reasons for believing", and *absolutely conclusive reasons* means something like "reasons sufficiently strong to rule out every counter-possibility." So we have some choices about how to characterize our pretense. One option is to suppose that what is pretended is that one's evidence, in being sufficiently strong to rule out certain counter-possibilities, is sufficiently strong to rule out *every* counter-possibility. A second option is that what is pretended is that only *some specified few* propositions are counter-possibilities in the first place. (This might be because the pretense is to the effect that *logical relations* among propositions are such as to have only some specified few propositions imply the falsity of p, or because the pretense is to the effect that only some specified few propositions might *ever* be true. The latter position won't have it that we pretend lots of logical falsehoods are true, and so is the more desirable way of fleshing out the second option.) On the first option the pretense is to the effect that one's evidence is more powerful, and on the second, that the world is less threatening.

Going either way, the central idea of pretense semantics remains—namely, that in our knowledge ascriptions, "To know is to rule out all counter-possibilities" is a demand we pretend to respect. The difference between the two options boils down to how we pretend to respect this demand: on the first option, for every counter-possibility, q, ruling out q is needed for knowing that p, and we pretend that ruling out every q is something one's evidence *can* do; while on the second, we pretend of some counter-possibilities that they are *not* counter-possibilities, and so don't need ruling out in the first place.

There are probably still more ways to specify a workable pretense, and a fuller exploration of our options merits discussion, though I won't make such exploration here. One reason for preferring the second option, it seems to me, is that it makes better sense of typical reactions we have to challenges to our knowledge ascriptions that strike us as out of line. In key cases, we don't react in the manner of "look, you're not paying attention! My evidence ruled that out already", but rather, "come on! Where'd you get the idea *that* mattered?" I'll return to this point below.

Here then is a partial characterization of Kurt and Steven's conversational pretense along the lines of the second option:

Foundational propositions	Principles of generation
Vacations cost money All our money is in the bank	The counter-possibilities in need of ruling out are *that we have more money in the bank than we thought, that we'll get a raise soon, that the vacation is cheap enough to be within our means*

The principle of generation specified tells Kurt and Steven that in ascribing knowledge, they can ignore various counter-possibilities, such as the possibility of winning the lottery, coming into a large inheritance, finding a bag of money on the street, and so on. They're pretending that these are not counter-possibilities. Since they can ignore these possibilities, and Kurt's evidence is sufficient to tell against the only counter-possibilities that the pretense recognizes concerning their affording the vacation (he has checked their bank statement for accuracy, already asked about a raise, and so forth), Kurt's utterance (4) is true.

In saying (4), the proposition Kurt makes as if to express is

(5) I have absolutely conclusive reasons for believing we cannot afford that vacation

which is quite a strong claim. In fact, his utterance does not have as its truth-condition (5). Were (5) to capture the truth-condition of his utterance, what he says would be false (as the skeptic patiently reminds us). After all, Kurt can't rule out that they might receive a large inheritance from an unknown relative. Kurt makes as if to express the proposition (5), but only in the service of communicating the proposition

(6) I have every reason to believe we cannot afford that vacation, given how much money we have in the bank, and how much we earn in our paychecks, and how much that vacation costs

It sounds like Kurt is committed to (5) because this is what he makes as if to say. But (6) is what he is committed to. The conditions under which Kurt's utterance (4) is true in the conversational pretense are given by (6). Since these conditions are met, his utterance is true—he knows they can't afford the vacation.[21]

On the pretense account of how knowledge claims come to be true, each conversational game determines how what one makes as if to say determines a communicated proposition. The communicated proposition is what one is committed to, and its truth or falsity determines the truth or falsity of one's utterance "I know that *p*."

6. How pretense semantics dissolves the puzzle

Let us return to the puzzle with which we began. We observed that our ascriptions of knowledge display an apparent tension between context-sensitivity and insensitivity. Although we ascribe knowledge as if "knows" were in some way context-sensitive, we routinely resist ascriptions of knowledge that would be licensed were the semantics for "knows" context-sensitive in any of the standard ways. More generally, when one claims to know, one makes no mention of the context-sensitivity of the truth of one's claim, and one's claim to know must stand the test of subsequent challenges as though its content were absolute. How does the pretense account resolve this tension?

I will give a short and a long answer to this question. The short answer is this: according to the pretense semantic account, "knows" has an invariant linguistic meaning—something like "has absolutely conclusive reasons for believing."[22] Since we grasp the meaning of "knows", we resist saying things such as "he knew in these circumstances (or when we had this or that in mind, or when the stakes were such and such), but now that circumstances have changed he doesn't know." Since the meaning of "knows" does not involve a parameter for an evidential standard, or any other sort of parameter, such sayings are not well-formed. (Saying such things is not how we play the game of knowledge attribution.) The invariance of the meaning of "knows" is a straightforward explanation of facts (b), (c), and (d). But what of the fact (a) above, that we ascribe knowledge as if "knows" were context-sensitive? Here, our explanation is also straightforward. We do ascribe knowledge as if the meaning of "knows" were context-sensitive—but only as if it were. Because each conversational game determines the truth conditions of a knowledge claim, a claim of the form *S knows that p* can be true when made in one setting, but not when made in another, even though nothing about the putative knower's evidence changes. Differences in conversational principles account for differences in truth conditions. So it is as if "knows" meant something different from one occasion to the next. It is only as if this were so, but that is enough to account for the appearance of context-sensitive meaning.

The longer answer to the question of how the pretense account handles the tension is this: Recall our initial example of Rob and Kate. Rob says to Kate:

(7) I know that it's a Diebenkorn

thereby making as if to say

(8) I have absolutely conclusive reasons for believing that it's a Diebenkorn

and so communicating the proposition

(9) I have every reason to believe that it's a Diebenkorn, if it's a major modern artist

The first thing we want explained is why Rob's utterance (7) is *true* when he makes it to Kate, but why Rob won't repeat his claim when talking to the curator. Rob resists saying to the curator, "I know that it's a Diebenkorn." He may even say to the curator

(10) I don't know that it is a Diebenkorn

The point is that (7) and (10) are both *true*. This is the context-sensitivity we wanted explained.

The second thing we wanted explained is why Rob won't say to Kate

(11) Well, I knew before, when I was talking to you, but now I don't know

In fact, he may say

(12) I didn't know, when I said it was a Diebenkorn

As noted above, making a knowledge claim, one makes no mention of the context-sensitivity of the truth of one's claim, and one's claim to know must stand the test of subsequent challenges as though its content were absolute—one's earlier claim will be rejected if later one won't claim to know. These utterances illustrate the context-insensitivity that we wanted explained.

Now to our explanation of these data. Start with this observation: the pretense account explains the context-sensitivity of knowledge attribution in such a way that the following holds: Rob's token utterance (7) is true, but another token utterance of the same type would be false if made by Rob later, talking to the curator. Rob says (10) later, talking to the curator, and (10) is true. How can (7) and (10) both be true? The answer is that these are utterance tokens, and their truth owes to the truth of the proposition they communicate in the course of a conversational pretense. And (7) and (10) don't communicate contradictory propositions, on the pretense semantic account. With (10) one makes as if to say

(13) I do not have conclusive reasons for believing that is a Diebenkorn.

And thereby communicates the proposition

(14) I do not have every reason to think that it is a Diebenkorn, if it might be a forgery

Now recall the proposition that (7) communicates is (9). And (9) is consistent with (14). So utterances of (7) and (10) can both be true without contradiction. Thus the pretense account accommodates the context-sensitivity of knowledge ascription.

Now turn to context-insensitivity. Why won't Rob say (11), and why will he say (12)? As I noted above, given the meaning of "knows", saying (11) borders on the non-sensical. On an analogy with another term whose meaning is insensitive to features of context, saying (11) would be like saying, "I was 40 years old when I was talking with you, but now that the stakes have gone up, I'm not." That is not the sort of remark we can make sense of.

The more difficult feature of context-insensitivity is revealed with (12). With this utterance, Rob denies his earlier claim to know. If his denial is true, then how can his earlier utterance (7) also be true? In answer, Rob's utterance (12) communicates a proposition only with respect to rules governing the conversational pretense in which it is uttered. Since the stakes have gone up, a claim now to know or have known demands that more counter-possibilities be ruled out. And to now deny knowing or having known is to affirm now that one does not or did not rule out these newly important counter-possibilities. Thus (12) communicates

(15) I did not, when I said it was a Diebenkorn, have every reason to believe it a Diebenkorn, if it might be a forgery

Now we can see, once again, since the proposition that (7) communicates is (9) and (9) is consistent with (15), there is no problem about how both (7) and (12) can both be true utterances.[23]

It is perhaps worth pausing to focus on this fact. On the account I have given, (7) and (12) can both be true. Now, the relativist might want to reply, But then isn't the self-same utterance (7) true (when made) and false (now that stakes have changed)? The reason why not is this. The utterance Rob made earlier to Kate (7) "I know that it's a Diebenkorn" was true. And it *still is* true. The utterance was true because the proposition it communicated, (9), was true, and that proposition *still is* true. It's just that Rob can't communicate *that* proposition anymore by using "knows"; he can't communicate that proposition anymore, using a token of the same type as (7) that he once used to communicate it.[24]

Thus we have explanations of the sensitivity and insensitivity phenomena we wanted explained. The pretense semantic account for "knows that" handles the puzzling tension in our usage nicely.[25]

No defense of a semantics for "knows that" is compelling without an account of how it handles important features of skeptical argument. So I will close with a brief consideration of the much-discussed "skeptical paradox." It will illustrate further the explanatory power of the pretense account.

7. Pretense semantics and the skeptical paradox

Here is the skeptical paradox, re-framed this time in its so-called "lottery" paradoxical form: Kurt makes the claim

(16) I know we can't afford that vacation

and, so the argument goes, Kurt will also be ready to claim

(17) If I know we can't afford that vacation, then I know we won't win the lottery

But of course, Kurt finds it difficult to accept that he can really know in advance that he will lose a fair lottery. So he will deny the claim

(18) I know we won't win the lottery

That is the paradox, in its "lottery" form. Now, think about claim (17). Will Kurt really be ready to make this claim, on having claimed (16)? It is a natural reaction to hesitate over (17), and only agree to it when one's interlocutor talks one around to it, for instance, by saying, "Come on, winning the lottery would make the vacation affordable, right? So you must know you won't win, if you know you can't afford the vacation", or some such.

I think it is an important fact that one first resists claim (17), and only agrees to it after conversational coercion. The pretense account helps us understand this important fact. Imagine Kurt and Steven are talking about possible vacations, calculating their savings, their future expenditures and so forth. Their conversation has proceeded in terms characterized by principles of generation on which only certain possibilities are counter-possibilities in need of ruling out. Lotteries, unexpected inheritances, and the like, are not counter-possibilities in their pretense, and so have nothing to do with determining the truth-conditions of knowledge claims.[26] Now suppose Kurt says "Let's take some of these off the table—I know we can't afford that one." If Steven were to say "Oh, don't take it off the table—after all, maybe we'll win the lottery", it will sound like a sorry joke at best. His utterance contravenes one of the principles of generation of their conversational game, by treating this as a counter-possibility. So Kurt might laugh or roll his eyes, but he won't feel compelled to retract what he said. Steven's utterance violates one of the principles to which they have both presumably sought to conform their conversational contributions, and in light of which their utterances take on truth conditions. That is why Kurt resists (17).

The pretense account explains why we baulk at saying such things, and often feel a trick is being played on us by an interlocutor (like the skeptic) who wants to force us to accept claims such as (17). It is worth noting here that Kurt's reaction speaks in favor of the second of the two options canvassed above for specifying the pretense. Kurt's reaction to Steven is not on a par with the reaction he would have were Steven to bring up a possibility that Kurt's evidence had already ruled out: If Steven said, "but maybe you'll get a raise", Kurt might say, "you haven't been paying attention! I told you I asked about that" or simply, "I already asked for one." But Kurt does not say "I already ruled out winning the lottery." Rather, when Steven speaks of the possibility, he shrugs or rolls his eyes.

What makes our resistance to such conversational moves important? It suggests that the paradox itself might be resisted. One resists (17) because it violates principles of generation for one's conversation. Consequently, one resists the inference that would carry one to (18).[27]

An objection to such a suggestion about the paradox is not far away, however: Doesn't it just sound odd, the objection goes, to deny (17)?[28] Aren't we committed thereby to an "abominable conjunction"—namely, "I know we can't afford the vacation but I don't know that we won't win the lottery"?[29]

This objection has proved powerful, and has moved many to reject any resolution of the paradox that would deny (17). I think the pretense account has a ready response. But matters here are delicate. They are delicate because Kurt may in fact say such things as, "I don't know that we won't win the lottery"—he may even say this and ask Steven to buy him a ticket, as he continues to plan for a cheap vacation visiting relatives, because he knows they can't afford a better one. So what is really abominable about the conjunction? There *is* something odd about saying, "I know we can't afford the vacation, although I don't know that we won't win the lottery", certainly. But there is nothing odd about being in a position to say each conjunct, and act on each conjunct, in the same stretch of rational activity. So whatever is odd about the abominable conjunction, it is not that it is self-refuting.[30]

What, then, is odd about saying "I know we can't afford the vacation but I don't know that we won't win the lottery"? Can the pretense account explain the oddity of such a claim? Here is one suggestion that a pretense account can give. With such an utterance, one brings a possibility pretended to *not* be a counter-possibility squarely into view. Since the possibility is in fact a logical contrary to the proposition purportedly known, mentioning it cannot but have the effect of making plain its status as *pretended away*. The fact that pretense alone is excluding it from consideration as a counter-possibility, and as bearing on one's knowledge claims, is now also squarely in view. These facts give the utterance an odd feeling. The utterance is not outright self-refuting, but it does cause certain sorts of unhelpful reflection on its conditions of use and truthfulness. Moreover, it is easy to imagine that our conversations about knowledge are guided by a presumption that salient counter-possibilities should *not* be pretended away. If so, then the making salient of this counter-possibility undercuts the game as it's been played up 'til now.[31]

On this suggestion, the pretense account has it that the abominable conjunction undercuts the conversational pretense that governs one's knowledge claim. Such a claim will be resisted, then. So, in resisting such claims as (17), we do not find ourselves committed to uttering abominable conjunctions, either.[32]

Having come this far, it is easy to imagine someone complaining, "But you haven't answered the skeptic at all, then—you've only said that we resist talking certain ways!" I agree. To answer the skeptic, one would also have to defend the claim that it is *reasonable* to resist talking in these ways, and I have not defended this claim. One's disappointment at this response will depend upon how much one believes a semantic account of "knows" can do, all by itself, in answering skepticism. By itself, I think, a semantic account of "knows" cannot answer the skeptic (and if *answering* means *silencing forever*, I'm not sure any account can answer the skeptic). The value of a semantic account of knowledge attribution to the discussion of skepticism is of a different kind. I want to close by focusing on the value of the pretense account in this regard.

8. The lasting power of skepticism

One of the greatest advantages of the pretense account is that it offers a compelling characterization of skepticism and its power to challenge us. The pretense account provides an explanation of skepticism's lasting power.

Too often, discussion of the skeptical paradox proceeds as though skepticism amounted to the claim that all or most of our ordinary knowledge claims were false. (And, correlatively, as if to answer the skeptic amounted simply to showing how most of our ordinary knowledge claims might be true.) If that were the right characterization, it isn't clear why skepticism should ever have bothered us. I think a deeper characterization of skepticism is required, both to make sense of its lasting appeal, and also, someday, to manage really to speak to skeptical challenges.

With the pretense account, we characterize one important kind of skeptical challenge as a challenge to our practices of knowledge ascription. Our practice involves cooperative pretenses according to which certain possibilities not ruled out by our evidence are ignored. So we might imagine what the skeptic says is not, "your knowledge claims are all false" but rather, "your choice of rules for games of knowledge ascription is ultimately arbitrary—why ignore these possibilities instead of those—why ignore any?" Alternatively, we might imagine the skeptic says, "These rules for talking about knowledge are just like yours, why play by your rules?"

If this is the better characterization of skepticism, does the pretense semantic account answer this skeptic?

No. But I think the account points toward a way to meet the challenge. As I noted, responding to skepticism requires an additional account of what makes it reasonable to play by some rules rather than others, and also sometimes to refuse conversational overtures (especially coming from a skeptic). Have we anything to say in defense of playing by some conversational rules rather than others? One answer that won't do is to make the reply that *we* speak this way, using these principles. Another answer that won't do is to say, these are the rules we always have played by. One answer that seems on the right track is to point to the fact that using our conversational principles and not the skeptic's lets us ascribe knowledge in such a way that we can engage in important work. Playing by our rules, we convey to each other important information about which claims we take ourselves to have sufficient reason to believe and to act on. (And one might add that it is only for doing such work that we have the concept of knowledge in the first place.)

J.L. Austin's remarks about knowledge suggest how we might further develop this response to the skeptic. Austin reminds us that our intents and purposes frame our conversations, when it comes to ascribing knowledge. If Rob claims to know that the painting is a Diebenkorn, Kate may object that his evidence is insufficient: "What you say is not enough, it doesn't prove your claim." But in such a case, Austin reminds us,

> Enough is enough. It doesn't mean everything. Enough means enough to show that (within reason, and for present intents and purposes) it 'can't' be anything else, there is no room for an alternative, competing, description . . .[33]

Austin's remark here suggests an answer to our question about what makes it reasonable to resist skeptical conversational overtures. The answer is that *reasonable* conversational principles are those that *answer to our purposes* in ascribing knowledge.

A full defense along these lines against the skeptic is of course a separate task. What can be said here, I think, is that the value of the semantic pretense account is that it makes possible the foregoing characterization of the skeptical challenge. It is a characterization that does justice to the lasting interest and importance of skepticism. And it points in the direction of a solution, if any solution is to be had. Overall, that is not bad for a semantic account.[34]

Notes

1. This section covers ground that's been thoughtfully explored by John Hawthorne (2003) and John McFarlane (2005). Variant species of the views discussed below are possible (for some, see MacFarlane), but for our purposes here, they can safely be grouped with other members of their genus.
2. J.L. Austin (1979) and Thompson Clarke (1972) originally explored the idea that knowledge ascriptions are context-sensitive. What I call "contextualism" (with a lower-case "c") is fully articulated in its recent form by Stewart Cohen (1988),(2000). David Lewis (1996) makes important contributions to contextualism. Philosophers of language know an entirely different sort of view by the name "Contextualism" (with a capital "C"), for instance in the work of Francois Recanati (2004), about which more below. Recanati's Contextualism owes to Barwise & Perry (1983) and Austin (1979). The suggestion that I will put forward in this paper is, broadly speaking, capital-C-Contextualist.
3. I will remain neutral about what epistemic standards are, relying on a rough understanding to the effect that a standard governs how good one's evidence must be. This leaves much undecided, as for instance whether it is best to try to capture the job such standards do in terms of isolating possible *defeaters* in need of *ruling out*, and so on. These are topics for another paper. Different versions of contextualism may emphasize different aspects of the ascriber's state as settling the standards on knowledge.
4. In further defense of taking "knows" to be ascriber-sensitive, the contextualist points to the tidy resolution we can thereby provide for the so-called "skeptical paradox." Cohen (1988) originated the skeptical paradox, as well as offering the basic contextualist solution. I will discuss the skeptical paradox in section 7.
5. Hawthorne (2003).
6. Hawthorne is not sanguine about salience doing the work here—see his chapter 4 section 2 for interesting discussion.
7. Stewart Cohen's example, cited in Hawthorne (p. 180)
8. As MacFarlane notes, "the evidence suggests that at any given context of use, we hold the standards one must meet in order to count as 'knowing' constant over all circumstances of evaluation." p. 7 manuscript
9. See for instance, Unger (1975). There are further alternatives here, too: for instance one could say with Schaffer (2004) that ordinary knowledge claims are pragmatically assertible though false, because they are cases of hyperbole. Such a view will imply systematic error on the part of speakers, however, since we don't take ourselves to be exaggerating when we make knowledge claims. See Hawthorne and MacFarlane for discussion of related attempts to save sensitive invariantism and contextualism by invoking conversational pragmatics.
10. As MacFarlane (2005) notes.

11. Schiffer (1996).
12. See Richard (2004) and MacFarlane (2005).
13. It seems the relativist will have to appeal to an error theory to explain why we are uncomfortable at hearing others apparently disagree with our knowledge claims, and that we take genuine disagreement to be involved. Perhaps Kate and John hear in each other's claim a genuine although implicit challenge concerning the appropriateness of their own context of assessment, and mistake it for a disagreement about the truth? See Richard (2004).
14. At the end of the day, whether the account I am about to offer is correct in its details is of less importance than that there should be some way of defending a view that incorporates these two features: invariance about meaning with context-sensitivity of truth-conditions.
15. A *true* claim to know also demands that the proposition known be *true*, of course (i.e. knowledge is factive). Here and in what follows, I will suppress mention of this requirement on knowledge claims, in order to allow formulations that focus exclusively on the (more troublesome) justification component. (Note also, debate is possible over this particular way of putting the justification component, and I won't defend it here, but will use it as a rough guide, since my main point is that "knows" need not have a sensitive meaning. My intention is not to give an analysis of knowledge.)
16. Walton (1990), Hills (1997), and Crimmins (1998).
17. I only include part of the story we'd need to tell here, about how Sarah's utterance comes to express what it does, in order to focus on just those features that will be relevant for our account of the semantics of "knows"—specifically, I focus on how principles of generation permit certain possibilities to be ignored in the determination of truth-conditions.
18. Someone might want to argue that there are two truth-conditions here: an utterance has pretense-derived truth-conditions, and real truth-conditions. I believe we should resist this way of talking: we might distinguish *propositions one makes as if to express* and *communicated propositions*, but only the communicated proposition matters for determining the truth of one's utterance. Also note: I do not mean to suggest that the *proposition one makes as if to express* must in some sense be generated first, and worked over cognitively *before* participants in conversational games arrive at the *communicated proposition*. There is every reason to think we arrive at the communicated proposition first, and the availability of the proposition one makes as if to express is the result of further cognitive work.
19. The full story of how this proposition (3) is generated would have to include more principles of generation no doubt. I focus only on that governing the nature of milk, so as to give a feeling for core idea of *truth-conditional ignoring of possibilities*.
20. See Crimmins p. 7ff. See also Recanati (2004) for further argument in favor of utterance truth-conditions being determined by conversational purposes.
21. As I noted above (note 15), since knowledge is factive, and a claim to know is only true if the proposition known is true, we would also have to add to (6) a clause to the effect that Kurt and Steven in fact cannot afford the vacation, and say that what Kurt says is true if that clause is also satisfied. For simplicity, I focus only on the justification component, and suppress these extra clauses.

22. In order to resolve the apparent tension in our usage, then, I believe that we have to advocate what Recanati calls "moderate Contextualism"—or "syncretism"—since I say the meaning of "knows" is invariant. More radical Contextualist views are possible, on which the meaning of knows is itself determined by pragmatic processes. Whether such views could provide an explanation of the tension is a matter for further discussion.
23. A note about embedded knowledge claims. Suppose Rob says,

    (12*) I didn't know, when I said it was a Diebenkorn, but *I thought I knew*

    The utterance (12*) contains an embedded use of "knows" within the scope of an attitude report. What does the pretense account say about such embedded uses? We might think that with (12*) Rob communicates

    (15*) I did not have every reason to believe it a Diebenkorn, if it might be a forgery, when I said it was a Diebenkorn, but I thought I did.

    However (15*) gets something wrong, since forgery was not a counter-possibility before, and so not even on Rob's mind before. Rob did not believe (then) that he had (then) reason to rule out forgery, and is not reporting (now) on the falsity of that earlier belief. What Rob communicates is

    (15**) I did not have every reason to believe it a Diebenkorn, if it might be a forgery, when I said it was a Diebenkorn, but I thought I had conclusive reasons.

    The error that he means to ascribe himself concerns his getting it wrong about what should have counted as conclusive reasons.
24. A further point worth observing is that when Rob is challenged by Kate regarding his earlier utterance, he may say (12), but he will also stand by the proposition he communicated, namely (9). And he *will* try to reformulate this claim (contra MacFarlane (manuscript p. 8)). That is, we can imagine that he won't simply blush and stammer, and say (12) at all—rather, he'll stand by his earlier utterance—not by making an utterance of the same type as (7) over again; now, of course, it is not open to him to stand by his earlier utterance this way—rather, he will find a way to re-express the proposition that his former utterance expressed. A relativist might complain that we don't seem to have systematic means in the language for such re-expressions, and for standing by our earlier claims. But I believe we do. One systematic means of standing by earlier claims is to reformulate with appeal to the principles by which the former conversation was governed: e.g. "Well, if it's a major modern artist, then it's a Diebenkorn."
25. That it does so counts in favor of the idea that some form of Contextualism is correct.
26. That is to say, nothing to do with the justification component of their knowledge claims—should they actually win the lottery, the proposition that they cannot afford the vacation is false. Again, here, as elsewhere I ignore the factive aspect of knowledge to highlight issues about the justification of our claims.

27. Someone might object: "But how can one resist (17)? Doesn't it just follow from a principle of *epistemic closure*? Kurt can certainly know that it is a logical implication of not being able to afford the vacation that they do not win the lottery. And if he knows that, then he should be willing to assert (17)." In fact, I believe that epistemic closure, at least in a form strong enough to generate the skeptical paradox, is false (see my (2005)), and so it need not be the case that Kurt should be willing to assert (17) on such grounds. However, I also believe that accepting the pretense semantic account does not *require* that one reject epistemic closure.
28. It is an important point to bear in mind that when one resists making an utterance, as Kurt resists (17), one does not thereby become committed to uttering its denial. But let us consider the challenge that follows in any case.
29. See Keith DeRose's introduction in DeRose (1999)
30. In this way, the abominable conjunction is like Moore's claim, "It's raining, but I don't believe it." Each conjunct might be true, but saying the conjunction is odd.
31. Much more might be said on the topic of the pragmatic demands on how our conversational pretenses are framed. For present purposes, since we just want a candidate pretense-based explanation of the oddity of the abominable conjunction, we can leave the matter with this rough suggestion, that the salience of a counter-possibility forces its consideration. No doubt we'd want something weaker, to capture how actual conversations about knowledge work.
32. A further objection to the account is this: a lone cogitator could consider the propositions of the paradox. What can the pretense account tell us about how such a cogitator's thoughts are framed? A full answer here is outside the scope of this paper, but a brief suggestion is that, insofar as thoughts have propositional content, mechanisms for ignoring certain possibilities must also come into play in the lone cogitator's cognitive economy.
33. Austin (1979), "Other Minds", p. 84
34. Thanks to Mark Crimmins, David Hills and John Hawthorne for comments on earlier drafts. I presented a version of this paper at the Ohio State University Philosophy Department in November 2004. Many thanks to the audience there for lively discussion.

References

Austin, J. L. (1979). *Philosophical Papers*. Oxford, Clarendon.

Barwise, J. and Perry, J. (1983). *Situations and Attitudes*. Cambridge, MA, MIT Press.

Clarke, T. (1972). "The Legacy of Skepticism." *Journal of Philosophy* 69: 754–769.

Cohen, S. (1988). "How to be a Fallibilist." *Philosophical Perspectives*. Tomberlin. 2: 581–605.

———. (2000). "Contextualism and Skepticism." *Skepticism*. S. a. Villanueva. Boston, Blackwell.

Crimmins, M. (1998). "Hesperus and Phosphorus: Sense, Pretense and Reference." *Philosophical Review* 107(1): 1–47.

DeRose, K. (1999). (ed) *Skepticism: A Contemporary Reader*. Oxford, Oxford University Press.

Hawthorne, J. (2003). *Knowledge and Lotteries*. Oxford, Oxford University Press.

Hills, D. (1997). "Aptness and Truth in Verbal Metaphor." *Philosophical Topics* 25(1): 117–153.

Lawlor, K. (2005). "Living without Closure." (forthcoming) in *Contextualism*, Grazer Philosophische Studien.

Lewis, D. (1996). "Elusive Knowledge." *Australian Journal of Philosophy* 74: 549–567.

MacFarlane, J. (2005). "The Assessment Sensitivity of Knowledge Attributions." *(forthcoming) Oxford Studies in Epistemology*. Oxford, Oxford University Press.
Recanati, F. (2004). *Literal Meaning*. Cambridge, Cambridge University Press.
Richard, M. (2004). "Contextualism and Relativism." *Philosophical Studies* 119: 215–242.
Schaffer, J. (2004). "Skepticism, Contextualism and Discrimination." *Philosophy and Phenomenological Research* 69: 138–155.
Unger, P. (1975). *Ignorance: A Case for Skepticism*. Oxford, Oxford University Press.
Walton, K. (1990). *Mimesis as Make-Believe*. Cambridge, MA, Harvard University Press.

Philosophical Perspectives, 19, Epistemology, 2005

PERCEPTUAL BELIEF AND NONEXPERIENTIAL LOOKS

Jack Lyons
Department of Philosophy, University of Arkansas

How things look (or sound, taste, smell, etc.) plays two important roles in the epistemology of perception.[1] First, our perceptual beliefs are epistemically justified, at least in part, in virtue of how things look. Second, whether a given belief is a perceptual belief, as opposed to, say, an inferential belief, is also at least partly a matter of how things look. Together, these yield an epistemically significant sense of 'looks'. A standard view is that "how things look", in this epistemically significant sense, is a matter of one's present perceptual phenomenology, of what nondoxastic experiential state one is in. On this standard view, these experiential states (a) determine which of my beliefs are perceptual beliefs and (b) are centrally involved in justifying these beliefs.

As an alternative to this view, I want to argue that there is a nonexperiential sense of 'look' as well and that this sense of 'look' is at least as epistemically significant a sense as any experiential sense. That is, the connection between what an agent is justified in believing and how things look to her in this nonexperiential sense is more direct than the connection between what she is justified in believing and how things look in any experiential sense. In addition, this same nonexperiential sense of looks can be used to solve the classic problem of distinguishing perception from inference.

I won't actually be arguing against the standard view; the goal is mainly to articulate an alternative. If, however, the epistemologically interesting sense of 'looks' is the one that is most directly connected to justified belief and/or to perceptual belief, then the epistemologically interesting sense is not an experiential sense. The existence of nonexperiential 'looks', 'sounds', and the like serves to undercut an important source of motivation for the standard view. So although I won't try to show that the standard view is false, I will show that there is considerably less reason to believe it than is usually assumed.

A Short Taxonomy of Looks

There are notoriously many different senses of 'looks'. Chisholm (1957, 1966) famously distinguished between comparative and noncomparative uses of '*x* looks *F* to *S*'. To believe that *x* looks—in the comparative sense—*F* to me is to believe that *x* looks to me the way that *F* things normally look.[2] Such a belief cannot be epistemologically basic, for it depends on additional beliefs, viz., beliefs about how *x* looks and how *F* things normally look. Chisholm argues that these additional beliefs must involve 'look' in the noncomparative sense, as a description of the intrinsic character of the state, not its relation to other states. It is common to add to these two senses epistemic and/or doxastic senses of 'looks' (e.g., Alston 2002), but we must be careful to distinguish purely epistemic or doxastic senses from those that make an essential reference to an experiential state. According to the experiential-epistemic sense, *x* looks *F* to *S* iff the way *x* looks to *S* prima facie justifies *S* in believing that *x* is *F*; the purely epistemic sense allows that *x* looks *F* to *S* iff *S* is prima facie justified in believing that *x* is *F*. Similarly, according to the experiential-doxastic sense, *x* looks *F* to *S* iff the way *x* looks to *S* disposes *S* to believe that *x* is *F*, while according to the purely doxastic sense *x* looks *F* to *S* iff *S* is disposed to believe that *x* is *F*.[3] The difference between the pure and the experiential senses is that the latter explicitly involve the agent's perceptual phenomenology. Thus, the reference to "the way *x* looks to *S*" is to be read as picking out a particular experiential state.

The comparative, noncomparative, experiential-doxastic, and experiential-epistemic senses of 'looks' are all experiential senses; they make essential reference to the agent's experiential states. They are literally about how things look. It is clear that the purely epistemic and doxastic senses of 'look', 'appear' and the like, on the other hand, are metaphorical and really have little if anything to do with looking or appearing. If I say that it looks as if the Republicans are going to win this election, I'm using either the purely epistemic or the purely doxastic sense; I am clearly not making any claims about *vision*.[4] What makes these metaphorical senses metaphorical, however, is *not* that they make no essential reference to visual *experience* but, rather, that they make no essential reference to *vision*. There is another sense of 'looks', which makes no essential reference to experiential states either, but which is a literal sense nonetheless.

According to what I will call the "perceptual output sense" of 'looks', *x* looks *F* to *S* iff one of *S*'s visual systems is outputting an identification of *x* as *F* (likewise, *mutatis mutandis*, for perceptual output senses of 'sounds', 'smells', etc.). This is an important sense of 'looks', and it describes neither the intrinsic nature of an experiential state nor a relationally characterized fact about the experiential state. Something can (perceptual-output-)look different ways to different agents who have the same visual experience, and something can (perceptual-output-)look a certain way to an agent who has no visual experiences at all. Nonetheless, this is a literal and epistemically significant sense of 'look'.

So we have three basic kinds of 'looks' locutions: (i) those that describe an experiential state, (ii) the metaphorical uses like the purely doxastic or epistemic senses, and (iii) a literal yet nonexperiential use that describes the output of a perceptual system. This last kind has been overlooked, so to speak, and I want to remedy that now.

Perceptual Systems and Their Outputs

I need to explain what is meant by the claim that a visual system is outputting an identification of *x* as *F*. To do so I will have to make a number of theoretical cognitive scientific assumptions, which I think are plausible but which cannot be defended here.

I presume, first of all, that the mind consists of or at least contains a number of modules, or cognitive systems. Fodor (1983), of course, has made the concept of a cognitive module a familiar one. Fodor's own understanding of modularity, though setting the stage for most subsequent discussion, is quite restrictive, especially in its assumptions of innateness and informational encapsulation.[5] Many authors opt instead for a kind of "weak modularity", which relaxes the more restrictive of Fodor's conditions.

I have tried elsewhere (2001) to clarify this notion of weak modularity: the conception in question is the cognitive neuroscientific understanding of a cognitive system. On this view, all modules in Fodor's sense are systems, but not all systems are modules in Fodor's restrictive sense. To mention just a few features incompatible with Fodorian modularity, some cognitive systems might very well fall short of total encapsulation (they may have partially but not fully restricted information trade with other systems), and some systems may result from learning (Elman, et al. 1996). Nor need cognitive systems be domain specific in any very robust sense. The term 'module' is a handy one, however, and I will retain it, though I will use it interchangeably with the term 'cognitive system' and will use it for this weak notion of modularity, rather than the strong Fodorian one. On my view, a cognitive system for some task is an isolable cognitive mechanism that specializes in that task and exhibits a kind of functional unity. I will summarize the basic view here; the argument for it, along with a good deal of elaboration, can be found in my (2001).

Systems must be isolable in the sense of being independently capable of performing those tasks in which they specialize, in the absence of other mechanisms. This feature is illustrated by the cognitive neuroscientific methodology of double dissociation. If some disease or brain lesion produces an impairment with respect to task *A* but leaves performance spared with respect to task *B*, that is some reason for thinking that *A* and *B* are subserved by distinct systems. However, such a single dissociation of *A* from *B* is compatible with *A* and *B*'s being handled by the same system if *A* is more difficult, the damaged system continuing to perform normally on the easy tasks but exhibiting deficits on the difficult ones. Suppose, for instance, we discover a patient with prosopagnosia: a selective deficit for recognizing faces, even while ordinary object identification is (relatively) unimpaired. Does this mean that there is a distinct face recognition system, or merely that face recognition is more difficult and thus more sensitive to injury? A double dissociation, where one population is impaired on *A* but not *B* and another population is impaired on *B* but not *A*, resolves this question. If *A* dissociates from *B* and *B* from *A*, it must be that different cognitive systems underlie performance of the different tasks, the one system being damaged in the one population, the other system in the other.[6]

All cognitive mechanisms, qua cognitive, effect a mapping of representational states.[7] Cognitive systems are said to be systems, or modules, *for* something. There is a module *for* face recognition (equivalently: there is a face recognition module) only if there is a module that specializes in face recognition, i.e., it does little or nothing else. If face recognition is performed by a more general purpose visual module and not a separable component, then there is nothing that specializes in face recognition and consequently no system *for* face recognition. This is not a substantive requirement that systems be domain specific; it is instead a constraint on nomenclature: we can't properly *call it* a face recognition system unless that's all (or pretty much all) the system does.[8]

Finally, suppose there is a system for face recognition, and suppose also that there is a system for gustation. It clearly does not follow from this that there is a system for gustation-or-face-recognition. Cognitive systems must exhibit a certain functional unity; not just any gerrymandered collection of systems is itself a system. The task must be unitary with respect to the implementing mechanisms in the sense that no proper part of the implementing mechanism performs any part of the task.[9]

Clarifying the concept of a cognitive system, or module, takes us part of the way toward an understanding of perceptual systems, but we will need to know what the difference is between perceptual and nonperceptual modules. By 'perceptual system', or 'perceptual module', I intend whatever it is that contemporary cognitive science means by the terms. Thus an account of perceptual systems, like the account of cognitive systems more generally, should aim at capturing the conception operative in cognitive science. Given the role I am reserving for perceptual systems, I clearly cannot delineate the class of perceptual systems in epistemological or phenomenological terms. Fortunately, cognitive science is notoriously unconcerned with either epistemology or phenomenology. A theory that captures current cognitive scientific assumptions about perceptual systems will be a theory that proceeds in terms of representations and computational processes, not in terms of reasons or raw feels.

What distinguishes perceptual from nonperceptual systems, I think, is this: perceptual systems take their inputs from the world and not from the larger organism. A perceptual system is a cognitive system that starts with the stimulation of sense organs by physical energy as input and processes information about the current environment, where none of the inputs to any of the subsystems are under the direct voluntary control of the larger organism. Delineating perceptual systems thus, on the basis of their inputs, yields a characterization of perceptual systems that is neutral with respect to their phenomenological properties. Similarly, what distinguishes one kind of perceptual system from another, e.g., auditory from visual systems, is the kind of information they process rather than any phenomenal experiences they produce.

It is important that cognitive systems can be assembled out of simpler subsystems; in fact, this appears to be commonplace. Vision, for instance, seems to comprise a number of distinct systems, many of which sum together to form larger visual systems. Visual processing splits fairly early on into the famous "what" and "where" systems (Ungerleider and Mishkin 1982; Goodale and Milner 1992). These systems contain a number of subsystems, including a system for the detection and analysis of motion, systems for computing object boundaries from surface discontinuities, and the like. Color vision is handled separately by a different system. Yet these systems "come together again" to bind object color, location, and identity into a single comprehensive representation. Slightly different visual systems are known to exist in the different hemispheres, at least in the ventral pathways, with the left being thought to specialize in relatively abstract visual information and the right in relatively specific information; alternatively the left may be engaged in "entry level" categorization, while the right is engaged in subordinate level categorization (Marsolek 1999). (The entry level is the level at which subjects tend to spontaneously identify perceptually presented objects, e.g., 'apple' 'chair' [Jolicoeur, et al. 1984]. It is to be contrasted with subordinate levels, e.g., 'Granny Smith', 'Macintosh', and superordinate levels, e.g., 'fruit', 'furniture', 'object'.) Thus, face recognition is normally subserved by the right hemisphere, general visual object recognition by the left.

Accurate boxologies of these things are exceedingly complex, but a simplified and fictionalized depiction appears in Figure 1. Boxes are drawn to indicate some of the relevant systems. The upper box that takes retinal irradiation as input and returns objection identifications as outputs corresponds (roughly) to one theory (Biederman 1990) about the computational nature of the left

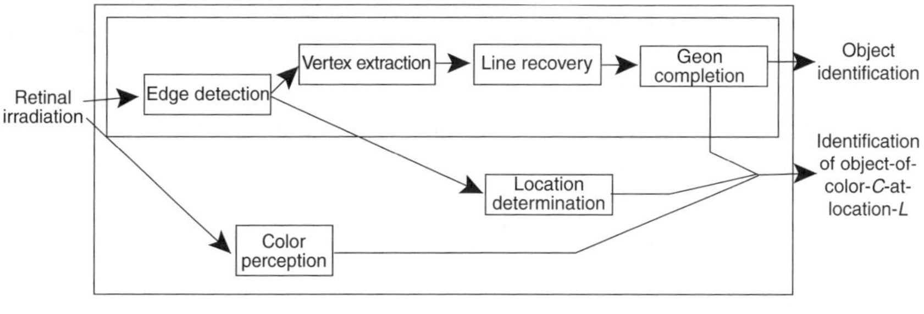

Figure 1

hemispheric ventral pathway; the location determination system corresponds to the dorsal pathway; and the color perception box corresponds to a system involving cortical area V4. The ventral system by itself computes object identities, but in conjunction with the dorsal system produces representations of object-location pairs. These two, in conjunction with color perception, yield object-color-location triples: e.g., 'there is a red ball in front of me and to the left.'

Thus, several perceptual systems are represented in Figure 1, including an edge detection system, a color perception system, an object identification system, etc. The picture that emerges is one in which several smaller systems working relatively independently of each other add up to form larger perceptual systems. These systems may very well interact, despite their being independent of each other—no one doubts that it is possible to go blind without going deaf, the ventriloquism effect notwithstanding. The perceptual systems start with the transduction of energy by the sense organs and feed their outputs into more central, nonperceptual systems: practical and theoretical reasoning systems, the various memory systems, and so forth.

Though the basic functional architecture of the perceptual systems may be innately specified, the actual operation of such systems is patently affected by learning. My face recognition system can't identify someone as my mother unless it knows what my mother looks like, and this is clearly not innate. Expertise often brings with it changes in the outputs of perceptual systems. Though I am following convention in calling it a "face recognition system", it is quite possible that the system in question is responsible for additional fine-grained judgements, not just those concerning faces. An expert bird watcher with prosopagnosia lost the ability to visually recognize bird species, and a farmer with the disorder could no longer tell which of his cows was which (Farah 1990). It is likely that such beliefs were also outputs of this perceptual system.

Perceptual systems frequently produce lower level outputs, among which are sensations and the various experiential states, but the highest level outputs are generally representations of objects as having certain properties and/or belonging to certain categories. I will call such high level outputs of perceptual systems "identifications". These identifications are, at least in the unmarked case, doxastic; i.e., these outputs are beliefs. Though the term 'belief' is used very rarely in these areas of cognitive science, this is the most straightforward way of reading the talk in the literature about object recognition and the like: to recognize an object, to categorize it, to identify it, is at least typically to *judge* it to be a member of a certain category.

Of course, we don't always accept the outputs of our perceptual systems; we don't always believe what they tell us. My visual system is classifying this stimulus as a chicken, even though I know it's a rubber toy. Does this mean that the high level outputs of the perceptual systems were not beliefs after all? No. A belief, on a standard view, is a mental representation with a certain functional role. An identification with a certain familiar causal role counts as a belief; one that lacks that causal role is not a belief. The property of being a belief is not an essential property of a mental state but one that the state can gain or lose over time. Thus, when the output of the visual system is accepted or otherwise allowed to play the cognitive role definitive of belief, that output representation *is* the belief that there's a chicken in front of me; otherwise, it merely *looks*—in the perceptual output sense—as if there is a chicken in front of me.

It is imperative that the account just sketched makes no appeal to phenomenology or experiential states of any sort. A creature could have perceptual systems in the present sense without there being anything it is like to be that creature, without the creature having anything that would count as *experiences* at all. Still, as I have defined the perceptual output sense of 'look', things might nevertheless *look* a certain way to that creature. Though experiential states are commonly among the outputs of normal perceptual systems, this is not a defining feature of perceptual systems, nor is this sort of output the sort relevant to the perceptual output sense of 'look', 'sound', and the rest.

How Things Can Look Different, Even Though They Look the Same

Having explained the nonexperiential, perceptual output sense of 'look', I now must try to show that this is not a mere stipulation, but a real and natural sense of the term. Learning frequently results in a change in how things look in the perceptual output sense, without necessarily changing how they look in any experiential sense. Perceptual learning does sometimes affect what nondoxastic experiential states one has: what used to sound (in some experiential sense or other of the term) like an uninterrupted stream of phonemes now sounds (in this same sense) like a sequence of words, with pauses in between them that weren't heard before. What is important, however, is that learning does not always affect the experiential state. Thus, two agents (or two different time-slices of the same agent) can have identical experiential states but different perceptual outputs. Consider a few representative examples:

(a) You and I have identical visual experiences, but the face looks like Joe to you and just looks like a face to me.
(b) Walking through a field, you and I come across a copperhead. I'm a professional herpetologist, and it looks like a copperhead to me, though only like a snake to you (it also, of course, looks like a snake to me). Nonetheless, you and I have identical visual experiences.
(c) I can now hear the difference between a melodic minor scale and a diminished scale; they sound quite different to me. Several years ago, they sounded the same as each other to me (i.e., I couldn't tell the

difference), though neither sounds any different now than it ever did (i.e., the experiential state itself seems to be the same).

(d) *X* is an expert chicken sexer. Some chicks look male to *X* and some look female, even though the experiential states do not differ in any articulable way; nor do they differ from those of a novice.

(c) and (d) are paradigm cases of what a psychologist would count as perceptual learning; (a) involves learning, but it differs from the more interesting kinds of perceptual learning in that it doesn't require repeated exposure and subsequent enhancement of discriminatory abilities. (b) is a sort of intermediate case, though I suspect it's closer to (c) and (d) than to (a).

In each case the experiential states are the same, despite the fact that things *look* different. Consequently, there must be a nonexperiential sense of 'look'. This, I suggest, is the perceptual output sense. The claim that it *looks* like Joe to you but not me in (a) amounts to the claim that your face recognition system produces an 'it's Joe' output, while mine does not. Its looking like a copperhead to me but a snake to you in (b) is a matter of my visual system delivering the belief that there's a copperhead in our path, while yours delivers the belief that there's a snake in the path. To say that minor and diminished scales sound different to me, though they used to sound the same (c), is to say that my auditory system now yields identifications of diminished scales and of minor scales, where it used to output identifications of "dark-sounding" scales. And if the chicken sexer and the novice have identical experiential states, yet a particular chick looks male to the expert and not to the novice (d), then the best explanation for this is that the expert's visual system classifies distal stimuli as male or female, while the novice's does not.

Note that the sense of 'look' that is being evoked here is not a purely doxastic or purely epistemic sense. Nor is it in any way metaphorical. The examples crucially involve a particular sense modality. Even the experiential-doxastic and experiential-epistemic senses of 'look' are less strictly concerned with vision than the current examples. My current visual experience might dispose me to (justifiably) believe that I'm confronted with Bruce's favorite venomous reptile, but clearly it is only in a relatively extended and metaphorical sense that anything could *look* to me like Bruce's favorite venomous reptile. Even if the snake in (b) looks in an experiential-epistemic or experiential-doxastic sense like a copperhead, it also looks like a copperhead in some important, more restrictive sense of 'looks'. This is the perceptual output sense.

My argument requires only that cases (a)–(d) are possible, but I think a stronger claim can be supported. I think that cases like this are not only possible, but actual, and in fact quite common. Some of the cases might require a more careful formulation before this is at all obvious. In the face recognition case, for instance, it is clear enough that faces don't look—experientially—any different on becoming familiar ones, but it is tempting to think that whatever learning occurs does so outside of the perceptual system. If the belief glossed as 'it's Joe' is the belief that the person here *is named* "Joe", then of course this is not the output of a perceptual system, and the learning involved does indeed take place outside the perceptual system. However, to count as a face recognition system, the system must in some sense attribute identities to faces. To visually recognize or identify someone is not necessarily to be able to specify the person's name (or occupation or connection to oneself, etc.), which presumably takes place outside the face recognition system, but rather to activate some minimal representation of the individual. This must occur within the face recognition system in order for it to count as a face recognition system.

What, though, is my evidence for thinking that the experiences are the same in the sorts of examples under discussion? In the chicken sexing case, it is mostly conjecture, based on the fact that chicken sexers are unable to specify what cues they are using. They will certainly claim that males "look different" from females, but it would be question-begging to infer from this alone that males cause different experiential states than females. In the other cases, I have introspection to go on, in diachronic, within-agent versions of the relevant sorts of cases. Introspection is a dubious source of information about the workings of the mind, but here the issue is how things seem, and it is unlikely that we will get more reliable information from some other source. And cases (a)–(c) above represent the way it seems to me that things seem to me. The people I met yesterday don't look (experientially) different than they did yesterday when I saw them for the first time, though now I recognize them and then I didn't. Copperheads don't look any different to me now than they used to, but now they look copperheady, and before they just looked snaky. Likewise with the musical/auditory case, and it seems that similar phenomena occur in other modalities as well. Developing a more discriminating palate does not, as far as I can introspect, alter the gustatory qualia in the way that, say, quitting smoking does; it alters one's psychological responses—including one's classificatory and discriminatory responses—to the relevant stimuli.

One might insist that the experiential aspects do change in the kinds of cases at issue. Even if this is true, it is clear that they change very little, not enough to fully account for the drastic change in classificatory capacity. These sorts of cases are, after all, quite different from the case of learning a new language. Even if copperheads somehow produce in me a different experiential state than they used to, this experiential difference is too slight to amount to much; the difference that really matters and that perceptual learning produces is the higher level change in identification capacities. If distal stimuli were suddenly to begin causing in me the same kinds of experiential states they do in an ornithologist, I doubt I would notice the difference. But even if I did, without an accompanying change in identifications (i.e., a change in the doxastic/classificatory outputs of my perceptual systems), there would be no epistemologically significant sense in which some object suddenly now *looks* like a two-year-old ivory billed woodpecker.

Again, it is worth repeating that all that's really needed here is that the cases as described are possible. And they clearly are. In fact, far more extreme possibilities obtain. Consider a proprietary sense of 'zombie' according to which zombies not only lack qualia, but lack experiential states altogether; they are otherwise just like us. Suppose two such zombies are walking through a field. A snake in the grass reflects photons into the eyes of both zombies, activating their perceptual systems, all of which produces in one of them the cognitively spontaneous belief that there's a snake, and in the other (a professional herpetologist zombie) the cognitively spontaneous belief that there's a copperhead. The latter zombie would be inclined, despite the fact that she has no experiential states, to say that it looked copperheady to her. And, I submit, she would be right.

A slight air of paradox is bound to attend the claim that things look certain ways to zombies, or that there are nonexperiential senses of 'sound', 'taste' and the like. This air is dispelled, however, by the essential role of perceptual systems. To say that *x* looks red to me—in this sense of 'looks'—is to say that the belief that *x* is red (or something very much like a belief) is the output of one of my perceptual systems, in particular, one of my visual systems. There is nothing metaphorical about this use of 'look'. Even subtracting out the experiential component, there is a vast difference between 'that looks like Joe' and 'it looks like someone has broken into your house and stolen your VCR'. When I say that something sounds like a diminished scale, I don't (typically) mean merely that I think it's a diminished scale or that I have some reason to think it is a diminished scale, and I am not (or not merely) reporting the contents of my experience. I am describing a belief, but a certain kind of belief, one that has a very tight connection with perception, in particular, audition. That connection is that the belief is the output of an auditory system.

Thus, I think that the perceptual output sense of 'looks' captures a real and natural usage of the 'looks' locution. Because the understanding of cognitive systems appealed to here is more elaborate than our folk concepts of faculties and the like, the perceptual output sense of 'looks' developed here will be more detailed and precise than the version employed by the folk. Nonetheless, the intuitive appeal of the examples illustrates that there really is some already existing folk notion that is being explicated.

Nonexperiential Looks and the Justification of Perceptual Beliefs

I promised to argue that this perceptual output sense of 'looks' is epistemically significant. The fact that it looks like Joe to you and not to me has a lot to do with why you are justified in believing it's Joe and I'm not. The snake's looking copperheady to me is a large part of what justifies me in believing that it's a copperhead. But the only obvious sense in which something looks like Joe to you or like a copperhead to me is the perceptual output sense.

Compare this with the main epistemological alternative. "Experientialism" is the view that nondoxastic experiential states can serve as evidence to justify beliefs. Such states are intended to provide a solution to the famous regress problem by serving to confer justification without being themselves in need of it. On this view, my being appeared to redly—that is, the nondoxastic state of being appeared to redly—justifies my belief that I'm appeared to redly and, on certain versions of experientialism, also justifies my belief that there's something red nearby. These latter versions of experientialism, sometimes classified as direct realist theories, allow perceptual beliefs about external objects to be epistemologically basic, while more traditional versions (e.g., Descartes 1984; Chisholm 1966) do not.[10]

"Cognitive essentialism" (Pollock 1986) is the view that evidential relations hold necessarily; this conjoined with experientialism entails that which experiential states justify which beliefs is a necessary matter. A cognitive essentialist who also embraces experientialism and direct realism will hold that there are true epistemic principles of the following form (Pollock 1986; Huemer 2001):

> *S*'s being appeared to ϕ-ly is sufficient for *S*'s being prima facie justified in believing that there is something ϕ nearby.

Other experientialists deny cognitive essentialism and hold that something else is needed to make being appeared to ϕ-ly a prima facie reason to believe that there is something ϕ nearby. Alston (1988) requires that the experiential state be a reliable indicator of the truth of the belief; Steup (2000) requires that the agent have evidence for thinking that the experiential state be a reliable indicator of the truth of the belief; Markie (2004) requires that the agent be following her own (contingent) epistemic norms in believing that there is something ϕ nearby on the basis of her being appeared to ϕ-ly. What these views all have in common is that each claims that (a) how things look determines at least in part whether a perceptual belief is prima facie justified, and (b) how things look, in this sense, is a matter of what nondoxastic experiential state the agent is in.

It is plausible to hold that the beliefs we have been discussing are basic beliefs; that is, those beliefs about copperheads and Joe and the like do not depend on evidential relations to other beliefs for their prima facie justification. If this is right, then the experientialist must endorse direct realism, and the current examples show that the cognitive essentialist versions of such a view are false. For the examples show that you and I might have the same sensory experience, even though what perceptual beliefs are justified for us differs. So the experientialist must abandon either cognitive essentialism or direct realism.

Nonessentialists claim that there is some factor in addition to the experiential state, which determines which beliefs that state justifies. But if this is true, then the connection between how things look and what we are justified in believing is considerably weakened. It is now this additional factor—reliability, evidence of reliability, or what have you—that is doing nearly all the work. The experiences themselves no longer need to have any intrinsic connection to the belief; all that is required is that the experiences be in some sense discriminable; the real epistemic work is being done by the additional factor.

An alternative is to reject direct realism, insisting that the basic beliefs are restricted to beliefs about our experiential states and that perceptual beliefs are justified on the basis of these, rather than directly on the basis of the experiential states themselves. It is obvious, however, that such a move results in an even further attenuated connection between how things look and which of our perceptual beliefs (these being beliefs about external objects) are justified.

If there is a reasonably close connection between how things look and what we are perceptually justified in believing, then the connection is between belief and perceptual output looks, not between belief and experiential looks. You are justified in believing that Joe's here because the face looks—in the perceptual output sense—like Joe to you; I am justified in believing that a diminished scale is being played because it sounds—in the perceptual output sense—like a diminished scale to me. If it hadn't (perceptual-output-)sounded that way, I wouldn't be justified in believing it was a diminished scale. Thus, while there is no necessary or even very close connection between nondoxastic experiential states and prima facie justified perceptual beliefs, there may yet be a tight, and perhaps even necessary, connection between perceptual system outputs and prima facie justified perceptual beliefs. Not only is the perceptual output sense of 'look' and its ilk an epistemically significant sense, it is more epistemically relevant, or at least more directly epistemically relevant, than any experiential sense.

Perceptual output looks, however, are epistemically significant in a very different way than experiential looks are standardly held to be. On the experientialist view, the way things look serves as a nondoxastic body of evidence for the perceptual belief. On the perceptual output view, however, how things look is not to be construed as something distinct from and causally antecedent to the perceptual belief; it is not a ground on which the belief is based. To say that the look justifies the belief is merely to say that the belief's being the output of a perceptual system is (a part of) what justifies the belief. Experiential looks are supposed to justify beliefs by serving as grounds, or evidence, for them. By contrast, the perceptual etiology of the belief contributes to that belief's justification by virtue of the fact that beliefs with such an etiology are prima facie justified. Perceptual output looks thereby justify beliefs by figuring into that on which the beliefs's justification supervenes, not by serving as evidence.

The first major epistemological role ascribed to how things look is captured by what we might call the "Looks Principle": our perceptual beliefs are epistemically justified, at least in part, because of how things look, sound, taste, smell, or feel to us. The intuitive appeal of this principle can lend a specious plausibility to experientialism. It is natural to take the Looks Principle as claiming that perceptual beliefs receive their justification from the corresponding experiential states. This latter claim might be true, but it does not follow from the Looks Principle, for the Looks Principle, as stated, fails to distinguish between experiential looks and perceptual output looks. Thus we cannot infer experientialism from the Looks Principle. The existence of nonexperiential looks undercuts this important motivation for experientialism.

Perception, Inference, and How Things Look

There is a second major epistemological role attributed to how things look; this is to help delineate between perception and inference. Perception is connected to how things look in a way that inferential belief is not. Looking around the room, I form a number of beliefs: my coffee cup is to the left of a pile of CDs; the light on the printer is on, and it is green; the dog is asleep, and the carpet needs to be vacuumed. I look at the clock, and find myself with the following beliefs: that there's a white round thing near me with black markings and two narrow black rectangular bars forming an acute angle; that there's a clock in front of me; that it's currently 10:55 (pm). I hear a familiar sound and form the belief that my telephone is ringing. I answer it and form a number of beliefs: Jane is talking to me; my sister is talking to me; the youngest of my three sisters wants to know what my summer plans are. Which of these beliefs are perceptual beliefs and which are inferential?

The perception/inference distinction is typically framed in terms of such factive states as seeing *F* or seeing that *p*, but I want to focus on the nonfactive state of having the perceptual belief that *p*. One can have the false perceptual belief that there's a cat in the room, though one cannot falsely *see* that there's a cat in the room. Taking the target to be perceptual belief rather than perception allows us to focus on the perceptuality rather than the factivity.

A natural and straightforward account of perceptual belief is this: my belief that *p* is a perceptual belief if and only if I believe that *p* because things look (sound, smell, etc.) as if *p*. My belief that it's cold in here counts as a perceptual belief if I hold it because it feels cold, but not if I hold it because someone I trust tells me it's cold. My belief that it's Jane on the phone is intuitively a perceptual belief, because it sounds like Jane; my belief that the youngest of my three sisters is on the phone is intuitively not a perceptual belief, because there is no obvious literal sense in which it *sounds* like the youngest of my three sisters on the phone.

This natural suggestion can be cashed out in at least two different ways. The experientialist version is this:

> My belief that *p* is a perceptual belief iff my belief that *p* is based on a perceptual experiential state with the content that *p*.[11]

The restriction to perceptual experience is essential, as many epistemologists believe in nonperceptual experiences, such as mnemonic experiences (Pollock

1986; Audi 1998) or even purely intellectual experiences (Plantinga 1993; Pust 2000), and surely being based on nonperceptual experiences is not sufficient for being a perceptual belief. How easy or difficult it will be to draw the distinction between perceptual and nonperceptual experiences is unclear. Rather than worry about this, however, I want to explore an alternative approach, one that invokes an already specified conception of perceptual output looks:

> My belief that *p* is a perceptual belief iff my belief that *p* is the output of one of my perceptual systems.

This latter approach gives us a "Perceptual System Theory" of perceptual belief.

Which beliefs do we intuitively want to count as perceptual beliefs? The class of perceptual beliefs cannot be specified merely by the contents of those beliefs. My belief that it's raining may result from my looking out the window, or it may result from my listening to the weather report on the radio. In the former case it's presumably a perceptual belief; in the latter case it is not. Still, our perceptual beliefs are beliefs about chairs, desks, apples, and other entry level categories, as well as their locations, colors, sizes, motions, etc., but also more subordinate level categories, like face identifications, individual objects, and the like. 'There is something red in front of me', 'the book is on the desk', and 'Susan is wearing a blue shirt' will be among the sorts of propositions that are sometimes perceptually believed by normal people. Propositions like 'the Edsel was only produced for three model years' or 'it's going to snow a lot next winter' are never perceptually believed, at least not by normal humans. These are largely contingent facts about us; creatures with different sense organs have perceptual access to information that for us is only available inferentially.

The Perceptual System Theory (PST) nicely captures these facts, while doing justice to the intuition that which beliefs are perceptual beliefs is determined by how things look. Beliefs about entry level categories and their properties, though not about the production history of Edsels, are sometimes the outputs of perceptual systems. When they are, they are intuitively perceptual beliefs; when they are not, they are intuitively not perceptual beliefs.

This, however, does little to differentiate PST from its experientialist rival. Where PST distinguishes itself is in cases like those described in the previous section. Intuitively, where the face looks like Joe to you but just like a face to me, even though we have the same experiential states, your belief that it's Joe is a perceptual belief. Though I might happen to believe that it's Joe, this belief is not a perceptual belief for me. The novice chicken sexer has the same experiential state as the expert. Both believe they are looking at a male, and they base this belief on their experiential state. But this belief is a perceptual belief for the expert; the novice, by contrast, is simply guessing.

What propositions I am capable of perceptually believing depends on the nature of my perceptual systems, but it does not seem to depend on the nature of my perceptual experiences. A decent mechanic can just *see* (a fortiori, perceptually believe) that a nut is a 17 mm nut; I have to either guess or figure it out by trying various wrenches. This difference between us is not obviously a difference in experiential state. The mechanic's perceptual systems produce finer-grained outputs in this domain than mine do, but this need not be reflected by any experiential difference. Similarly, the professional herpetologist's belief that there's a copperhead is a perceptual belief, and perhaps the ornithologist's belief that there's a two-year-old ivory billed woodpecker is a perceptual belief. Finally, it seems to me to be intuitively plausible to hold that zombies in our proprietary sense can have perceptual beliefs—they aren't necessarily *blind*, after all.

One interesting feature of PST, and I take this to be a virtue of the theory, is that it allows us to turn to the cognitive sciences to resolve certain difficult questions about whether a given belief is a perceptual belief or not. Consider another example. While looking at Jane I form the belief that Jane is in front of me, and intuitively, this is a perceptual belief. However, I also form the belief that a sibling of mine is in front of me. Is this belief also a perceptual belief? My personal guess is that the sibling belief is not the output of any perceptual system but is instead in the same camp with the belief that the person in front of me is named 'Jane'. If so, the belief will count as inferential rather than perceptual. On the other hand, my belief that there's a conspecific in front of me might be the output of a perceptual system and thus count as a perceptual belief. The idea, roughly, is that while *conspecific* might be a perceptual kind, *sibling* most likely isn't. Things *look* like conspecifics (in the perceptual output sense), but they don't *look* like siblings to me. Rather, they look like Pat, Ann, Jane, or Mike, whom I know to be my siblings, thus allowing me to infer that one of my sibs is nearby. I don't need to identify someone first, however, to be justified in believing he or she is a conspecific.[12]

Now I don't mean to suggest that *sibling* couldn't be a perceptual kind. For all I know some species recognize siblings by scent, for instance: some mice might, as it were, "smell like a brother" to other mice. Even the claim that things don't look like sibs to me is intended merely as a fact about *my* siblings; yours may be different, and some visual systems may have access to that fact.

In saying all this, I am expressing my hunch about how the science is going to turn out, about how the perceptual systems actually work. My guess is that our perceptual systems classify things as humans, and even as particular individuals, though not as siblings. This guess is based in part on the fact that there is a set of visually accessible features that reliably, even if imperfectly, distinguishes humans from other things and a set of visually accessible properties that the different views of an individual person have in common, which pretty reliably distinguishes that individual from others, but there is not a set of visually accessible features that reliably distinguishes siblings from other things. In any case, this hunch of mine is something that scientific research can in principle confirm or refute. In such an event, we should modify our inventory or perceptual beliefs accordingly.

Which of an agent's beliefs could be perceptual beliefs depends not merely on the agent's innate perceptual capacities but on its learning history. Perceptual learning is surely bounded and constrained, but in a way that is impossible to fully delimit *a priori*. Churchland famously discusses a group of hypothetical perceivers, who are trained to see by a group of future scientists. "They do not observe the western sky redden as the Sun sets. They observe the wavelength distribution of incoming solar radiation shift towards the longer wavelengths (about 0.7×10^{-6} m) as the shorter are increasingly scattered away from the lengthening atmospheric path they must take as terrestrial rotation turns us slowly away from their source" (1979, 29). Though it is an empirical issue, I am doubtful of the nomological possibility of such a scenario. It is important, however, to see exactly where the doubt lies.

One crucial difference between Churchland and me is that his scenario is laid out in terms of children being taught certain speech dispositions until these dispositions become spontaneous. However, even if it is possible for children to be trained in the way Churchland describes, this would not indicate a *perceptual* change. On my view, the effect would not count as genuinely perceptual unless it occurred at the level of the perceptual system and not merely at the level of spontaneous verbal reports. The latter would be a different kind of learning from perceptual learning, and I don't think we should classify its effects as altering the way they *see*; it wouldn't change their perceptual beliefs but merely the way they spontaneously reported these beliefs.

I am quite willing to grant—indeed, insist—that learning changes how/what we see, in the sense that it changes what perceptual beliefs we have and are capable of. Nonetheless, I want to reserve such a description for a particular kind of change, and not just any old change that comes as a result of expertise and not just any change in those beliefs that are caused by the stimulations of sense organs. It is an empirical question which changes are perceptual and which are not, and my guess is that in the end we will want to distinguish cases like the physicist "seeing" a proton in a cloud chamber from cases like the histologist seeing an abnormal cell growth. As the scare quotes indicate, I am predicting that it is not the output of the physicist's *visual* system that has changed, but some inferential capacity outside the visual system. In the histologist's case, however, it is likely that the changes really are changes to the outputs of the visual system; if so, the change is genuinely a perceptual change.

In any case, PST will allow us to adjudicate such issues. What perceptual systems a creature has and what they produce as outputs are questions that can in principle be empirically answered. Thus PST offers hope of a principled solution to such perennial problems as whether the physicist sees or merely infers a proton in a cloud chamber.

PST offers such a natural response to the problem of distinguishing perception from inference that it might seem trivial in one of two ways. First, it may seem circular to claim that perceptual beliefs are those beliefs that are produced by perceptual systems. But I have argued that perceptual systems can be understood in nonepistemic terms, and more generally, can be understood independently of understanding what perceptual beliefs are. So there is no circularity here. Second, PST might sound trivial in the sense of being too obvious to bother defending. For some reason, however, PST is not obvious to everyone. In fact, it seems to be a minority view; to my knowledge I am the only one who holds it.[13] Though many epistemologists are regrettably silent on what they take perceptual beliefs to be, the received view seems to be a kind of experientialism; experiences certainly play a major role in classic treatments of perceiving (e.g., Chisholm 1957; Jackson 1977). So PST calls for extended defense.

Conclusion

How things look was supposed to be relevant to the epistemology of perception in two important ways: first, looks were supposed to figure into the justification of our perceptual beliefs; second, looks were supposed to figure into the delineation of our perceptual beliefs by separating perceptual from inferential beliefs. I have tried to explicate a nonexperiential sense of 'looks' and the like, namely, the perceptual output sense. I have argued that perceptual output looks are at least as epistemologically significant as experiential looks. How things look in the perceptual output sense is a better predictor of what one is justified in believing than is how things look in some experiential sense. And how things look in this perceptual output sense provides a better demarcation principle for distinguishing perception and inference than does how things look in an experiential sense.

It is intuitively plausible that looks are epistemologically significant, but experientialist theories of the justification of perceptual beliefs, or of the delineation of perceptual beliefs, are not the only way to capture this central fact. The existence of nonexperiential looks undermines any quick inference from this obvious fact about the epistemic significance of looks to any controversial thesis about the epistemological role of nondoxastic experiential states.[14]

Notes

1. For expository convenience I formulate issues in terms of how things look. Standard disclaimers apply. The present formulation only fits comfortably with nonhallucinatory cases, where there really is something that looks some way; however, nothing of any significance will ride on this. Also, I follow common practice by focusing mainly on vision, though what I will say about vision will apply to the other sense modalities as well.
2. '*x*' occurs in this discussion transparently and is not taken to have ontological import; see note 1. Nor do I mean to be making any substantive commitments to

the metaphysics of perception; I use the 'looks' rather than the 'appeared-to' idiom simply because it is less obtrusive in the present context.

3. This is not, of course, intended to be an exhaustive classification of 'looks' locutions.
4. Of course, these metaphorical senses are generally compatible with the literal senses. If I say, in the purely doxastic sense, that the tower looks round from here, this doesn't rule out the tower's looking round to me in one or more of the experiential senses.
5. Fodor (1983) has either five (pp. 36–7) or nine (pp. 47–101) diagnostic criteria for modularity, depending on how (and where) you count. Many of these are quite controversial. Fodor explicitly denies that he is defining the term 'module', and it is best to read him not as offering an account of what modules are but as propounding a high-level empirical theory: that cognitive capacities exhibiting some of these five or nine properties tend to have most or all of the rest of them.
6. Such an inference requires a number of assumptions, including one of premorbid uniformity of cognitive architecture and localization across subjects. This has been much discussed elsewhere, and I have nothing to add to that discussion here.
7. That is, a cognitive mechanism computes a function which has representational states as its range or domain (or both).
8. To claim that a system is domain specific is not merely to claim that the system specializes in some task or other but that this task is sufficiently narrow or constrained.
9. A part of a task is to be construed as a subset of the ordered input-output pairs that constitute the task. This is not the same as a subtask, which is a task computed on the way toward computing the overarching task. Vertex extraction is presumably a subtask of visual object recognition, while visually recognizing puppies is a part of visual object recognition. Again, a more detailed treatment is in my (2001).
10. By 'direct realism' here I mean an epistemological view. The relation between such a view and a direct realist theory of the metaphysics of perception is far from clear. Allowing beliefs about external objects to be epistemologically basic does not obviously commit one to any particular view about sense data and the like.
11. Experientialists who hold that experiential states have neither conceptual nor propositional content will have to develop a more elaborate account than the natural one suggested here, since beliefs have both conceptual and propositional content. Claiming that experiential states have nonconceptual content, of course, does not preclude their having conceptual content as well.
12. Translating the outputs of perceptual systems into English is a difficult matter, as is the case with translating any beliefs into English, though the difficulty may be more a matter of getting the pragmatics right than of getting the semantics right. Perhaps it would be better to say that the visual system classifies distal stimuli as humans, or better yet people, rather than conspecifics. One need not have a concept answering exactly to *conspecific* in order to engage in the relevant classification. Nothing hinges on my describing the output as conspecific detection; I do so only because this is how the cognitive scientists are prone to talk,

ethologists especially, even though nonhumans presumably lack the concept *conspecific*. Nonetheless, it should be perfectly clear what is meant by saying that the pigeon or its visual system classifies some distal object as a conspecific but not as a sib.

13. Fodor *seems* to be presupposing something like PST in a well-known exchange with Churchland concerning observation (Fodor 1984, 1988). However, this is not a thesis he argues for, nor does he develop observation as an especially epistemological notion in the way that perceptual belief is here. Furthermore, on closer examination, it is not obvious that it really is PST that Fodor is presupposing. He does think that what one observes is determined by one's perceptual modules. But this is like saying that how things look is determined by one's perceptual modules. Because of the ambiguity central to the present paper, such a claim is quite compatible with experientialism. In fact, Fodor seems to hold that the outputs of the perceptual modules are ipso fact nondoxastic, and this view is actually incompatible with PST; it is likely experientialism, rather than PST that Fodor is presupposing, after all. I do follow Fodor in thinking that the modules are important, but I differ with him concerning *how* they are important.
14. Versions of this paper were presented at the Midsouth Philosophy Conference and to the philosophy department at the University of Arkansas. Thanks to those audiences for helpful comments.

References

Alston, W. P. (1988). An internalist externalism. *Synthese* 74, 265–283.

Alston, W. P. (2002). Sellars and the myth of the given. *Philosophy and Phenomenological Research* 65, 69–86.

Audi, R. (1998) *Epistemology: a contemporary introduction to the theory of knowledge*. New York: Routledge.

Biederman, I. (1990). Higher-level vision. In D. N. Osherson, S. M. Kosslyn & J. M Hollerbach, eds. *An invitation to cognitive science, vol. 2: Visual cognition and action*. Cambridge, MA: MIT Press.

Chisholm, R. (1957). *Perceiving* Ithaca, NY: Cornell UP.

Chisholm, R. (1966). *Theory of knowledge*. Englewood Cliffs, NJ: Prentice Hall.

Churchland, P. M. (1979). *Scientific realism and the plasticity of mind*. Cambridge: Cambridge UP.

Descartes, R. (1984) *The Philosophical Writings of Descartes*. J. Cottingham, R. Stoothoff, & D. Murdoch, trans. Cambridge: Cambridge UP.

Elman, J. L., E. A. Bates, M. H. Johnson, A. Karmiloff-Smith, D. Parisi, & K. Plunkett (1996). *Rethinking innateness: a connectionist perspective on development*. Cambridge, MA: MIT Press.

Farah, M. J. (1990). *Visual agnosia: Disorders of object recognition and what they tell us about normal vision*. Cambridge, MA: MIT Press.

Fodor, J. A. (1983). *Modularity of mind*. Cambridge, MA: MIT Press.

Fodor, J. A. (1984). Observation reconsidered. *Philosophy of Science* 51, 22–43.

Fodor, J. A. (1988). A reply to Churchland's "Perceptual plasticity and theory neutrality". *Philosophy of Science* 55, 188–94.

Goodale, M. A. & Milner, A. D. 1992: Separate visual pathways for perception and action. *Trends in Neurosciences* 15, 20–25.

Huemer, M. (2001). *Skepticism and the veil of perception.* Lanham, MD: Rowman and Littlefield.

Jackson, F. (1977). *Perception.* Cambridge: Cambridge UP.

Jolicoeur, P., M. A. Gluck, & S. M. Kosslyn (1984). Pictures and names: Making the connection. *Cognitive Psychology* 16, 243–275.

Lyons, J. C. (2001). Carving the mind at its (not necessarily modular) joints. *British Journal for the Philosophy of Science* 52, 277–302.

Markie, P. J. (2004). Nondoxastic perceptual evidence. *Philosophy and Phenomenological Research* 68, 530–553.

Marsolek, C. J. (1999). Dissociable neural subsystems underlie abstract and specific object recognition. *Psychological Science* 10, 111–118.

Plantinga, A. (1993). *Warrant and proper function.* New York: Oxford University Press.

Pollock, J. (1986). *Contemporary theories of knowledge.* Savage, MD: Rowman & Littlefield.

Pust, J. (2000). *Intuitions as evidence.* New York: Routledge.

Steup, M. (2000). Unrestricted foundationalism and the Sellarsian dilemma. *Grazer Philosophische Studien* 60, 75–98.

Ungerleider, L. G. & M. Mishkin (1982) Two cortical visual systems. In D. J. Ingle, M. A. Goodale, & R. J. W. Mansfield, eds., *Analysis of visual behavior.* Cambridge, MA: MIT Press.

Philosophical Perspectives, 19, Epistemology, 2005

THE EPISTEMOLOGICAL ARGUMENT FOR CONTENT EXTERNALISM*

Brad Majors
University of Wisconsin-Madison

Sarah Sawyer
University of Nebraska-Lincoln

1. Introduction

Over the past 30 years, much of the philosophical community has become persuaded of the truth of content externalism, the view that the intentional contents of certain of a subject's thoughts are to be individuated with essential reference to her environment. This conversion is due in large measure to arguments set forth by Hilary Putnam and Tyler Burge, arguments which notoriously appeal to Twin-Earth style thought experiments.[1] We do not dispute these arguments or the methodology they employ; nevertheless, both remain controversial. Our aim in this paper is to show that the truth of content externalism can be grounded in purely epistemological considerations in which no appeal is made to Twin-Earth style cases.

We begin with a dilemma concerning the notion of justification. We argue that internalist and externalist theories of justification alike are problematic. Internalist theories cannot account for the constitutive connection between justification and truth; and externalist theories cannot account for the fact that reliability is unnecessary for justification. However, we contend that the problem facing externalist theories of justification can be overcome by invoking, in addition but essentially, the anti-individualistic individuation conditions of the psychological states they concern. This solution requires and hence provides support for the truth of content externalism. The argument for content externalism, then, is indirect; but pending an alternative solution to our dilemma we take it to be rationally persuasive.

There are gestures—and in some cases more than a gesture—toward an argument from epistemological considerations to content externalism in the literature. John McDowell has emphasized the epistemological problems which beset a notion of content conceived as radically divorced from the nature of the empirical world (1995, p. 409). Bill Brewer has claimed to follow McDowell here, arguing that there are epistemic requirements upon the very possibility of empirical belief (1999, pp. 21–22).[2] Christopher Peacocke has repeatedly made the point that only if content is externally individuated will taking experience at face value be justified and lead to knowledge (1999, p. 94; 2004, pp. 123–6). And Burge himself has recently invoked content externalism in providing an account of our entitlement to perceptual belief (2003, pp. 530–7).[3] Nevertheless, to date no one has either set out in detail an argument of the sort we give in this paper, or connected—as we attempt to—the relevant considerations to existing work in the theory of justification.

Our discussion begins with the aforementioned dilemma. We then move on to discuss classical forms of internalism with respect to justification in section 3, contemporary forms of internalism in section 4, and externalist theories of justification in section 5. In each case it is argued that the theory of justification under consideration is unsatisfactory. Section 6 sets out our own theory of justification. The paper as a whole amounts to an argument for content externalism.

2. Justification and Truth

Epistemologists generally agree that there is a constitutive relation between epistemic justification and truth. Stewart Cohen (1984, p. 279) has emphasized that an essential connection with truth is what distinguishes specifically epistemic justification from other forms of justification. Laurence BonJour states that "if finding epistemically justified beliefs did not substantially increase the likelihood of finding true ones, then epistemic justification would be irrelevant to our main cognitive goal and of dubious worth" (1985, p. 8). A final way of coming to the thesis that justification requires a constitutive relation to truth is by noting, first, that belief necessarily aims at truth; and second, that justification, as a property of belief, is an epistemic good.

In his (1984), Cohen argues that issues concerning this constitutive connection between justification and truth present epistemologists with a dilemma: theories of justification that ignore the connection incur an explanatory deficit, but theories that try to explain it are problematic in other respects. As noted, Cohen points out that it is precisely its close connection with truth that distinguishes epistemic justification from other sorts of justification. In accordance with at least one strand of Cohen's important discussion, we believe that the constitutive connection between justification and truth places a tremendously important constraint upon any adequate theory of justification. Theories which ignore this connection are not merely explanatorily deficient; they are *eo ipso* inadequate. We aim to show that the second horn of Cohen's dilemma can be avoided by basing a theory of justification on a formulation of the truth-connection that appeals to the anti-individualistic individuation conditions of psychological states—that is, one that appeals to content externalism.

To give structure to the issues (and the paper), we offer here a dilemma of our own, loosely based on the second horn of Cohen's original dilemma. Justification can be understood either as an internalist notion or as an externalist notion. If justification is an internalist notion, any putative connection with truth will occur merely at the subjective level, and hence—we will argue—the constitutive connection between justification and truth will not be accounted for. Externalist theories of justification, in contrast, have the virtue of maintaining an actual, objective connection between justification and truth. However, externalist theories of justification are problematic, inasmuch as actual reliability is not necessary for epistemic justification. This is shown by what has become known as the 'New Evil Demon Problem': the belief-forming processes of an envatted twin who shares all of the reader's experiences will be almost completely unreliable; nevertheless, it is highly unintuitive to regard him or her as unjustified. This is a problem specifically for forms of reliabilism.

The dilemma facing theories of justification, then—our dilemma, which is related to but distinct from Cohen's—is this: one cannot, it would appear, account for the necessary connection between justification and truth, and at the same time provide an adequate response to the New Evil Demon Problem.[4] Internalist theories of justification cannot account for the constitutive connection between justification and truth; extant externalist theories cannot account for the fact that actual reliability is not necessary for justification.

Use of the term "justification" in the literature is far from uniform. We intend the term to refer to a positive epistemic property of beliefs, but to remain neutral—at least initially—with regard to how the notion is to be analyzed. Note also that the concern throughout is with perceptual justification.[5]

3. Classical Internalism

A primary source of classical internalism is Descartes, who has been interpreted as holding that justification entails truth. Clearly this Cartesian account has the virtue of upholding the constitutive connection between justification and truth.[6] Indeed, there could be no stronger such connection. This sort of Cartesian internalism, however, in implying that no false belief can be justified, is inadequate as a theory of justification.

We will not dwell on this account here since, while there may be advocates of Cartesian internalism, it is no longer prominent in the literature.[7] Instead, we turn to a more prominent version of classical internalism—that found in the early writings of BonJour:

> The distinguishing characteristic of epistemic justification is thus its essential or internal relation to the cognitive goal of truth. It follows that one's cognitive

> endeavours are epistemically justified only if and to the extent that they are aimed at this goal, which means very roughly that one accepts all and only those beliefs which one has good reason to think are true ... To accept a belief in the absence of such a reason, however appealing or even mandatory such acceptance might be from some other standpoint, is to neglect the pursuit of truth; such acceptance is, one might say, epistemically irresponsible. My contention here is that the idea of avoiding such irresponsibility, of being epistemically responsible in one's believings, is the core of the notion of epistemic justification (1985, p. 8).

As we saw in section 2, BonJour appears to be committed to the existence of a constitutive connection between justification and truth. However, his theory of epistemic justification connects it not to truth but to apparent truth. The connection in his theory lies purely at the subjective level; one's epistemic methods are said to be justified not in so far as they are actually likely to lead to the truth, but rather just in case *one has reason to believe* that they are likely to lead to the truth. The theory of epistemic justification BonJour advocated at this time is a classical version of deontologism, which we formulate as follows:

> (D) *Deontologism*: Justification consists in being epistemically responsible in one's believings.

The problem then becomes clear: one may be epistemically responsible without it being the case that one's epistemic methods are truth conducive even in one's normal environment; indeed without it being the case that there is any constitutive connection whatever between the methods and the truth. To put the point slightly differently—one may be doing all that can reasonably be expected of one epistemically, while holding beliefs for which there is nonetheless little or no genuine support.

To illustrate this fault in deontologism we borrow an example from James Pryor (2001). Pryor asks us to imagine a hapless individual who has been taught poor epistemic standards. In particular, the individual has been taught to reason statistically in such a way that he cannot distinguish between the likelihood that a test will yield a false negative, and the likelihood that it will yield a false positive. The hapless individual does not recall how he first acquired the standards, and is intellectually incapable of discerning their defects. Nevertheless, he is scrupulous about applying the standards he has been taught. As Pryor says, "Our subject is doing the best he can, and the best that can reasonably be demanded of him. That seems a good reason to say he's violating no epistemic obligations. Yet the beliefs he forms on the basis of statistical reasoning will be seriously defective; and for that reason it's natural to regard those beliefs as *unjustified.* Hence it appears that a subject can sometimes be blameless for holding unjustified beliefs" (pp. 114–5).

A natural explanation for our intuitions concerning this sort of case is that the hapless individual is unjustified precisely because his beliefs do not connect in the right kind of way with truth.[8] Such cases illustrate the fact that being epistemically responsible is not sufficient for justification. A way of diagnosing the problem with (D) is to note that there is no constitutive connection between epistemic responsibility and truth. This is presumably why our intuitions concerning the hapless but epistemically responsible subject are as they are. The kind of classical deontologism once advocated by BonJour, therefore, cannot account for the necessary connection between justification and truth.

It is worth noting at this point that internalist theories generally have a core of agreement. The core of internalist theories can be construed in terms of a supervenience thesis, according to which the facts upon which justification supervenes are accessible in some special way to the believing subject. A stronger version of this core claim holds in addition that whether the subject is justified must be similarly accessible. Classical versions of internalism tended to endorse the stronger version. Thus it is the stronger view that Kent Bach has in mind when he says "internalism ... treats justifiedness as a purely internal matter: if p is justified for S, then S must be aware (or at least be immediately capable of being aware) of what makes it justified *and why*" (1985, p. 250, emphasis added). Similarly, speaking of internalism as an approach to traditional epistemological questions, Roderick Chisholm says "the internalist assumes that, merely by reflecting upon his own conscious state, he can formulate a set of epistemic principles that will enable him to find out, with respect to any possible belief he has, whether he is justified in having that belief. ... [O]ne needs only consider one's own state of mind" (1988, p. 286).

It is these supervenience theses that people tend to have in mind when they speak of 'access internalism', the supervenience theses generating weak access internalism and strong access internalism, respectively. We do not discuss access internalism in its own right simply because we do not consider it a theory of justification, so much as a thesis which offers an ostensibly necessary condition for a subject's being justified in believing that p; a necessary condition that is agreed upon by (most) internalists of different varieties. We deal with particular varieties of internalism instead.[9] Nevertheless, the problem with access internalism considered as a theory of justification is plain: one does not have access, in the relevant sense, to the truth; it is therefore difficult to see how justification, which must be constitutively tied to truth, could itself be a matter solely of that to which one has special access.[10]

4. Contemporary Internalism

In this section we discuss four contemporary versions of internalism. We start with a theory of justification offered by Richard Feldman and Earl Conee: evidentialism. According to Feldman and Conee (1985), what one is justified in believing is determined by what evidence one has.[11] They put forward the following thesis (p. 404):

(EJ) *Evidentialism*: Justification consists in believing propositions which fit one's evidence.

As Feldman and Conee emphasize, (EJ) "has no implication about the actions one must take in a rational pursuit of the truth. It is about the epistemic evaluation of attitudes given the evidence one does have, however one came to possess that evidence" (p. 409). Consequently, there is no reason to believe that the evidentialist's notion of justification is constitutively connected to the truth in the way that epistemic justification must be. After all, the evidence in one's possession might be wildly inappropriate given one's situation—if one's cognitive equipment were seriously defective, for example—and hence highly unlikely to lead one to the truth, even in normal circumstances.

In a footnote (p. 416), Feldman and Conee address this issue, mentioning Cohen's dilemma and the truth-connection explicitly. They concede that (EJ) does "not explain how having an epistemically justified or well-founded belief is connected to the truth of that belief", but try to mitigate the significance of this fact in two ways. First, they offer the following as a principle which the evidentialist can 'safely' assert about the connection between justification and truth: "evidence that makes believing p justified is evidence on which it is *epistemically* probable that p is true." However, the term 'true' occurs here only obliquely. To say that it is epistemically probable that p is true is to say no more than that it seems to the subject, perhaps on careful reflection, that p is true. This is not a connection between evidence and truth, but a connection between evidence and perceived truth. It could be epistemically probable that p, for a given subject, without there being any relevant objective connection between the belief and the truth.

Second, Feldman and Conee claim that Cohen has not argued for an incompatibility between evidentialism and the constitutive connection between justification and truth, but has merely shown that evidentialists have work left to do in explicating what the connection could consist in on the evidentialist view. There is clearly a burden of proof issue here; but since, as Feldman and Conee readily admit, evidentialism provides no reason to think one's evidence more likely to be appropriate to the situation than not, it provides no reason to think the beliefs which it deems justified more likely true than not. Feldman and Conee do not explain how evidentialism accounts for the constitutive connection between justification and truth, and in the absence of such an explanation we see no reason to think that it can do so. Indeed, there is positive reason to think that it cannot.

Pryor, in his (2000), defends an alternative internalist theory of justification which rests on the claim that having a perceptual experience as of p's being the case gives one immediate (prima facie) justification for believing that p. This position, which he calls 'dogmatism', is distinctive in allowing that a subject can be justified in believing certain propositions without being able to defend her beliefs in a non-question-begging way: merely having certain experiences justifies one in having certain beliefs.[12] It is a form of internalism, according to Pryor, since the justifying states (the experiences) are internal to the subject; but it is of the weak variety mentioned toward the end of section 3, since the justificatory connection between the experiences and the beliefs need not itself be accessible to the subject. Pryor's main concern is to show how the dogmatist can respond to scepticism about perceptual justification by exposing a false assumption underlying the sceptic's reasoning: the sceptic says that if you are justified in believing that things are as they perceptually seem to you to be, you need antecedent reason to believe that you're not in certain sceptical scenarios; the dogmatist denies this.

Dogmatism, taken as an approach toward dealing with scepticism, is an interesting position, and one to which we are attracted. However, it is inadequate as a theory of perceptual justification unless supplemented by an account of just how the relevant experiences justify the perceptual beliefs on which they are based. While this is not Pryor's main concern, he is clearly aware of the need to explain the justificatory relation, and offers the following brief remark: "In my view ... it's the peculiar 'phenomenal force' or way our experiences have of presenting propositions to us ... which explains why our experiences give us the immediate justification they do" (2000, p. 547). We formulate Pryor's view thus:

(P) *Phenomenalism*: Perceptual justification consists in the peculiar phenomenal force of experiences when presenting propositions to us.

The problem with this is that the presence of a peculiar phenomenal force is neither sufficient nor necessary for epistemic justification.[13] Imagine a perceiving subject who is not connected to the world in the way that we are. His perceptual faculties are very poorly suited to obtaining information about his surroundings. We may imagine that these faculties are completely unreliable in normal circumstances. Suppose, however, that the subject nevertheless enjoys exactly the same phenomenology as we do when we have a perception as of a tree in epistemically unproblematic conditions. It seems clear that his consequent belief that there is a tree before him is not justified. If this is so then Pryor's 'peculiar phenomenal force' is not sufficient for justification.

Now suppose that we are confronted with a perceiving subject who is connected to the world in precisely the same way we are, but who nevertheless lacks the relevant phenomenology. We may suppose that this is the only difference between her and us. Here it seems clear that the subject *is* justified in forming the belief that there is a tree in front of her. If this is correct, then the phenomenal force in question is not necessary for justification.

Pryor may object that his concern is not to give an analysis of the notion of perceptual justification so much as to indicate what it is, in beings more or less like us, which seems special about immediate perceptual justification. It isn't being able to construct an apodictic argument for the truth of one's perceptual belief—we have seen that Pryor thinks (surely correctly) that this is unnecessary in such cases. And it isn't the reliability of the belief-forming process—for, again quite plausibly, the subject could be transported to a demon-world, in which she would be unreliable but still justified. So what could it be? One salient aspect of the relevant class of perceptual beliefs is the way one feels in forming them. Thus (P).

The trouble here is that on almost every contemporary view of justification members of the relevant class of beliefs of normal human beings tend to be justified. And so, while Pryor's examples are quite plausible, it seems to be the tacit reference to normality—'in beings more or less like us'—which is doing all the work. Phenomenal force would appear to be quite beside the point. The explanatory question remains: *why* are our basic perceptual beliefs immediately (prima facie) justified? A correct, non-trivial answer to this question must connect those beliefs with truth.

Ralph Wedgwood has offered an internalist account of justification which he takes to account for the constitutive connection between justification and truth by means of an appeal to rules of rationality. Indeed, Wedgwood's primary concern in his (1999) is to reconcile two ideas that he takes to be intuitively plausible: first, that the rationality of a belief or decision is an internal matter; and second, that the aim of rationality is an external matter, such as forming a true belief or arriving at a good decision.[14] In this context, the first principle amounts to the advocation of an internalist theory of justification; the second to an acknowledgement that justification is constitutively tied to truth.

According to Wedgwood, rationality has two components. The first is deontological. Thus, we are told that a genuine rule of rationality "must be such that following [it] is a way for the thinker to be doing all that can be reasonably expected in order to achieve the required external aim"; and that "a belief is rational if and only if the thinker has done all that can reasonably be expected to ensure that the belief in question is true" (pp. 116–7). This deontological component motivates the claim that rationality is an internal matter, since doing what can reasonably be expected of one is itself an internal matter. As a deontological account, without supplement, it faces the same problem as that which plagues BonJour's deontological account, discussed above.[15] To his credit, Wedgwood recognizes this. The second component, then, is brought in to provide the requisite connection between justification and truth missing from a purely deontological account.

The second component concerns rules of rationality which it is metaphysically necessary for creatures with certain cognitive capacities to follow. The rationality of a belief depends upon how it is formed and maintained; a rational belief is consequently seen as one that is based on the thinker's following rules of rationality. Given the infinite number of rules one might follow in forming and maintaining one's beliefs, clearly we need an account of what makes a rule a genuine rule of rationality—one that is, in the requisite sense, constitutively tied to the truth. Summarizing his view, Wedgwood says:

> ... there are two kinds of rules of rationality: there are derivative, non-basic rules, which it is rational for the thinker to follow only because it is rational for her to believe (by means of following *other* rules) that the rules in question are reliable; and there are basic rules, which it is rational for the thinker to follow because it is necessary that any thinker capable of asking the questions that the thinker is actually capable of asking will be inclined to follow the rules when the opportunity arises (1999, p. 131).

It is rational for us to follow non-basic rules, then, in so far as we believe them to be reliable; and it is rational for us to follow basic rules because it is a metaphysical necessity that we are immediately inclined to do so, in virtue of possessing the relevant concepts.[16] The basic rules of rationality are nonetheless ones we are justified in following, and the beliefs formed on the basis of these basic rules of rationality are consequently themselves justified. According to Wedgwood we are "fully warranted in following these rules; for in following them, we are pursuing the aim of having a true belief ... in the only way available for anyone who can even ask the questions that we are considering" (p. 131). These rules are ones which, as a matter of metaphysical necessity, we could not but follow given the kinds of enquiry in which we are engaged.

We formulate Wedgwood's conception of justification as follows:

(RR) *Rules of Rationality*: Justification consists (ultimately) in following rules in accordance with which we are metaphysically compelled to judge.

What, then, is wrong with Wedgwood's account? The error occurs in the move from the claim that we cannot but help follow certain rules to the claim that we are justified in doing so, and from thence to the claim that beliefs formed on the basis of such rules are themselves justified. The fact, if it is a fact,[17] that one is metaphysically compelled to follow certain rules does not make those rules likely to lead to true beliefs. It is easy to imagine a believing subject who judges as he must, given his concepts, but who is nevertheless so poorly adapted to his normal environment that he is completely unreliable in it. (One can imagine, relatedly but in addition, a variation upon Pryor's hapless reasoner which would serve to disconfirm Wedgwood's account.) Consequently, (RR) fails to account for the constitutive connection between justification and truth.

The final contemporary internalist account we consider is offered by Fred Dretske in his (2000). Following Burge, Dretske distinguishes justification from entitlement. Burgean entitlements are epistemic warrants to believe that need not be understood by or accessible to the subject; justifications are justifications 'in the narrow sense', which involve reasons cognitive agents have and have access to.[18]

On the face of it, the very notion of entitlement in this sense is a peculiarly externalist one. However, we believe Dretske's account is more properly classified as internalist, and he apparently agrees, referring to his theory as "my internalism ... about entitlement" (p. 596).[19] Certainly there are significant similarities between his account and the weak internalist account of justification presented by Pryor. According to Pryor, it will be recalled, experiences provide immediate prima facie justification for perceptual beliefs, and the justificatory status of the latter does not require that the subject be able to defend her beliefs in a non-question-begging way. Pryor takes himself to be an internalist because the facts upon which perceptual justification supervenes—the experiences—are accessible to the believing subject. Dretske explicitly endorses such a supervenience thesis: "Entitlements supervene on the subjective resources of the believer—facts the believer either is, or can be made, aware of" (p. 597). While Pryor talks of justification and Dretske talks of entitlement, the notions are very nearly identical.[20] The similarity allows each to identify the same error in the sceptic's reasoning: a subject need not be able to provide reasons for her belief in order for it to be justified, in the broad sense. For the sake of continuity with the discussion above, we will continue to use the term 'justification' in this broad sense to cover Dretske's internalist notion of an entitlement.

A further reason to regard Dretske's view as internalist is that he endorses the supervenience thesis mentioned in order to accommodate an intuition which motivates internalist theories in general. Dretske writes:

> I can imagine some benighted soul—a brain in a vat will do—whose beliefs are false but whose total evidence—both the evidence he has and the evidence he can by assiduous effort obtain—is the same as mine. If his beliefs are false and mine are true, it nonetheless strikes me that he has the right to believe whatever I have the right to believe (p. 595).

Finally, there is in addition a strong deontological element in Dretske's account, an element characteristic of—though not invariably associated with—internalist theories of justification.[21]

What, then, is Dretske's account of how experiences justify perceptual beliefs? He holds that a subject is justified in believing that p if she is epistemically responsible, and has no choice whether to believe that p; she has no choice whether to believe that p if there is nothing she can do to prevent herself from being caused to form the belief that p; and there is nothing she can do to prevent herself from being caused to form the belief that p if there is nothing she should do, as an epistemically responsible agent, which would prevent her from forming the belief. Dretske does not hold, then, that a subject is justified in believing that p only if it is *logically impossible* for her to prevent herself from forming the belief that p; rather, she is justified only if there is nothing she *should* do, *qua* epistemically responsible agent, to prevent herself from forming the belief that p (p. 603). We formulate his thesis as follows:

(IT) *Inescapability Theory*: A subject is justified in believing that p if she is epistemically responsible, and there is nothing she should do to prevent herself from forming the belief that p.

It follows that the epistemically responsible brain in a vat is justified in believing on the basis of his experience as of a green object that there is a green object before him because he could do nothing to discover his error.

The problem with (IT) is that one can imagine a non-demonized, non-envatted, epistemically responsible subject who is nevertheless cognitively limited in such a way that she could not prevent herself from forming the beliefs she does. We have already shown that being epistemically responsible is insufficient for epistemic justification. In addition, whether or not there is anything one can do to prevent oneself from forming the belief that p is quite irrelevant to the question whether there obtains between the belief and its subject matter the requisite alethic connection. The cognitively limited subject might be completely unreliable even under normal circumstances. (IT) cannot account for the constitutive connection between justification and truth.

This is in fact acknowledged by Dretske, though he evidently does not see it as a mark against the account. Indeed, one explicit aim of his paper is to reject our guiding assumption that justification must be connected to truth. He says, "I will ... reject [the] idea ... that it is only a relation to the truth ... that can render a belief ... apt" (p. 594); and goes on to say that there are other sources, other grounds, for epistemic rights. Again, later on, he writes: "On this account of entitlement, there is no way to demonstrate ... that entitled beliefs are more likely to be true than false" (p. 603). *Contra* Dretske, we have argued that an adequate account must connect justification constitutively with truth. We will see in the next section, moreover, that Dretske has abandoned the connection unnecessarily.

5. Reliabilism and the New Evil Demon Problem

We have argued above that internalist theories of justification cannot account for the constitutive connection between justification and truth. In contrast, externalist theories fare well on this front. Reliabilism is the archetypical externalist theory of justification, and its classical version can be formulated as follows:

(CR) *Classical Reliabilism*: Justification consists in reliability in the world a subject happens to inhabit.

Thus a subject's belief is justified if and only if it was formed by a belief-forming process that is in fact reliable; a process which is more likely than not to yield true beliefs. (CR), however, faces a well-known problem: the New Evil Demon Problem.[22] As noted earlier, the New Evil Demon Problem is the problem of how to accommodate the fact that reliability is not necessary for justification. Here is the intuition as presented by Ernest Sosa:

> What if twins of ours in another possible world were given mental lives just like ours down to the most minute detail of experience or thought, etc., though they were also totally in error about the nature of their surroundings, and their perceptual and inferential processes of belief acquisition accomplished very little except to sink them more and more deeply and systematically into error? Shall we say that we are justified in our beliefs while our twins are not? They are quite wrong in their beliefs, of course, but it seems somehow very implausible to suppose that they are unjustified (1991, p. 132).

The intuition expressed in this passage is a commonly shared one. Indeed, contemporary internalist theories of justification are typically motivated expressly to accommodate it. Cohen explicitly argues against reliabilism on the grounds that it cannot accommodate such intuitions about the epistemic worth of the beliefs of certain deluded subjects (1984, pp. 281–284); it is Wedgwood's reason for claiming that "rationality is an *internalist* standard; [that] the rationality of an attitude is determined solely by the contents of the thinker's mind" (1999, p. 118); it is Dretske's reason for rejecting reliabilism and endorsing instead the internalist claim that entitlements supervene on the subjective resources of the believer (2000, pp. 595–596); and Pryor claims that it is precisely such considerations that incline him to an internalist account of justification (2001, p. 117). In common with these philosophers, we take it to be an essential feature of justification that one does not lose justification merely by virtue of finding oneself in unfortunate circumstances.

In our view, each of these thinkers has fallen victim to a fallacy, which we call 'The Internalist Fallacy': it consists in inferring from the fact that reliability is not necessary for justification that there is, or can be, no necessary or constitutive connection between justification and truth. That this is a fallacious line of reasoning will be shown in section 6, when we outline our theory of justification.

How, then, might an externalist accommodate the fact that reliability is not necessary for justification? Alvin Goldman has attempted to solve the New Evil Demon Problem within the framework of reliabilism. He acknowledges that justification does not consist in reliability in the world the subject happens to inhabit, and proposes instead the thesis that justification consists in reliability in 'normal worlds'.

(NR) *Neoclassical Reliabilism*: Justification consists in reliability in normal worlds.

Thus, according to Goldman, a process that is in fact unreliable, as perceptual processes are for subjects in a demonic world, may nevertheless be reliable in normal worlds; thus rendering beliefs formed on the basis of such processes justified for all subjects—even deluded subjects in a demonic world.[23]

The important question, of course, is how to mark out the set of normal worlds. Goldman offers the following by way of definition:

> We have a large set of common beliefs about the actual world: general beliefs about the sorts of objects, events, and changes that occur in it. We have beliefs about the kinds of things that, realistically, do and can happen. Our beliefs on this score generate what I shall call the set of *normal worlds*. These are worlds consistent with our *general* beliefs about the actual world. ... Our concept of justification is constructed against the backdrop of such a set of normal worlds. My proposal is that, according to our ordinary conception of justifiedness, a rule system is right in any world W just in case it has a sufficiently high truth ratio in *normal worlds* ... Rightness of rules—and hence justifiedness—displays normal-world chauvinism (1986, p. 107).

On the face of it this is an important improvement over classical reliabilism. It does, after all, accommodate the relevant intuition: the beliefs of our twins in the demonic world are justified just in case their belief-forming mechanisms are reliable in worlds such as we take the actual world to be. And the twins in the relevant sort of thought experiment satisfy this condition.

However, Goldman's neoclassical reliabilism is inadequate as a theory of justification for the following two reasons. First, it has the result that our general beliefs about the world are trivially justified. This is not plausible. As Peacocke notes (2004, p. 113), the question of whether our general beliefs about the sorts of things that there are in the world are justified is a substantive normative question on our ordinary concept of justification, and hence one that it is reasonable—and, *a fortiori*, possible—for us to raise. Second, Goldman's account yields an intuitively unacceptable result for certain subjects who live in non-normal worlds. Imagine a subject who lives in a non-normal world to which she is nevertheless well-adapted, and who consequently relies on belief-forming mechanisms which yield a high ratio of true to false beliefs when assessed relative to her world. Such processes would, we are supposing, serve the subject well in her home environment, rendering her intuitively justified; but they may nevertheless be wildly unreliable in normal worlds. These are crippling difficulties for the view.

The New Evil Demon Problem shows that actual reliability is not necessary for justification. Goldman's claim that justification consists in reliability in normal worlds, however, cannot be correct. The claim is inconsistent with very strong and widely shared intuitions concerning when a subject is justified, as well as ruling out the very possibility of meaningful inquiry into the epistemic status of our most general beliefs. We suggest that these problems stem ultimately from the fact that the privilege accorded the set of normal worlds lacks independent motivation. Taking note of the failures we find in Goldman's account, we develop and motivate in the next section the view that the reliability of a belief-forming mechanism needs to be assessed relative to a cognitive subject's *home environment*, where one's home environment is not necessarily the environment one inhabits. Before expanding on these claims, we look briefly at two alternative attempts to solve the New Evil Demon Problem: Goldman's later view, which draws a distinction between strong and weak justification; and Sosa's relativistic approach to justification.

Abandoning an appeal to normal worlds to ground a notion of justification adequate to solve the New Evil Demon Problem, Goldman (1988) appeals instead to a distinction between strong and weak justification. Very roughly, the former is reliability, and the latter unreliable but responsible belief. This suggests the following account:

(S/W) *Strong/Weak Justification*: Justification consists either in reliability in the world the subject happens to inhabit (strong justification), or in unreliable but cognitively responsible belief (weak justification).

On this account, the subject in the demon world lacks strong justification, but possesses weak justification nonetheless. According to Goldman's proposal, then, it is the fact that the deluded subject is responsible which accounts for our intuition that she is epistemically justified. Our response to this proposal will occasion no surprise. It was shown in section 3 above that responsibility of the relevant sort bears no essential connection to truth. That is to say, Goldman's 'weak justification' is no form of epistemic justification at all. At best it is mere blamelessness, which is now widely recognized to be insufficient for epistemic justification.[24] And since the subject in the demon world is not strongly justified, the New Evil Demon Problem remains unsolved. (S/W) does not provide for a satisfactory solution to the problem at hand.

Finally, Sosa has claimed not only that reliability is relative—this is common ground—but that justification itself is a relative notion. Thus he says:

> Relative to our actual environment A, our automatic experience-belief mechanisms count as virtues that yield much truth and justification. Of course relative to the demonic environment D such mechanisms are not virtuous and yield neither truth nor justification. It follows that relative to D the demon's victims are not justified, and yet relative to A their beliefs are justified (1991, p. 144).

This, however, does not accommodate the initial intuition that deluded subjects may have justified beliefs, but instead gives it up. To treat justification as relative, as Sosa does, is in effect to eradicate the distinction between justified and unjustified beliefs, and hence to lose sight of the significance of the notion of justification. After all, virtually every belief will on this view count as justified relative to some world or other, since for virtually any given belief-forming process, no matter how wild and crazy, one can locate a possible world in which employing that method is more likely than not to yield true beliefs. If every belief is justified relative to some set of worlds, and unjustified relative to a different set of worlds, then how are we to distinguish between epistemically good methods of belief-acquisition, and epistemically poor methods? Why is a subject who accepts the deliverances of astrology in any worse a position, in general, than one who employs scientific methods?

To deny that this distinction is of any importance is, it seems to us, to give up on the very notion of justification.[25] Justification is a non-relative notion. We do not think that our twins in the demonic world have beliefs that are justified merely relative to a given world (in this case the actual world); we think their beliefs are justified *simpliciter*. As far as we can see, nothing short of an outright conflation of justification (or epistemic virtue) with reliability could lead one to think otherwise.[26]

In this respect Goldman's first proposal [(NR)] is much more satisfactory—for all its faults, it leaves room for a distinction between the justified and the unjustified. However, Goldman's theory yields the wrong results, and hence we are still in need of an adequate solution to the New Evil Demon Problem. We know that reliability is a relative affair; we have also argued, in effect, that reliability (of some sort or other) is necessary for justification—only it can provide for the constitutive connection with truth. The question is, *relative to what world or set of worlds does reliability yield justification*? It is to this question that we now turn. Answering it satisfactorily will crucially involve appeal to content externalism.[27]

6. Content Externalism and Justification

We have argued that internalist theories of justification cannot account for the constitutive connection between justification and truth, and that extant externalist theories of justification violate widely shared intuitions concerning when a subject's beliefs are justified. In this penultimate section we argue that only by appealing to externalism about content can one provide for an effective and principled restriction upon the set of worlds relative to which one must be reliable in order for one's perceptual beliefs to be justified.

We begin with a brief reminder of where we are. Classical reliabilism takes justification to consist in reliability in the world the subject inhabits. This account runs up against the problem that such reliability is not necessary for justification. In order to accommodate this fact, Goldman's neoclassical reliabilism takes justification to consist rather in reliability in normal worlds.

Neoclassical reliabilism, however, runs up against a different problem. A subject who is well-adapted to her environment, and (consequently) relies on belief-forming mechanisms that are highly reliable within this environment, is surely a subject whose beliefs are justified. But if the subject is relying—as she may well be—upon belief-forming mechanisms that would be highly unreliable in normal worlds, as defined above, Goldman's account renders her beliefs *ipso facto* unjustified. Moreover, neoclassical reliabilism renders meaningless the question whether our most general beliefs are justified. Goldman abandoned (what we are calling) neoclassical reliabilism in favour of the distinction between strong and weak justification. The former notion runs headlong into the New Evil Demon Problem, and the latter notion, we have argued, is no kind of justification at all—precisely because it fails to connect 'weakly justified' beliefs with truth.

The problem with classical reliabilism lies in its privileging the world the subject happens to inhabit; the problem with neoclassical reliabilism lies in its privileging so-called normal worlds; but the lesson from Sosa—and from the failure of internalism—is that some world or set thereof *must* be privileged. The question is which set. Here is our proposal:

(HWR) *Home World Reliabilism*: Justification consists in reliability in the subject's home world.[28]

Three tasks confront us at this point: first, we must define the notion of a home world. Second, we must show how (HWR) handles the cases. Third, we need to provide a rationale for the privileging of the subject's home world.

We offer here a provisional definition of 'home world' sufficient to discuss the way in which the view treats the problematic cases. A subject's home world is defined as that set of environments relative to which the natures of her intentional contents are individuated. The world (or proper part thereof) in which the subject actually develops cognitively is one such environment. The others are those worlds or world-portions which are 'relevantly similar' to this world; similar in the sense that each of them possesses the same relevant content-determining features. A home world, then, is not a possible world but a set of relevantly similar parts of worlds. The definition depends essentially upon content externalism; content internalism denies that environmental conditions play any role in the individuation of content. A more complete understanding of 'home world' will emerge once we provide the rationale for the view, although the notion will still require further development. It should be noted that a home world is not merely a set of content-determining properties, but rather a set of environments—a set of configurations of content-determining properties together with relations to the subject.[29]

Our view, then, is that justification consists in reliability in the sort of environment that serves to individuate one's perceptual states and beliefs; typically, the sort of environment in which one developed into a mature cognitive being. The first point to note is that justification according to (HWR) is a non-relative notion. Beings that are justified in believing that p are justified *simpliciter*—justified in any world to which they might be transported.[30]

This leads us to the problematic cases. Consider once again the New Evil Demon Problem. It is a consequence of (HWR) that subjects who share a mental life thereby share a home world. This follows from the definition of 'home world', and from the anti-individualistic individuation conditions of representational states upon which it depends. Further, trivially, any given belief-forming method will either be reliable in a given world or be unreliable in that world. Consequently, for every set of subjects who share a mental life, and hence a home world, and for any given belief-forming method, that method will serve to justify the beliefs of either all of the members of the set or none. This is because, according to (HWR), justification consists in reliability in the home world. Consequently, no two individuals who share a mental life and employ the same belief-forming methods *could* have beliefs that differed in their epistemic status. Now consider the unfortunate inhabitant of a demon world and her non-deluded twin. Two assumptions drive the intuition that the beliefs of each subject are equally justified: first, the assumption that the subjects have the same total evidence—the same mental lives; second, the assumption that they are employing the same methods of belief-formation. But, as stated above, the assumption that the subjects have the same mental lives in conjunction with the assumption that they are employing the same methods of belief-formation entails, if (HWR) is correct, that the beliefs of the subject's have the same epistemic status. Since (HWR), together with the two assumptions, entails that the subjects have beliefs with the same epistemic status, (HWR) solves the New Evil Demon Problem. We take it as further confirmation of (HWR) that if either one of the assumptions driving the initial intuition is revoked, not only does the intuition of sameness of epistemic status change, but the implication of sameness of epistemic status that (HWR) predicts changes along with it.

The cases which bedevil Goldman's neoclassical reliabilism are also no problem for (HWR). We deal with these in reverse order. The second of the objections concerned a subject living in a non-normal world to which she is nevertheless well-adapted, and whose belief-forming mechanisms are consequently highly reliable relative to her non-normal world even though highly unreliable relative to the set of normal worlds. Goldman's (NR) renders the unintuitive result that such a subject is unjustified. (HWR), in contrast, accords with intuition in this case. A subject who inhabits a world wildly different from the way we take our world to be may nonetheless have justified beliefs, so long as those beliefs are produced by mechanisms that are reliable relative to her home world. The supposition that the subject is well-adapted to her non-normal world is, we take it, tantamount to the claim that her non-normal world is (part of) her home world. Consequently, (HWR) implies that the subject in this particular case is justified.

The first objection concerned the possibility of meaningful inquiry into the justification of our most general beliefs. More fully, since justification is claimed to be reliability in normal worlds, and the notion of a normal world is characterized by reference to a certain class of general beliefs, Goldman's view implies that these general beliefs are trivially justified. It might be thought that (HWR) suffers from a similar problem. Since justification, according to (HWR), is reliability in the home world, and the notion of a home world is characterized by reference to the individuation of representational states, it might be thought that (HWR) implies that our beliefs about the individuation of representational states are trivially justified. In fact, (HWR) has no such implication. One's home world is not constituted by the set of worlds in which one's beliefs about content individuation are true. If it were, then we would face a version of Goldman's problem. The claim is rather that one's home world is that set of environments relative to which the contents of one's perceptual beliefs are individuated. The way in which content is actually determined is one thing; the way in which we take it to be determined—and our justification for so taking it—is another. The two can certainly come apart.

This concludes our discussion of the problematic cases in the literature: Home World Reliabilism appears to give the correct verdicts. It has yet to be shown that the restriction upon the worlds in which one must be reliable in order to count as justified is principled; and consequently it has yet to be made clear that content externalism is required for an adequate account of justification. We now turn to this task.[31]

As noted in the discussion of Sosa above, every relevant belief-forming process is reliable in some possible world. It is clear in addition that no relevant belief-forming process is reliable in all possible worlds. Epistemic justification, however, requires not merely reliability, but non-accidental reliability. Merely happening to be reliable in a given world is not sufficient for the justification of the beliefs yielded by a process, any more than a belief which merely happens to be true can amount to knowledge. Justification requires, not merely a connection with truth, but a non-accidental connection. For a connection between a belief-forming process and the truth to be non-accidental is for there to obtain between them a constitutive or explanatory connection. The connection between the truth—the environment—and the relevant class of beliefs is mediated by perceptual states. But the natures of perceptual beliefs and perceptual states alike are given by their contents, which they possess essentially.

Reliability in some world or other is insufficient for justification, we can now see, because such reliability is accidental relative to the natures of the relevant intentional states; states which are, again, typed by their contents. If the connection between content and environment is not to be thus accidental then a constitutive connection must obtain between them. Such a connection will be provided only if the environment or world plays a role in determining the nature of the content; that is, only if it helps to make it what it is, to individuate it. But then the content must be individuated at least partly in terms of the environment, which is to say that it must be externally individuated. Only if the contents of perceptual states are externally individuated will their connections with the environment—and the connections of the correlative perceptual beliefs—be non-accidental. Since, again, non-accidental reliability is necessary for justification, external individuation must be added to reliability if justification is to result.

We assume it is clear that a certain expedient is unavailable to the theorist who wishes to avoid content externalism. One might seek to appropriate the view of justification which underlies (HWR), without making commitment to the view that content is externally individuated. Such a theorist might find attractive the way in which the view handles the relevant problematic cases—and, relatedly, the way in which it provides for a constitutive connection between justification and truth—but desire not to be committed to content externalism. This sort of move cannot be made precisely because the view that content is externally individuated is built into the very definition of 'home world', and thus into (HWR).

To summarize: Only if content is externally individuated will there be a constitutive or explanatory connection between perceptual states and beliefs, on the one hand, and a set of environments or worlds, on the other. Without such a connection, moreover, the reliability of a belief-forming process relative to a given world can be only accidental. And accidental connections do not contribute to epistemic justification. Insofar as our perceptual beliefs are justified, therefore, their contents must be externally individuated.

We close with discussion of a potential objection. It may be supposed that content individuation is doing all the work in our account, and that, therefore, the view is not properly classified as a version of reliabilism. To put the point another way: if the constitutive connection between the contents of perceptual states and beliefs, on the one hand, and one's home world, on the other, were sufficient for justification, then our appeal to reliability (in one's home world) would be misconceived. But external individuation is only one necessary component of justified perceptual belief. As Burge (2003, p. 533) notes, the external individuation of a perceptual content makes belief in that content epistemically evaluable. It determines the nature of the related perceptual competence, and hence what are the norms which govern the proper exercising of the competence. However, in order to judge and believe in accordance with these norms—that is, in order to be epistemically justified—one must in addition be reliable in the relevant sorts of context. One can imagine a type of creature whose perceptual contents are externally individuated, but whose beliefs (or precursors to belief) are highly unreliable—perhaps certain lower animals are examples. Such creatures would not be epistemically justified. Hence external individuation alone is not sufficient for justification.

7. Conclusion

We have argued that extant theories of justification either fail to connect justification with truth, or fail to provide both an adequate and a principled restriction upon the set of possible worlds in which one must be reliable in order to count as justified. Justification can be connected with truth only by making reliability of some sort a necessary condition upon justification. But reliability in the world the subject inhabits, reliability in some world or other, and reliability in 'normal worlds', are each inadequate to the task. We contend that what is crucial to justification is reliability in a subject's home world. And this view crucially involves commitment to content externalism.

The dialectical situation here is complex. We began by suggesting that there is a route to content externalism which does not require consideration of Twin-Earth style thought experiments. One who is sceptical of such argumentative devices, we claim, ought still to endorse the view that content is externally individuated. But the justificatory force that runs between (HWR) and content externalism travels in both directions. We take it that content externalism is very well grounded by the more traditional Twin-Earth style considerations. If this is so, then the kind of epistemological view promoted here gains additional support thereby.

Notes

* For helpful comments and discussion thanks to Al Casullo, Juan Comesaña, Sanford Goldberg, Richard Fumerton, A.C. Genova, John Hawthorne, and Joseph Mendola. The paper is fully collaborative; authors are listed alphabetically.

1. See Putnam (1975) and Burge (1979) for the classic arguments.
2. Brewer's case is complicated by the fact that he is not an externalist about content—his notion of 'unitary concepts' involves him in a species of narrow content. Indeed, Brewer's argument may be viewed as nearly the direct opposite of ours: he in effect argues from a radical epistemological internalism to a version of content internalism. By contrast, our strategy is to argue that an adequate theory of justification must be externalist, and then that an adequate externalist theory of justification requires content externalism.
3. We make use of a central aspect of Burge's strategy in section 6.
4. Actual reliability is in addition not sufficient for epistemic justification. This requires that externalist theories of justification solve not only the New Evil Demon Problem but also the Meta-Incoherence Problem. [See Sosa (1991) for this terminology.] In this paper we concentrate on the former problem, but we believe—and argue in Majors and Sawyer (manuscript)—that the solution to it we propose in section 6 can be adapted to solve as well the latter problem.
5. While the basic form of perceptual justification is the justification that attaches to perceptual demonstrative beliefs, we do not mark out the category of perceptual demonstrative belief for special treatment. We take such beliefs to have the form of open sentences that are potentially applicable to different objects; we do

not take such beliefs to be object-dependent or to have the form of singular propositions. The considerations we offer in the body of the text apply equally to the conceptual component of context-dependent (demonstrative) beliefs, and to context-independent beliefs.

6. Cartesian internalism (so characterized) is, so far as we can see, the only internalist account which can explain the connection between justification and truth. This creates a tension within the Cartesian framework, and could even be taken to provide support for the claim that the Cartesian view is a form of epistemic externalism.
7. A position close to Cartesian internalism, according to which knowledge effectively requires certainty, is advocated by Peter Unger. See for example Unger (1975).
8. One can even imagine a class of cases in which a subject's ability to reason is so poor that his being epistemically responsible actually hinders his ability to form true beliefs. Such an individual would be better served by random guessing.
9. Another reason to deal with particular internalist theories is that, as we will see, not all those who consider themselves internalists think that there is an access requirement on justification. See Feldman and Conee (1985), which we discuss below.
10. The objection applies to weak and strong access internalism alike. Our point, then, is not merely that one might have access to the states that justify a belief, those states might be objectively connected to the truth, and yet the fact that such a connection obtains would nonetheless be inaccessible to the subject. This claim, being consistent with weak access internalism, would undermine strong access internalism only. Rather, the fact that such a connection obtains is not built into either version of access internalism as a requirement on justification. Consequently, the justificatory status of any given belief is independent of its connection to truth. Thanks to Al Casullo for prompting clarification on this point.
11. Page references in the text are to their (1985); for more extended defense of the view, see Conee and Feldman (2004). In our formulation of (EJ) we have altered Feldman and Conee's terminology slightly.
12. But see also Dretske (2000), which we discuss below.
13. One is reminded here of Wittgenstein's objections to the claim that understanding a word consists in having an image before one's mind; see, e.g., Wittgenstein (1953, §§665–681).
14. See Wedgwood (1999) for the account of rules of rationality. See his (2002) for further defence of the claim that the rationality of a belief revision supervenes either on facts that supervene on one's non-factive mental states, or on facts about the explanatory relations between such internal facts.
15. At (1999, p. 118, n.9) Wedgwood affirms that his topic is justification in the sense of blamelessness. In his (2002) he gives up this view of justification, but continues to take rationality to be an internal matter.
16. Wedgwood's account of concepts bears a striking similarity to that offered earlier in Peacocke (1992). Where Peacocke speaks of a primitive compulsion to make certain inferences or judgements as being constitutive of possessing a

given concept, Wedgwood talks of being immediately inclined to follow a given rule.

17. It is questionable whether there are any concepts which are such that one must follow certain rules in order to possess them. See Burge (1986) and Williamson (2003).
18. See Burge (1993, especially pp. 458–459). [Cf. Burge (2003, p. 509), where Burge contrasts his notion of warrant with that of Plantinga (1993).] There are in fact crucial differences between Burge's account of the distinction and Dretske's. Some of these will become clear as we proceed.
19. We should point out that Dretske does add the partial disclaimer "if that is what it is".
20. Dretske chooses the latter because he wishes explicitly to mark the distinction between justified beliefs (in the broad sense) for which a subject is unable to provide reasons, and justified beliefs (in the narrow sense) for which she can provide reasons.
21. For instance he says "if you cannot do otherwise, it surely can't be true ... that you ought to do otherwise" (p. 598); and "if there is nothing an epistemically responsible agent could have done to avoid believing P, that agent has the right to believe P. There are absolutely no grounds for criticizing him. He is *entitled* to the belief" (p. 601).
22. Reliabilism also notoriously faces a problem concerning the individuation of processes—the Generality Problem. While we do not discuss this problem here, we are broadly sympathetic to the treatment in Alston (1995).
23. For a similar proposal, see Alston (1995).
24. See Pryor (2001). Note that Goldman actually uses 'blameless' and 'non-culpable' as glosses on his notion of weak justification (1988, p. 59). Also note that (S/W) is not strictly speaking an externalist account of justification.
25. We are in agreement with Goldman (1992) when he notes that there is no indication in ordinary practice—what he calls the practice of 'the folk'—that justification is a relative notion.
26. Our criticism of Sosa might be thought unfair on the grounds that we ignore an important distinction within his epistemology. Sosa introduces a distinction analogous to Goldman's distinction between strong and weak justification and proposes to deal with the New Evil Demon Problem by appeal to it (1991, pp. 134–8). Since Sosa's proposal is not significantly different in the relevant respects from (S/W), it suffers the same defect, and we need not provide independent discussion of it here.
27. Peacocke (2004, p. 13) proposes that justification requires reliability in worlds of a kind one has a prima facie defeasible entitlement to believe one is in. On the face of it this is circular; but the real concern is Peacocke's commitment to the view that explaining entitlement requires refuting scepticism. We follow Burge (1993) and Pryor (2000) in rejecting this view.
28. The key idea behind this view is taken from Burge (2003, sec. VI).
29. A home world cannot be characterized merely as a set of content-determining properties. If it were so characterized, it would run into the following problem. A set of properties is such that its members can be jointly instantiated in numerous different ways. Any given possible joint instantiation would constitute

an environment; but there is no subject, even one who is fully justified in the relevant respects, who would be reliable in or well-adapted to every such environment. An environment to which a justified subject is not well-adapted, however, should not count as part of her home world, even if that environment contains instantiations of all and only those properties which feature in the determination of her representational states. Thanks to Richard Fumerton and John Hawthorne for emphasizing the unacceptability of defining a home world as a set of properties.

30. A complication arises given that the environment to which a subject is transported might after a while come to serve to individuate her representational states. This is a case in which the subject's home world changes over time. Justification is not thereby rendered a relative notion, however; the absolute justificatory status of the subject's beliefs is subsequently determined by appeal to reliability in her new home world.
31. In what follows we are again indebted to Burge (2003, sec.VI).

References

William Alston (1995) "How to Think about Reliability", *Philosophical Topics* 23: 1–29.

Kent Bach (1985) "A Rationale for Reliabilism", *The Monist* 68: 246–263.

Laurence BonJour (1985) *The Structure of Empirical Knowledge* (Cambridge, MA: Harvard University Press).

Bill Brewer (1999) *Perception and Reason* (Oxford: Oxford University Press).

Tyler Burge (1979) "Individualism and the Mental", in P. French, T. Uehling, and H. Wettstein, (eds) *Midwest Studies in Philosophy* 4 (Minnesota: University of Minnesota Press).

Tyler Burge (1986) "Intellectual Norms and Foundations of Mind", *Journal of Philosophy* 83: 697–720.

Tyler Burge (1993) "Content Preservation", *Philosophical Review* 103: 457–488.

Tyler Burge (2003) "Perceptual Entitlement", *Philosophy and Phenomenological Research* 67: 503–548.

Roderick Chisholm (1988) "The Indispensability of Internal Justification", *Synthese* 74: 285–296.

Stewart Cohen (1984) "Justification and Truth", *Philosophical Studies* 46: 279–295.

Earl Conee and Richard Feldman (2004) *Evidentialism: Essays in Epistemology* (Oxford: Oxford University Press).

Fred Dretske (2000) "Entitlements: Epistemic Rights Without Epistemic Duties?", *Philosophy and Phenomenological Research* 60: 591–606.

Richard Feldman and Earl Conee (1985) "Evidentialism", *Philosophical Studies* 48: 404–416.

Alvin Goldman (1986) *Epistemology and Cognition* (Cambridge, MA: Harvard University Press).

Alvin Goldman (1988) "Strong and Weak Justification", *Philosophical Perspectives 2: Epistemology*, James Tomberlin (ed.).

Alvin Goldman (1992) "Epistemic Folkways and Scientific Epistemology", reprinted in his *Liaisons: Philosophy Meets the Cognitive and Social Sciences* (Cambridge, MA: Harvard University Press).

John McDowell (1995) "Knowledge and the Internal", *Philosophy and Phenomenological Research* 55: 877–893.

Brad Majors and Sarah Sawyer (manuscript) "Home World Reliabilism".

Christopher Peacocke (1992) *A Study of Concepts* (Cambridge, MA: MIT Press).

Christopher Peacocke (1999) *Being Known* (Oxford: Oxford University Press).

Christopher Peacocke (2004) *The Realm of Reason* (Oxford: Oxford University Press).

Alvin Plantinga (1993) *Warrant: The Current Debate* (Oxford: Oxford University Press).

James Pryor (2000) "The Skeptic and the Dogmatist", *Noûs* 34: 517–549.

James Pryor (2001) "Recent Highlights of Epistemology", *The British Journal for the Philosophy of Science* 52: 95–124.

Hilary Putnam (1975) "The Meaning of 'Meaning'", reprinted in his *Mind, Language, and Reality: Philosophical Papers*, Vol. II (Cambridge: Cambridge University Press, 1975): 215–72.

Ernest Sosa (1991) "Reliabilism and Intellectual Virtue", from E. Sosa, *Knowledge in Perspective: Selected Essays in Epistemology* (Cambridge: Cambridge University Press).

Peter Unger (1975) *Ignorance: A Case for Scepticism* (Oxford: Oxford University Press).

Ralph Wedgwood (1999) "The A Priori Rules of Rationality", *Philosophy and Phenomenological Research* 59: 113–131.

Ralph Wedgwood (2002) "Internalism Explained", *Philosophy and Phenomenological Research* 65: 349–369.

Timothy Williamson (2003) "Understanding and Inference", *Proceedings of the Aristotelian Society, Supplemental Volume* 77: 249–93.

Ludwig Wittgenstein (1953) *Philosophical Investigations*, translated by G.E.M. Anscombe (Blackwell: Oxford University Press).

Philosophical Perspectives, 19, Epistemology, 2005

THREE PROPOSALS REGARDING A THEORY OF CHANCE

Christopher J. G. Meacham
Rutgers University

1. Introduction

Probability is used to model the actual likelihoods, or *chances*, of various possibilities. Probability is also used to model the degrees of belief, or *credences* a reasonable subject has in various possibilities. Now it seems there should be a relation between the two: if a subject believes that an event has a given chance of occurring, this should have some bearing on her credence that the event will occur.

The canonical account of this relation is that of David Lewis (1986). Lewis proposes that the correct relation between chance and credence is given by his Principal Principle. Lewis's account is not just an account of the chance-credence relation, however; it is partially a theory of chance as well. (A theory *of* chance, not a chance theory; I take a chance theory to be a physical theory that employs chance, such as statistical mechanics or quantum mechanics.) Worries about the compatibility of the Principal Principle and Humean supervenience have led to variations of Lewis' original principle, but the general nature of these principles and the notion of chance they employ have remained the same. I'll call Lewis's theory and these variants the *Lewisian theories of chance*.

Ceteris paribus it seems your credences should agree with your chances. If you believe that a coin has a .5 chance of coming up heads, then all else being equal you should have a .5 credence that the coin will come up heads. But you don't always want your credences to accord with the chances. Suppose you are in possession of a crystal ball which reliably depicts the future, and the crystal ball shows you that heads will come up. Then your credence in the coin coming up heads should be near 1, not .5. So it seems you should only let the chances guide your credences in an outcome when you're not possession of illicit or *inadmissible* evidence.

With the notion of admissibility in hand, the relation between chance and credence falls into place: your credences should accord with what you think the chances are unless you're in possession of inadmissible evidence. This is Lewis's Principal Principle. (Lewis later abandoned the Principal Principle in favor of a variant.[1] The details of this new principle need not concern us; any points I make assuming Lewis' original principle will apply *mutatis mutandis* to this variant.)

The Lewisian accounts also make assumptions about the objects and arguments of chance. They take the objects of chance to be *de dicto* propositions.[2] Following Lewis, we can take these propositions to be sets of possible worlds, and understand the chance of these propositions as the chance of one of those worlds obtaining. Chance distributions are functions of two arguments on the Lewisian accounts. The first argument is a set of chance laws, the second is a history up to a time at some world where those chance laws hold. So on the Lewisian accounts every chance distribution is entailed by a set of chance laws and a history.

These arguments can be picked out by a world and a time. The chance laws are picked out by the world, and the history up to a time is picked out by the world and the time. So we can also treat chance distributions as functions of a world and time. In the rest of the paper, when I speak of the 'past', 'future', etc., I'll always be speaking relative to the time associated with a chance distribution. For example, a 'past event' will be an event that occurs at a time before the time associated with the relevant chance distribution.[3]

In his original paper, Lewis made two further claims about chance. The first is that the past is no longer chancy; i.e., that a chance distribution assigns only trivial chances (0 or 1) to events in its past. The second is that determinism and chance are incompatible. Both of these claims can be derived from the Lewisian theories given some additional assumptions. The first requires that the arguments of a chance distribution are admissible. The second requires that anything entailed by the laws must be assigned a chance of 1.[4] Proponents of the Lewisian accounts have generally rejected these assumptions due to worries regarding the compatibility of chance and Humeanism. Instead, they have adopted these two claims as further, independent assumptions about the nature of chance.

Despite their popularity, there are several problems with the Lewisian theories of chance. First, they are time asymmetric, and these asymmetries are incompatible with some of the chance theories considered in physics. Second, they are incompatible with statistical mechanical chances. Third, the content of Lewis's Principal Principle depends on how admissibility is cashed out, but there is no agreement as to what a precise characterization of admissible evidence should be.

In this paper I will make three proposals regarding a theory of chance. The first two proposals address these three problems by amending the problematic parts of the Lewisian theories.[5] The third proposal offers an account of some of the common features shared by the chance theories of physics. Since the third proposal isn't needed to resolve any particular problems, it's less motivated than the first two proposals. The three proposals are independent, however, so those wary of the third proposal can adopt the first two by themselves.

The rest of this paper will proceed as follows. In the second section I motivate the first proposal in two steps. In the first part of the second section I'll look at the temporal asymmetries of the Lewisian accounts, and show how they conflict with some of the chance theories considered in physics. In the second part of the second section I'll show how the Lewisian accounts are incompatible with statistical mechanical chances, and argue that the only tenable account of statistical mechanical probabilities on offer is that they're chances. In the third section I motivate the second proposal. I'll look at whether Lewis's chance-credence principle needs an admissibility clause, and argue that we should adopt a chance-credence principle which does not make use of admissibility. In the fourth section I'll present the third proposal, and apply it to two of our physical theories. In the fifth section I'll present two problems that remain, and sketch some possible responses. I'll conclude in the sixth section.

Much of the discussion of the Lewisian accounts of chance has focused on the compatibility of chance and Humean supervenience. The work done in this paper largely crosscuts these issues. Unfortunately, the issue of Humeanism so pervades the literature on chance that it is impossible to avoid it completely. In this paper I attempt the following compromise: in the body of the paper I sidestep issues regarding Humeanism, and I leave a discussion of the (lack of) implications my proposals have on Humeanism to an appendix.

2. The First Proposal

2.1. Time Asymmetry

There are two temporal asymmetries in the Lewisian theories of chance. First, there is the assumption that the second argument of chance distributions are histories. Second, there is the claim that the past is no longer chancy. These asymmetries make the Lewisian accounts incompatible with some of the chance theories considered in physics, such as the Aharonov, Bergmann and Lebowitz (ABL) theory of quantum mechanics and classical statistical mechanics.[6]

Lewis recognized that the temporal asymmetry of his account was a deficit: "Any serious physicist, if he remains at least open-minded both about the shape of the cosmos and about the existence of chance processes, ought to do better."[7] I propose to do better: I propose to allow the second argument of chance distributions to be propositions other than histories up to a time, and to reject the claim that the past is no longer chancy.

We will see how the asymmetries of the Lewisian accounts conflict with classical statistical mechanics in the next subsection. In this subsection we will look at how these asymmetries rule out the ABL theory.

In standard theories of quantum mechanics the chance of a measurement result at t_1 is determined by the state of the wave function prior to the measurement, the prior wave function being pre-selected by an earlier measurement at t_0. According to the ABL theory, these chances are incomplete. On the ABL theory, the chance of a given outcome at t_1 is determined by the wave functions prior *and* posterior to the t_1 measurement, the prior and posterior wave functions being pre and post-selected by an earlier measurement at t_0 and a later measurement at t_2.[8]

Say the ABL theory assigns non-trivial chances to the possible outcomes of a measurement at t_1. On the Lewisian accounts the arguments of this chance distribution will be the ABL laws and a history up to a time. But a history up to what time? The ABL laws and this history must entail the chance distribution on the Lewisian accounts. Since the distribution depends on the results of the earlier (t_0) and later (t_2) measurements, histories up to t_0 or t_1 aren't enough to entail the distribution. To obtain the desired distribution the history must run up to t_2. But on the Lewisian accounts the past is no longer chancy: events which occur before the time associated with the chance distribution—the time the associated history runs up to—receive trivial chances. If the second argument of the chance distribution is a history up to t_2, then the distribution must assign trivial chances to the possible outcomes of the t_1 measurement. Since the ABL theory assigns a non-trivial chance to the outcome of the t_1 measurement, the Lewisian can't accomodate the chances of the ABL theory.

We can hold on to these asymmetries and reject theories like the ABL theory, but I think we should be wary of outlawing proposed physical theories on contentious metaphysical grounds. I think a better option is to reject the asymmetric components of the Lewisian theories of chance.

Note that once we reject the Lewisian account of the arguments of chance distributions, it's hard to make sense of the claim that the past isn't chancy. The claim that the past is no longer chancy presupposes that chance distributions can be associated with a time, relative to which some events are in the past. On the Lewisian accounts chance distributions can be associated with a time because they're functions of chance laws and histories, and chance laws and histories can be picked out by a world and a time. But once we allow the second argument to be propositions other than histories up to a time, we're no longer guaranteed that a world and time will pick out what the second argument is. So once we reject the Lewisian account of the arguments of chance we're no longer guaranteed a way to associate a time with chance distributions, and a way to make sense of the claim that the past is no longer chancy.

2.2. Statistical Mechanics

Statistical mechanical theories also pose a problem for the Lewisian theories of chance. I'll draw out some of these problems by looking at a particular statistical mechanical theory, classical statistical mechanics. Since it will be useful to have a concrete theory to work with in the rest of this paper, I will sketch the theory in some detail. For simplicity, I will ignore electrodynamics and assume that all masses are point particles.

Central to statistical mechanics is the notion of a *state space*. A state space is a space of possible states of the world at a time. All of the possibilities in a classical mechanical state space are alike with regards to certain static properties, such as the spatiotemporal dimensions of the system, the number of particles, and the masses of these particles. The individual elements of this space are picked out by certain dynamic properties, the locations and momenta of the particles.[9]

In classical statistical mechanics these static and dynamic properties determine the state of the world at a time. Classical mechanics is deterministic: the state of the world at a time determines the history of the system.[10] So in classical statistical mechanics each point in the state space corresponds to a unique history, i.e., to a possible world. We can therefore take a state space to be a set of possible worlds, and the state space and its subsets to be propositions. The state spaces form a partition of the classical statistical mechanical worlds, dividing the classical statistical mechanical worlds into groups of worlds that share the relevant static properties.

Given a state space, we can provide the classical statistical mechanical probabilities. Let m be the Liouville measure, the Lebesgue measure over the canonical representation of the state space, and let K be a subset of the state space. The classical statistical mechanical probability of A relative to K is $m(A \cap K)/m(K)$.

Note that statistical mechanical probabilities aren't defined for all object propositions A and relative propositions K. Given the above formula, two conditions must be satisfied for the chance of A relative to K to be defined. Both $m(A \cap K)$ and $m(K)$ must be defined, and the ratio of $m(A \cap K)$ to $m(K)$ must be defined.

Despite the superficial similarity, the statistical mechanical probability of A relative to K is not a conditional probability. If it were, we could define the probability of A '*simpliciter*' as m(A), and retrieve the formula for the probability of A relative to K using the definition of conditional probability. The reason we can't do this is that the Liouville measure m is not a probability measure; unlike probability measures, there is no upper bound on the value a Liouville measure can take. We only obtain a probability distribution after we take the ratio of $m(A \cap K)$ and $m(K)$; since $m(A \cap K) \leq m(K)$, the ratio of the two terms will always fall in the range of acceptable values, [0,1].

Now, how should we understand statistical mechanical probabilities? A satisfactory account must preserve their explanatory power and normative force. For example, classical mechanics has solutions where ice cubes grow larger when placed in hot water, as well as solutions where ice cubes melt when placed in hot water. Why is it that we only see ice cubes melt when placed in hot water? Statistical mechanics provides the standard explanation. When we look at systems of cups of hot water with ice cubes in them, we find that according to the Liouville measure the vast majority of them quickly develop into cups of lukewarm water, and only a few develop into cups of even hotter water with larger ice cubes. The explanation for why we always see ice cubes melt, then, is that it's *overwhelmingly likely* that they'll melt instead of grow, given the statistical mechanical probabilities. In addition to explanatory power, we take statistical mechanical probabilities to have normative force: it seems irrational to believe that ice cubes are likely to grow when placed in hot water.

The natural account of statistical mechanical probabilities is to take them to be chances. On this account, statistical mechanical probabilities have the explanatory power they do because they're chances; they represent lawful, empirical and contingent features of the world. Likewise, statistical mechanical probabilities have normative force because they're chances, and chances normatively constrain our credences via something like the Principal Principle.

But statistical mechanical probabilities cannot be chances on the Lewisian accounts. First, classical statistical mechanical chances are compatible with classical mechanics, a deterministic theory. But on the Lewisian accounts determinism and chance are incompatible.

Second, classical statistical mechanics is time symmetric like the ABL theory, and is incompatible with the Lewisian accounts for similar reasons. Consider two propositions, A and K, where A is the proposition that the temperature of the world at t_1 is T_1, and K is the proposition that the temperature of the world at t_0 and t_2 is T_0 and T_2. Consider the chance of A relative to K. On the Lewisian accounts the arguments of the relevant chance distribution will be the classical statistical mechanical laws and a history up to a time. But a history up to what time? The statistical mechanical laws and this history entail the chance distribution on the Lewisian accounts. The distribution depends on the relative state K, and a history must run up to t_2 to entail K, so we need a history up to t_2 to obtain the desired distribution. Since the past is no longer chancy, the chance of any proposition entailed by the history up to t_2, including A, must be trivial. But the statistical mechanical chance of A is generally not trivial, so the Lewisian account cannot accommodate such chances.

Third, the Lewisian restriction of the second argument of chance distributions to histories is too narrow to accommodate statistical mechanical chances. Consider the case just given, where A is a proposition about the temperature of the world at t_1 and K a proposition about the temperature of the world at t_0 and t_2. Consider also a third proposition K′, that the temperature of the world at t_0, $t_{1.5}$ and t_2 is T_0, $T_{1.5}$ and T_2, respectively. On the Lewisian accounts it looks like the chance of A relative to K and the chance of A relative to K′ will have the same arguments: the statistical mechanical laws and a history up to t_2. But for many values of $T_{1.5}$, statistical mechanics will assign different chances to A relative to K and A relative to K′.

It's not surprising that the Lewisian account of the arguments of chance distributions is at odds with statistical mechanical chances. It's natural to take classical statistical mechanics T and the relative state K to be the arguments of statistical mechanical distributions, since T and K alone entail these distributions. But taking T and K to be the arguments conflicts with the Lewisian accounts, since while K can be a history up to a time, often it is not.

So the Lewisian accounts are committed to denying that statistical mechanical probabilities are chances. Instead, they take them to be subjective values of some kind. There's a long tradition of treating statistical mechanical probabilities this way, taking them to represent the degrees of belief a rational agent should have in a particular state of ignorance. Focusing on classical statistical mechanics, it proceeds along the following lines.

Start with the intuition that some version of the Indifference Principle—the principle that you should have equal credences in possibilities you're epistemically 'indifferent' between—should be a constraint on the beliefs of rational beings. There are generally too many possibilities in statistical mechanical cases—an uncountably infinite number—to apply the standard Indifference Principle to. But given the intuition behind indifference, it seems we can adopt a modified version of the Indifference Principle: when faced with a continuum number of possibilities that you're epistemically indifferent between, your degrees of belief in these possibilities should match the values assigned to them by an appropriately uniform measure. The properties of the Lebesgue measure make it a natural candidate for this measure. Granting this, it seems the statistical mechanical probabilities fall out of principles of rationality: if you only know K about the world, then your credence that the world is in some set of states A should be equal to the proportion (according to the Lebesgue measure) of K states that are A states. Thus it seems we recover the normative force of statistical mechanical probabilities without having to posit chances.

However, as Albert (2001), Loewer (2000), and others have argued, this account of statistical mechanical probabilities is untenable. First, the account suffers from a technical problem. The representation of the state space determines the Lebesgue measure of a set of states, and there are an infinite number of ways to represent the state space. So there are an infinite number of ways to 'uniformly' assign credences to the space of possibilities. Classical statistical mechanics uses the Lebesgue measure over the canonical representation of the state space, the Liouville measure, but no compelling argument has been given for why *this* is the right way to represent the space of possibilities when we're trying to quantify our ignorance. So it doesn't seem that we can recover statistical mechanical probabilities from intuitions regarding indifference after all.

Second, the kinds of values this account provides can't play the explanatory role we take statistical mechanical probabilities to play. On this account statistical mechanical probabilities don't come from the laws. Rather, they're *a priori* necessary facts about what it's rational to believe when in a certain state of ignorance. But if these facts are *a priori* and *necessary*, they're incapable of explaining *a posteriori* and *contingent* facts about our world, like why ice cubes usually melt when placed in hot water. Furthermore, as a purely normative principle, the Indifference Principle isn't the kind of thing that could explain the success of statistical mechanics. Grant that *a priori* it's rational to believe that ice cubes will usually melt when placed in hot water: that does nothing to explain why in fact ice cubes *do* usually melt when placed in hot water.

The indifference account of statistical mechanical probabilities is untenable. The only viable account of statistical mechanical probabilities on offer is that they are chances, and the Lewisian theories of chance are incompatible with statistical mechanical chances. I propose to amend the Lewisian theories so that they are compatible with physical theories like classical statistical mechanics and the ABL theory of quantum mechanics.

The first proposal is to allow the second argument of chance distributions to be propositions other than histories, and to reject the two additional claims about chance the Lewisian theories make: that the past is no longer chancy, and that determinism and chance are incompatible. The two additional claims of the Lewisian theories stipulate properties of chance distributions that are incompatible with time symmetric and deterministic chances; by rejecting these two additional claims, we eliminate these stipulated incompatibilities. By allowing the second argument to be propositions other than histories, we can incorporate the time symmetric arguments needed for theories like the ABL theory and the more varied arguments needed for statistical mechanical theories.

3. The Second Proposal

On the Lewisian theories, the relation that should hold between credence and chance is captured by the Principal Principle. Roughly, the Principal Principle claims that your credences should accord with what you think the chances are unless you're in possession of inadmissible evidence. The content of this principle depends on how admissibility is cashed out. If nothing is admissible the principle is vacuous, if everything is admissible the principle is inconsistent. Unfortunately, there is no agreement as to what a precise characterization of admissible evidence should be. So the content of the Principal Principle is unclear.

If a satisfactory chance-credence principle requires something like an admissibility clause, there's a pressing need to figure out what admissibility is. But it's not clear that a satisfactory chance-credence principle does require an admissibility clause. Let's try to construct such a principle, and look to see why admissibility is needed.

Intuitively, a subject who knows what the chances are should have credences which line up with those chances. Let G stand for the arguments of a chance distribution. G entails the chances it's the argument of, so a subject whose total evidence is G should have credences that line up with the chances that G entails. If we let '$ch_G(\cdot)$' stand for the chance distribution entailed by G, and let '$cr_G(\cdot)$' stand for the credences of a subject whose total evidence is G, we can express this as

(1) $cr_G(A) = ch_G(A)$, if $ch_G(A)$ is defined.

The added clause is needed because for some arguments and object propositions $ch_G(A)$ won't be defined. On the Lewisian accounts, for example, $ch_G(A)$ won't be defined if G isn't a complete chance theory and a history up to a time.

If we assume Bayesianism, we can translate (1) into a constraint on reasonable initial credence functions, or *hypothetical priors*. (Hypothetical priors are 'prior' because they represent the subject's credences prior to the receipt of any evidence, and 'hypothetical' because it is unlikely that one ever is in such a state.) Bayesianism states that a subject whose total evidence is G should have credences equal to their hypothetical priors conditional on G. Letting '$hp(\cdot)$' stand for the hypothetical priors of a subject, we can express Bayesianism as

(2) $cr_G(A) = hp(A|G)$, if $hp(A|G)$ is defined

The added clause is needed here because $hp(A|G)$ won't be defined if $hp(G) = 0$.

Using (2), we can present (1) as the following chance-credence principle:[11]

(3) $hp(A|G) = ch_G(A)$, if $hp(A|G)$ and $ch_G(A)$ are defined.

This is similar to the rule that Lewis proposes, but without a clause regarding admissibility. If we add such a clause, we get the following principle:

(4) $hp(A|GE) = ch_G(A)$, if GE is admissible relative to $ch_G(A)$, and $hp(A|G)$ and $ch_G(A)$ are defined.

This is a version of Lewis's Principal Principle.

Why is (4) preferable to (3)? I.e., why is (3) inadequate without an admissibility clause? If we assume that the arguments of a distribution are admissible, as Lewis originally did, then (4) is a strictly stronger principle than (3). We get (3) as a special case of (4) when E is a tautology. So if we're worried about (3), we should be worried that (3) isn't strong enough without an admissibility clause: it doesn't give us all the relations between chance and credence that we intuitively think should hold.

(3) and (4) by themselves don't tell us anything about our current credences if we have evidence. For (3) or (4) to have a bearing on our current credences, we

need to employ a rule which relates our hypothetical priors to our credences, like Bayesianism. So let's assume that Bayesianism holds.

In the first section, I motivated the introduction of admissibility with the following story:

> *Ceteris paribus* it seems your credences should agree with your chances. If you believe that a coin has a .5 chance of coming up heads, then all else being equal you should have a .5 credence that the coin will come up heads. But you don't always want your credences to accord with the chances. Suppose you are in possession of a crystal ball which reliably depicts the future, and the crystal ball shows you that heads will come up. Then your credence in the coin coming up heads should be near 1, not .5. So it seems you should only let the chances guide your credences in an outcome when you're not possession of illicit or *inadmissible* evidence.

Now, it's true that you don't always want your credences to accord with the *same* chances. If your total evidence is G, then your credence in heads should line up with $ch_G(H)$. If a crystal ball then gives you some new evidence E, and $ch_{GE}(H) \neq ch_G(H)$, then your credences should no longer line up with $ch_G(H)$. But this doesn't raise any problems for (3). (3) only requires that your credences line up with the chances when your total evidence is the same as the arguments of those chances. As your evidence changes, so do the chances (3) requires your credences to line up with.

But we might worry about cases where our total evidence doesn't equal the arguments of any chance distribution. On the Lewisian picture of the arguments of chance distributions, for example, the crystal ball's evidence might be such as to leave us with a chance theory and a *partial* history up to a time as our total evidence E. Since E isn't the argument of a chance distribution, it's not clear what constraints (3) will place on our credences. With the worry that (3) is too weak in mind, it's natural to worry that (3) doesn't tell us enough about what our credences should be in these cases.

If we assume Bayesianism, though, then (3) is strong enough to capture all of the relations between chance and credence that we think should hold. We can divide our uncertainty into two kinds, uncertainty about the outcome of chance events and uncertainty about other things. We should only expect chances to have a bearing on our uncertainty about the outcome of chance events. But once we eliminate our uncertainty about other things, (3) and Bayesianism are enough to completely fix our credences in the outcomes of chance events. So no admissibility clause is needed to strengthen (3).

To see that (3) and Bayesianism fix our credences, let's look at a simple case. Assume with the Lewisian that chance distributions are functions of chance laws and histories. Consider a world where there are only three chance events, three fair coin flips, that take place at times t_1 through t_3, respectively. Consider a subject at this world who knows the laws T and the history up to t_0,

H_0. Let T and H_0 entail everything about the world except how the coin tosses come up, so the subject knows everything about the world except the outcome of these chance events.

In this case the subject knows she's in one of eight possible worlds. (3) and Bayesianism entail that her credences in each world should be 1/8. If the subject learns the history up to t_1, H_1, then she'll be left with four worlds, and (3) and Bayesianism will entail that her credences in each of these remaining worlds should be 1/4. Now consider the case we were worried about: what if she gets evidence such that her total evidence E consists of the laws and a *partial* history up to t_1?

We know this new evidence will leave her with at least four worlds. Precisely how many and which worlds are left will depend on what her new evidence is. But once we're told what the new evidence is, it's trivial to determine what her new credences should be. She should set her credence in the worlds incompatible with the evidence to 0, and normalize her credences in the rest. That is, like any good Bayesian she should conditionalize.

Call (3) the Basic Principle. The second proposal is to discard the admissibility clause that Lewis built into the Principal Principle, and to adopt something like the Basic Principle instead.[12] An admissibility-free chance-credence principle like the Basic Principle and an updating rule like Bayesianism tell us all we need to know about the relation between credence and chance. In section four I will use the Basic Principle to show how our credences are constrained by the chances of some of our actual chance theories. I will sketch the chances of two of the complete chance theories considered in physics, classical statistical mechanics and statistical Bohmian mechanics, and then sketch the acceptable priors of a subject with respect to these theories.

4. The Third Proposal

The third proposal is an account of the arguments and objects for which chance distributions are defined, and of their relation to the values assigned by chance theories. Unlike the first two proposals, the third proposal is not motivated by any particular problems. As such, it is more tentative than the first two. In support of the third proposal, I offer the following: it is compatible with the chance theories considered in physics, and, if true, it explains several similarities between the chance theories that physics considers that would otherwise be accidental.

The three proposals are largely independent, so those who reject the third proposal can still accept the first two. In any case, the third proposal provides a useful framework for working with the chance theories of physics, and *a fortiori* for figuring out the constraints that these theories place on our credences. If all three of the proposals are correct, we can say quite a lot about chance, chance theories, and the chance-credence relation. I do not claim, however, that this provides a complete theory of chance. Among other things, the proposals leave two issues unresolved; issues which come into the spotlight once we look closely at the chance theories of physics. In the next section I will briefly present these issues, and sketch some possible responses.

The third proposal is that every chance theory T has the following structure. First, the worlds of the chance theory can be partitioned into *coarse sets*. The coarse sets are the broadest regions of possibility to which the theory assigns well defined chances. In classical statistical mechanics the coarse sets are the state spaces; i.e., sets of classical statistical mechanical worlds which share the relevant static properties.

Second, the coarse sets can be partitioned into *fine sets*. The fine sets provide the smallest units of possibility to which the theory assigns well defined chances. In classical statistical mechanics the fine sets are the points of the state spaces; i.e., individual possible worlds.

Third, each coarse set is associated with a countably additive measure. Each measure is defined on an algebra S over the associated coarse set C, where S includes all of the fine sets of C but no proper subsets of these sets except the empty set.[13] These measures encode the chances of the theory, although they themselves need not be probability measures. In classical statistical mechanics these measures are the Liouville measures over the state spaces.

Given this structure, I propose that the chances of the theory T are as follows: For any propositions A and K, either (i) $ch_{TK}(A) = m(A \cap K)/m(K)$, where m is the measure T associates with a coarse set C that contains K, or (ii) $ch_{TK}(A)$ is undefined, if the above prescription fails to pick out a unique well-defined value. This entails that $ch_{TK}(A)$ is defined *iff* (a) T is a complete chance theory and K is a subset of a coarse set C of T, (b) the ratio of $m(A \cap K)$ to m(K) is defined, and (c) $A \cap K$ and K are elements of S, the algebra over which m is defined. As we saw in section two, this lines up with the chances that classical statistical mechanics assigns and the conditions under which the classical statistical mechanics chances are defined.

With this picture of chance theories in hand, let's turn to the question of how our priors should be constrained by the chances according to an admissibility free chance-credence rule like the Basic Principle. There may be a number of objective constraints on one's priors, but in this context we're only interested in those imposed by the chances. So let us assume a version of subjective Bayesianism on which the Basic Principle is the only objective constraint on our priors.

Given the structure outlined above, we can divide up the space of possible worlds into smaller and smaller regions by applying finer and finer partitions. We can partition the space of possible worlds into chance theories T_i, partition the chance theories into coarse sets C_j, partition the coarse sets into fine sets F_k, and partition the fine sets into individual worlds W_l. Now consider an arbitrary proposition, A. We know that if some sets X_i form a partition of A, we can express hp(A) as

$$(5)\quad hp(A) = \sum_i hp(A \wedge X_i) = \sum_i hp(X_i)hp(A|X_i)$$

By applying (5) repeatedly for each of the above partitions, we can express hp(A) as

$$\begin{aligned} hp(A) &= \sum_i hp(T_i)hp(A|T_i) \\ &= \sum_{i,j} hp(T_i)hp(C_j|T_i)hp(A|T_iC_j) \\ &= \sum_{i,j,k} hp(T_i)hp(C_j|T_i)hp(F_k|T_iC_j)hp(A|T_iC_jF_k) \\ &= \sum_{i,j,k,l} hp(T_i)hp(C_j|T_i)hp(F_k|T_iC_j)hp(W_l|T_iC_jF_k)hp(A|T_iC_jF_kW_l) \\ (6)\qquad &= \sum_{i,j,k,l} hp(T_i)hp(C_j|T_i)hp(F_k|C_j)hp(W_l|F_k)hp(A|W_l) \end{aligned}$$

So we can determine the value of hp(A) by figuring out the values of the five sets of terms in (6).[14]

The first set of terms are of the form $hp(T_i)$, and represent our prior in a chance theory. Since we need to assume that a particular chance theory holds before we can get any chances, how we should divide our priors among chance theories is beyond the scope of chance. So our priors in the first set of terms will be determined by subjective considerations. The second set of terms are of the form $hp(C_j|T_i)$, and represent our prior in a coarse set given a chance theory. Since we need to fix on a coarse set before a theory can assign chances, how we should divide our prior in a chance theory among its coarse sets is also beyond the scope of chance. So our priors in the second set of terms will also be determined subjectively.

The third set of terms are of the form $hp(F_k|C_j)$, and represent our prior in a fine set given a coarse set. This is the regime where chances come in. If $hp(C_j) > 0$ and $ch_{Ti,Cj}(F_k)$ is defined, then the Basic Principle applies and $hp(F_k|C_j) = ch_{Ti,Cj}(F_k)$. So our priors in these terms will generally be fixed by the chances. If $hp(C_j) = 0$ or $ch_{Ti,Cj}(F_k)$ is not defined, then the Basic Principle won't apply. In these cases, $hp(F_k|C_j)$ is unconstrained by the chances, and will be determined subjectively.

The fourth set of terms are of the form $hp(W_l|F_k)$, and represent our priors in an individual world given a fine set. Since the fine sets are the smallest units to which chances are assigned, once we've fixed on a fine set the chances have nothing more to say. So as with the first two sets of terms, our priors in the fourth set of terms will be determined subjectively. The fifth set of terms are of the form $hp(A|W_l)$, and represent our priors in A given an individual world. These are trivial to determine. If $W_l \in A$ then $hp(A|W_l) = 1$, if $W_l \notin A$ then $hp(A|W_l) = 0$.

Given the third proposal, it's clear where and to what extent the chances constrain our priors. Likewise, it's clear how to determine what our priors are in the worlds of a given chance theory. We subjectively determine our priors in the chance theory and its coarse sets, align our priors in the fine sets of these coarse sets using the chances, and then subjectively determine our priors in individual possible worlds. So to determine our priors in the classical statistical mechanical worlds, we determine our subjective prior in classical statistical mechanics, divide this subjectively among the state spaces, and divide our prior in each state space among its points in accordance with the statistical mechanical chances. Since the points of state space are individual possible worlds, we don't need to divide our priors any further.

We've seen how the third proposal works for classical statistical mechanics. Let's look at how the proposal works for a different chance theory, statistical Bohmian mechanics, the complete chance theory encompassing Bohmian mechanics and quantum statistical mechanics. Unlike classical statistical mechanics, the chances of statistical Bohmian mechanics are generally segregated into the chances of Bohmian mechanics and the chances of quantum statistical mechanics. To apply the third proposal to statistical Bohmian mechanics we need to glue the chances of Bohmian mechanics and quantum statistical mechanics together, and fit them into the framework given above.

Fortunately, this framework makes this easy to do, since it can be applied to Bohmian mechanics and quantum statistical mechanics independently. It then becomes clear how to merge the two theories into a single theory.

I will first give a brief description of quantum statistical mechanics and Bohmian mechanics. To avoid a lengthy discussion of these theories, I won't present them in as much detail as I presented classical statistical mechanics. Instead, I will simply give a gloss of their relevant features, and then sketch how each fits into the above framework.

As with classical statistical mechanics, quantum statistical mechanics considers spaces of possibilities that share certain static properties, such as spatio-temporal dimensions of the system, the number of particles, etc. The elements of these spaces are picked out by certain dynamic properties, in this case the property of having the same wave function at a given time. Quantum statistical mechanics assigns a canonical measure over these possibilities from which the chances are derived.[15]

Bohmian mechanics is an interpretation of quantum mechanics that adds hidden variables to the formalism, in this case the positions of the particles. In Bohmian mechanics a complete description of a system at a time is given by the static properties considered above and the wave function and particle positions of the system. Both the wavefunction and the particles evolve deterministically, so a complete description of the system at a time fixes the history of the system. Bohmian chances come in when we consider possibilities that have the same wave function and relevant static properties but differ in particle positions. Bohmian mechanics assigns a special measure over this space which determines the chances.[16]

The framework given above straightforwardly applies to each of these theories. In quantum statistical mechanics the coarse sets are sets of possibilities that share the relevant static properties, and its fine sets are the sets of possiblities with the same wave function. In Bohmian mechanics the coarse sets are sets of possibilities that share the relevant static properties and have the same wave function, and its fine sets are the sets of possiblities with the same particle positions. Since the relevant static properties, wave function, and particle positions at a time determine the history of a system, these fine sets are individual possible worlds.

Since the fine sets of quantum statistical mechanics are the coarse sets of Bohmian mechanics, gluing the two theories together is simple. Let the coarse sets of quantum statistical mechanics be the coarse sets of the combined theory, and let the fine sets of Bohmian mechanics be the fine sets of the combined theory. Then we get the appropriate measures for the combined theory, statistical Bohmian mechanics, by essentially taking the product of the quantum statistical mechanical measures and the Bohmian mechanical measures.

With statistical Bohmian mechanics formulated in terms of the above framework, we can sketch what our priors should be in the manner given above. First we determine our subjective prior in statistical Bohmian mechanics, and divide this subjectively among the coarse sets of the theory. Then we divide our prior in each coarse set among its fine sets in accordance with the chances. Since in this case the fine sets are individual possible worlds, we don't need to divide our priors any further.

Although we've considered the combination of quantum statistical mechanics and Bohmian mechanics, a similar procedure can be used to obtain the complete chance theory of quantum statistical mechanics and other quantum mechanical interpretations.[17] For genuinely indeterministic interpretations, for example, we can obtain the chances histories that share the relevant static properties by essentially taking the product of the quantum statistical mechanical chances for their initial wave functions and the stochastic chances of their histories given those initial wave functions.

5. Two Problems

These three proposals leave a number of issues unresolved. Two of these issues become particularly urgent when we look closely at the chance theories of physics. In this section I will raise these two issues, and sketch some possible responses.

5.1. The First Problem

The first problem concerns the tie between credence and chance. Assume that, like Lewis, we formulate our chance-credence principle in terms of hypothetical priors. The problem then is that our priors for chance theories like classical statistical mechanics only end up being constrained by trivial chances. That is, the values of the non-trivial statistical mechanical chances are epistemically irrelevant, since they have no effect on our priors.

A rigorous derivation of this result is given in Appendix B.3, but the following is a rough sketch of how the problem arises. If the relative state K of a statistical mechanical chance is of infinite measure, then that chance will be trivial or undefined.[18] So the relative state K of a non-trivial chance must be of finite measure. Now, any prior you have in a classical mechanical state space is required by the chances to be spread uniformly over that space in accordance with the Liouville measure. Since the state spaces of classical statistical mechanics are of infinite measure, any finite measure region of such a space will be assigned a 0 prior.[19] So the relative state K of a non-trivial chance will be assigned a 0 prior. But the Basic Principle only applies if one's prior in the arguments TK of the chance distribution are non-zero, since otherwise hp(A|TK) is undefined. Since one's prior in the relative state K of any non-trivial chance will be 0, it follows that the Basic Principle never applies to non-trivial statistical mechanical chances.

We saw the source of the problem in section two. The problem arises because chance-credence principles like (3) and (4) attempt to equate statistical mechanical chances with conditional priors. But as we saw in section two, we can't understand the statistical mechanical chance of A relative to K as a conditional probability. To do so would require us to make sense of the probability of A *simpliciter*, where the probability of A *simpliciter* is set equal to the Liouville measure of A. But the Liouville measure is not a probability measure, since there is no upper bound to the values it can assign. So these values generally won't make sense as probabilities. The clauses in (3) and (4) that require hp(A|TK) and $ch_{TK}(A)$ to be defined prevent contradictions by severing the chance-credence connection in problematic cases. But after severing the problematic chance-credence connections we find that most statistical mechanical chances don't have an effect on our priors, and those that do are trivial.

One way to respond to this problem is to adopt a chance-credence principle like (1) that equates chances with credence-given-total-evidence. Since this principle doesn't attempt to equate chances with conditional probabilities, it avoids the problems that (3) and (4) run into. But if, like many Bayesians, we would like to encode the constraints on how we should update our hypothetical priors, then we would like our chance-credence principle to be formulated in terms of priors.

A second way to respond to this problem is to adopt Alan Hajek's (2003) proposal to reject the standard definition of conditional probabilities. Hajek proposes that we take conditional probabilities to be primitive, and understand the formula $p(A|K) = p(A \wedge K)/p(K)$ to be a constraint on the values of conditional probabilities when $p(K) > 0$. Adopting Hajek's proposal avoids the problem because $hp(K) = 0$ no longer entails that $hp(A|TK)$ is undefined, and thus (3) can still apply when $ch_{TK}(A)$ is non-trivial. If we adopt this response, we can keep something like (3) as our chance-credence principle.

5.2. The Second Problem

The second problem concerns how we understand the objects of chances. The problem arises for chance theories whose models have certain physical symmetries. Consider an example of this problem in classical statistical mechanics. Take a classical statistical mechanical state space S. Consider two disjoint regions in S of finite and equal Liouville measure that are related by a symmetry transformation. That is, the points in the first region map to the points in the second by a rotation about a given axis, a spatial translation, or some other symmetry of the relevant systems. Let A_1 and A_2 be the first and second regions, and let K be the union of these regions. What is the statistical mechanical chance of A_1 relative to K? Since the Liouville measure of A_1 is half that of K, the chance of A_1 relative to K should be 1/2. Likewise, the chance of K relative to K should be 1.

Now, the objects of statistical mechanical chances are regions of state space. We have been assuming that the objects of chances are *de dicto* propositions, i.e., sets of possible worlds. So it needs to be the case that we can take regions of state space to correspond to sets of possible worlds. In situations with symmetries like the one sketched above, it's hard to see what set of worlds to associate with a region of state space like A_1. The worlds in A_1 are qualitatively identical to the worlds in A_2, and qualitatively identical worlds are generally thought to be numerically identical. So if we say A_1 contains a world if any of its state space points correspond to that world, then it will contain the same worlds as A_2 and K. But if A_1 and K are the same proposition, then the chance of A_1 relative to K should be the same as the chance of K relative to K, which it is not. Alternatively, if we say A_1 contains a world if it contains all of the state space points that correspond to that world, then A_1 will contain no worlds. But if A_1 is the empty set, then it follows from the probability axioms that $ch_{TK}(A_1) = 0$, which it does not.[20]

The problem stems from the tension between three individually plausible assumptions. The first assumption is that our chance theories successfully assign the chances they seem to assign. The second assumption is that there are no non-qualitative differences between possible worlds. This assumption addresses the intuitive difficulty of making sense of qualitatively identical but distinct possible worlds. The third assumption is that the objects of chances are *de dicto* propositions. This captures the intuition that chances are about the way the world could be. In these terms, the problem is that our chance theories seem to assign chances which are hard to make sense of if we take the objects of chance to be sets of possible worlds and take qualitatively identical worlds to be identical.

A natural response to this problem is to reject one of these three assumptions. One option is to reject the first assumption, and reject as unintelligible any apparent chance assignments whose objects or arguments don't neatly correspond to sets of possible worlds. In the context of classical statistical mechanics, this constraint will be that the object and relative state of a chance assignment must contain either all of the state space points corresponding to a world or none of them. In the above example, this gets around the problem of making sense of the chance of A_1 relative to K by denying that such chances are intelligible.

Another option is to reject the second assumption, and use *haecceities* to individuate between qualitatively identical worlds. With *haecceities* we can distinguish between worlds related by symmetry transformations, and make sense of chances with these worlds as objects. In the above example, this makes analyzing the chance of A_1 relative to K straightforward, since A_1 and K represent distinct and well-defined sets of possible worlds.

A third option is to reject the third assumption and take the objects of chances to be something other than (*de dicto*) propositions. On this approach A_1 would not correspond to a set of possible worlds; instead, the chance of A_1 relative to K would be made intelligible by resorting to an alternative account of the relevant space of possibilities. This option is more open ended then the first two. In addition to providing a different account of the objects of chance, this response requires a different chance-credence principle. Chance-credence principles like the Basic Principle and the Principal Principle equate values associated with the same objects; i.e., equate the chance of a proposition with a credence in a proposition. Changing the objects of chance from propositions to non-propositions requires a modification of the chance-credence principle to account for this. Either the chance-credence principle must be modified to account for how chances in non-propositions link up with credences in propositions, or the chance-credence principle must be modified so that chances in non-propositions are linked up with credences in non-propositions and an account of credence in these non-propositions must be provided.

6. Conclusion

I have made three proposals regarding a theory of chance. The first proposal amends the Lewisian theory to accommodate physical theories like statistical mechanics and the ABL theory of quantum mechanics. I suggest we allow the second argument of chance distributions to be propositions other than histories up to a time, and to reject the two further claims about chance that the Lewisian accounts make: that the past is no longer chancy and that determinism and chance are incompatible. The second proposal disambiguates the relation between credence and chance. Here, I suggest we adopt a chance-credence principle without an admissibility clause, such as the Basic Principle. The third proposal is a partial account of the structure of chance theories, and the relation between the values of chance and the arguments and objects of chance distributions. I suggest each chance theory should be associated with coarse sets, fine sets, and countably additive measures over the coarse sets which determine the theories' chances.

Although I am optimistic that this makes some progress toward a complete theory of chance, further work remains to be done. I will end by noting three issues that require investigation. First, we need to clarify and analyze the possible responses to the problems raised in section five. I have briefly sketched some possible responses, but more needs to be done to see what other options are available, and to evaluate which of these responses we should adopt. Second, I've assumed that the objects of belief are *de dicto* propositions. Work may need to be done to see if, and how, chance-credence rules like the Basic Principle need to be modified when we consider *de se* and *de re* beliefs.[21] Third, I have presented the third proposal as tentative because I think it possible, if not likely, that some of the details of this proposal will be changed in a satisfactory final theory. One possible modification, for example, would be an extension of the proposal to accomodate non-standard probability spaces.[22] It is an open question what form the third proposal will eventually take.[23]

Appendices

A. Humeanism

Much of the literature on chance has focused on the compatibility of a satisfactory chance-credence principle and Humean supervenience. My three proposals have little bearing on this issue, as I will show. The majority of this section will look at the impact of adopting an admissibility-free chance-credence principle on the debate over Humeanism. I will end with a quick note on the bearing of my other two proposals on this debate.

Lewis (1994) and others have noted that at worlds where Humean supervenience holds, a chance theory T will generally assign a positive chance to $\neg$T. Consider a simple Humean theory, frequentism. On this account, the chance of a chance event is determined by (i) assigning a chance to outcomes equal to the actual frequency (past and future) of these outcomes, while (ii) treating these events as independent and identically distributed. Now consider a world where frequentism is true, and where there are only two chance events, two coin flips, one which comes up heads and one which comes up tails. Then the chance of a coin flip coming up heads is 1/2, and the chance of two coin flips coming up heads is 1/4. But if the coin came up heads twice, then frequentism would assign chance 1 to the coin toss coming up heads. So it seems that Humean chances *undermine* themselves: they assign a positive chance to an outcome on which they wouldn't be the correct chances. More generally, they assign a positive chance to some other chance theory being true.

Given Lewis' Principal Principle, this appears to lead to a contradiction:

$$(7)\ \ 0 < ch_{TH}(\neg T) = hp(\neg T|TH) = 0$$

where the middle equality is furnished by the Principal Principle. On further inspection, this does not lead to a contradiction because Lewis' Principal Principle is equipped with an admissibility clause. The admissibilty clause can be used to disrupt the middle equality of (7) and prevent a contradiction. But we only avoid a contradiction by making so much inadmissible that the Principal Principle is useless.

How does the Basic Principle fare? The Basic Principle leads to the same apparent contradiction as the Principal Principle, and since the Basic Principle has no admissibility clause, admissibility cannot be used to disrupt the middle equality of (7). So given the Basic Principle, undermining does appear to lead to a contradiction. Regardless of whether we adopt the Principal Principle or the Basic Principle, the Humean seems to be in bad shape.

Lewis (1994) later tried to avoid this problem by adopting an alternate principle:

$$(8)\ \ hp(A|THE) = ch_{TH}(A|T), \text{ if THE is admissible relative to } ch_{TH}(A|T), \text{ and } hp(A|THE) \text{ and } ch_{TH}(A|T) \text{ are defined.}$$

Since $ch_{TH}(\neg T|T) = 0$ even on a Humean account of chance, adopting (8) escapes the problem. A similarly modified version of the Basic Principle avoids the problem in the same way.

In either case, the move Lewis proposes is questionable. First, Arntzenius and Hall (2003) have shown that adopting this principle leads to highly counterintuitive consequences. Second, as Vranas (2002) shows, the problem that motivated Lewis's adoption of (8) is only apparent.

Take a world w at which both Humean supervenience S and the chance theory T hold. Let H be an *undermining history* of w relative to T, such that $S \wedge H \Rightarrow \neg T$. T will generally assign a positive chance to w, and so a positive chance to S. Likewise, T will generally assign positive chances to some histories like H, histories that would entail $\neg$ T if they held at a world where S held. But it doesn't follow from this that T must assign a positive chance to *both* H and S being true, and thus a positive chance to $\neg$ T. T can assign a positive chance to H and a positive chance to S while assigning a 0 chance to the conjunction of H and S. So Humean chances don't need to undermine themselves. And this is true regardless of whether the chance-credence principle has an admissibility clause.[24]

The proposal to adopt an admissibility-free chance credence principle has little bearing on the issue of Humeanism. The proposal to revise the Lewisian account of the arguments of chance and to reject the two additional claims the Lewisian theories make also has little bearing on the issue. What about the third proposal? At first the third proposal seems at odds with Humeanism. In presenting the third proposal I implicitly assume that the measures associated with chance theories are assigned over the worlds where that theory holds; as a consequence, chance theories will always assign themselves a chance of 1. Since it appears that on Humeanism the chance a chance theory assigns to itself is generally less than one, this seems like an anti-Humean assumption. But as Vranas has shown us, this is a mistake; this assumption is not incompatible with Humeanism. So neither of these proposals have much bearing on the issue of Humean supervenience.

B. Derivations

B.1. The Past is no Longer Chancy

Let T be a complete theory of chance at a world, and H any history up to a time t at that world. Let E be any proposition about the past (relative to t). Since E is about the past, H entails either E or its negation.

Now, if H entails E, and $ch_{TH}(E)$ is defined, then:

$$(9) \qquad ch_{TH}(E) = hp(E|TH) = \frac{hp(ETH)}{hp(TH)} = \frac{hp(TH)}{hp(TH)} = 1$$

The first line follows from the Principal Principle (see section three) and the assumption that the arguments of a distribution are always admissible relative to its chances.

On the other hand, if H entails $\neg$ E, and $ch_{TH}(E)$ is defined, then:

$$(10) \qquad ch_{TH}(E) = hp(E|TH) = \frac{hp(ETH)}{hp(TH)} = \frac{hp(\neg EETH)}{hp(TH)} = 0$$

As before, the first line follows from the Principal Principle and the assumption that the arguments of a distribution are always admissible relative to its chances.

So if $ch_{TH}(E)$ is defined, $ch_{TH}(E) = 1$ or 0. Since this is true for any proposition E about the past, it follows that the past is no longer (non-trivially) chancy.

B.2. Determinism and Chance are Incompatible

Let L be the laws at a deterministic world, and T the complete chance theory at that world. Let H be any history up to a time at this world, and A be any proposition. If L is deterministic, then either $LH \Rightarrow A$ or $LH \Rightarrow \neg A$, since deterministic laws and a complete history up to a time entail everything. Equivalently, either $L \Rightarrow A \vee \neg H$ or $L \Rightarrow \neg A \vee \neg H$.

Suppose $L \Rightarrow A \vee \neg H$ and $ch_{TH}(A)$ is defined. Then:

$$\text{(11)} \quad \begin{aligned} 1 &= ch_{TH}(A \vee \neg H) \\ &= hp(A \vee \neg H | TH) \\ &= \frac{hp((A \vee \neg H) \wedge TH)}{hp(TH)} \\ &= \frac{hp(ATH)}{hp(TH)} \\ &= hp(A|TH) \\ &= ch_{TH}(A) \end{aligned}$$

The first line follows from the Lewisian account of the arguments of chance and the assumption that anything the laws entail gets assigned a chance of 1 by the chance laws. The latter fact also ensures that $ch_{TH}(A \vee \neg H)$ will be defined. The second and last steps follow from the Principal Principle (see section three) and the assumption that the arguments of a distribution are always admissible relative to its chances.

So if $L \Rightarrow A \vee \neg H$ and $ch_{TH}(A)$ is defined, then $ch_{TH}(A) = 1$. If $L \Rightarrow \neg A \vee \neg H$ and $ch_{TH}(A)$ is defined, then an identical derivation yields $ch_{TH}(\neg A) = 1$, i.e., $ch_{TH}(A) = 0$. So for any history H and any proposition A, if $ch_{TH}(A)$ is defined, $ch_{TH}(A) = 1$ or 0. I.e., all of the chance distributions associated with T assign only trivial chances. Since this is true for any chance theory of a deterministic world, it follows that determinism and (non-trivial) chances are incompatible.

B.3. The First Problem

If we formulate the chance-credence principle in terms of hypothetical priors, then we find that for chance theories like classical statistical mechanics, our priors only end up being constrained by trivial chances.

To see this, assume that (3) is our chance-credence principle. Now consider the Liouville measure of a state space S. If there are no particles in the systems of a state space, then the space will consist of a single point, and the associated chances will be trivial.[25] So let's confine our attention to state spaces whose systems have at least one particle. In classical mechanics there's no upper bound on the velocity of a particle, so the Liouville measure of any state space with particles will be infinite.

Assume the extended real number line and the standard extension of the arithmetical operators over it; in particular, that $x/\infty = 0$ if x is finite, and ∞/∞ and $x/0$ are undefined. Now consider the chance of A relative to K, for some arbitrary propositions $A, K \subset S$. If $m(K) = \infty$ then $ch_{TK}(A)$ will either be undefined (if $m(A \cap K) = \infty$) or 0 (if $m(A \cap K) \neq \infty$). If $m(K) \neq \infty$, on the other hand, then $ch_{TK}(A)$ can take on non-trivial values. But if $m(K) \neq \infty$, then the chances require $hp(A|K)$ to be undefined, and (3) won't hook up our priors to these chances.

To see that the chances require $hp(A|K)$ to be undefined, suppose otherwise, i.e., suppose that $hp(K) > 0$. The chance of K relative to S will be

$$(12)\ ch_{TS}(K) = \frac{m(K \cap S)}{m(S)} = 0,$$

since $m(K \cap S)$ is finite and $m(S)$ infinite. And if $hp(K) > 0$ then $hp(S) > 0$, since $K \subset S$, so $hp(K|S)$ is defined. Since both $hp(K|S)$ and $ch_{TS}(K)$ are well defined, (3) applies, and

$$\begin{aligned}(13)\quad ch_{TS}(K) &= 0\\ hp(K|S) &=\\ \frac{hp(K \cap S)}{hp(S)} &=\\ \frac{hp(K)}{hp(S)} &=\\ &\Rightarrow hp(K) = 0\end{aligned}$$

contradicting our supposition.

Notes

1. Lewis's switch was motivated by worries about the compatibility of the Principal Principle and Humean supervenience; see Lewis (1999). I discuss these matters more in appendix A. Although Lewis's (1999) New Principle and Hall's (1994) New Principle are often spoken of interchangeably, I take them to be distinct. The comments I make apply to the former.

2. See Lewis (2004), p. 14.
3. We can say an event occurs at t *iff* it's entailed by a history up to t and is not entailed by any history up to $t' < t$.
4. These two derivations are provided in Appendix B. Note that neither assumption entails the other. The first assumption, that a distribution's arguments are admissible, entails that anything the chance laws entail is assigned a chance of 1. But the complete laws at a world might entail more than the chance laws. The second assumption, that anything the laws entail is assigned a chance of 1, does entail that anything the chance laws entail is assigned a chance of 1. But the second assumption does not entail (as the first one does) that, for example, whatever is entailed by the historical argument of a distribution must be assigned a chance of 1.
5. Ned Hall has independently proposed that we get rid of admissibility in a recent paper; see Hall (2004). Frank Arntzenius has independently proposed revisions similar to my first two proposals in an unpublished paper.
6. Aharonov, Bergmann and Lebowitz (1964), Aharonov and Vaidman (1991). Note that their theory is not a *complete* theory; it doesn't include a particular solution to the measurement problem, for example.
7. Lewis (1986), p. 94
8. More generally, the ABL theory assigns chances given pre-measurements, given post-measurements, and given pre and post-measurements. In this context, I restrict myself to the latter chances.
9. In versions of classical statistical mechanics like that proposed by Albert (2000), one of the statistical mechanical laws is a constraint on the initial entropy of the universe. On such theories the space of classical statistical mechanical worlds (and the state spaces that partition it) will only contain worlds whose initial macroconditions are of a suitably low entropy.
10. Earman (1986), Xia (1992), Norton (2003) and others have offered counterexamples to the claim that classical mechanics is deterministic. These results have been by and large ignored by the physics literature on statistical mechanics, and I will follow suit. Two comments are in order, however. First, these cases spell trouble for the standard distinction between dynamic and static properties employed by classical statistical mechanics. For example, in some of these cases new particles will unpredictably zoom in from infinity. Since this leads to a change in the number of particles in the system, it would seem the number of particles cannot be properly understood as a static property. Second, although no proof of this exists, prevailing opinion is that these indeterministic cases form a set of Lebesque measure zero. If so, we can ignore these cases in this context, since their exclusion will have no effect on the probabilities classical statistical mechanics assigns.
11. Strictly speaking, (3) is not a reformulation of (1), since (3) is slightly weaker than (1). (3) will fail to apply when $hp(A|G)$ is defined, whereas (1) does not have this limitation. In section five we will see that problems with the standard definition of conditional probability will motivate the adoption of primitive conditional probabilities. With this adoption $hp(A|G)$ will always be defined, and (1) and (3) will be equivalent.

12. Although admissibility is no longer needed to decipher the relation between credence and chance, admissibility-free principles like the Basic Principle provide us with the means to provide a precise characterization of what admissibility is. For example, we can characterize 'admissible evidence' as used in (4) as follows: GE is admissible relative to $ch_G(A)$ *iff* the priors (4) would then assign are the same as the priors recommended by (3); i.e., $hp(A|GE) = hp(A|G)$. With a characterization of admissibility in hand, the Principal Principle is no longer vague. But since we only eliminate this vagueness by using the Basic Principle, the Basic Principle is the more fundamental of the two. For another way of cashing out admissibility, see Hall (2004).
13. A *countably additive measure* over (C,S) is a function $m{:}S \Rightarrow [0,\infty]$, where S is a sigma algebra over C, such that $m(\emptyset) = 0$, and such that if $s_i \in S$ are disjoint, then $m(\cup_{i=1}^{\infty} s_i) = \sum_{i=1}^{\infty} m(s_i)$. A *sigma algebra* S over C is a non-empty family of subsets of C which is closed under complementation and countable unions.
14. I'm implicitly assuming that the indices i, j, k, and l range over countably infinite members at most. Strictly speaking, this assumption should be discarded and these sums should be replaced by integrals over the appropriate probability densities.
15. In quantum statistical mechanics one generally works with probability density operators, not probability measures over states, and the density operators underdetermine the probability measures that could be used to justify it. But a satisfactory justification for the density matrix used in quantum statistical mechanics can (and perhaps must) be obtained from a measure over states. For one way to do this, see Tumulka and Zanghi (2005).
16. See Berndl, Daumer, Durr, Goldstein and Zanghi (1995).
17. By this I mean *complete* quantum mechanical interpretations, not interpretations whose content hangs on vague terminology or which are otherwise imprecise. I take it that I am under no obligation to provide a precise account of the chances of chance theories which are not themselves precise.

    On some quantum mechanical interpretations the status of quantum statistical mechanics changes to the extent that a procedure for gluing quantum mechanics to quantum statistical mechanics isn't needed. For example, Albert (2001) has argued that if we adopt the GRW interpretation of quantum mechanics an additional statistical theory isn't needed to explain 'statistical mechanical' phenomena.
18. I'm assuming the extended real number line and the standard extension of the arithmetical operators over it; in particular, that $x/\infty = 0$ if x is finite, and ∞/∞ and $x/0$ are undefined.
19. There is one state space of finite measure, the trivial state space of a system with no particles. But since the chances associated with this space are trivial, we can safely ignore it.
20. That $ch_G(\cdot)$ is a probablity function over possible worlds follows from the criteria laid out in section four and the assumption that the objects of chances are sets of possible worlds.
21. See Lewis (1983). The Basic Principle can be used without modification in the context of *de se* beliefs. The Basic Principle is then a constraint on a special subset of *de se* beliefs: beliefs in centered propositions that contain all and only those centered worlds that correspond to some set of possible worlds. Interestingly, recent literature on the sleeping beauty problem has looked,

in part, at the interaction between *de se* beliefs and the admissibility of chances (see Elga (2000), Lewis (2001), Dorr (2002), Halpern (2004), Meacham (2003)). If the Basic Principle is adopted without modification in the context of *de se* beliefs, it entails the position defended by Halpern (2004) and Meacham (2003).

22. See Halpern (2001) for a discussion of some of these possibilities.
23. I'd like to thank Frank Arntzenius, Maya Eddon, Ned Hall, John Hawthorne, Tim Maudlin and Jonathan Weisberg for valuable comments and discussion.
24. Note that while the revised theory is compatible with the truth of Humean supervenience at this world, it's incompatible with the more ambitious claim that Humean supervenience is metaphysically or nomologically necessary.

    Frank Arntzenius has pointed out that Vranas' treatment still leads to counter-intuitive results for subjects who are confident that Humeanism obtains. Given this, it seems none of the Humean responses to the undermining problem are without cost.
25. I follow Tolman (1979) here in not taking the total energy to be one of the relevant static properties. If we do adopt the total energy as one of these properties, then some of the details will be different.

References

Aharonov, Y., Bergman, P. G. and Lebowitz, J. L. (1964) "Time Symmetry in the Quantum Process of Measurement", *Phys. Rev. B* 134, pp. 1410–1416.

Aharonov, Y. and Vaidman, L. (1991) "Complete Description of a Quantum State at a Given Time", *J. Phys. A* 24, pp. 2313–2328.

Albert, D. (2001) *Time and Chance*, Harvard University Press.

Arntzenius, F. and Hall, N. (2003) "On What We Know About Chance", *Brit. J. Phil. Sci.* 54, pp. 171–179.

Berndl, K., Daumer, M., Durr, D, Goldstein, S. and Zanghi, N. (1995) "A Survey of Bohmian Mechanics", *Il Nuovo Cimento* 110, pp. 737–750.

Dorr, C. (2002) "Sleeping Beauty: In Defense of Elga", *Analysis* 62, pp. 292–296.

Earman, J. (1986) *A Primer on Determinism*, Kluwer Academic Publishers.

Elga, A. (2000) "Self-locating Belief and the Sleeping Beauty problem", *Analysis* 60, pp. 143–147.

Hajek, A. (2003) "What Conditional Probabilities Could Not Be", *Synthese* 137, pp. 273–323.

Hall, N. (1994) "Correcting the Guide to Objective Chance", *Mind* 103, pp. 505–517.

Hall, N. (2004) "Two Mistakes About Credence and Chance", *Australasian Journal of Philosophy* 82, pp. 93–111.

Halpern, J. Y. (2001) "Lexicographic Probability, Conditional Probability, and Nonstandard Probability", *Proceedings of the Eighth Conference on Theoretical Aspects of Rationality and Knowledge*, Morgan Kaufmann Publishers.

Halpern, J. (2004) "Sleeping Beauty Reconsidered: Conditioning and Reflection in Asynchronous Systems", *Proceedings of the Twentieth Conference on Uncertainty in AI*, AUAI Press.

Lewis, D. (1983) "Attitudes *De Dicto* and *De Se*", *Philosophical Papers, Volume I*, Oxford University Press.

Lewis, D. (1986) "A Subjectivist's Guide to Objective Chance", *Philosophical Papers*, Volume II, Oxford University Press.

Lewis, D. (1999) "Humean Supervenience Debugged" *Papers in Metaphysics and Epistemology*, Cambridge University Press.

Lewis, D. (2001) "Sleeping Beauty: Reply to Elga", *Analysis* 61, pp. 171–176.

Lewis, D. (2004) "How Many Lives Has Schrodinger's Cat?", *Australasian Journal of Philosophy* 82, pp. 3–22.

Loewer, B. (2001) "Determinism and Chance", *Studies in the History of Modern Physics* 32, pp 609–620.

Meacham, C. J. G. (2003) "Sleeping Beauty and the Dynamics of *De Se* Beliefs", manuscript.

Norton, J. D. (2003) "Causation as Folk Science", *Philosopher's Imprint* 3, pp.1–22.

Tolman, R. C. (1979) *The Principles of Statistical Mechanics*, Dover Publications.

Tumulka, R. and Zanghi, N. (2005) *Thermal Equilibrium Distribution of Wavefunctions*, arXiv: quant-ph/0309021v2.

Vranas, P. (2002) "Who's Afraid of Undermining? Why the Principal Principle might not contradict Humean Supervenience", *Erkenntnis* 57, pp. 151–174.

Xia, Z. (1992) "The Existence of Noncollision Singularities in the N-body Problem", *Annals of Mathematics* 135, pp. 411–468.

Philosophical Perspectives, 19, Epistemology, 2005

VISION, KNOWLEDGE, AND THE MYSTERY LINK

John L. Pollock[1]
University of Arizona

Iris Oved[2]
Rutgers University

1. Perceptual Knowledge

Imagine yourself sitting on your front porch, sipping your morning coffee and admiring the scene before you. You see trees, houses, people, automobiles; you see a cat running across the road, and a bee buzzing among the flowers. You see that the flowers are yellow, and blowing in the wind. You see that the people are moving about, many of them on bicycles. You see that the houses are painted different colors, mostly earth tones, and most are one-story but a few are two-story. It is a beautiful morning. Thus the world interfaces with your mind through your senses.

There is a strong intuition that we are not disconnected from the world. We and the other things we see around us are part of a continuous whole, and we have direct access to them through vision, touch, etc. However, the philosophical tradition tries to drive a wedge between us and the world by insisting that the information we get from perception is the result of inference from indirect evidence that is about how things look and feel to us. The philosophical problem of perception is then to explain what justifies these inferences.

We will focus on visual perception. Figure 1 presents a crude diagram of the cognitive system of an agent capable of forming beliefs on the basis of visual perception. Cognition begins with the stimulation of the rods and cones on the retina. From that physical input, some kind of visual processing produces an introspectible visual image. In response to the production of the visual image, the cognizer forms beliefs about his or her surroundings. Some beliefs—the *perceptual beliefs*—are formed as direct responses to the visual input, and other beliefs are inferred from the perceptual beliefs. The perceptual beliefs are, at the very least, caused or causally influenced by having the image. This is signified by the dashed arrow marked with a large question mark. We will refer to this as the *mystery link*.

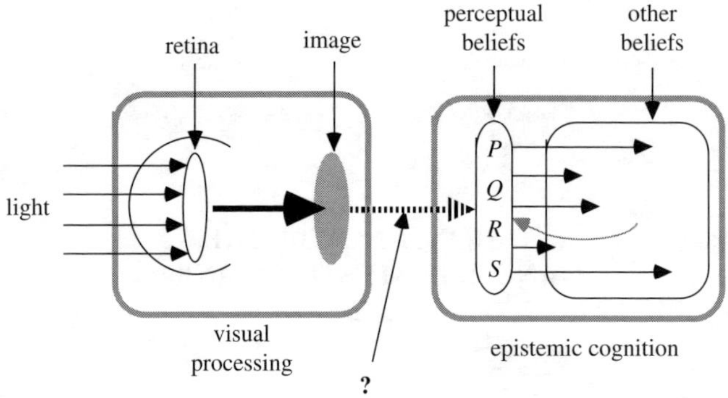

Figure 1. Knowledge, perception, and the mystery link

Figure 1 makes it apparent that in order to fully understand how knowledge is based on perception, we need three different theories. First, we need a psychological theory of visual processing that explains how the introspectible visual image is produced from the stimulation by light of the rods and cones on the retina. Second, we need a philosophical theory of higher-level epistemic cognition, explaining how beliefs influence each other rationally. We think of this as an epistemological theory of reasoning. We will assume without argument that it involves some kind of defeasible reasoning.[3] These first two theories are familiar sorts of theories. To these we must add a third theory—a theory of the mystery link that connects visual processing to epistemic cognition. Philosophers have usually had little to say about the mystery link, contenting themselves with waving their hands and pronouncing that it is a causal process producing input to epistemic cognition. However, the main contention of this paper will be that there is much more to be said about the mystery link, and a correct understanding of it severely constrains what kinds of epistemological theories of perceptual knowledge can be correct.

This paper will begin by looking briefly at epistemological theories of perceptual knowledge. We will present an argument for "direct realism", which we endorse, and then raise a difficulty for direct realism. This will lead us into a closer examination of vision and the way it encodes information. From that we will derive an account of the mystery link. It will be shown that this theory of the mystery link provides machinery for constructing a modified version of direct realism that avoids the difficulty and makes visual knowledge of the world explicable.

2. Direct Realism

Historically, most epistemological theories were *doxastic theories*, in the sense that they endorsed the *doxastic assumption*. That is the assumption that the justifiability of a cognizer's belief is a function exclusively of what beliefs she holds. Nothing but beliefs can enter into the determination of justification. The doxastic assumption has unfortunate consequences when applied to perception. Perceptual beliefs—the first beliefs formed on the basis of perception—are by their very nature not obtained by inference from previously held beliefs. Perception gives us new information that we could not get by inference alone. As perceptual beliefs are not inferred from other beliefs, that cannot be the source of their justification. But on a doxastic theory, the justification of a belief cannot depend on anything other than the cognizer's beliefs. Thus perceptual beliefs must be *self-justified* in the sense that they are justified (at least defeasibly) by the mere fact that the cognizer holds them. On a doxastic theory, this is the only alternative to their being inferred from other beliefs, because nothing other than beliefs can be relevant.

Historical foundations theories tried to make this plausible by taking perceptual beliefs to be about the cognizer's perceptual experience. The trouble is, perceptual beliefs, as the first beliefs the agent forms on the basis of perception, are not generally about appearances. It is rare to have any beliefs at all about how things look to you. You normally just form beliefs about ordinary physical objects. You see a table and judge that it is round, you see an apple on the table and judge that it is red, etc. Can such beliefs be self-justified? They cannot. The difficulty is that the very same beliefs can be held for non-perceptual reasons. While blindfolded, you can believe there is a red apple on a round table before you because someone tells you that there is, or because you looked in other rooms before entering this one and saw tables with apples on them. Worse, you can hold such beliefs unjustifiably by believing them for inadequate reasons. Wishful thinking might lead to such a belief, or hasty generalization. These are not cases in which you have good reasons that are defeated. These are cases in which you lack good reasons from the start. If, in the absence of defeaters, these beliefs can be unjustified, it follows that they are not self-justified.

It seems clear that what makes perceptual beliefs justified in the absence of inferential support from other beliefs is that they *are* perceptual beliefs. That is, they are believed on the basis of perceptual input. The same belief can be held on the basis of perceptual input or on the basis of inference from other beliefs. When it is held on the basis of perceptual input, that makes it justified unless the agent has a reason for regarding the input as non-veridical or otherwise dubious in this particular case. But this is not the same thing as being self-justified. Self-justified beliefs are justified without any support at all, perceptual or inferential. These beliefs need support, so they are not self-justified.

What is it about my perceptual experience that justifies me in believing, for example, that the apple is red? It seems clear that the belief is justified by the fact that the apple looks red to me. In general, there are various states of affairs P for which visual experience gives us direct evidence. Let us say that the relevant visual experience is that of *being appeared to as if P*. Then *direct realism* is the following principle:

(DR) For appropriate P's, if S believes P on the basis of being appeared to as if P, S is defeasibly justified in doing so.

Direct realism is “direct” in the sense that our beliefs about our physical surroundings are the first beliefs produced by cognition in response to perceptual input, and they are not inferred from lower-level beliefs about the perceptual input itself. But, according to direct realism, these beliefs are not self-justified either. Their justification depends upon having the appropriate perceptual experiences. Thus the doxastic assumption is false.

Direct realism is, in part, a theory about the mystery link. It tells us, first, that perceptual beliefs are ordinary physical-object beliefs, and second that the mystery link is not just a causal connection—it conveys justification to the perceptual beliefs. It does not, however, tell us how the latter is accomplished. For the most part, it leaves the mystery link as mysterious as it ever was. This gives rise to an objection that is often leveled at direct realism. The objection is that perceptual beliefs involve concepts, but the visual image is non-conceptual, so how can the image give support to the perceptual belief?[4] We are not sure what it means to say that the image is or is not conceptual, but this objection can be met in a preliminary way without addressing that question. If there is a problem here, it is not a problem specifically for direct realism. It is really a problem about the mystery link. If it is correct to say that the image is non-conceptual but beliefs are conceptual, then on *every* theory of perceptual knowledge, what is on the left of the mystery link is non-conceptual and what is on the right is conceptual. The problem is then, how does the mystery link work to get us from the one to the other? This is just as much a problem for the foundationalist who thinks that perceptual beliefs are about the image, because we still want an explanation for how cognition gets us from the image to the beliefs, be they about the image or about objects in the world. Clearly it does, so this cannot be a decisive objection to any theory of perceptual knowledge, and it has nothing particular to do with direct realism. It is instead a puzzle about how the mystery link works. Hopefully, it will be less puzzling by the end of the paper.

Direct realism has had occasional supporters in the history of philosophy, perhaps most notably Peter John Olivi in the 13th century and Thomas Reid in the 18th century. But the theory was largely ignored by contemporary epistemologists until Pollock (1971, 1974, 1986) resurrected it on the basis of the preceding argument. The name of the theory was suggested by Anthony Quinton (1973), although he did not endorse the theory. In recent years, direct realism has gained a small following.[5] The argument just given in its defense seems to us to be strong. However, in the next section we will raise a difficulty for the theory. That will lead us to a closer examination of the mystery link, and ultimately to a formulation of direct realism that avoids the difficulty.

3. A Problem for Direct Realism

The argument for direct realism seems quite compelling. Surely it is true that perceptual beliefs are justified by being perceptual beliefs. That is, they are justified *by being* beliefs that are held on the basis of appropriately related perceptual experiences. And it appears that this is what (DR) says. (DR) has most commonly been illustrated by appealing to the following instance:

(RED) If *S* believes that *x* is red on the basis of its looking to *S* as if *x* is red, *S* is defeasibly justified in doing so.

However, it now appears to us that the principle (RED) cannot possibly be true. Let us begin by distinguishing between precise shades of red ("color determinates") and the generic color red ("color determinables", composed of a disjunction of color determinates). The principle (RED), if true, should be true regardless of whether we take it to be about precise shades of red or generic redness. The problems are basically the same for both, but they are more dramatic for the case of precise shades of red.

The principle (RED) relates the concept *red* to a way of looking—an *apparent color*. It tells us that something's having that apparent color gives defeasible support for the conclusion that it is red. Defeasible support arises without requiring an independent argument. Thus if (RED) is to be a correct description of our epistemological access to whether objects are red, it must describe an essential feature of the concept *red*. That is, there must be an apparent color (a way of looking) that is logically or essentially connected to the concept *red*.

To most philosophers, this will not seem to be a surprising requirement. It is quite common for philosophers to think that the concept *red* has as an essential feature a specification of how red things look. For instance, Colin McGinn (1983) writes, "To grasp the concept of red it is necessary to know what it is for something to look red." However, for reasons now to be given, this seems to us to be false.

In the philosophy of mind there has been much discussion of the so-called "inverted spectrum problem", and debate about whether it is possible. We want to call attention here to a variant of this that is not only possible but common. This is the "sliding spectrum". Some years ago, one of us (not Iris) underwent cataract surgery. In this surgery, the clouded lens is surgically removed from the eye and replaced by an implanted silicon lens similar to a contact lens. When the operation was performed on the right eye, the subject was amazed to discover that everything looked blue through that eye. Upon questioning the surgeon, it was learned that this is normal. In everyone, the lens yellows with the passage of time. In effect, people grow a brownish-yellow filter in their eye, which affects all apparent colors, shifting them towards yellow. This phenomenon is so common that it has a name in vision research. It is called "photoxic lens brunescence" (Lindsey and Brown 2002). For a while after the surgery, everything looked blue through the right eye and, by contrast, yellow through the left eye. Then when the cataract-clouded lens was removed from the second eye a few weeks later, everything looked blue through both eyes. But now, with the passage of time, everything seems normal.

Immediately following surgery, white things look blue and red things look purple to a cataract patient. After the passage of time, the patient no longer notices anything out of the ordinary. What has happened? The simplest explanation is that the subject has simply become used to the change, and now takes things to look red when they look the way red things now look to him. On this account, in everyone, the way red things look changes slowly over time as the eye tissues yellow, but because the change is slow, the subject does not notice it. Then if the subject undergoes cataract surgery, the way red things look changes back abruptly, and the subject notices that. But after a while he gets used to it, and forgets how red things looked before the operation. However, one could maintain instead that the brain somehow compensates so that colors continue to look the same as one ages. Which is right? It turns out that there is hard scientific data supporting the conclusion that brunescence alters the way things look to us, even if we don't notice the effects. Brunescence lowers discrimination between blues and purples (Fairchild 1998). Consequently, people suffering from brunescence cannot discriminate as many different phenomenal appearances in that range of colors. But this means that their phenomenal experience is different from what it was before brunescence. Hence the phenomenal appearance of colors has changed.

There are other kinds of color shifts to which human perception is subject. In what is called the *Bezold-Brücke effect*, when levels of illumination are increased, there is a shift of perceived hues such that most colors appear less red or green and more blue or yellow. The result is that the apparent colors of red things differ in different light even when the relative energy distribution across the spectrum remains unchanged.

There are numerous other well-known phenomena. In what is known as *simultaneous color contrast*, the apparent colors of objects vary as the color of the background changes. In *chromatic adaptation*, looking at one color and then looking at a contrasting color changes the second apparent color. This is illustrated by afterimages.

These psychological phenomena produce variations within a single subject. But just thinking about all the things that can affect how colors look makes it extremely unlikely that red things will normally look the same to different subjects. Between-subject variations seem likely if for no other reason than that there are individual differences between different people's perceptual hardware and neural wiring. No two cognizers are exactly the same, so why should we think things are going to look exactly the same to them? We need not merely speculate. There is experimental data that strongly suggests they do not. This turns upon the notion of a *unique hue*. Byrne and Hilbert (2003) observe,

> There is a shade of red ("unique red") that is neither yellowish nor bluish, and similarly for the three other *unique hues*—yellow, green, and blue. This is nicely shown in experiments summarized by Hurvich (1981, Ch. 5): a normal observer looking at a stimulus produced by two monochromators is able to adjust one of

> them until he reports seeing a yellow stimulus that is not at all reddish or greenish. In contrast, every shade of purple is both reddish and bluish, and similarly for the other three *binary hues* (orange, olive, and turquoise).

But what is more interesting for our purposes is that different people classify different colors in this way. As Byrne and Hilbert go on to observe:

> There is a surprising amount of variation in the color vision of people classified on standard tests ... as having "normal" color vision. Hurvich et al. (1968) found that the location of "unique green" for spectral lights among 50 subjects varied from 590 to 520 nm. This is a large range: 15 nm either side of unique green looks distinctly bluish or yellowish. ... A more recent study of color matching results among 50 males discovered that they divided into two broad groups, with the difference between the groups traceable to a polymorphism in the L-cone photopigment gene (Merbs & Nathans 1992). Because the L-cone photopigment genes are on the X chromosome, the distribution of the two photopigments varies significantly between men and women (Neitz & Neitz 1998).

The upshot of the preceding observations is that there is no way of looking—call it *looking red*—such that objects are typically red iff they look red. In fact, for any apparent color we choose, it is likely that objects that are red will typically *not* look that color. If our judgments of color were based on principles like (RED), we would almost always be led to conclude defeasibly that red objects are not red. Furthermore, it follows from direct realism that there would be no possible way for us to correct these judgments by discovering that they are unreliable, because any other source of knowledge about redness would have to be justified inductively by reference to objects judged red using the principle (RED). It seems apparent that the principle (RED) cannot be a correct account of how we judge the colors of objects. But (RED) also seems to be a stereotypical instance of direct realism. It is certainly the standard example that Pollock (1986) and Pollock & Cruz (1999) used throughout their defense of direct realism. Thus (DR) itself seems to be in doubt.

It might be supposed that there is something funny about color concepts, and these problems will not recur if we consider some of the other kinds of properties about which we make perceptual judgments. These would include shapes, spatial orientations, the straightness of lines, the relative lengths of lines, etc. But in fact, analogues of the above problems arise for all of these supposedly perceivable properties. For example, anyone who was very nearsighted as a child and whose eyes were changing rapidly has probably had the experience of getting new glasses and finding that straight lines looked curved and when they walked forwards it looked to them like they were stepping into a hole. This is a geometric analogue of brunescence. Less dramatically, most of us suffer from varying degrees of astigmatism, which has the result that straight lines are projected unevenly onto the surface of the retina, with presumed consequences for our phenomenal experience. Furthermore, the severity of the astigmatism changes over time. In addition, the lenses in our eyes are not very good lenses from an optical point of view. They would flunk as camera lenses. In particular, they suffer from large amounts of barrel distortion, where parallel lines are projected onto the retina as curved lines that are farther apart close to the center of the eye. The amount of barrel distortion varies from subject to subject, so very likely the looks of geometric figures, straight lines, etc., vary as well.

4. The Visual Image

Our solution to this problem is going to be that there is a way of understanding the principle (DR) of direct realism that makes both it and (RED) true. The above problem arises from a misunderstanding of what it is to be "appeared to as if *P*", and in particular what it is for it to look to one as if an object is red. To defend this claim, we turn to an examination of the visual image. We will investigate what the visual image actually consists of, and how it can give rise to perceptual beliefs.

The classical picture of the visual image was, in effect, that it is a two-dimensional array of colored pixels—a bitmap image.[6] Then the epistemological problem of perception was conceived as being that of justifying inferences from this image to beliefs about the way the world is. We can, in fact, think of the input to the visual system in this way. The input consists of the stimulation of the individual rods and cones arrayed on the retina. Each rod or cone is a binary (on/off) device responding to light of the appropriate intensity (and in the case of cones, light of the appropriate color). A bitmap image represents the pattern of stimulation. Philosophers sometimes refer to this bitmap as "the retinal representation", but for present purposes we will reserve the term "representation" for higher-level mental items, including various constituents of the visual image.

Although this may be a good way to think of the input to the visual system, it does not follow that its output—the introspectible visual image—has the same form. Early twentieth century philosophers (and indeed, most early twentieth century psychologists) thought of the optic nerve as simply passing the pattern of stimulation on the retina down a line of synaptic connections to a "mental screen" where it is redisplayed for the perusal of epistemic cognition. Of course, this makes no literal sense. How does epistemic cognition peruse the mental screen—using a mental "eye" inside the brain? This picture is really just a reflection of the fact that people had no idea how vision works. It is the mystery link that takes us from the visual image to epistemic cognition, so what they were doing was packing all the interesting stuff into the mystery link and leaving its operation a complete mystery.

The inadequacy of the "pass-through" conception of the visual image is obvious when we reflect on the fact that we have just one visual image but two eyes. This is illustrated in Figure 2. The single image is constructed on the basis of the two separate retinal bitmaps. The two bitmaps cannot simply be laid on top of one another, as in Figure 3, because by virtue of being from different vantage points they are not quite the same. Nor can they be laid side by side in the mind. Then we would have two images. In fact, the visual system uses the difference between the two bitmaps to compute depth, and this is an important part of why we can see three-dimensional relationships between the objects we see. This highlights the fact that the visual image is not a two-dimensional pattern at all. It is three-dimensional. On the one hand, it has to be, because there would be no way to merge the bitmaps from the two retinas into a single two-dimensional image. But on the other hand, in order to get a three-dimensional image out of two two-dimensional bitmaps, a great deal of sophisticated computation is required. So far be it from mimicking the retinal bitmap, the visual image is the result of sophisticated computations that take the two separate retinal bitmaps as input. If the visual image is more sophisticated than the retinal bitmaps in this way, why shouldn't it profit from other sorts of computational massaging of the input data?

Figure 2. Two retinal bitmaps

Figure 3. Laying the bitmaps on top of one another.

In fact, it does. A second illustration of this is that the visual system does not compute the visual image on the basis of a single momentary retinal bitmap. We have high visual acuity over only a small region in the center of the retina called the *fovea*. In your visual field, the region of high visual acuity is the size of your thumbnail held at arm's length. To see this, fix your eyes on a single word on this page, and notice how fuzzy the other words on the page look. Now allow your eyes to roam around the page, as when looking at it normally, and notice how much richer and sharper your whole visual image becomes. In normal vision your eyes rarely remain still. The eyes make tiny movements (saccades) as the viewer scans the scene, and multiple saccades are the input for a single visual image. For another example of this, attend to your own eye movements as you are standing face to face with someone and talking to them. You will find your eyes roaming around your interlocutor's face, and you will have a sharp image of the face. Now focus on the tip of the nose and force your eyes to remain still. You will have a sharp image of the nose, but the rest of the face will be very fuzzy.

The visual image is the product of a number of retinal bitmaps resulting from multiple saccades. Think about what this involves. The visual system must somehow merge the information contained in these multiple bitmaps. This is known as the "correspondence problem" of visual perception. The bitmaps cannot simply be laid on top of each other, because they are the result of pointing the eyes in different directions. Saccades involve movements of the eyes, which means that the occulomotor system that detects and controls these movements must provide spatial information to the visual system. Without such input, the visual system would not be able to merge the bitmaps. To illustrate this, jiggle one of your eyes by pulling on the outer corner of your eyelid with your finger, and notice that your visual image is shaky and blurry. Since the visual system is not taking into account the eye motions that result from your manual jiggling, the resulting motion across the retina affects the visual representation.

The visual system must make use of multiple saccades to get high resolution over more than a minute portion of the visual image, which means that the image is not computed on the basis of the momentary retinal bitmap. This is the reason we do not notice the retinal "blind spot" (the spot on the retina that carries no information because it contains the opening of the optic nerve). Another dramatic illustration of this occurs when you are riding in a car alongside a fence consisting of vertical slats with small openings between them. When you are stationary you cannot see what is behind the fence, but when your are moving you may have a very clear image of the scene behind it. Momentary states of the retinal bitmap are the same whether you are stationary or moving. The fact that you can see through the fence when you are moving indicates that your visual representations are computed on the basis of a stream of retinal bitmaps extending over some interval of time.

The study of vision has developed into an interdisciplinary field combining work in psychology, computer science, and neuroscience. Contemporary vision scientists now know a great deal about how vision works. Most contemporary theories of vision are examples of what are called "computational theories of vision", an approach first suggested in the work of J. J. Gibson (1966) and David Marr (1982), and developed in more recent literature by Irving Biederman (1985), Oliver Faugeras (1993), Shimon Ullman (1996), and others. On this approach, the visual system is viewed as an information processor that takes inputs from the rods and cones on the retinas and outputs the visual image as a structured array of mental representations. Along the way representations are computed for edges, corners, motion, parts of objects, objects, etc. For our purposes, the most important idea these theories share is that visual processing produces *representations* of edges, corners, surfaces, objects, parts of objects, etc., and throws away most of the rest of the information contained in the retinal bitmap.

Computational theories of vision differ in their details, and no existing theory is able to handle all of the subtleties of the human visual system. But what we want to take away from these theories and use for our purposes is fairly general. First, all theories agree that there is a great deal of complex processing involved in getting from the pattern of stimulation on the retina to the introspectible visual image in terms of which we see the world. Not even the simplest parts of the visual image can be read off the retinal bitmaps directly. For epistemological purposes, what is most important about these theories is that the end product is an image that is parsed into representations of objects exemplifying various properties and standing in various spatial relations to one another. The image is not just an uninterpreted bitmap—a swirling morass of colors and shades. The hard work of picking out objects and their properties is already done by the visual system before anything even gets to the system of epistemic cognition. The first thing the agent has introspective access to is the fully parsed image. The epistemological problem begins with this image, not with an uninterpreted bitmap. As we will see, this makes the epistemological problem vastly simpler.

But why, the epistemologist might ask, does the visual system do all the dirty work for us? Is there something rationally suspect here? There are purely computational reasons that at least suggest that this could not be otherwise. There are 130 million rods and 7 million cones in each eye, so the number of possible patterns of stimulation on the two retinas is $2^{274,000,000}$, which is approximately $10^{82,482,219}$. That is an unbelievably large number. Compare it with the estimated number of elementary particles in the universe, which is 10^{78}. Could a real agent be built in such a way that it could respond differentially in some practically useful way to more patterns of retinal stimulation than there are elementary particles in the universe? That seems unlikely. If you divide $10^{82,482,219}$ by 10^{x} for any $x < 78$, the result is still greater than $10^{82,482,141}$. So less than 1 out of $10^{82,482,141}$ differences between patterns can make any difference to the visual processing system. In other words, almost all the information in the initial bitmap must be ignored by the visual system. This explains why the human visual system works by performing simple initial computations on the retinal bitmap, discarding the rest of the information, and then uses the results of those computations to compute the final image.

The crucial observation that will lead us to an account of the mystery link is that when we perceive a scene replete with objects and their perceivable properties and interrelationships, perception itself gives us a way of thinking of these objects and properties. For instance, if you see an apple on a table, you can look at it and think to yourself, "That is red". The apple is represented in your thought by the visual image of the apple. You do not think of the apple under a description like "the thing this is an image of", because that would require your thought to be about the image, and as we remarked above, people do not usually have thoughts about their visual images. Usually, the first thoughts we get in response to perception are thoughts about the objects perceived, not thoughts about visual images. For a thought to be about something, it must contain a representation of the item it is about. In perceptual beliefs, physical objects can be represented by representations that are provided by perception itself.

We will call perceptual representations of objects *percepts*. The claim is then that the visual image provides the perceiver with percepts of the objects perceived, and those percepts can play the role of representations in perceptual beliefs.[7] That is, they can occupy the "subject position" in such thoughts.[8]

5. Seeing Properties

The visual image does not just contain representations of objects. It also represents objects as having properties and as standing in relationships to one another. Consider the scene depicted in Figure 4, and imagine seeing it in real life with both eyes. What do you see? Presumably you see the Marajó pot (from Marajó island at the mouth of the Amazon River), the Costa Rican dancer, the

Figure 4. Scene.

Inuit soapstone statue, and the ruler. You also *see that* a number of things are true of them. For instance you see that the dancer is behind the ruler. In saying this, we do not mean to imply that you see that the dancer is a dancer or that the ruler is a ruler (although you might). We are using the referential terms in "see that" indirectly, so that what we mean by saying "You see that the dancer is behind the ruler" is "You see what is in fact the dancer, and you see what is in fact the ruler, and you see that the first is behind the second." So it is only the property attributions we are interested in here.

With this understanding, you might see that any of the following are true:

(1) The pot is to the left of the soapstone statue.
(2) The dancer is behind the ruler.
(3) The end of the line marked "6" on the ruler coincides with the point on the base of the dancer.
(4) The contour on the top of the dancer's skirt is concave.
(5) The pot has two handles.
(6) The base of the pot is roughly spherical.

You *might* see that the following are true:

(7) The pot is from Amazonia.
(8) The point on the base of the dancer is six inches to the right of the pot.
(9) The soapstone figure depicts a boy holding a seal.

When you *see that* something is true of an object, you are seeing that the object has a property. However, the different property attributions in these *see-that* claims have different statuses. Some are based directly on the presentations of the visual system, while others require considerable additional knowledge of the world. The visual system, by itself, cannot provide you with the information that the pot is from Amazonia, or that the dancer is six inches from the pot. If you are an expert on such matters, you might *recognize* that the pot is from Amazonia, but the visual system does not represent the pot *as being* from Amazonia. This is an important distinction. Much of what we know from vision is a matter of recognizing, on the basis of visual clues, that things we see have or lack various properties, where such recognition normally involves a skill that the cognizer acquires. The skill is not a simple exercise of built-in features of the visual system, and may depend upon having contextual information that is not provided directly by vision. By contrast, it is very plausible to suppose that the visual system itself *represents* the pot *as being* to the left of the soapstone statue, represents the contour on the top of the soapstone statue's head *as being* convex, etc.

When something that we see is represented as having a certain property, the visual system computes that information and stores it as part of the perceptual representation of the item seen. It is part of the specification of how the perceived object looks. When this happens, the visual system is computing a representation of the object as having the property. We will call such properties *perceptible properties*. Just to have some convenient terminology, we will call this kind of seeing-that *direct seeing-that*, as opposed to *recognizing-that*.

The distinction between direct-seeing and visual recognition turns on whether the visual system itself provides the representation of the property or the visual system merely provides the evidence on the basis of which we come to ascribe a property that we think about in some other way. For instance, we can recognize cats visually. However, cats look many ways. They can be curled up in a ball, or stretched full length across a bed, they can be crouched for pouncing, or running high speed after a bird, they can have long hair or short, they can have vastly different markings, etc. There is no such thing as *the* look of a cat. Cats have many looks.

Furthermore, these looks are only contingently related to being a cat. As you learn more about cats, you learn more ways they can look and you acquire the ability to visually recognize them in more ways. In acquiring such knowledge, you are relying upon having a prior way of thinking of cats. Nor does the representation of cats that you employ in thinking about them change as a result of your learning to recognize cats visually. This follows from the fact that the appearance of cats can change and that does not make it impossible for you to continue thinking about them. Imagine a virus that spread world-wide and resulted in all cats losing their fur. Furthermore, it affects their genetic material so all future cats will be born bald. One who was not around cats while this was occurring would probably find it impossible to visually recognize the newly bald cats as cats, although this would not affect her ability to think about cats, or to subsequently learn that cats have become bald. So the visual appearance of cats is not the representation we employ when thinking about cats. We have some other way of thinking about cats, and learn (or discover inductively) that things looking a certain way are generally cats.

Direct realism has traditionally been focused on direct-seeing, and that will be the focus of the rest of this section. However, we feel that visual recognition is of more fundamental importance than has generally been realized. Accordingly, it will be discussed further in section seven.

It is an empirical matter just what properties are represented by the visual system and recorded as properties of perceived objects. We cannot decide this *a priori*, but we can suggest some constraints. When properties are represented by the visual system and stored as properties of perceived objects, they form part of the look of the object. As such, there must be a characteristic look that objects with these properties can be (defeasibly) expected to have. This rules out such properties as "being from Amazonia", but it is less clear what to say about some other properties.

In deciding whether the visual system has a way of encoding a property, we must not assume that the encoding itself has a structure that mirrors what we may think of as the logical analysis of the property. Perhaps the clearest instance of this is motion. It would be natural to suppose that we *infer* motion by sequential observation of objects in different spatial locations, but perception does not work that way. One conclusion that vision scientists generally agree upon is that representations of motion are computed prior to computing object representations. This is because information about motion is used in computing object representations. For example, motion parallax plays an important role in parsing the visual image into objects. Motion parallax consists of nearby objects traversing your visual field faster than distant objects. The importance of motion in perceiving objects is easily illustrated. Consider looking for a well-camouflaged insect on a tree leaf surrounded by other tree leaves. You may be looking directly at it but be unable to see it until it moves. The motion is indispensable to your visual system parsing the image so that the insect is represented as a separate object. The important thing about this example is that although motion can be logically analyzed in terms of sequential positions, the representation of motion is not similarly compound. It does not have a structure. This is further illustrated by the "apparent motion" illusion. For example, after strenuous aerobic exercise, if you look at a blank blue sky it is common for it to seem to be moving, despite the fact that there are no object representations in the visual field that are changing apparent position. From a functional perspective, your visual image simply stores a tag "motion" at a certain location. There is no way to take that tag apart into logical or functional components. It is just a tag. It may be *caused* by other components of the visual image, but it does not *consist* of them.

Consider another example. According to most computational theories of vision, representations of convexity and concavity are computed fairly early and play an important role in the computation of other representations. We can talk about convexity and concavity in either two dimensions or three dimensions. In two dimensions, the convexity of a part of the visual contour (the outline) of a perceived object plays an important role in computing shape representations, but for present purposes it is more illuminating to consider three-dimensional convexity and concavity. For example, note how obvious the convexity of the "plumbing fixtures" on the front of the statue in Figure 5 appear.[9] The convexity has a clear visual representation in your image. Contrast this with Figure 6, which is a photograph of the same statue in different light. Now the plumbing fixtures appear clearly concave. In fact, they really are concave, but it is almost impossible to see them that way in Figure 5, and it is very difficult to see them as convex in Figure 6. So three-dimensional convexity and concavity have characteristic "looks" (but, of course, these looks are not always veridical). The percepts represent objects as having concave or convex features. It does not take much thought to realize that these looks are *sui generis*. The phenomenal quality that constitutes the look does not have an analysis. It is *caused by* (computed on the basis of) all sorts of lower-level features of the visual image, but it does not simply consist of those lower-level features. Once again, from a functional point of view this simply amounts to storing a tag of some sort in

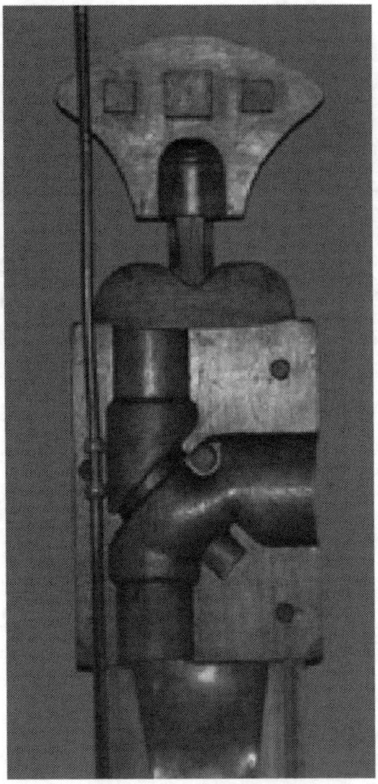

Figure 5. Convex

relation to the percept. We can usefully think of the percept as a data-structure. Data-structures have "fields" at which information is stored. When the appropriate field of the percept is occupied by the appropriate tag, the object is perceived as convex. This is despite the fact that convexity has a logical analysis in terms of other kinds of spatial properties of objects.

Obviously, we can perceive relative spatial positions and the juxtaposition of objects we see, and it is generally acknowledged that we can see the orientation of surfaces in three dimensions. All of this is illustrated by Figure 4. Note particularly the visual representation of the orientation of the floor. Three-dimensional orientation is perceived partly on the basis of stereopsis, but it can also be perceived without the aid of stereopsis, as in Figure 4.

6. Direct-Seeing and the Mystery Link

Now let us return to direct realism. Direct realism is intended to capture the intuition that our perceptual apparatus connects us to the world "directly", without our having to think about our visual image and make inferences from it. The key to understanding this is to realize that the visual image is

Figure 6. Concave

representational. Perception constructs perceptual representations of our surroundings, and these are passed to our system of epistemic cognition to produce beliefs about the world. The latter are our "perceptual beliefs"—the first beliefs produced in response to perceptual input—and they are about physical objects and their properties, not about appearances, qualia, and the like.

These observations can be used to make a first pass at explaining the mystery link. In broad outline, our proposal will be that perception computes representations of objects and their perceivable properties. The objects are represented as having those properties. This is the information that is passed to epistemic cognition. The belief that is constructed in response to the perceptual input is built out of those perceptual representations of the object and of the property attributed to it. Let us see if we can make this a bit more precise.

In section one we formulated direct realism as follows:

(DR) For appropriate *P*'s, if *S* believes *P* on the basis of being appeared to as if *P*, *S* is defeasibly justified in doing so.

We still want to endorse a principle of this form, but now we are in a position to say what counts as an appropriate *P*. Our suggestion is that *P* should simply be a reformulation of the information computed by the visual system.

More precisely, suppose the cognizer sees a physical object. Then his visual system computes a visual representation *O* of the object—a percept. The visual system may represent the object as having a perceptible property. This means that the visual system also constructs a representation *F* of the property and stores it in the appropriate field of the percept. *O* and *F* are visual representations, and hence mental representations. As mental representations, the cognizer can use them in thinking about the object and the property. In other words, the cognizer can have the thought ⌜*O* has the property *F*⌝. This is not a thought about *O* and *F*—it is a thought about what *O* and *F* represent. We are using the corner quotes here much as they are used in ordinary logic. So to say that *S* has the thought ⌜*O* has the property *F*⌝ is to say that *S* has a thought of the form "*x* has the property *y*" in which "*x*" is replaced by *O* and "*y*" is replaced by *F*. Having the visual representation *O* that purports to represent an object as having the property F enables the cognizer to form the thought ⌜*O* has the property *F*⌝, and our claim is that the perceptual experience defeasibly justifies the cognizer in doxastically endorsing this thought, i.e., believing it.

This account removes the veil of mystery from the mystery link. The mystery link is the process by which a thought is constructed out of a visual image. It appeared mysterious because the thought and the visual image are logically different kinds of things. In particular, some philosophers have been tempted to say that the thought is conceptual but the visual image is not. So how can you get from the one to the other? But now we can see that this puzzlement derives from an inadequate appreciation of the structure of the visual image. It has a very rich representational structure. We are not sure what to say about whether it is conceptual. We are not sure what that means. But whatever it means, it doesn't seem to be relevant. The transformation of certain parts of the visual image into thoughts is a purely syntactical transformation. It takes a perceptual representation *O*, extracts a representation *F* of a property from one of the fields of the representation, and then constructs a thought by putting the *O* in the subject position and *F* in the predicate position. There is no mystery here.

The key to understanding this aspect of the mystery link is the observation that our thought about a perceived object can be about that object by virtue of containing the percept of the object that is contained in the visual image. That is what the percept is—a mental representation of an object—and as its role is to represent an object, it can do so in thought as well as in perception. To have a thought about a perceived object, we need not somehow construct a different representation out of the perceptual representation. We can just reuse the perceptual representation. There is no "mysterious inference" involved in the mystery link. It is a simple matter of constructing one type of mental object out of another. We will refer to this process as the *direct encoding of visual information.*

It will turn out that this is not yet a complete account of the mystery link, but it is useful to diagram what we have so far as in Figure 7. Several comments are in order. First, note the role of attention in Figure 7. Our visual image is very rich and contains much more information than we actually use on any one occasion. We can think of the visual image as a transient database of perceptual representations, and we can abstractly regard a data-structure as having fields in which various information is encoded. In the case of a perceptual representation, there must be a field recording the kind of representation (e.g., edge, line,

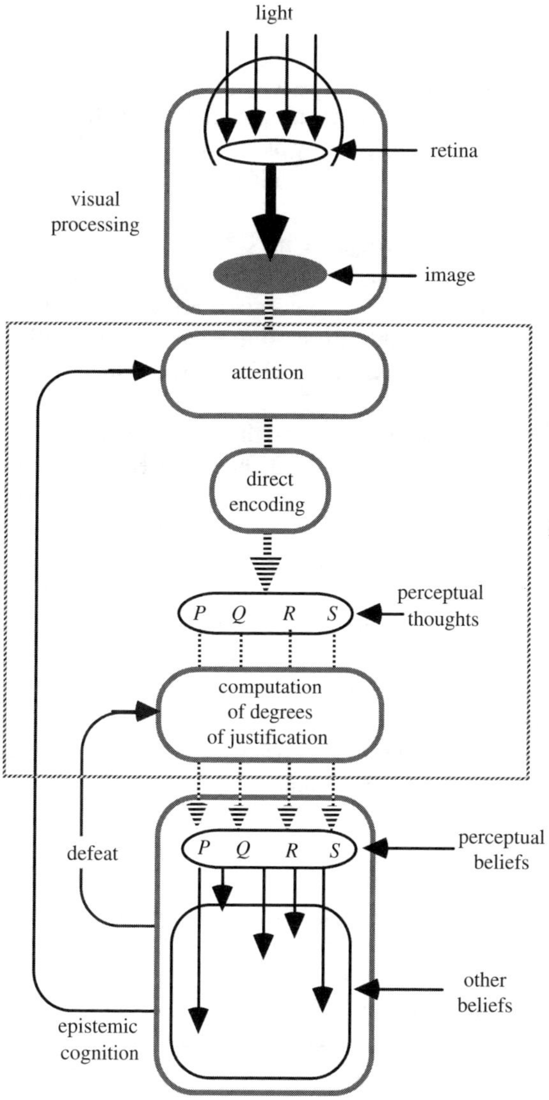

Figure 7. A first pass at explaining the mystery link

surface, object-part, object, etc.) and there must be fields recording the information about the perceived object that is provided directly by perception. When we perceive the apple, we perceive it as having apparent color and shape properties, so the visual image contains a perceptual representation of the apple—a percept—and the apple percept contains fields for color and shape information. If we see that the apple is sitting on the table, we also perceive the apple's spatial relationship to the table, so that information must be stored in both the apple percept and the table percept, each making reference to the other percept.

So on our view, the visual image is a transient database of data-structures—visual representations. It is transient because it changes continuously as the things we see change and move about. It is produced automatically by our perceptual system, and contains much more information than the agent has any use for at any one time. However, any of the information in the visual image is, presumably, of potential use. So our cognitive architecture provides attention mechanisms for dipping into this rich database and retrieving specific bits of information to be put to higher cognitive uses. Attention is a complex phenomenon, part of it being susceptible to logical analysis, but other parts of it succumbing only to a psychological description. Some perceptual events, like abrupt motions or flashes of light, attract our attention automatically. Others are more cognitively driven and are susceptible to logical analysis deriving from the fact that our reasoning is "interest driven", in the sense of Pollock (1995). Practical problems pose specific questions that the cognizer tries to answer. Various kinds of backward reasoning lead the cognizer to become interested in questions that can potentially be answered on the basis of perception, and this in turn leads the cognizer, through low-level practical cognition, to put herself in a position and direct her eyes in such a way that her visual system will produce visual representations relevant to the questions at issue. Interest in the earlier questions then leads the cognizer to extract information from the visual image and form thoughts that provide answers to the questions. For instance, you might want to know the color of Joan's blouse. This interest leads you to direct your eyes in the appropriate direction, and to attend to the perceptual representation you get of Joan's blouse, and particularly to the representation of the color. The visual image you get by looking in Joan's direction contains much more than the information you are seeking, but attention allows you to extract just the information of use in answering the question you are interested in.[10] The use of attention to select specific bits of information encoded in the visual image is a mechanism for avoiding swamping our cognition with too much information. Perceptual processing is a feedforward process that starts with the retinal bitmap and automatically produces much of the very rich visual image. Making it automatic makes it more efficient. But it also results in its producing more information than we need. So epistemic cognition needs a mechanism for selecting which bits of that information should be passed on for further processing, and that is the role of attention.

Figure 7 also makes a distinction between perceptual *thoughts* and perceptual *beliefs*. On the basis of the visual image and driven by attention, we construct a thought employing perceptual representations to think about the objects we are seeing and the properties we are attributing to them. However, we need not endorse the thought that is produced in this way. For instance, if you walk into the seminar room and have the visual experience of seeming to see a six-foot tall transparent pink elephant floating in the air five feet above the seminar table, you are not apt to form the belief that such a thing is really there. The visual experience leads you to entertain the thought, but the thought never gets endorsed.

This should not be surprising. Compare reasoning. When we form beliefs on the basis of reasoning (rather than perception), the reasoning is a process of mechanical manipulation. However, beliefs come in degrees. Some beliefs are better justified than others, and this is relevant to what beliefs we should form on the basis of the reasoning. The mere fact that a conclusion can be drawn on the basis of reasoning from beliefs we already hold does not ensure that we should believe the conclusion. After all, we might also have an argument for its negation. For instance, Jones may tell us that it is raining outside, and Smith may tell us that it is not. Both of these conclusions are inferred from things we believe, viz., that Jones said that it is raining and Smith said that it is not. But we do not want to endorse both conclusions. Having done the reasoning, we still have to decide what to believe and how strongly to believe it. Getting this right is the hardest part of constructing a theory of defeasible reasoning.[11]

It is apparent that when we engage in reasoning, forming beliefs is a two-step process. First, we construct the conclusions (thoughts) that are candidates for doxastic endorsement, and then we decide whether to endorse them and how strongly to endorse them. The same thing should be true when we form beliefs on the basis of perception. First we construct the thoughts by extracting them from the perceptual image, and then we decide whether to endorse them and how strongly to endorse them. This process should be at least very similar to the evaluation step employed when we form beliefs on the basis of reasoning. Thus when you seem to see a pink elephant, you have the thought that there is a pink elephant floating in the air before you, but when that thought is evaluated, background information provides defeaters that prevent it from being endorsed.

7. What Can't We See?

7.1 Seeing Colors

Now let us consider colors again. This was the original motivation for trying to make direct realism clearer. We see that objects have various colors. For example, when we see a London bus, we see that it is red. Is *red* a perceptible property? Does the visual system represent perceived objects as being red? Most philosophers have thought so. For example, Thompson *et al* (1992) claim, "That color should be the content of chromatic perceptual states is a criterion of adequacy for any theory of perceptual content." But let us consider this matter more carefully.

We certainly can see that a physical object is red. But as we have noted, this could either be a matter of directly seeing that it is red (in which case vision represents the object as red), or a matter of the cognizer visually recognizing that it is red. What is at issue is whether the visual system itself can provide the information that it is red, or if the recognition of colors is a learned skill making use of a lot of contextual information over and above that provided by the visual system. For the visual system to provide the information that something is red, it must have a way of representing the color universal. If vision provides representations of color universals, how does it do that? We have a mental color space, and different points on a perceived surface are "marked" with points from that color space. This is part of their look.

We will refer to the points in this color space as *color values*. It is natural to suppose that the color values that are used to mark points on a perceived surface represent color universals, and hence marking a surface or patch of surface with such a color value amounts to perceiving it as having that color. This is probably the standard philosophical preconception, and is responsible for the idea that colors have characteristic appearances that are partly constitutive of their being the colors they are.

However, the discussion of brunescence in section three strongly suggests that this philosophical preconception is mistaken. If color values (points in color space) represented color universals, it would turn out that objects having a particular objective color will hardly ever be represented by percepts marked with the corresponding color value. What then would make it the case that a particular color value represents a particular color universal? For that matter, we need not rely upon anything as exotic as brunescence to make this point. Simply stand in a room whose walls are painted some uniform color but unevenly illuminated by a bright window, and look at the color. Notice how much variation there is in the apparent color. The differences are not just differences of shading. For example, if the wall is a pale blue, some areas will look distinctly more yellow than others. In fact, in one real life case, the effect was so pronounced that we were unconvinced the wall really was a uniform color, and we tested it by moving a matching paint chip around the surface. It matched everywhere. So when we see the wall, we are seeing the same objective color everywhere—the same color universal is instantiated by every point on the wall. But in our visual image the representation of the wall is marked by widely varying color values. Which of these color values is the "right" color value? Does that make any sense? Surely not.

A single color looks very different under different circumstances. Which circumstances define "looking that color"? We imagine that some philosophers will be tempted to say that the right color value is the one we experience when we view the color in white light. But this just exhibits ignorance about the wide variety of things that can affect how colors look. It is not just the color of the light that affects how a color looks. It is affected by the brightness of the illumination (the Bezold-Brücke effect), simultaneous color contrast, chromatic adaptation, brunescence, and the sensitivity of one's photopigments, and there are probably many other factors that affect how colors look as well.[12] There is no such thing as a "normal" perceiver.

Apparently we cannot directly see that objects have particular colors. We can visually recognize things as exemplifying specific color universals, but that is different from directly seeing the colors.

If color values are not representations of color universals, what are they for? The answer is simple. They are part of what makes up the look of the object. The look of the object does not contain a representation of a color universal, but it is nevertheless a large part of the basis upon which we recognize what color the object is. Such recognition would be particularly simple if each color value represented a unique color universal, but as we have seen, because of the variability in how colors look under different circumstances, there is no way for the visual system to achieve that. So color recognition must instead take account of both the look of the object and the context in which the object looks that way. Because red does not have a characteristic look, there is no way the visual system can represent objects as being red. To see that an object is red must be to exercise a (partially) learned capacity to recognize that objects are red.

To recapitulate, percepts do three things. First, the percept is a mental representation of the object perceived. Second, it represents the object as having certain perceptible properties or as standing in certain perceptible relations to objects represented by other percepts. Third, it encodes the look of the object perceived. The latter is different from representing the object as having perceptible properties (unless we want to count looking that way as a perceptible property). Looks are important, because they can provide the evidence on the basis of which we ascribe non-perceptible properties to objects. That is what goes on in visual recognition.

7.2 Seeing Shapes

In response to the preceding, some may be tempted to say, "So what? We always knew colors were strange anyway. They are mere secondary qualities, maybe not real properties at all." It is interesting then that similar observations can be made about many shape properties. We can certainly recognize shapes visually, but it is less clear that we see them directly. For example, consider the circles and ellipses on the side of the monolith in Figure 8. When we are looking at them from a perpendicular angle, it is easy to tell which are which. This might suggest that circularity is represented in the visual image much as convexity is. It is popularly alleged that circles look like circles and not like ellipses even when

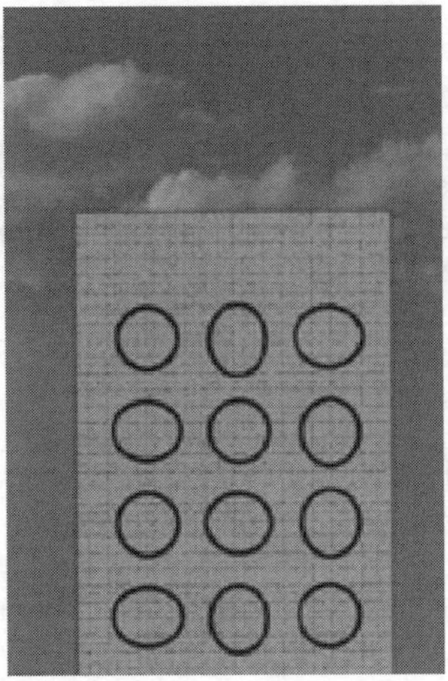

Figure 8. Circles at a right angle.

seen from an angle. If this were right, it would support the suggestion that circularity is seen directly. But we doubt that it is right. The same circles and ellipses that appear in Figure 8 appear again on both sides of the monolith in Figure 9. Do some of them look circular and others elliptical? That does not seem to us to be the case. This suggests that one cannot see directly that a shape is circular.

Figure 9. Circles at an oblique angle

It might be suggested that there is no need for us to be able to directly see that objects have particular shapes, because shape properties have definitions in terms of simpler perceptible spatial properties. The thinking would be that we can judge shapes in terms of those definitions. But two considerations suggest that this is not an adequate account of our ability to judge shapes. First, children can judge shapes without knowing the definition of *square* or *circle*. In fact, these definitions were only discovered fairly late in human history by the Greek geometers. Second, the standard definitions presuppose Euclidean geometry, but our best current physics tells us that space is not Euclidean. In a non-Euclidean space (such as the one we actually reside in), you cannot employ the familiar Euclidean definitions of *square* or *circle*. So it seems clear that they do not provide the basis for our judgments.

How then do we judge shapes? One suggestion is that, because one can directly see the orientation of surfaces and one can easily see that a shape is circular when it is viewed from a perpendicular angle, the property of being a circle oriented at a right angle to us is a perceptible property. Similarly for squares. Then other shape judgments could be parasitic on the perceptual judgments made at a right angle. This is just a tentative suggestion, however. These are issues that require further investigation.

8. Visual Recognition

8.1 Recognizing Cats and Kings

We observed above that there is an important distinction between a cognizer being able to visually recognize that an object has a property and his being able to directly see that it does. The latter requires that the object be visually represented as having the property. For this to be possible, the property must have a visual representation—a characteristic look that can be encoded in the percept. Such properties have been called "perceptible properties". As thus far explained, direct realism can only accommodate judgments attributing perceptible properties to perceived objects. However, most of our visual judgments are not like that. When you walk into the room you see that your cat is sprawled out on your easy chair. In seeing this you see an object and recognize it as a cat, and as your cat. You see a second object and recognize it as a chair, and as a particular chair. The spatial relationship consisting of the first object being on the second is something you can see directly.

Consider recognizing something as a cat. This does not seem to be the result of an explicit inference from other simpler beliefs. We defined *perceptual beliefs* to be the initial beliefs that we form on the basis of perception. Your belief that what you see before you is a cat is a perceptual belief just as much as is the belief that it is on the second object (the chair). But this is not a belief attributing a perceptible property to an object.

There may be nothing in common between two images of cats. Different cats, seen in different circumstances, can look very different, but by virtue of having learned to recognize cats visually, we can relate them all to the category *cat*. The first point at which there is something common to all cases of recognizing cats is when our recognition issues in the thought "That is a cat". By contrast, in all cases of seeing movement or seeing three-dimensional convexity, there is something common already at the level of the introspectible image that is responsible for our having the thought "That is moving" or "That is convex".

Recognition is also context dependent. Consider recognizing a person that you know only slightly, e.g., a student in one of your classes. In the context of the class, you can recognize him reliably. But if you run into him in the grocery store, you may have no idea who he is. So recognition is cognitively penetrable, i.e., it is influenced by our beliefs.

On the other hand, a vast amount of psychological evidence strongly supports the thesis that the production of the visual image is not cognitively penetrable (Pylyshyn 1999). This is illustrated by perceptual illusions. Consider again the statue in figures five and six. Knowing that the front of the statue is actually concave does not enable you to see it that way. Your other beliefs can prevent your perceptually derived thought from being endorsed as a belief, but they cannot affect what thought you entertain as the product of perception.

So visually recognizing and directly seeing are quite different in some ways, but alike in other epistemologically important respects. It is beliefs based on recognition, rather than beliefs based on directly seeing, that usually provide our initial epistemological access to our surroundings. Direct realism was originally defended by observing that the beliefs we get directly from perception are usually about the physical world around us and not about our own inner states. Philosophers inclined to endorse this observation have nevertheless tended to assume that the beliefs we get on the basis of perception involve only perceptible properties. The assumption has been that you cannot literally see that something is a cat or a table—only that it is shaped and colored in various ways. Now we are going one step further and noticing that perceptual beliefs are not usually beliefs attributing perceptible properties to perceived objects. We don't form beliefs about colors and shapes much more often than we form beliefs about apparent colors and apparent shapes. What we believe on the basis of perception is, for example, that the cat is sitting on the dinner table licking the dirty plates. It never occurs to us to believe that an object with a certain highly complex shape and mottled pattern of colors is spatially juxtaposed with and above an object with a different somewhat simpler shape and pattern of colors.

If one doubts that cognition proceeds directly from perception to beliefs about cats, plates, and dinner tables, they must suppose that we first form beliefs about there being objects having complex shapes and colors and then make inferences to beliefs about cats. Perhaps we just make the transition so rapidly that we do not notice the first belief. But the implausibility of this hypothesis is manifest when we realize that we have no precise idea what it is about the look of a cat that makes us think it is a cat. We can say things like, "It is about a foot long, furry, with pointy ears and a long tail, and has a mottled brown color". But note, first, that these are not perceptible properties any more than *cat* is. They are still too high level. And second, even if they were perceptible properties, they would not suffice to distinguish cats from a host of other small furry creatures. We can recognize cats, but we cannot say how we do it.

Consider an even simpler example—the infamous chicken sexers. These are people who learn to identify the gender of newborn chicks on the basis of their visual appearance, the purpose being to keep only the females for their future egg-laying capabilities. Some people can learn to do this reliably, but they generally have no idea how they do it. Newborn male and female chicks do not look very different. There must be a difference, but the chicken sexers themselves are unsure what it is, and so they are certainly not first forming a belief about that difference and then inferring that what they are seeing is a female chick. As they do not know what the difference is, they do not have a belief to the effect that the chick they are observing displays that difference.

An example of this that should be familiar to everyone is face recognition. We are very good at recognizing people on the basis of their faces, but imagine trying to say what it is about a person's face that makes you think it is them. Face recognition turns on very subtle visual clues, and we often have no idea what they are.

How is it possible to recognize something as a cat without inferring that from something simpler you can see directly? We do not have a complete answer to give, but we can propose the beginnings of an answer. Consider connectionist networks (so-called "neural nets"). In their infancy, these were proposed as models of human neurons, but it is now generally recognized that existing connectionist networks are only remotely similar to systems of neurons. Nevertheless, they exhibit impressive performance on some kinds of tasks. They are perhaps most impressive in pattern recognition. A rather small network can be trained to recognize crude cat silhouettes and distinguish them from crude dog silhouettes. Larger connectionist networks have proven to be impressive pattern recognizers in a number of applications.

What does this show? It doesn't show that we are chock full of little connectionist networks. What connectionist networks are is efficient statistical analysis machines. They do a very good job of finding and encoding statistical regularities. Although it is not plausible to suppose that we are full of little connectionist networks, it is eminently plausible to suppose that our neurological structure is able to implement something with similar capabilities.[13] And such capabilities are what are involved in visual recognition. Experience has the effect of training category recognizers in us. These can, in principle, take anything accessible to the system as input. In particular, they can be sensitive to data from the visual image and also to beliefs about the current context. Thus there can be many different looks that, in different contexts, fire the "cat-detector". We aren't built with cat-detectors—we acquire them through learning, much as a connectionist network learns to recognize cat silhouettes. Furthermore, different people may learn to recognize cats differently. A person who has never seen a manx cat may not recognize one as a cat because it has no tail.

What makes visual recognition possible is the fact that cat-detectors can be sensitive to facts about the visual image and not just to the cognizer's beliefs. We do not have to have beliefs about how the cat looks in order to recognize it as a cat. The move from the image to the judgment that it is a cat can be just as direct as the move from the image to the belief that one object is on top of another. The difference is just that the latter move is built-in rather than learned, while the ability to recognize cats is learned from experience.

We assume that the look of a cat is incidental to being a cat. From a logical point of view, learning how cats look could be a simple matter of statistical induction. We could discover inductively that things that look a certain way in a certain context tend to be cats. This information could then be used to identify cats by applying the statistical syllogism. Roughly, the statistical syllogism licenses a defeasible inference from "This looks such-and-such, and the probability is high that if something looks such-and-such then it is a cat" to "This is a cat".

Inductive reasoning is difficult for a cognizer with human-like resource constraints. In particular, to engage in explicit inductive reasoning we would have to remember a huge amount of data. Outside of science, humans rarely do that. Instead, we are equipped with special purpose modules that summarize the data as we go along, without our having to keep track of it, and do induction at the same time.[14] Such modules can occasionally lead us astray, but on the whole it is essential for real cognitive agents to employ such short-cut procedures for inductive reasoning.

We can imagine cognitive agents that do not have cat-detectors, relying instead upon such induction modules to learn generalizations of the form "Things that look this way under these circumstances tend to be cats". They could then use those generalizations to detect cats. But there would remain an important difference between the way they detect cats and the way humans detect cats. Those agents would have to form beliefs about how objects look and then explicitly infer that they are cats. As we have noted, although humans *can* reason that way, they don't have to. Humans can recognize cats simply by having appropriate perceptual experiences, without forming beliefs about those perceptual experiences.

Logically, visual detectors should work like an explicit appeal to statistical induction and the statistical syllogism, but they make cognition more efficient by simplifying the inductive reasoning and shortcutting the need to form beliefs about appearances. The effect of this is to complicate the mystery link. The mystery link now represents two somewhat different ways to move from the visual image to beliefs about the world. First, we can do that by directly encoding some of the contents of the image into thoughts. Second, we can do this by acquiring visual detectors through learning and using them to attribute non-perceptible properties to the things we see. Thus we can expand Figure 7 as in Figure 10.

Direct realism must be extended to accommodate these observations and give visual recognition a central role in the formation of perceptual beliefs. Recall that (DR) was formulated as follows:

(DR) For appropriate *P*'s, if *S* believes *P* on the basis of being appeared to as if *P*, *S* is defeasibly justified in doing so.

We will henceforth interpret "being appeared to as if *P*" as a matter of either (1) having a visual image part of which can be directly encoded to produce

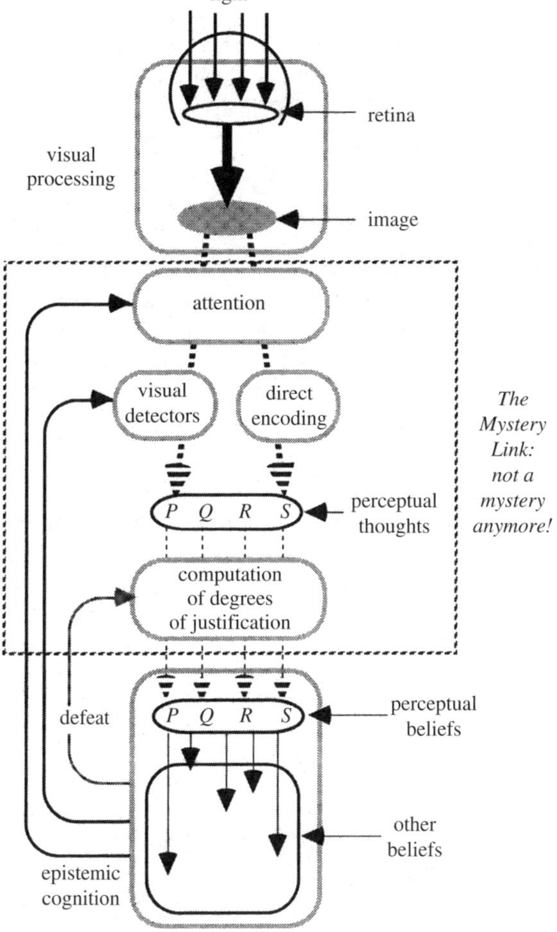

Figure 10. Explaining the mystery link

the thought that *P*, or (2) having a visual image or sequence of visual images that fires a *P*-detector. Appropriate *P*'s are simply those that can either result from direct encoding or for which the cognizer can learn a *P*-detector. We will thus understand direct realism as embracing both direct encoding and visual detection.

In the previous paragraph we implicitly noted that visual detectors can appeal to a sequence of visual images rather than a single momentary image. Thus, for example, in identifying something as a cat when it is curled up in a furry ball and sound asleep, it may help a lot to walk around it and view it from different angles. Note also that if it is purring, this may decide the issue. This indicates that it is a bit simplistic to talk about exclusively *visual* detectors. We should really be talking about *perceptual* detectors, or perhaps something even broader, because the input can be cross-modal. However, for simplicity we will continue to use our present terminology.

Visual detectors can produce recognition with varying degrees of conviction. If you see the curled-up cat from across the room, you may recognize it only tentatively as a cat. If you examine it up close and from different angles, you may be fairly confident that it is a cat. If you also hear it purring, you may be certain. So we should think of visual detectors as producing outputs with differing degrees of defeasible justification depending upon just what inputs are being employed.

The incorporation of visual detection into (DR) enables it to handle perceptual beliefs that are not the product of direct encoding of the visual image, but this also changes the character of (DR) in an important respect. In Pollock (1986) and Pollock & Cruz (1999), (DR) was taken to formulate a logical relationship between *P* and being appeared to as if *P*. The claim was that this defeasible reasoning scheme is partly constitutive of the conceptual role of *P*, and hence it is a necessary truth that (DR) holds for *P*. However, *P*-detectors are only contingently connected with *P*. We generally have to learn what it looks like for *P* to be true, and different people can learn different *P*-detectors. The acquisition of a *P*-detector depends on a (generally implicit) statistical analysis. In effect, *P*-detectors are based on inductive reasoning. Thus (DR) itself remains a necessary truth, but for many *P*'s, what it is to be appeared to as if *P* is something that an agent must discover inductively.

8.2 The Mechanics of Visual Detectors

We have been intentionally vague about the way visual detectors work, just saying that they involve a statistical analysis of how things look. The human cognitive architecture may include a lot of built-in structure that facilitates this process. For example, Biederman (1985) makes the observation that many kinds of things may be recognized in terms of their parts. Consider cats. They have a number of movable parts, including legs, tails, heads, ears, eyes, etc. Because these parts can stand in many different spatial relations to one another, cats can have many different looks. But the parts have more stereotyped looks. So Biederman suggests that we may first recognize the parts in terms of their appearances and then recognize cats in terms of how the parts fit together. If Biederman is right, this amounts to saying that the human cognitive architecture makes preferential use of certain kinds of regularities in learning visual detectors. This seems very plausible.

There is at least one case in which it seems undeniable that humans employ special purpose cognitive machinery in learning visual detectors. Humans and most higher mammals are very good at recognizing other members of their species on the basis of their faces. This seems to involve skills that go beyond ordinary object recognition. Some of the evidence for this derives from the fact that damage to the medial occipitotemporal cortex can cause people to lose this ability without losing other recognitional abilities. The resulting disability is known as *prosopagnosia* or "face blindness". Hoffman (1998) reports an example from Pallis (1995):

> After his stroke, Mr. P still had outstanding memory and intelligence. He could still read and talk, and mixed well with the other patients on his ward. His vision was in most respects normal—with one notable exception: he couldn't recognize the faces of people or animals. As he put it himself, "I can see the eyes, nose, and mouth quite clearly, but they just don't add up. They all seem chalked in, like on a blackboard. . . . I have to tell by the clothes or by the voice whether it is a man or a woman. . . . The hair may help a lot, or if there is a mustache . . ." Even his own face, seen in a mirror, looked to him strange and unfamiliar.

The internet is a rich source of first-person accounts of prosopagnosia.

Vision scientists often fail to distinguish between visual recognition and the computation of the visual image. For example, both Marr and Biederman include the recognition of objects as the final stage of visual processing. But this is somewhat misleading. There is little that is explicitly visual about visual recognition. We noted above that the process should be viewed as multi-modal because it can be responsive to non-visual perceptual information too, like the purr of a cat. It may in fact be best to strike "visual" from "visual recognition" altogether, and just talk about recognition. Recognition is a general cognitive process that can take any information at all as input. Much of it employs visual information, but not all of it, and it seems to be essentially the same process whether visual information is used or not. For example, we often recognize people by their voices. This is a case of auditory recognition, with no visual input. For a more complex case of auditory recognition, note that it is common for a person to be able to recognize the composer of a piece of music even when they have never heard the music before. Mozart, for instance, is easy to recognize. Furthermore, there are cases of recognition that are completely non-perceptual. Just as you may recognize the composer of a piece of music, you may recognize the author of a literary work without having previously read it. There is nothing perceptual about this case at all, but it does not seem to work differently from other more perceptual varieties of recognition. The general cognitive process is recognition. Visual recognition is just recognition that is based partly on visual input. Vision provides the input, but vision does not do the recognizing.

8.3 Recognizing Colors

In section one we observed that direct realism has often been illustrated by appealing to the following putative instance of (DR):

(RED) If *S* believes that *x* is red on the basis of its looking to *S* as if *x* is red, *S* is defeasibly justified in doing so.

We noted, however, that the principle (RED) seemed to assume that there is a way of looking—*looking red*—that is logically connected with being red. It was argued that unless red objects generally look that way, (RED) will usually lead us to conclude that red objects are not red. We assume that this result would be unacceptable. However, the sliding spectrum argument shows that there is no way that red objects characteristically look to all persons and at all times, nor is there any sensible set of "normal viewing conditions". This was illustrated by a variety of phenomena, including brunescence, the Bezold-Brücke effect, simultaneous color contrast, and chromatic adaptation, plus the observation that individual differences in perceptual hardware and neural wiring (e.g., the sensitivity of photopigments) lead colored objects to look different to different people. To have a collective name for all of these phenomena, let us call them cases of *color variability*.

The preceding considerations seemed initially to constitute a counterexample to direct realism in general and to (RED) in particular. However, in light of the preceding section, we are now understanding (DR) in a more liberal way—as including reference to *P*-detectors. And we can understand (RED) analogously. What color variability indicates is that *red* is not a perceptible property. These psychological phenomena illustrate that there is no fixed way of looking that is associated, for all people and all time, with being red. Hence there is no way for the visual system to compute a fixed representation for the property of being red, i.e., it cannot represent a perceived object *as being* red. So we cannot directly see that something is red. However, we clearly do see that things are red, so this must be a case of visual recognition. *Red* is like *cat* in that we can visually recognize things as red, but this is not a matter of directly encoding aspects of the visual image. Because red things look different to different people, each person has to learn for herself how red things look, and hence how to visually identify red things. For each cognizer, red things do have typical looks, described in terms of the cognizer's mental color space. That is what the color space is for—to enable the cognizer to identify colors. But the identification cannot be direct, because we cannot fix beforehand what region of the cognizer's color space corresponds to a particular objective color universal.

How would it be possible to acquire red-detectors through learning? Compare them to cat-detectors. Cat-detectors are just doing a statistical analysis of the looks of a pre-existing category of things, viz., cats. For red-detectors to work similarly, there must be a pre-existing category—*red*—that we can access independently of red-detectors and investigate statistically. But how can we access color categories without color-detectors? One possibility is to appeal to the fact that *red* is an interpersonal category, enshrined in public language. It denotes a range of color universals. Many ranges of color universals might constitute useful categories, and there is no reason to expect that every linguistic culture will have words for the same ranges. For instance, Lindsey and Brown (2002) indicates that many languages lack a word for "blue" because the adults in that linguistic community suffer from pronounced brunescence:

> Many languages have no basic color term for "blue". Instead, they call short-wavelength stimuli "green" or "dark". The article shows that this cultural, linguistic phenomenon could result from accelerated aging of the eye because of high, chronic exposure to ultraviolet-B (UV-B) in sunlight (e.g., phototoxic lens brunescence). Reviewing 203 world languages, a significant relationship was found between UV dosage and color naming: In low-UV localities, languages generally have the word "blue"; in high-UV areas, languages without "blue" prevail. Furthermore, speakers of these non-"blue" languages often show blue-yellow color vision deficiency.

Children certainly learn the *word* "red" from other members of their culture. This *might* be the way they learn the category *red*. This would make it entirely conventional. However, this is not the only way to learn new color categories. For example, many cars are now painted with a metallic paint that is roughly the color of old pewter. This has become a fairly familiar color, although the authors do not know a name for it. It probably has a name, but we did not learn to identify this color by having it pointed out by name. For current purposes, let us call it "pewter". Instead of having this color pointed out by name, we observed a number of cars painted that color, and mentally constructed that category and began thinking in terms of it.

How is it possible to learn new color categories in this way? To do this we must be able to think about colors and ranges of colors and we must be able to tell when an object has a color falling within a particular range so that we can inductively generalize about what such objects look like. We assume that the concept of color (but not the concept of any particular color) is innate. More generally, our cognitive architecture equips us with a number of innate concepts like *object*, *edge*, *part*, *color*, etc. These concepts do not have logical analyses.

They are characterized by the role they play in cognition. If the concept of color plays this kind of role in our cognitive architecture, how do we reason about colors, and how does that enable us to learn color categories?

Color categories pick out continuous ranges of color—*color continua*. We have the concept of two colors being more or less similar (another innate concept), and a color continuum is a range of colors satisfying the condition that if x and y are in the range, and z is a color that is more similar to both x and y than they are to each other, then z is also in the range. We typically judge the similarity of two colors on the basis of their looking similar, i.e., their eliciting nearby color values in our phenomenal color space. This amounts to saying that color similarity is a perceptible relation, and we can make judgments about it by employing the following defeasible inference scheme, which is an instance of (DR):

(COLOR) If S believes that two simultaneously perceived objects x and y have the same (or similar) colors on the basis of their looking to S as if they have the same (or similar) colors, S is defeasibly justified in doing so.

Color variability prevents colors from having predetermined fixed looks, but it does not similarly prevent color similarity from having a predetermined fixed look. Changes in lighting, or physical changes like brunescence may change how a color looks to a person, but they will tend to change all colors in the same way. Hence they will leave perceived similarity (closeness in the color space) relatively unchanged. Hence *this* can be a perceptible relation, even though color categories themselves are not perceptible properties.

If we can pick out a set O of similarly colored objects, we can then pick out a range of colors—a color category C—by stipulating that a color falls in the category C iff it is sufficiently similar to the color of one of the objects in O. So color categories get defined by reference to sets of objects. For this reasoning to be possible, we must be able to pick a set O in such a way that it consists of similarly colored objects. For this approach to be non-circular, we must be able to tell that objects are similarly colored without categorizing them as, e.g., pewter. Our proposal is that this can be done by appealing to two epistemic principles. The first is the aforementioned principle (COLOR).

By appealing to (COLOR) we can judge whether two objects seen at the same time are similarly colored. But we need more than that to acquire a color category like *pewter* and learn a color-detector for it. A statistical analysis of how pewter-colored things look under different circumstances will require identifying an object as being of that color and then examining it under varying conditions. To do that we have to know that it remains the same color while we vary other conditions. This is not something that we can determine by using (COLOR), because it only applies to objects seen at the same time—not to temporally separated objects or temporally separated stages of the same object.

Can we simply generalize the principle (COLOR) to apply to objects perceived at different times? Not exactly, because (COLOR) appeals to its being the case that the percepts of x and y represent x and y as having similar colors, and that requires that perception itself marks the percept of x and the percept of y as similarly colored. For that to be possible, the cognitive agent must have simultaneous percepts of x and y. But we might propose a somewhat similar principle according to which, if we can remember how x and y looked when we are no longer perceiving one or both, then if their apparent colors were similar, that gives us defeasible justification for believing that they are (objectively) similarly colored. One difficulty for applying such a principle is that we are not very good at remembering how things looked. But even if we could remember apparent colors reliably, this principle would lead us to make incorrect judgments in cases of color variability. In doing a statistical analysis of the look of a color under various circumstances, our objective is to discover when the same color looks different. But if we reasoned about colors using a principle like this one, we would be led to conclude that the colors are changing rather than that a single color is looking different.

What we need instead is the assumption that the colors of objects tend to be fairly stable, so that when we vary the lighting conditions, although the look of the color changes the color does not. This is an instance of a more general principle that is known as *temporal projection*. Temporal projection is a familiar principle in the artificial intelligence literature (Sandewall 1972, McDermott 1982, McCarthy 1986, Pollock 1998), but it has been largely overlooked in philosophical epistemology. It is basically a defeasible assumption that most "logically simple" properties of objects are relatively stable. If an object has such a property at one time, this gives us a defeasible reason for thinking it will continue to have it at a later time, although the strength of the reason decreases as the time interval increases. Pollock (1998) formulates this more precisely as follows:

> If P is temporally projectible, then P's being true at time t_0 gives us a defeasible reason for expecting P to be true at a later time t, the strength of the reason being a monotonic decreasing function of the time difference $(t - t_0)$.

This is also known as the "commonsense law of inertia". The temporal projectibility constraint reflects the fact that this principle does not hold for some choices of P. For instance, its being 3 o'clock at one time does not give us a reason for expecting it to be 3 o'clock ten minutes later.

What justifies temporal projection? It is not an empirical discovery about the world. Any cognitive agent must employ some such principle if it is to be able to use perception to build a comprehensive account of the world. The problem is that perception is essentially a sampling technique. It samples disparate bits and pieces of the world at different times, and if we are to be able to make use of multiple facts obtained from perception, we must be able to assume that they remain true for a while. For instance, suppose your task is to read two meters and record which has the higher reading, but the meters are separated so that you cannot see both at once. You look at one and note that it reads "4.7". Then you look at the other and note that it reads "3.4". This does not yet allow you to complete your task, because you do not know that after you turned away from the first meter it continued to read "4.7". Obviously, humans solve this problem by assuming that things stay fixed for awhile. The logical credentials of this assumption are discussed further in Pollock (1998).

By employing (COLOR) and temporal projection in unison we can create new color categories. For instance, by employing (COLOR) we can observe that two cars are similarly colored. Later we might note that one of them is similarly colored to a third car. By temporal projection we can infer that the color of the first has not changed, so the third car is similarly colored to both of the original two cars. In this way, the set of similarly colored cars can grow, and we can stipulate that something has the color *pewter* iff it is similarly colored to the cars in this set. On the assumption that the cars tend to retain their colors, we can go on to investigate how the color looks under various circumstances, thus establishing a pewter-detector. Or, more realistically, having observed the set of similarly colored cars, a pewter-detector will be learned automatically.

Note that we appeal to the set of similarly colored cars to fix the reference of the term "pewter", not to define its meaning. It could turn out that we were mistaken about one of the cars being the same color as the others—we saw it in peculiar lighting conditions. Thus it cannot be a necessary truth that the cars in the set are pewter-colored. We appeal to them simply as a way of fixing our thought on a color range we take them to exemplify.

So it seems that it should be possible to learn all of our color-detectors from experience. And it is clear that we have to learn, to some extent, how red things look to us. They look different under different circumstances, and they may well look different to each person. However, this does not imply that red-detectors cannot be innate. There are three kinds of considerations that affect how a red thing looks to a person. First, there are transitory variations in illumination, background contrast, etc. Second, there are interpersonal variations resulting from differences in perceptual hardware and neural wiring that are present "right out of the box". Third, there are long-term variations resulting from changes to perceptual hardware and neural wiring. Brunescence is an example of the latter. Transitory variations can be accommodated by, at least initially, having a red-detector attach only low degrees of justification to conclusions based on momentary perceptual experiences. It seems likely that red-detectors could be constructed so that they are unaffected by out-of-the-box hardware variations. The neural pathways leading from red-sensitive cones to the look of the image are determined by the initial neurological structure of the cognizer, and a color-detector could be innately designed to respond to whatever range of looks is in fact wired to those cones. Thus the first two classes of variations could be accommodated reasonably well using an innately configured red-detector. However, the third class of variations has the effect that things may not stay the way they were originally. To accommodate these variations, even if the cognizer has an innate red-detector, she must be able to modify its detection properties in light of experience. Even without long term changes, this will be desirable to allow people to become more sophisticated in detecting colors so that they can take account of things like the difference between tungsten and fluorescent lighting (or even firelight). This is also going to be desirable because, although we cannot always place great reliance on color judgments based on momentary visual images, it seems that often we can. We are able to learn that under some circumstances, a glance is enough to tell the color of something, but under other circumstances we must examine things more carefully to judge their colors. So even if there are innate color-detectors, they should be tunable by experience.

We don't need innate color-detectors, but it might be useful to have them. Do we? This can only be answered by empirical investigation. There is, however, some evidence (albeit controversial) suggesting that we do have innate color-detectors specifically for the primary colors. It turns out that infants can discriminate primary colors by four months of age (Bornstein, Kessen & Weiskopf 1976). It is pretty unlikely that they have learned these categories in that short amount of time, so they probably have innate detectors for the primary colors. On the other hand, it is also clear that we can acquire color-detectors for new color categories like *pewter* through learning.

8.4 Color Variability

This entire paper was motivated by the inability of traditional philosophical views about color to handle the way we reason about phenomena like brunescence. Let us see if the present account can do better. Consider four cases:

(1) We see a white cube against a black background. Then a blue filter is put over our eyes and the cube looks blue. Then the filter is removed and the cube looks white again. In this case we want to be able to conclude that the cube did not change color—it just looked different.

(2) Unbeknownst to us, scientists have discovered a new electromagnetic phenomenon. By imposing an oscillating electromagnetic field of a certain frequency, they can permanently change the color of an object. The effect is analogous to painting the object, but it alters the surface properties of the material rather than covering it with a different material. We observe the field being applied to the white cube in the laboratory. Then the scientists go home for the day, leaving the cube sitting on its pedestal unattended. When the field was applied, the cube began to look blue, and it continues to do so forever more. In this case we want to conclude that the cube really did change color. This is just like painting it.

(3) Brunescence: a membrane in our eye yellows very slowly—so slowly that we do not notice it. The look of all objects slowly changes, but we cannot remember how they looked earlier, so we are unaware of the change. Then the membrane is surgically removed, and objects look bluer than they did before the surgery. We look at the white cube, and it now looks blue. It continues to do so forever more. In this case we want to conclude that things did not really change color. Rather, colors changed appearance.

(4) A blue filter is surgically implanted in our eyes, so everything comes to look bluer than it did before. We look at the white cube, and it now looks blue. It continues to do so forever more. This is a cleaner version of case (3). The difference between this and case (1) is that, like case (2), the change is permanent. But unlike case (2), we want to conclude that things did not really change color.

In case (1) we want to judge that the cube did not change color. This seems to be based on temporal projection. Suppose we have a strong reason for thinking that the cube is white at t_0. By temporal projection, we can infer that it is still white at a later time t, although the strength of the reason decreases as the interval $(t - t_0)$ increases. Meanwhile, the cube's looking blue at time t gives us a reason for thinking it is blue. If we assume that momentary perception gives us a weaker reason for thinking it is blue than we originally had for thinking it was white, then when $(t - t_0)$ is small, temporal projection gives us a stronger reason for thinking the cube is still white than momentary perception gives us for thinking it is now blue. But when $(t - t_0)$ becomes large enough, perception overwhelms temporal projection. In case (1), we can make the appearance switch quickly by placing the filter over our eyes and removing it. So temporal projection swamps momentary perception, and we conclude that the cube has not changed color.

To make this reasoning work, it must be the case that momentary perception does not give us as good a reason for thinking that the cube is blue as we had originally for thinking it was white. It was remarked above that it seems to be a general characteristic of visual detectors that recognition based on more observations gives us more confidence (a higher degree of justification) in the recognition. For instance, if your cat is moving about, or if you move around it and see it from different angles, this increases your confidence that you are seeing a cat. Similarly, if you observe the color of an object over an extended period, in various lighting conditions and from different angles, you will be more confident about its color. So case (1) seems to be unproblematic on the current theory.

In case (2), when the cube appears to change color, temporal projection initially gives us a rebutting defeater, just as in case (1). But the fact that the change is permanent will eventually make us reconsider. This is explained by noting that as the interval $(t - t_0)$ increases, temporal projection gives us a systematically weaker reason for thinking that the cube is still white. At some point that reason becomes significantly weaker than the reason momentary perception gives us for thinking it is blue, so at that point the application of (DR) overwhelms temporal projection. Thus it becomes reasonable to think that the cube is blue. We can then inductively generalize about the change, learning that subjecting an object to such an electromagnetic field changes its color. In this way we can acquire an undercutting defeater for future applications of temporal projection in such cases.

The crucial difference between cases (3) and (4) and case (2) seems to be that *everything* changes apparent color. To handle cases (3) and (4) we have to think about how the color detector works. Acquiring a blue-detector through learning is logically analogous to confirming by statistical induction that when things look a certain way they tend to be blue. Let us pretend for the moment that this is how we acquire the blue-detector. Then it is based on an initial evidence set *E*. *E* will consist of many blue things that look a certain way, many non-blue things that do not look that way, and perhaps a few non-blue things that do look that way. Suppose, suddenly, everything looks bluer than it did, and in particular things that were previously white all look blue. By temporal projection we can conclude that those white things are still white but just look blue—this is like case (1). From this we can infer inductively that white things now look blue. We can also infer by temporal projection that most of the non-blue things in *E* are still non-blue. But we can also conclude, from our inductive generalization, that many of them now look blue. This undercuts the earlier statistical induction supporting the establishment of the generalization that when things look a certain way they tend to be blue. Thus the fact that everything looks bluer now than it did before gives us no reason for thinking that things really are bluer, and temporal projection gives us a reason for thinking they are not. Hence it is reasonable to conclude that colored things no longer look the same way they did. In fact, we have confirmed inductively that the way they look has shifted towards the blue. This provides the basis for new (or modified) color-detectors.

Of course, the preceding is based on the pretense that color detectors are established by explicit statistical confirmation. They aren't really. They are the product of a psychological learning process that goes on without any direction from the cognizer. But the logic of the use of such color detectors should be the same as if they were the product of statistical confirmation. This indicates that if we notice that everything seems to have changed apparent color, this should defeat color judgments based on the application of (DR) and our color-detectors. Initially, we will conclude by induction that apparent colors have changed, and so we will reason about colors by thinking about apparent colors—something we ordinarily avoid. As one of us can attest from personal experience, this is in fact exactly what patients do after cataract surgery. But after a while our color detectors will adjust, and we will no longer have to think about how things look. We can go back to making automatic judgments on the basis of having the visual image, unmediated by beliefs about the visual image.

Our conclusion is that the present theory—a refined version of direct realism—is able to handle variations in the appearance of colors in ways that earlier theories could not. Earlier theories assumed that every color has a characteristic appearance that is an essential and unchangeable feature of it. The connection between colors and appearances must be looser, and the present theory accommodates that by understanding principles like (RED) in terms of color-detectors rather than direct encoding. So these examples do not constitute a threat to direct realism.

9. Conclusions

The mystery link is the process by which information is moved from the visual image into epistemic cognition. A constraint on psychological theories of vision and philosophical theories of knowledge is that they must fit together via some account of the mystery link. The contemporary epistemological problem of perception has been strongly conditioned by the view of the visual image that was prevalent at the start of the 20th century. That view took the visual image to be an undifferentiated morass of colors and shades corresponding directly to the bitmap of retinal stimulation. Contemporary scientific theories of perception insist instead that the visual image is the product of computational processing that produces visual representations of physical objects and some of their properties and relations. This rich array of preprocessed visual information is the input to the kind of epistemic cognition that is the topic of epistemological theorizing. Epistemology begins with the visual image, not the retinal bitmap.

We have argued that this is done in two distinct ways. The simplest is direct encoding, wherein representations are retrieved from perception and inserted into thoughts. However, only the simplest perceptual beliefs can be produced in this way. More sophisticated cognition requires visual recognition, wherein we learn to recognize properties on the basis of their appearances. This is what is involved in seeing colors.

These have been remarks about how vision and the mystery link work. They are about the structure of visual cognition. What, one might ask, has this to do with the justifiedness of our perceptual beliefs? We do not have the space to discuss this issue at length, but a brief answer is that our interest is in the procedural concept of epistemic justification developed first in Pollock (1986) and further in Pollock and Cruz (1999). This concerns the epistemic norms that are built into our cognitive architecture, and their structure is to be elucidated by investigating how cognition works. See Pollock (2006) for the most recent incarnation of this view.

Notes

1. Supported by NSF grants nos. IRI-IIS-080888 and IIS-0412791.
2. Supported by a grant from Rutgers University.

3. See Pollock (1995) and (2002) for accounts of our preferred theory of defeasible reasoning. One version of this theory has been implemented in OSCAR. For up to date information on OSCAR and the implementation of the architecture, go to http://www.u.arizona.edu/~pollock.
4. This objection is often associated with Sellars (1963). See also Sosa (1981) and Davidson (1983).
5. See, for example, Pryor (2000) and Huemer (2001).
6. This view has recently been endorsed again, at least tentatively, by Bonjour (2001), and also by Kosslyn (1983).
7. This view was advanced in Pollock (1986). For some related earlier accounts, see Kent Bach (1982), Romane Clark (1973), and David Woodruff Smith (1984,1986).
8. Here we are unabashedly assuming at least a weak version of the language of thought hypothesis (Fodor 1975), according to which thoughts can be viewed as having syntactic structure.
9. The statue is the work of Tony de Castro, of Tiradentes, Brazil.
10. This "cognitive" view of attention contrasts strongly with the familiar "mental spotlight" view, according to which attention picks out a region of the visual field and we attend to everything in it. That is not a correct account of attention in general because, for example, I can attend to the color of the apple without attending to its shape.
11. John Pollock has been pursuing this question for thirty years. For his most recent proposal, see Pollock (2002).
12. It seems obvious to us that colors do not have unique "correct" looks, but Michael Tye (2000) commits himself to the view that if a color looks different to different people then at most one of them can have it right.
13. For some recent work along these lines, see Duygulu et al. (2002), Barnard et al. (2003), Barnard et al (2003a), Belongie et al. (2002), Yu *et al.* (2001).
14. These are Q&I ("quick and inflexible") modules, in the sense of Pollock (1989), (1995), and Pollock & Cruz (1999). Their role in induction has been discussed in all these places.

References

Bach, Kent 1982 "De re belief and methodological solipsism". In *Thought and Object: Essays on Intentionality*, ed. Andrew Woodfield. Oxford: Oxford University Press.

Barnard, Kobus, Pinar Duygulu, Nando de Freitas, David Forsyth, David Blei, and Michael I. Jordan 2003 "Matching Words and Pictures," *Journal of Machine Learning Research*, Vol. 3, pp 1107–1135.

Barnard, Kobus, Pinar Duygulu, Raghavendra Guru, Prasad Gabbur, and David Forsyth 2003a "The effects of segmentation and feature choice in a translation model of object recognition", in Danielle Martin (ed), *Computer Vision and Pattern Recognition*, vol II, 675–684. IEEE Press.

Belongie, Serge, Jitendra Malik, and Jan Puzicha 2002 "Shape matching and object recognition using shape contexts", *IEEE Trans. on Pattern Analysis and Machine Intelligence* 24, 509–522.

Biederman, I. 1985 "Human image understanding: Recent research and a theory." *Computer Vision, Graphics, and Image Processing* 32: 29–73.

Bonjour, Lawrence 2001 "Toward a defense of empirical foundationalism", in Michael R. Depaul (ed.), *Resurrecting Old-Fashioned Foundationalism.* Lanham, Maryland: Rowman and Littlefield.

Bornstein, M. H., Kessen, W., & Weiskopf, S. 1976 "Color vision and hue categorization in young human infants". *Journal of Experimental Psychology: Human Perception & Performance*, 2(1), 115–129.

Byrne, Alex and David R. Hilbert 2003 "Color realism and color science", *Behavioral and Brain Sciences* 26.

Clark, Romane 1973 "Sensuous judgments". *Nous* 7, 45–56.

Davidson, Donald 1983 "A coherentist theory of truth and knowledge". D. Henrich (ed.), *Kant oder Hegel.* Suttgart: Klett-Cotta.

Duygulu, Pinar, Kobus Barnard, Nando de Freitas, and David Forsyth 2002 "Object recognition as machine translation: Learning a lexicon for a fixed image vocabulary", *Seventh European Conference on Computer Vision*, pp IV:97–112.

Fairchild, Mark D. 1998 *Color Appearance Models.* Reading, Mass: Addison-Wesley.

Faugeras, O. 1993 *Three-Dimensional Computer Vision: A Geometric Viewpoint.* Cambridge, MA: MIT Press.

Fodor, J. A. 1975 *The Language of Thought.* Cambridge: Harvard University Press.

Gibson, J. 1966 *The Senses considered as Perceptual Systems.* Boston: Houghton Mifflin.

Hoffman, D. 1998 *Visual Intelligence: How We Create What We See.* New York. W.W. Norton & Company.

Huemer, Michael 2001 *Skepticism and the Veil of Perception.* Lanham, Maryland: Rowman and Littlefield.

Hurvich, L M. 1981 *Color Vision.* Sinauer Associates Inc.

Hurvich, L. M., D. Jameson & J. Cohen 1968 "The experimental determination of unique green in the spectrum". *Perception and Psychophysics* 4, 65–68.

Kosslyn, S. M. 1983 *Ghosts in the Mind's Machine*, New York: Norton.

Lindsey, D. T., & Brown, A. M. 2002 "Color naming and the phototoxic effects of sunlight on the eye". *Psychological Science*, 13(6), 506–512.

Marr, D. 1982 *Vision.* San Francisco: Freeman.

McCarthy, John 1986 "Applications of circumscription to formalizing common sense knowledge." *Artificial Intelligence* 26, 89–116.

McDermott, Drew 1982 "A temporal logic for reasoning about processes and plans", *Cognitive Science* 6, 101–155.

McGinn, C. 1983 *The Subjective View: Secondary Qualities and Indexical Thoughts.* Oxford University Press: Oxford.

Merbs, S. L. and J. Nathans 1992 "Absorption spectra of human cone pigments" *Nature* 356, 433–35.

Neitz, M. and J. Neitz 1998 "Molecular genetics and the biological basis of color vision". In *Color Vision: Perspectives from Different Disciplines*, (eds) W. Backhaus, R. Kliegl and J. S. Werner. Walter de Gruyter.

Pallis, C. A. 1995 "Impaired identification of faces and places with agnosia for colors". *Journal of Neurology, Neurosurgery and Psychiatry* 18, 218–224.

Pollock, John 1971 "Perceptual Knowledge", *Philosophical Review* 80, 287–319.

1974 *Knowledge and Justification*, Princeton University Press.

1986 *Contemporary Theories of Knowledge*, Rowman and Littlefield.

1989 *How to Build a Person*, Cambridge, MA: Bradford/MIT Press.

1995 *Cognitive Carpentry*, MIT Press.

1998 "Perceiving and reasoning about a changing world", *Computational Intelligence* 14, 498–562.

2002 "Defeasible reasoning with variable degrees of justification", *Artificial Intelligence* 133, 233–282.

2006 "Irrationality and cognition", in *Topics in Contemporary Philosophy*, ed. Joseph Campbell and Michael O'Rourke, MIT Press.

Pollock, John, and Joseph Cruz 1999 *Contemporary Theories of Knowledge*, 2nd edition, Lanham, Maryland: Rowman and Littlefield.

Pryor, James 2000 "The skeptic and the dogmatist", *Noûs* 34, 517–549.

Pylyshyn, Zenon 1999 "Is vision continuous with cognition? The case for Cognitive impenetrability of visual perception", *Behavioral and Brain Sciences* 22, 341–423.

Quinton, Anthony 1973 *The Nature of Things*, London: Routledge and Kegan Paul.

Sandewall, Erik 1972 "An approach to the frame problem and its implementation". In B. Metzer & D. Michie (eds.), *Machine Intelligence 7*. Edinburgh: Edinburgh University Press.

Sellars, Wilfrid 1963 "Empiricism and the philosophy of mind." Reprinted in *Science, Perception, and Reality*, New York: Humanities Press; London: Routledge & Kegan Paul.

Smith, David Woodruff 1984 "Content and context of perception". *Synthese* 61, 61–87.

1986 "The ins and outs of perception". *Philosophical Studies* 49, 187–212.

Sosa, Ernest 1981 The raft and the pyramid: coherence versus foundations in the theory of knowledge. *Midwest Studies in Philosophy*, vol. 5, pp. 3–26. Minneapolis: University of Minnesota Press.

Thompson, E. A., A. Palacios & F. J. Varela 1992 "Ways of coloring: Comparative color vision as a case study for cognitive science". *Behavioral and Brain Sciences* 15, 1–74.

Tye, Michael 2000 *Consciousness, Color, and Content*. Cambridge: MIT Press.

Ullman, S. 1996 *High-level Vision: Object Recognition and Visual Cognition*. Cambridge, MA: MIT Press.

Yu, Yizhou, Andras Ferencz, and Jitendra Malik 2001 *IEEE Trans. on Visualization and Computer Graphics* 7, 351–364.

Philosophical Perspectives, 19, Epistemology, 2005

CONTENT ASCRIPTIONS AND THE REVERSIBILITY CONSTRAINT

Richard Price
All Souls College, University of Oxford

We often make content ascriptions to subjects that are assertable despite being literally false, in the sense that the subject does not literally have the content that we are ascribing to them. The ascriptions are close enough to the truth, and in the conversational context it is convenient to be a little loose in one's content ascriptions. In this paper, I shall give some examples of one kind of non-literal content ascription, and then propose a constraint, which I call the reversibility constraint, which distinguishes instances of this kind of non-literal content ascription from literal content ascriptions. I will then apply this constraint to looks-statements, and argue that the reversibility constraint can help us decide which looks-statements report the contents of visual experiences, and which do not. I will argue for the conclusion that 'that apple looks to the left of me' does not report the content of my visual experience when I do not see myself.

I.

In this section I discuss examples of non-literal content ascriptions.

I might know that Peter, who is not in the conversation, believes that the UK has a population of 60 million. It might be salient to you and me in the conversational context that France has a population of 60 million. If you ask me 'what does Peter believe the population of the UK is?', I might trade on the established link in the conversation between the figure of 60 million and the population of France and answer 'Peter believes that the UK has the same population as France', even though we both understand that I am not trying to communicate that Peter believes the proposition that the UK has the same population as France. Here I am using the phrase 'same population as France' as a way of picking out the population that Peter believes the UK to have. What you understand me as communicating is really that the population of France is what Peter believes the population of the UK to be.

I am assuming here that the only reading of the sentence 'Peter believes that the UK has the same population as France' is the one on which Peter believes the proposition expressed by its embedded sentence, i.e. the proposition that the UK has the same population as France. Call this the *de dicto* reading of the content ascription. One might wonder whether 'Peter believes that the UK has the same population as France' has as a literal reading 'The population of France is the same as what Peter believes the population of the UK to be'. Call the latter reading the *de re* reading of the content ascription. I will be assuming in what follows that 'Peter believes that the UK has the same population as France' has *only* the de dicto reading, and therefore is literally false in the context described above. If you think that 'Peter believes that the UK has the same population as France' has a de re reading, then you should understand my claim as being that that sentence does not have, in the specified context, a true de dicto reading. The same goes for the examples I give below. And instead of understanding the constraint I will develop as I do, namely as a way of distinguishing instances of one kind of non-literal content ascription from literal content ascriptions, you should understand it as distinguishing instances of one kind of content ascription which do not have true de dicto readings from content ascriptions that do have true de dicto readings.

I will now give a series of other examples of content ascriptions that I take to be literally false. The first is very similar to the one above. If it is salient to us that Bill Clinton thinks that the population of France is 60 million, then when you ask 'What population does Peter think that the UK has?', in response to your question I might say 'Peter believes that the UK has the same population as Bill Clinton thinks France has'. Again in saying that I may not think that Peter has any views about the population that Bill Clinton thinks France has. What you understand me as communicating is really that the population that Bill Clinton thinks France has is the population that Peter believes that the UK has.

Let's say that we both know that Peter only lets short people into his car, say a Mini, and I know that Peter believes that Mary is 170 cm tall. We have been discussing Clive, whom we both know Peter has never heard of. It has come up in discussion between us that Clive is 160 cm tall. Since you know Peter, you tell me that Clive is too tall a person for Peter to allow in his car. You ask me whether Peter would let Mary into his car. I know that Peter thinks that Mary is 170 cm tall, and I respond to your question by saying 'No, Peter wouldn't let Mary into his car, because he believes that Mary is taller than Clive'. When I say this, we both understand that I do not intend to communicate that Peter believes the proposition that Mary is taller than Clive. Rather, given that you know that Peter has never heard of Clive, you understand me as communicating that Clive's height is less than the height that Peter believes that Mary has. My belief report gives you enough information to answer your question, namely whether Peter would let Mary into his car, but not so much as to tell you the specific height property that Peter believes Mary to have.

I might know that Peter thinks that Mary is very generous. To be poetic and dramatic, I might report what Peter believes by saying 'Peter believes that Mary is more generous than Santa Claus', even though I do not mean to convey that Peter believes the proposition that Mary is more generous than Santa Claus. You understand me as communicating that Santa Claus is less generous than Peter believes Mary to be.

Let us say that we need to know where Peter thinks his son is, because we know that Peter will travel to where he thinks his son is, and we need to get in touch with Peter. The two options that we are considering for where Peter believes his son to be are: at the playground, and near The Cutty Sark. I know that Peter believes that his son is at the harbor. Since the harbor is, in fact, near The Cutty Sark, I choose not to report Peter's belief precisely, but to adopt the terminology of the conversation, and I say 'Peter believes his son is near The Cutty Sark'. I choose to report Peter's belief content quite roughly because there is no practical risk involved; a more literal belief report would produce the same course of action as my actual report, and my actual report fits with the established terminology of the conversation. If everyone understands that, when there is no practical risk involved, specific belief contents might get expressed loosely, then when they hear my belief report, they will understand me as communicating that a place near The Cutty Sark is where Peter believes that his son to be.

We can imagine a case just like the one in the paragraph above except where the options for where Peter thinks his son is are Oxford and London. I may know that Peter believes that his son is in Leicester Square, which is in London, and I might report that by saying 'Peter believes that his son is in London', even though, for all I know, Peter might not have a view on whether Leicester Square is in London.

We can use examples similar to those above to generate non-literal assertion reports, or desire reports, or intention reports. When Peter said that the population of the UK is 60 million, and it is salient in the conversational context to both of us that France has a population of 60 million, I might trade on this link and say 'Peter said that the population of the UK was the same as the population of France'. When Peter said that Mary was 170 cm tall, and it is salient between us that Clive is 160 cm tall, then I might say 'Peter won't let Mary into his car because he said that Mary was taller than Clive'. As long as it is understood by everyone that Peter has never heard of Clive, what I will be understood as communicating is that Clive's height is less than the height that Peter said Mary had. If Peter wants Mary to be very generous, I might say, in a dramatic way, 'Peter wanted Mary to be more generous than Santa Claus'.

II.

I have given examples of one kind of non-literal content ascription, and in this paper I shall focus only on this kind. I will now argue for a constraint that distinguishes instances of this kind of non-literal content ascription from literal content ascriptions. Consider the situation above in which Peter believes that Mary is 170 cm tall, and given the salience of Clive's height in the conversational context, I report Peter's belief by saying 'Peter believes that Mary is taller than Clive'. What demonstrates that this is a non-literal belief report is that, although Mary is believed by Peter to be some way, it is not the case that Clive is believed by Peter to be some way. The thought here is that if Peter really believes that Mary is taller than Clive, then Mary is believed by Peter to be some way (i.e. taller than Clive), and Clive is believed by Peter to be some way (i.e. such that Mary is taller than him). The fact that this constraint is not met in the context when I utter 'Peter believes that Mary is taller than Clive' demonstrates that the content ascription is not literally true (I am assuming that the content ascription does not have a de re reading, though, if you thought that it did, you should understand the point of the constraint as demonstrating that the content ascription does not have a true de dicto reading).

In general, then, the constraint is this: if Peter believes that A bears relation R to B, then A is believed by Peter to be some way, and B is believed by Peter to be some way. We can use this constraint to show why the other belief reports discussed in section I are non-literal. Consider the example where Peter believes that the UK has a population of 60 million, and, trading on the established link in the conversation between the figure of 60 million and the population of France, I report what Peter believes by saying 'Peter believes that the UK has the same population as France'. In this case, although the UK is believed to be some way by Peter, it is not the case that France is believed to be some way by Peter. If 'Peter believes that the UK has the same population as France' was a literal belief report in this context, the UK would be believed by Peter to be some way, and France would be believed by Peter to be some way.

In another example, although I know that Peter believes that his son is at the harbor, trading on certain facts about the conversational context, I say 'Peter believes that his son is near The Cutty Sark'. What demonstrates that this is a non-literal belief report is that it is not the case that The Cutty Sark is believed by Peter to be such that his son is near it.

As we saw, for all the cases of non-literal belief reports, there are cases of non-literal assertion reports that work in just the same way. A similar explanation can be given of why these assertion reports are also non-literal. For instance, when Peter said that the population of the UK was 60 million, and trading on certain facts about the conversational context, I say 'Peter said that the UK had the same population as France', what demonstrates this to be a non-literal assertion report is that, although the UK was said by Peter to be some way, it is not the case that France was said by Peter to be some way.

The constraint that we have identified seems to hold for all representational content, and I formulate it below as such. This is a reason to think that the constraint holds for all representational content, and I formulate it below as such. The main aim of this paper is to apply the constraint to the contents of perceptual experiences to explore what consequences it has for those contents. I express the constraint as follows:

> **Reversibility Constraint**: Necessarily, if A is represented as bearing R to B, then B is represented as being such that A bears R to it.

The way I am understanding this constraint is as follows. 'A' and 'B' here are singular terms. In the phrase 'A is represented as bearing R to B', 'A' is outside of the scope of 'is represented', and in the phrase 'B is represented as being such that A bears R to it', 'B' is outside of the scope of 'is represented'. It is important that 'A' and 'B' in the constraint are singular terms, since the constraint would not hold if they were definite or indefinite descriptions. For instance, suppose that Katie is believed by David to have visited a foreign country; from this it does not follow that a foreign country is believed by David to be such that Katie has visited it, where 'a foreign country' is outside of the scope of 'is believed'; for a foreign country to be believed by David to be such that Katie has visited it, where 'foreign country' is outside the scope of 'is believed', it would follow that a foreign country exists, whereas it does not follow from Katie's believing that David has visited a foreign country that a foreign country exists.

III.

In this section I shall apply the reversibility constraint to looks-statements. I assume that there are at least some looks-statements that report the contents of visual experiences. In fact, the most natural way to introduce the phrase 'the contents of visual experiences' is by appealing to the notion of the ways objects look. An object can look a certain way to a subject, and if the object is the way it looks to the subject, then we say that the subject's experience is veridical, and if the object is not the way it looks to the subject, we say that the subject's experience is non-veridical.

There is a question concerning which looks-statements report the contents of visual experiences. It is plausible, for instance, that 'O looks square to S' can report the content of a particular experience of S. It is also very intuitive that some looks-statements do not report the content of experience. For instance, occasionally we use perceptual verbs even when we are having no experiences of the relevant sense-modality. Derek and Jody might be arguing in the dark, and Jody says to Derek 'it looks as though you are in agreement with Russell' and Derek replies 'I see what you mean'. Here the perceptual verbs are being used to report acts of understanding and not the contents of Derek's and Jody's visual experiences. Derek might be listening to the radio, and on the basis of the radio report say 'it looks as though there are going to be elections in Afghanistan';

again the looks-statement here seems to have nothing in particular to do with the contents of Derek's visual experience at the time.

Given that there are looks-statements that do seem to report the contents of visual experiences, and those that do not, the question arises as to how to decide which ones do and which ones do not. The presence of a perceptual verb in the report is clearly not the deciding factor. And although in some cases it might be intuitively clear whether the looks-statement reports the content of experience, in many cases it is highly contentious. Some philosophers, for instance Christopher Peacocke (1983), think that 'O looks to Adam to be a tomato' can report the content of Adam's visual experience (Siegel (2005) is sympathetic to this view as well), and other philosophers, for instance Colin McGinn (1982), Tyler Burge (2002), and Alan Millar (2000) disagree.

Philosophers in the latter camp take the view that the only looks-statements that report the contents of visual experience are those that concern a very sparse range of properties, for instance, color, shape, location and size properties. Philosophers in the former camp think that looks-statements concerning a much richer range of properties can report the contents of visual experiences (I should make it clear that, in this paper, I am using the word 'report' in the sense that, if a looks-statement reports the content of S's visual experience, then that looks-statement correctly reports the content of S's visual experience). For instance, a philosopher in this camp might hold that visual experiences could represent natural kind properties, such as the property of being water, artificial kind properties, such as the property of being a table, semantic properties, such as the property of meaning *bachelor*, moral properties, such as the property of being good, mental state properties, such as the property of being in pain, and aesthetic properties, such as the property of being beautiful.

There is also a question as to what restrictions there might be on experience representing relations. For instance, suppose that you are looking at two chairs, and you say 'this chair looks to me the same height as that chair'. In a second case, suppose that you are looking at a building in front of you, and do not see the Eiffel Tower, and you say 'this building looks to me the same height as the Eiffel Tower'. Both of these are relational looks-statements, but in one case you see both the relata, and in the other case you see only one of the relata; and the question is whether they both report the content of your visual experience in the above contexts. In the rest of this paper I will be arguing that the second looks-statement does not report the content of your experience in the above context, on the grounds that you do not see both the relata in question. I will then discuss the implications of this point for the debate over which looks-statements report the content of experience and which do not.

We saw above that the reversibility constraint applies to the contents of beliefs, desires, assertions and intentions, and we noted that, given its broad application, there is a reason to think that it applies to all cases of representational content, including the contents of perceptual experiences. One might try to argue that, since the content of experience is non-conceptual, and the content of beliefs and desires is conceptual, terms which I will define below, one should not expect experiences and beliefs to obey the same constraints. This argument would be powerful if it could be shown that there was an explanatory connection between a content's being conceptual and the content's satisfying the reversibility constraint. This would challenge the presumption that the contents of perceptual experiences, which are arguably non-conceptual, satisfy the reversibility constraint. However, in the absence of such an explanatory connection between conceptualism and reversibility, the presumption that the reversibility constraint applies to the contents of perceptual experiences, given that it applies to all other kinds of content we have considered, should remain.

In fact, there is good reason to deny any link between a state's satisfying the reversibility constraint and its having conceptual content. On the standard definition, a state has conceptual content iff being in that state requires the subject of the state to possess the concepts that canonically characterize that content. For this way of thinking about conceptual content, see Gareth Evans (1982, p 159), Adrian Cussins (1990, p 382–383). According to this definition, there is at least one kind of state that satisfies the reversibility constraint and is, arguably, non-conceptual, namely the state of saying that p. On one view, you can say that p without having the concepts that characterize the content that p. For instance, consider someone who falsely thinks the word 'red' means *green*, and who does not have the concept *red*. When they point at a green tablecloth and say 'that tablecloth is red', of course what they *mean* to say is that the tablecloth is green, but according to this view, what they actually say is that the tablecloth is red. This is why we are inclined, according to this view, to say that what they said is false. If this view is correct, and it does seem plausible, then the subject does not have the concepts that characterize what they said, and hence the state of saying what they in fact said is a non-conceptual state. And if the state of saying that p is a non-conceptual state, then, given that assertions satisfy the reversibility constraint, there is no essential connection between a state satisfying the reversibility constraint and a state having conceptual content.

Let us now apply the reversibility constraint to the two relational looks-statements that you utter:

1) 'this chair looks to me the same height as that chair' (where you see both chairs)
2) 'this building looks to me the same height as the Eiffel Tower' (where you see what is referred to by 'this building', but do not see the Eiffel Tower).

I am assuming here that 'The Eiffel Tower' is a name, and so the reversibility constraint, which applies only to content-ascriptions involving singular terms, does indeed apply to 2.). The reversibility constraint entails that 2.) does not report the content of your visual experience. This is because for the looks-statement to satisfy the reversibility constraint, it must be possible to reverse the order of the relata in the looks-statement and say how the second relatum looks to you to be. That is, if it is true that this building looks to you the same height as the Eiffel Tower, it must be true that the Eiffel Tower looks to you such that this building is the same height as it. However, when you do not see the Eiffel Tower, the Eiffel Tower does not look any way to you at all. Let us call this the 'seeing rule': if x looks F to S, and 'x' is outside the scope of the 'looks', then S sees x. The seeing rule seems intuitively plausible, and in this paper I shall assume that it is correct. If there was an analogue of the seeing rule for beliefs it would be this: if x is believed by S to be F, and 'x' is outside the scope of the 'is believed', then S is *acquainted* with x. But I will not be relying on this rule about belief being correct, because the notion of acquaintance is hard to spell out.

Since 2.) does not satisfy the reversibility constraint, it does not report the content of your visual experience. 1.), by contrast, is reversible. Since you see both chairs, you can reverse the order of the relata in the looks-statement and say how the second chair looks to you to be; you can say 'that chair looks to me to be such that this chair is the same height as it'. So it is an open possibility that 1.) reports the content of your visual experience.

One might respond at this stage and say that the correct way of reporting the contents of visual experiences is by using the operators 'it looks to me to be the case that', 'it is seen by me to be the case that', or 'I see that' (for this application the latter two operators would have to be understood, non-standardly, as non-factive, to allow for the possibility of non-veridical visual contents). So, for instance, 2.) would be re-phrased as 'I see that this building is the same height as the Eiffel Tower'. And one might argue that that this statement is reversible within the scope of the 'I see that' operator. For instance, one can reverse the order of the relata within the scope of the 'I see that' operator and say 'I see that the Eiffel Tower is the same height as this building'.

However, this is not an application of the reversibility constraint as formulated, but rather a weaker version of it. If Jane believes that A bears relation R to B, the requirements of the reversibility constraint are that one can say how each relatum is believed to be, not simply that one can reverse the order of the relata within the scope of the 'believes that' operator. That is, if Jane believes that A bears relation R to B, then A must be believed by Jane to be some way, and B must be believed by Jane to be some way. Recall the example above in which I say 'Peter believes that Mary is taller than Clive', when Peter has never heard of Clive. Nothing I have said rules out the possibility that, in the same conversational context, I could reverse the order of the relata within the scope of the 'believes that' operator and say 'Peter believes that Clive is shorter than Mary', where this second belief report would still be a non-literal one. I do not want to take a stand on whether this kind of reversal within the scope of the 'believes that' operator is possible for non-literal belief reports. What I am claiming is that if Jane believes that A bears relation R to B, then A is believed by Jane to be some way, and B is believed by Jane to be some way.

So, let us suppose that one's preferred way of reporting the contents of visual experiences was by using the operator 'I see that'. If you see that A bears a relation R to B, then the reversibility constraint entails that A is seen by you to be some way, and B is seen by you to be some way. So, the correct application of the reversibility constraint shows that, when you do not see the Eiffel Tower, the sentence 'I see that this building is the same height as the Eiffel Tower' does not report the content of your visual experience, since the Eiffel Tower is not seen by you to be any way at all.

IV.

In this section I shall discuss some further applications of the reversibility constraint. I shall argue that the reversibility constraint rules out, in most cases, one's experiences from representing objects as having observer-relative properties. An observer-relative property is a property of bearing a certain relation to the observer. For instance, if I am the observer, such properties include the property of being to the left of me, the property of being in front of me, the property of being far away from me, and the property of being circular and at a slant from me. Although it is very natural to think that visual experiences do represent these properties, I shall argue that in most circumstances they do not.

Consider the relational looks-statement 'this apple looks to me to the left of me'. According to the reversibility constraint, this looks-statement reports the content of a visual experience only if one can reverse the relata and say 'I look to me to be such that this apple is to the left of me'. However, if I do not see myself, then I do not look any way to myself at all. So, in those cases in which I do not see myself, 'this apple looks to the left of me' is ruled out from reporting the content of my visual experience. The reversibility constraint also entails that 'this apple looks to me far away from me' is ruled out from reporting the content of my experience when I do not see myself. The same points apply to the looks-statements 'this apple looks in front of me', 'this coin looks to me circular and at a slant from me' and 'this apple looks 120 degrees from me'; when I do not see myself, none of these looks-statements are reversible, and so do not report the contents of my visual experiences.

One might think that the reversibility constraint allows the sentence 'A looks further away than B' to report the content of experience, if A and B are both seen. But in fact this statement is elliptical for 'A looks further away *from me* than B', and this statement is not reversible if I do not see myself. Similarly, if one sees A and B, one might think that 'A looks to the left of B' can report the content of experience; however, this sentence is elliptical for 'A looks further to *my* left than B', and this statement is not reversible if I do not see myself.

The reversibility constraint rules out all observer-relative properties from featuring in the content of one's visual experience when one does not see oneself. This conclusion raises a question about what position properties visual experience does represent, since it is very intuitive that visual experience does indeed represent position properties; for instance, sometimes a red square looks in a different position at t_1 and t_2. I do not address this question in this paper, but leave it to further work.

V.

In this section I shall consider some objections to the argument in the above two sections. Different objections focus on different aspects of the argument. The first objection concerns the way in which I have applied the reversibility constraint to derive the conclusion that objects do not look to the left of me when I do not see myself. My argument was that, when I do not see myself, the statement 'this apple looks to me to the left of me' does not report the content of my visual experience because the looks-statement is not reversible: it is not the case that I look to myself to be such that this apple is to the left of me. The objector agrees that, when I do not see myself, I do not look to myself to be such that this apple is to the left of me. However, the objector claims that I am proprioceptively perceived by myself to be such that this apple is to the left of me. In other words, although I am not seen to be any way at all, when I do not see myself, I am proprioceptively perceived by myself to be such that this apple is to the left of me.

It may well be true that I am proprioceptively perceived by myself to be such that this apple is to the left of me. However, this will not enable the looks-statement 'this apple looks to the left of me' to report the content of my visual experience. The reversibility constraint requires that if, say, Peter believes that the US is larger than the UK, then the US is believed by Peter to be some way, and the UK is believed by Peter to be some way. It is not enough for the reversibility constraint to be met in this case that the UK be merely hoped to be some way, or seen to be some way, or otherwise represented to be some way; the UK has to be *believed* to be some way. Similarly, for 'this apple looks to me to the left of me' to satisfy the reversibility constraint, it is not sufficient that I be somehow represented to myself to be such that this apple is to the left of me; rather I have to look to myself to be such that this object is to the left of me. The reversed attitude-ascription has to involve the same attitude as the original, unreversed attitude-ascription.

A second objection agrees with my conclusion that objects do not look to the left of me when I do not see myself, but argues that there is a fall-back option, namely that objects look to me (monadically) to the left, or in front, or at a certain distance. The proponent of this objection does not hold that there exists a property of being to the left. Rather, the objection is that the state of affairs of something's being to the left of me has two modes of presentation in visual experience, a monadic mode of presentation and a relational mode of presentation. Under the monadic mode of presentation, the object is simply presented as to the left. Under the relational mode of presentation, the object is presented as being to the left of me. The objector is suggesting that experience represents objects as being simply to the left, but this monadic mode of presentation determines a relational veridicality-condition, namely being to the left of me. The suggestion that objects look to the left *simpliciter* is made by John Campbell (1994, p119); the use of modes of presentation is my development of the suggestion.

One way of thinking of these modes of presentation is along Fregean lines. These modes of presentation are Fregean senses that appear elsewhere in the contents of thoughts. This would be an unattractive way of developing the idea, since there are powerful arguments for thinking that the content of perceptual experiences is non-conceptual (see Evans (1982), Peacocke (2001), Heck (2000), Campbell (2002)). To avoid a conflict with these arguments, the modes of presentation should be taken to be non-conceptual modes of presentation.

How should we decide whether a given relational state of affairs has two non-conceptual modes of presentation or not? Frege gave a sufficient condition for introducing modes of presentation, according to which, if you could rationally doubt that Hesperus was Phosphorus, it followed that 'Hesperus' and 'Phosphorus' had different modes of presentation. However, assuming that the content of experience is non-conceptual, then what you can rationally doubt will not be a constraint on the contents of your experiences. The proponent of this objection would need some equivalent criterion that we could use to decide when to introduce non-conceptual modes of presentation. One option is that they draw on the reversibility constraint. They could argue that, when we are apprised of all the relevant facts, if we are prepared to assert 'A looks to bear R to B', and we do not see B, then the state of affairs of A bearing R to B is being visually represented in a monadic way. In other words, a more accurate report of how things look would be to say 'A looks R-ish', where 'R-ish' is a non-conceptual mode of presentation that picks out the state of affairs of bearing R to B.

This proposal cannot be right, since, recalling an example we considered above, Derek and Jody might be arguing in the dark, and Jody might say to Derek 'it looks as though you are in agreement with Russell'; it is clear here that the combination of this sentence being uttered when the speaker is apprised of all the relevant facts, together with the fact that Russell is not seen, does not entail that Jody's visual experience represents via a monadic mode of presentation the state of affairs of being in agreement with Russell; quite apart from anything else, Jody may not be having any visual experiences at all at the time.

Another criterion for introducing non-conceptual modes of presentation that the proponent of non-conceptual modes of presentation could offer is this: if there can be phenomenally different ways in which a visual experience can represent a given property, then this is sufficient for there to be non-conceptual modes of presentation of this property in visual experience. Let us consider an example. Suppose that you can visually represent someone as being taller*, where the non-conceptual mode of presentation taller* picks out the state of affairs of being taller than Tony Blair. Suppose now that you in fact see Bill Clinton and Tony Blair standing next to each other. The challenge to the proponent of non-conceptual modes of presentation is to say what the perceptual difference is between representing the scene before you via the relational mode of presentation, and representing the scene before you via the monadic mode of presentation. That is, as you look at the scene before you, containing Bill Clinton and Tony Blair, the challenge is to explain what sort of phenomenal difference in your experiences we might expect to occur as your experiences go from representing this state of affairs via the monadic mode of representation, taller*, to representing the state of affairs via the relational mode of presentation, taller than Tony Blair.

The proponent of non-conceptual modes of presentation could argue that no such change is possible, since whenever you represent the relational mode of presentation you represent the relevant monadic mode of presentation too. This would be a slightly odd consequence, since it would mean that one could never represent the particular state of affairs in question purely relationally. A stronger objection, however, is that, even if representing the relational mode of presentation entails representing the monadic mode of presentation, they are still distinct modes of presentation, and when they are both present, we should be able to distinguish them as different features of our experience. So the perceptual difference objection presented in the previous paragraph does not require something as strong as the possibility of representing the relational mode of presentation *without* representing the monadic mode of presentation. In fact all that the perceptual difference objection requires is that when the two modes of presentation are present together, one should be able to say what the perceptual difference is between them. Indeed, since we think we have fairly reliable introspective access to the contents of our experiences, it should be obvious to us what this perceptual difference is. The lack of any obvious perceptual difference between these modes of presentation in our experiences is therefore evidence against the hypothesis that they are there.

Similar points can be made for the case where 'taller*' is replaced by 'to the left'; the parallel challenge would then be to say, when an apple is to the left of S, and S sees both the apple *and* herself, what the perceptual difference is between S's representing the state of affairs of the apple being to the left of her via a relational mode of presentation, and representing that state of affairs via a monadic mode of presentation. I should make it clear that this is not a general argument against the existence of non-conceptual modes of presentation; it is just an argument that, in this particular case, there is a challenge facing the person who wants to introduce them.

A third objection to my argument concerns the applicability of the reversibility constraint to the content of experience at all. The objector argues as follows. There must be a time index in the content of experience. After all, if my experience represents that this apple is green, my experience is not made veridical by this apple being green at some time in the past or future. My experience is veridical only if the apple is green now. Therefore my experience represents that this apple is green now. And 'now' picks out a relation to a time. Therefore the lengthened version of the content of my experience is: this apple is green at t. 't' here refers to the time of the experience. So we can say that 'this apple looks green at t' reports the content of my experience. But, the objection continues, this looks-statement is not reversible. We cannot reverse it and say that t looks to me to be such that this apple is green at it. Therefore, the objection continues, the reversibility constraint does not apply to visual experience.

One way to respond to this challenge would be to allow that my experience represents that this apple is green now, but deny that 'now' picks out a relation to a time. One could be a nominalist and continue to describe events as happening 'now', but deny that there are entities, times, that things stand in the 'at' relation to.

However, I will not pursue this nominalist line of response. My answer to this challenge is to deny that the content of experience involves reference to a time. By 'the content of experience', we mean the way things look. And it seems a very intuitive idea that we can ask of this apple 'was it yesterday the way it now looks?'. The intelligibility of this question requires that the way the apple now looks does not include a reference to a time. If it did include a reference to a time, such as green today, then asking, of the apple yesterday, whether it was green today, would get us the wrong results. Yesterday, the apple was green today just in case it is green today. How the apple is *today* is not the question that was being asked by 'was the apple yesterday the way it now looks?'. The meaning of the question left it open that the apple might have been yesterday the way it now looks even though it is not today the way it now looks. For the question to be intelligible in this way, the properties that the apple looks to have cannot include a time index.

The objector's motivation for introducing temporal properties into the content of experience was to prevent the content of experience being made accidentally veridical by the apple being green at some point in the past or future. However, this problem is removed if we use the notion of 'is the way it looks' instead of 'veridical'. For we can ask 'is the apple the way it looks?', where we are explicitly asking whether the apple has *now* the set of properties that it looks to have, and so there is no danger of how the apple was yesterday or two years ago affecting the answer to this question. In other words, one can avoid the problem of accidental veridicality by being careful about how we use the notion of something's being the way it looks. We can ask whether an apple is the way it looks, or whether it was the way it looks, or whether it will be the way it looks. Each question will receive an answer that is unaffected by the answers to the other questions, thereby avoiding the accidental veridicality problem.

A fourth way of responding to my argument is to accept the result of the reversibility constraint that my visual experiences do not represent the property of being to the left of me, when I do not see myself, but argue that there is a fall-back option. Perhaps visual experience represents the property of being to the left of the observer at the center of *this* region of space, where 'this' picks out a region of space of which the observer is at the center, and which, according to the suggestion, the observer does indeed see. Of course, we need some answer to the question of exactly which region of space this is, and we need to be convinced that the observer does indeed see it. But the key point, as far as the reversibility constraint is concerned, is that the observer is picked out with a description, rather than with a singular term. And given that the reversibility constraint applies only to looks-statements that involve singular terms, if a particular cup looks to me to be to the left of the observer at the center of this region of space, it is not required by the reversibility constraint that the observer at the center of this region of space look to me to be such that the cup is to the left of it. All that is required by the reversibility constraint is that this region of space looks to me to be some way.

In responding to this suggestion I shall focus on the more general question that this suggestion raises. The more general question concerns what one should say about cases in which x looks to S to bear a relation R to the F, where 'the F' is a definite description and what it picks out is not seen by S. A related question concerns what one should say about cases in which x looks to S to bear a relation R to an F, where an F is not seen by S. Given that we are interested in which looks-statements report the contents of experiences, the general issue here is whether visual experience has quantificational content. I will present an argument that there are certain quantificational contents that experiences do not have as part of their *non-conceptual* contents, and so there are certain looks-statements of the form 'x looks to S to bear a relation R to the F/an F', where the F/an F is not seen by S, that do not report the non-conceptual content of S's experience. In particular, I will argue that the looks-statement that is being offered by the proponent of the fourth objection does not report the non-conceptual contents of visual experience.

I want to distinguish at the outset two ways in which one might be tempted to think that experience has quantificational content. If one thinks that hallucinatory experiences have contents, one might be tempted to think that they have quantificational, existential contents, since they cannot have singular contents, because nothing is seen by the subject. According to this view, for instance, a given hallucination might represent that a red square is next to a green circle. Call this kind of content 'qualitative quantificational content'; I will explain the terminology below. A second way in which one might be tempted to ascribe quantificational contents to visual experiences is due to looks-statements such as 'Claire looks to me to be near the red boat', where the red boat is not seen by me (perhaps Claire is wearing a distinctive uniform), or 'Claire looks to me to be near a red boat', where a red boat is not seen by me. Call this 'non-qualitative quantificational content'. The qualitative and the non-qualitative kinds of quantificational content are distinct. Hallucinations, which we are supposing might have qualitative quantificational content, are qualitatively similar to experiences one has when objects one sees look to one to be certain ways. For instance, a case in which one hallucinates a red square next to a green circle is qualitatively similar to a case in which there are two objects, A and B, and A looks red and square to you and it looks to you to be next to B that looks green and circular to you. If any experiences have non-qualitative quantificational content, they are not like this. If Claire looks to me to be near the red boat, and the red boat is not seen by me, the experience that I am having at the time need be not at all qualitatively similar to the experience I have when I see Claire as being next to something that I see and that looks to me to be a red boat. When Claire looks to me to be near the red boat, and the red boat is not seen by me, there need be no reddish quality to my experiences at all, whereas when I hallucinate a red square next to a green circle, there is a reddish quality to my experience.

My main thesis, as far as the fourth objection goes, is that it is not possible for experience to have non-qualitative quantificational contents as part of its non-conceptual content. So it is not possible for looks-statements of the form 'Claire looks to me to be near the red boat', where the red boat is not seen by me, to report the non-conceptual contents of my visual experience, where the non-conceptual contents are those that your experiences can have without you, as the subject, having the concepts that canonically characterize them. I have four reasons for thinking this. Firstly, when there exists an object that looks red to me, I am having a suitable experience on the basis of which I could acquire the concept *red*. Similarly, a hallucination with qualitative quantificational content might well be a suitable experience on the basis of which I could acquire the concept *red*. But it seems that the sort of experience I am having when Claire looks to me to be near the red boat, and the red boat is not seen by me, is not the kind of experience on the basis of which I could acquire the concept *red*. The natural explanation of this is that for Claire to look to me to be near the red boat, where the red boat is not seen by me, I must have the concept *red* (and the concept *boat*) already. A second, related, reason is that it does not seem that 'Claire looks to me to be near the red boat', where the red boat is not seen by me, could be true unless previously some particular object had looked red to me, or I had had an experience with a qualitative quantificational content involving the property of being red. The natural explanation of this seems to be that the previous occasions of an object looking red to me, or me hallucinating something red, are necessary for me to acquire the concept *red*, which in turn I need to possess if some object is going to look to me to be near the red boat, when the red boat is not seen by me.

Thirdly, when it is appropriate to assert 'Claire looks to me to be near the red boat', when the red boat is not seen by me, there is always some story to be told about what I know or think that enables that looks-statement to be assertable. For instance, I might know that the uniform that Claire is wearing is the uniform that people from the red boat wear. Knowledge or thoughts of this kind about the red boat seem necessary for Claire to look to me to be near the red boat in the case described. To the extent that such knowledge is necessary for 'Claire looks to me to be near the red boat' to be true in the case described, that looks-statement cannot report the non-conceptual content of experience in that case. Fourthly, when I see something as red, I always see it as being some particular shade of red. Similarly, if you hallucinate a red square, you always hallucinate the square as being some particular shade of red. However, the same is not true for non-qualitative quantificational contents. When Claire looks to me to be near the red boat, it does not follow that there is some shade of red, red*, such that Claire looks to me to be near the red* boat. One could argue that there is a general ban on non-qualitative quantificational contents containing determinate color properties such as particular shades of red. But this strategy seems implausible. If you are a color expert, you might well say that Claire looks to you to be near the yellow ochre boat, when you do not see the yellow ochre boat. A better explanation of the frequent lack of determinacy in non-qualitative quantificational contents is that the story about the subject's beliefs or states of knowledge, described in the third reason above, that one has to tell in order to make the looks-statement in question assertable, does not usually involve the subject having thoughts or knowledge about determinate color properties that the un-seen object has. To the extent that this is the explanation for the frequent lack of determinacy in looks-statements involving non-qualitative quantificational content, it follows that 'Claire looks to me to be near the red boat' does not report the non-conceptual content of my experience in the case described.

These four reasons make it plausible that Claire can only look to me to be near the red boat, in the context described above, if I have the concept *red boat*, and therefore the sentence 'Claire looks to be near the red boat', uttered in that context, cannot report the non-conceptual content of my visual experience. We are now in a position to answer the fourth objection. The sentence 'this apple looks to me to be to the left of the observer at the center of this region of space', uttered when I do not see myself, and where the content being ascribed to me is a non-qualitatively quantificational one, does not report the non-conceptual content of my visual experience.

A consequence of saying that the non-conceptual contents of visual experience do not contain non-qualitative quantificational contents is that looks-statements such as 'this tomato looks to Glenn to have a back', where a back is not seen by Glenn, do not report the non-conceptual content of Glenn's experience (because looks-statements such as these ascribe to Glenn non-qualitative quantificational contents), and hence Glenn's visual experience does not non-conceptually represent the tomato as having a back. If Glenn's visual experience does not non-conceptually represent the tomato as having a back, then there is a case for saying that Glenn's visual experience does not non-conceptually represent the object as a tomato. This is because an intuitive condition of representing something as a tomato is representing it as a three-dimensional object, and an intuitive condition of representing something as a three-dimensional object is representing it as having a back. Thus, to the extent that Glenn's visual experience does not non-conceptually represent the tomato as having a back, it does not non-conceptually represent the tomato as being a tomato. Perhaps there is a position in logical space for the view on which one's visual experiences can non-conceptually represent something as being a tomato without representing it as having a back, but it seems that if the non-conceptual contents of visual experiences are so sparse as to include not even the property of having a back, it is not clear what motivation would remain for saying that the non-conceptual contents of visual experiences include the property of being a tomato.

A fifth objection to the conclusion that observer-relative properties do not feature in the content of experience when we do not see ourselves is that this is such a counter-intuitive conclusion that it constitutes a *reductio ad absurdum* of the applicability of the reversibility constraint to the content of experience. I do agree that the validity of a constraint should be assessed against the plausibility of its consequences, but in this particular case, I believe that the conclusion that observer-relative properties do not feature in the content of experience to be independently justified by at least two other arguments, which I give below.

The problem of defining 'the observer'

Let us call the informal idea that objects can look to the right of you, or to the left of you the 'observer-relative' view. There is a question about what the best construal of the observer-relative view is: whether the view should be that objects look to the left of *you*, your *head*, or your *eyes*. I will present some arguments for thinking that the best construal of the observer-relative view is that objects look to the left of the axis that extends from the center of your pupils. However, this construal leads to a problem. If it is indeed the case that the spatial contents of experience refer to specific physiological properties of the eye, then that implausibly rules out beings with slightly different physiologies from ours from having veridical experiences with the same spatial contents as ours.

First, I will argue that we should avoid saying that objects look to the left of *you*. Call S_1 the situation in which object O, against a plain white background, moves from your left to your right, and you keep your head still. Call S_2 the situation in which O stays still, and you move your head from right to left. From a purely visual point of view, S_1 and S_2 seem qualitatively identical. The change in look of O in S_1 is identical with the change in look of O in S_2. Of course, you may be able know whether you are in S_1 or S_2 by proprioception, since proprioception may tell you whether you have moved your head. But if we focus on the purely visual aspects of S_1 and S_2 (to do this, we can imagine that your proprioceptive awareness has been numbed), it seems hard to deny that O's change in look in S_1 is identical with its change in look in S_2. If we say that, in S_1, the object comes to look to your right, then we have to say that in S_2 as well.

But if we say that in S_2, we are committed to saying that your experience is illusory, since O remains to your left!

One could get round this implausible consequence by saying that, in S_1 and S_2, O comes to look to the right of your *head*, rather than you. If we said this, then the experience in S_2 would be veridical, since when you swing your head round to the left, O does come to be to the right of your head.

However, this construal of the view is problematic as well. Imagine a situation, S_3, in which O remains to your left, and, instead of swinging your head round from right to left, you keep your head still, and swing your eyes round from right to left. It seems that the change in look of O in S_3 will be qualitatively identical with the change in look of O in S_1 and S_2 (and the only way of distinguishing S_3 from S_1 and S_2 would be through proprioception, which we are imagining is numbed at present). If we say that, in S_3, O comes to look to the right of your head as your eyes swing round from right to left, then we are committed to saying that your experience is illusory, since O remains to the left of your head.

We can avoid this implausible consequence by saying that O comes to look to the right of your eyes, rather than your head. But what is it to be to the right of one's eyes? The notion of one's eyes having a right and left depends on them having a front and back. The front of the eyes would presumably be where the pupil is, and the right of the eye would presumably be to the right of the axis that extends out from the center of the pupil. So, this, I contend, is the best construal of the observer-relative view: that objects look to the left of the axis extending from the center of my pupils (because I have two pupils, perhaps the axis should be taken to be in the middle of the two axes that extend from the center of my two pupils).

This view, on which the spatial contents of perception include certain physiological properties of the eye, has implausible consequences concerning whether other animals with very slightly different physiologies could have experiences with the same veridical spatial contents as ours. For instance, imagine a race of Martians that are physiologically identical to humans, except that they have photo-sensitive cells on one side of their pupils, so that if they wanted to see something straight ahead, they had to angle their eyes slightly to the right. Such a race of animals seems easy to imagine. It also seems intuitive that objects could, in principle, be visually represented to them in the same way as they are to us, including in all spatial aspects. However, if we say that the way we represent objects spatially is by representing them as having such properties as being to the left of the axis extending from the center of the pupils, then there will be cases in which we will be committed to saying that the Martians' similar experiences are non-veridical, whilst ours are veridical, and this seems deeply implausible.

An instance of this problem occurs when one considers the Martian seeing something that we would normally describe as straight ahead. On the observer-relative view, object O looking to one to lie straight ahead is a matter of O looking to lie directly on the axis that extends from the center of one's pupils. If the Martian can have experiences with the same spatial contents as ours, then when he sees an object as straight ahead, the object will, on the observer-relative view, look to lie directly on the axis that extends from the center of his pupils. But of course, because he is a Martian, his eyes are angled slightly to the right, so the object doesn't lie directly on the axis that extends from the center of his pupils! Hence his experience is an illusion. This consequence seems extremely implausible, not least because the Martian has as much right to say that he is the one having veridical experiences, and we are the ones that are having illusory experiences.

One way for the observer-relative view to avoid this conclusion is to say that the Martian has different spatial contents from us, because of the different physiology of his eyes. But this seems implausible too. It seems that we could have had experiences with the same spatial contents if we had been born with photo-sensitive cells on the sides of our pupils.

This is the case against the observer-relative view: the view is forced to a position that has implausible consequences for the spatial contents of the experiences of animals with different physiologies from us. One could try to respond to the argument by appealing to locational non-conceptual modes of presentation. On this view, a subject's locational non-conceptual mode of presentation picks out whatever state of affairs normally causes the subject's experiences containing that type of non-conceptual mode of presentation. So in the example of the Martians and the humans, the same locational non-conceptual mode of presentation present in Martians' and humans' experiences would pick out different states of affairs, hence allowing qualitatively identical Martians' and humans' experiences to be made veridical by different kinds of states of affairs.

In this proposal non-conceptual modes of presentation are playing exactly the role that qualia play in *causal externalist* theories of perceptual representation of certain other properties, such as color properties. For instance, causal externalists about color properties hold that visual experiences have certain non-representational qualitative properties, and these experiences acquire their content by their standing in certain causal relations with properties in the world (see Chalmers (2005) for such a view). So, it would be legitimate to regard the locational non-conceptual modes of presentation introduced above as location qualia.

As opposed to answering the fundamental question that the argument that visual experience does not represent observer-relative properties raises, the causal externalist merely forces it to be asked in different terms. The question facing the person who denies that visual experience represents observer-relative properties is what location properties visual experiences do represent. The parallel question facing the causal externalist is how to characterize the locational qualitative properties that partly constitute the qualitative character of visual experience. The causal externalist might offer the suggestion that there are left-ish and right-ish qualia, but this suggestion is implausible (see the considerations in the argument below). So, even if one was attracted by the causal externalist position, the fundamental question raised by the argument in this section, namely what a proper account is of locational qualitative properties, would need to be addressed. Indeed, the principal difference between the causal externalist and the opposing view is that the opposing view thinks that qualitative properties *are* representational properties, and the causal externalist denies this. So both positions need to give an account of locational qualitative properties. The difference between the positions emerges only after one has given such an account, namely over the issue of whether, in giving an account of these qualitative properties, one has thereby given an account of representational properties.

360 degree vision

I shall now present a second argument for the claim that objects do not look to the left of me. Imagine that, at t_1, I am looking straight ahead and a cup is to my right. In this situation, the observer-relative view holds that the cup looks to my right (or "to the right of my eyes"; all the points made below will apply to this construal of the observer-relative view too). Now imagine that, between t_1 and t_2, the physical angle that I see gradually increases, so that at t_2 I come to have 360 degree vision all around. Let us imagine further that I come to be able to walk in the direction that I used to call 'backwards'. I am now a relatively symmetrical being along two axes: the axis I used to call front/back, and the axis I used to call right/left.

When I have become symmetrical in this way, there will be no way of distinguishing my front from my back, and, since the notions of right and left are essentially connected with the notions of front and back, no way of distinguishing my right from my left. Intuitively given that there is no such thing as my front, there would be no such thing as looking to be in front of me, as opposed to the back of me. It follows from this that there would be no such thing as looking to my right or to my left. It also seems that, in the process of my coming to have a wider and wider angle of vision, and therefore coming to see a wider range of objects, the apparent location of the cup that I see need not change. The simple fact that I can see more objects around the back of me does not seem to require that the apparent location of the cup change.

If the above reasoning is sound, then we can construct the following argument:

1. At t_2, the cup does not look to my right.
2. There is no change in the apparent location of the cup between t_1 and t_2.
3. At t_1, the cup does not look to my right.

This is the second argument (not including the argument from the reversibility constraint) against the view that objects look to our left and right. Certain features of this argument connect with the causal externalist position above. I claimed that the causal externalist position had to include an account of the location properties that are part of the qualitative character of visual experience. If the argument from 1. to 3. is sound, the proposal that there are right-ish and left-ish qualia seems implausible. 1. says that at t_2, when I no longer have a front or back, objects would not look to the front of me, as opposed to the back of me. This suggests that my experiences of objects would not have a front-ish qualitative character, as opposed to a back-ish qualitative character, and therefore neither a right-ish as opposed to a left-ish qualitative character (intuitively this idea explains our acceptance of 1.). This claim is entirely consistent with saying that the locational qualitative character of my experience will vary as objects move around me; what is being denied is that any given locational qualitative property is essentially front-ish or back-ish. Similar claims can be made about auditory perception. If we were symmetrical, and had no front or back, it seems plausible that, although the locational qualitative character of our auditory experiences may vary as objects making noises move around us, we would not continue to describe objects as sounding in front of us, or behind us. This thought suggests that the locational qualitative properties in auditory experience are neither essentially front-ish nor back-ish. This concludes my discussion of the two further arguments for the conclusion that visual experience does not represent observer-relative properties, the aim of which was to rebut the objection that the counter-intuitiveness of this conclusion ought to count as a *reductio ad absurdum* of the reversibility constraint.

The central argument of this paper has been the development of the reversibility constraint and its consequences. I have argued that the reversibility constraint is a general constraint on representational content. On the assumption that some looks-statements report the contents of visual experiences, the reversibility constraint, when applied to looks-statements, has the consequence that visual experiences do not represent observer-relative properties, such as the property of being to the left of you, the property of being to the right of you, the property of being in front of you, the property of being far away from you, and the property of being circular and at a slant from you, when you do not see yourself. This consequence of the reversibility constraint, that visual experience does not represent observer-relative properties when you do not see yourself, raises a question about what sorts of position properties visual experience, in general, does represent. I intend to address this question in further work. A subsidiary argument in the paper, which formed the response to one of the objections, was that visual experience does not have non-qualitative quantificational content in its non-conceptual content, which has the consequence that visual experience does not non-conceptually represent objects as having backs.[1]

Notes

1. I am very grateful to the following people for the helpful conversations I have had with them about the arguments in this paper: Wylie Breckenridge, Bill Brewer, Naomi Eilan, John Hawthorne, Stephen Kearns, Maria Lasonen, Geoffrey Lee, Hemdat Lerman, Rory Madden, Ofra Magidor, Sarah Moss, Anders Nes, Kranti Saran, Tim Williamson, and audiences at graduate conferences at Warwick and Harvard/MIT.

References

Campbell, J. 1994, *Past, Space and Self*, Cambridge, Mass: MIT Press.

Campbell, J. 2002, *Reference and Consciousness*, Oxford: Oxford University Press.

Chalmers, D. 2005, 'Perception and the Fall from Eden' in *Perceptual Experience*, eds. J. Hawthorne and T. Gendler-Szabo. Oxford: Oxford University Press.

Cussins, A. 1991, 'The Connectionist Constructionist of Concepts'. In *Readings on The Philosophy of Artificial Intelligence*, ed. M. Boden. Oxford: Oxford University Press.

Evans, G. 1982, *The Varieties of Reference*, Oxford: Oxford University Press.

Heck, R. 2000. 'Nonconceptual Content and the 'Space of Reasons'', *The Philosophical Review*, Vol. *109*, (4), 483–522.

McGinn, C. 1982, *The Character of Mind*, Oxford: Oxford University Press.

Peacocke, C. 1983. *Sense and content: Experience, Thought, and Their Relations*. Oxford: Oxford University Press.

Siegel, S. 2005, 'Which Properties Are Represented in Perception?', in *Perceptual Experience*, eds. J. Hawthorne and T. Gendler-Szabo. Oxford: Oxford University Press.

Philosophical Perspectives, 19, Epistemology, 2005

DECEPTION AND EVIDENCE[1]

Nicholas Silins
New York University

Introduction

Suppose that, whenever Gary has an experience as of two bananas in a bowl, Barry does too, and suppose that, whenever Gary believes that there are two bananas in the bowl, reasoning that there will be a banana left if he takes one, Barry does too. In general, whenever Gary or Barry has some non-factive attitude to a proposition—an attitude one can bear to a proposition even if it is false—the other does too. They are what can be called "internal twins".

Suppose that Gary and Barry still differ in a dramatic way. Although Gary is now and then mistaken about some matter of fact, Barry is a radically deceived brain in a vat, as deceived as can be given that he has the same non-factive mental states as Gary.

Gary is in the good case; Barry is in the bad case—do they have the same evidence nevertheless? That is the question I will address in this paper.

According to proponents of what I'll call *Evidential Internalism* (such as Bonjour 1999 or Audi 2001), the answer to my question is "yes". According to proponents of *Evidential Externalism* (such as McDowell 1982, 1995 or Williamson 2000), the answer to my question is "no".

My main aim is to evaluate the case for Evidential Internalism. Although I have some sympathy for the externalist view, I want to understand why one might find the opposing view attractive. Evidential internalists should not take their view for granted, and evidential externalists should be aware of what else they might have to deny when they deny the claim. Since arguments for Evidential Internalism have been challenged, it is especially important to understand why one might endorse the view, since one might otherwise mistakenly conclude that it is unmotivated.

There is a further reason to evaluate the case for Evidential Internalism: the view plays a key role in skeptical arguments. Thus, the denial of Evidential Internalism provides a reply to some skeptical arguments, and the acceptance of

Evidential Internalism will commit one to skeptical conclusions, if no further response to the arguments can be devised.

The plan of the paper is as follows. I will start by formulating and clarifying the respective views (section 1). I will then state and evaluate two lines of argument for Evidential Internalism. The first line of argument appeals to considerations about one's access to one's evidence (section 2), the second appeals to a supervenience thesis about the equal justification of internal twins (section 3).[2] My conclusion will be that the second line of argument, once thoroughly pursued, is the best line of defense for the view. The main problem for Evidential Externalism will turn out to be that, if the view is true, then one's beliefs are sometimes *less* justified in the *good* case than in the bad case. I will close by discussing whether, as one might suspect, the evidential externalist has some advantage in responding to skepticism (section 4). Here I will conclude that she does not.

A further task is to evaluate the overall case against Evidential Internalism. Although I will address some objections to the view in what follows, I do not have the space to take on that task here.

I. Formulations

The specific thesis I will evaluate is this:

(Evidential Internalism): Necessarily, if A and B are internal twins, then A and B have the same evidence.

I will start by clarifying what Evidential Internalism says, and will then make some points about what it does not say.

Evidential Internalism is a particular version of internalism in epistemology. It is an internalist thesis because it entails that, once the contents of one's internal states are fixed, what evidence one has does not depend in any further way on how one's environment is. Provided that two subjects are internal twins, their evidence will be the same, regardless of how different their environments may otherwise be.[3]

One might wonder what is meant here by "evidence". An initial suggestion would be "whatever plays a role in explaining why a subject has justification to hold a belief". This suggestion may be too generous. That Myla lacks a certain defeater may well help to explain why she is justified in holding a certain belief, without itself standing as evidence for what she believes. The intuitive notion I have in mind is that of a reason which provides one with justification to hold a belief, rather than merely explaining a belief. I leave open the question of whether only reasons can provide one with justification to hold a belief, and will not hazard any further explication of "evidence" here.[4]

On the use of "internal" I follow, two people are internal twins just in case they have the same non-factive mental states to the same degree—the same beliefs, apparent experiences, apparent memories, and so on (cf. Wedgwood 2002).[5] What is crucial on this reading is that internal twins be the same in all representational respects. It is not crucial on this reading that internal twins have the same intrinsic properties—presumably two subjects can be the same in all representational respects without being the same in all intrinsic respects.

It's worth clarifying what sorts of mental states can count as "internal" on the use I follow. Evidential Internalism is compatible with the claim that there are "broad" mental states, mental states such that being in them does not supervene on one's intrinsic properties, but instead can depend on one's relations to other speakers or the environment. Evidential Internalism is compatible with the claim that there are object-dependent mental states, states such that one is in them only if objects represented by the states exist. In particular, being an internal twin of a person can require sharing broad mental states or object-dependent states with that person, if those states are themselves non-factive. For example, if Gary has a broad belief that bananas are yellow, someone will be an internal twin of Gary only if he shares that broad belief. I take it that, since beliefs are a primary object of epistemic appraisal, we should count two people as internal twins only if they at least have the same beliefs.[6]

Others might use different readings of "internal", and propose narrower supervenience bases for two thinkers to have the same evidence. For example, an internalist might say that "internal" mental states are just those non-factive mental states which are consciously accessible, or an internalist might say that "internal" mental states are just narrow mental states, states such that being in them does supervene on the intrinsic properties of a thinker.[7] However, these philosophers will not reject the version of Evidential Internalism I address: the mental states they count as "internal" are still not factive. Also, one might accept the version of Evidential Internalism I consider, and reject versions of Evidential Internalism in terms of a narrower supervenience base. Thus, by focusing on the version of Evidential Internalism in terms of non-factive mental states, we may address our attention to the most general version of the view.[8]

Evidential Internalism says that internal twins have the same evidence; it does not say what their evidence consists of. The thesis does not address detailed questions about the content and the ontology of evidence. One might think that the claim at least entails some particular view about what evidence we have; I will return to the issue later in the paper.

Evidential Internalism is not what we may call an *access thesis* in epistemology. Access theses place epistemic constraints on what it takes for something to be in one's evidence, or more generally on what it takes for something to justify one in believing this or that. The epistemic constraints can themselves be stated in terms of knowledge, justified belief, or other terms. According to the access theorist, something provides one with justification to hold a belief only if some further constraint is satisfied about one's access to the justifier, or to one's possession of the justifier.[9]

Evidential Internalism also does not concern the property of being justified, as opposed to the possession of evidence. It leaves open the question of whether, if a person's belief has the property of being justified, then the belief stands in some suitable relation to evidence the person has. The thesis is compatible with the possibility of non-evidential justification. It also leaves open the question of whether, if two people are the same with respect to their evidence, then they are the same with respect to how justified their beliefs are.

What Evidential Internalism tells us is that internal twins have the same evidence, whatever their evidence may exactly be, and whatever the relation between evidence and justification may exactly be.

According to the opponent of Evidential Internalism, the following claim is instead true:

> (Evidential Externalism): It's possible that: A and B are internal twins and A and B do not have the same evidence.

Evidential Externalism, like Evidential Internalism, is not itself a view about what evidence one has. An externalist might accept the thesis, defended in Williamson (2000: ch. 9), that one's (propositional) evidence is what one knows.[10] On this line of thought, assuming that propositions are what one knows, one's evidence includes a proposition P if and only if one knows P. But the thesis that one's propositional evidence is what one knows is a strong one, and there is room for versions of Evidential Externalism which are weaker than it. For example, an evidential externalist might accept the weaker thesis that one's propositional evidence is what one justifiedly and truly believes. Or she might accept the foundationalist thesis that one's evidence includes a proposition P if and only if one perceives P. And so on. According to the most straightforward versions of Evidential Externalism—those I will focus on in this paper—one's body of evidence includes P just in case one has some privileged factive attitude to P. Since here it can be easy for one to be in possession of evidence which obviously entails contingent propositions about the environment, we can think of this variant of Evidential Externalism as Entailing Evidence Externalism.[11]

Evidential Externalism is a version of externalism in epistemology. On this view, even when we have fixed the representational contents of one's non-factive states, what evidence one has is still sensitive to the environment one is in. Indeed, Evidential Externalism is arguably the best version of externalism in epistemology. An advantage of the claim is that it does not entail reliabilist views, which I take to be the most familiar versions of externalism in epistemology. According to the reliabilist views I have in mind, a belief is justified if some salient process (or perhaps method) whereby the belief is formed or maintained is reliable. Someone can meet the sufficient condition proposed, yet fail to appreciate the reliability of the salient source of her belief. So one common objection is that something unrecognized by the thinker cannot make a positive contribution to the justification of a belief (Bonjour 1980). According to another common objection, such views face a "generality problem" in properly specifying the salient processes by which one's belief is formed or maintained (Conee and Feldman 1998).

There are versions of Evidential Externalism which are not vulnerable to the above complaints about reliabilism. Even if one's evidence is sensitive to what environment one is in, it does not follow that unrecognized factors make a positive contribution to the justification of one's beliefs. For example, an evidential externalist such as Williamson (2000) says both that one's evidence is what one knows, and that only one's evidence justifies belief. This view fares well with the demand that one must have access to what justifies one's beliefs, since on this view *only* what is known justifies belief.[12] Also, the evidential externalist need not face any problem in specifying what one's evidence is: one's evidence will be what one knows, or justifiedly and truly believes, etc. The upshot is that versions of Evidential Externalism escape some standard objections to reliabilism, making those versions of Evidential Externalism promising theses for an externalist in epistemology to accept.

We now have clarified the positions of the evidential internalist and of her rival. It is time to consider how one might argue for the internalist view.

II. Access Arguments

According to the first line of argument I will consider, Evidential Internalism is entailed by some true access thesis in epistemology, even though the view is not itself an access thesis. Before we look at the strategy in more detail, we should bear in mind that some access theses are compatible with Evidential Externalism. For example, as we just saw, it might be that only known propositions justify beliefs. On this sort of view, Evidential Internalism is false, but some access thesis is nevertheless correct. To argue for Evidential Internalism from access theses in epistemology, then, one will have to be very clear about which access thesis one invokes, and why that thesis should rule out the externalist view.

The kind of access thesis I will consider concerns one's knowing whether one has such-and-such a piece of evidence. For example, if one's evidence includes the proposition that the wall looks white, the relevant access thesis will concern one's knowledge that one's evidence includes the proposition that the wall looks white, as opposed to one's knowledge simply that the wall looks white.

I will consider two access arguments. The first is not novel, and I will pass over it quickly. The second argument is novel, and I will set it out in much more detail, finally explaining why I think it is flawed.[13]

The first access argument is stated and critiqued in Williamson (2000: ch. 8). It uses the following thesis:

> (Transparency): For any proposition P, if one is suitably alert and conceptually sophisticated, then one is in a position to know whether or not one's evidence includes P.

If Transparency is true, and Evidential Internalism is false, some reflective subject in the bad casee should be able to work out that she is not in the good case. Since she will know that she is in the good case only if she has a certain piece of evidence, and she will know that she does not have the piece of evidence, she will be in a position to know that she is not in the good case. Since no subject in the bad case can figure out that she is not in the good case, the proponent of the Transparency argument concludes that Evidential Internalism is true.

We can all agree that Transparency is a very strong claim about one's access to one's evidence. Williamson (2000) sets out an extended argument to show that the Transparency thesis is false. Further, according to Williamson, Evidential Internalism is unmotivated once we have shown Transparency to be false:

> If something like this argument [from Transparency] is not the reason for which skeptics and others think that one has the same evidence in the two cases, it is not at all clear what is (2000: 173).

On this line of thought, the Transparency argument is unsound, and there is no other argument in sight for Evidential Internalism. The upshot is presumably supposed to be that Evidential Internalism is unmotivated.

I set aside the question of how Williamson argues against the Transparency thesis, and whether his argument succeeds.[14] I also set aside the question of whether there is a true weakening of Transparency which can do the work of the stronger claim.[15] What I want to emphasize is that there is a novel access argument which uses a very different thesis, one which is not touched by Williamson's argument against Transparency. Since there is a good deal of discussion in the literature of Williamson's line of argument against Transparency, and no discussion of the new argument, it is worth taking the trouble to set it out.

The Transparency argument focuses on the bad case, using a claim about *when* one is in a position to know what one's evidence is. One can set up a different access argument, focusing on the good case, with a claim about *how* one can know what one's evidence is. According to the new argument, Evidential Externalism is false because it has unacceptable consequences about what one can know from the armchair.

To set out the argument, we will need a grip on what "armchair knowledge" means. One has armchair knowledge of a proposition when one knows it, and one's justification for believing the proposition does not *constitutively* depend on one's having had any particular sense experience or type of sense experience. Thus, one can have armchair knowledge of a proposition, even if a background condition for having that knowledge is that one has had a certain experience or type of experience. For example, one might have armchair knowledge that redness is a color, even if one knows that proposition only if one has had experiences of redness (Kitcher 1980: 5; Burge 1993: 459–60).

The key access thesis for the new argument is the following one:

(Armchair Access): It is sometimes the case that: one's evidence includes some proposition E, and one knows from the armchair that one's evidence includes E.

According to Armchair Access, one sometimes knows by reflection that one has a certain piece of evidence. The claim should be plausible. Although I may be fallible about what evidence I have, it still seems that I sometimes know what evidence I have simply by reflecting on my situation, rather than by relying on sense experience. Of course, it might be that I have the piece of evidence only if I have had some particular experience—the evidence might itself consist of some sense experience. But my justification for believing that I have the evidence need not constitutively depend on my having had the experience. The source of my knowledge remains reflection rather than sense experience. Analogously, I know that I am having a certain sense experience only if I am having the sense experience, but that does not show that I lack armchair knowledge that I am having the experience. The source of my knowledge is arguably still reflection instead of experience.

To set out the problem for the evidential externalist, we can focus on an example of a thoughtful subject in the good case. Suppose Gary sees that the dial reads 0.4, and considers what evidence he has and what his having certain evidence entails. If Evidential Externalism is true, then in the good case he has as a piece of evidence that the dial reads 0.4, and in the bad case he at best has the evidence that it seems that the dial reads 0.4. That's just the sort of asymmetry between the cases we should expect if the view is true.[16]

In particular, if Evidential Externalism is true, we should expect that Gary knows from the armchair that his evidence includes the proposition that the dial reads 0.4. It would be ad hoc for the externalist to accept that we sometimes have armchair access to our evidence, yet insist that we never have armchair access to our environmentally sensitive evidence. After all, it would be ad hoc for a content externalist to say, we have privileged access to some of our mental states, just not to any of our environmentally sensitive mental states. No such restrictions are built into the plausible thoughts about how we can access our evidence or our mental states.

We should also expect that, if Evidential Externalism is true, then one's evidence includes any proposition P only if P is true. After all, if the view is true, then what evidence one has depends on how the environment is—the most straightforward way for this to happen is for attributions of propositional evidence to be factive. Given that Gary is thinking about the matter, he knows this from the armchair if we do.

So far Gary knows two things from the armchair if Evidential Externalism is true: that his evidence includes the proposition that the dial reads 0.4, and that, if his evidence includes the proposition that the dial reads 0.4, then the dial reads 0.4.

We should also expect that, if Gary puts the two pieces of armchair knowledge together, and infers what they entail, he will also have armchair knowledge of what follows from the two pieces of armchair knowledge. Granted a suitable closure principle for armchair knowledge, Gary is in a position to know, still from the armchair, that the dial reads 0.4!

According to the proponent of the access argument, although Gary can know what the dial reads, he cannot know such a proposition through armchair reflection. In general, if a proposition concerns how the world is, and is not guaranteed to be true by the concepts which figure in it, one's justification for believing the proposition must constitutively depend on one's experience. The problem is not restricted to contingent propositions—it is also not possible to have armchair knowledge of a necessary proposition such as the proposition that water is H20.

According to the proponent of the argument, Evidential Externalism is itself false, since it has false consequences about how one can have knowledge of the world.

We can sum up the problem for the evidential externalist by sketching the following argument:

(1) Gary has armchair knowledge that his evidence includes the proposition that the dial reads 0.4.

(2) Gary has armchair knowledge that, if his evidence includes the proposition that the dial reads 0.4, then the dial reads 0.4.

So,

(3) Gary is in a position to have armchair knowledge that the dial reads 0.4.

The evidential externalist must either identify the flaw with the argument, or explain away the implausibility of its conclusion. In particular, the challenge is either to reconcile the externalist view about evidence with our having special access to our evidence, or else to show we don't have the special access to our evidence after all.[17]

On one line of externalist response, the argument's conclusion is unobjectionable, given that the source of Gary's evidence is itself his experience. Here Gary at most has an armchair route to a claim he already empirically knows—no new knowledge is supplied. But we can raise a special problem for the externalist thesis that one's evidence includes P only if one knows P. Consider the following argument:

(4) Gary has armchair knowledge that his evidence includes the proposition that there is a dial in the room.

(5) Gary has armchair knowledge that, if his evidence includes the proposition that there is a dial in the room, then there are no fake dials around.

So,

(6) Gary is in a position to have armchair knowledge that there are no fake dials around.

We can know from the armchair that, in order to know that there is a dial (or barn) around, it had better not be true that there are fake dials (or fake barns) around. It seems to be an a priori matter of epistemology that knowledge excludes such a possibility of error. But it still seems too demanding to ask that, in order to know that there is a dial around, one must *know* that there are no fake dials around. Someone could know that there is a dial around without even believing, and hence not knowing, that there are no fake dials around. Thus, if Gary is in a position to know from the armchair that there are no fake dials around, he is in a position to gain armchair knowledge of something he did not already know. The previous response to the armchair argument does not help with the current problem.

We can also make the current problem vivid without using the notion of armchair knowledge.[18] On the one hand, when one has a piece of evidence which supports some proposition Q, it's plausible that one could know Q by reflecting on one's possession of the piece of evidence. On the other hand, when one has a piece of evidence which does *not* support some proposition Q, it's implausible that one could know Q by reflecting on one's possession of the piece of evidence. The relevant piece of evidence in the current case—that there is a dial in the room—does not itself support the conclusion that there are no fake dials around. However, it seems that, if one's evidence includes P only if one knows P, then, by knowing that one's evidence includes that there is a dial in the room, one can know that there are no fake dials around. Here reflection on evidence which does not justify a proposition still can provide knowledge of that proposition. Whether the case is one of armchair knowledge or not, the externalist owes us some therapy.

We have now seen that the Transparency argument is not the only access argument against Evidential Externalism. There is another argument against the view which appeals to a different access thesis, focusing on the way in which we can know what our evidence is.

The new access argument raises a prima facie problem for the evidential externalist. I still take it that the internalist should seek an independent argument for her view. We can bring out the difficulty by comparing the second access argument with the much-discussed, and still unresolved, McKinsey problem (McKinsey 1991).[19] The problem concerns the compatibility of externalism regarding the contents of our mental states with our having privileged access to our mental states. If certain content externalist theses are true, then one's being in some mental states depends on the environment being a certain way. However, if we have privileged access to our mental states, we sometimes have armchair knowledge of what mental states we are in. Thus there is a worry that, if content externalism is true (and armchair knowable), and we have privileged access to our mental states, then we can also have armchair knowledge of how the environment is.

The new access argument concerns the compatibility of externalism regarding our evidence with our having privileged access to our evidence. Given the close parallel between the new access argument and the McKinsey problem, we should expect a wide variety of the potential solutions to the McKinsey problem to be available to the evidential externalist. In particular, one might deny that closure holds for armchair knowledge, as does Schiffer (2005), or one might allow that one can have armchair knowledge of the world, as is discussed in Sawyer (1998), Hawthorne (2002), or Weatherson (2005). My own sympathies lie with the compatibilist line of response to both problems. At any rate, since the McKinsey problem has yet to supply a compelling objection against the content externalist, we should not expect the second access argument to supply a more compelling objection against the evidential externalist. Just as the McKinsey argument poses a puzzle for the content externalist, rather than a strong objection to the view, the new access argument poses a puzzle for the evidential externalist, rather than a strong objection to the view.[20]

Given the limitations of the new access argument, I now set the access strategy aside, and turn to what I take to be the most promising line of defense of Evidential Internalism. The further argument does not invoke any claim about access to evidence, and apparently does not otherwise rely on any such claim.

III. Supervenience Arguments

We may start with a sketch of the overall strategy:

(7) If Evidential Internalism is not true, then internal twins are not equally justified.
(8) Internal twins are equally justified.
So,
(9) Evidential Internalism is true.

The evidential externalist may well be happy to deny that internal twins are equally justified. My aim is to show how problematic the commitment is for the view, by examining exactly why the view has the commitment. I will start by explaining and motivating the thesis that internal twins are equally justified. I will then discuss the best way to argue from that thesis to Evidential Internalism itself. My main point will be that, if Evidential Externalism is true, then there are violations of equal justification that even the externalist should find implausible: the view implies that the radically deceived subject is sometimes more justified than her twin who is not deceived.[21]

> We can formulate the equal justification thesis as follows:
>
> (Equal Justification): Necessarily, if A and B are internal twins, then A is justified to degree n1 in believing P to degree n2 just in case B is justified to degree n1 in believing P to degree n2.

Notice that we can consider the degree to which a given belief is justified, or whether the belief is justified simpliciter. Equal Justification concerns the degree of justification of internal twins' partial beliefs, and not just whether internal twins are outright justified in believing the same propositions. Further, Equal Justification is what we might call an *evaluative* thesis, rather than an *explanatory* thesis. It says that internal twins have the same degree of justification for their partial beliefs, but says nothing about what provides their partial beliefs with the degree of justification that they have. Of course, one might think that the fan of Equal Justification is committed to some specific view about what evidence we have. I will return to the issue later.[22]

There are at least two distinct readings of Equal Justification. One reading of the thesis is focused on what is commonly called "propositional justification." According to this reading, internal twins are, in terms of what they have justification to believe, equally well-positioned with respect to the same propositions. The twins might still fail to have any attitudes towards the propositions, or have attitudes towards them, though not on the basis of the justifications available to them. We can call this the *propositional reading* of the Equal Justification thesis, since it is silent about the status of the attitudes internal twins actually hold. Another reading of Equal Justification is focused on what is commonly called "doxastic justification". According to this reading, internal twins are equally justified in holding the degrees of confidence they actually hold. We can call this the *doxastic reading* of the Equal Justification thesis, since it is not silent about the epistemic status of the attitudes internal twins actually hold.

As far as I can tell, the doxastic and propositional readings entail each other, given that internal twins are the same with respect to the causal relations between their internal mental states. However, I take the doxastic reading to be the most natural reading of Equal Justification. In what follows, my emphasis will be on that reading of the claim.

I now turn to the motivation of the Equal Justification thesis, on its doxastic reading. I take it that Equal Justification is extremely plausible when we consider instances of the claim. Suppose that both Gary and Barry are confident to degree .9 that there is a dial in the room. Intuitively, they are justified to the same degree in being confident in that proposition to that degree, even though one person is radically deceived and the other is not. Even when the question of whether they are both outright justified in the belief is distinguished from the question of whether they are both justified to the same degree, I take it that the plausible answer to both questions is "yes". This consideration in favor of Equal Justification could of course be outweighed by other considerations, or otherwise undermined, but it is a consideration in favor of Equal Justification nonetheless.

It is important that Equal Justification is supported by intuitive judgments about cases. The upshot is that the motivation of the claim is not based on theoretical judgments about one's access to one's evidence, or indeed on any other premises. In order to motivate Equal Justification, then, one need not invoke Transparency or indeed any thesis concerning one's access to one's evidence.

I take us to be non-inferentially justified in believing instances of Equal Justification. One might claim that, even if the motivation for Equal Justification does not invoke a claim like Transparency as a premise, Equal Justification is plausible only if one accepts some such claim (Williamson 2004b: 315). Disputes about the underlying commitments of a thesis are of course difficult to adjudicate. Some evidence that the claims are independent is that there are philosophers who accept Equal Justification without yet accepting Transparency, such as Conee and Feldman (2001). I also find it plausible that, if one is a coherentist about justification, one will be committed to Equal Justification, while also being committed to rejecting claims like Transparency, since one might fail to be in a position to access subtle facts about the coherence of one's overall belief set.

Taking it that Equal Justification can be motivated independently of considerations about access to evidence, I now turn to the incompatibility of the claim with Evidential Externalism.

As far as propositional justification is concerned, the evidential externalist should allow that internal twins can have different degrees of justification for their beliefs. Suppose an externalist said that, even though internal twins have different evidence, they are equally justified in their beliefs. Perhaps, given that one is not certain of what evidence one has in the good case, the differences between the evidence one has in each case end up washing out. On this sort of externalist position, however, evidential differences between internal twins are epistemically idle. Evidential differences here would not even explain differences in knowledge—it seems that one can have knowledge in the good case even if one has the same evidence in the bad case. However, I take it that evidential differences between internal twins are interesting and important only if those differences can generate differences in propositional justification between twins. So I take it that, if Evidential Externalism is true, then internal twins can fail to have the same degree of propositional justification.[23]

One might also be convinced that Evidential Externalism will conflict with Equal Justification on its doxastic reading. What is less clear is where exactly the conflicts will arise. By attending closely to the matter, we'll best bring out just how surprising and implausible the consequences are of Evidential Externalism, as well as gain a sharper understanding of its relation to Equal Justification.

I will start with a cautionary observation about a consequence Evidential Externalism does not have. I will then show how, if Evidential Externalism is true, one is sometimes more justified in the good case than in the bad case. I will finally illustrate what I take to be the worst consequence of Evidential Externalism: that one is sometimes more justified in the bad case than in the good case.

In the arguments I set out, I will need to use some assumptions about the relation between the evidence that one has and the degrees of confidence that one ought to have. For the sake of simplicity and vividness, I will use the following assumptions. The first is that, if the probability of P on one's evidence is n, then one's degree of confidence in P ought to be n. For example, if the probability on one's evidence that Jones committed the murder is .8, then one's degree of confidence that Jones committed the murder ought to be .8. The assumption is fairly plausible, since I take it that evidential probabilities should determine how confident one ought to be, and the most straightforward way for them to determine how confident one ought to be is if one's credence ought to match them.

The second assumption I will use is that, if one's degree of confidence ought to be n, and one's actual degree of confidence diverges from n, then one's actual degree of confidence is less than fully justified insofar as it diverges from what it ought to be. This is not to say that, if one's degree of confidence is not exactly what it ought to be, then one's degree of confidence is not outright doxastically justified. This is also not to say that, if one's degree of confidence is exactly what it ought to be, then it is outright doxastically justified: one might have the appropriate degree of confidence for the wrong reason. The key point is instead that, other things being equal, if A's degree of confidence in P is placed where it ought to be, and B's degree of confidence in P is not, then B's partial belief in P is less justified than A's.

One might reject the assumptions I use.[24] But my arguments should go through with weaker assumptions. In particular, they should go through as long as the externalist accepts that, if A has entailing evidence for P, and B does not, then A ought to be more confident in P than B. One of the most striking features of Evidential Externalism is that it allows one to have entailing evidence in the good case which one lacks in the bad case. This feature of the view is toothless if it does not imply that one should be more confident in some propositions in the good case. Nevertheless, I will use the stronger assumptions stated above to make the problems for the externalist as vivid as possible.

I will now look at some examples in more detail.

A natural thought one might start with is that any counterexample to Evidential Internalism is a counterexample to Equal Justification: if two internal twins do not have the same evidence for some proposition P, then it follows automatically that they are not equally doxastically justified in believing P. The thought turns out to be wrong.

We can illustrate the mistake with the following sort of example. If Evidential Internalism is false, it will transpire that Gary has entailing evidence for some proposition P, whereas his internal twin Barry only has good but non-entailing evidence for P. I take it that the probability of P on Gary's entailing evidence will be 1. The probability of P on Barry's evidence will itself be less than 1, let us say

.9. As far as their degrees of confidence are concerned, however, they may both be confident to degree .95 in P. Their situation will then be as follows:

	Degree of Confidence in P	*Probability of P on Total Evidence*
Gary	.95	1
Barry	.95	.9

We may now consider the degree of doxastic justification of their partial beliefs. It seems that Gary and Barry are not quite as confident in C as they should be, given their evidence. However, the difference between their actual degrees of confidence and the degrees of confidence they should have is the same—0.05. Even if Gary and Barry do not have the same evidence in this case, they remain doxastically justified to the same degree. The upshot is that counterexamples to Evidential Internalism are not automatically counterexamples to Equal Justification.

It is natural to expect that, if Evidential Internalism is false, one will sometimes be more doxastically justified in the good case, given that in the good case one will have evidence which one lacks in the bad case. I will now illustrate this consequence of the externalist view.

First, consider the claim that one does not have entailing evidence that one is not a brain in a vat or otherwise radically deceived. If Evidential Internalism is false, then the claim is mistaken. For example, sometimes one's evidence in the good case will include the proposition that a spider is black, and one's twin in the bad case will merely have the evidence that there seems to be a black spider. Now, the proposition that there is a black spider, as opposed to the proposition that there seems to be a black spider, entails the negation of BIV, the proposition that [one is a radically deceived brain in a vat and it merely seems to be the case that there is a black spider]. Thus, if Evidential Internalism is false, one will sometimes have evidence which entails that one is not in a skeptical scenario.

Second, suppose that Gary and Barry are confident in ~BIV to degree .999. If Evidential Internalism is false, the probability of ~BIV on Gary's evidence will be 1. The probability of ~BIV on Barry's evidence will be less than 1, and will plausibly be less than .99. Thus,

	Degree of Confidence in ~BIV	*Probability of ~BIV on Total Evidence*
Gary	.999	1
Barry	.999	<.99

Even though Gary's confidence in the good case in ~BIV may be slightly misplaced, Barry's confidence in the bad case in ~BIV is more distant from where it ought to be. The upshot is that one can be more justified in the good case than the bad case, if Evidential Externalism is true.

We have now seen a specific case in which Evidential Externalism yields a counterexample to Equal Justification. Since there is reason to believe Equal Justification, there is already reason to believe that Evidential Externalism is false.

A complication for the objection is that, as far as the evidential externalist is concerned, it is no disadvantage that her view allows for greater doxastic justification in the good case. Indeed, she might think that an advantage of her view is that it allows for greater doxastic justification in the good case. I now want to explore an unexpected problem for her view. Although it is natural to think that, if Evidential Externalism is true, then one can be better off only in the good case, that natural thought is wrong.

The further difficulty arises given that, just as in the bad case one will sometimes overestimate one's evidence, in the good case one will sometimes underestimate one's evidence. For example, suppose that Gary remembers and knows B, that he had a banana with breakfast yesterday, but is not fully confident in B, given that he also knows that his memory is not entirely reliable about such matters. We thus may have it that in the good case he is confident to degree .9 in B, where the probability of the proposition on his evidence is in fact 1. In the bad case, however, Barry's evidence is something like the proposition that he seems to remember that he had a banana with breakfast yesterday. It seems fair to say that the probability of B on his evidence is .9. Thus,

	Degree of Confidence in B	*Probability of B on Total Evidence*
Gary	.9	1
Barry	.9	.9

If Evidential Externalism is true, it turns out that Gary's partial belief in B is misplaced by a wide margin, whereas Barry's partial belief in B is not misplaced at all. Indeed, Barry's confidence is causally based, in the right way, on the weaker evidence he has, whereas Gary's fails to be adequately adjusted to his stronger evidence. Since Gary underestimates his evidence, and Barry's partial belief is properly adjusted to his own evidence, the subject in the good case is less justified in believing B.

We arguably knew from the start that the externalist will have to deny Equal Justification, and the externalist may well be happy to do so. But here is another plausible thesis:

> (The Bad Case is Never Better): Necessarily, if B is in the bad case and A is an internal twin of B in the good case, B is not more justified in believing P than A.

In having to deny this attractive claim, the externalist has a problem beyond denying Equal Justification—no one expected that one is sometimes more justified in the bad case than the good case. Even if one is willing to accept the result that one is sometimes more justified in the good case, it is harder to live with the claim that one is sometimes more justified in the bad case. In particular, many reliabilists will be happy to deny Equal Justification, but I take it that no ordinary reliabilist will be happy to say that one is something better off in the bad case. The consequence that one is sometimes more justified in the bad case should be unwelcome to all.

The externalist might protest that, since the consequence arises because one has greater propositional justification in the good case, the consequence is in fact benign. After all, the issue is not that one has too little propositional justification in the good case, but instead that one has a great deal of propositional justification in the good case—what could be wrong with that?

We can sharpen the problem for the externalist by setting aside the comparison of cases, and considering the good case in its own right.

One strike against the externalist might be that, if the view is true, one has *too much* propositional justification in the good case, more than was expected or plausible. But I'll set that question aside. The point I want to emphasize is that, if Evidential Externalism is true, then counterintuitive assessments of beliefs in the good case turn out to be correct. Intuitively, our ordinary partial beliefs are just fine as they are: we are neither more nor less confident in our ordinary beliefs than we should be. If Evidential Externalism is true, however, we are sometimes less confident than we should be, given our evidence. Although the view does not have skeptical consequences, it implies that there are flaws in places where apparently there are none.

If the externalist view is true, it may even turn out that we are *typically* more cautious than we should be, given our evidence. If one's evidence includes anything one knows, presumably a subject will have an abundance of entailing evidence in the good case, while only rarely being as confident as she should be given her superb evidence. Here the externalist might have to conclude that most of our ordinary partial beliefs are somewhat at fault, despite the fact that our ordinary beliefs seem fine as they are.

As we saw, not every counterexample to Evidential Internalism is a counterexample to Equal Justification. Sometimes internal twins will have evidence of different strengths, but will proportion their confidence to their evidence equally well. As we also saw, Evidential Externalism does predict that one is sometimes more justified in the good case. Sometimes the confidence of someone in the good case will be better proportioned than the confidence of her twin in the bad case. Most importantly, we saw that Evidential Externalism predicts that one is sometimes more justified in the bad case. Sometimes one will have greater propositional justification in the good case, but greater doxastic justification in the bad case, since one's confidence will be better proportioned to one's evidence in the bad case. This last consequence of the externalist view is one that even the externalist should find wrong.

To make vivid the problems for Evidential Externalism, I used the strong assumption that, if the probability of P on one's evidence is n, then one's credence in P ought to be n. It's worth repeating that the arguments can go through without the assumption. As long as one ought to be more confident in some propositions in the good case than in the bad case, one will sometimes underestimate one's evidence in the good case, and overestimate one's evidence in the bad case. In particular, cautious subjects will sometimes be more justified in the bad case, and aggressive subjects will sometimes be more justified in the good case.[25]

According to the proponent of the supervenience argument, the consequences of Evidential Externalism are false. We have reason to reject Evidential Externalism, both because it is incompatible with Equal Justification, and because of the particular kind of counterexamples it yields to Equal Justification.

I will now sketch some ways the externalist might respond to the overall argument, and address one line of response in detail.

According to the first line of response, Equal Justification is false and the supervenience argument is unsound. Since most of the arguments against Equal Justification I am aware of are themselves direct arguments for Evidential Externalism, I set this line of response aside. Surveying the case for the view is beyond the scope of the paper.[26]

According to the second line of response, the Equal Justification thesis expresses a truth in some contexts of utterance and a falsehood in others. This line of response can be developed either in terms of an ambiguity in the expression "justified" and its cognates, or in terms of some context-sensitivity of the expressions.[27] In either case, the supervenience argument shows that Evidential Internalism expresses a truth in some contexts of utterance, not that it expresses a truth in all contexts of utterance. The ambiguity and contextualist views in question deserve further explanation and attention. However, since they concede so much to the evidential internalist, I will not discuss them further here.

According to a third line of response, which I will consider in detail, Equal Justification is unmotivated and the supervenience argument is unconvincing. In particular, although we have reason to believe some claim weaker than Equal Justification, we do not have reason to believe Equal Justification itself. Thus, provided that Evidential Externalism is compatible with the weaker claim, that Evidential Externalism is incompatible with the stronger claim is no reason to believe that Evidential Externalism is false. On this line of thought there is some *surrogate* for Equal Justification which undermines the supervenience argument.

The challenge for this line of response is to identify a suitable surrogate for the claim. I will now consider some attempts to meet the challenge.

According to one proposal, we have good reason to believe only the following weaker thesis, which does not concern epistemic justification:

> (Equal Blamelessness): Necessarily, if A and B are internal twins, then A is epistemically blameless in believing P just in case B is epistemically blameless in believing P.

According to the weaker thesis, it cannot be that a person is deserving of (epistemic) criticism for holding a particular belief when an internal twin of the person is not. This weaker thesis seems to be perfectly compatible with Evidential Externalism. According to the objector, it is confused to think that anything more than this claim is plausible upon the comparison of internal twins.[28]

The problem with this response is that we can argue for a supervenience thesis which is stronger than Equal Blamelessness. The stronger thesis concerns outright justification rather than degrees of justification. It says that internal twins are outright justified in believing the same propositions. Since the argument for the stronger thesis is, as far as I know, novel, it is especially useful to set the argument out.[29]

Just as one's belief or disbelief in a proposition can be epistemically evaluated, one's suspension of judgment regarding a proposition can also be epistemically evaluated. In particular, we can provide a simple sufficient condition for one to be justified in suspending judgment:

> (Suspension): Necessarily, if one lacks justification to believe P, and one lacks justification to believe ~P, then one has justification to suspend judgment in P.

We can use the Suspension principle to argue for a weakening of Equal Justification. First, it's never the case that one person has justification to believe P, and some internal twin of that person has justification to believe ~P. Even one's radically deceived internal twins do not have justification to believe the negations of what one is justified in believing, since part of what it is to be radically deceived is to lack justification to suspect that one is. Given the Suspension principle, if Barry lacks justification to believe that there is a dial in front of him, or lacks justification to believe any other proposition that Gary is justified in believing, then Barry will have positive justification to suspend judgment in those propositions. But suppose Barry did suspend judgment in the proposition that there is a dial in front of him, despite the fact that there seems to be a dial in front of him, and despite the fact that no defeating evidence is available to him. I take it to be very implausible that Barry would be justified in suspending judgment in the matter. Thus, given that Barry also does not have justification to deny the proposition, and given the Suspension principle, it follows that he does have justification to believe the proposition.

We can sum up the argument as follows:

(16) It's not possible that, A is justified in believing P, and B is justified in believing ~P, where A is in the good case and B is A's internal twin in the bad case.

(17) It's not possible that, A is justified in believing P, and B is justified in suspending judgment in P, where A is in the good case and B is A's internal twin in the bad case.

(18) Necessarily, if one lacks justification to believe P, and one lacks justification to suspend judgment in P, then one has justification to believe P.

So,

(19) It's not possible that, A is justified in believing P, and B is not justified in believing P, where A is in the good case and B is A's internal twin in the bad case.

The new argument supports a weaker counterpart of Equal Justification:

> (Outright Equal Justification): Necessarily, if A and B are internal twins, then A is justified simpliciter in having an outright belief in P just in case B is justified simpliciter in having an outright belief in P.

The weaker thesis is set out neither in terms of degrees of confidence nor in terms of degrees of justification. We are simply considering the outright justification of outright beliefs (while keeping the focus on doxastic justification rather than propositional justification). According to the minimal thesis, either internal twins are both justified in holding a given outright belief, or neither is. They are not merely equally blameless in their beliefs. The upshot is that the proposed surrogate for Equal Justification—the mere claim that internal twins are equally blameless—will not do.[30]

Outright Equal Justification, unlike Equal Justification itself, might be compatible with Evidential Externalism. The evidential externalist must deny that internal twins have the same evidence, but the evidential externalist might be able to allow that one's twin in the bad case has evidence, albeit weaker evidence, for her beliefs. In particular, the externalist might be able to say that, although internal twins are equally outright justified in their beliefs, they still are not justified to the same degree in their beliefs. In response to the supervenience argument, then, the externalist could insist that the weaker thesis is the plausible core of the stronger claim. After all, the Suspension argument does support Outright Equal Justification, but apparently does not support Equal Justification itself.

Let me now evaluate the retreat to Outright Equal Justification. One problem is that Evidential Externalism is not obviously compatible even with Outright Equal Justification. We have not yet seen any guarantee that the externalist will be able to hold on to the weaker claim. Another problem is that the response fails to appreciate the force of the intuitions which support Equal Justification. If Outright Equal Justification is the plausible core of the stronger claim, then the supervenience argument shouldn't have seemed to bring out any problem for the evidential externalist. But it did. So Equal Justification must itself be plausible after all. The fact that the supervenience argument requires a response reveals that the retreat to Outright Equal Justification does not work.

If we are shown how to explain away the intuitive appeal of Equal Justification, the supervenience argument is undermined. We have not yet been shown how to explain away the intuitive appeal of Equal Justification. So the supervenience argument provides us with some reason to believe that Evidential Internalism is itself true. Given that the argument also does not fall prey to worries about the access argument, I take it that we have spelt out the most promising line of argument for the view.

Now that we have seen how the supervenience argument is best set out, I want to conclude by clarifying what the argument does not show. So far we have simply considered whether internal twins have the same evidence, whatever exactly it may consist of. It is time to consider what Equal Justification might imply about what their evidence can be. I will argue that, if one endorses Equal Justification and Evidential Internalism, one is still relatively uncommitted regarding what evidence one has. The upshot is that the internalist is not yet vulnerable to the following sort of objection:

> That one has the same evidence in the good and bad cases is a severe constraint on the nature of evidence ... [Evidential Internalism] drives evidence towards the purely phenomenal (Williamson 2000: 173).[31]

A tempting thought is that, if Equal Justification and Evidential Internalism are true, then some mentalist conception of evidence is correct. According to mentalist conceptions of evidence, one's evidence consists only of one's mental states or facts about one's mental states. On these views, if P does not concern one's mental state, then one's evidence does not include P. One might think that the internalist is committed to some such view, and one might find the view implausible for that reason.[32]

We can flesh out the line of thought as follows. The key step is that, if a person has a piece of non-mental evidence, then some internal twin of that person does not have that non-mental evidence. For instance, since Gary is in the good case, that a spider is black may well be evidence Gary has that an arthropod is black. However, since Barry is in the bad case, in which it is false that a spider is black, that a spider is black is not evidence Barry has that there is an arthropod is black. Thus, if one can have non-mental evidence, internal twins do not have the same evidence. But then, if one can have non-mental evidence, internal twins are not equally justified either.

Let's now evaluate the argument that Equal Justification entails some mentalist conception of evidence. The argument relies on the claim that, if someone has a piece of non-mental evidence, then some internal twin of the person lacks that evidence. There are at least two worries about the claim.

One potential problem is the assumption that one's evidence can consist only of true propositions or of states that one is in. This assumption might be mistaken. If it is wrong, then internal twins could be equally justified, yet have evidence which consists of false propositions which do not concern their mental state. For instance, it might be that one's (propositional) evidence consists of those propositions one is justified in believing, whether or not they are true. This non-mentalist view is plainly compatible with Evidential Internalism and Equal Justification. Further, this view respects the datum that, when one forms a belief on the basis of reasoning, one does not takes one's reason to be that one believes this or that, but instead to be what one believes. Given how we reason and think about our reasons, it is plausible to think of the evidence at least for our inferential beliefs as the contents of our beliefs, rather than as belief states themselves.[33]

One might protest that one's evidence can consist only of true propositions or of states that one is in. It would still not be true that a mentalist conception of evidence follows from the Equal Justification thesis. One way to bring this out is by considering necessary propositions. Although some contingent propositions will be true in the good case though false in the bad case, no such scenario can arise for any necessary proposition. Thus, internal twins can have non-mental evidence which consists of necessary propositions, concerning logic or mathematics or even their environment, as with a posteriori necessary truths. Another way to bring out the problem is by considering some contingent non-mental truths. Suppose it seems to Gary as though *that* spider is black, and he believes that *that* spider is black. Second, suppose that the contents of his mental states are object-dependent: if anyone has a mental state with those contents, it follows that the spider exists in their world. What follows is that, if Gary and Barry have exactly the same beliefs, then the spider exists in Barry's world as well. More generally, assuming that some non-factive mental states have object-dependent contents, the environments of people in those mental states must be alike in certain respects. Since the spider exists in both cases, and the twins have the same apparent experiences of the spider in both cases, there's no reason to deny that some facts about the spider can be evidence for their beliefs.

In sum, the Equal Justification thesis does not force us into any mentalist conception of evidence. We can bring this out either by considering that one's evidence might include false propositions, or by considering that the truth of many propositions, perhaps even of some contingent propositions, supervenes on the non-factive mental states of internal twins.

The points just made generalize to Evidential Internalism as well. Even if internal twins have the same evidence, it does not follow that they only have mental evidence. Evidential Internalism, like Equal Justification, leaves open the question of what evidence it is that internal twins share. The upshot is that, even if it is a mistake to endorse a mentalist conception of evidence, the view does not yet force us to make any such mistake.

IV. Skepticism and Evidence

Having discussed the motivation for Evidential Internalism in some detail, I now want to address a particular line of worry about the claim. According to this line of worry, one plays into the hands of the skeptic if one accepts Evidential Internalism. That is, there is a skeptical argument such that the externalist can undermine it and the internalist can't. By addressing the best argument which is a candidate for an externalist response, I will show that the worry is unmotivated. Despite what one might think, the externalist does not have any advantage in responding to skepticism.

The skeptical argument I will address tries to show that one is not justified in disbelieving certain radical skeptical hypotheses. For concreteness, I will focus on the hypothesis that you are a brain in a vat such that, although you are in all the non-factive mental states you would be in if you were in the good case, your beliefs are wherever possible false rather than true. I will take it for granted that, if you are not justified in disbelieving the skeptical hypothesis, then you are not justified in believing any proposition obviously incompatible with it.

The argument runs as follows.[34]

First, if you are justified in believing that you are not a BIV, then either you are experientially justified in believing that you are not a BIV, or you are non-experientially justified in believing that you are not a BIV. That is, either some experience or experiences of yours are part of what makes you justified in disbelieving the hypothesis, or something which excludes your experiences makes you justified in disbelieving the hypothesis. Assuming that something makes you justified in disbelieving the hypothesis if you are justified in disbelieving it at all, this first claim is correct.

Second, you are not experientially justified in believing that you are not a BIV. To motivate this claim, the skeptic may stress that the hypothesis entails that you have the experiences you do. In particular, since the skeptical hypothesis predicts that you have an experience as of having hands, you should respond to your experience as of having hands by raising your confidence in the skeptical hypothesis, just as you should increase your confidence in any hypothesis when you discover that something it predicts is true. And given that you should raise your confidence that the skeptical hypothesis is true in response to your experience, your experience does not provide you with justification to believe that the skeptical hypothesis is false.

Third, you are not non-experientially justified in believing that you are not a BIV. To motivate this claim, the skeptic may insist that the proposition that you are not a BIV is a worldly proposition, not guaranteed to be true by the concepts which figure in it.[35] Here the skeptic may rely on the empiricist thought, already mentioned above, that for any worldly proposition, justification for believing such a proposition must rest on one's course of experience.

There is much more to be said about how to refine the argument I have sketched, and there is much more to be said about various lines of potential response. But we have said enough to clarify how the evidential externalist will respond to the argument, and it is the externalist way with the argument which is of interest here.

According to the externalist, the claim that one is not experientially justified in believing that one is not a BIV is unmotivated and false. The claim is supposed to be unmotivated because the argument for it relies on an internalist description of my evidence for the proposition that I have hands. The skeptical hypothesis indeed does entail that I have an experience as of having hands. However, my strongest evidence (on the basis of which I believe) that I have hands is that I see my hands, or see that I have hands. My being in these perceptual states is not entailed by the skeptical hypothesis, but instead entails that the skeptical hypothesis is false. So it's false that my perceptual evidence is predicted by the skeptical hypothesis. Further, I am experientially justified in believing that I am not a BIV. Given that my perceptual evidence is incompatible with the skeptical hypothesis, it also provides me with justification to believe that I am not a BIV. The further details of exactly how I am justified in disbelieving the hypothesis remain to be worked out, but the thought is that there is no principled problem here for the externalist.

According to the evidential externalist, an advantage of their view is that it makes available a Moorean story about how one is justified in disbelieving radical skeptical hypotheses. On this line of thought, the evidential internalist is not in a position to provide a Moorean story of how one is justified in believing that one is not a BIV, or at least cannot provide as simple a Moorean story about how one is justified in believing that one is not a BIV. After all, the internalist would need to provide us with a principled reason to deny that, when one discovers that a prediction of a hypothesis obtains, one ought to increase one's confidence in the hypothesis. That seems hard to do.

I'll now discuss how Evidential Externalism fails to have the advantage it might seem to have. The problem I will explore is that the response envisaged by the externalist does not apply in the bad case. I set aside the question of whether the externalist response even works in the good case.

We can clarify and sharpen the problem as a dilemma. One option for the externalist is to deny that, in the bad case, one has outright justification to disbelieve the BIV hypothesis. Another option is to allow that, in the bad case, one has outright justification to disbelieve the hypothesis.

The externalist might say that the thinker in the bad case is not justified in disbelieving the skeptical hypothesis. Perhaps part of what is so bad about a scenario of radical deception is that, when one is in it, one is not justified in believing that one is not in it. This suggestion requires rejecting a claim already seen above:

> (Outright Equal Justification): Necessarily, if A and B are internal twins, then A is justified simpliciter in having an outright belief in P just in case B is justified simpliciter in having an outright belief in P.

This minimal thesis allows that one might have a greater degree of justification in the good case or the bad case. Thus, even if the externalist provides a reason to deny the stronger Equal Justification thesis, and explains away the plausibility of the stronger claim, the externalist will still need to provide a special treatment of Outright Equal Justification. A further complication is that I set out a further argument for Outright Equal Justification—the further argument will also have to be undermined.

The other option for the externalist is to grant that one is justified in the bad case in believing that one is not a BIV. Since their Moorean story is not applicable in the bad case, they will have to accept some story which is available to the internalist, which applies in the good case as well. Here the internalist is as well positioned as the externalist to hold that one is justified in believing that the skeptical hypothesis is false. The externalist will simply add that one enjoys an extra justification in the good case. However, it is no advantage for the externalist to grant us an extra anti-skeptical justification in the good case. The extra justification available in the good case is not required for one to be outright justified in disbelieving the hypothesis. The extra justification also is not required to explain how one knows that the skeptical hypothesis is false: one's belief in the good case is not inferred from a false premise, and it seems that one is not otherwise in danger of having justified true belief without knowledge.[36]

On the one option, the externalist has a burden the internalist lacks, namely of showing that Outright Equal Justification is false and explaining why it seemed true. This problem is an extra problem for the externalist position, on top of the problem of being incompatible with Equal Justification. On the other option, one need not endorse Evidential Externalism to explain how one is justified in disbelieving skeptical hypotheses, or even to explain how one knows they are false. Either way, the externalist has no special advantage in responding to the argument.

With respect to the skeptical argument we have considered—what I take to be the best skeptical argument one might give an externalist response—Evidential Externalism does not have the upper hand. Indeed, given the costs of some externalist responses to the argument, it might be that Evidential Internalism itself has the upper hand. In any case, the view cannot be fairly accused of playing into the hands of the skeptic.

Conclusion

We have now surveyed two lines of argument for Evidential Internalism. One strategy appeals to considerations about one's access to one's evidence, focusing either on when one can know what one's evidence is, or on how one can know what one's evidence is. Another strategy appeals to considerations about the Equal Justification of internal twins. I hope to have shown that the second strategy has the best prospects, while remaining clear about how much the strategy leaves open about exactly what evidence internal twins share. I also hope to have shown that, as far as responding to skepticism is concerned, the evidential externalist is no better off than the internalist. The overall case for

Evidential Externalism might turn out to be stronger, but the case for Evidential Internalism is not weak.

Notes

1. I'm grateful for helpful comments from Stewart Cohen, Adam Elga, Greg Epstein, Matt Kotzen, Anna-Sara Malmgren, Ram Neta, James Pryor, Stephen Schiffer, Declan Smithies, Ralph Wedgwood, Roger White, and Timothy Williamson, as well as participants in an NYU seminar.
2. A further line of argument for internalism appeals to considerations about the psychological explanation of internal twins' beliefs. I won't discuss that sort of argument here.
3. Evidential Internalism might be best understood as the claim that, if A and B are internal twins, then they have the same type of evidence. It might be that two internal twins have evidence which consists of their token experiences, and fail to share the same token experiences, although they do have experiences of the same type. A view which allows for this possibility need not conflict with the spirit of Evidential Internalism.
4. I also use the term "justification" broadly, so that I won't attend to distinctions that others might try to capture with terms such as "entitlement" or "warrant".
5. An evidential internalist should also require that the causal explanatory relations between their internal states are the same.
6. It may well be that, if I have a belief that I am F, someone is an internal twin of me only if he is identical with me. In that case Barry will just be Gary in another possible world.
7. The two suggestions seem to fail to be equivalent: broad mental states probably are consciously accessible, and narrow mental states probably are not consciously accessible.
8. One might insist that, if the version of Evidential Internalism formulated in terms of non-factive states is true, some version formulated in terms of a narrower supervenience base is true, and more basic. I won't be able to pursue the issue here.
9. Conee and Feldman (2001) helpfully distinguish between "accessibilism" and other forms of internalism. For useful discussion of distinctions between various access theses one might propose, see Pryor (2001: 105–8).
10. Similar theses can be found in early responses to the Gettier problem, as in Meyers and Stern (1973: 152) or Armstrong (1973: 152). For related claims formulated in terms of "reasons", see also Unger (1975) or Hyman (1999). Since Unger (1975) denies that one knows anything, he is not an evidential externalist in that work.
11. As James Pryor pointed out to me, someone might endorse Evidential Externalism while rejecting the claim that one can have evidence which obviously entails contingent propositions about the environment. For example, two internal twins might be in the same perceptual states, where being in those perceptual states fails to entail their propositional contents. Still, the internal

twins might have different evidence since their perceptual states differ with respect to how reliably they indicate the truth. We can think of this variant of Evidential Externalism as Indicator Evidence Externalism. (There may well be other versions of Evidential Externalism which diverge from Entailing Evidence Externalism, but I'm not aware of them).

Following Alston (1989: Essay 9), I find it natural to distinguish between the grounds of a subject's beliefs, and the adequacy of those grounds, or the evidence a subject possesses, and the strength of that evidence. As far as the above example of perceptual evidence is concerned, I take it that the evidence of the two twins is the same, even if the strength of their evidence is different. In general, I will take it that, if Evidential Externalism is true, then Entailing Evidence Externalism is true. Although it is important that one might turn out to be able to sever Evidential Externalism from Entailing Evidence Externalism, I won't provide any separate treatment of Indicator Evidence Externalism and related views in what follows.

12. This sort of point can also be found in Williamson (forthcoming, section 3).
13. For discussion of an access argument for an internalist claim which is stronger than Evidential Internalism, see Goldman (1999). For some responses to Goldman, see Bonjour (2001) or Feldman and Conee (2001).
14. For some relevant discussion, see Brueckner and Oreste Fiocco (2002) or Neta and Rohrbaugh (2004).
15. Relevant here is Fumerton (2000), Hawthorne (2004), and Williamson (2004a).
16. On any reasonable version of Evidential Externalism, there will be evidence one has in the good case but lacks in the bad case. On some, but not all, versions of the view, there will also be evidence one has in the bad case but lacks in the good case. For example, on some metaphysical views about experiences, there is no (visual) experiential state in common between someone who sees a parrot and anyone who hallucinates a parrot (Hinton 1973 or McDowell 1982). Here there may be experiential evidence that one has in the bad case but lacks in the good case, as well as experiential evidence that one has in the good case but lacks in the bad case. Since there is no experiential state in common between the cases there is no experiential evidence in common between the cases either. Discussions with Greg Epstein were helpful here.
17. According to one line of response, the evidential externalist need not allow that we can have evidence which obviously entails proposition about the environment. For some discussion of this line of response, see n. 11.
18. Discussions with Matt Kotzen were helpful here.
19. For a selection of approaches to the problem, see Ludlow and Martin (1998) or Nuccetelli (2003).
20. I explore the puzzle for Evidential Externalism in more detail in my dissertation, "Reasons and Armchair Knowledge."
21. A similar line of argument—often called the "new evil demon problem"—is used against proposals of necessary conditions for justification in terms of reliability. Such proposals seem to imply that one's internal twin in the bad case is not justified in her beliefs. See Cohen (1984: 280–4), Foley (1984: 113–4), or Luper-Foy (1985: 215–6). The problem for the externalist is importantly different from the problem for the reliabilist. It is open to the externalist to claim that one's

twin in the bad case does have evidence, albeit less evidence than oneself. The initial argument against Evidential Externalism will thus need to concern the degree of justification of internal twins' beliefs, whereas the argument against reliabilism can simply consider the outright justification of internal twins' beliefs. Also, Evidential Externalism will turn out to imply that one is sometimes epistemically better off when one is radically deceived, whereas reliabilism seems only to imply that one is sometimes better off in the good case.

22. The epistemology literature is often unclear about the distinction between evaluative and explanatory claims. For an exception, see Sidelle (2001: 170–2).
23. For a technical discussion of the relation between Evidential Internalism and the claim that the evidential probabilities in the good case and the bad case are the same, see Williamson (2004b: 313–4). The discussion is orthogonal to my own, since my emphasis is on doxastic justification.
24. For example, Williamson writes that "we should question the association between evidential probability 1 and absolute certainty (2000: 213)." Hawthorne also writes that "such an equation [on which it is rational to be confident in p to degree n iff the epistemic probability of p is n] will not likely be palatable to a nonskeptic who thinks that knowledge entails epistemic probability of 1, assuming that rational confidence of degree 1 in p bring with it a rational disposition to be at any odds on p (2004: 29, n. 72)." The further details of Williamson's account of evidential probability are to be found in his (2000: ch. 10).
25. Notice that the argument is insensitive to the difference between evidential externalists who allow that one can have evidence which obviously entails propositions about the environment, and those who don't.
26. For some recent work which supplies considerations against Equal Justification, without arguing directly for Evidential Externalism, see Sutton (forthcoming). One should bear in mind, when assessing Equal Justification, that internal twins are in the same non-factive mental states throughout their careers. The proponent of Equal Justification thus can allow that two people are in the same non-factive mental states at a given time, yet fail to be equally justified at that time, since one may have forgotten evidence that the other never had (cf. Sosa 1999 or Greco 2005). Given the reading we are using of "internal twin", such a case is not a counterexample to Equal Justification. The point can also be found in Feldman (2005).
27. For a contextualist treatment of ascriptions of evidence, see Neta (2003). For a view one might describe as an ambiguity view, see Sosa in BonJour and Sosa (2003: 153–5).
28. This sort of move is suggested in a different context by Byrne (2005: 246–7).
29. Another objection could be that, since being epistemically blameless just is being epistemically justified, Equal Blamelessness is not a substitute for any thesis in terms of epistemic justification. I follow other philosophers in denying that being justified is a matter of being blameless. See Pryor (2001: 114–5), Conee and Feldman (2001: 240), or Wedgwood (2002: 351). The simplest way to make the point is to stress that being justified is a matter of degree whereas being blameless is not. Notice that it is a separate question whether being epistemically *praiseworthy* entails being epistemically justified.

30. Strictly speaking, the conclusion of the Suspension argument is that, if one has sufficient propositional justification in the good case to have an outright belief in P, then one has sufficient propositional justification in the bad case to have an outright belief in P. That's because the Suspension principle is best understood in terms of propositional justification. I assume it to follow that, if one is doxastically justified in the good case in believing P, then one is doxastically justified in the bad case in believing P. I also assume that, if one is doxastically justified in the bad case, then one is doxastically justified in the good case. Finally, I assume that one's internal twins who are not radically deceived require no special treatment here.
31. Williamson's specific objection is that, if Evidential Internalism is true, then one's evidence can consist only of "those conditions, whatever they are, which rational subjects can know themselves to be in whenever they are in them (173)." By showing that one need not invoke a claim like Transparency to motivate the internalist view, I hope to have already addressed this particular objection. The more general question remains of whether the internalist is committed to a mentalist conception of evidence.
32. For useful discussion of mentalist views of reasons for action, and more discussion of what reasons might be, see Dancy (2000).
33. On the view that one's evidence is what one is justified in believing, we also have an abundance of entailing evidence if we have lots of justified beliefs. One might protest that, if it was supposed to be problematic for the externalist to allow us a wealth of entailing evidence, it should also be problematic for the internalist to allow us a wealth of entailing evidence. However, the internalist can allow that, even if the probability of H on entailing E is 1, we should discount how confident one should be by how confident one should be in E itself. The externalist is not allowed to make this move, since it presumably would undermine the claim that one should be more confident in the good case than the bad case. So the internalist might escape the objection to externalism.
34. Here I draw on Pollock (1974), Pryor (2000), Schiffer (2004), and White (forthcoming).
35. The skeptical hypothesis in question is one in which one has the mental contents that one would in the good case. It thus is not open to the response to skepticism set out in Putnam (1981).
36. If one accepts the thesis that only knowledge justifies belief, it's not clear how to explain that a subject is justified in the bad case in believing that she is not in the bad case, since it seems possible for such a subject to fail to have knowledge which justifies that belief. She might for example merely hold the belief on the basis of an inference from the false premise that she has hands. Here the externalist might have to abandon the stronger thesis that only knowledge justifies belief—thereby allowing for non-evidential justification—and retreat to the weaker claim that only what one knows is evidence.

References

Alston, W.P. 1989: *Epistemic Justification: Essays in the Theory of Knowledge*. Cornell University Press.

Armstrong, A. 1973: *Belief, Truth, and Knowledge*. Cambridge University Press.

Audi, R. 2001: An Internalist Theory of Normative Grounds, *Philosophical Topics* (29): 31–45.

BonJour, L. 1999: Foundationalism and the External World, in J. Tomberlin, ed., *Philosophical Perspectives, 13: Epistemology*, Blackwell.

——2001: The Indispensability of Internalism, *Philosophical Topics* (29): 47–65.

—— and Sosa, E. 2003: *Epistemic Justification: Internalism vs. Externalism, Foundations vs. Virtues*. Blackwell.

Brewer, B. 1999: *Perception and Reason*. Oxford University Press.

Brueckner, A., and M. Oreste Fiocco. 2002: Williamson's Anti-Luminosity Argument. *Philosophical Studies* (110): 285–293.

Burge, T. 1993: Content Preservation, *Journal of Philosophy* (102): 457–488.

Byrne, A. 2005: Perception and Conceptual Content, in M. Steup and E. Sosa, eds., *Contemporary Debates in Epistemology*, Blackwell.

Cohen, S. 1984: Justification and Truth, *Philosophical Studies* (46): 279–95.

Conee, E. and Feldman, R. 1998: The Generality Problem for Reliabilism, *Philosophical Studies* (89): 1–29.

——2001: Internalism Defended, *American Philosophical Quarterly* (38): 1–18. Also in their *Evidentialism*, Oxford University Press, 2004.

Dancy, J. 2000: *Practical Reality*. Oxford University Press.

Feldman, R. 2005: Justification is Internal, in M. Steup and E. Sosa, eds., *Contemporary Debates in Epistemology*, Blackwell.

Foley, R. 1984: Epistemic Luck and the Purely Epistemic, *American Philosophical Quarterly* (21): 113–124.

Fumerton, R. 2000: Williamson on Skepticism and Evidence, *Philosophy and Phenomenological Research* (60): 629–35.

Goldman, A. 1999: Internalism Exposed, *Journal of Philosophy* (96): 271–93.

Greco, J. 2005: Justification is Not Internal, in M. Steup and E. Sosa, eds., *Contemporary Debates in Epistemology*, Blackwell.

Hawthorne, J. 2002: Deeply Contingent A Priori Knowledge, *Philosophy and Phenomenological Research* (65): 247–69.

Hinton, J. 1973: *Experiences*. Clarendon Press.

Hyman, J. 1999: How Knowledge Works, *Philosophical Quarterly* (49): 433–51.

Kitcher, P. 1980: A Priori Knowledge, *Philosophical Review* (89): 3–23.

Ludlow, P. and Martin, N. 1998: *Externalism and Self-Knowledge*, CSLI Publications.

Luper-Foy, S. 1985: The Reliabilist Theory of Rational Belief, *The Monist* (68): 203–225.

McDowell, J. 1982: Criteria, Defeasibility, and Knowledge, *Proceedings of the British Academy* (68): 455–79. Also in J. Dancy, ed., *Perceptual Knowledge*, Oxford University Press, 1988.

——1995: Knowledge and the Internal, *Philosophy and Phenomenological Research* (55): 877–93.

McKinsey, M. 1998: Anti-Individualism and Privileged Access, *Analysis* (51): 9–16. Also in Ludlow and Martin (1998).

Meyers, R., and Stern, K. 1973: Knowledge Without Paradox, *The Journal of Philosophy* (70): 147–60.

Neta, R. 2003: Contextualism and the Problem of the External World, *Philosophy and Phenomenological Research* (66): 1–31.

—— and Rohrbaugh, G. 2004: Luminosity and the Safety of Knowledge, *Pacific Philosophical Quarterly* (85): 396–406.

Nuccetelli, S. 2003: *New Essays on Semantic Externalism and Self-Knowledge*. MIT Press.
Pollock, J. 1974: *Knowledge and Justification*. Princeton University Press.
Pryor, J. 2000: The Skeptic and the Dogmatist, *Noûs* (34): 517–49.
———2001: Highlights of Recent Epistemology, *British Journal of Philosophy of Science* (52): 95–124.
Putnam, H. 1981: *Reason, Truth, and History*. Cambridge University Press.
Sawyer, S. 1998: Privileged Access to the World, *Australasian Journal of Philosophy* (76): 523–33.
Schiffer, S. 2005: Paradox and the A Priori, to appear in J. Hawthorne and T. Gendler, eds., *Oxford Studies in Epistemology*, Oxford University Press. Available at <http://www.nyu.edu/gsas/dept/philo/faculty/schiffer/papers/ParadoxAPriori.pdf>.
Sidelle, A. 2001: An Argument that Internalism Requires Infallibility, *Philosophy and Phenomenological Research* (63): 163–79.
Sosa, E. 1999: Skepticism and the Internal/External Divide, in M. Steup and E. Sosa, eds., *Contemporary Debates in Epistemology*, Blackwell.
Sutton, J. forthcoming: Stick to What You Know, to appear in *Noûs*. Available at <http://www.faculty.smu.edu/jsutton/obligation.pdf>.
Unger, P. 1975: *Ignorance: A Case for Skepticism*. Oxford University Press.
Weatherson, B. 2005: Skepticism, Rationalism, and Externalism, to appear in J. Hawthorne and T. Gendler, eds., *Oxford Studies in Epistemology*, Oxford University Press. Available at <http://www.brian.weatherson.net/papers.html>.
Wedgwood, R. 2002: Internalism Explained, *Philosophy and Phenomenological Research* (65): 349–69.
White, R. forthcoming: Problems for Dogmatism, to appear in *Philosophical Studies*. Available at <http://www.nyu.edu/gsas/dept/philo/faculty/white/papers/dogmatism.pdf>.
Williamson, T. 2000: *Knowledge and Its Limits*. Oxford University Press.
———2004a: Replies to Commentators, *Philosophical Books* (45): 313–23.
———2004b: Replies to Commentators, *Philosophy and Phenomenological Research*.
———forthcoming: On Being Justified in One's Head, to appear in a festschrift for Robert Audi. Available at <http://www.philosophy.ox.ac.uk/faculty/members/index_tw.htm>.

Philosophical Perspectives, 19, Epistemology, 2005

KNOWLEDGE FROM FALSEHOOD

Ted A. Warfield
University of Notre Dame

I am interested in a variety of situations in which one apparently knows something despite the existence of something non-ideal in the epistemic pedigree of the belief in question (examples: faulty reasoning, false premise, problematic testimony). In this paper I begin a discussion of the 'knowledge from falsehood' part of this project.

Consider the following claim:

(1) Inferential knowledge of a conclusion requires known relevant premises.[1]

One consequence of (1) is:

(1a) Inferential knowledge of a conclusion requires true relevant premises.

I will focus my critical attention on (1a).[2] I will now offer some charitable interpretation of parts of (1a), interpretations that help us dodge obvious counterexamples. I'll then briefly explain some ways of motivating (1a) before beginning my critical engagement with it.

Clarifications of 'inferential knowledge' and 'relevant' will enable us to sidestep what might seem to be obvious counterexamples to (1a). I make these clarifications in reverse order. First, the restriction to 'relevant' premises avoids simple counterexamples involving overdetermination. I reason (having seen each enter the room a minute ago)—'Jerry Fodor is in the room, Steve Stich is in the room, Colin McGinn is in the room, Brian McLaughlin is in the room; therefore, at least one Rutgers philosopher of mind is in the room.' Assume that my premises are all true except one: McGinn has, after entering, stepped out to take a phone call. I know my conclusion despite the false premise about McGinn. Here's a first pass at an explanation: the McGinn premise is not 'relevant' in this case to the particular conclusion. I will address further issues about the proper unpacking of 'relevant' when they arise in the discussion of my counterexamples to (1a).

Second, in evaluating (1a) let us charitably understand 'inferential knowledge' so that our attention is restricted to cases in which every path to the conclusion in question is an inferential path. Otherwise we would likely find counterexamples in cases where one both sees that P, and infers (through a falsehood) that P, but where one knows because one sees and one's seeing epistemically dominates the inference. Having been told falsely but authoritatively that Barry Loewer never leaves this room, I reason (through the suppressed conditional 'If Loewer never leaves this room then he's here today') to the conclusion that Loewer is here today. As I complete this reasoning, I see Loewer standing in front of me. I know that Loewer is here despite reasoning through a falsehood to my conclusion.[3]

In the interest of further simplification, let's focus on cases in which one has exactly one 'inferential argument' for one's conclusion and one's inferential argument consists of a single material premise and a suppressed conditional linking the premise to the conclusion via simple modus ponens. This simplification does not require taking a stand on the question of whether coherentist or other 'holistic' features play a justificatory role nor does the simplification involve taking a stand on the epistemic role of 'the background' or anything else. In simplifying in this way, we simply attend to inferences where the surface form of reasoning involved is quite perspicuous. Simplify the discussion still further by focusing on the *formation* of the belief via this modus ponens inference (and the epistemic status of the belief at the time of formation) and leave belief 'sustenance' issues aside.[4]

Turning from clarification to motivation, I now briefly present some ways of motivating (1a). Here are three quick points followed by a fourth and more fully explored point.[5] First, (1a) partly reflects widespread preference for sound arguments over merely valid arguments. Second, inferential knowledge requires that the conjunction of one's premises constitutes a 'good reason' for accepting one's conclusion and falsity suffices for the badness of a reason. Third, with a false premise in one's inferential argument, it appears that luck of some sort is needed to get one to a truth at one's conclusion.[6] Compare the luck apparently involved in reaching a true conclusion via valid inference from a *false* premise with the *guarantee* of truth in the conclusion when one's inferential argument to that conclusion is sound. Turn now to a fourth point that seemingly motivates (1a): a natural line of thought has it that Gettier issues suggest that (1a) is correct.

Begin with some Gettier lessons. I see what looks like a dog out in the yard. I reason (on this occasion) as follows: there's a dog in the yard, so there's at least one animal in the yard. As it happens, my premise is false (there's a realistic looking toy in the yard and that is what I see in the dog-less yard). But my conclusion is true because concealed behind some brush is a squirrel. I don't know my conclusion despite its truth and the valid argument leading to it. The falsity of my premise is, perhaps, what has gone wrong in the case. In studying the Gettier problem, we learn fairly early on that 'reasoning through a falsehood' is not an essential element in constructing a Gettier case. One typically learns this from a 'stopped clock case'. At what I correctly judge to be 5 minutes' walking distance from my classroom, I see a clock face reading 1:00. Relying wholly on that reading of the clock for my estimate of the time, I reason: it's 1:00; so, I'm not late for my 1:10 class. It is in fact 1:00 but the clock I am reading stopped working days ago. I don't know I'm not late for my 1:10 class. Reasoning through a relevant falsehood is not necessary for generating Gettier cases. Reflection on the dog/yard/squirrel case, however, leaves many thinking that reasoning through a relevant falsehood is sufficient for generating a Gettier case. Because Gettiered conclusions aren't knowledge, (1a) would seem to follow.

We thus have non-trivial motivation for (1a). Any rejection of (1a) should surely include some commentary explaining why and how these four motivations for (1a) are safely rejected. I will return to this task after providing and discussing some counterexamples to (1a), and rejecting anticipated resistance to the counterexamples.

I turn now to some examples. (1a) cannot be sustained. Begin with this counterexample.

> **Example #1.** My doctor has ordered that I get at least 8 hours sleep per night. I knowingly go to bed at 11pm. I wake up and see the clock reading "2:30am". I reason: (premise) I've been asleep 3½ hours, so (conclusion) I haven't slept the mandated 8 hours. My premise is false. I've forgotten that it's the night of the (Fall) time change and I have a clock that automatically resets in the appropriate way at the appropriate time and it has already done this. So I've been asleep 4½ hours (we're at "2:30am" for the 2nd time). Despite all of this complexity (and, indeed, partly because of it) I still know my conclusion.[7]

Additional counterexamples to (1a) are easy to find. Not all of the examples I'll present are equally compelling and perhaps some are similar enough to others that they add nothing of substance to the investigation. I provide a range of examples so that non-essential features of one example don't inappropriately dominate the analysis and so that distinct types of counterexamples (if distinct types exist) can perhaps be identified. Here's another example.

> **Example #2.** With hopes of getting him to attend a party in Providence on Saturday night, Jaegwon Kim asks Christopher Hill what he's doing on Saturday. Hill replies 'I'm flying to Fayetteville on Saturday night' and the conversation ends. Kim, recalling that Hill taught for many years in Fayetteville, Arkansas, reasons as follows: 'Hill will be in Arkansas on Saturday night; so, he won't be at my party Saturday night'. Kim knows his conclusion, but his premise is false: Hill is flying to Fayetteville, *North Carolina*.[8]

And here, in abbreviated form, are three more to round out the example set:

> **Example #3**. Counting with some care the number of people present at my talk, I reason: 'There are 53 people at my talk; therefore my 100 handout copies are

sufficient'. My premise is false. There are 52 people in attendance—I double counted one person who changed seats during the count. And yet I know my conclusion.

Example #4. CNN breaks in with a live report. The headline is 'The President is speaking now to supporters in Utah'. I reason: 'The President is in Utah; therefore he is not attending today's NATO talks in Brussels'. I know my conclusion but my premise is false: the President is in Nevada—he is speaking at a 'border rally' at the border of those two states and the speaking platform on which he is standing is in Nevada. The crowd listening to the speech is in Utah.

Example #5. I have a 7pm meeting and extreme confidence in the accuracy of my fancy watch. Having lost track of the time and wanting to arrive on time for the meeting, I look carefully at my watch. I reason: 'It is exactly 2:58pm; therefore I am not late for my 7pm meeting'. Again I know my conclusion, but as it happens it's exactly 2:56pm, not 2:58pm.

With five apparent counterexamples to (1a) before us, I should clarify the overall dialectical situation and then look at possible responses to the counterexamples from those who don't want to concede the falsity of (1a). The examples are at least apparent counterexamples to (1a) because it seems that:

(i) the examples involve inferential knowledge of a conclusion

and

(ii) the examples involve a false relevant premise.

In defense of (i) there is nothing to do except appeal to clear and widely shared intuitions about the cases. In defense of (ii), the falsity of the premise in each argument is properly stipulated in each example and the 'relevance' of that false premise is suggested by the fact that the premise is the sole material premise in the inferential episode leading to the conclusion. If the sole substantive premise isn't relevant then someone has some explaining to do about the notion of 'relevance' involved in (1a).

In light of the examples and these observations, I prefer the following straightforward evaluation of the situation. We have counterexamples to (1a) and so (1a) is false. The cases are cases of '*knowledge from falsehood*' and so we must integrate this fact, carefully no doubt, into our overall epistemological thinking. As a starting point for this, note that in the examples the truth of the conclusion and the path to it seem quite stable despite the relevant falsehoods in the examples. Metaphorically, we do not seem to be kicked off the path to inferential knowledge of our conclusion in these examples by the falsehood. This seems to be because the falsehood, to leave things unanalyzed for now, seems to do the job (of taking us to knowledge) quite well.

If everyone would agree with this initial reaction to the counterexamples, I would move forward immediately to unpack my metaphorical diagnostic language and to revisit the motivations for believing (1a) to explain how they led us astray. Strangely enough, however, not everyone believes that we should reject (1a). Many would like to resist this conclusion. Any resistance to a counterexample to (1a) must make one of two claims. Either the resistance must claim that the agent in the example does not know the conclusion or the resistance must claim that the falsehood involved in the example is not 'relevant' in the sense involved in (1a). Though the examples are not of precisely equal plausibility, I think it is safe to exclude the first approach (denying knowledge) as a *general* response to the range of examples.[9] The resistance must therefore make at least partial use of the other available response: denying that the involved falsehood is a 'relevant' falsehood.

Those favoring this approach should be heartened by the fact that I have not provided an account of (or even a sufficient condition for) the 'relevance' of a premise in an inferential argument. In charitably rejecting simple overdetermination counterexamples to (1a), I rejected the simple idea that a sufficient condition for the relevance of a premise is that the premise actually is used in the inferential argument being examined.[10] This gestures at a familiar distinction between the causal and epistemic base of a belief and plausibly suggests that 'relevance' is a matter of epistemology. And a moment ago I suggested, but did not *argue*, that in the one premise arguments we are considering, the fact that the false premise is the sole premise seems to suffice for its relevance. The resistance should seize upon this inexactness and attempt to understand the examples in such a way that though knowledge of the conclusion is indeed present, the falsehood involved is not relevant. If successful, the resistance could fairly describe the examples as 'knowledge *despite* falsehood' (knowledge despite an involved, though not epistemically relevant, falsehood) rather than 'knowledge *from* falsehood' as I would have it.

There are several ways one might attempt to work out a detailed resistance strategy.[11] But all possible resistance strategies must make the following claims about each counterexample in which knowledge of the conclusion is conceded:

(i) though there is a falsehood *involved* in the inferential argument, the falsehood is not *relevant*.
(ii) a truth (not the falsehood) in the example plays the central epistemizing role.

Point (ii) is the substantive point that downplays the role of the falsehoods in the examples. The falsehoods are involved in the examples, but perhaps they are not epistemically relevant. Let's see what the resistance might have in mind by returning to the examples. I begin with two clearly inadequate resistance strategies that help point the way to more serious resistance.

Most who have reflected on the five examples displayed earlier have noticed at least the following. In each example there seems to be at least one true proposition 'somewhere in the neighborhood' that seems well suited to playing an epistemizing role with respect to the conclusion. The propositions seem well suited because, at a minimum, it looks like they are strongly supported by the agent's evidence. Though individuals might identify different propositions in some cases, let's take note of some candidate resistance propositions (noting possible alternatives in brackets):

Example #1 - I've been asleep less than 5 hours. [alternatively 'about 3 ½ hours']
Example #2 - Hill will be out of town on Saturday. ['not in Providence']
Example #3 - There are approximately 53 people at my talk. ['fewer than 55']
Example #4 - The President is in the Western USA. ['is in or near Utah']
Example #5 - It's about 3:00 pm. ['several hours before my meeting']

The simplest resistance strategy would, having identified these true propositions in each of the proposed counterexamples, boldly suggest the following response to the counterexamples. The involved falsehoods in the examples are not relevant and so we have no counterexamples to (1a). Epistemization in each example is a product of the above identified propositions. These propositions are all true and the agent in each example seems to have good evidence for the proposition. I know that I haven't had the doctor-mandated eight hours of sleep, says this approach, not because of my justified belief that I've slept 3 ½ hours (that's false) but because of the nearby true proposition 'I've slept fewer than 5 hours' that is also justified for me.

This simplest resistance strategy moves too quickly. The strategy suggests that sufficient for knowledge in each case is there being a true proposition intuitively 'in the neighborhood' that serves to epistemize each example's conclusion. This simple approach fails. Notice that though we have identified true propositions intuitively 'in the neighborhood' of the examples for which the agents appear to have strong evidence, we have not even said that the agents believe the propositions. One wonders how the propositions identified are supposed to epistemize the conclusions if they are not even believed by the agents in the examples. Given the evidence that the agents seem to have for the identified proposition, it seems plausible that the agents would be disposed to believe the relevant proposition. But mere dispositions to believe cannot play an epistemizing role in an inferential argument: allowing them to do so grossly over-ascribes inferential knowledge.

This first resistance strategy suggests a second. Acknowledging that mere dispositions to believe can't play an epistemizing role, the resistance might claim that the agent in each example *at least* dispositionally believes the identified proposition. Dispositional beliefs (or stronger) surely can play an epistemizing role. The natural suggestion here is that one knows despite the involvement of a falsehood, if one has a justified dispositional belief suitable for epistemizing one's conclusion.

This second resistance strategy also clearly fails. Grant for purposes of criticism the controversial assumption that in all cases of the same type as the proposed counterexamples the agent at least dispositionally believes the identified proposition.[12] Proponents of this strategy encounter severe difficulty with standard 'basing relation' cases. The detective believes that Jones is the murderer. He accepts the contents of a forensic report indicating that DNA evidence strongly points to Jones. But the detective believes that Jones is the murderer not on the basis of the report but rather solely because he infers this from his delusional belief that Jones confessed to the killings. The standard and proper verdict in this case is that the detective does not know that Jones is the murderer. The second resistance strategy fails here, delivering the verdict that detective has knowledge. Despite the involved false belief about the confession, there is a true and evidentially supported dispositional belief in the neighborhood (about the contents of the forensic report) suitable for epistemizing the belief that Jones is the murderer. The second resistance strategy therefore says that the detective knows that Jones is the murderer in a case in which uncontroversially he does not know this. This fact eliminates the second resistance strategy from contention.

Once again, however, failure suggests another path. A third resistance strategy can be identified in an attempt to keep what is promising in the second strategy while distinguishing the cases in which we clearly want to ascribe knowledge (the counterexample cases at least) from the cases in which we clearly do not want this to happen (the 'no knowledge' standard basing relation cases). Notice that almost all of the truths pointed to in the alleged counterexamples are entailed by the key proposition falsely believed in the example. Notice further that for each example, there is at least one such entailed truth. The resistance might claim that it is the entailment of the justified and (at least) dispositionally believed truth by the involved falsehood that marks these cases as cases of knowledge despite the involvement of a falsehood in the inference.

The suggestion is that one has knowledge despite the presence of an involved falsehood if there is a justified and (at least) dispositionally believed truth entailed by the falsehood that serves as the premise in one's inferential argument. The truth is the epistemic basis though the falsehood is the causal basis. The truth is an appropriate epistemic basis (avoiding standard basing condition case worries) because of the entailment of the truth by the falsehood. Notice that the detective's false belief about a confession from Jones does not entail the proposition concerning the content of the forensic report. This shows how this approach would improve upon the second approach's mishandling of the detective case.

A variant on this proposal can be identified as a fourth possible resistance strategy. The resistance might not be best served by requiring that the dispositional belief being pressed into service as the purported epistemizer be *entailed* by the falsehood. Perhaps the resistance could make do with a less restrictive condition that manages to block the verdict that the resistance gets the detective case wrong. The resistance might suggest the following broader account. One has knowledge despite the presence of an involved falsehood if there is a justified and (at least) dispositionally believed truth evidentially supported by the evidence for the involved falsehood. Notice that just as with the third resistance strategy, the detective case is not a problem because the evidence for the confession belief does not epistemically support the belief concerning the forensic report's contents.

Here are two apparent advantages this fourth strategy may have over the third. This fourth strategy seems to avoid what resistance fans should think is an unsettling picture of the epistemology of the counterexample cases that emerges from the third resistance strategy. According to the third strategy, knowledge is reached in the conclusion but the falsehood seems to be playing an important epistemizing role: there is good evidence for the falsehood, which then entails the truth, which then epistemizes the conclusion. This picture seems to give the falsehood an important and apparently epistemic role to play, one that should offend the intuitions of fans of the resistance. The fourth strategy avoids this appearance. A second apparent advantage of the fourth resistance proposal is its breadth. This account seemingly covers a wider range of cases than the account requiring entailment: entailment is presumably only one kind of epistemic support relation between evidence and conclusion.

I evaluate (and reject) these more serious third and fourth resistance proposals together. Grant, once again, the assumption that in every counterexample case we will find dispositional beliefs entailed by the involved falsehood or epistemically supported by it. Both proposals fail catastrophically in Gettier cases. I seem to see a dog in the yard. On this occasion I form the belief that there is a dog in the yard and then reason as before to the conclusion that there is at least one animal in the yard. My belief is false (there is no dog, only the toy) and my conclusion though true, because of the squirrel behind the brush, is not known. The third and fourth resistance strategies get this clear 'no knowledge' case wrong. They both imply that I know that there's at least one animal in the yard. After all, there is a justified and dispositionally believed truth that is *both* evidentially supported by and entailed by my false belief that there is a dog in the yard: the truth is 'there is a dog or squirrel in the yard'. The third and fourth resistance strategies both rule that this belief epistemizes my conclusion. I therefore am judged to have knowledge in this case which goes against the standard and correct Gettier verdict. The sophisticated third and fourth resistance strategies fail and with them fails the resistance.

I see no way of maintaining that the knowledge present in the counterexample cases traces entirely to some truth. I think we need to take the cases at face value: they are cases of knowledge *from* falsehood, not cases of knowledge *despite* falsehood. We sometimes gain knowledge via inference from a false premise. And not merely in familiar enough cases where a falsehood is not essentially involved (in a non-epistemizing role). I think we need to accept that relevant falsehoods sometimes play a central epistemizing role in inference. As noted earlier, one taking my position owes responses to the motivations that seem to lead so many to embrace (1a). As we'll see momentarily, these responses raise complex and important questions about central epistemological issues. I can't deal adequately with all of these issues on this occasion. Here I'll restrict my focus to showing what issues need to be addressed by defending my position and by beginning to sketch my preferred strategy for dealing with these issues.[13]

Recall the motivations for (1a) rehearsed early in the paper:

(i) We have a reasonable preference for sound arguments over merely valid arguments.
(ii) A 'good reason' for accepting a conclusion must be a truth.
(iii) Luck is apparently involved, even when reasoning validly, in reaching a true conclusion from a false premise (compared with the *guarantee* of a true conclusion when reasoning validly from a truth). The luck involved is plausibly thought to be destructive of knowledge.
(iv) Gettier cases show that though reasoning through a falsehood isn't a necessary part of a Gettier case, reasoning through a relevant falsehood is sufficient for Gettier-eliminating the conclusion.

Points (i) and (ii) on their own are not substantive points. They seem to state a preference for (1a) but they provide no serious motivation for it. What force might be contained in these points is likely found in points (iii) and (iv) which are clearly more serious attempts to motivate (1a).[14]

The motivation coming from points (iii) and (iv) may well be the same. One possible diagnosis of what goes wrong in a Gettier case that involves reasoning through a falsehood (eg, the dog/yard/squirrel case) is that in reasoning through the falsehood in the case, one puts oneself in a situation where (knowledge-destroying) *luck* is needed to get back on the path to truth. That common explanation of this sort of Gettier scenario suggests that points (iii) and (iv) are intimately connected.

This point does not downplay the significance of the Gettier issue in raising worries about my rejection of (1a). One accepting my 'knowledge from falsehood' position does owe an alternative explanation of what has gone wrong in Gettier cases involving reasoning through a falsehood. One can't, obviously enough, explain the lack of knowledge simply by saying, 'the agent reasoned through a falsehood' because the 'knowledge from falsehood' position implies that such reasoning is consistent with inferential knowledge. This is indeed an important and complex issue. I have two points to make about the issue now.

First, though one taking my 'knowledge from falsehood' position does owe an explanation of what goes wrong in falsehood-involving Gettier cases, one taking my position does not have a special burden here. After all, the proposed counterexamples to (1a) should, whether ultimately judged successful or not, significantly worry those who take reasoning through a falsehood to be sufficient for generating a Gettier case. Philosophers on both sides of this overall debate need to reexamine the connection between falsehood and Gettier cases. Second, though the Gettier issues are indeed important and interesting, it seems that the relevant Gettier issues fold back into the issues raised by point (iii) above. If I can, in reply to point (iii), distinguish cases in which inference through a relevant falsehood generates or constitutes knowledge-destroying luck from cases in which it does not, the account will thereby separate out the 'no-knowledge' Gettier falsehood cases from the 'knowledge from falsehood' cases. I see no way to immediately provide a full account of this distinction. But I can, as promised, sketch and motivate my preferred strategy for dealing with this issue.

The key point in my sketch of a strategy made one brief appearance earlier in the paper. Recall that in each of the counterexamples to (1a) the inferential path from the falsehood to the known conclusion did not seem especially shaky or precarious. Indeed, the path from falsehood to truth in each example seemed remarkably stable and secure. It is no accident that the falsehood 'there are 53 people at my talk' gets me to the truth 'my 100 handout copies are sufficient' nor does it seem that I was epistemically lucky in concluding 'the President is not in Brussels' upon coming to (falsely) believe that he is in Utah based on CNN's accurate report of his 'speaking to supporters in Utah'. Given that both Fayetteville airports are far from Providence, Kim's path to knowledge that Hill will miss his party is quite secure given the evidence of Hill's statement that he is 'flying to Fayetteville'.

This notion of 'stability' that I am opposing with 'luck' is still at the level of metaphor and for now that's where it will have to stay. I do think that the main point is quite suggestive: falsehoods of a certain sort (or, better, of a certain sort in certain *overall* contexts) are well suited to take us to truth. Consider what is probably one (but not the only) sort of common situation in which the path from falsity to truth could not be happily described as 'lucky': approximation. One who falsely believes that pi rounded to the 11th decimal place is 3.14159265358 and uses this mistaken belief in reasoning about circumferences can surely be credited with knowing (with relevant further detail filled in) that the circumference of a one meter diameter circle is 'greater than 3.14 meters'.[15]

I'm not, I emphasize, claiming that approximation is what's involved in all possible counterexamples to (1a). It's one important feature involved in some of the examples and it's one that helpfully illustrates the mistake involved in thinking that all inferences through falsehoods involve knowledge-destroying luck. There is no hint of problematic 'luck' in the above inference to the circumference of the one meter circle.[16]

My sketch of a response to the initial motivations for (1a) and for articulating an account of when knowledge does and does not arise from falsehood is now in view. I emphasize the strength of the clear counterexamples to (1a). I identify, metaphorically for now, an 'anti-luck' component that all the apparent counterexamples share: 'stability' in the path from the falsehood to the known conclusion. And I illustrate one general and common form of reasoning involving falsehoods that one could profitably defend by appeal to this informal notion of stability. Filling in the details of this story is, as I've emphasized, in some ways a complex matter. The necessity of this project and the inevitability of its success are, however, strongly suggested by the central cases illustrating that we sometimes get knowledge from falsehood.[17]

Notes

1. (1) is used in a variety of defenses of 'knowledge foundationalism' and in other settings as well.
2. (1a) has been endorsed by, among others, Aristotle, Russell, Frege and many living philosophers.
3. For simplicity, and because it might be correct, let's assume that the case of two overdetermining inferential paths to a conclusion appearing to generate knowledge despite an involved falsehood in exactly one of the paths can be diagnosed in the same way as in the overdetermining premises case above (about the Rutgers philosophers of mind). In this case, rule that the path with the falsehood is 'irrelevant'.
4. Alternatively: think of the conclusion in question as being epistemically sustained by a continuous chanting of the premise of one's inferential argument combined with mental affirmation of the suppressed conditional.
5. Points two and three may well be only elaborations of part of the content of the first point.
6. Truth of the conclusion is of course a necessary condition for knowledge of the conclusion.
7. Notice that another consequence of (1) above is this claim:
   (1b) Inferential knowledge of a conclusion requires warranted relevant premises.
   As an aside, notice that in light of this first counterexample to (1a), (1b) seems to fall quickly. Some accept that warrant entails truth. If it does, the falsity of (1a) implies the falsity of (1b). Whether or not warrant entails truth, (1b) falls to an example that parallels the clock example just provided. For the parallel example, leave everything in the initial example the same except this: I have indeed slept 3 ½ hours (we're at 2:30am for the first time). My premise belief is true (but unwarranted due to the relevance of '4 ½ hours') and yet once again I clearly know my conclusion. I'll say no more about (1b) except to note that it has played a non-trivial role in many 'pro-foundationalist' arguments and that it clearly cannot serve in that capacity.
8. As my luggage has informed me, there are two 'Fayetteville' airports in the USA. For a counterexample to (1b) add that unbeknownst to Kim and Hill, Hill's flight will divert to Fayetteville, Arkansas on Saturday.
9. One might make this response for some particular cases and combine this with some other response to the cases conceded to contain a known conclusion.
10. I did this in rejecting the relevance of the premise 'McGinn is in the room' in the argument for the conclusion that 'at least one Rutgers philosopher of mind is present'.
11. Again, one might mix and match, combining more than one of these approaches and also possibly combining this sort of response with an application of the earlier 'reject knowledge' response mentioned a moment ago.

12. This assumption is controversial because it is a claim about *all* members of the class of counterexamples. Of course it's clear that in some of the counterexamples the suggested truth would be at least dispositionally believed. I see no reason to believe that this will be true of all cases in this class.
13. I intend to take up these additional issues on another occasion.
14. It is unlikely that any positive motivation could really come from point (ii). As I'll discuss shortly, approximations known to be false can surely provide 'good reasons' for accepting conclusions in a variety of situations.
15. The 12th decimal place is occupied by '9' and so we need to round up to 3.14159265359.
16. Part of the filling in of the case would be an explanation of why the agent involved would (reasonably) never make judgments of the circumference of the circles he's dealing with out beyond, say, the 6th decimal point. These points about approximation clearly apply to counterexamples #3 and #5. Perhaps they apply to #1 as well.
17. I presented some ideas from this paper in talks at Calvin College and at Notre Dame. Both audiences provided insightful feedback. I especially benefitted from comments from Joshua Armstrong, Robert Audi, Marian David, Michael DePaul, Stephen Grimm, Matt Halteman, Anja Jauernig, Jaegwon Kim, William Ramsey, Michael Schweiger, Leopold Stubenberg and Stephen Wykstra. Robert Audi and EJ Coffman have been extremely generous with feedback and assistance during the drafting of the written version of the paper. Discussions with Coffman, who commented at a conference on related work from Claudio de Almeida and Peter Klein, informed me that others were working on this topic and prompted me to write up my notes for publication.

Philosophical Perspectives, 19, Epistemology, 2005

CAN WE DO WITHOUT PRAGMATIC ENCROACHMENT?

Brian Weatherson
Cornell University

1. Introduction

Recently several authors have defended claims suggesting that there is a closer connection between practical interests and epistemic justification than has traditionally been countenanced. Jeremy Fantl and Matthew McGrath (2002) argue that there is a "pragmatic necessary condition on epistemic justification" (77), namely the following.

(PC) S is justified in believing that *p* only if S is rational to prefer as if *p*. (77)

And John Hawthorne (2004) and Jason Stanley (2005) have argued that what it takes to turn true belief into knowledge is sensitive to the practical environment the subject is in. These authors seem to be suggesting there is, to use Jonathan Kvanvig's phrase, "pragmatic encroachment" in epistemology. In this paper I'll argue that their arguments do not quite show this is true, and that concepts of epistemological justification need not be pragmatically sensitive. The aim here isn't to show that (PC) is (unambiguously) false, but rather that it shouldn't be described as a pragmatic condition on *justification*. Rather, it is best thought of as a pragmatic condition on *belief*. There are two ways to spell out the view I'm taking here. These are both massive simplifications, but they are close enough to the truth to show the kind of picture I'm aiming for.

First, imagine a philosopher who holds a very simplified version of functionalism about belief, call it (B).

(B) S believes that *p* iff S prefers as if *p*

Our philosopher one day starts thinking about justification, and decides that we can get a principle out of (B) by adding normative operators to both sides, inferring (JB).

(JB) S is justified in believing that *p* only if S is justified to prefer as if *p*

Now it would be a mistake to treat (JB) as a pragmatic condition on *justification* (rather than belief) if it was derived from (B) by this simple means. And if our philosopher goes on to infer (PC) from (JB), by replacing 'justified' with 'rational', and inferring the conditional from the biconditional, we still don't get a pragmatic condition on *justification.*

Second, Fantl and McGrath focus their efforts on attacking the following principle.

Evidentialism. For any two subjects S and S′, necessarily, if S and S′ have the same evidence for/against *p*, then S is justified in believing that *p* iff S′ is, too.

I agree, evidentialism is false. And I agree that there are counterexamples to evidentialism from subjects who are in different practical situations. What I don't agree is that we learn much about the role of pragmatic factors in *epistemology* properly defined from these counterexamples to evidentialism. Evidentialism follows from the following three principles.

Probabilistic Evidentialism. For any two subjects S and S′, and any degree of belief α necessarily, if S and S′ have the same evidence for/against *p*, then S is justified in believing that *p* to degree α iff S′ is, too.

Threshold View. For any two subjects S and S′, and any degree of belief α, if S and S′ both believe *p* to degree α, then S believes that *p* iff S′ does too.

Probabilistic Justification. For any S, S is justified in believing *p* iff there is some degree of belief α such that S is justified in believing *p* to degree α, and in S's situation, believing *p* to degree α suffices for believing *p*.

(Degrees of belief here are meant to be the subjective correlates of Keynesian probabilities. See Keynes 1921 for more details. They need not, and usually will not, be numerical values. The Threshold View is so-called because given some other plausible premises it implies that S believes that *p* iff S's degree of belief in *p* is above a threshold.)

I endorse Probabilistic Justification, and for present purposes at least I endorse Probabilistic Evidentialism. The reason I think Evidentialism fails is because the Threshold View is false. It is plausible that Probabilistic Justification and Probabilistic Evidentialism are epistemological principles, while the Threshold View is a principle from philosophy of mind. So this matches up with the earlier contention that the failure of Evidentialism tells us something interesting about the role of pragmatics in philosophy of mind, rather than something about the role of pragmatics in epistemology.

As noted, Hawthorne and Stanley are both more interested in knowledge than justification. So my discussion of their views will inevitably be somewhat distorting. I think what I say about justification here should carry over to a theory of knowledge, but space prevents a serious examination of that question. The primary bit of 'translation' I have to do to make their works relevant to a discussion of justification is to interpret their defences of the principle (KP) below as implying some support for (JP), which is obviously similar to (PC).

(KP) If *S* knows that *p*, then *S* is justified in using *p* as a premise in practical reasoning.

(JP) If *S* justifiably believes that *p*, then *S* is justified in using *p* as a premise in practical reasoning.

I think (JP) is just as plausible as (KP). In any case it is independently plausible whether or not Hawthorne and Stanley are committed to it. So I'll credit recognition of (JP)'s importance to a theory of justification to them, and hope that in doing so I'm not irrepairably damaging the public record.

The overall plan here is to use some philosophy of mind, specifically functionalist analyses of belief, to respond to some arguments in epistemology. But, as you can see from the role the Threshold View plays in the above argument, our starting point will be the question what is the relation between the credences decision theory deals with, and our traditional notion of a belief? I'll offer an analysis of this relation that supports my above claim that we should work with a pragmatic notion of belief rather than a pragmatic notion of justification. The analysis I offer has a hole in it concerning propositions that are not relevant to our current plans, and I'll fix the hole in section 3. Sections 4 and 5 concern the role that closure principles play in my theory, in particular the relationship between having probabilistically coherent degrees of belief and logically coherent beliefs. In this context, a closure principle is a principle that says probabilistic coherence implies logical coherence, at least in a certain domain. (It's called a closure principle because we usually discuss it by working out properties of probabilistically coherent agents, and show that their beliefs are closed under entailment in the relevant domain.) In section 4 I'll defend the theory against the objection, most commonly heard from those wielding the preface paradox, that we need not endorse as strong a closure principle as I do. In section 5 I'll defend the theory against those who would endorse an even stronger closure principle than is defended here. Once we've got a handle on the relationship between degrees of belief and belief *tout court*, we'll use that to examine the arguments for pragmatic encroachment. In section 6 I'll argue that we can explain the intuitions behind the cases that seem to support pragmatic encroachment, while actually keeping all of the pragmatic factors in our theory of belief. In section 7 I'll discuss how to endorse principles like (PC) and (JP) (as far as they can be endorsed) while keeping a non-pragmatic theory of probabilistic justification. The interesting cases here are ones where agents have mistaken and/or irrational beliefs about their practical environment, and intuitions in those cases are cloudy. But it seems the most natural path in these cases is to keep a pragmatically sensitive notion of belief, and a pragmatically insensitive notion of justification.

2. Belief and Degree of Belief

Traditional epistemology deals with beliefs and their justification. Bayesian epistemology deals with degrees of belief and their justification. In some sense they are both talking about the same thing, namely epistemic justification. Two questions naturally arise. Do we really have two subject matters here (degrees of belief and belief *tout court*) or two descriptions of the one subject matter? If just one subject matter, what relationship is there between the two modes of description of this subject matter?

The answer to the first question is I think rather easy. There is no evidence to believe that the mind contains two representational systems, one to represent things as being probable or improbable and the other to represent things as being true or false. The mind probably does contain a vast plurality of representational systems, but they don't divide up the doxastic duties this way. If there are distinct visual and auditory representational systems, they don't divide up duties between degrees of belief and belief *tout court*, for example. If there were two distinct systems, then we should imagine that they could vary independently, at least as much as is allowed by constitutive rationality. But such variation is hard to fathom. So I'll infer that the one representational system accounts for our credences and our categorical beliefs. (It follows from this that the question Bovens and Hawthorne (1999) ask, namely what beliefs *should* an agent have given her degrees of belief, doesn't have a non-trivial answer. If fixing the degrees of belief in an environment fixes all her doxastic attitudes, as I think it does, then there is no further question of what she should believe given these are her degrees of belief.)

The second question is much harder. It is tempting to say that S believes that p iff S's credence in p is greater than some salient number r, where r is made salient either by the context of belief ascription, or the context that S is in. I'm following Mark Kaplan (1996) in calling this the threshold view. There are two well-known problems with the threshold view, both of which seem fatal to me.

As Robert Stalnaker (1984: 91) emphasised, any number r is bound to seem arbitrary. Unless these numbers are made salient by the environment, there is no special difference between believing p to degree 0.9786 and believing it to degree 0.9875. But if r is 0.98755, this will be *the difference* between believing p and not believing it, which is an important difference. The usual response to this, as found in Foley (1993: Ch. 4) and Hunter (1996) is to say that the boundary is vague. But it's not clear how this helps. On an epistemic theory of vagueness, there is still a number such that degrees of belief above that count, and degrees below that do not, and any such number is bound to seem unimportant. On supervaluational theories, the same is true. There won't be a *determinate* number, to be sure, but there will be a number, and that seems false. My preferred degree of belief theory of vagueness, as set out in Weatherson (2005) has the same consequence. Hunter defends a version of the threshold view combined with a theory of vagueness based around fuzzy logic, which seems to be the only theory that could avoid the arbitrariness objection. But as Williamson (1994: Ch. 4) showed, there are deep and probably insurmountable difficulties with that position. So I think the vagueness response to the arbitrariness objection is (a) the only prima facie plausible response and (b) unsuccessful.

The second problem concerns conjunction. It is also set out clearly by Stalnaker.

> Reasoning in this way from accepted premises to their deductive consequences (*P*, also *Q*, therefore *R*) does seem perfectly straightforward. Someone may object to one of the premises, or to the validity of the argument, but one could not intelligibly agree that the premises are each acceptable and the argument valid, while objecting to the acceptability of the conclusion. (Stalnaker 1984: 92)

If categorical belief is having a credence above the threshold, then one can coherently do exactly this. Let x be a number between r and $r^{1/2}$, such that for an atom of type U has probability x of decaying within a time t, for some t and U. Assume our agent knows this fact, and is faced with two (isolated) atoms of U. Let p be that the first decays within t, and q be that the second decays within t. She should, given her evidence, believe p to degree x, q to degree x, and $p \wedge q$ to degree x^2. If she believed $p \wedge q$ to a degree greater than r, she'd have to either have credences that were not supported by her evidence, or credences that were incoherent. (Or, most likely, both.) So this theory violates the platitude. This is a well-known argument, so there are many responses to it, most of them involving something like appeal to the preface paradox. I'll argue in section 4 that the preface paradox doesn't in fact offer the threshold view proponent much support here. But even before we get to there, we should note that the arbitrariness objection gives us sufficient reason to reject the threshold view.

A better move is to start with the functionalist idea that to believe that p is to treat p as true for the purposes of practical reasoning. To believe p is to have preferences that make sense, by your own lights, in a world where p is true. So, if you prefer A to B and believe that p, you prefer A to B given p. For reasons that will become apparent below, we'll work in this paper with a notion of preference where *conditional* preferences are primary.[1] So the core insight we'll work with is the following:

> If you prefer A to B given q, and you believe that p, then you prefer A to B given $p \wedge q$

The bold suggestion here is that if that is true for all the A, B and q that matter, then you believe p. Put formally, where *Bel*(p) means that the agent believes that

p, and A $\geq_q$ B means that the agent thinks A is at least as good as B given q, we have the following

(1) $Bel(p) \leftrightarrow \forall A \forall B \forall q\ (A \geq_q B \leftrightarrow A \geq_{p \wedge q} B)$

In words, an agent believes that p iff conditionalizing on p doesn't change any conditional preferences over things that matter.[2] The left-to-right direction of this seems trivial, and the right-to-left direction seems to be a plausible way to operationalise the functionalist insight that belief is a functional state. There is some work to be done if (1) is to be interpreted as a truth though.

If we interpret the quantifiers in (1) as unrestricted, then we get the (false) conclusion that just about no one believes any contingent propositions. To prove this, consider a bet that wins iff the statue in front of me waves back at me due to random quantum effects when I wave at it. If I take the bet and win, I get to live forever in paradise. If I take the bet and lose, I lose a penny. Letting A be that I take the bet, B be that I decline the bet, q be a known tautology (so my preferences given q are my preferences *tout court*) and p be that the statue does not wave back, we have that I prefer A to B, but not A to B given p. So by this standard I don't believe that p. This is false—right now I believe that statues won't wave back at me when I wave at them.

This seems like a problem. But the solution to it is not to give up on functionalism, but to insist on its pragmatic foundations. The quantifiers in (1) should be restricted, with the restrictions motivated pragmatically. What is crucial to the theory is to say what the restrictions on A and B are, and what the restrictions on q are. We'll deal with these in order.

For better or worse, I don't right now have the option of taking that bet and hence spending eternity in paradise if the statue waves back at me. Taking or declining such unavailable bets are not open choices. For any option that is open to me, assuming that statues do not in fact wave does not change its utility. That's to say, I've already factored in the non-waving behavior of statues into my decision-making calculus. That's to say, I believe statues don't wave.

An action A is a live option for the agent if it is really possible for the agent to perform A. An action A is a salient option if it is an option the agent takes seriously in deliberation. Most of the time gambling large sums of money on internet gambling sites over my phone is a live option, but not a salient option. I know this option is suboptimal, and I don't have to recompute every time whether I should do it. Whenever I'm making a decision, I don't have to add in to the list of choices *bet thousands of dollars on internet gambling sites*, and then rerule that out every time. I just don't consider that option, and properly so. If I have a propensity to daydream, then becoming the centerfielder for the Boston Red Sox might be a salient option to me, but it certainly isn't a live option. We'll say the two initial quantifiers range over the options that are live and salient options for the agent.

Note that we *don't* say that the quantifiers range over the options that are live and salient for the person making the belief ascription. That would lead us to a form of contextualism for which we have little evidence. We also don't say that an option becomes salient for the agent iff they *should* be considering it. At this stage we are just saying what the agent does believe, not what they should believe, so we don't have any clauses involving normative concepts.

Now we'll look at the restrictions on the quantifier over propositions. Say a proposition is *relevant* if the agent is disposed to take seriously the question of whether it is true (whether or not she is currently considering that question) and conditionalizing on that proposition or its negation changes some of the agents *unconditional* preferences over live, salient options.[3] The first clause is designed to rule out wild hypotheses that the agent does not take at all seriously. If q is not such a proposition, if the agent is disposed to take it seriously, then it is relevant if there are live, salient A and B such that $A \geq_q B \leftrightarrow A \geq B$ is false. Say a proposition is *salient* if the agent is currently considering whether it is true. Finally, say a proposition is *active* relative to p iff it is a (possibly degenerate) conjunction of propositions such that each conjunct is either relevant or salient, and such that the conjunction is consistent with p. (By a degenerate conjunction I mean a conjunction with just one conjunct. The consistency requirement is there because it might be hard in some cases to make sense of preferences given inconsistencies.) Then the propositional quantifier in (1) ranges over active propositions.

We will expand and clarify this in the next section, but our current solution to the relationship between beliefs and degrees of belief is that degrees of belief determine an agent's preferences, and she believes that p iff the claim (1) about her preferences is true when the quantifiers over options are restricted to live, salient actions, and the quantifier over propositions is restricted to salient propositions. The simple view would be to say that the agent believes that p iff conditioning on p changes none of her preferences. The more complicated view here is that the agent believes that p iff conditioning on p changes none of her conditional preferences over live, salient options, where the conditions are also active relative to p.

3. Impractical Propositions

The theory sketched in the previous paragraph seems to me right in the vast majority of cases. It fits in well with a broadly functionalist view of the mind, and as we'll see it handles some otherwise difficult cases with aplomb. But it needs to be supplemented a little to handle beliefs about propositions that are practically irrelevant. I'll illustrate the problem, then note how I prefer to solve it.

I don't know what Julius Caeser had for breakfast the morning he crossed the Rubicon. But I think he would have had *some* breakfast. It is hard to be a good general without a good morning meal after all. Let p be the proposition that he had breakfast that morning. I believe p. But this makes remarkably little difference to my practical choices in most situations. True, I wouldn't have written this paragraph as I did without this belief, but it is rare that I have to write about Caeser's dietary habits. In general whether p is true makes no practical difference to me. This makes it hard to give a pragmatic account of whether I believe that p. Let's apply (1) to see whether I really believe that p.

(1) $Bel(p) \leftrightarrow \forall A \forall B \forall q\ (A \geq_q B \leftrightarrow A \geq_{p \wedge q} B)$

Since p makes no practical difference to any choice I have to make, the right hand side is true. So the left hand side is true, as desired. The problem is that the right hand side of (2) is also true here.

(2) $Bel(\neg p) \leftrightarrow \forall A \forall B \forall q\ (A \geq_q B \leftrightarrow A \geq_{\neg p \wedge q} B)$

Adding the assumption that Caeser had no breakfast that morning doesn't change any of my practical choices either. So I now seem to *inconsistently* believe both p and $\neg p$. I have some inconsistent beliefs, I'm sure, but those aren't among them. We need to clarify what (1) claims.

To do so, I supplement the theory sketched in section 2 with the following principles.

- A proposition p is *eligible for belief* if it satisfies $\forall A \forall B \forall q\ (A \geq_q B \leftrightarrow A \geq_{p \wedge q} B)$, where the first two quantifiers range over the open, salient actions in the sense described in section 2.
- For any proposition p, and any proposition q that is relevant or salient, among the actions that are (by stipulation!) open and salient with respect to p are *believing that p*, *believing that q*, *not believing that p* and *not believing that q*
- For any proposition, the subject prefers believing it to not believing it iff (a) it is eligible for belief and (b) the agent's degree of belief in the proposition is greater than ½.
- The previous stipulation holds both unconditionally and conditional on p, for any p.
- The agent believes that p iff $\forall A \forall B \forall q\ (A \geq_q B \leftrightarrow A \geq_{p \wedge q} B)$, where the first two quantifiers range over all actions that are either open and salient *tout court* (i.e. in the sense of section 2) or open and salient with respect to p (as described above).

This all looks moderately complicated, but I'll explain how it works in some detail as we go along. One simple consequence is that an agent only believes that p iff their degree of belief in p is greater than ½. Since my degree of belief in Caeser's foodless morning is not greater than ½, in fact it is considerably less, I don't believe $\neg p$. On the other hand, since my degree of belief in p is considerably greater than ½, I prefer to believe it than disbelieve it, so I believe it.

There are many possible objections to this position, which I'll address sequentially.

Objection: Even if I have a high degree of belief in p, I might prefer to not believe p because I think that belief in p is bad for some other reason. Perhaps, if p is a proposition about my brilliance, it might be immodest to believe that p.
Reply: Any of these kinds of considerations should be put into the credences. If it is immodest to believe that you are a great philosopher, it is equally immodest to believe to a high degree that you are a great philosopher.

Objection: Belief that p is not an action in the ordinary sense of the term.
Reply: True, which is why this is described as a supplement to the original theory, rather than just cashing out its consequences.

Objection: It is impossible to choose to believe or not believe something, so we shouldn't be applying these kinds of criteria.
Reply: I'm not as convinced of the impossibility of belief by choice as others are, but I won't push that for present purposes. Let's grant that beliefs are always involuntary. So these 'actions' aren't open actions in any interesting sense, and the theory is section 2 was really incomplete. As I said, this is a supplement to the theory in section 2.

This doesn't prevent us using principles of constitutive rationality, such as we prefer to believe p iff our credence in p is over ½. Indeed, on most occasions where we use constitutive rationality to infer that a person has some mental state, the mental state we attribute to them is one they could not fail to have. But functionalists are committed to constitutive rationality (Lewis 1994). So my approach here is consistent with a broadly functionalist outlook.

Objection: This just looks like a roundabout way of stipulating that to believe that p, your degree of belief in p has to be greater than ½. Why not just add that as an extra clause than going through these little understood detours about preferences about beliefs?
Reply: There are three reasons for doing things this way rather than adding such a clause.

First, it's nice to have a systematic theory rather than a theory with an ad hoc clause like that.

Second, the effect of this constraint is much more than to restrict belief to propositions whose credence is greater than ½. Consider a case where p and q and their conjunction are all salient, p and q are probabilistically independent, and the agent's credence in each is 0.7. Assume also that p, q and $p \wedge q$ are completely irrelevant to any practical deliberation the agent must make. Then the criteria above imply that the agent does not believe that p or that q. The reason is that the agent's credence in $p \wedge q$ is 0.49, so she prefers to not believe $p \wedge q$. But conditional on p, her credence in $p \wedge q$ is 0.7, so she prefers to believe it. So conditionalizing on p does change her preferences with respect to believing $p \wedge q$, so she doesn't believe p. So the effect of these stipulations rules out much more than just belief in propositions whose credence is below ½.

This suggests the third, and most important point. The problem with the threshold view was that it led to violations of closure. Given the theory as stated, we can prove the following theorem. Whenever p and q and their conjunction are all open or salient, and both are believed, and the agent is probabilistically coherent, the agent also believes $p \wedge q$. This is a quite restricted closure principle, but this is no reason to deny that it is *true*, as it fails to be true on the threshold view.

The proof of this theorem is a little complicated, but worth working through. First we'll prove that if the agent believes p, believes q, and p and q are both salient, then the agent prefers believing $p \wedge q$ to not believing it, if $p \wedge q$ is eligible for belief. In what follows $Pr(x \mid y)$ is the agent's conditional degree of belief in x given y. Since the agent is coherent, we'll assume this is a probability function (hence the name).

1. Since the agent believes that q, they prefer believing that q to not believing that q (by the criteria for belief)
2. So the agent prefers believing that q to not believing that q given p (From 1 and the fact that they believe that p, and that q is salient)
3. So $Pr(q \mid p) > ½$ (from 2)
4. $Pr(q \mid p) = Pr(p \wedge q \mid p)$ (by probability calculus)
5. So $Pr(p \wedge q \mid p) > ½$ (from 3, 4)
6. So, if $p \wedge q$ is eligible for belief, then the agent prefers believing that $p \wedge q$ to not believing it, given p (from 5)
7. So, if $p \wedge q$ is eligible for belief, the agent prefers believing that $p \wedge q$ to not believing it (from 6, and the fact that they believe that p, and $p \wedge q$ is salient)

So whenever, p, q and $p \wedge q$ are salient, and the agent believes each conjunct, the agent prefers believing the conjunction $p \wedge q$ to not believing it, if $p \wedge q$ is eligible. Now we have to prove that $p \wedge q$ is eligible for belief, to prove that it is actually believed. That is, we have to prove that (5) follows from (4) and (3), where the initial quantifiers range over actions that are open and salient *tout court*.

(3) $\forall A \forall B \forall r\, (A \geq_r B \leftrightarrow A \geq_{p \wedge r} B)$
(4) $\forall A \forall B \forall r\, (A \geq_r B \leftrightarrow A \geq_{q \wedge r} B)$
(5) $\forall A \forall B \forall r\, (A \geq_r B \leftrightarrow A \geq_{p \wedge q \wedge r} B)$

Assume that (5) isn't true. That is, there are A, B and s such that $\neg(A \geq_s B \leftrightarrow A \geq_{p \wedge q \wedge s} B)$. By hypothesis s is active, and consistent with $p \wedge q$. So it is the conjunction of relevant, salient propositions. Since q is salient, this means $q \wedge s$ is also active. Since s is consistent with $p \wedge q$, it follows that $q \wedge s$ is consistent with p. So $q \wedge s$ is a possible substitution instance for r in (3). Since (3) is true, it follows that $A \geq_{q \wedge s} B \leftrightarrow A \geq_{p \wedge q \wedge s} B$. By similar reasoning, it follows that s is a permissible substitution instance in (4), giving us $A \geq_s B \leftrightarrow A \geq_{q \wedge s} B$. Putting the last two biconditionals together we get $A \geq_s B \leftrightarrow A \geq_{p \wedge q \wedge s} B$, contradicting our hypothesis that there is a counterexample to (5). So whenever (3) and (4) are true, (5) is true as well, assuming p, q and $p \wedge q$ are all salient.

4. Defending Closure

So on my account of the connection between degrees of belief and belief *tout court*, probabilistic coherence implies logical coherence amongst salient propositions. The last qualification is necessary. It is possible for a probabilistically coherent agent to not believe the *non*-salient consequences of things they believe, and even for a probabilistically coherent agent to have inconsistent beliefs as long as not all the members of the inconsistent set are active. Some people argue that even this weak a closure principle is implausible. David Christensen (2005), for example, argues that the preface paradox provides a reason for doubting that beliefs must be closed under entailment, or even must be consistent. Here is his description of the case.

> We are to suppose that an apparently rational person has written a long nonfiction book—say, on history. The body of the book, as is typical, contains a large number of assertions. The author is highly confident in each of these assertions; moreover, she has no hesitation in making them unqualifiedly, and would describe herself (and be described by others) as believing each of the book's many claims. But she knows enough about the difficulties of historical scholarship to realize that it is almost inevitable that at least a few of the claims she makes in the book are mistaken. She modestly acknowledges this in her preface, by saying that she believes the book will be found to contain some errors, and she graciously invites those who discover the errors to set her straight. (Christensen 2005: 33–4)

Christensen thinks such an author might be rational in every one of her beliefs, even though these are all inconsistent. Although he does not say this, nothing in his discussion suggests that he is using the irrelevance of some of the propositions in the author's defence. So here is an argument that we should abandon closure amongst relevant beliefs.

Christensen's discussion, like other discussions of the preface paradox, makes frequent use of the fact that examples like these are quite common. We don't have to go to fake barn country to find a counterexample to closure. But it seems to me that we need two quite strong idealizations in order to get a real counterexample here.

The first of these is discussed in forthcoming work by Ishani Maitra, and is briefly mentioned by Christensen in setting out the problem. We only have a counterexample to closure if the author *believes* every thing she writes in her book. (Indeed, we only have a counterexample if she reasonably believes every one of them. But we'll assume a rational author who only believes what she ought to believe.) This seems unlikely to be true to me. An author of a historical book is like a detective who, when asked to put forward her best guess about what explains the evidence, says "If I had to guess, I'd say . . ." and then launches into spelling out her hypothesis. It seems clear that she need not *believe* the truth of her hypothesis. If she did that, she could not later learn it was true, because you can't learn the truth of something you already believe. And she wouldn't put any effort into investigating alternative suspects. But she can come to learn her hypothesis was true, and it would be rational to investigate other suspects. It seems to me (following here Maitra's discussion) that we should understand scholarly assertions as being governed by the same kind of rules that govern detectives making the kind of speech being contemplated here. And those rules don't require that the speaker believe the things they say without qualification. The picture is that the little prelude the detective explicitly says is implicit in all scholarly work.

There are three objections I know to this picture, none of them particularly conclusive. First, Christensen says that the author doesn't qualify their assertions. But neither does our detective qualify most individual sentences. Second, Christensen says that most people would describe our author as believing her assertions. But it is also natural to describe our detective as believing the things she says in her speech. It's natural to say things like "She thinks it was the butler, with the lead pipe," in reporting her hypothesis. Third, Timothy Williamson (2000) has argued that if speakers don't believe what they say, we won't have an explanation of why Moore's paradoxical sentences, like "The butler did it, but I don't believe the butler did it," are always defective. Whatever the explanation of the paradoxicality of these sentences might be, the alleged requirement that speakers believe what they say can't be it. For our detective cannot properly say "The butler did it, but I don't believe the butler did it" in setting out her hypothesis, even though *believing* the butler did it is not necessary for her to say "The butler did it" in setting out just that hypothesis.

It is plausible that for *some* kinds of books, the author should only say things they believe. This is probably true for travel guides, for example. Interestingly, casual observation suggests that authors of such books are much less likely to write modest prefaces. This makes some sense if those books can only include statements their authors believe, and the authors believe the conjunctions of what they believe.

The second idealisation is stressed by Simon Evnine in his paper "Believing Conjunctions". The following situation does not involve me believing anything inconsistent.

- I believe that what Manny just said, whatever it was, is false.
- Manny just said that the stands at Fenway Park are green.
- I believe that the stands at Fenway Park are green.

If we read the first claim *de dicto*, that I believe that Manny just said something false, then there is no inconsistency. (Unless I also believe that what Manny just said was that the stands in Fenway Park are green.) But if we read it *de re*, that the thing Manny just said is one of the things I believe to be false, then the situation does involve me being inconsistent. The same is true when the author believes that one of the things she says in her book is mistaken. If we understand what she says *de dicto*, there is no contradiction in her beliefs. It has to be understood *de re* before we get a logical problem. And the fact is that most authors do not have *de re* attitudes towards the claims made in their book. Most authors don't even remember everything that's in their books. (I'm not sure I remember how this section started, let alone this paper.) Some may argue that authors don't even have the capacity to consider a proposition as long and complicated as the conjunction of all the claims in their book. Christensen considers this objection, but says it isn't a serious problem.

> It is undoubtedly true that ordinary humans cannot entertain book-length conjunctions. But surely, agents who do not share this fairly *superficial* limitation are easily conceived. And it seems just as wrong to say of such agents that they are rationally required to believe in the inerrancy of the books they write. (38: my emphasis)

I'm not sure this is undoubtedly true; it isn't clear that propositions (as opposed to their representations) have lengths. And humans can believe propositions that *can* be represented by sentences as long as books. But even without that point, Christensen is right that there is an idealization here, since ordinary humans do not know exactly what is in a given book, and hence don't have *de re* attitudes towards the propositions expressed in the book.

I'm actually rather suspicious of the intuition that Christensen is pushing here, that idealizing in this way doesn't change intuitions about the case. The preface paradox gets a lot of its (apparent) force from intuitions about what attitude we should have towards real books. Once we make it clear that the real life cases are not relevant to the paradox, I find the intuitions become rather murky. But I won't press this point.

A more important point is that we believers in closure don't think that authors should think their books are inerrant. Rather, following Stalnaker (1984), we think that authors shouldn't unqualifiedly *believe* the individual statements in their book if they don't believe the conjunction of those statements. Rather, their attitude towards those propositions (or at least some of them) should be that they are probably true. (As Stalnaker puts it, they accept the story without believing it.) Proponents of the preface paradox know that this is a possible response, and tend to argue that it is impractical. Here is Christensen on this point.

> It is clear that our everyday binary way of talking about beliefs has immense practical advantages over a system which insisted on some more fine-grained reporting of degrees of confidence ... At a minimum, talking about people as believing, disbelieving, or withholding belief has at least as much point as do many of the imprecise ways we have of talking about things that can be described more precisely. (96)

Richard Foley makes a similar point.

> There are *deep* reasons for wanting an epistemology of beliefs, reasons that epistemologies of degrees of belief by their very nature cannot possibly accommodate. (Foley 1993: 170, my emphasis.)

It's easy to make too much of this point. It's a lot easier to triage propositions into TRUE, FALSE and NOT SURE and work with those categories than it is to work assign precise numerical probabilities to each proposition. But these are not the only options. Foley's discussion subsequent to the above quote sometimes suggests they are, especially when he contrasts the triage with "indicat[ing] as accurately as I can my degree of confidence in each assertion that I defend." (171) But really it isn't *much* harder to add two more categories, PROBABLY TRUE and PROBABLY FALSE to those three, and work with that five-way division rather than a three-way division. It's not clear that humans as they are actually constructed have a *strong* preference for the three-way over the five-way division, and even if they do, I'm not sure in what sense this is a 'deep' fact about them.

Once we have the five-way division, it is clear what authors should do if they want to respect closure. For any conjunction that they don't believe (i.e. classify as true), they should not believe one of the conjuncts. But of course they can classify every conjunct as probably true, even if they think the conjunction is false, or even certainly false. Still, might it not be considered something of an idealisation to say rational authors must make this five-way distinction amongst propositions they consider? Yes, but it's no more of an idealisation than we need to set up the preface paradox in the first place. To use the preface paradox to find an example of someone who reasonably violates closure, we need to insist on the following three constraints.

a) They are part of a research community where only asserting propositions you believe is compatible with active scholarship;
b) They know exactly what is in their book, so they are able to believe that one of the propositions in the book is mistaken, where this is understood *de re*; but
c) They are unable to effectively function if they have to effect a five-way, rather than a three-way, division amongst the propositions they consider.

Put more graphically, to motivate the preface paradox we have to think that our inability to have *de re* thoughts about the contents of books is a "superficial constraint", but our preference for working with a three-way rather than a five-way division is a "deep" fact about our cognitive system. Maybe each of these attitudes could be plausible taken on its own (though I'm sceptical of that) but the conjunction seems just absurd.

I'm not entirely sure an agent subject to exactly these constraints is even fully conceivable. (Such an agent is negatively conceivable, in David Chalmers's terminology, but I rather doubt they are positively conceivable.) But even if they are a genuine possibility, why the norms applicable to an agent satisfying that very gerrymandered set of constraints should be considered relevant norms for our state is far from clear. I'd go so far as to say it's clear that the applicability (or otherwise) of a given norm to such an odd agent is no reason whatsoever to say it applies to us. But since the preface paradox only provides a reason for just these kinds of agents to violate closure, we have no reason for ordinary humans to violate closure. So I see no reason here to say that we can have probabilistic coherence without logical coherence, as proponents of the threshold view insist we can have, but which I say we can't have *at least when the propositions involved are salient*. The more pressing question, given the failure of the preface paradox argument, is why I don't endorse a much stronger closure principle, one that drops the restriction to salient propositions. The next section will discuss that point.

I've used Christensen's book as a stalking horse in this section, because it is the clearest and best statement of the preface paradox. Since Christensen is a paradox-mongerer and I'm a paradox-denier, it might be thought we have a deep disagreement about the relevant epistemological issues. But actually I think our overall views are fairly close despite this. I favor an epistemological outlook I call "Probability First", the view that getting the epistemology of partial belief right is of the first importance, and everything else should flow from that. Christensen's view, reduced to a slogan, is "Probability First and Last". This section has been basically about the difference between those two slogans. It's an important dispute, but it's worth bearing in mind that it's a factional squabble within the Probability Party, not an outbreak of partisan warfare.

5. Too Little Closure?

In the previous section I defended the view that a coherent agent has beliefs that are deductively cogent with respect to salient propositions. Here I want to defend the importance of the qualification. Let's start with what I take to be the most important argument for closure, the passage from Stalnaker's *Inquiry* that I quoted above.

> Reasoning in this way from accepted premises to their deductive consequences (P, also Q, therefore R) does seem perfectly straightforward. Someone may object to one of the premises, or to the validity of the argument, but one could not intelligibly agree that the premises are each acceptable and the argument valid, while objecting to the acceptability of the conclusion. (Stalnaker 1984: 92)

Stalnaker's wording here is typically careful. The relevant question isn't whether we can accept *p*, accept *q*, accept *p* and *q* entail *r*, and reject *r*. As Christensen (2005: Ch. 4) notes, this is impossible even on the threshold view, as long as the threshold is above 2/3. The real question is whether we can accept *p*, accept *q*, accept *p* and *q* entail *r*, and *fail* to accept *r*. And this is always a live possibility on any threshold view, though it seems absurd at first that this could be coherent.

But it's important to note how *active* the verbs in Stalnaker's description are. When faced with a valid argument we have to *object* to one of the premises, or the validity of the argument. What we can't do is *agree* to the premises and the validity of the argument, while *objecting* to the conclusion. I agree. If we are really *agreeing* to some propositions, and *objecting* to others, then all those propositions are salient. And in that case closure, deductive coherence, is mandatory. This doesn't tell us what we have to do if we haven't previously made the propositions salient in the first place.

The position I endorse here is very similar in its conclusions to that endorsed by Gilbert Harman in *Change in View*. There Harman endorses the following principle. (At least he endorses it as true – he doesn't seem to think it is particularly explanatory because it is a special case of a more general interesting principle.)

> *Recognized Logical Implication Principle*. One has reason to believe *P* if one *recognizes* that *P* is logically implied by one's view. (Harman 1986: 17)

This seems right to me, both what it says and its implicature that the reason in question is not a conclusive reason. My main objection to those who use the preface paradox to argue against closure is that they give us a mistaken picture of what we have *to do* epistemically. When I have inconsistent beliefs, or I don't believe some consequence of my beliefs, that is something I have a reason to deal with at some stage, something I have to do. When we say that we have things to do, we don't mean that we have to do them *right now*, or instead of everything else. My current list of things to do includes cleaning my bathroom, yet here I am writing this paper, and (given the relevant deadlines) rightly so. We can have the job of cleaning up our epistemic house as something to do while recognizing that we can quite rightly do other things first. But it's a serious mistake to infer from the permissibility of doing other things that cleaning up our epistemic house (or our bathroom) isn't something to be done. The bathroom won't clean itself after all, and eventually this becomes a problem.

There is a possible complication when it comes to tasks that are very low priority. My attic is to be cleaned, or at least it could be cleaner, but there are no imaginable circumstances under which something else wouldn't be higher priority. Given that, should we really leave *clean the attic* on the list of things to be done? Similarly, there might be implications I haven't followed through that it couldn't possibly be worth my time to sort out. Are they things to be done? I think it's worthwhile recording them as such, because otherwise we might miss opportunities to deal with them in the process of doing something else. I don't need to put off anything else in order to clean the attic, but if I'm up there for independent reasons I should bring down some of the garbage. Similarly, I don't need to follow through implications mostly irrelevant to my interests, but if those propositions come up for independent reasons, I should deal with the fact that some things I believe imply something I don't believe. Having it be the case that all implications from things we believe to things we don't believe constitute jobs to do (possibly in the loose sense that cleaning my attic is something to do) has the right implications for what epistemic duties we do and don't have.

While waxing metaphorical, it seems time to pull out a rather helpful metaphor that Gilbert Ryle develops in *The Concept of Mind* at a point where he's covering what we'd now call the inference/implication distinction. (This is a large theme of chapter 9, see particularly pages 288ff.) Ryle's point in these passages, as it frequently is throughout the book, is to stress that minds are fundamentally active, and the activity of a mind cannot be easily recovered from its end state. Although Ryle doesn't use this language, his point is that we shouldn't confuse the difficult activity of drawing inferences with the smoothness and precision of a logical implication. The language Ryle does use is more picturesque. He compares the easy work a farmer does when sauntering down a path from the hard work he did when building the path. A good argument, in philosophy or mathematics or elsewhere, is like a well made path that permits sauntering from the start to finish without undue strain. But from that it doesn't follow that the task of coming up with that argument, of building that path in Ryle's metaphor, was easy work. The easiest paths to walk are often the hardest to build. Path-building, smoothing out our beliefs so they are consistent and closed under implication, is hard work, even when the finished results look clean and straightforward. Its work that we shouldn't do unless we need to. But making sure our beliefs are closed under entailment even with respect to irrelevant propositions is suspiciously like the activity of buildings paths between points without first checking you need to walk between them.

For a less metaphorical reason for doubting the wisdom of this unchecked commitment to closure, we might notice that theorists tend to get into all sorts of difficulties. Consider, for example, the view put forward by Mark Kaplan in *Decision Theory as Philosophy*. Here is his definition of belief.

> You count as believing P just if, were your sole aim to assert the truth (as it pertains to P), and your only options were to assert that P, assert that ~P or make neither assertion, you would prefer to assert that P. (109)

Kaplan notes that conditional definitions like this are prone to Shope's conditional fallacy. If my sole aim were to assert the truth, I might have different beliefs to what I now have. He addresses one version of this objection (namely that it appears to imply that everyone believes their sole desire is to assert the truth) but as we'll see presently he can't avoid all versions of it.

These arguments are making me thirsty. I'd like a beer. Or at least I think I would. But wait! On Kaplan's theory I can't think that I'd like a beer, for if my sole aim were to assert the truth as it pertains to my beer-desires, I wouldn't have beer desires. And then I'd prefer to assert that I wouldn't like a beer, I'd merely like to assert the truth as it pertains to my beer desires.

Even bracketing this concern, Kaplan ends up being committed to the view that I can (coherently!) believe that *p* even while regarding *p* as highly improbable. This looks like a refutation of the view to me, but Kaplan accepts it with some equanimity. He has two primary reasons for saying we should live with this. First, he says that it only looks like an absurd consequence if we are committed to the Threshold View. To this all I can say is that *I* don't believe the Threshold View, but it still seems absurd to me. Second, he says that any view is going to have to be revisionary to some extent, because our ordinary concept of belief is not "coherent" (142). His view is that, "Our ordinary notion of belief both construes belief as a state of confidence short of certainty and takes consistency of belief to be something that is at least possible and, perhaps, even desirable" and this is impossible. I think the view here interprets belief as a state less than confidence and allows for as much consistency as the folk view does (i.e. consistency amongst salient propositions), so this defence is unsuccessful as well.

None of the arguments here in favor of our restrictions on closure are completely conclusive. In part the argument at this stage rests on the lack of a plausible rival theory that doesn't interpret belief as certainty but implements a stronger closure principle. It's possible that tomorrow someone will come up with a theory that does just this. Until then, we'll stick with the account here, and see what its epistemological implications might be.

6. Examples of Pragmatic Encroachment

Fantl and McGrath's case for pragmatic encroachment starts with cases like the following. (The following case is not quite theirs, but is similar enough to suit their plan, and easier to explain in my framework.)

> *Local and Express*
> There are two kinds of trains that run from the city to the suburbs: the local, which stops at all stations, and the express, which skips the first eight stations. Harry and Louise want to go to the fifth station, so they shouldn't catch the Express. Though if they do it isn't too hard to catch a local back the other way, so it isn't usually a large cost. Unfortunately, the trains are not always clearly labelled. They see a particular train about to leave. If it's a local they are better off catching it, if it is an express they should wait for the next local, which they can see is already boarding passengers and will leave in a few minutes. While running towards the train, they hear a fellow passenger say "It's a local." This gives them good, but far from

> overwhelming, reason to believe that the train is a local. Passengers get this kind of thing wrong fairly frequently, but they don't have time to get more information. So each of them face a gamble, which they can take by getting on the train. If the train is a local, they will get home a few minutes early. If it is an express they will get home a few minutes later. For Louise, this is a low stakes gamble, as nothing much turns on whether she is a few minutes early or late, but she does have a weak preference for arriving earlier rather than later. But for Harry it is a high stakes gamble, because if he is late he won't make the start of his daughter's soccer game, which will highly upset her. There is no large payoff for Harry arriving early.

What should each of them do? What should each of them believe?

The first question is relatively easy. Louise should catch the train, and Harry should wait for the next. For each of them that's the utility-maximizing thing to do. The second one is harder. Fantl and McGrath suggest that, despite being in the same epistemic position with respect to everything except their interests, Louise is justified in believing the train is a local and Harry is not. I agree. (If you don't think the particular case fits this pattern, feel free to modify it so the difference in interests grounds a difference in what they are justified in believing.) Does this show that our notion of epistemic justification has to be pragmatically sensitive? I'll argue that it does not.

The fundamental assumption I'm making is that what is primarily subject to epistemic evaluation are degrees of belief, or what are more commonly called states of confidence in ordinary language. When we think about things this way, we see that Louise and Harry are justified in adopting *the very same degrees of belief*. Both of them should be confident, but not absolutely certain, that the train is a local. We don't have even the appearance of a counterexample to Probabilistic Evidentialism here. If we like putting this in numerical terms, we could say that each of them is justified in assigning a probability of around 0.9 to the proposition *That train is a local*.[4] So as long as we adopt a Probability First epistemology, where we in the first instance evaluate the probabilities that agents assign to propositions, Harry and Louise are evaluated alike iff they do the same thing.

How then can we say that Louise alone is justified in believing that the train is a local? Because that state of confidence they are justified in adopting, the state of being fairly confident but not absolutely certain that the train is a local, counts as believing that the train is a local given Louise's context but not Harry's context. Once Louise hears the other passenger's comment, conditionalizing on *That's a local* doesn't change any of her preferences over open, salient actions, including such 'actions' as believing or disbelieving propositions. But conditional on the train being a local, Harry prefers catching the train, which he actually does not prefer.

In cases like this, interests matter not because they affect the degree of confidence that an agent can reasonably have in a proposition's truth. (That is, not because they matter to epistemology.) Rather, interests matter because they affect whether those reasonable degrees of confidence amount to belief. (That is, because they matter to philosophy of mind.) There is no reason here to let pragmatic concerns into epistemology.

7. Justification and Practical Reasoning

The discussion in the last section obviously didn't show that there is no encroachment of pragmatics into epistemology. There are, in particular, two kinds of concerns one might have about the prospects for extending my style of argument to block all attempts at pragmatic encroachment. The biggest concern is that it might turn out to be impossible to defend a Probability First epistemology, particularly if we do not allow ourselves pragmatic concepts. For instance, it is crucial to this project that we have a notion of evidence that is not defined in terms of traditional epistemic concepts (e.g. as knowledge), or in terms of interests. This is an enormous project, and I'm not going to attempt to tackle it here. The second concern is that we won't be able to generalize the discussion of that example to explain the plausibility of (JP) without conceding something to the defenders of pragmatic encroachment.

(JP) If *S* justifiably believes that *p*, then *S* is justified in using *p* as a premise in practical reasoning.

And that's what we will look at in this section. To start, we need to clarify exactly what (JP) means. Much of this discussion will be indebted to Fantl and McGrath's discussion of various ways of making (JP) more precise. To see some of the complications at issue, consider a simple case of a bet on a reasonably well established historical proposition. The agent has a lot of evidence that supports *p*, and is offered a bet that returns \$1 if *p* is true, and loses \$500 if *p* is false. Since her evidence doesn't support *that* much confidence in *p*, she properly declines the bet. One might try to reason intuitively as follows. Assume that she justifiably believed that *p*. Then she'd be in a position to make the following argument.

p
If *p*, then I should take the bet
So, I should take the bet

Since she isn't in a position to draw the conclusion, she must not be in a position to endorse both of the premises. Hence (arguably) she isn't justified in believing that *p*. But we have to be careful here. If we assume also that *p* is true (as Fantl and McGrath do, because they are mostly concerned with knowledge rather than justified belief), then the second premise is clearly false, since it is a conditional with a true antecedent and a false consequent. So the fact that she can't draw the conclusion of this argument only shows that she can't endorse *both* of the premises, and that's not surprising since one of the premises is most likely false. (I'm not assuming here that the conditional is true iff it has a true antecendent or a false consequent, just that it is only true if it has a false antecedent or a true consequent.)

In order to get around this problem, Fantl and McGrath suggest a few other ways that our agent might reason to the bet. They suggest each of the following principles.

> S knows that p only if, for any act A, if S knows that if p, then A is the best thing she can do, then S is rational to do A. (72)
>
> S knows that p only if, for any states of affairs A and B, if S knows that if p, then A is better for her than B, then S is rational to prefer A to B. (74)
>
> (PC) S is justified in believing that p only if S is rational to prefer as if p. (77)

Hawthorne (2004: 174–181) appears to endorse the second of these principles. He considers an agent who endorses the following implication concerning a proposed sell of a lottery ticket for a cent, which is well below its actuarially fair value.

> I will lose the lottery.
> If I keep the ticket, I will get nothing.
> If I sell the ticket, I will get a cent.
> So I ought to sell the ticket. (174)

(To make this fully explicit, it helps to add the tacit premise that a cent is better than nothing.) Hawthorne says that this is intuitively a *bad* argument, and concludes that the agent who attempts to use it is not in a position to know its first premise. But that conclusion only follows if we assume that the argument form is acceptable. So it is plausible to conclude that he endorses Fantl and McGrath's second principle.

The interesting question here is whether the theory endorsed in this paper can validate the true principles that Fantl and McGrath articulate. (Or, more precisely, we can validate the equivalent true principles concerning justified belief, since knowledge is outside the scope of the paper.) I'll argue that it can in the following way. First, I'll just note that given the fact that the theory here implies the closure principles we outlined in section 5, we can easily enough endorse Fantl and McGrath's first two principles. This is good, since they seem true. The longer part of the argument involves arguing that their principle (PC), which doesn't hold on the theory endorsed here, is in fact incorrect.

One might worry that the qualification on the closure principles in section 5 mean that we can't fully endorse the principles Fantl and McGrath endorse. In particular, it might be worried that there could be an agent who believes that *p*, believes that if *p*, then A is better than B, but doesn't put these two beliefs together to infer that A is better than B. This is certainly a possibility given the qualifications listed above. But note that in this position, if those two beliefs were justified, the agent would certainly be *rational* to conclude that A is better than B, and hence rational to prefer A to B. So the constraints on the closure principles don't affect our ability to endorse these two principles.

The real issue is (PC). Fantl and McGrath offer a lot of cases where (PC) holds, as well as arguing that it is plausibly true given the role of implications in practical reasoning. What's at issue is that (PC) is stronger than a deductive closure principle. It is, in effect, equivalent to endorsing the following schema as a valid principle of implication.

> *p*
> Given *p*, A is preferable to B
> So, A is preferable to B

I call this Practical Modus Ponens, or PMP. The middle premise in PMP is *not* a conditional. It is not to be read as *If p, then A is preferable to B*. Conditional valuations are not conditionals. To see this, again consider the proposed bet on (true) *p* at exorbitant odds, where A is the act of taking the bet, and B the act of declining the bet. It's true that given *p*, A is preferable to B. But it's not true that if *p*, then A is preferable to B. Even if we restrict our attention to cases where the preferences in question are perfectly valid, this is a case where PMP is invalid. Both premises are true, and the conclusion is false. It might nevertheless be true that whenever an agent is justified in believing both of the premises, she is justified in believing the conclusion. To argue against this, we need a *very* complicated case, involving embedded bets and three separate agents, Quentin, Robby and Thom. All of them have received the same evidence, and all of them are faced with the same complex bet, with the following properties.

- *p* is an historical proposition that is well (but not conclusively) supported by their evidence, and happens to be true. All the agents have a high credence in *p*, which is exactly what the evidence supports.
- The bet A, which they are offered, wins if *p* is true, and loses if *p* is false.
- If they win the bet, the prize is the bet B.
- *s* is also an historical proposition, but the evidence tells equally for and against it. All the agents regard *s* as being about as likely as not. Moreover, *s* turns out to be false.
- The bet B is worth $2 if *s* is true, and worth -$1 if *s* is false. Although it is actually a losing bet, the agents all rationally value it at around 50 cents.
- How much A costs is determined by which proposition from the partition {*q*, *r*, *s*} is true.

- If q is true, A costs \$2
- If r is true, A costs \$500
- If t is true, A costs \$1
- The evidence the agents has strongly supports r, though t is in fact true
- Quentin believes q
- Robby believes r
- Thom believes t

All of the agents make the utility calculations that their beliefs support, so Quentin and Thom take the bet and lose a dollar, while Robby declines it. Although Robby has a lot of evidence in favor of p, he correctly decides that it would be unwise to bet on p at effective odds of 1000 to 1 against. I'll now argue that both Quentin and Thom are potential counterexamples to (PC). There are three possibilities for what we can say about those two.

First, we could say that they are justified in believing p, and rational to take the bet. The problem with this position is that if they had rational beliefs about the partition $\{q, r, t\}$ they would realize that taking the bet does not maximize expected utility. If we take rational decisions to be those that maximize expected utility given a rational response to the evidence, then the decisions are clearly not rational.

Second, we could say that although Quentin and Thom are not rational in accepting the bet, nor are they justified in believing that p. This doesn't seem particularly plausible for several reasons. The irrationality in their belief systems concerns whether q, r or t is true, not whether p is true. If Thom suddenly got a lot of evidence that t is true, then all of his (salient) beliefs would be well supported by the evidence. But it is bizarre to think that whether his belief in p is rational turns on how much evidence he has for t. Finally, even if we accept that agents in higher stakes situations need more evidence to have justified beliefs, the fact is that the agents are in a low-risk situation, since t is actually true, so the most they could lose is \$1.

So it seems like the natural thing to say is that Quentin and Thom *are* justified in believing that p, and are justified in believing that given p, it maximizes expected utility to take the bet, but they are not rational to take the bet. (At least, in the version of the story where they are thinking about which of q, r and t are correct given their evidence when thinking about whether to take the bet they are counterexamples to (PC).) Against this, one might respond that if belief in p is justified, there are arguments one might make to the conclusion that the bet should be taken. So it is inconsistent to say that the belief is justified, but the decision to take the bet is not rational. The problem is finding a premise that goes along with p to get the conclusion that taking the bet is rational. Let's look at some of the premises the agent might use.

- If p, then the best thing to do is to take the bet.

This isn't true (p is true, but the best thing to do isn't to take the bet). More importantly, the agents think this is only true if s is true, and they think s is a 50/50 proposition. So they don't believe this premise, and it would not be rational to believe it.

- If p, then probably the best thing to do is to take the bet.

Again this isn't true, and it isn't well supported, and it doesn't even support the conclusion, for it doesn't follow from the fact that x is probably the best thing to do that x should be done.

- If p, then taking the bet maximizes rational expected utility.

This isn't true—it is a conditional with a true antecedent and a false consequent. Moreover, if Quentin and Thom were rational, like Robby, they would recognize this.

- If p, then taking the bet maximizes expected utility relative to their beliefs.

This is true, and even reasonable to believe, but it doesn't imply that they should take the bet. It doesn't follow from the fact that doing something maximizes expected utility relative to my crazy beliefs that I should do that thing.

- Given p, taking the bet maximizes rational expected utility.

This is true, and even reasonable to believe, but it isn't clear that it supports the conclusion that the agents should take the bet. The implication appealed to here is PMP, and in this context that's close enough to equivalent to (PC). If we think that this case is a prima facie problem for (PC), as I think is intuitively plausible, then we can't use (PC) to show that it *doesn't* pose a problem. We could obviously continue for a while, but it should be clear it will be very hard to find a way to justify taking the bet even spotting the agents p as a premise they can use in rational deliberation. So it seems to me that (PC) is not in general true, which is good because as we'll see in cases like this one the theory outlined here does not support it.

The theory we have been working with says that belief that p is justified iff the agent's degree of belief in p is sufficient to amount to belief in their context, and they are justified in believing p to that degree. Since by hypothesis Quentin and Thom are justified in believing p to the degree that they do, the only question left is whether this amounts to belief. This turns out not to be settled by the details of the case as yet specified. At first glance, assuming there are no other relevant decisions, we might think they believe that p because (a) they prefer (in the relevant sense) believing p to not believing p, and (b) conditionalizing on p doesn't change their attitude towards the bet. (They prefer taking the bet to declining it, both unconditionally and conditional on p.)

But that isn't all there is to the definition of belief *tout court*. We must also ask whether conditionalising on p changes any preferences conditional on any active proposition. And that may well be true. Conditional on r, Quentin and Thom prefer not taking the bet to taking it. But conditional on r and p, they prefer taking the bet to not taking it. So if r is an active proposition, they don't believe that p. If r is not active, they do believe it. In more colloquial terms, if they are concerned about the possible truth of r (if it is salient, or at least not taken for granted to be false) then p becomes a potentially high-stakes proposition, so they don't believe it without extraordinary evidence (which they don't have). Hence they are only a counterexample to (PC) if r is not active. But if r is not active, our theory predicts that they are a counterexample to (PC), which is what we argued above is intuitively correct.

Still, the importance of r suggests a way of saving (PC). Above I relied on the position that if Quentin and Thom are not maximising rational expected utility, then they are being irrational. This is perhaps too harsh. There is a position we could take, derived from some suggestions made by Gilbert Harman in *Change in View*, that an agent can rationally rely on their beliefs, even if those beliefs were not rationally formed, if they cannot be expected to have kept track of the evidence they used to form that belief. If we adopt this view, then we might be able to say that (PC) is compatible with the correct normative judgments about this case.

To make this compatibility explicit, let's adjust the case so Quentin takes q for granted, and cannot be reasonably expected to have remembered the evidence for q. Thom, on the other hand, forms the belief that t rather than r is true in the course of thinking through his evidence that bears on the rationality of taking or declining the bet. (In more familiar terms, t is part of the inference Thom uses in coming to conclude that he should take the bet, though it is not part of the final implication he endorses whose conclusion is that he should take the bet.) Neither Quentin nor Thom is a counterexample to (PC) thus understood. (That is, with the notion of rationality in (PC) understood as Harman suggests that it should be.) Quentin is not a counterexample, because he is *rational* in taking the bet. And Thom is not a counterexample, because in his context, where r is active, his credence in p does not amount to belief in p, so he is not justified in believing p.

We have now two readings of (PC). On the strict reading, where a rational choice is one that maximises rational expected utility, the principle is subject to counterexample, and seems generally to be implausible. On the loose reading, where we allow agents to rely on beliefs formed irrationally in the past in rational decision making, (PC) *is* plausible. Happily, the theory sketched here agrees with (PC) on the plausible loose reading, but not on the implausible strict reading. In the previous section I argued that the theory also accounts for intuitions about particular cases like *Local and Express*. And now we've seen that the theory accounts for our considered opinions about which principles connecting justified belief to rational decision making we should endorse. So it seems at this stage that we can account for the intuitions behind the pragmatic encroachment view while keeping a concept of probabilistic epistemic justification that is free of pragmatic considerations.

8. Conclusions

Given a pragmatic account of belief, we don't need to have a pragmatic account of justification in order to explain the intuitions that whether *S* justifiably believes that *p* might depend on pragmatic factors. My focus here has been on sketching a theory of belief on which it is the belief part of the concept of a justified belief which is pragmatically sensitive. I haven't said much about why we should prefer to take that option than say that the notion of epistemic justification is a pragmatic notion. I've mainly been aiming to show that a particular position is an open possibility, namely that we can accept that whether a particular agent is justified in believing *p* can be sensitive to their practical environment without thinking that the primary epistemic concepts are themselves pragmatically sensitive.[5]

Notes

1. To say the agent prefers A to B given *q* is not to say that if the agent were to learn *q*, she would prefer A to B. It's rather to say that she prefers the state of the world where she does A and *q* is true to the state of the world where she does B and *q* is true. These two will come apart in cases where learning *q* changes the agent's preferences. We'll return to this issue below.
2. This might seem *much* too simple, especially when compared to all the bells and whistles that functionalists usually put in their theories to (further) distinguish themselves from crude versions of behaviourism. The reason we don't need to include those complications here is that they will all be included in the analysis of *preference*. Indeed, the theory here is compatible with a thoroughly anti-functionalist treatment of preference. The claim is not that we can offer a functional analysis of belief in terms of non-mental concepts, just that we can offer a functionalist reduction of belief to other mental concepts. The threshold view is *also* such a reduction, but it is such a crude reduction that it doesn't obviously fall into any category.
3. Conditionalizing on the proposition *There are space aliens about to come down and kill all the people writing epistemology papers* will make me prefer to stop writing this paper, and perhaps grab some old metaphysics papers I could be working on. So that proposition satisfies the second clause of the definition of relevance. But it clearly doesn't satisfy the first clause. This part of the definition

of relevance won't do much work until the discussion of agents with mistaken environmental beliefs in section 7.

4. I think putting things numerically is misleading because it suggests that the kind of bets we usually use to measure degrees of belief are open, salient options for Louise and Harry. But if those bets were open and salient, they wouldn't *believe* the train is a local. Using qualitative rather than quantitative language to describe them is just as accurate, and doesn't have misleading implications about their practical environment.
5. Thanks to Michael Almeida, Tamar Szabó Gendler, Peter Gerdes, Jon Kvanvig, Barry Lam, Ishani Maitra, Robert Stalnaker, Jason Stanley, Matthew Weiner for helpful discussions, and especially to Matthew McGrath for correcting many mistakes in an earlier draft of this paper.

References

Bovens, Luc and James Hawthorne (1999) "The Preface, the Lottery, and the Logic of Belief" 108(430): 241–264.

Christensen, David (2005) *Putting Logic in Its Place*. Oxford: Oxford University Press

Evnine, Simon (1999) "Believing Conjunctions" *Synthese* 118: 201–227.

Fantl, Jeremy and Matthew McGrath (2002) "Evidence, Pragmatics, and Justification" *Philosophical Review* 111: 67–94.

Foley, Richard (1993) *Working Without a Net*. Oxford: Oxford University Press.

Harman, Gilbert (1986) *Change in View*. Cambridge, MA: Bradford.

Hawthorne, John (2004) *Knowledge and Lotteries*. Oxford: Oxford University Press.

Hunter, Daniel (1996) "On the Relation Between Categorical and Probabilistic Belief," *Noûs* 30:75–98.

Kaplan, Mark (1996) *Decision Theory as Philosophy*. Cambridge: Cambridge University Press.

Keynes, John Maynard (1921) *A Treatise on Probability*. London: Macmillan

Lewis, David (1994) "Reduction of Mind" in Guttenplan, S. (ed.) *A Companion to the Philosophy of Mind*, Oxford, Blackwell, pp. 412–31.

Ryle, Gilbert (1949) *The Concept of Mind*. New York: Barnes and Noble.

Stalnaker, Robert (1984) *Inquiry*. Cambridge, MA: MIT Press.

Stanley, Jason (2005) *Knowledge and Practical Interests*. Oxford: Oxford University Press.

Weatherson, Brian (2005) "True Truer Truest" *Philosophical Studies* 123: 47–70.

Williamson, Timothy (1994) *Vagueness*. London: Routledge.

Williamson, Timothy (2000) *Knowledge and Its Limits*. Oxford: Oxford University Press.

Philosophical Perspectives, 19, Epistemology, 2005

EPISTEMIC PERMISSIVENESS

Roger White
New York University

A rational person doesn't believe just anything. There are limits on what it is rational to believe. How wide are these limits? That's the main question that interests me here. But a secondary question immediately arises: What factors impose these limits? A first stab is to say that one's *evidence* determines what it is epistemically permissible for one to believe. Many will claim that there are further, non-evidentiary factors relevant to the epistemic rationality of belief. I will be ignoring the details of alternative answers in order to focus on the question of what kind of rational constraints one's evidence puts on belief. Our main question concerns how far epistemic *permission* and *obligation* can come apart.[1] Suppose I am epistemically permitted to believe P, i.e., it would not be irrational for me to believe it. Am I thereby obliged to believe P, or are other options rationally available to me?[2] Might I be equally rational in remaining agnostic about P, or even believing not-P? Or could even a slightly stronger or weaker degree of confidence be just as reasonable?

1. Examples and Motivations for Permissive Epistemology

Following Feldman (forthcoming) we can call the negative answer the Uniqueness thesis.

> **Uniqueness:** Given one's total evidence, there is a unique rational doxastic attitude that one can take to any proposition.[3]

I call positions that depart from Uniqueness "permissive" as they entail that epistemic rationality permits a range of alternative doxastic attitudes. Many philosophers hold permissive epistemologies. Rejection of Uniqueness is prominent in Bas van Fraassen's (1984, 1989, 2002) epistemology. Proponents of Conservatism (Harman 1986, Lycan 1988) suggest that you are prima facie justified in maintaining your beliefs until you have a reason to abandon them.

So had you drawn a different conclusion from the same evidence, you would be fully rational in continuing to hold it, at least until challenged. According to Richard Foley (1987), a belief is epistemically rational if upon sufficient reflection you would think that holding that belief was an effective means to achieving the goal of believing just what is true. This condition fails to single out a unique set of beliefs for any given evidence. It seems that the method of seeking Reflective Equilibrium (Rawls 1999, Goodman 1955) need not terminate in a unique set of convictions. So if that is the ultimate standard of rationality, Uniqueness is false. According to the Subjectivist version of Bayesianism, the only rational constraint on one's initial degrees of belief is conformity to the probability calculus. While some Bayesians are uncomfortable with this degree of permissiveness, the constraints that they are willing to add fall far short of Uniqueness.[4] Any coherence theory of rational belief would appear to be at odds with Uniqueness. For however we understand coherence there will be multiple ways of achieving it that involve different attitudes to various propositions.

Doubts about Uniqueness may arise from reflection on persistent and widespread disagreement among apparently rational inquirers.[5] According to Gideon Rosen (2001)

> It should be obvious that reasonable people can disagree, even when confronted with the same body of evidence. When a jury or a court is divided in a difficult case, the mere fact of disagreement does not mean that someone is being unreasonable. (p. 71)

In a criminal trial we have a large, complex body of evidence, some of which appears to link the defendant with the crime, some which suggests that he had nothing to do with it. Figuring out what to believe is a matter of weighing various considerations as we try to fit all the pieces together. Difficult cases like this tend to produce sharp disagreement even among the most diligent inquirers. Some may be tempted to give up and conclude that there is no telling who's right. But many of us retain our conviction that having earnestly wrestled with the evidence our conclusions are correct. Now a proponent of Uniqueness will have to insist that those who disagree have failed to respond to the evidence rationally. For if the parties in the dispute have the same evidence, and one's total evidence uniquely determines what one can rationally believe, then they should all be in agreement.[6] But this can be an awkward position to maintain. Why should I trust my own estimate of the probative force of the evidence, when equally intelligent people judge it differently? One initially appealing way to escape this worry is to join Rosen in insisting that those who disagree needn't display any failure of rationality.

Examples and motivations for permissivism can be multiplied. There are many important differences among permissive epistemologies. For instance, many permissive views will identify some other non-evidential factor which "takes up the slack" in fully determining what one should believe. And these extra factors will vary among different views. Differences such as these may crucially affect how a permissivist can best respond to the objections that I present. But in order to get out the basic worries that I have without too much fuss, I will ignore these distinctions and treat these permissive views as a generic position. I think there is much to be said for these and other challenges to Uniqueness. But my purpose here will be to raise trouble for permissive views by displaying some difficulties we get into by denying Uniqueness.

2. Objections to Extreme Permissivism

Let's begin by considering the following radical rejection of Uniqueness:

> **Extreme Permissivism:** There are possible cases in which you rationally believe P, yet it is consistent with your being fully rational and possessing your current evidence that you believe not-P instead.

My main objection to Extreme Permissivism will take some work to develop. I will begin with a quick-and-dirty preliminary one. I am on a jury with the task of deciding whether the defendant Smith is guilty. Prior to considering any evidence it would be quite unreasonable to have any opinion as to Smith's guilt or innocence. Perhaps there are some propositions that one can rationally believe without evidence, but the guilt or innocence of a criminal defendant is not one of them. How could evaluation of the evidence render me rational in believing that Smith is guilty, if it is not reasonable to believe this already? Surely only if the total evidence *supports Smith's guilt*. And likewise only evidence supporting his innocence could *make it* rational to believe that he is innocent. Evidence that has no bearing on whether Smith is guilty is no better than no evidence at all.

But the evidence cannot support both Smith's innocence *and* his guilt. Whatever is evidence *for* P is evidence for the falsity of not-P and hence is evidence *against* not-P. Of course, certain elements of or aspects of the total body of evidence might suggest that Smith is guilty, while others suggest the opposite. But it is incoherent to suppose that a whole body of evidence could count both for and against a hypothesis. So then it is impossible that my examination of the evidence makes it rational for me to believe that Smith is guilty but also rational to believe instead that he is innocent. And since neither view was rational apart from any evidence, the proposed radical departure from Uniqueness cannot be right.

While I think it is right, the argument above might seem a little too quick. The following considerations go into more depth. First consider the following situation. Once again, prior to being presented with the evidence I haven't a clue as to whether Smith is guilty. But I have a couple of magical belief-inducing pills. One, when swallowed, will give me a true belief on the matter, the other a false belief. I have no idea which one is the Truth pill, so it is clearly irresponsible to take either, given that my purpose is to discern the truth. But I pick one at random and take it, finding myself with the conviction that Smith is guilty, without being aware of any reason to think so. Now perhaps we can rationally retain beliefs after we have lost track of the reasons that led us first to hold them. But in this case I can recall that my belief was not based on evidence pointing to Smith's guilt, but is rather the result of an arbitrarily chosen pill. If I am rational, recognition of this fact should surely undermine my conviction in Smith's guilt. Prior to taking the pill my credence that I would soon hold a true belief should have been about 1/2. I cannot coherently maintain a conviction that Smith is guilty while being entirely uncertain as to whether my belief that Smith is guilty is true. And it would be perverse to reason backward as follows: Even though I had a only fifty-fifty chance of taking the Truth Pill, since I have formed the belief that Smith is guilty, and indeed he is guilty, I now see that I must have got lucky in choosing the right pill! If it is not already obvious enough that this would be absurd, imagine the following. I take lots of these pills, arbitrarily forming hundreds of beliefs on matters about which I had no clue beforehand. If I retain the resulting beliefs then I will have to conclude that by some extraordinary coincidence I managed to pick a Truth pill each time. And if this were reasonable, then it should make no difference if the pills were selected from a collection 99% of which were Falsity Pills. Surely instead the only reasonable response to reflection on my pill popping is to slip back into agnosticism about Smith's guilt.

Now let's suppose instead that I have not taken a pill, but that under the influence of a permissive epistemologist I come to believe that Extreme Permissivism applies to the matter of Smith's guilt given the available evidence. That is, I believe that upon considering the evidence in court one could rationally conclude that Smith is guilty, but there is an alternative path that one's reasoning could take arriving instead at the rational conclusion that he is innocent. Supposing this is so, is there any advantage, from the point of view of pursuing the truth, in carefully weighing the evidence to draw a conclusion, rather than just taking a belief-inducing pill? Surely I have no better chance of forming a true belief either way. If my permissive assumption is correct, carefully weighing the evidence in an impeccably rational manner will not determine what I end up believing; for by hypothesis, the evidence does not determine a unique rational conclusion. So whatever I do end up believing upon rational deliberation will depend, if not on blind chance, on some arbitrary factor having no bearing on the matter in question.

It might be suggested that rationally evaluating the evidence is a fairly reliable means of coming to the correct conclusion as to whether P, even if that evidence does not determine that a particular conclusion is rational. But it is very hard to see how it could. Of course often one's total evidence does favor a conclusion of P over not-P, and its doing so is a fairly reliable guide to the truth.

Evidence can be misleading—i.e. point us to the wrong conclusion—but this is not common. So there is no problem in this sort of non-permissive case in seeing how rational assessment of evidence is a reliable means to the truth. The probative force of the evidence is a reliable guide to the truth, and a rational inquirer is sensitive to this force, forming his beliefs accordingly. But in any case in which the evidence does favor one conclusion over another, it is *not* equally rational to draw either conclusion. A rational person when confronted with evidence favoring P does not believe not-P. So a case—if there could be such—in which a rational person can believe P or believe not-P instead, must be one in which the evidence favors neither conclusion.

Even if it is granted that a rational person needn't suspend judgment in such a situation, just how rational evaluation of the evidence could reliably lead us to the truth in such a case is entirely mysterious. It would have to be by virtue of some property of the evidence whose reliable link to the truth is inaccessible to the inquirer. For if an inquirer is aware that the evidence has feature F, which is reliably linked to the truth of P, then surely it would be unreasonable to believe not-P. It is hard to imagine what such a truth-conducive feature could be, let alone how it could act on an inquirer's mind directing him to the truth. Furthermore, it is not enough for forming beliefs in response to evidence to have a rational advantage over pill-popping, that it just so happens that the former is a reliable route to the truth without the inquirer recognizing this. For all I can tell, the Truth pill might be a little stickier, so that randomly fetching one from the bag and taking it will usually yield a true belief. But for all I can tell it might be quite the opposite: I may have a tendency to pick the Falsity pill. Only if I could reasonably suppose that arbitrarily selecting a pill will most likely lead to the truth would this be a way to form beliefs that can rationally survive recognition of having been formed this way. We certainly have no reason to expect that rational assessment of the evidence reliably leads to the truth in a way that is inaccessible to an inquirer, even if we allow for this as a possibility. So forming beliefs in response to evidence that does not determine a rational conclusion seems no better than taking belief-inducing pills.

Perhaps the following will drive home the point further. I might examine all the evidence without drawing a conclusion as to whether Smith is guilty. But I do draw the epistemological conclusion that either verdict could be rationally held given this evidence. Perhaps if I were to judge that a particular verdict was rationally obligatory, I couldn't help but draw that conclusion. But as the evidence doesn't strike me as pointing clearly in one direction—if it did, I couldn't judge it to be equally rational to believe the opposite—I am psychologically capable of suspending judgment. But if I really do judge that believing P in this situation would be rational, as would believing not-P, then there should be nothing wrong with my bringing it about that I have some belief or other on the matter. But then it surely cannot matter how I go about choosing which belief to hold, whether by choosing a belief that I'd like to hold, or flipping a coin, or whatever.

Now I have argued that reflection on my having taken a pill to believe that Smith is guilty should undermine all my conviction on the matter. So likewise, if I have concluded on the basis of the evidence that Smith is guilty, my conviction should be undermined if I really think that a belief in Smith's innocence is also rationally permissible in the light of this evidence. For if I believe this, then I should judge myself no more likely to have arrived at the truth than a random pill-popper. So we have reached the conclusion that I cannot rationally accept the extreme permissivist thesis with respect to one of my own beliefs. That is, believing P is not rationally compatible with believing that one could just as rationally have believed not-P given the same evidence.

To be careful, we should note that there are some logical loopholes available to the permissivist here, even granting my argument thus far. For instance, *I* might maintain that it is rationally permissible for *you* either to believe P or to believe not-P, given your evidence, but deny that the same liberal standards apply to me. But this would be obviously *ad hoc* and unmotivated. It is hard to imagine any reason I could have to accept a permissive view of rationality that exempts myself. Another move would be to suggest that Extreme Permissivism is true but epistemically destructive if known: In some cases one can rationally believe P or believe not-P given one's evidence, but *only* as long as one mistakenly thinks that one's current attitude to P is rationally obligatory given one's evidence. This strikes me as an odd position, for it seems natural to suppose that a belief can always rationally survive learning the epistemic value of one's evidence. That is, if it is rational to believe P given evidence E, then it is rational to believe P given E & E′, where E′ correctly states what attitudes to P are rationally permissible given E. But in any event, this position makes it very difficult for us to rationally believe Extreme Permissivism, for the knowledge that it applies in a particular case is self-undermining: By the arguments above, if I believe that both a belief in P and a belief in not-P are each rationally permitted by my evidence, then I should conclude that neither belief is rationally permissible. Hence if I am to believe anything, then for each belief I should hold that it is the only rational attitude that I can take given my evidence. Furthermore, if Extreme Permissivism were plausible with respect to many matters, then surely it could plausibly be applied to itself. That is, Extreme Permissivists should hold that the usual evidence available to philosophers does not determine whether one should believe or disbelieve Extreme Permissivism. After all, plenty of apparently reasonable people deny Extreme Permissivism. But then by the arguments above, Extreme Permissivism cannot rationally be believed on our evidence.

This still seems to leave room for a coherent permissive position. Call a case in which my evidence rationally permits me to believe P or to believe not-P, a *permissive case*. We could maintain that there are possible (and even actual) permissive cases, but that these are very rare, and one cannot tell, for any case, that it is a permissive one. So my attitude with regard to each case considered individually should be that it is not permissive, while I may maintain that some rare cases are permissive.[7] (There is an obvious parallel here with the so-called Preface Paradox, where I believe regarding each of my beliefs individually, that it is true, while maintaining that at least some of my beliefs are false). But while this position may be coherent and escape the objections thus far, I doubt that anyone holds such a view, as it is hard to see what could motivate it. Typical permissive epistemologies such as Subjectivist Bayesianism entail that permissive cases are quite pervasive, and hence cannot easily avoid the problems I have raised.

3. Alternative Permissible Standards?

Here is an objection that one might make to the main argument that I've put forth.[8] A crucial step in my case was the claim that if you believe P but maintain that you could have rationally believed not-P on the same evidence, then you should take the means by which you arrived at your belief in P to be no better than arbitrarily popping a belief-inducing pill. This might be a point of resistance for a permissivist. He might insist that he has come to his conviction in P by means that are very conducive to forming true beliefs, namely by assessing the evidence according to the appropriate epistemic standards. This is not at all like randomly popping a belief-inducing pill. He might claim that such standards are not permissive ones presenting subjects with alternative options for belief, but rather they state uniquely what is to be believed given certain evidence. Even before assessing the evidence, if someone accepts such standards of evidence assessment, then he should judge it very likely that he will arrive at the truth by their application. For the standards will sanction only those beliefs that according to the standards, are well supported by the evidence, and hence likely to be true. So far this doesn't seem like a permissive position. For given his acceptance of standards that sanction only a belief in P given his evidence, then he shouldn't just believe not-P instead. However, the permissivist that I'm imagining might maintain he could have adopted a different set of standards that sanction very different attitudes given the same evidence. This possibility, he might suggest, is consistent with his being fully rational and possessing his current evidence; and were he to accept standards sanctioning a belief in not-P, he would be rational in doing so. In this way the subtle permissivist tries to have his cake and eat it too. On the one hand he can proudly maintain that he is responsibly forming beliefs in a manner that he takes to be reliable in attaining the truth. On the other, he denies that he is bound by rationality to form just his current opinions on his evidence. Likewise, he needn't accuse those who share his evidence but differ in their conclusions of any irrationality, provided their views are in accord with their own alternative epistemic standards.

I think we ought to be suspicious of this position for similar reasons as before. First note that if our permissivist takes his own standards to be a reliable guide to the truth, then since the alternative standards deliver very different conclusions, he must judge them to be rather unreliable. So he should judge himself very lucky to have adopted truth-conducive standards, since with full rationality he could have followed ones that would lead him wildly into error. We see here that the same worries about arbitrariness just arise at a different position. How have I come to hold the epistemic standards which lead me from my evidence to conclude that P? According to this permissivist it was not by virtue of being rational, since it is consistent with my being rational that I adhere to rather different standards that would have me believe not-P instead. But then it seems that my applying the correct standards and hence arriving at the right conclusion is just a matter of dumb luck, much like popping a pill. And hence I ought to doubt that I really have been lucky enough to do so.

To make the situation more vivid, let's fill in the details with a make-believe story about how we come to adhere to certain epistemic standards. Suppose it is just a matter of education. I follow standards S because I was inculcated with them at MIT. But had I attended Berkeley, I would have been inculcated with standards S′ instead. Given my total evidence as input, S and S′ deliver the conclusions P, and not-P respectively. (The story may be far-fetched, but nothing hinges on the details. And if my being rational is compatible with adopting either set of standards, then there is *some* further factor which led me to hold S rather than S′.) Now I can imagine myself in a counterfactual situation before graduate school where my sole motive for study is to answer the question whether P. I have all the available relevant evidence, I'm just not sure yet what to make of it. Now I learn that if I attend MIT I will inevitably inherit standards S from my mentors, which given the evidence will lead me to believe P. Attending Berkeley will result in my adhering to standards S′ and hence arriving at the conclusion not-P. Now surely the prospect of several years of graduate school will seem rather pointless no matter how passionately curious I am as to whether P. Indeed my prospects for answering whether P to my satisfaction should seem dim. I might as well choose a grad school to attend and hence opinions to hold by a preference for Massachusetts weather, or by flipping a coin. Once I have filled out the enrollment form for MIT say, I will know that unless something gets in the way, in a few years I will be of the opinion that P. If I am a permissivist, I should take it that I will soon *rationally* believe P. If this is so, why shouldn't I just believe it now and save myself the time and trouble? But of course it would be absurd to form an opinion on the matter by an arbitrary choice when I don't even know what to make of the evidence. If this is the sorry state I find myself in with respect to answering whether P before I begin my inquiry, then I should judge myself no better off having arrived at a conclusion, if I judge that my adoption of epistemic standards was such an arbitrary matter.[9]

4. Moderate Permissivism and Practical Deliberation

I have been considering an extreme rejection of Uniqueness that might appeal only to the most permissive epistemologists. We can back off from this level of permissiveness without going all the way to Uniqueness. Many will find it easier to accept that rationality allows for a more restricted range of differences of opinion. Perhaps there are cases in which a reasonable assessment of the evidence rules out a belief that not-P, but does not dictate whether one should believe that P or suspend judgment. Or more cautiously still, there may at least be some leeway in the *degree* of conviction that is rationally permissible given one's evidence.

These moderately permissive positions still run into trouble. Suppose that having carefully considered the evidence, my conviction in Smith's guilt is strong enough to warrant voting Guilty. Surely this is what I should do--to let him go free given that I am (rationally) confident that he's guilty would be grossly irresponsible. If I had more substantial doubts it would be appropriate to vote Not Guilty, even if I strongly suspected that he was guilty. Now let's try to suppose that the range of rationally permissible degrees of confidence in Smith's guilt is just broad enough to include my own conviction as well as a degree of doubt that would make a vote of Not Guilty appropriate.[10] It appears that if this were so I should have no qualms about letting Smith go free, even though I'm sure he's a murderer.[11] For suppose that before considering the evidence I am persuaded that there is this range of rationally permissible degrees of conviction. If I am correct in really thinking this, then there should be nothing wrong with arbitrarily choosing a verdict without bothering to look at the evidence. For there should be nothing wrong with my arbitrarily choosing a degree of conviction (induced perhaps by a magic pill) that is within the rationally permissible range. And given such a degree of conviction, I should vote accordingly, whatever it is. I can do no better by examining the evidence, forming a view and voting in accordance with it—to suppose otherwise involves denying the permissive view. For assuming that rationality and evidence do not determine a unique degree of conviction, then even if I am perfectly rational, there is no predicting what my degree of conviction will be upon evaluating the evidence. And hence there is no predicting how I will vote, whether Smith is guilty or not. Justice is no more likely to be done given that I examine the evidence than if I just vote however I like.

Now if this is an appropriate way to proceed before considering the evidence, then I can reason similarly once I have viewed it and have become convinced that Smith is guilty:

> Given the same evidence I could no less rationally have had significant doubts about Smith's guilt, given which I could responsibly vote Not Guilty. That I happen to lack these doubts is either a result of chance or some arbitrary causal factor. So I would be doing no better with respect to the goal of securing a just verdict by voting with my convictions. For what ultimately matters for justice is the correspondence between the verdict and whether Smith *is* guilty. What I happen believe and how strongly I believe it makes no difference to the justice of the verdict. My rationally forming an opinion in the light of the evidence is just

> the *means* by which I try to attain a just outcome. But however good I am at assessing the probative force of the evidence, it is entirely open whether my degree of rational conviction will fall within the Guilty or Not Guilty range. As long as my vote corresponds to an attitude that is within the bounds of rationally permissible conviction, I have done as well as I possibly can given the available evidence to attain a just verdict. So although I'm sure that Smith is guilty, I'll vote Not Guilty just because I happen to like the guy.

But of course it can't be right to try to let someone go free when you are rationally persuaded that he is a murderer. Perhaps it is obligatory to vote Not Guilty, if I know that one might have rational doubts about Smith's guilt. For any evidence that it is rational to have doubts may itself cast enough doubt on Smith's guilt to make a Guilty vote inappropriate. But in this case I should not retain my conviction that he is guilty. Holding this moderately permissive view either leads to the absurd consequence that it is appropriate to vote against one's convictions, or it is self-undermining.

Here is a related worry. Instead of immediately inducing a degree of conviction, a magic pill might ensure that I rationally respond to the evidence to arrive at that conviction. We are supposing for the sake of argument that there is a certain range of rationally permissible degrees of confidence in Smith's guilt, given the evidence. So among the possible worlds in which I respond to the same evidence in a perfectly rational manner, there are some in which I'm sure he's guilty and others in which I have doubts. The pill simply ensures that one of the latter worlds obtains. Taking such a pill at random is not essentially different from evaluating the evidence without it. In either case, some factor other than the evidence or my ability to rationally respond to it causes me to form a degree of conviction—why not take charge of these arbitrary influencing factors as I choose? But since which pill I take determines how sure I will be, which in turn will determine how I vote, taking a pill is tantamount to arbitrarily choosing how to vote with no evidence at all. But this cannot be the right thing to do.

5. Responsiveness to New Evidence

A rational person is responsive to new evidence. My confidence in a proposition given certain evidence should depend partly on my confidence prior to obtaining this evidence, and partly on the strength of the evidence.[12] The problem I want to raise is that to the extent that we reject Uniqueness, it is hard to see why one's convictions ought always to be responsive to confirming evidence. Suppose that you and I share our total evidence E. My subjective probability for P is x, and yours is lower at y. We each now obtain additional evidence E′, which supports P. My confidence in P rises to x' and yours to y', which happens to be equal to the x that I held prior to obtaining E′. We have each updated our convictions appropriately in response to the new evidence. But now let's suppose that we were each fully rational in holding our different degrees of belief x and y given just evidence E. Although I've been a little more confident than you, I would have been no less rational in sharing your doubts. Why then shouldn't I just keep my confidence in P at x, if it suits me? After all, that is where I would have ended up had I enjoyed your lower degree of confidence prior to obtaining E′. If that degree of doubt would have been rational for me back then, what could be wrong with the corresponding lower credence now? Perhaps in between obtaining E′ and responding to it, I take one of those pills shifting my confidence down to yours at y. Then recognizing the significance of E′, my confidence rises appropriately to x. There should be nothing wrong with taking such a pill given that the resulting conviction is no less rational. But the net effect is that I remain entirely unmoved by E′, even thought I correctly recognize that it confirms P.

This can't be right. Imagine a juror who is on the fence, undecided as to whether Smith is guilty. He receives new evidence and correctly recognizes that it confirms Smith's guilt. But our juror remains unmoved, not the slightest bit more inclined toward a guilty verdict. Such a person is not epistemically competent to serve on a jury.

6. Rationality and First-person Deliberation

The arguments of Sections 4 and 5 suggest that a permissive account of rationality introduces a kind of arbitrariness to our beliefs that can infect both practical and theoretical deliberations. We can roughly pose the general challenge in terms of outright belief as follows. If my current beliefs are not rationally obligatory for me, why should I take propositions that I *actually* believe as a basis for action and reasoning, rather than some others that I don't believe, but would be rational in believing? Why should *my* beliefs be privileged in my practical and theoretical deliberations, over equally rational alternative beliefs? Suppose that due to a bump on the head, I lose my belief in P and forget that I ever held it. The Epistemology Oracle informs me that believing P is just one of a range of epistemically permissible options for me given my evidence. In figuring out what to believe now, surely the fact that *I used to believe P* is entirely irrelevant; I might just as well start over again and form a new rational belief. Why then should it be any different if I still happen to believe P?

Here is a possible response. To vote Not Guilty when I'm rightly sure that Smith committed murder amounts to deliberately trying to bring about an injustice. This is surely wrong regardless of whether a different degree of conviction would be equally rational. Similarly, to reason from propositions one takes to be false, is to purposely undermine the aim of inquiry, namely to reach the truth. And taking pills that change one's beliefs is not a rational option, even if the resulting beliefs are such that one could have rationally held them given one's evidence. For taking such a pill amounts to attempting to deceive one's self. To induce a belief that one takes to be false violates the aim of believing only what is true.

What this reply suggests is that I have inappropriately been taking a "third-person" approach in questioning the relevance of *what my beliefs happen to be* if alternative attitudes are permissible. Rather, what I must ask myself in my deliberations is *whether P*. Since I can't help but answer from my own perspective, my answer will correspond to what I happen to believe. But it is the (apparent) fact *that P* which is relevant, not the fact that *I* happen to believe it. If my aim is to convict Smith if and only if he is guilty, then the question I must answer is *whether he is guilty*. If I answer that yes he is guilty, then of course I should I vote accordingly, for a guilty person should be convicted. From my perspective, it is the fact (as I take it) that he is guilty that is a sufficient reason to convict him, not the fact that I happen to believe that he's guilty. So whether or not the beliefs that I happen to hold are epistemically obligatory is just not relevant to whether I should act on them or reason from them.

I don't find this response entirely satisfying. For it seems that at least in some cases my assessment of the epistemic status of a belief can legitimately override my own take on the facts in theoretical and practical deliberation. Suppose that due to irrational fears, I can't help but think that my plane will crash. Yet I'm well aware that the statistical data make it unreasonable to believe this. It is not that I take myself to have some special insight that can override the regular evidence. I realize that my belief is irrational, but I just can't manage to abandon it. Admittedly, this is a very odd state to be in. It is crucial to this case that I genuinely expect the plane to crash (I don't merely fear that it will), while genuinely recognizing the epstemic irrationality of my attitude (I don't merely recognize that according to typical epistemological theories, it would count as irrational). But I would suggest that it is at least possible to get into such a state, even if it involves severe cognitive dissonance.

It seems to me that in this situation it would be quite reasonable just to force myself to board the plane, or perhaps ask someone to drag me on. Depending how urgent my flight was, it might be irresponsible not to do so. Similarly, it may be appropriate to take a pill to help me believe that the plane is safe. If my faculties were functioning as they should, my recognition of the irrationality of my belief would cause me to abandon this belief and attain the rational conviction that the plane will not crash. As I'm aware of this, but still can't come to my senses, a magic pill may be useful to nudge my beliefs into order.

Now in a sense, forcing myself on the plane while believing it will crash almost amounts to attempting suicide. I may not intend to die, but I'm acting in a way that I fully expect to have this consequence. Similarly, if I take the pill to induce the belief that the plane is safe, I am trying to adopt a view that I take to be false. Nevertheless, it seems quite appropriate to do so in this case. Instead of acting on what I take to be the facts, I step outside my own perspective, so to speak, and let my epistemological convictions guide me. Even though I expect the plane to crash, and take the belief that it won't to be false, I correctly take the *rationality* of the belief that the plane is safe as the best guide in action. For rationality is the best guide to the truth, and when it conflicts with my own view on things, it is best that rationality wins out.

Now if my epistemic convictions can legitimately overrule my beliefs in a case where they *conflict*, it is hard to see why this should not be appropriate if rationality neither conflicts with my beliefs nor *dictates* what they should be. I should be able to consider my views from the outside, as it were, and recognize that as far as rationality is concerned, they are on a par with various competing views. As there is no better guide to the truth than a rational assessment of the evidence, I should see that there is no advantage to acting on, or reasoning from my actual beliefs rather than other rational alternatives. But as I have argued, this leads to various absurdities.

7. Conclusion

I have been drawing out some of the difficulties we face by being epistemically permissive to various degrees. These arguments should tend to push us toward a less permissive account of rationality, and perhaps all the way to Uniqueness. This will have consequences both for our general theory of rationality and specific issues such as what impact disagreement with peers should have on our convictions. Perhaps whether or not Uniqueness is tolerable, all things considered, is yet to be seen.[13]

Notes

1. I'm following Rosen (2001) in the use of these terms. There is a natural analogue with permissible/obligatory action. But they should not be understood as involving a commitment to a deontological conception of rationality according to which believing rationally is entirely a matter of fulfilling certain epistemic duties.
2. For practical reasons such as clutter avoidance (Harman 1986) it might be wiser to take no attitude to P at all, even though one's evidence adequately supports P. We could refine our question as 'If I am to take any doxastic attitude to P, is believing P the only rational option?'
3. Feldman takes the options to be just belief, disbelief and suspension of belief. I am understanding it as covering degrees of belief, or subjective probabilities. Distracting complications arise here. The relation between outright belief and degrees of belief is controversial. Also, perhaps our convictions do not, and even should not come in precise degrees, but rather cover vague ranges. I will ignore these matters as they are not crucial here.
4. See Earman (1992) for a survey of more and less permissive versions of Bayesianism.

5. See van Inwagen (1996), Kelly (forthcoming), Feldman (forthcoming), and Christensen (unpublished mss.).
6. Whether jurors really do possess the same evidence in a case like this is questionable. Even if they have seen the same data presented in court, different judgments may be due to different background beliefs, which in turn are due to different past experiences. So the relation between epistemic permissiveness and the possibility of rational disagreement is not so simple.
7. I believe it was either Ralph Wedgwood, or Jason Stanley, or both, or someone else who suggested this as a coherent position.
8. Adam Elga and Ralph Wedgwood each raised the kind of worry that I'm responding to here. Apologies if I haven't fully captured their concerns.
9. The issues raised here are related to ones considered by Adam Elga (unpublished ms.). Here, as elsewhere, I have benefited much from discussions with Elga.
10. The case is complicated by the fact that one's vote is supposed to depend on whether it is "beyond reasonable doubt" that the defendant is guilty. Suppose I am convinced beyond a shadow of a doubt that Smith is guilty, correctly judge that my conviction is reasonable, and yet allow that one might reasonably have doubts. Does this count as judging it to be beyond reasonable doubt that he's guilty? Let's avoid this complication by pretending that one's vote should be based just on one's own convictions. In voting one judges: if it were up to me to determine the verdict, this would be my decision.
11. No more qualms that is, than someone who has reasonable doubts about Smith's guilt and votes Not Guilty. Such a person may worry that he is letting a murderer go free, but he can be sure that he has acted responsibly.
12. The standard rule for updating one's degrees of belief is Bayesian Conditionalization. But the problem that I'm raising should apply to any account of rational updating. Thanks to Adam Elga (who in turn gives the credit to Alan Hájek) for suggesting that I state the problem more generally than in the context of Bayesianism.
13. Thanks to Karen Bennett, Paul Boghossian, Liz Camp, David Christensen, Adam Elga, Alan Hájek, Liz Harman, Tom Kelly, Jill North, Karl Schafer, Nico Silins, Ted Sider, Jason Stanley, Michael Strevens, and Ralph Wedgwood for helpful discussion and feedback on this topic. Versions of this material were presented at the Analytic Philosophy Summer School, Venice, July 2004, the Corridor group, an NYU graduate seminar, the Australasian Association of Philosophy Conference July 2005 and the Bellingham summer philosophy conference, August 2005. I'm grateful for the questions and comments I received on these occasions.

References

Christensen, D. "Epistemology of Disagreement: The Good News" unpublished manuscript.

Earman, J. 1992. *Bayes or Bust?* Cambridge, Mass.: MIT Press.

Elga, A. "The Problem of Arbitrary Factors" unpublished manuscript.

Feldman, R. "Reasonable Religious Disagreements" forthcoming in L. Antony ed. *Philosophers without God*

Foley, R. 1987. *The Theory of Epistemic Rationality*, Cambridge: Harvard University Press.

Goodman, N. 1955. *Fact, Fiction, and Forecast*, Cambridge, Mass.: Harvard University Press.

Harman, G. 1986. *Change in View: Principles of Reasoning*, Cambridge, Mass.: MIT Press.

Kelly, T. "The Epistemic Significance of Disagreement" forthcoming in J. Hawthorne, and T. Gendler eds. *Oxford Studies in Epistemology* (Oxford University Press)

Lycan, W. 1988. *Judgment and Justification*, Cambridge, Cambridge University Press.

Rawls, J. 1999. *A Theory of Justice Revised Edition*, Cambridge, Mass.: Harvard University Press.

Rosen, G. 2001. "Nominalism, Naturalism, Epistemic Relativism" *Philosophical Perspectives* 15: 69–91.

van Fraassen, B. 1984. "Belief and the Will" *Journal of Philosophy* 81: 235–256.

———, 1989. *Laws and Symmetry*, Oxford: Clarendon Press.

———, 2002. *The Empirical Stance*, New Haven: Yale University Press.

van Inwagen, P. 1996. "It is Wrong, Always, Everywhere, and for Anyone, to Believe Anything, Upon Insufficient Evidence" in J. Jordan and D. Howard-Snyder eds. *Faith, Freedom, and Rationality*, Hanham, MD: Rowman and Littlefield, pp. 137–154.